Volume **2**

FUNDAMENTAL
Accounting Principles

ELEVENTH CANADIAN EDITION

Kermit D. Larson
University of Texas – Austin

Tilly Jensen
Northern Alberta Institute of Technology

 **McGraw-Hill**
Ryerson

Toronto Montréal Boston Burr Ridge, IL Dubuque, IA Madison, WI
New York San Francisco St. Louis Bangkok Bogotá Caracas
Kuala Lumpur Lisbon London Madrid Mexico City Milan
New Delhi Santiago Seoul Singapore Sydney Taipei

McGraw-Hill
Ryerson

Fundamental Accounting Principles
Volume 2
Eleventh Canadian Edition

ISBN: 0-07-091649-7

1 2 3 4 5 6 7 8 9 10   TCP   0 9 8 7 6 5

Care has been taken to trace ownership of copyright material contained in this text; however, the publisher will welcome any information that enables them to rectify any reference or credit for subsequent editions.

Vice President and Editorial Director: *Pat Ferrier*
Executive Sponsoring Editor: *Nicole Lukach*
Developmental Editor: *Brook Nymark*
Director of Marketing: *Jeff MacLean*
Marketing Manager: *Kim Verhaeghe*
Manager, Editorial Services: *Kelly Dickson*
Senior Supervising Editor: *Margaret Henderson*
Copy Editor: *Laurel Sparrow*
Senior Production Coordinator: *Madeleine Harrington*
Composition: *Bookman Typesetting Co.*
Cover Design: *Dianna Little*
Cover Photos: *Oliver Strewe/Gettyimages*
Printer: *Transcontinental Printing Group*

Printed in Canada

Larson, Kermit D.
    Fundamental accounting principles / Kermit D. Larson, Tilly Jensen. —
11th Canadian ed.

Includes bibliographical references and index.
Contents: v. 1.   Chapters 1–11 — v. 2.   Chapters 12–20 —
    v. 3.   Chapters 21–28 / Kermit D. Larson, Suresh Kalagnanam.

ISBN 0-07-091649-7 (v. 1).—ISBN 0-07-091652-7 (v. 2).—-
ISBN 0-07-091653-5 (v. 3)

1. Accounting.   2. Accounting—Problems, exercises, etc.
I. Jensen, Tilly   II. Kalagnanam, Suresh Subbarao   III. Title.

HF5635.L343 2003   657   C2003-906284-8

Brief Contents

Preface

VOLUME 1

VOLUME 2

VOLUME 3

Contents

THE ACCOUNTING STANDARD

The Larson Advantage

We may have raised the bar for pedagogical excellence with the Tenth Canadian Edition, but we have achieved even higher standards this time out. The Eleventh Canadian Edition includes even more real-world examples, innovative pedagogical features, and thought-provoking examples.

Very well done … gives non-accounting students an intro into the benefits of accounting to businesses. I like it much better than other texts.

Real-World Emphasis

Instructors asked for more real-life examples, so we interviewed real business people and incorporated their perspectives on accounting into the text.

Social responsibility is important in the real world. Through the Did You Know? feature, FAP describes accounting's role in social responsibility by both reporting and assessing its impact.

Annual Reports

The features and assignments that highlight companies like WestJet and Leon's show accounting in a modern, global context. FAP challenges students to apply learned knowledge in practical and diverse ways with analytical problems, research requirements, and communication exercises.

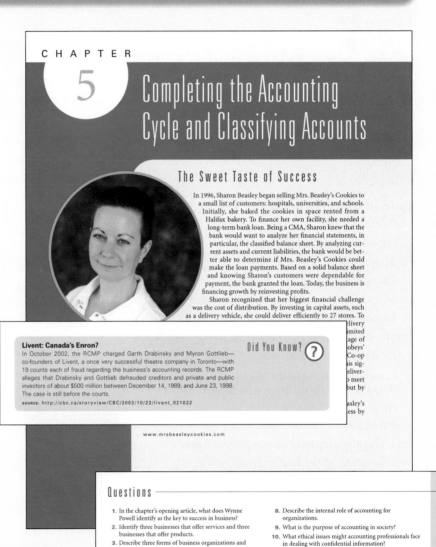

CHAPTER 5

Completing the Accounting Cycle and Classifying Accounts

The Sweet Taste of Success

In 1996, Sharon Beasley began selling Mrs. Beasley's Cookies to a small list of customers: hospitals, universities, and schools. Initially, she baked the cookies in space rented from a Halifax bakery. To finance her own facility, she needed a long-term bank loan. Being a CMA, Sharon knew that the bank would want to analyze her financial statements, in particular, the classified balance sheet. By analyzing current assets and current liabilities, the bank would be better able to determine if Mrs. Beasley's Cookies could make the loan payments. Based on a solid balance sheet and knowing Sharon's customers were dependable for payment, the bank granted the loan. Today, the business is financing growth by reinvesting profits.

Sharon recognized that her biggest financial challenge was the cost of distribution. By investing in capital assets, such as a delivery vehicle, she could deliver efficiently to 27 stores. To [...] delivery [...]

Did You Know? ?

Livent: Canada's Enron?
In October 2002, the RCMP charged Garth Drabinsky and Myron Gottlieb—co-founders of Livent, a once very successful theatre company in Toronto—with 19 counts each of fraud regarding the business's accounting records. The RCMP alleges that Drabinsky and Gottlieb defrauded creditors and private and public investors of about $500 million between December 14, 1989, and June 23, 1998. The case is still before the courts.
SOURCE: http://cbc.ca/storyview/CBC/2002/10/22/livent_021022

www.mrsbeasleycookies.com

Questions

1. In the chapter's opening article, what does Wynne Powell identify as the key to success in business?
2. Identify three businesses that offer services and three businesses that offer products.
3. Describe three forms of business organizations and their characteristics.
4. Identify the two organizations for which accounting information is available in Appendix I at the end of the book.
8. Describe the internal role of accounting for organizations.
9. What is the purpose of accounting in society?
10. What ethical issues might accounting professionals face in dealing with confidential information?
11. Technology is increasingly used to process accounting data. Why, then, should we study accounting?
12. What is the relation between accounting and technology?
13. Identify four managerial accounting tasks performed by both private and government accountants.

The advantage of the Larson text is the language used, which is easy for students to understand. They can relate to the material because they see businesses like these every day—in the news and at home.

Preparing a Trial Balance

Preparing a trial balance involves five steps:

Extend Your Knowledge

3-3

1. Identify each account balance from the ledger.
2. List each account and its balance (in the same order as the Chart of Accounts). Debit balances are entered in the Debit column and credit balances in the Credit column.[8]
3. Compute the total of debit balances.
4. Compute the total of credit balances.
5. Verify that total debit balances equal total credit balances.

New **Extend Your Knowledge**

New to the Larson/Jensen Eleventh Canadian Edition, supplementary material expanding on the text coverage is now available through the Online Learning Centre at www.mcgrawhill.ca/college/larson.

Learning Objectives

LO¹ Describe and prepare a work sheet and explain its usefulness.

LO² Describe the closing process and explain why temporary accounts are closed each period.

LO³ Prepare closing entries.

LO⁴ Explain and prepare a post-closing trial balance.

LO⁵ Describe the steps in the accounting cycle.

Focus on Financial Statements

FFS 2-1

Glenrose Servicing began operations on June 1, 2005. The transactions for the first two months follow:

2005
June 1 The owner, Diane Towbell, invested $20,000 cash and office equipment with a value of $6,000.
      5 Glenrose Servicing performed $3,000 of services for a client on account.
      7 Paid rent for June in the amount of $1,500.
      9 Collected $1,000 from the customer of June 5.
     15 Paid $5,000 of mid-month wages to part-time employees.
     17 Provided $2,000 of services to a client and collected the cash immediately.
     29 Received the $300 June utilities bill. It will be paid in July.
     30 Paid $1,500 in wages to part-time employees.
July 5 Did work for a customer on account; $3,500.
      8 Collected $2,000 from credit customers.

A new series of problems called **Focus on Financial Statements** have been created to address the comments of several reviewers who were concerned that after learning the accounting cycle, students tend to study accounting at the micro level rather than refocusing on the big picture, namely, the incorporation of new concepts into the financial statements.

Entrepreneur
You and a friend have developed a new design for mountain bikes that improves speed and performance by a remarkable 25% to 40%. You are planning to form a small business to manufacture and market these bikes. You and your friend are concerned about potential lawsuits from individuals who may become injured because of using the speed feature of the bikes with reckless abandon. What form of organization do you set up?

Judgement Call

Answer—p. 19

The Judgement Call feature requires you to make accounting and business decisions. It uses role-playing to show the interaction of judgement, the need for business awareness, and the impact of decisions.

The **Judgement Call** feature requires students to make accounting and business decisions. It uses role-playing to show the interaction of judgement, the need for business awareness, and the impact of decisions. Guidance answers are provided.

REAL-WORLD EMPHASIS

THE ACCOUNTING STANDARD

More than ever, Larson/Jensen strives to be the optimal learning tool for student success. This edition has focussed upon innovative pedagogy and new ways to get students excited to learn financial accounting.

> *I love the new format in terms of introducing the features of the text. This is an excellent way to start the students off…. Showing exactly how and why the features are presented.*

Chapter Walkthrough

Instructors raised the issue that many students couldn't remember or didn't understand some of the features associated with the textbook. To this end, Chapter 1 was rewritten to accomplish two goals: to introduce accounting *and,* to introduce and explain textbook features at their first occurrence through the use of marginal descriptors.

Chapter 1   Accounting: The Key to Success

Chapter Preview

A Chapter Preview introduces the importance and relevance of the material, and also links these materials to the opening article to motivate you, the reader.

Accounting is at the heart of business: accounting information pulsates throughout an organization, feeding decision makers with details needed to give them an edge over competitors. Because of new technologies, the increasing speed and quantity of information available makes the task for accountants like Wynne Powell an ever-increasing challenge. Decision makers like Wynne cannot rely on hunches and guesses. Decision makers depend on their knowledge of accounting principles and practices to help identify and take advantage of opportunities discovered from reviewing large volumes of information. Through your studies of this book, you will learn about many of the accounting concepts, procedures, and analyses common to both small and large businesses. This knowledge will provide you with the basics necessary to make better business decisions.

This first chapter serves a dual role. First, it introduces the subject of accounting. It describes accounting, the users and uses of accounting information, the importance of ethics and social responsibility, and opportunities in accounting. This chapter provides a foundation for those students who have little or no understanding of business or the role of accounting in business. Chapter 2 will build on this foundation by focusing on transactions and financial statements.

Chapter 1 also introduces you to each of the learning features found in most chapters. For example, immediately to the left of the first paragraph above is an explanation of purpose regarding the Chapter Preview, and two additional features are described in the lower left margin. Some of the features refer to the "OLC," the Online Learning Centre, located on the Web at www.mcgrawhill.ca/college/larson. Take the time in this chapter to explore and learn the value of these additional resources.

What is Accounting?

Boldfaced words or phrases represent new terminology that is explained here and defined in the glossary at the end of the chapter.

Accounting knowledge is a powerful tool; it is your key to success, according to Wynne Powell. How does accounting knowledge give you power? What exactly is the focus of accounting? This section answers these fundamental questions.

Power of Accounting

LO¹ Describe accounting and its goals and uses.

Accounting is an information system that identifies, measures, records and communicates relevant, reliable, consistent and comparable information about an organization's economic activities, as shown in Exhibit 1.1. Its objective is to help people make better decisions. It also helps people better assess opportunities, products, investments, and social and community responsibilities. In addition to reporting on the performance of a business, what the business owns, and what it owes, accounting opens our eyes to new and exciting possibilities.

Each chapter is separated into chunks of information called learning objectives (LO). Each LO tells you what needs to be mastered in that section of reading.

A series of Flashbacks in the chapter reinforce the immediately preceding materials. Flashbacks allow the reader to stop momentarily and reflect on the topics described. They give immediate feedback on the reader's comprehension before going on to new topics. Answers are provided.

1. Describe a company's annual reporting period.
2. Why do companies prepare interim financial statements?
3. What accounting principles most directly lead to the adjusting process?
4. Is cash basis accounting consistent with generally accepted accounting principles?

⋯ Flashback

Answers—pp. 158–159

GUIDANCE ANSWERS TO   ⋯ Flashback

1. An annual reporting (or accounting) period covers one year and refers to the preparation of annual financial statements. The annual reporting period can follow the calendar year or a fiscal year. The fiscal year can follow the business's natural business year.

2. Interim (less than one year) financial statements are prepared to provide decision makers with information frequently and promptly.

provides more complete information than simply reporting a net amount.

7. An accrued expense refers to costs incurred in a period that are both unpaid and unrecorded prior to adjusting entries. One example is salaries earned by employees but not yet paid at the end of a period.

8. An unearned revenue arises when cash (or other assets) is received from a customer before the services and prod-

In terms of problem material, Larson/Jensen still sets the standard for quantity and quality of end-of-chapter question material. Over 150 new questions have been added, and even more have been modified and updated.

There is an excellent variety of assignment material from which to choose and enough questions to assign supplemental extra questions to students who may need the extra practice.

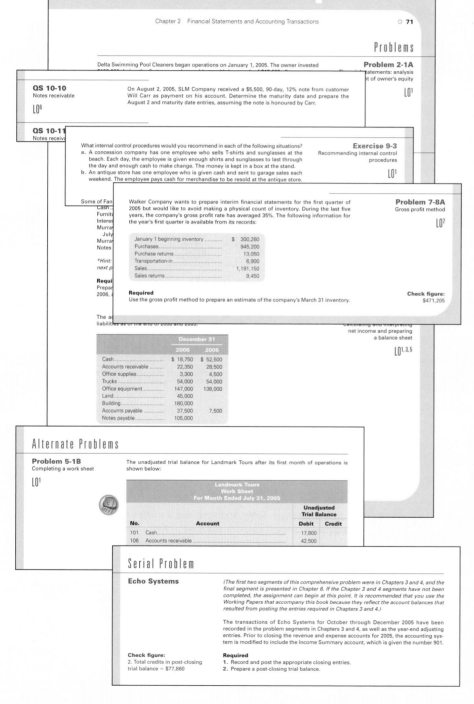

Chapter 2   Financial Statements and Accounting Transactions   ○ **71**

Problems

Delta Swimming Pool Cleaners began operations on January 1, 2005. The owner invested

Problem 2-1A
Financial statements: analysis
of owner's equity
LO¹

QS 10-10
Notes receivable
LO⁶

On August 2, 2005, SLM Company received a $5,500, 90-day, 12% note from customer Will Carr as payment on his account. Determine the maturity date and prepare the August 2 and maturity date entries, assuming the note is honoured by Carr.

QS 10-11
Notes receivable

What internal control procedures would you recommend in each of the following situations?
a. A concession company has one employee who sells T-shirts and sunglasses at the beach. Each day, the employee is given enough shirts and sunglasses to last through the day and enough cash to make change. The money is kept in a box at the stand.
b. An antique store has one employee who is given cash and sent to garage sales each weekend. The employee pays cash for merchandise to be resold at the antique store.

Exercise 9-3
Recommending internal control
procedures
LO¹

Some of Fan...
Cash ...
Furnit...
Interes...
Murray...
July...
Murray...
Notes ...

Hint:
next p...

Requi...
Prepar...
2006, ...

Walker Company wants to prepare interim financial statements for the first quarter of 2005 but would like to avoid making a physical count of inventory. During the last five years, the company's gross profit rate has averaged 35%. The following information for the year's first quarter is available from its records:

January 1 beginning inventory	$ 300,260
Purchases	945,200
Purchase returns	13,050
Transportation-in	6,900
Sales	1,191,150
Sales returns	9,450

Required
Use the gross profit method to prepare an estimate of the company's March 31 inventory.

Problem 7-8A
Gross profit method
LO⁷

Check figure:
$471,205

The a...
liabilities as of the end of 2006 and 2005.

Calculating and interpreting
net income and preparing
a balance sheet
LO¹,³,⁵

	December 31	
	2006	**2005**
Cash	$ 18,750	$ 52,500
Accounts receivable	22,350	28,500
Office supplies	3,300	4,500
Trucks	54,000	54,000
Office equipment	147,000	138,000
Land	45,000	
Building	180,000	
Accounts payable	37,500	7,500
Notes payable	105,000	

Alternate Problems

Problem 5-1B
Completing a work sheet
LO¹

The unadjusted trial balance for Landmark Tours after its first month of operations is shown below:

	Landmark Tours		
	Work Sheet		
	For Month Ended July 31, 2005		
		Unadjusted Trial Balance	
No.	**Account**	**Debit**	**Credit**
101	Cash	17,800	
106	Accounts receivable	42,500	

Serial Problem

Echo Systems

(The first two segments of this comprehensive problem were in Chapters 3 and 4, and the final segment is presented in Chapter 6. If the Chapter 3 and 4 segments have not been completed, the assignment can begin at this point. It is recommended that you use the Working Papers that accompany this book because they reflect the account balances that resulted from posting the entries required in Chapters 3 and 4.)

The transactions of Echo Systems for October through December 2005 have been recorded in the problem segments in Chapters 3 and 4, as well as the year-end adjusting entries. Prior to closing the revenue and expense accounts for 2005, the accounting system is modified to include the Income Summary account, which is given the number 901.

Check figure:
2. Total credits in post-closing
trial balance = $77,860

Required
1. Record and post the appropriate closing entries.
2. Prepare a post-closing trial balance.

Confidence-Building Problem Material

Starting with the basic concepts, Larson/Jensen move students through Questions and Quick Study material that cover definitions and concepts. Once these are completed, Exercises focus on practice of single concepts, thus preparing the way for the multi-concept Problems. Tied to the Learning Objectives and with Check Figures available, students have the resources they need to stay on track and stay motivated to finish assignments.

In keeping with the growing exposure of technology in accounting and the classroom, we have updated and expanded the Excel® templates. Questions with these templates are indicated with a marginal icon.

Alongside the new end-of-chapter material are perennial favourites— updated or re-written to reflect the changing scope of accounting as well as the changing needs of our learners.

THE ACCOUNTING STANDARD

What you said—what we did

In focus groups, via emails, on the telephone and in your reviews, you have told us what you want—and we listened. In all, we received feedback from over 150 faculty members—representing tens of thousands of students! Students gave suggestions, too, and you have all been heard! Here are some examples.

> *I know that sole proprietorship is the way most instructors teach at this level, but I would like my students to have exposure to both sole proprietorship and Corporations.... I would like to see more information on corporations along with problems at the end of the earlier chapters.*

You said it— we did it.

With the Corporate Supplement, faculty now have the option of covering sole proprietorships or corporations, or they can integrate both. In addition to presenting the methodology of both types, we have added to and enriched the problem material in each supplement. Corporate supplements for chapters 2, 3, and 5 are available at no extra cost to students on the Larson Online Learning Centre.

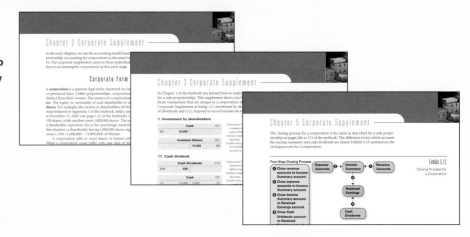

> *A problem we have in the industry is the number of names you can have for the same thing. I know that the basic idea is that the students may see other names later in other courses, but do we really need so many names for things at this level? I'd rather they were left out.*

This comment was often heard in both focus groups and reviews. In the Eleventh Canadian Edition, there are countless situations throughout the book where we deleted or added words and sentences to improve readability.

> *Things are presented in an orderly fashion. Some textbooks use a scatter-gun approach, and you cover one topic about three or four times in the book. That is not the case here. The topic is brought up, dealt with, and then on to the next topic; it's clean.*

What you said—what we did

In light of current business events and the criticisms of the accounting profession, it may be appropriate to include a greater discussion of ethics along with Web sites or quotes from the specific codes of conduct of individual professional accounting associations.

Excerpts from the codes of ethics and professional conduct were moved from an appendix at the end of the textbook to Chapter 1. In an effort to place greater emphasis on ethics, Canadian examples of unethical practices were also added to Chapter 1 as well as the addition of "Ethics Challenge" problems to the end-of-chapter material.

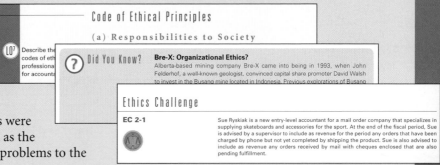

The thing that I really like about the Ethics questions is that I can finally have a class discussion. So much of accounting is black and white. Ethics is more shades of grey.

… The current treatment (of perpetual and periodic) makes it difficult to teach Periodic Inventory.…

I want my students to have more exposure to the periodic inventory method than your text offers.… We need more problems and more detail.

To better satisfy those reviewers wanting to use the periodic system, we expanded the appendix in Chapter 6 to include a mid-chapter and end-of-chapter demonstration problem plus increased the amount of problem material beyond what was added in the Tenth Canadian Edition.

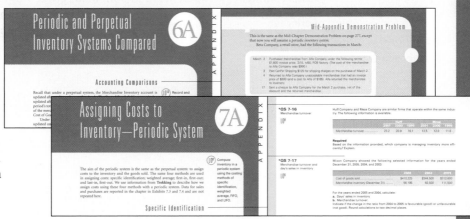

THE ACCOUNTING STANDARD

The Accounting Standard

We listened! In addition to obtaining individual reviewer comments, we held focus groups in cities throughout Canada to hear the issues and concerns instructors like you have about the materials you use to teach introductory financial accounting. Tilly Jensen attended every session to listen and ask questions. We received excellent feedback, and she has integrated the benefit of your comments and experience into the Eleventh Canadian Edition. We were the first textbook to go to these lengths for market research, and we do more every year. We think you'll like what you see.

Throughout the Textbook

In every chapter, the text has been carefully considered and reworded to achieve maximum readability. The end-of-chapter material has been fine-tuned and tightened, and overall we have added over 150 new end-of-chapter entries.

Chapter 12

New chapter opening vignette

Chapter updated for changes in *CICA Handbook* regarding Capital Assets and Goodwill

Chapter 13

New chapter opening vignette

Payroll chapter added to OLC for those who teach it in Volume 2

Numerous wording changes and exhibit enhancements

Chapter 14

Exhibits 14.4, 14.6, and 14.7 changed from 50/50 sharing of remainder to an unequal amount

Streamlined section on withdrawal of a partner

Linked liquidation calculation to journal entries

Chapter 15

Motivation for preferred shares moved from middle to beginning of chapter

Real-world examples updated

Numerous wording changes

Chapter 16

Section on accounting changes improved

Chapter 17

Streamlined

Exhibits 17.10, 17.11, 17.16, 17.17, 17.19, and 17.20 shortened to simplify

Chapter 18

Examples updated

Content streamlined

Chapter 19

New chapter opening vignette

Indirect method moved to appendix

More than 10 new preparation of cash flow statement problems

Chapter 20

New style of ratio problems added

Appendix I—Financial Statements

ClubLink replaced with Leon's

WestJet statements have been updated

Appendix II—Chart of Accounts

Was Appendix III

Technology Solutions To Meet Your Every Need

In North America alone, over 200,000 post-secondary educators use the Internet in their respective courses. Some are just getting started, while others are eager to embrace the very latest advances in educational Content-Delivery and Course Management.

That's why McGraw-Hill Ryerson supports instructors and students alike with the most complete range of digital solutions. Your students can use our complete Online Learning Centre (OLC), access Mobile Resources and Premium Content areas, or work with assessment solutions such as GradeSummit and Lyryx/LIFA.

In addition to an Instructor's CD-ROM, faculty have access to nearly every supplement online. These assets range from the Instructor's Resource Manual and Microsoft® PowerPoint® slides, to the powerful supplements integration guide and a range of course-management systems, including PageOut, McGraw-Hill's proprietary system.

McGraw-Hill has always set the standard as a leader in bringing helpful technology into the classroom. With Larson/Jensen, your class gets all the benefits of the digital age without any set-up issues or confusion.

> *Larson has a very strong technological advantage in that it integrates several computer applications, such as Excel spreadsheets, LIFA software, etc. This is becoming an important issue as more courses are converted to on-line learning, hybrid format and laptop environments.*

LYRYX LEARNING INC
Online Learning and Assessment
lyryx.com

www.blackboard.com

Create a custom course Website with **PageOut**, free with every McGraw-Hill Ryerson textbook.

To learn more, contact your McGraw-Hill Ryerson publisher's representative or visit www.mhhe.com/solutions

courses · campus · community

THE ACCOUNTING STANDARD

Online Learning Centre

The Larson/Jensen Online Learning Centre holds a wealth of resources unmatched in educational publishing. With valuable study tools, fingertip availability of teaching aids, and a little fun to help the learning process, the Online Learning Centre for *Fundamental Accounting Principles* has resources for every teaching and learning style.

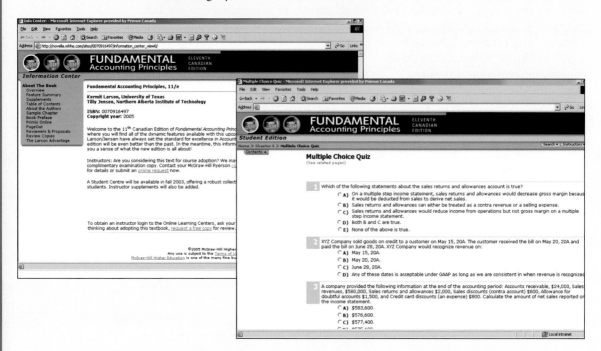

Students have more research and practice opportunities than ever before, with

- Extend Your Knowledge links for further study,
- practice quizzes,
- searchable glossary,
- and even a crossword puzzle to practice the key terms for each chapter.

As usual, instructors will have all supplements available online (with the exception of the test bank), as well as a digital repository of selected exhibits and tables.

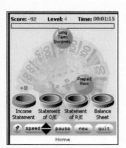

New to the Eleventh Canadian Edition, Larson/Jensen now offers the Online Learning Advantage: a fully integrated, premium Web site featuring

- mobile versions of almost all OLC content, sized to fit a laptop or PDA
- **TetrAccounting**, the accounting videogame
- interactive journal entries and trial balance tutorials
- animated conceptual objects that visually reinforce textbook material
- PowerWeb and PowerWeb-to-Go: the latest news and worldwide developments—right at your fingertips!

I think that the Online Learning Centre is a great study tool for reviewing the concepts presented in the textbook. Doing the true/false, multiple-choice, and fill-in-the-blank questions have helped me to grasp all the concepts from the text.

GradeSummit

GradeSummit is a self-assessment, diagnostic service that helps students make the most efficient use of their study time. This Internet service provides a variety of ways for students to analyze what they know and what they don't. GradeSummit reveals subject strengths and weaknesses, and provides feedback and direction, which enables students to focus their study time on those areas.

My students are giving rave reviews about GradeSummit. One student in particular attributes his rise in grades from a D to a B to GradeSummit!

The ability to create automatically graded, multiple-choice quizzes provides a vehicle to you, the instructor, to make accountable homework assignments.

GradeSummit's diagnostic reports yield valuable data about student understanding of the course material.

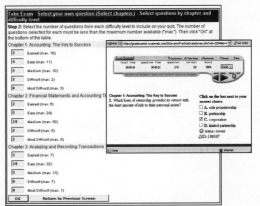

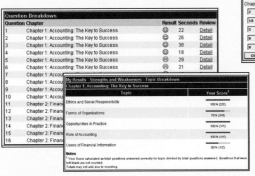

Before I had GradeSummit, I re-read and studied the entire chapter before taking exams. With GradeSummit information …I now focus on areas where I'm not already strong. It has helped me do better.

With as little as one hour per term, you can create graded homework assignments, use a variety of reporting features, download homework scores to use with your existing grade book, and know you've given your students a service they will thank you for. Try it today at www.gradesummit.com, or for more information contact us at info@gradesummit.com.

GradeSummit was easy to navigate with straightforward instructions. It helped me focus my studies and concentrate on questions I had most difficulties with, resulting in higher grades.

THE ACCOUNTING STANDARD

LYRYX LEARNING INC
Online Learning and Assessment
lyryx.com

Teaching/learning technology at its best ... LIFA!

> *"LIFA is an excellent tool and it has greatly helped my learning. More courses should have similar programs."*
>
> —*Student feedback from the LIFA pilot*

LIFA—Lyryx Interactive Financial Accounting is a Web-based teaching/learning tool that has captured the attention of post-secondary institutions across the country. Offering significant benefits not only to the student but *also* to the instructor, LIFA has instant appeal because it parallels the classroom environment.

Each chapter is broken down into several Lessons, condensed versions of the material in the textbook.

Each Lesson is supported by a self-correcting Exploration that allows the student to practice the concept just learned in the Lesson. Because Explorations are algorithmically generated, the student can try them as many times as they like and always get a different question on the same topic.

Once the student has mastered the Exploration, an instructor can set a homework assignment called a Lab. Algorithmically generated and automatically graded, students get instant grades and feedback—no need to wait until the next class to find out how well you did!

Grades are instantly recorded in a grade book that the student can view. Instructors can view the grades of all students, which means less time spent marking, but with the pedagogical advantages of marked assignments—a dream come true!

Students are motivated to do their LIFA *Labs* for two reasons: first, because it can be **tied to assessment**, and second, because they can try the *Lab* as many times as they wish prior to the due date with only their best grade being recorded. Instructors know from experience that if students are doing their accounting homework, they will be successful in the course. Recent research regarding the use of LIFA has shown that when *Labs* are tied to assessment, even if worth only a small percentage of the total grade for the course, **students WILL do their homework—and MORE THAN ONCE!!**

> *"I found that by doing these labs was pretty much the only way I learned."*

Mobile Learning

The businesses and companies of today want their new employees to be adept in all aspects of the changing business environment. They are quick to tell us they want graduates with the skills of tomorrow . . . today. From laptops to cell phones to PDAs, the new medium is mobility.

As a leader in technology and innovation, McGraw-Hill Ryerson has developed material providing students with optimum flexibility for use anytime, anywhere they need to study—whether with a laptop, PDA or tablet. These innovations provide instructors with a number of exciting ways to integrate technology into the learning process.

We have integrated several wireless activities as a part of our Online Learning Centre. Now, whether you are waiting in line, riding on transit, or just filling some spare time, homework and practice are just a click away. **Study to Go** allows you to access quizzes from your PDA, and **PowerWeb to Go** provides a link to our research library from anywhere!

Interactive Journal Entries These problems can be assigned as homework on the go or just for practice.

TetrAccounting Practice your Debits and Credits, and your financial statements in an exciting, interactive videogame: you score points, gain levels, and improve your accounting knowledge. Who said accounting couldn't be fun?!

Streaming Video Download informative, education interviews with experts from the field. Watch them in your spare time.

Using such innovations as wireless communication, Personal Digital Assistants (PDAs), digital content from textbooks, and more, we are providing a dynamic learning environment and laying the framework for more exploration into the fusion of education and technology.

THE ACCOUNTING STANDARD

For the Student

Working Papers

Updated for the Eleventh Canadian Edition, these volumes match end-of-chapter assignment material. They include papers that can be used to solve all of the Quick Studies, Exercises, and Problems. Each chapter contains papers for both the A-Problems and the B-Problems.

Study Guide

An essential study aid for students, the Study Guide volumes review the Learning Objectives and the summaries, outline the chapter, and provide a variety of practice problems and solutions.

Student Solutions Manual

This manual provides the solutions to the odd-numbered exercises and problems in the text.

Excel® Templates (SPATS)

Selected end-of-chapter exercises and problems, marked in the text with an icon, can be solved using these Microsoft® Excel® templates, located on the Online Learning Centre.

GradeSummit

Take your grades to the next level. One of the premier academic practice and assessment tools available anywhere, GradeSummit provides you with thousands of practice questions and targeting assessment. You find out what you know and what you need to practice. Contact your bookstore for more details, or go directly to www.GradeSummit.com and try a sample chapter.

New Lyryx: LIFA

LYRYX LEARNING INC
Online Learning and Assessment
lyryx.com

Lyryx Interactive Financial Accounting (LIFA) is a Web-based teaching/learning tool that has captured the attention of post-secondary institutions across the country. Offering significant benefits not only to the student but *also* to the instructor, LIFA has instant appeal because it parallels the classroom environment. More than just questions and problems, LIFA mixes interactive tutorials with problems and labs that guide you through each step of the accounting process. Algorithmically generated and automatically graded, you get feedback tutoring on the spot. Plus, the problems and practice material are always new, so you can practice as much as you need to—with out ever repeating the same question. Try it out at http://lifa.lyryx.com (guest username: **student1** guest password: **student1**).

PowerWeb and PowerWeb-to-Go

POWERWEB

Bombardier, Enron, Nortel, or Air Canada—for both successes and scandals, PowerWeb keeps you on top of the ever-changing world of accounting and business news and events. Continuously updated, PowerWeb is a rich, dynamic source of what is happening right now, all over the world. Visit www.dushkin.com/powerweb for more details.

Practice Sets

Need something that brings the whole picture together? McGraw-Hill Ryerson publishes a number of dynamic and useful practice sets to help students practice any number of scenarios over the course of several weeks of study. For more information on these and other accounting resources, visit www.mcgrawhill.ca/college/accounting.

For the Instructor

Instructor's Resource CD-ROM (ICD)

This CD-ROM contains materials for managing an active learning environment. In addition to the core supplements below, the ICD includes a Lecture Outline, a chart linking Learning Objectives to end-of-chapter material, and transparency masters. For instructors' convenience, student copies of these visuals are provided in the Study Guide. If students do not acquire the Study Guide, adopters are permitted to duplicate these visuals for distribution.

Solutions Manual

Larson/Jensen sets the standard in quality control: six different instructors technically checked the Solutions Manuals at three different stages of development. The manuals contain solutions for all text questions, exercises, and problems.

Test Bank and Computerized Testbank

The Test Bank has been revamped and expanded to reflect the changes of the text, and to improve the quality of this core supplement. A significant number of the questions are new in the Eleventh Canadian Edition. Volumes 1 and 2 are available in both hard copy, and a computerized version is available for all three volumes. Grouped according to Learning Objectives, the Test Bank contains a wide variety of questions—including true/false, multiple choice, matching, short essay, quantitative problems, and completion problems of varying levels of difficulty.

PowerPoint® Presentation Slides

The Microsoft® PowerPoint® Presentation slides have been re-developed in their entirety to better illustrate chapter concepts. This package is available on the Instructor CD or as a download from the OLC.

Supplements Integrator

New

This pioneering instructional resource from McGraw-Hill Ryerson is your road map to all the other elements of your text's support package. Keyed to the chapters and topics of your McGraw-Hill Ryerson textbook, the integrator ties together all of the elements in your resource package, guiding you to where you'll find corresponding coverage in each of the related support package components!

Transition Guides

New

Moving to a new textbook or edition is that much easier with the Larson/Jensen Advantage. New to the Eleventh Canadian Edition are transition guides that make it easy to adapt your notes and assignments to this new edition.

Exhibits Database

New

A number of the text exhibits have been saved in an easy to use JPG format so you can use them when creating classroom presentations and reference materials. These images are available on both the Instructor's CD-ROM and the Online Learning Centre.

Course Management

For faculty requiring online content, Larson/Jensen is available in three of the most popular delivery platforms: WebCT, Blackboard, and Desire2Learn. These platforms are designed for instructors who want complete control over course content and how it is presented to students. This format provides instructors with more user-friendly and highly flexible teaching tools that enhance interaction between students and faculty. In addition, PageOut, McGraw-Hill's proprietary course-management system, is available free to all adopters.

SUPERIOR SERVICE

Superior Service

Service takes on a whole new meaning with McGraw-Hill Ryerson and Larson/Jensen. More than just bringing you the textbook, we have consistently raised the bar in terms of innovation and educational research—both in accounting and in education in general. These investments in learning and the education community have helped us to understand the needs of students and educators across the country, and allowed us to foster the growth of truly innovative, integrated learning.

Integrated Learning

Your Integrated Learning Sales Specialist is a McGraw-Hill Ryerson representative who has the experience, product knowledge, training, and support to help you assess and integrate any of our products, technology, and services into your course for optimum teaching and learning performance. Whether it's using our test bank software, helping your students improve their grades, or putting your entire course online, your *i*-Learning Sales Specialist is there to help you do it. Contact your local *i*-Learning Sales Specialist today to learn how to maximize all of McGraw-Hill Ryerson's resources!

i-Learning Services Program

McGraw-Hill Ryerson offers a unique *i*Services package designed for Canadian faculty. Our mission is to equip providers of higher education with superior tools and resources required for excellence in teaching. For additional information, visit www.mcgrawhill.ca/highereducation/eservices.

Teaching, Technology & Learning Conference Series

The educational environment has changed tremendously in recent years, and McGraw-Hill Ryerson continues to be committed to helping you acquire the skills you need to succeed in this new milieu. Our innovative Teaching, Technology & Learning Conference Series brings faculty together from across Canada with 3M Teaching Excellence award winners to share teaching and learning best practices in a collaborative and stimulating environment. Pre-conference workshops on general topics, such as teaching large classes and technology integration, will also be offered.

We will also work with you at your own institution to customize workshops that best suit the needs of your faculty at your institution. These include our **Teaching Excellence** and **Accounting Innovation** symposium series.

Research Reports into Mobile Learning and Student Success

These landmark reports, undertaken in conjunction with academic and private-sector advisory boards, are the result of research studies into the challenges professors face in helping students succeed and the opportunities that new technology presents to impact teaching and learning.

Reviewers

The unprecedented review process and success of this revision of Larson/Jensen is the result of an ongoing process that has gone beyond the scope of a single edition. In the Tenth Canadian Edition, we went to instructors and students from across Canada, and their feedback launched the rigorous research and investigative process that made this edition what it is.

Eleventh Edition Reviewers

Cecile Ashman	*Algonquin College*	Geraldine Joosse	*Lethbridge Community College*
Les Barnhouse	*Athabasca University*	Barbara Jordan	*Cambrian College*
Keith Barrett	*Humber College*	Jane Kaake-Nemeth	*Durham College*
Maria Belanger	*Algonquin College*	Dave Kennedy	*Lethbridge Community College*
Gary Biggs	*Grant MacEwan College*	Val Kinnear	*Mount Royal College*
Mark Binder	*Red River College*	Laurette Korman	*Kwantlen University College*
Dave Bopara	*Toronto School of Business*	Rafik Kurji	*Mount Royal College*
Rick Boyack	*Southern Alberta Institute of Technology*	Douglas Leatherdale	*Georgian College*
		Michael Lee	*Humber College*
Walt Burton	*Okanagan University College*	Cynthia Lone	*Red River College*
Cheryl Christoff	*Toronto School of Business*	Marie Madill-Payne	*George Brown College*
Alice Cleveland	*Nova Scotia Community College*	Michael Malkoun	*St. Clair College*
Louise Connors	*Nova Scotia Community College*	Patricia Margeson	*New Brunswick Community College*
Joan Conrod	*Dalhousie University*		
Suzanne Coombs	*Kwantlen University College*	Bonnie Martel	*Niagara College*
William Cormier	*St Francis Xavier University*	Dani Moss	*Durham College*
John Currie	*Humber College*	Jan Nyholdt	*Southern Alberta Institute of Technology*
John Daye	*New Brunswick Community College*		
		Penny Parker	*Fanshawe College*
Randy Dickson	*Red Deer Community College*	Clifton Philpott	*Kwantlen University College*
Chaman Doma	*Centennial College*	Joe Pidutti	*Durham College*
Carolyn Doni	*Cambrian College*	Sharon Ramstad	*Grant MacEwan College*
Dave Eliason	*Southern Alberta Institute of Technology*	Traven Reed	*Canadore College*
		Clara Reid	*Lethbridge Community College*
Sheila Elworthy	*Camosun College*	Doug Ringrose	*Grant MacEwan College*
Albert Ferris	*University of Prince Edward Island*	David Sale	*Kwantlen University College*
		Giuseppina Salvaggio	*Dawson College*
David Fleming	*George Brown College*	Michael Sirtonski	*Assiniboine College*
Amanda Flint	*Trinity Western University*	Melbourne Sparks	*Lambton College*
Jeremy Frape	*Humber College*	Greg Streich	*DeVry Institute of Technology (Calgary)*
Henry Funk	*Red River College*		
Jack Halliday	*Northern Alberta Institute of Technology*	Selina Tang	*Douglas College*
		Marie Templeton	*Southern Alberta Institute of Technology*
Ern Harley	*Sheridan Institute of Technology and Advanced Learning*		
		John Varga	*George Brown College*
Elizabeth Hicks	*Douglas College*	John Vermeer	*Humber College*
Michael Hockenstein	*Vanier College*	Jeannine Wall	*Red River College*
Sue Hogan	*Capilano College*	Brenda Warner	*Conestoga College*
Pat Humphreys	*Medicine Hat College*	Dennis Wilson	*Centennial College*
Stephanie Ibach	*Northern Alberta Institute of Technology*	Richard Wright	*Fanshawe College*
		Brian Zwicker	*Grant MacEwan College*
Connie Johl	*Douglas College*		

Capital Assets and Goodwill

Cameco

The Canadian Mining and Energy Company became Cameco in 1988, as a result of the merger of a provincial Crown Corporation, Saskatchewan Mining Development Corporation, and a federal Crown Corporation, Eldorado Nuclear Limited. With its head office in Saskatoon, Saskatchewan, Cameco is not only the world's largest producer of uranium but also tops the list in terms of being the world's principal supplier of combined uranium and conversion services—showing revenues of $748 million for the year ended December 31, 2002. Cameco's uranium products are used to generate emissions-free electricity in nuclear power plants around the world, including in Ontario's Bruce Power nuclear facility. In addition to having controlling ownership of the largest high-grade uranium reserves in the world (located at McArthur River and Cigar Lake in northern Saskatchewan), the company has uranium mining operations in the U.S., uranium processing/conversion operations in Ontario, and is operator and one-third owner of a mid-sized gold mine in Kyrgyzstan, Central Asia.

Mining operations require significant investments in capital assets. As at December 31, 2002, Cameco's balance sheet showed $2 billion of property, plant, and equipment after accumulated amortization of $1.2 billion. Amortization expense, calculated primarily using the units-of-production method, totalled $112 million for the year ended December 31, 2002—about 17% of the year's total operating expenses. Additions to property, plant, and equipment during 2002 were $90 million, with sales of capital assets of $0.1 million.

Cameco's operations involve sensitive environmental matters that require special accounting issues such as the treatment of decommissioning and reclamation costs (the costs to wind down mine operations once all reserves are depleted plus costs to restore the mine site to its original state). The challenging job of maintaining the accounting records related to Cameco's capital assets is charged to three capital accountants. These individuals are responsible for ensuring that the accounting information regarding all aspects of the capital assets is current and accurate … not a small task considering that Cameco's capital assets represent more than 67% of its total assets.

www.cameco.com

Learning Objectives

LO¹ Describe capital assets and issues in accounting for them.

LO² Apply the cost principle to calculate the cost of capital assets.

LO³ Explain, record, and calculate amortization using the methods of straight-line, units-of-production, and double-declining-balance.

LO⁴ Explain and calculate amortization for partial years.

LO⁵ Explain and calculate revised amortization.

LO⁶ Account for asset disposal through discarding, selling, or exchanging an asset.

LO⁷ Account for natural resources and their amortization.

LO⁸ Account for intangible capital assets and their amortization.

LO⁹ Account for goodwill.

*APPENDIX 12A

*LO¹⁰ Explain and account for exchanging dissimilar and similar assets.

Chapter Preview

This chapter focuses on long-term assets used in the operation of a company: *capital assets* and *goodwill*.[1] Recall from Chapter 5 that property, plant, and equipment and intangible assets other than goodwill are referred to collectively as *capital assets*.[2] Capital assets represent a major investment for most companies and make up a large portion of assets on the balance sheet. They also affect the income statement because their costs are charged to amortization expense, often one of the largest expenses on the income statement. This chapter will describe the purchase and use of these assets. We also explain what distinguishes capital assets from other types of assets, how to determine their cost, how to allocate their costs to periods benefiting from their use, and how to record their disposal.

Capital Assets

 Describe capital assets and issues in accounting for them.

Capital assets are assets used in the operations of a company and have a useful life of more than one accounting period. Capital assets are divided into two groups:

1. Tangible capital assets known as property, plant, and equipment[3] and

2. Intangible capital assets (which excludes goodwill).[4]

Property, plant, and equipment (PPE), sometimes referred to as **fixed assets**, includes land, buildings, equipment, machinery, leasehold improvements, and natural resources. For instance, WestJet's $605,124,000 of capital assets as at December 31, 2002, includes aircraft, property and equipment, buildings, leasehold improvements, and other capital assets as detailed in Note 2 of the financial statements located in Appendix I at the end of the text. **Intangible assets** lack physical substance and include patents, copyrights, leaseholds, and trademarks. Goodwill is also an intangible asset but it is shown on the balance sheet separately from capital assets.

For many companies, capital assets make up the single largest asset category on the balance sheet. For example, on its February 1, 2003, balance sheet, Reitmans (Canada) Limited shows total assets of $419,570,000 with capital assets comprising $159,044,000 of this amount. TransCanada Pipelines Limited showed $17,496 million of property, plant, and equipment at December 31, 2002, representing 88% of total assets. The Hudson's Bay Company uses the term *fixed assets* on its January 31, 2003, balance sheet to describe its $1,205,333,000 of property, plant, and equipment; total assets on this date were $4,275,687,000.

Capital assets are set apart from other assets by two important features:

Extend Your Knowledge

12-1

> **1.** *They are used in business operations to help generate revenue.* This makes them different from *inventory*, for instance, which is an asset that is *not used* in operations but rather held for the purpose of resale. A company that purchases a computer for the purpose of selling it reports the computer on the balance sheet as inventory. But if the same company purchases this computer for use in operations, it is classified as a capital asset.

---

[1] Section 3060 of the *CICA Handbook*, "Capital Assets," was superseded (displaced) effective December 31, 2002.
[2] *CICA Handbook*, Section 3061, "Property, Plant and Equipment," par. .04.
[3] *CICA Handbook*, Section 3061, "Property, Plant and Equipment."
[4] *CICA Handbook*, Section 3062, "Goodwill and Other Intangible Assets."

> **2.** *Capital assets have useful lives extending over more than one accounting period.* This makes capital assets different from *current assets* such as *supplies* that are usually consumed soon after they are placed in use. The cost of current assets is assigned to a single period when they are used.

Accounting for capital assets reflects these two important features. We must measure capital assets (balance sheet focus) and match their cost to periods benefiting from their use (income statement focus).

Exhibit 12.1 shows the three main accounting issues with capital assets. They are:

> **1.** Calculating and accounting for the initial and subsequent costs of capital assets
> **2.** Allocating the costs of capital assets against revenues for the periods they benefit
> **3.** Recording the disposal of capital assets.

This chapter focuses on the decisions and factors surrounding these three important issues.

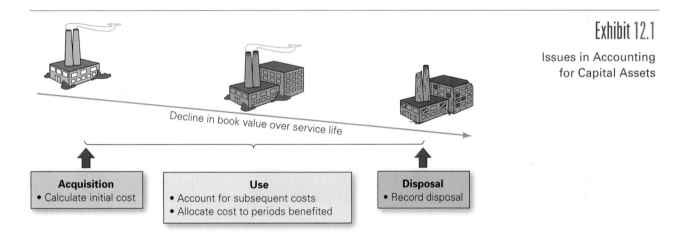

Exhibit 12.1

Issues in Accounting for Capital Assets

Decline in book value over service life

Acquisition	Use	Disposal
• Calculate initial cost	• Account for subsequent costs • Allocate cost to periods benefited	• Record disposal

Cost of Capital Assets

Consistent with the *cost principle* P.41, capital assets are recorded at **cost**, which includes all normal and reasonable expenditures necessary to get the asset in place and ready for its intended use.[5] The cost of a factory machine, for instance, includes its invoice price, less any cash discount for early payment, plus freight, unpacking, assembling costs, and non-refundable sales taxes (PST). The cost of a capital asset also includes the necessary costs of installing and testing a machine before placing it in use. Examples are the costs of building a base or foundation for a machine, of providing electrical hook-ups, and of adjusting the machine before using it in operations. These are all examples of *capital expenditures.*

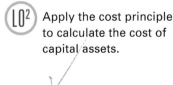

LO2 Apply the cost principle to calculate the cost of capital assets.

---

[5] *CICA Handbook*, Section 3061, "Property, plant and equipment," par. .05.

Capital expenditures are costs of capital assets that provide material benefits extending beyond the current period. They are debited to capital asset accounts and reported on the balance sheet.

When expenditures regarding capital assets are *not* considered a normal part of getting the asset ready for its intended use, they are charged to another account. For example, if a machine is damaged during unpacking, the **repairs** are recorded as an expense. Also, a traffic fine paid for moving heavy machinery on city streets without a proper permit is an expense and *not* part of the machinery's cost. These are **revenue expenditures**: costs that maintain an asset but do not materially increase the asset's life or productive capabilities. They are recorded as expenses and deducted from revenues in the current period's income statement. Consistent with this rule, Air Canada reports:

> Maintenance and repair costs are charged to operating expenses as incurred. Significant modification costs are capitalized and amortized over the remaining service lives of the assets.
>
> **SOURCE:** Air Canada

Subsequent Expenditures

When a capital asset is acquired and put into service, additional or *subsequent* expenditures often are incurred after the acquisition to operate, maintain, repair, and improve it. In recording these subsequent expenditures, we must decide whether they are to be accounted for as a *capital* or *revenue* expenditure. Exhibit 12.2 can be used to determine if a subsequent expenditure is capital or revenue in nature. Subsequent expenditures that would be capitalized or debited to the related capital asset account are sometimes referred to as **betterments**. Examples include roofing replacement, plant expansion, and major overhauls of machinery and equipment. Examples of subsequent expenditures that would be classified as

Exhibit 12.2

Is It a Capital or Revenue Expenditure?

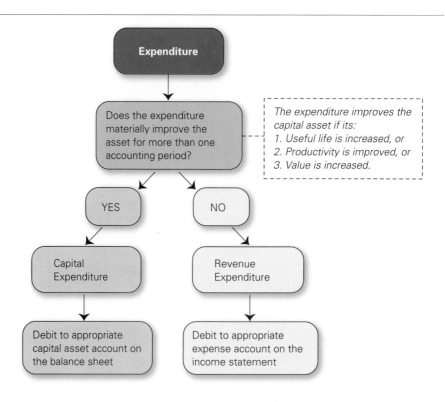

revenue expenditures and recorded as an expense on the income statement are supplies, fuel, lubricants and electric power. For example, the installation of a new battery in a car is a revenue expenditure and is recorded as an expense. Revenue expenditures like the purchase of the battery do not materially improve the capital asset but rather *maintain* it, keeping it in good working order over its estimated useful life. However, putting a new engine in a car *is* an improvement because the useful life of the car is extended. Therefore, the new engine is recorded as a capital expenditure. A betterment does not always increase an asset's useful life. An example is replacing manual controls on a machine with automatic controls to reduce labour costs. This machine will still wear out just as fast as it would with manual controls but because the automatic controls improve the machine's efficiency in terms of labour cost savings, it is a capital expenditure.

Financial statements P. 34 are affected for several years as a result of the choice between recording costs as revenue expenditures or as capital expenditures. Therefore, managers must be careful when classifying costs.

Capital Asset Subledger

For accounts payable and accounts receivable, we discussed and illustrated the benefits in maintaining both a control account in the General Ledger and a corresponding subledger. In the case of accounts receivable, the subledger recorded the detailed transactions by customer. Many companies also keep a subledger for capital assets. The Capital Asset Subledger details information such as cost, salvage value, estimated useful life, date of purchase, amortization P. 143, serial number, and other relevant data for each capital asset or group of capital assets. This information is useful in recording amortization but is also a valuable form of internal control P. 12 over capital assets. The subledger can be used to verify recorded capital assets against a physical count.

Low Cost Asset Purchases

Maintaining individual capital asset records can be expensive, even in the most advanced system. For that reason, many companies do not keep detailed records for assets costing less than some minimum amount such as $100. Instead, these low cost capital assets are treated as revenue expenditures. This means their costs are directly charged to an expense account at the time of purchase. This practice is acceptable under the *materiality principle* P. 347. Treating immaterial capital expenditures as revenue expenditures is unlikely to mislead users of financial statements. As an example, in a recent annual report Coca-Cola disclosed that it only capitalizes *major* or material betterments:

> Additions and major replacements or betterments are added to the assets at cost. Maintenance and repair costs and minor replacements are charged to expense when incurred.
>
> SOURCE: Coca-Cola

Mechanic

You are a mechanic who recently opened your own auto service centre. Because of a cash shortage, you are preparing financial statements in the hope of getting a short-term loan from the bank. A friend of yours suggests that you treat as many expenses as possible like a capital expenditure. What are the effects on financial statements of treating expenses as capital expenditures? What do you think of your friend's proposal?

Judgement Call

Answer—p. 639

1. What is included in the cost of a capital asset?

2. Explain the difference between revenue expenditures and capital expenditures and how they are recorded.

3. What is a betterment? How is a betterment recorded?

In the remainder of this section we explain how to determine the capital costs for each of five types of tangible capital assets: land (property), land improvements, buildings (plant), leasehold improvements, and machinery and equipment. Natural resources, also a tangible capital asset, are discussed in a separate section.

Land

When land is purchased for a building site, its cost includes the total amount paid for the land, including any real estate commissions, fees for insuring the title, legal fees, and any accrued property taxes paid by the purchaser. Payments for surveying, clearing, grading, draining, and landscaping[6] are also included in the cost of land. Other costs of land include assessments by the local government, whether incurred at the time of purchase or later, for items such as roadways, sewers, and sidewalks. These assessments are included because they permanently add to the land's value.

Land purchased as a building site sometimes includes a building or other obstructions that must be removed. In such cases, the total purchase price is charged to the Land account along with the cost of removing the building, less any amounts recovered through sale of salvaged materials. To illustrate, assume a company bought land for a retail store for $170,000. This land contains an old service garage that is removed at a net cost of $15,000 ($20,000 in costs less $5,000 proceeds from salvaged materials). Additional closing costs totalled $10,000, and consisted of brokerage fees ($8,000), legal fees ($1,500), and title costs ($500). The cost of this land is $195,000, calculated as:

Net cash price of land	$ 170,000
Net cost of garage removal	15,000
Closing costs	10,000
Cost of Land	**$195,000**

Land Improvements

Because land has an unlimited life and is not consumed when used, it is not subject to amortization. But **land improvements** such as parking lot surfaces, driveways, fences, and lighting systems have limited useful lives. While these costs increase the usefulness of the land, they are charged to a separate capital asset account called Land Improvements so their costs can be allocated to the periods they benefit.

Buildings

A Building account is charged for the costs of purchasing or constructing a building when it is used in operations. When purchased, the costs of a building usually

---

[6] Landscaping is included in the cost of land if it is considered permanent in nature. Landscaping costs with a finite life of greater than one accounting period are included in Land Improvements.

include its purchase price, brokerage fees, taxes, title fees, and legal costs. Its costs also include all expenditures to make it ready for its intended use, such as repairs or renovations that include wiring, lighting, flooring, and wall coverings.

When a building, or any capital asset, is constructed by a company for its own use, its cost includes materials and labour plus a reasonable amount of amortization on machinery, heat, lighting, and power used to construct the asset. Cost of construction also includes design fees, building permits, and insurance during construction. But insurance costs for coverage *after* the asset is placed in use are an operating expense.

Leasehold Improvements

Property is rented under a contract called a **lease**. The property's owner grants the lease and is called the **lessor**. The one who secures the right to possess and use the property is called the **lessee**. Long-term leases sometimes require the lessee to pay for alterations or improvements to the leased property—such as partitions, painting, and storefronts—called **leasehold improvements**. Leasehold improvements become part of the property and revert to the lessor at the end of the lease. These costs are debited to a *Leasehold Improvements* account and amortized over the life of the lease or the life of the improvements, whichever is shorter. In its notes to the financial statements found in Appendix I of the text, WestJet reports leasehold improvements at December 31, 2002, of $4,514,000, at cost, amortized using the straight-line method over the term of the lease.

Machinery and Equipment

The cost of machinery and equipment consists of all costs normal and necessary to purchase it and prepare it for its intended use. It includes the purchase price, less discounts, plus non-refundable sales taxes, transportation charges, insurance while in transit, and the installing, assembling, and testing of machinery and equipment.

Lump-Sum Asset Purchase

A **lump-sum purchase**, also called a **basket purchase**, is the purchase of capital assets in a group with a single transaction for a lump-sum price. When this occurs, we allocate the cost of the purchase among the different types of assets acquired based on their *relative market values*. Their market values P. 144 can be estimated by appraisal or by using the tax-assessed valuations of the assets. To illustrate, Cola Company paid $90,000 cash to acquire land appraised at $30,000, land improvements appraised at $10,000, and a building appraised at $60,000. The $90,000 cost was allocated on the basis of appraised values as shown in Exhibit 12.3:

	Appraised Value	Percent of Total	Apportioned Cost
Land...................................	$ 30,000	30% ($30,000/$100,000)	**$27,000** ($90,000 × 30%)
Land improvements..........	10,000	10 ($10,000/$100,000)	**9,000** ($90,000 × 10%)
Building............................	60,000	60 ($60,000/$100,000)	**54,000** ($90,000 × 60%)
Totals................................	$100,000	100%	**$90,000**

Exhibit 12.3

Calculating Costs in a Lump-Sum Purchase

Flashback

Answers—p. 640

4. Identify the account charged for each of the following expenditures: (a) purchase price of a vacant lot, (b) cost of paving that vacant lot.

5. What amount is recorded as the cost of a new machine given the following items related to its purchase: gross purchase price, $700,000; sales tax, $49,000; purchase discount taken, $21,000; freight to move machine to plant, $3,500; assembly costs, $3,000; cost of foundation for machine, $2,500; cost of spare parts used in maintaining the machine, $4,200?

Amortization

LO³ Explain, record, and calculate amortization using the methods of straight-line, units-of-production, and double-declining-balance.

Because capital assets (except for land) wear out or decline in usefulness as they are used, an expense must be recorded. **Amortization**[7] is the process of matching (or allocating) the cost of the capital asset over the time that the asset is used. The cost of capital assets should be amortized over their useful lives in a rational and systematic manner.[8]

To illustrate, assume a delivery van is purchased for $40,000 on January 1, 2005. It is estimated that the van will help generate $30,000 in revenues each year for four years. At the end of the four-year period, it is estimated that the van will be worthless. We could record the $40,000 as an expense in the year it was purchased as illustrated in Exhibit 12.4. However, income is distorted because we have not matched the expense of the delivery van over the four years that it is creating revenue. The treatment in Exhibit 12.4 is therefore not in conformance with GAAP.

Exhibit 12.4

Cost of the Delivery Van Recorded as an Expense in Year of Purchase

	2005	2006	2007	2008
Revenues	$30,000	$30,000	$30,000	$30,000
Expense	40,000	-0-	-0-	-0-
Income (Loss)	($10,000)	$30,000	$30,000	$30,000

Estimated four-year life of the delivery van.

If instead we apply the matching principle and allocate the cost of the delivery van against the periods it generates revenue, we achieve a more accurate reflection of performance across time, as Exhibit 12.5 illustrates.

Exhibit 12.5

Cost of the Delivery Van Matched Against Revenues Generated Over Its Four-Year Useful Life

	2005	2006	2007	2008
Revenues	$30,000	$30,000	$30,000	$30,000
Expense	10,000*	10,000*	10,000*	10,000*
Income (Loss)	$20,000	$20,000	$20,000	$20,000

Estimated four-year life of the delivery van.

*$40,000 ÷ 4 years = $10,000 per year.

---

[7] In many countries, such as the United States, the term **depreciation** is used to describe the allocation of the cost of a tangible asset over its useful life; *amortization* is used to describe the allocation of the cost of an intangible asset; and **depletion** is used to describe the allocation of the cost of a natural resource over its useful life.

[8] *CICA Handbook*, Section 3061, "Property, plant and equipment," par. .28.

This allocation of the delivery van's cost is *amortization*.

Note that amortization is a process of cost allocation, not asset valuation. *Amortization does not measure the decline in the van's market value each period.* Nor does it measure the physical deterioration of the van. Amortization is a process of allocating a capital asset's cost to expense over its useful life, nothing more. Because amortization reflects the cost of using a capital asset, we do not begin recording amortization charges until the asset is actually put into use. The next sections describe the reporting of amortization, the factors in calculating amortization, the amortization methods used, amortization for partial periods, and revisions in amortization.

Reporting Amortization on Assets

Both the cost and accumulated amortization of capital assets are reported on the balance sheet. Alcan reports the following on its December 31, 2002, balance sheet:

(in millions of US $)	2002	2001
Property, plant and equipment, net (Note 14)		
Cost (excluding construction work in progress)	$17,798	$16,225
Construction work in progress	573	613
Less: Accumulated amortization	8,138	7,136
	$10,233	$ 9,702

Many companies show capital assets on one line at the net amount of cost less *accumulated amortization.* When this is done, the amount of accumulated amortization P.144 is disclosed in a footnote. WestJet, whose annual report is found in Appendix I to the text, reports only the net amount of its property and equipment in its balance sheet. To satisfy the *full disclosure principle*[9] P.358, WestJet also describes its amortization methods in Note 1(h) and the net book values of individual capital assets in Note 2.

Flint Energy Services Ltd., for instance, reported the following in Note 5 of its December 31, 2002, balance sheet:

5. Property, Plant and Equipment

December 31, 2002	Cost	Accumulated Amortization	Net Book Value
Land	$ 8,863	$ –0–	$ 8,863
Buildings and improvements	39,642	6,373	33,269
Construction and automotive equipment	187,899	64,450	123,449
Office furniture and equipment	20,590	4,820	15,770
	$256,994	$75,643	$181,351

Reporting both the cost and accumulated amortization of capital assets helps balance sheet readers compare the assets of different companies. For example, a company holding assets costing $50,000 and accumulated amortization of $40,000 is likely in a different situation than a company with new assets costing $10,000. The **book value** (original cost of the capital asset less its accumulated amortization) is the same in both cases, but the first company may have more productive capacity available and likely is facing the need to replace older assets.

---

[9] *CICA Handbook*, Section 3061, "Property, plant and equipment," par. .38.

We emphasize that amortization is a process of cost allocation. Capital assets are reported on a balance sheet at their book values, not at market values. This emphasis on costs rather than market values is based on the *going concern principle* P.41. This principle states that, unless there is evidence to the contrary, we assume that a company will continue in business. This implies that capital assets are held and used long enough to recover their cost through the sale of products and services. Market values of capital assets are not reported in the financial statements since capital assets are not intended to be sold until they are no longer useful. Instead, assets are reported on a balance sheet at cost less accumulated amortization. This is the remaining portion of the cost that is expected to benefit future periods.

Factors in Calculating Amortization

Three factors are relevant in determining amortization. They are:

1. Cost,
2. Salvage value, and
3. Useful life.

1. Cost

The *cost* of a capital asset, as described earlier in this chapter, consists of all necessary and reasonable expenditures to acquire it and to prepare the asset for its intended use.

2. Salvage Value

Salvage value, also called *residual value* or *scrap value*, is an estimate of the amount we expect to receive from selling the asset or trading it in at the end of its useful life or benefit period. The total amount of amortization to be expensed over an asset's benefit period equals the asset's cost minus its estimated salvage value. For example, the cost and estimated salvage value of the delivery van in Exhibit 12.5 were $40,000 and $0 respectively. Therefore, the total amount of amortization to be expensed over the van's useful life is $40,000 (= $40,000 − $0). If we expect an asset to be traded in on a new asset, its salvage value is the expected trade-in value.

3. Useful (Service) Life

The **useful life** of an asset is the length of time it is productively used in a company's operations. Useful life, also called **service life**, is not necessarily as long as the asset's total productive life. As an example, the productive life of a computer may be four years. Yet some companies trade in old computers for new ones every two years. In this case, these computers have a two-year useful life. This means the cost of these computers (less their expected trade-in value) is charged to amortization expense over a two-year period.

Several variables often make the useful life of an asset hard to predict, such as wear and tear from use in operations, *inadequacy*, and *obsolescence*. When a company grows more rapidly than expected, its assets sometimes do not meet the company's productive demands. **Inadequacy** refers to the condition where the capacity of a company's capital assets is too small to meet the company's productive demands. **Obsolescence** refers to a condition where, because of new inventions and improvements, a capital asset is no longer useful in producing goods or services with a competitive advantage. A company usually disposes of an obsolete asset before it wears out. Obsolescence, like inadequacy, is hard to predict.

To predict the useful life of a new asset, a company uses its past experience or, when it has no experience with a type of asset, it relies on the experience of others or on engineering studies and judgement. In Note 1 of its 2002 annual report, Call-Net Enterprises Inc. reported that amortization is calculated on a straight-line basis based on the following useful lives:

Multiplex and telephone switch equipment................	10 years
Fibre optic cable	20 years
Computer equipment and software...........................	3 years
Buildings	15 to 40 years
Leasehold improvements	Term of the lease
Furniture and fixtures	5 years

Did You Know? ?

The life expectancy of capital assets is often in the eye of the beholder. Take Imperial Oil and Suncor Energy, for instance. Both compete in the oil industry, yet their refineries' life expectancies are quite different. Imperial amortizes its refineries over 25 years, but Suncor amortizes its refineries over an average of 32 years. Such differences can dramatically impact their financial statement numbers.

Amortization Methods

There are many *amortization methods* for allocating a capital asset's cost over the accounting periods in its useful life. We explain three methods in this section:

1. Straight-line, the most frequently used method of amortization,
2. Units-of-production, and
3. Double-declining-balance, an accelerated method.

The calculations in this section use information from an athletic shoe manufacturer. In particular, we look at equipment used for inspecting shoes before packaging. This equipment is used by manufacturers such as Beta, Converse, Reebok, Adidas, and L.A. Gear, and its data for amortization are shown in Exhibit 12.6.

Straight-Line Method

Straight-line amortization P.144 charges the same amount to expense for each period of the asset's useful life. A two-step process is used to calculate expense.

Exhibit 12.6

Data for Shoe-Inspection Equipment

Cost...	$10,000
Estimated salvage value...........................	1,000
Cost to be amortized.................................	$ 9,000
Estimated useful life:	
Accounting periods..............................	5 years
Units inspected....................................	36,000 shoes

1. First calculate the *cost to be amortized* over the asset's life by subtracting the asset's salvage value from its total cost.
2. Second, divide the cost to be amortized by the asset's useful life.

Total cost to be amortized
= Cost − Salvage

The formula and calculation for straight-line amortization of the inspection equipment just described is shown in Exhibit 12.7.

Exhibit 12.7

Straight-Line Amortization Formula

$$\frac{\text{Cost} - \text{Estimated salvage value}}{\text{Estimated useful life in years}} = \frac{\$10{,}000 - \$1{,}000}{5\ \text{years}} = \$1{,}800\ \text{per year}$$

If this equipment is purchased on January 1, 2005, and used throughout its predicted useful life of five years, the straight-line method allocates an equal amount of amortization to each of the years 2005 through 2009. We make the following adjusting entry P.141 at the end of each of these five years to record straight-line amortization of this equipment:

Dec. 31	Amortization Expense......................................	1,800	
	Accumulated Amortization, Equipment....		1,800
	To record annual amortization over its five-year useful life.		

The $1,800 Amortization Expense appears on the income statement among operating expenses. This entry credits Accumulated Amortization, a contra account P.144 to the Equipment account in the balance sheet.

The net balance sheet amounts are the asset's book values for each of those years and are calculated as the asset's original cost less its accumulated amortization. At the end of year two, its book value is $6,400 and is reported in the capital asset section of the balance sheet as shown in Exhibit 12.8:

$$\text{Book value} = \text{Cost} - \text{Accumulated amortization}$$

Exhibit 12.8

Balance Sheet Presentation After Two Years of Amortization

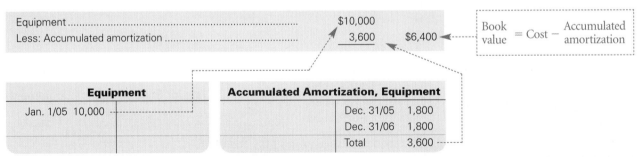

Instead of listing the cost less accumulated amortization, many balance sheets show capital assets *net* of accumulated amortization. The *net* means *after* accumulated amortization has been subtracted from the cost of the asset. Recall that cost less accumulated amortization is *book value*. Exhibit 12.9 shows this alternative form of presentation for the equipment of Exhibit 12.8 (cost of $10,000 less accumulated amortization of $3,600).

Exhibit 12.9

Alternative Balance Sheet Presentation

Equipment (net)... $6,400

The graphs in Exhibit 12.10 show: (1) why this method is called straight-line amortization, and (2) the decline in book value by $1,800 amortization each year.

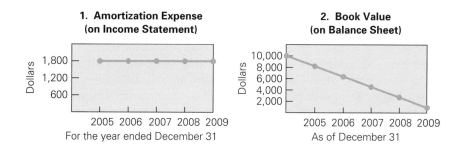

Exhibit 12.10

Financial Statement Effects of Straight-Line Amortization

The straight-line amortization *rate* is calculated as 100% divided by the number of periods in the asset's useful life. In the case of our inspection equipment, this rate is 20% (100% ÷ 5 years). We use this rate and other information on the equipment to calculate the machine's *straight-line amortization schedule* shown in Exhibit 12.11.

| | Amortization for the Period | | | End of Period | |
Period	Cost to be Amortized	Amortization Rate	Amortization Expense	Accumulated Amortization	Book Value
	—	—	—	—	10,000*
2005	$9,000**	20%	**$1,800**	$1,800	8,200
2006	9,000	20	**1,800**	3,600	6,400
2007	9,000	20	**1,800**	5,400	4,600
2008	9,000	20	**1,800**	7,200	2,800
2009	9,000	20	**1,800**	9,000	**1,000**

Exhibit 12.11

Straight-Line Amortization Schedule

 * Cost on January 1, 2005
** $10,000 − $1,000

Note three items in this schedule:

1. Amortization expense is the same each period.
2. Accumulated amortization is the sum of current and prior periods' amortization expense.
3. Book value declines each period until it equals salvage value at the end of its useful life.

Straight-line is by far the most frequently applied amortization method in financial reporting. Bombardier, for instance, in each year's annual report, discloses that it uses this method of amortization:

Amortization is computed under the straight-line method over the...estimated useful lives.

SOURCE: Bombardier

Units-of-Production Method

If capital assets are used about the same amount in each accounting period, the straight-line method produces a reasonable matching of expenses with revenues. Yet the use of some capital assets varies greatly from one accounting period to the next. A builder, for instance, may use a piece of construction equipment for a month and then not use it again for several months.

When use of equipment varies from period to period, the units-of-production amortization method can provide a better matching of expenses with revenues than straight-line amortization. **Units-of-production amortization** charges a varying amount to expense for each period of an asset's useful life depending on its usage.

A two-step process is used to calculate units-of-production amortization:

1. Calculate the amortization per unit by subtracting the asset's salvage value from its total cost, and then dividing by the total number of units expected to be produced during its useful life. Units of production can be expressed in units of product or in any other unit of measure such as hours used or kilometres driven. This gives us the amount of amortization per unit of service provided by the asset.
2. Calculate amortization expense for the period by multiplying the units used in the period by the amortization per unit.

Exhibit 12.12 shows the formula and calculation for units-of-production amortization for the inspection equipment described in Exhibit 12.6 (assume 7,000 shoes inspected in 2005).

Exhibit 12.12

Units-of-Production
Amortization Formula

Step 1:

$$\text{Amortization per unit} = \frac{\text{Cost} - \text{Estimated salvage value}}{\text{Total estimated units of production}} = \frac{\$10,000 - \$1,000}{36,000 \text{ units}}$$

$$= \$0.25 \text{ per shoe}$$

Step 2:

Amortization expense =	Amortization per unit	×	Units used in period	
	0.25 per shoe	×	7,000 shoes	= **$1,750**

Using the production estimates for the equipment, we calculate the *units-of-production amortization schedule* shown in Exhibit 12.13. If the equipment inspects 7,000 shoes in 2005, its first year, amortization for 2005 is $1,750 (7,000 shoes at $0.25 per shoe). If the equipment inspects 8,000 shoes in 2006, amortization for 2006 is 8,000 shoes times $0.25 per shoe, or $2,000.

| | Amortization for the Period | | | End of Period | |
Period	Number of Units	Amortization per Unit	Amortization Expense	Accumulated Amortization	Book Value
	—	—	—	—	$10,000*
2005	7,000	$0.25	**$1,750**	$1,750	8,250
2006	8,000	0.25	**2,000**	3,750	6,250
2007	9,000	0.25	**2,250**	6,000	4,000
2008	7,000	0.25	**1,750**	7,750	2,250
2009	6,000**	0.25	**1,250***	9,000	**1,000**

Exhibit 12.13

Units-of-Production
Amortization Schedule

* Cost on January 1, 2005

** 6,000 units were actually inspected, but the maximum number of units on which amortization can be calculated in 2009 is 5,000 [36,000 total estimated units less 31,000 units amortized to date (7,000 + 8,000 + 9,000 + 7,000)]. Recall that an asset must not be amortized below its salvage value.

*** 5,000 × 0.25 = 1,250

Note that amortization expense depends on unit output, that accumulated amortization is the sum of current and prior periods' amortization expense, and book value declines each period until it equals salvage value at the end of the asset's useful life.

The units-of-production amortization method is not as frequently applied as straight-line. Suncor Energy Inc. uses units-of-production and reported in its December 31, 2002, annual report:

> Acquisition costs of proved properties are depleted using the unit-of-production method based on proved reserves.
>
> SOURCE: Suncor Energy Inc.

Declining-Balance Method

An **accelerated amortization method** yields larger amortization expenses in the early years of an asset's life and smaller charges in later years. While several accelerated methods are used in financial reporting, the most common is the **declining-balance method** of amortization, which uses an amortization rate of up to twice the straight-line rate and applies it to the asset's beginning-of-period book value. Because book value *declines* each period, the amount of amortization also declines each period.

The **double-declining-balance method** (DDB) is applied in two steps:[10]

1. Calculate the double-declining-balance rate (= 2 ÷ Estimated years of useful life), and
2. Calculate amortization expense by multiplying the rate to the asset's beginning-of-period book value.

Note that salvage value is not used in these calculations.

---

[10] The double-declining-balance method is also described as being *twice the straight-line rate* because it can be alternatively applied as follows to get the same results:
1. Calculate the asset's straight-line amortization rate (100% ÷ Estimated useful life in years),
2. Double it, and
3. Calculate amortization expense by multiplying this rate to the asset's beginning-of-period book value.

Returning to the shoe inspection equipment, we can apply the double-declining-balance method to calculate its amortization expense. Exhibit 12.14 shows this formula and its first-year calculation for the inspection equipment. The abbreviated two-step process is:

1. 2 divided by the estimated useful life of 5 years to get a declining-balance rate of 0.40 or 40% per year, and

2. Calculate annual amortization expense as the declining-balance rate multiplied by the book value at the beginning of each period (see Exhibit 12.15).

Exhibit 12.14

Double-Declining-Balance Amortization Formula

Maximum accumulated amortization*
= Cost − Salvage
OR
(another way to describe the same thing)
Minimum book value*
= Salvage value
**regardless of method*

Step 1:
Double-declining-balance rate = 2 ÷ Estimated useful life = 2 ÷ 5 years = 0.40 or 40%

Step 2:
Amortization expense = Double-declining-balance rate × Beginning period book value
= 40% × \$10,000 = **\$4,000**

The *double-declining-balance amortization schedule* is shown in Exhibit 12.15. The schedule follows the formula except in the year 2009, when amortization expense is \$296. The \$296 is calculated by subtracting the \$1,000 salvage value from the \$1,296 book value at the beginning of the fifth year. This is done because an asset is never amortized below its salvage value. If we had used the \$518.40 (40% × \$1,296) for amortization expense in 2009, then ending book value would equal \$777.60, which is less than the \$1,000 salvage value.

Exhibit 12.15

Double-Declining-Balance Amortization Schedule

| | Amortization for the Period | | | End of Period | |
| | Beginning-of-Period Book Value | Amortization Rate | Amortization Expense | Accumulated Amortization | Book Value |
Period					
	—	—	—	—	10,000*
2005	\$10,000	40%	**\$4,000**	\$4,000	6,000
2006	6,000	40	**2,400**	6,400	3,600
2007	3,600	40	**1,440**	7,840	2,160
2008	2,160	40	**864**	8,704	1,296
2009	1,296	40	**296****	9,000**	**1,000**

* Cost on January 1, 2005
** Year 2009 amortization is \$1,296 − \$1,000 = \$296. This is because maximum accumulated amortization equals cost minus salvage (or book value cannot be less than salvage value).

Comparing Amortization Methods

Exhibit 12.16 shows amortization expense for the shoe inspection equipment under each of the three amortization methods.

Exhibit 12.16

Amortization Methods Compared

Period	Straight-Line	Units-of-Production	Double-Declining-Balance
2005	\$ 1,800	\$ 1,750	\$ 4,000
2006	1,800	2,000	2,400
2007	1,800	2,250	1,440
2008	1,800	1,750	864
2009	1,800	1,250	296
	\$9,000	**\$9,000**	**\$9,000**

While the amount of amortization expense per period is different for different methods, *total* amortization expense is the same ($9,000) for the machine's useful life. Each method starts with a total cost of $10,000 and ends with a salvage value of $1,000. The difference is the *pattern* in amortization expense over the useful life. This pattern is graphically represented in Exhibit 12.17. The book value of the asset when using straight-line is always greater than book value from using double-declining-balance, except at the beginning and end of an asset's useful life. Also, the straight-line method yields a steady pattern of amortization expense, while units-of-production does not because it depends on the number of units produced. But all of these methods are acceptable as they allocate cost in a rational and systematic manner.[11]

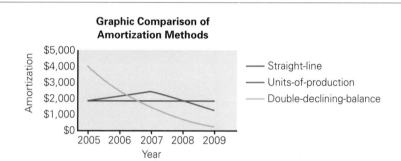

Graphic Comparison of Amortization Methods

— Straight-line
— Units-of-production
— Double-declining-balance

Exhibit 12.17

Graphic Comparison of Amortization Methods

6. On January 1, 2005, a company pays $77,000 to purchase office furniture with a salvage value of zero. The furniture's useful life is somewhere between 7 and 10 years. What is the 2005 straight-line amortization on the furniture using: (a) a 7-year useful life, and (b) a 10-year useful life?

7. What is the meaning of the term *amortization* in accounting?

8. A company purchases a new machine for $96,000 on January 1, 2005. Its predicted useful life is five years or 100,000 units of product, and its salvage value is $8,000. During 2005, 10,000 units of product are produced. Calculate the book value of this machine on December 31, 2005, assuming: (a) straight-line amortization, and (b) units-of-production amortization.

Flashback

Answers—p. 640

Amortization for Tax Reporting

The rules a company follows for financial accounting P.10 purposes are usually different from the rules it follows for tax accounting purposes. Financial accounting aims to report useful information on financial performance and position, whereas tax accounting reflects government objectives in raising revenues. Differences between these two accounting systems are normal and expected. Amortization is a common example of one of the differences.

The *Income Tax Act* requires that companies use a declining-balance method for calculating the maximum *capital cost allowance* that may be claimed in any period. **Capital cost allowance (CCA)** is the term used to describe amortization for tax purposes. CCA reduces taxable income in the early years of an asset's life because amortization is greatest in the early years. The company's goal here is to postpone its tax payments. The *Income Tax Act* permits the use of CCA to encourage capital investment. The money a company saves in taxes in the early years

---

[11] Ibid.

means a company has the resources to earn additional profit. The *Income Tax Act* specifies the rates for various groups of assets. For example, a rate of 20% would be used for general machinery and equipment, and a rate of 4% for most buildings. Provincial Acts are also involved in setting capital cost allowances as a means of encouraging investment in various provincial jurisdictions. Further discussion of the details of tax accounting for capital assets is deferred to a more advanced course.

Partial-Year Amortization

LO⁴ Explain and calculate amortization for partial years.

Assets are purchased and disposed of at various times during a period. When an asset is purchased (or disposed of) at a time other than the beginning or end of an accounting period, amortization is recorded for part of a year. This is to make sure that the year of purchase or the year of disposal is charged with its share of the asset's amortization. There are different ways to account for the amortization for partial years. We are going to look at two methods:

> 1. Nearest whole month, and
> 2. Half-year rule.

Nearest Whole Month

When calculating amortization for partial years to the nearest whole month, amortization for a month is calculated if the asset was in use for more than half of that month. To illustrate, let's return to the shoe inspection equipment. Assume this equipment is purchased and placed in service on April 8, 2005, and the annual accounting period ends on December 31. This equipment costs $10,000, has a useful life of five years, and a salvage value of $1,000. Because this equipment is purchased and used for more than half of April plus all of May through December in 2005, the amount of amortization reported is based on nine months (if the purchase date had been April 28, the amortization would have been calculated for eight months since the asset was not in use for more than half of April). Amortization is not calculated by taking into account specific days of use because this would imply that amortization is precise, when in fact it is based on estimates of the useful life and salvage values. Using straight-line amortization, we calculate nine months' amortization of $1,350 as follows:

$$\frac{\text{Cost} - \text{Estimated salvage value}}{\text{Estimated useful life in years}} = \frac{\text{Amortization}}{\text{per year}} \times \frac{\text{Fraction}}{\text{of year}} \qquad \frac{\$10,000 - \$1,000}{5 \text{ years}} = \$1,800/\text{year} \times \frac{9}{12} = \mathbf{\$1,350}$$

A similar calculation is necessary when disposal of an asset occurs during a year. As an example, let's suppose the equipment described above is sold on June 4, 2009. Amortization for 2009 is recorded for the period January 1 through June 4, or five months. Because the asset was held for less than half of June, amortization is not calculated for June. This partial year's amortization, calculated to the nearest whole month, is:

$$\frac{\$10,000 - \$1,000}{5 \text{ years}} = \$1,800/\text{year} \times \frac{5}{12} = \mathbf{\$750}$$

Exhibit 12.18 demonstrates the calculations for partial years' amortization to the nearest month for the units-of-production and double-declining-balance methods. *Notice that the amortization expense calculation for units-of-production is not affected by the partial year.* This is because the units-of-production method is a function of use, not of time.

Date of Purchase	Units-of-Production	Double-Declining-Balance
April 8, 2005	$\dfrac{\$10{,}000 - \$1{,}000}{36{,}000 \text{ units}}$ $= \$0.25/\text{unit} \times 7{,}000 \text{ units} = \textbf{\$1,750}$	Rate $= \dfrac{2}{5} = 0.40$ or 40% $40\% \times \$10{,}000$ $= \$4{,}000/\text{year} \times \dfrac{9}{12} = \textbf{\$3,000}$

Exhibit 12.18

Partial Year's Amortization Calculated to Nearest Month Under the Units-of-Production and Double-Declining-Balance Methods

Half-Year Rule

For companies that have a large number of capital asset expenditures year after year, tracking when individual assets were put into use and then calculating amortization to the nearest month can be a costly process. Because this kind of accuracy would not necessarily increase the usefulness of information related to amortization, the *materiality principle* P.347 allows us the flexibility to use a method more appropriate for the situation, such as the *half-year rule*.[12] When calculating amortization for partial years using the **half-year rule**, six months' amortization is recorded for the partial period regardless of when during the period the asset was acquired or disposed of. Exhibit 12.19 illustrates the application of the half-year rule assuming the shoe inspection equipment was purchased and put into use on April 8, 2005.

Exhibit 12.19

Partial Year's Amortization Calculated Using the Half-Year Rule Under the Straight-Line, Units-of-Production, and Double-Declining-Balance Methods

Date of Purchase	Straight-Line	Units-of-Production	Double-Declining-Balance
April 8, 2005	$\dfrac{\$10{,}000 - \$1{,}000}{5 \text{ years}}$ $= \$1{,}800/\text{year} \times \dfrac{6}{12} = \textbf{\$900}$	$\dfrac{\$10{,}000 - \$1{,}000}{36{,}000 \text{ units}}$ $= \$0.25/\text{unit} \times 7{,}000 \text{ units} = \textbf{\$1,750}$	Rate $= \dfrac{2}{5} = 0.40$ or 40% $40\% \times \$10{,}000$ $= \$4{,}000/\text{year} \times \dfrac{6}{12} = \textbf{\$2,000}$

Notice again that the calculation of units-of-production is not affected by partial years.

Revising Amortization Rates

Amortization is based on the original cost of an asset, estimated salvage value, and estimated useful life. If the cost of the asset changes because of a betterment or if the estimates for salvage value and/or useful life are adjusted, *revised amortization* for current and future periods must be calculated.

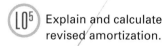 Explain and calculate revised amortization.

---

[12] The half-year rule is used for tax purposes to calculate CCA in the first year of the asset's life.

Revising Amortization Rates When There is a Change in the Estimated Salvage Value and/or Estimated Useful Life

Because amortization is based on predictions of salvage value and useful life, amortization expense is an estimate. If our estimate of an asset's useful life and/or salvage value changes, we use the new estimate(s) to calculate **revised amortization** for current and future periods. This means we revise the amortization expense calculation by spreading the cost that has not yet been amortized over the remaining useful life. This approach is used for all amortization methods.

Let's return to our shoe inspection equipment using straight-line amortization. At the beginning of this asset's third year, its book value is $6,400, calculated as:

Cost..	$10,000
Less: Two years' accumulated amortization........	3,600
Book value...	$ 6,400

At the beginning of its third year, the predicted number of years remaining in its useful life changes from three to four years and its estimate of salvage value changes from $1,000 to $400. Amortization for each of the equipment's four remaining years is calculated as shown in Exhibit 12.20.

Exhibit 12.20

Calculating Revised Amortization Rates

$$\frac{\text{Remaining book value} - \text{Revised salvage value}}{\text{Revised remaining useful life}} = \frac{\$6,400 - \$400}{4 \text{ years}} = \textbf{\$1,500 per year}$$

This means $1,500 of amortization expense is recorded for the equipment at the end of the third through sixth years of its remaining useful life.

Since this asset was amortized at the rate of $1,800 per year for the first two years, it is tempting to conclude that amortization expense was overstated in these first two years. But these expenses reflected the best information available at that time.

Revising estimates of the useful life or salvage value of an asset is referred to as a **change in an accounting estimate**. A change in an accounting estimate results from "the exercise of judgement and reappraisal as new events occur, as more experience is acquired, or as additional information is obtained."[13] A change in an accounting estimate is given prospective treatment. This means that it is reflected in current and future financial statements, and not in prior statements.[14]

Revising Amortization Rates When There is a Betterment

We also calculate revised amortization if the cost of the asset changes because of a betterment, such as the installation of a new engine. Revised amortization would be calculated from the date of the betterment. Study Part 3 of the Mid-Chapter Demonstration Problem, which illustrates the calculations for this type of situation.

---

[13] *CICA Handbook*, Section 1506, "Accounting Changes," par. .22.
[14] Ibid. par. .25.

9. In early January 2005, a company acquires equipment at a cost of $3,800. The company estimates this equipment to have a useful life of three years and a salvage value of $200. Early in 2007, the company changes its estimate to a total four-year useful life and zero salvage value. Using straight-line amortization, what is amortization expense on this equipment for the year ended 2007?

Flashback
Answer—p. 640

Controller

You are the controller for Fascar Company. Fascar has struggled financially for more than two years, and there are no signs of improvement. Fascar's operations require major investments in equipment, and amortization is a large item in calculating income. Fascar's industry normally requires frequent replacements of equipment, and equipment is typically amortized over three years. Your company's president recently instructed you to revise estimated useful lives of equipment from three to six years and to use a six-year life on all new equipment. You suspect this instruction is motivated by a desire to improve reported income. What actions do you take?

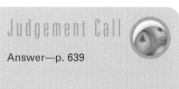

Judgement Call
Answer—p. 639

Mid-Chapter Demonstration Problem

Part 1

Exeter Consulting purchased equipment for cash of $160,000 on September 3, 2005. The estimated life of the equipment is 10 years but due to technological advances, Exeter expects to replace the equipment in five years. The salvage value is estimated to be $40,000. Exeter's year-end is December 31.

Required

Complete a schedule similar to the following for each year of the asset's estimated useful life using the (a) straight-line, and (b) double-declining-balance methods (round calculations to the nearest whole dollar).

	2005	2006	2007	2008	2009	2010
Cost..						
Less: Accumulated amortization.......						
Book value						
Amortization expense						

Part 2

Exeter Consulting purchased a vehicle for $30,000 on August 21, 2005. The company planned to use it for 100,000 kilometres or about three years and then trade it in for $10,000. The actual kilometres driven were:

2005	10,250
2006	33,700
2007	37,980
2008	19,710

Required

Complete a schedule similar to that required in Part 1 using the units-of-production method.

Part 3

On January 4, 2005, Exeter purchased a machine for $48,120 and it was estimated to have a useful life of six years and a salvage value of $15,000. On October 4, 2007, the motor in the machine was replaced at a total cost of $7,685. It was determined that with the new motor, the total useful life of the machine should be revised to eight years and the salvage value would increase by $2,000.

Required

Record amortization expense on the machine for the year ended December 31, 2007.

SOLUTION TO Mid-Chapter Demonstration Problem

Part 1

a. Straight-line

	2005	2006	2007	2008	2009	2010
Cost	160,000	160,000	160,000	160,000	160,000	160,000
Less: Accumulated amortization	8,000[1]	32,000[2]	56,000	80,000	104,000	120,000
Book value	152,000	128,000	104,000	80,000	56,000	40,000
Amortization expense	8,000[1]	24,000[3]	24,000	24,000	24,000	16,000[4]

[1] $(160,000 - 40,000)/5 = 24,000\text{/year} \times \dfrac{4}{12} = 8,000$

[2] $8,000 + 24,000 = 32,000$

[3] $(160,000 - 40,000)/5 = 24,000\text{/year}$

[4] $(160,000 - 40,000)/5 = 24,000\text{/year} \times \dfrac{8}{12} = 16,000$

b. Double-declining-balance

	2005	2006	2007	2008	2009	2010
Cost..	160,000	160,000	160,000	160,000	160,000	160,000
Less: Accumulated amortization.......	21,333	76,800[2]	110,080	120,000	120,000	120,000
Book value	138,667	83,200	49,920	40,000	40,000	40,000
Amortization expense	21,333[1]	55,467[3]	33,280[4]	9,920[5]	-0-	-0-

[1] $40\% \times 160,000 = 64,000 \times \dfrac{4}{12} = 21,333$

[2] $21,333 + 55,467 = 76,800$

[3] $40\% \times 138,667 = 55,467$

[4] $40\% \times 83,200 = 33,280$

[5] $40\% \times 49,920 = 19,968$. However, this exceeds the maximum accumulated amortization allowed of 120,000 (cost less salvage of 160,000 − 40,000). Therefore, the maximum amortization expense is 9,920 (= 120,000 maximum allowable accumulated amortization less 110,080 accumulated amortization to date).

Part 2

	2005	2006	2007	2008
Cost..	30,000	30,000	30,000	30,000
Less: Accumulated amortization.......	2,050	8,790[2]	16,386	20,000
Book value	27,950	21,210	13,614	10,000
Amortization expense	2,050[1]	6,740[3]	7,596[4]	3,614[5]

[1] (30,000 − 10,000)/100,000 = \$0.20/km;
10,250 km × \$0.20/km = \$2,050

[2] \$2,050 + \$6,740 = \$8,790

[3] 33,700 km × \$0.20/km = \$6,740

[4] 37,980 km × \$0.20/km = \$7,596

[5] 19,710 km × \$0.20/km = \$3,942. However, this would exceed the maximum allowed accumulated amortization of \$20,000 (= \$30,000 − \$10,000). Therefore, amortization expense is limited to \$3,614 (= \$20,000 − 16,386).

Part 3

2007			
Dec. 31	Amortization Expense, Equipment	5,265[5]	
	Accumulated Amortization, Equipment....		5,265
	To record revised amortization.		

Calculations:

1. Revised amortization =

$$\dfrac{(48,120 + 7,685) - 15,180^2 - (15,000 + 2,000)}{8 - 2\frac{9}{12} = 5.25 \text{ years}} = 4,500/\text{year} \times \frac{3}{12} = \$1,125 \text{ for Oct. 4/07 to Dec. 31/07}$$

2. Accumulated amortization at October 4, 2007 =
   \$5,520[3] (2005) + \$5,520 (2006) + \$4,140[4] (Jan. 1/07 to Oct. 4/07) = \$15,180

3. (48,120 − 15,000)/6 = 5,520/year

4. $5,520/\text{year} \times \dfrac{9}{12} = 4,140$ for Jan. 1/07 to Oct. 4/07

5.   \$4,140[4]   +   \$1,125[1]   =   \$5,265
      for Jan. 1/07 to Oct. 4/07   for Oct. 4/07 to Dec. 31/07   total for 2007

Disposals of Capital Assets

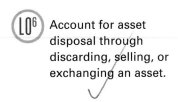

LO⁶ Account for asset disposal through discarding, selling, or exchanging an asset.

Assets are disposed of for several reasons. Many assets eventually wear out or become obsolete. Other assets are sold because of changing business plans. Sometimes an asset is discarded or sold because it is damaged by fire or accident. Regardless of the cause, disposals of capital assets occur in one of three ways: discarding, sale, or exchange. The accounting for disposals of capital assets is described in Exhibit 12.21.

Exhibit 12.21

Accounting for Disposals of Capital Assets

1. Record amortization expense up to the date of disposal. This updates the accumulated amortization account.
2.* Remove the balances of the disposed asset and related accumulated amortization accounts. *Why? If the asset is gone, all accounts related to the asset (the asset account and its related accumulated amortization) must be taken off the books as well.*
3.* Record any cash (and other assets) received or paid in the disposal.
4.* Compare the asset's book value with the net amount received or paid at disposal and record any resulting gain or loss.

*Steps 2, 3, and 4 are recorded in one journal entry.

Discarding Capital Assets

A capital asset is *discarded* when it is no longer useful to the company and it has no market value. To illustrate, assume a machine costing $9,000 with accumulated amortization of $9,000 is discarded on June 5. When accumulated amortization equals the asset's cost, the asset is fully amortized and the entry to record the discarding of this asset is:

June 5	Accumulated Amortization, Machinery.............	9,000	
	Machinery		9,000
	To record the discarding of fully amortized machinery.		

This entry reflects all four steps of Exhibit 12.21. Step 1 is not needed since the machine is fully amortized. Step 2 is shown in the debit to *Accumulated Amortization* and credit to *Machinery*. Since no cash is involved, Step 3 is irrelevant. Since book value is zero and no cash is involved, no gain or loss is recorded in Step 4.

How do we account for discarding an asset that is not fully amortized or whose amortization is not up to date? Consider equipment costing $8,000 with accumulated amortization of $6,000 on December 31, 2005. This equipment is being amortized using the straight-line method over eight years with zero salvage value. On July 1, 2006, it is discarded. Step 1 is to bring amortization expense up to date:

July 1	Amortization Expense, Equipment	500	
	Accumulated Amortization, Equipment....		500
	To record six months' amortization;		
	Jan. 1/06 to July 1/06; $1,000 × $\frac{6}{12}$.		

The July 1 balance in the Accumulated Amortization, Equipment account after posting this entry is:

Accumulated Amortization, Equipment					Acct. No. 168
Date	Explanation	PR	Debit	Credit	Balance
2005 Dec. 31	Balance	✔			6,000
2006 July 1		G8		500	6,500

The second and final entry reflects Steps 2 to 4 of Exhibit 12.21.

2006			
July 1	Accumulated Amortization, Equipment...........	6,500	
	Loss on Disposal of Equipment......................	1,500	
	Equipment...		8,000
	To record the discarding of machinery having a $1,500 book value.		

The loss is calculated by comparing the equipment's book value of $1,500 (= $8,000 − $6,500) with the zero net cash proceeds. The loss on disposal is reported in the *Other Revenues and Expenses* section of the income statement.

Gain (loss) on disposal* = Cash proceeds − Book value

A gain occurs when proceeds are greater than book value; a loss occurs when proceeds are less than book value.

Selling Capital Assets

To illustrate the accounting for selling assets, we consider SportsWorld's April 1, 2006, sale of its delivery equipment costing $16,000 with accumulated amortization of $12,000 on December 31, 2005. Annual amortization on this equipment is $4,000 calculated using straight-line amortization. The entry (Step 1) to record amortization expense and update accumulated amortization to April 1 is:

2006			
April 1	Amortization Expense, Equipment..................	1,000	
	Accumulated Amortization, Equipment....		1,000
	To record three months' amortization;		
	Jan. 1/06 to April 1/06; $4,000 × $\frac{3}{12}$.		

The April 1 balance in the Accumulated Amortization, Equipment account after posting this entry is:

Accumulated Amortization, Equipment					Acct. No. 168
Date	Explanation	PR	Debit	Credit	Balance
2005 Dec. 31	Balance	✔			12,000
2006 Apr. 1		G11		1,000	13,000

The second entry to reflect Steps 2 to 4 of Exhibit 12.21 depends on the amount received in the sale. We consider three different possibilities:

	Sale at Book Value		**Book Value = $16,000 − $13,000 = $3,000** **Sale Above Book Value** **(Cash Proceeds = $7,000)**		**Sale Below Book Value** **(Cash Proceeds = $2,500)**	
2006 Apr. 1	Cash..	3,000	Cash..	7,000	Cash...	2,500
	Accum. Amort., Equip.............	13,000	Accum. Amort., Equip	13,000	Accum. Amort., Equip	13,000
	Equipment	16,000	Gain on Disposal of Equip..	4,000	Loss on Disposal of Equip	500
	To record the sale of		Equipment	16,000	Equipment...........................	16,000
	equipment for $3,000.		*To record the sale of*		*To record the sale of*	
			equipment for $7,000.		*equipment for $2,500.*	

Exchanging Capital Assets

Many assets such as machinery, automobiles, and office equipment are disposed of by exchanging them for new assets. The acquisition of a new asset by exchanging a used asset is called a trade-in. In a typical exchange of capital assets, a trade-in allowance is received on the old asset and the balance is paid in cash. Typically, the exchange is viewed as both a sale of the old asset and a purchase of a new asset. Both the cost and related accumulated amortization of the old asset must be removed from the books. In Canadian practice most exchanges involve gains and losses that are recognized when recording the exchange transactions.[15]

To illustrate, assume that on Jan. 2, 2005, Crandell Company exchanges an automobile for a trailer that has a fair market value of $40,000. The original cost of the automobile was $30,000 and related accumulated amortization was $12,000 up to the date of the exchange, resulting in a book value of $18,000 (= $30,000 − $12,000). Crandell received a trade-in-allowance of $19,000 and paid the balance in cash. The entry to record this transaction is as follows:

2005 Jan. 2	Trailer...	40,000	
	Accumulated Amortization, Automobile	12,000	
	Automobile...		30,000
	Cash		21,000
	Gain on Asset Exchange		1,000
	To record exchange of automobile and *cash for trailer; gain = $19,000 − $18,000.*		

In effect, the $19,000 trade-in allowance is considered to be the sales price of the automobile. The difference between this $19,000 and the $18,000 book value of the automobile is recorded as a $1,000 gain on the exchange.

If the trade-in-allowance is less than the book value of the asset given up, a loss must be recognized on the exchange. For example, if in the previous example the trade-in-allowance had been $16,000 instead of $19,000, the exchange would have been recorded as follows:

2005 Jan. 2	Trailer...	40,000	
	Accumulated Amortization, Automobile	12,000	
	Loss on Asset Exchange	2,000	
	Automobile...		30,000
	Cash		24,000
	To record exchange of automobile and *cash for trailer; loss = $16,000 − $18,000.*		

---

[15] When dealing with the exchange of *similar* assets as discussed in Appendix 12A, gains and losses are not always recognized.

10. A company acquires equipment on January 10, 2005, at a cost of $42,000. Straight-line amortization is used assuming a five-year life and $7,000 salvage value. On June 27, 2006, the company sells this equipment for $32,000. Prepare the entry or entries for June 27, 2006.

11. A company trades an old truck for a new tractor. The original cost of the old truck is $30,000, and its accumulated amortization at the time of the trade is $23,400. The new tractor has a cash price of $45,000. Prepare entries to record the trade under two different assumptions where the company receives: (a) a $3,000 trade-in allowance, or (b) a $7,000 trade-in allowance.

Flashback

Answers—p. 640

Natural Resources

Natural resources are tangible capital assets that are physically consumed when used, and include items such as standing timber, mineral deposits, and oil and gas fields. Because they are consumed when used, they are often called *wasting assets*. The natural state of these assets represents inventories of raw materials that will be converted into a product by cutting, mining, or pumping. But until that conversion takes place, they are non-current assets and reported in a balance sheet using titles such as Timberlands, Mineral deposits, or Oil reserves. These natural resources are reported under capital assets or as a separate category. Suncor Energy Inc. reports its natural resources under the balance sheet title *Capital assets*. In the related note to the financial statements, Suncor reports separate amounts for *Oil Sands* and *Exploration and Production Properties*.

LO7 Account for natural resources and their amortization.

Acquisition Cost and Amortization

Natural resources are initially recorded at cost. Cost includes all expenditures necessary to acquire the resource and prepare it for its intended use. Amortization is the process of allocating the cost of natural resources to periods when they are consumed, known as the resource's *useful life*. Natural resources are reported on the balance sheet at cost less *accumulated amortization*. The amount these assets are amortized each year by cutting, mining, or pumping is usually based on units extracted or depleted. This is similar to units-of-production amortization. Imperial Oil uses this approach to amortize the costs of discovering and operating its oil wells.

To illustrate amortization of natural resources, let's consider a mineral deposit with an estimated 500,000 tonnes of available ore. It is purchased for $500,000 and we expect zero salvage value. The amortization charge is calculated in Exhibit 12.22, assuming 85,000 tonnes of ore are extracted during the period.

Step 1:

$$\text{Amortization per unit} = \frac{\text{Cost} - \text{Salvage value}}{\text{Total units of capacity}} = \frac{\$500,000 - \$\text{-}0\text{-}}{500,000 \text{ tonnes}} = \$1 \text{ per tonne}$$

Step 2:

$$\text{Amortization expense} = \text{Amortization per unit} \times \text{Units extracted in period}$$
$$= \$1 \times 85,000 = \$85,000$$

Exhibit 12.22

Amortization Formula and Calculations

Amortization expense is recorded as:

Dec. 31	Amortization Expense, Mineral Deposit	85,000	
	Accumulated Amortization,		
	Mineral Deposit		85,000
	To record amortization of the		
	mineral deposit.		

The balance sheet at the end of this first year reports the deposit as shown in Exhibit 12.23.

Exhibit 12.23

Balance Sheet Presentation of Natural Resources

Balance Sheet Presentation of Natural Resorces		
Mineral deposit	$500,000	
Less: Accumulated amortization	85,000	$415,000

Because the 85,000 tonnes of mined ore are sold in the year, the entire $85,000 amortization charge is reported on the income statement. But if some of the ore remains unsold at year-end, the amortization cost related to the unsold ore is carried forward on the balance sheet and reported as Unsold Ore Inventory, which is a current asset.

Recall that natural resource assets are tangible capital assets and are therefore shown on the balance sheet as part of property, plant, and equipment.[16] For example, Talisman Energy Inc. shows $10,042 million of property, plant, and equipment on its December 31, 2002, balance sheet. Natural resources represent $5,934 million of this amount, as detailed in the following note to its financial statements:

5. Property, plant and equipment			
December 31, 2002	**Cost**	**Accumulated amortization**	**Net book value**
Oil and gas properties.................................	$10,198	$4,264	$ 5,934
Gas plants, pipelines and production equipment	5,576	1,547	4,029
Corporate assets..	213	134	79
	$15,987	$5,945	$10,042

Capital Assets Used in Extracting Resources

The conversion of natural resources by mining, cutting, or pumping usually requires machinery, equipment, and buildings. When the usefulness of these assets is directly related to the amortization of the natural resource, amortization is calculated using the units-of-production method in proportion to the natural resource's amortization charges. For example, if a machine is permanently installed in a mine and one-eighth of the mine's ore is mined and sold in the year, then one-eighth of the machine's cost (less salvage value) is charged to amortization expense. The same procedure is applied if the machine is abandoned once the resources are fully extracted. But if this machine will be moved to another site when extraction is complete, then it is amortized over its useful life.

---

[16] *CICA Handbook*, Section "Property, plant and equipment," par. .08 and .11.

12. Give an example of a natural resource.

13. A mining company pays $650,000 for an ore deposit. The deposit is estimated to have 325,000 tonnes of ore that will be fully mined over the next 10 years. During the current year, 91,000 tonnes are mined, processed, and sold. What is the current year's amortization expense?

Flashback

Answers—p. 640

Intangible Assets

 Account for intangible capital assets and their amortization.

Intangible capital assets are rights, privileges, and competitive advantages to the owner of capital assets that have no physical substance and are used in operations. Examples are patents, copyrights, leaseholds, and trademarks. *Goodwill is an intangible asset but it is not a capital asset; it is shown separately on the balance sheet.* Lack of physical substance is not sufficient for an asset to be an intangible. Accounts receivable, for instance, lack physical substance but are not used in operations to produce products or services. Assets without physical substance that are not used in operations are reported as either current assets or investments.

Accounting for Intangible Capital Assets

Accounting for intangible capital assets is similar to that for all other capital assets. An intangible capital asset is recorded at cost when purchased. Its cost must be systematically allocated to expense over its estimated useful life through the process of amortization.[17] The amortization period for other intangible assets is based on legal, regulatory, contractual, competitive, economic, or other factors that might limit its useful life.[18] Disposal of an intangible capital asset involves removing its book value, recording any asset received, and recognizing any gain or loss for the difference.

Intangible capital assets are amortized in a similar manner to other capital assets except for two differences:

1. Only the straight-line method is used *unless* the company can show that another method is preferred, and

2. Amortization is usually *credited directly* to the intangible capital asset account (resulting in no accumulated amortization account).

Intangible capital assets are shown on the balance sheet separately from property, plant, and equipment. For example, Molson Inc.'s March 31, 2003, balance sheet shows the following:

(Dollars in millions)	2003	2002
Property, plant and equipment	$1,026.9	$1,188.5
Intangible assets, excluding goodwill	1,552.5	1,690.4
Goodwill	770.4	981.3

[17] Section 3062 of the *CICA Handbook*, "Goodwill and other intangible assets," discusses special circumstances when amortization is not applied to intangible capital assets. For simplicity in this introductory course, we will assume that all intangible capital assets are amortized.

[18] *CICA Handbook*, section 3062, "Goodwill and other intangible assets," par. .15.

Patents

The federal government grants patents to encourage the invention of new machines, mechanical devices, and production processes. A **patent** is an exclusive right granted to its owner to manufacture and sell a patented machine or device, or to use a process, for 20 years. When patent rights are purchased, the cost of acquiring the rights is debited to an account called *Patents*. If the owner successfully engages in lawsuits to defend a patent, the cost of lawsuits is debited to the Patents account. The costs of research and development leading to a new patent are expensed when incurred.[19]

While a patent gives its owner exclusive rights to it for 20 years, its cost is amortized over the shorter of its legal life of 20 years or estimated useful life. If we purchase a patent costing $25,000 with a useful life of 10 years, the following entries are made to record the acquisition of the patent and the annual adjusting entry over the 10-year period to amortize one-tenth of its cost:

Jan. 2	Patents...	25,000	
	Cash		25,000
	To record purchase of patents.		
Dec. 31	Amortization Expense, Patents........................	2,500	
	Patents		2,500
	To write off patent cost over its 10-year useful life.		

The debit of $2,500 to Amortization Expense appears on the income statement as a cost of the product or service provided under the protection of the patent. This entry uses the common practice of crediting the Patents account rather than using a contra account.

Copyrights

A copyright is granted by the federal government or by international agreement. A **copyright** gives its owner the exclusive right to publish and sell a musical, literary, or artistic work during the life of the creator plus 50 years. Yet the useful life of most copyrights is much shorter. The costs of a copyright are amortized over its useful life. The only identifiable cost of many copyrights is the fee paid to the Copyright Office and if immaterial, the cost is charged directly to an expense account; if material, such as the cost of purchasing the copyrights to songs by the Beatles, they are capitalized and periodically amortized by debiting an account called *Amortization Expense, Copyrights.*

Trademarks and Trade Names

Companies often adopt unique symbols or select unique names and brands in marketing their products. A **trademark** or *trade name* is a symbol, name, phrase, or jingle identified with a company, product, or service. Examples are Speedy Muffler, Tim Hortons, Second Cup, Coca-Cola, and Honda. Ownership and exclusive right to use a trademark or trade name are often established by showing that one company used it before another. But ownership is best established by registering a trademark or trade name with the government's Patent Office. The cost of developing, maintaining, or enhancing the value of a trademark or trade name by means such as advertising is charged to expense when incurred. But if a trademark or trade name is purchased, its cost is debited to an asset account and amortized.

---

[19] *CICA Handbook*, section 3450, "Research and Development," par. .16 & .18.

Leaseholds

A **leasehold** refers to the rights granted to the lessee to use a specific asset by the lessor in the lease. A leasehold is an intangible asset for the lessee if a long-term lease requires the lessee to pay a bonus in advance.[20] The resulting debit to a Leasehold account is amortized over the term of the lease by debiting Rent Expense and crediting Leaseholds.

Accounting for Goodwill

Goodwill,[21] an intangible asset, is the amount by which the price paid for a company exceeds the fair market value of this company's net assets (assets minus liabilities) if purchased separately. This usually implies that the company has certain valuable attributes not measured among its net assets. These can include superior management, skilled workforce, superior supplier and customer relations, quality products or services, excellent location, or other competitive advantages. Goodwill is a major part of many company purchases. For instance, Flint Energy Services Ltd. shows goodwill on its December 31, 2002, balance sheet of $204,086,000.

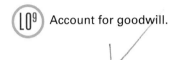

LO9 Account for goodwill.

GAAP do not permit firms to record internally generated goodwill. Permission to do so could lead to abuse and values arrived at would lack objectivity. The purchase transaction provides objective evidence that goodwill exists. The purchase of a business is recorded by debiting the assets acquired and crediting the liabilities assumed at fair market values. Cash is credited for the purchase price of the business acquired and goodwill is debited for the amount that the purchase price exceeds the fair value of the net assets. To illustrate, assume that on January 2, 2005, Canadian Tire acquired Best Tools for $8,000,000. The market value of Best Tools' assets was $7,000,000 and its liabilities were valued at $2,000,000. Goodwill is calculated at $3,000,000 as follows:

Purchase price to acquire Best Tools		$8,000,000
Total market value of Best Tools' assets	$7,000,000	
Less: Liabilities assumed	2,000,000	
Net assets purchased		5,000,000
Goodwill		**$3,000,000**

Canadian Tire's entry to record the purchase is:

2005			
Jan. 2	Assets (shown individually)	7,000,000	
	Goodwill	3,000,000	
	Liabilities (shown individually)		2,000,000
	Cash		8,000,000
	To record purchase of Best Tools and to record goodwill equal to the excess of the purchase price over the net assets.		

---

[20] Some long-term leases give the lessee essentially the same rights as a purchaser and result in tangible assets and liabilities reported by the lessee. The details of this advanced topic are left to an intermediate accounting course.

[21] The excess of the cost of the purchase price over the net of the amounts assigned to assets acquired and liabilities assumed should be reflected as goodwill. (CICA 1581 par. 40).

Goodwill is not amortized. Instead, goodwill is decreased only if its value has been determined by management to be impaired.[22] **Impairment of goodwill** results when the current value of goodwill (fair value of the organization less the fair value of its net assets) is less than the carrying value of goodwill.

The entry to record the impairment is:

Reported on the income statement ┈┈┈┈┈┈┈┈┈┈┈┈▶ Loss on impairment of goodwill   XX

Goodwill   XX

Causes of impairment might include ongoing past or potential cash flow losses or negative changes in variables supporting original calculations of goodwill. Testing for impairment should be done at least annually.

? Did You Know?   Goodwill write-offs decrease income on the income statement and also decrease assets and equity on the balance sheet. Corel, BCE Inc., and Celistica are examples of Canadian companies that recently each recorded multimillion-dollar write-offs of goodwill. In the multibillion U.S. dollar range of goodwill write-offs are Nortel with $15 billion, JDS Uniphase at $50 billion, and AOL with $100 billion.

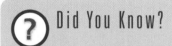

Flashback

Answer—p. 640

14. On January 6, 2005, a company pays $120,000 for a patent with a 20-year legal life to produce a toy that is expected to be marketable for about three years. Prepare entries to record its acquisition and the December 31, 2005, adjustment.

──────────

[22] *CICA Handbook* paragraphs 3062.22, 3062.23, and 3062.25.

Summary

LO1 **Describe capital assets and issues in accounting for them.** Capital assets are set apart from other assets by two important features: (1) they are used in the operations of a company, and (2) they have a useful life of more than one accounting period. There are three main accounting issues with capital assets: (1) calculating and accounting for their initial and subsequent costs, (2) allocating their costs to the periods they benefit, and (3) recording their disposal.

LO2 **Apply the cost principle to calculate the cost of capital assets.** Capital assets are recorded at cost when purchased. Cost includes all normal and reasonable expenditures necessary to get the asset in place and ready for its intended use. Revenue expenditures expire in the current period and are debited to expense accounts. Ordinary repairs are an example of revenue expenditures. Capital expenditures benefit future periods and are debited to asset accounts. The cost of a lump-sum purchase is

allocated among its individual assets based on their relative market values.

LO3 **Explain, record, and calculate amortization using the methods of straight-line, units-of-production, and double-declining-balance.** Amortization is the process of allocating to expense the cost of a capital asset over the accounting periods benefiting from use of the capital asset. Amortization does not measure the decline in a capital asset's market value, nor does it measure the asset's physical deterioration. Three factors determine amortization: cost, salvage value, and useful life. Salvage value is an estimate of the asset's value at the end of its benefit period. Useful (service) life is the length of time an asset is productively used in operations. The straight-line method of amortization divides the cost less salvage value by the number of periods in the asset's useful life to determine amortization expense for each period. The units-of-production method divides the cost less salvage value by the estimated number of units the asset will produce to determine the amortization per unit. The double-declining-balance (DDB) method multiplies the asset's book value by a rate that is double the straight-line rate. The amount of amortization expense per period is usually different for different methods but total amortization expense is the same. The difference is in the pattern in amortization expense over the asset's useful life. The straight-line method yields a steady pattern of amortization expense, while units-of-production does not because it depends on the number of units produced. DDB is an accelerated amortization method.

LO4 Explain and calculate amortization for partial years. When capital assets are bought and sold throughout the year, amortization can be calculated either to the nearest whole month *or* by applying the half-year rule.

LO5 Explain and calculate revised amortization. Amortization is revised when material changes occur in the estimated salvage value and/or useful life and/or there is a betterment. Revised amortization is calculated by spreading the *remaining* cost to be amortized over the remaining useful life of the asset.

LO6 Account for asset disposal through discarding, selling, or exchanging an asset. When a capital asset is discarded, sold, or exchanged, its cost and accumulated amortization are removed from the accounts. Any cash proceeds from discarding or selling an asset are recorded and compared to the asset's book value to determine a gain or loss. When assets are exchanged, the new asset is recorded at its fair value, and any gain or loss on disposal is recognized.

LO7 Account for natural resources and their amortization. The cost of a natural resource is recorded in an asset account and amortization is recorded by allocating its cost to expense normally using the units-of-production method. Amortization is credited to an Accumulated Amortization account.

LO8 Account for intangible capital assets and their amortization. An intangible capital asset is recorded at the cost incurred to purchase the asset. Amortization is normally recorded using the straight-line method with a credit made directly to the asset account instead of a contra account. Intangible capital assets include patents, copyrights, leaseholds, franchises, and trademarks. Goodwill is an intangible asset but is *not* an intangible capital asset.

LO9 Account for goodwill. Goodwill is an intangible asset. It is the amount by which the price paid for a company exceeds the fair market value of the purchased company's net assets. Goodwill is not amortized but is instead decreased if its value has been impaired.

GUIDANCE ANSWERS TO Judgement Call

Mechanic

Treating an expense as a capital expenditure results in lower reported expenses and higher income. This is because, unlike an expense, a capital expenditure is not expensed immediately. Instead, the cost of a capital expenditure is spread out over the asset's life. Treating an expense as a capital expenditure also means asset and equity totals are reported at a larger amount. This continues until the asset is fully amortized. Your friend is probably trying to help, but the suggestion hints at unethical behaviour. You must remember that only an expenditure benefiting future periods is a capital expenditure. If an item is truly an "expense" not benefiting future periods, then it must not be treated as a capital expenditure.

Controller

Before you conclude that this instruction is unethical, you might tell the president of your concern that the longer estimate doesn't seem realistic in light of past experience with three-year replacements. You might ask if the change implies a new replacement plan. Depending on the president's response, such a conversation might eliminate your concern. It is possible the president's decision to change estimated useful life reflects an honest and reasonable prediction of the future. Since the company is struggling financially, the president may have concluded that the normal pattern of replacing assets every three years can't continue. Perhaps the strategy is to avoid costs of frequent replacements and stretch use of the equipment a few years longer until financial conditions improve. Even if you doubt the company will be able to use the equipment for six years, you should consider the possibility that the president has a more complete understanding of the situation and honestly believes a six-year life is a good estimate.

On the downside, you may be correct in suspecting that the president is acting unethically. If you conclude the president's decision is unethical, you might confront the president with your opinion that it is unethical to change the prediction just to increase income. This is a personally risky course of action and you may want to remind the president of her own ethical responsibility. Another possibility is to wait and see if the auditor will insist on not changing the estimate. You should always insist the statements be based on reasonable estimates.

GUIDANCE ANSWERS TO  Flashback

1. Consistent with the cost principle, capital assets are recorded at cost, which includes all normal and reasonable expenditures needed to get the asset ready for use.

2. A revenue expenditure benefits only the current period and should be charged to expense of the current period. A capital expenditure has a benefit that extends beyond the end of the current period and should be charged to an asset.

3. A betterment involves enhancing an existing capital asset, usually by replacing part of the asset with an improved or superior part. A betterment should be debited to the improved asset's account.

4. (a) Land

   (b) Land Improvements

5. $700,000 + $49,000 − $21,000 + $3,500 + $3,000 + $2,500 = $737,000

6. (a) Straight-line with 7-year life: ($77,000/7) = $11,000

   (b) Straight-line with 10-year life: ($77,000/10) = $7,700

7. Amortization is a process of allocating and charging the cost of capital assets to the accounting periods that benefit from the assets' use.

8. (a) Book value using straight-line amortization:

   $96,000 − [($96,000 − $8,000)/5] = $78,400

   (b) Book value using units of production:

   $96,000 − [($96,000 − $8,000) × (10,000/100,000)] = $87,200

9. ($3,800 − $200)/3 = $1,200
   $1,200 × 2 = $2,400
   ($3,800 − $2,400)/2 = $700

10.

Jan. 27	Amortization Expense	3,500	
	Accum. Amortization		3,500

27	Cash	32,000	
	Accum. Amortization	10,500	
	Gain on Sale of Equip.		500
	Equipment		42,000

11. (a)

Mar. 3	Tractor (new)	45,000	
	Loss on Trade-In	3,600	
	Accum. Amortization (old)	23,400	
	Truck (old)		30,000
	Cash		42,000

(b)

Mar. 3	Tractor (new)	45,000	
	Accum. Amortization (old)	23,400	
	Truck (old)		30,000
	Cash		38,000
	Gain on Trade-In		400

12. Examples of natural resources are timberlands, mineral deposits and oil reserves.

13. $650,000 × (91,000/325,000) = $182,000

14.

Jan. 6	Patents	120,000	
	Cash		120,000
Dec. 31	Amortization Expense	40,000	
	Patents		40,000
	[Amortization calculation:		
	$120,000/3 = $40,000]		

Demonstration Problem

QLT Services purchased a machine on March 2, 2005, for $62,000 cash. It had an estimated useful life of five years and a salvage value of $14,000. On February 25, 2008, the machine was disposed of. QLT's year-end is December 31, and it calculates amortization to the nearest whole month.

Required

1. Prepare the entry to record the disposal under each of the following independent assumptions:

   a. The machine was sold for $26,000 cash.

   b. The machine was sold for $33,200 cash.

   c. The machine was sold for $34,180 cash.

   d. The old machine was exchanged for tools with a market value of $88,000. A trade-in allowance of $25,000 was offered on the old machine and the balance was paid in cash.

Additional company transactions to account for dealing with capital assets:

2. On January 4, 2008, the company purchases with cash a patent for $100,000. The company estimates the useful life of the patent to be 10 years. Journalize the patent acquisition and amortization for the year.

3. On October 17, 2008, the company makes its final addition to property and equipment with the acquisition of an ore deposit for $600,000 cash. Access roads and shafts are added for an additional cost of $80,000 cash. Salvage value of the mine is estimated to be $20,000. The company estimates 330,000 tonnes of available ore. Only 10,000 tonnes of ore are mined and sold before the end of the year. Journalize the mine's acquisition and first year's amortization.

Planning the Solution

o Remember that all amortization must be recorded before removing a disposed asset from the books. Calculate and record the amortization expense for 2005 through to 2008 using the straight-line method calculated to the nearest whole month. Record the gain/loss on the disposal as well as the removal of the asset and its related accumulated amortization from the books.

o Record the patent as an intangible asset for its purchase price. Use straight-line amortization over the years of useful life to calculate amortization expense. Remember that no accumulated amortization account is used in recording amortization expense; instead the intangible asset account is credited directly.

o Record the ore deposit as a natural resource asset including all additional costs to ready the mine for use. Calculate amortization per tonne using the units-of-production amortization formula. Multiply the amortization amount per tonne by the number of tonnes mined since the acquisition to calculate the appropriate amortization expense for the current year.

SOLUTION TO Demonstration Problem

1a.

2008			
Feb. 25	Amortization Expense, Machine.....................	1,600	
	Accumulated Amortization, Machine......		1,600
	To update amortization to date of sale.		
25	Accumulated Amortization, Machine[1]..............	28,800	
	Cash	26,000	
	Loss on Disposal[2]	7,200	
	Machine		62,000
	To record sale of machine.		

1b.

Feb. 25	Amortization Expense, Machine.....................	1,600	
	Accumulated Amortization, Machine......		1,600
	To update amortization to date of sale.		
25	Accumulated Amortization, Machine...............	28,800	
	Cash	33,200	
	Machine		62,000
	To record sale of machine.		

1c.

Feb. 25	Amortization Expense, Machine.....................	1,600	
	Accumulated Amortization, Machine......		1,600
	To update amortization to date of sale.		
25	Accumulated Amortization, Machine...............	28,800	
	Cash	34,180	
	Machine		62,000
	Gain on Disposal[3]		980
	To record sale of machine.		

1d.

Feb. 25	Amortization Expense, Machine.....................	1,600	
	Accumulated Amortization, Machine......		1,600
	To update amortization to date of exchange.		
25	Accumulated Amortization, Machine...............	28,800	
	Tools	88,000	
	Loss on Disposal[4]	8,200	
	Machine		62,000
	Cash		63,000
	To record exchange of machine.		

[1] 2005: $(62,000 - 14,000)/5 \times 10/12$ = 8,000
   2006: $(62,000 - 14,000)/5$ = 9,600
   2007:   = 9,600
   2008: $(62,000 - 14,000)/5 \times 2/12$ = 1,600
   Accumulated Amortization   28,800

[2] Gain (loss)   = Proceeds − Book value
       = 26,000 − (62,000 − 28,800) = (7,200)

[3] Gain (loss)   = 34,180 − (62,000 − 28,800)   = 980

[4] Gain (loss)   = 88,000 − [63,000 + (62,000 − 28,800)] = (8,200)

2.

	2008			
	Jan. 4	Patent	100,000	
		Cash		100,000
		To record patent acquisition.		
	Dec. 31	Amortization Expense, Patent	10,000	
		Patent..		10,000
		To record amortization expense		
		($100,00/10 years = $10,000).		

3.

	2008			
	Oct. 17	Ore Deposit	680,000	
		Cash		680,000
		To record ore deposit aquisition and		
		related costs.		
	Dec. 31	Amortization Expense, Ore Deposit	20,000	
		Accumulated Amortization,		
		Ore Deposit...		20,000
		To record amortization expense		
		[($680,000 − $20,000)/ 330,000 tonnes		
		available] = $2.00 per tonne;		
		10,000 tonnes mined and sold × $2.00		
		= $20,000 amortization.		

Exchanging Dissimilar and Similar Assets

 Explain and account for exchanging dissimilar and similar assets.

We mentioned in the body of Chapter 12 that many capital assets such as machinery, automobiles, and office equipment are disposed of by exchanging them for new assets. This appendix builds on that material by introducing the concepts of similar and dissimilar assets. Similar assets are assets of the same general type that perform the same function in the same kind of business. Trading an old truck for a new truck is an exchange of similar assets, whereas trading a truck for a machine is an exchange of dissimilar assets. The recognition of gains and losses on exchanging capital assets is shown in Exhibit 12A.1.

Exhibit 12A.1

Gains and Losses on Capital Asset Exchanges

Assets Exchanged	Losses Recognized	Gains Recognized
Dissimilar	Yes	Yes
Similar—Monetary	Yes	Yes
Similar—Non-monetary......	**No**	**No**

Exchanging Dissimilar Assets

If a company exchanges a capital asset for another asset that is dissimilar in use or purpose, any gain or loss on the exchange is recorded. Any gain or loss is calculated by comparing the book value of the asset given up with the fair market value of the asset received (or trade-in allowance). These entries were illustrated in Chapter 12 on page 632.

Exchanging Similar Assets—Monetary

In general, accounting for exchanges of similar assets depends on whether the amount of cash involved is more or less than 10% of the *total consideration* given up or received.[23] If fair values are not known or lack objectivity, the total consideration given up can be calculated as the book value of the asset given up plus the cash paid or minus any cash received. If the amount of cash exchanged on a trade-in of capital assets is *more than 10%*, the transaction is a monetary transaction and a gain or loss on the exchange is recorded in the same manner as for exchanges of dissimilar assets.

---

[23] *CICA Handbook*, Section 3830, "Non-Monetary Transactions," par. .04(e).

Exchanging Similar Assets—Non-Monetary

If the amount of cash exchanged on a trade-in of capital assets is *less than 10%*, the transaction is a non-monetary transaction and a gain or loss on the exchange is normally not recorded. There are three possibilities. First, no cash is paid or received and the assets are simply traded for each other. Second, a small amount of cash is *paid*. And third, a small amount of cash is *received*.

Case 1: No Cash Paid or Received

Let's assume a company exchanges its old equipment for new equipment and no cash is paid or received. The old equipment originally cost $36,000 and has accumulated amortization of $20,000 at the time of exchange. The new equipment received has a fair market value of $19,000. This would be considered a non-monetary exchange because the cash involved is less than 10% of the value of the total consideration [Total consideration = ($36,000 − $20,000) ± $0 = $16,000]. The cost of the new equipment is adjusted to equal the value of the total consideration. The historical cost principle requires that an asset be recorded at the cash or cash equivalent amount given in exchange, not to exceed the fair market value of the asset received. The entry to record this exchange is:

Jan. 3	Equipment (**new**)	16,000	
	Accumulated Amortization, Equipment	20,000	
	Equipment (**old**)		36,000
	To record exchange of old equipment for new equipment.		

Case 2: $1,000 Cash Received

Let's assume the same information as for Case 1 except that cash of $1,000 is received in the exchange. This is a non-monetary exchange because the cash involved is *less than 10%* of the value of the total consideration [Total consideration = ($36,000 − $20,000) − $1,000 = $15,000]. The cost of the new equipment is adjusted to equal the value of the total consideration. The entry to record this exchange is:

Jan. 3	Cash	1,000	
	Equipment (**new**)	15,000	
	Accumulated Amortization, Equipment	20,000	
	Equipment (**old**)		36,000
	To record exchange of old equipment for new equipment plus cash.		

Case 3: $1,000 Cash Paid

Let's assume the same information as for Case 1, except that cash of $1,000 is paid in the exchange. This is considered a non-monetary exchange because the cash involved is *less than 10%* of the value of the total consideration [Total consideration = ($36,000 − $20,000) + $1,000 = $17,000]. The cost of the new equipment is adjusted to equal the value of the total consideration.

The entry to record this exchange is:

Jan. 3	Equipment (**new**)	17,000	
	Accumulated Amortization, Equipment	20,000	
	Equipment (**old**)		36,000
	Cash		1,000
	To record exchange of old equipment for new equipment and payment of cash.		

Exhibit 12A.2 summarizes the cost at which the new asset is recorded under each of the three possibilities just discussed.

Exhibit 12A.2

Cost Basis of New Asset when Gain is Not Recognized

	Case 1	Case 2	Case 3
Cost of old equipment	$36,000	$36,000	$36,000
Less: Accumulated amortization	20,000	20,000	20,000
Book value of old equipment	16,000	16,000	16,000
Cash (received) paid	nil	(1,000)	1,000
Cost recorded for new equipment	$16,000	$15,000	$17,000

Although the general rule is that no gains or losses should be recorded on non-monetary exchanges of similar assets, the *CICA Handbook* discusses the accounting treatment for uncommon exceptions. These are beyond the scope of this textbook.[24]

---

[24] *CICA Handbook*, section 3830, "Non-Monetary Transactions," par. .10.

Summary of Appendix

LO10 **Explain and account for exchanging dissimilar and similar assets.** When a capital asset is exchanged, the cost of the old asset and related accumulated amortization are removed from the accounts. When dissimilar and similar monetary assets are exchanged, the new asset is recorded at its fair value, and any gain or loss on disposal is recognized. When similar non-monetary assets are exchanged, gains or losses are normally not recognized, and the new asset account is debited for the book value of the old asset plus/minus any cash paid/received.

Glossary

Accelerated amortization method An amortization method that produces larger amortization charges during the early years of an asset's life and smaller charges in the later years. (p. 621)

Amortization A process of systematically allocating the cost of a capital asset to expense over its estimated useful life. (p. 614)

Basket purchase See *lump-sum purchase.* (p. 613)

Betterment An expenditure to make a capital asset more efficient or productive and/or extend the useful life of a capital asset beyond original expectations; also called an improvement. Betterments are debited to a capital asset account. (p. 610)

Book value The original cost of a capital asset less its accumulated amortization. (p. 615)

Capital assets Tangible and intangible assets (excluding goodwill) used in the operations of a company that have a useful life of more than one accounting period. (p. 608)

Capital cost allowance (CCA) The system of amortization required by federal income tax law. (p. 623)

Capital expenditures Costs of capital assets that provide material benefits extending beyond the current period. They are debited to capital asset accounts and reported on the balance sheet. (p. 610)

Change in an accounting estimate A change in a calculated amount used in the financial statements that results from new information or subsequent developments and from better insight or improved judgement. (p. 626)

Copyright A right granted by the federal government or by international agreement giving the owner the exclusive privilege to publish and sell musical, literary, or artistic work during the life of the creator plus 50 years. (p. 636)

Cost Includes all normal and reasonable expenditures necessary to get a capital asset in place and ready for its intended use. (p. 609)

Declining-balance amortization An amortization method in which a capital asset's amortization charge for the period is determined by applying a constant amortization rate (up to twice the straight-line rate) each year to the asset's book value at the beginning of the year. (p. 621)

Depletion The process of allocating the cost of natural resources to the periods in which they are consumed. Another term for *amortization* of natural resources. (p. 614)

Depreciation An American term used to describe amortization. See *amortization.* (p. 614)

Double-declining-balance amortization An amortization method in which amortization is determined at twice the straight-line rate. (p. 621)

Fixed assets See *property, plant, and equipment.* (p. 608)

Goodwill The amount by which the value of a company exceeds the fair market value of the company's net assets if purchased separately; goodwill is an intangible asset; it is *not* a capital asset; goodwill is *not* amortized but is instead subject to impairment. (p. 637)

Half-year rule A method of calculating amortization for partial periods. Six months' amortization is taken for the partial period regardless of when the asset was acquired or disposed of. The half-year rule is used to calculate CCA in the first year of an asset's life for tax purposes. (p. 625)

Impairment of goodwill Results when the current value of goodwill is less than its carrying value. (p. 638)

Inadequacy A condition in which the capacity of the company's capital assets is too small to meet the company's productive demands. (p. 616)

Intangible assets Rights, privileges, and competitive advantages to the owner of assets used in operations that have a useful life of more than one accounting period but have no physical substance; examples include patents, copyrights, leaseholds, franchises, and trademarks. Goodwill is an intangible asset. (p. 608)

Intangible capital assets Intangible assets that include patents, copyrights, leaseholds, franchises, and trademarks. Goodwill is an intangible asset but it is *not* a capital asset. (p. 635)

Land improvements Assets that increase the usefulness of land but that have a limited useful life and are subject to amortization. (p. 612)

Lease A contract allowing property rental. (p. 613)

Leasehold A name for the rights granted to the lessee by the lessor in a lease. (p. 637)

Leasehold improvement An asset resulting from a lessee paying for alterations or improvements to the leased property. (p. 613)

Lessee The party to a lease that secures the right to possess and use the property. (p. 613)

Lessor The party to a lease that grants to another the right to possess and use property. (p. 613)

Lump-sum purchase Purchase of capital assets in a group with a single transaction for a lump-sum price. The cost of the purchase must be allocated to individual asset accounts; also called a *basket purchase.* (p. 613)

Natural resources Assets that are physically consumed when used; examples include timber, mineral deposits, and oil and gas fields; also called wasting assets. (p. 633)

Obsolescence A condition in which, because of new inventions and improvements, a capital asset can no longer be used to produce goods or services with a competitive advantage. (p. 616)

Patent An exclusive right granted to its owner by the federal government to manufacture and sell a machine or device, or to use a process, for 20 years. (p. 636)

PPE A common abbreviation for *property, plant, and equipment.* (p. 608)

Property, plant, and equipment Tangible capital assets used in the operations of a company that have a useful life of more than one accounting period; often abbreviated as *PPE*; sometimes referred to as fixed assets. (p. 608)

Repairs Expenditures made to keep a capital asset in normal, good operating condition; treated as a revenue expenditure. (p. 610)

Revenue expenditure An expenditure that should appear on the current income statement as an expense and be deducted from the period's revenues because it does not provide a material benefit in future periods. (p. 610)

Revised amortization Recalculating amortization because of a change in cost, salvage value, or useful life. (p. 626)

Salvage value Management's estimate of the amount that will be recovered at the end of a capital asset's useful life through a sale or as a trade-in allowance on the purchase of a new asset; also called residual or scrap value. (p. 616)

Service life See *useful life*. (p. 616)

Straight-line amortization A method that allocates an equal portion of the total amortization for a capital asset (cost minus salvage) to each accounting period in its useful life. (p. 617)

Trademark A symbol, name, phrase, or jingle identified with a company, product, or service. Also referred to as trade name. (p. 636)

Units-of-production amortization A method that charges a varying amount to expense for each period of an asset's useful life depending on its usage; expense is calculated by taking the cost of the asset less its salvage value and dividing by the total number of units expected to be produced during its useful life. (p. 620)

Useful life The length of time in which a capital asset will be productively used in the operations of the business; also called *service life*. (p. 616)

For more study tools, quizzes, and problem material,
refer to the Online Learning Centre at
www.mcgrawhill.ca/college/larson

Questions

1. What characteristics of a capital asset make it different from other assets?

2. What is the balance sheet classification of land held for future expansion? Why is the land not classified as a capital asset?

3. In general, what is included in the cost of a capital asset?

4. What is the difference between land and land improvements?

5. Does the balance of the Accumulated Amortization, Machinery account represent funds accumulated to replace the machinery when it wears out?

6. What is the difference between an ordinary repair and a betterment and how should they be recorded?

7. What accounting principle justifies charging the $75 cost of a capital asset immediately to an expense account?

8. Refer to the balance sheet for WestJet in Appendix I. On what basis are aircraft amortized: straight-line, units-of-production, or double-declining-balance?

9. What are some of the events that might lead to the disposal of a capital asset?

10. What is the name for the process of allocating the cost of natural resources to expense as the natural resources are used?

11. What are the characteristics of an intangible capital asset?

12. Is the declining-balance method an acceptable means of calculating amortization of natural resources?

13. What general procedures are followed in accounting for intangible capital assets?

14. When does a business have goodwill?

15. A company bought an established business and paid for goodwill. If the company plans to incur substantial advertising and promotional costs each year to maintain the value of the goodwill, must the company also amortize the goodwill?

*16. Should a gain on an exchange of capital assets be recorded?

An asterisk (*) identifies assignment material based on Appendix 12A.

Sydney Lanes installed automatic scorekeeping equipment. The electrical work required to prepare for the installation was $18,000. The invoice price of the equipment was $180,000. Additional costs were $3,000 for delivery and $600 for insurance during transportation. During the installation, a component of the equipment was damaged because it was carelessly left on a lane and hit by the automatic lane cleaning machine during a daily maintenance run. The cost of repairing the component was $2,250. What is the cost of the automatic scorekeeping equipment?

QS 12-1
Cost of capital assets

1. Classify the following expenditures as revenue (R) or capital expenditures (C):
   a. The monthly replacement cost of filters on an air conditioning system, $120.
   b. The cost of replacing a compressor for a meat packing firm's refrigeration system that extends the estimated life of the system by four years, $40,000.
   c. The cost of annual tune-ups for delivery trucks, $200.
   d. The cost of $175,000 for an addition of a new wing on an office building.
2. Prepare the journal entry to record each of the above (assume all transactions occurred on March 15, 2005, and were for cash).

QS 12-2
Revenue and capital expenditures

On April 14, 2005, Lestok Company purchased land and a building for a total price of $540,000, paying cash of $85,000 and borrowing the balance from the bank. The bank appraised the land at $320,000 and the building at $180,000. Prepare the entry to record the purchase.

QS 12-3
Lump sum purchase

Capital Asset	(a) Appraised Values	(b) Ratio of Individual Appraised Value to Total Appraised Value (a) ÷ Total Appraised Value	(c) Cost Allocation (b) × Total Actual Cost
Land			
Building			
Totals			

TechCom has provided the following selected account information, in alphabetical order, from its adjusted trial balance at October 31, 2005 (assume normal balances):

QS 12-4
Balance sheet presentation

Accounts receivable	$16,400
Accumulated amortization, equipment	3,800
Accumulated amortization, vehicles	13,800
Allowance for doubtful accounts	800
Cash	9,000
Equipment	25,000
Land	48,000
Patent*	17,000
Vehicles	62,000

*Net of $3,100 accumulated amortization

Prepare the asset section of the balance sheet at October 31, 2005.

On January 2, 2005, Crossfire acquired sound equipment for concert performances at a cost of $55,900. The rock band estimated that it would use this equipment for four years, and then sell the equipment for $1,900. Calculate amortization for each year of the sound equipment's estimated life using the straight-line method. Crossfire's year-end is December 31.

QS 12-5
Calculating amortization—straight-line

QS 12-6
Calculating amortization—
units-of-production

LO³

Delta Company purchased a photocopier costing $45,000 on January 1, 2005. The equipment is expected to produce a total of 4,000,000 copies over its productive life. Its salvage value at the end of its useful life is estimated to be $5,000. The equipment actually produced: 650,000 copies in 2005; 798,000 copies in 2006; 424,000 copies in 2007; 935,000 copies in 2008; and 1,193,000 copies in 2009. Calculate amortization for 2005 through to 2009 using the units-of-production method. Delta's year-end is December 31.

QS 12-7
Calculating amortization—
double-declining balance

LO³

Wimberly Holdings acquired a delivery truck on January 1, 2005, for $86,000. It is expected to last five years and then sell for about $16,000. Calculate amortization for each year of the truck's life using the double-declining-balance method. Wimberly's year-end is December 31.

QS 12-8
Calculating amortization—
partial periods

LO³,⁴

Refer to the information in QS 12-5. Assuming the sound equipment was purchased on March 6, 2005, calculate amortization for 2005:
a. to the nearest whole month.
b. using the half-year rule.

QS 12-9
Calculating amortization—
partial periods

LO³,⁴

Refer to the information in QS 12-6. Assuming the photocopier was purchased on February 2, 2005, calculate amortization for 2005:
a. to the nearest whole month.
b. using the half-year rule.

QS 12-10
Calculating amortization—
partial periods

LO³,⁴

Refer to the information in QS 12-7. Assuming the delivery truck was purchased on November 17, 2005, calculate amortization for 2005:
a. to the nearest whole month.
b. using the half-year rule.

QS 12-11
Revised amortization—change
in useful life and salvage value

LO⁵

On January 1, 2005, Kaldex Company purchased for $35,720 equipment with an estimated useful life of eight years and an estimated salvage value at the end of its life of $4,200. Early in January of 2008, it was determined that the total estimated useful life on the equipment should be 10 years with a revised estimated salvage value of $1,570. Kaldex uses the straight-line method to calculate amortization and its year-end is December 31. Calculate revised amortization for 2008.

QS 12-12
Revised amortization—betterment

LO⁵

On January 1, 2005, Pyongyang Servicing purchased for $25,000 machinery with an estimated useful life of four years and an estimated salvage value of $5,000. On January 2, 2008, a new motor costing $12,000 was installed in the machinery, which extended its useful life to eight years with no change in the salvage value. Pyongyang uses the straight-line method to calculate amortization and its year-end is December 31. Record the amortization for the year ended December 31, 2008.

QS 12-13
Disposal of capital assets

LO⁶

Dorsier Company showed the following adjusted account balances on September 30, 2005:

Equipment	$ 56,000
Accumulated amortization, equipment	39,000
Machinery	109,000
Accumulated amortization, machinery	96,000
Delivery truck	48,000
Accumulated amortization, delivery truck	33,000

Prepare the entry to record the sale on October 1, 2005, of the:
a. equipment for cash of $17,000.
b. machinery for cash of $27,000.
c. delivery truck for cash of $11,000.

Refer to the information in QS 12-13. Assume that on October 1, 2005, Dorsier Company scrapped the equipment. Prepare the entry.

QS 12-14
Disposal of a capital asset

LO^6

Dean Carpet Stores owned an automobile with a $15,000 cost that had $13,500 accumulated amortization as of December 31, 2005. On the same day, Dean exchanged this auto for a computer with a fair market value of $4,500. Dean was required to pay an additional $2,750 cash. Prepare the entry to record this transaction for Dean.

QS 12-15
Exchanging an asset

LO^6

Sudbury Industries acquired a mine on May 4, 2005, at a cost of $1,300,000 cash. On the same day, the company had to pay an additional $200,000 cash to access the mine. The mine is estimated to hold 500,000 tonnes of ore and the estimated value of the land after the ore is removed is $150,000.
a. Prepare the entry to record the acquisition.
b. Prepare the year-end adjusting entry at December 31, assuming that 90,000 tonnes of ore were mined in 2005.

QS 12-16
Natural resources and amortization

LO^7

On January 4, 2005, Amber's Boutique paid cash of $95,000 for a ten-year franchise. Prepare the entry to record the purchase of the franchise and the adjusting entry at December 31, 2005.

QS 12-17
Intangible assets and amortization

LO^8

On February 2, 2005, the accounting records of Neon Company showed a machine that cost $75,000 and had accumulated amortization of $47,000. It was exchanged for a similar machine with a fair value of $40,000. Neon also paid $2,500 cash. Record the exchange.

*QS 12-18
Exchange of similar non-monetary assets

LO^{10}

Exercises

Santiago Co. purchased a machine for $11,500, terms 2/10, n/60, FOB shipping point. The seller prepaid the freight charges, $260, adding the amount to the invoice and bringing its total to $11,760. The machine required a special steel mounting and power connections costing $795, and another $375 was paid to assemble the machine and get it into operation. In moving the machine onto its steel mounting, it was dropped and damaged. The repairs cost $190. Later, $30 of raw materials were consumed in adjusting the machine so that it would produce a satisfactory product. The adjustments were normal for this type of machine and were not the result of the damage. However, the items produced while the adjustments were being made were not saleable. Prepare a calculation to show the cost of this machine for accounting purposes. (Assume Santiago pays for the purchase within the discount period.)

Exercise 12-1
Cost of a capital asset

LO^2

Check figure:
Total acquisition costs = $12,730

Exercise 12-2
Recording costs of real estate

LO²

Check figure:
Dr Land $430,500

After planning to build a new plant, Jammers Manufacturing purchased a large lot on which a small building was located. The negotiated purchase price for this real estate was $225,000 for the lot plus $120,000 for the building. The company paid $34,500 to have the old building torn down and $51,000 for levelling the lot. Finally, it paid $1,440,000 in construction costs, which included the cost of a new building plus $85,500 for lighting and paving a parking lot next to the building. Present a single journal entry to record the costs incurred by Jammers, all of which were paid in cash (assume a date of March 10, 2005, for your entry).

Exercise 12-3
Lump-sum purchase

LO²

Check figure:
Dr Land $162,897

On April 12, 2005, Horizon Company paid cash of $368,250 for real estate plus $19,600 cash in closing costs. The real estate included: land appraised at $166,320; land improvements appraised at $55,440; and a building appraised at $174,240. Prepare a calculation similar to QS 12-3 showing the allocation of the total cost among the three purchased assets and present the journal entry to record the purchase.

Exercise 12-4
Lump-sum purchase

LO²

Check figure:
Dr Tools $162,000

On January 1, 2005, Gear Research Institute purchased land, a building, equipment, and tools for a total price of $1,800,000, paying cash of $460,000 and borrowing the balance from the bank. The bank appraiser valued the assets as follows: $480,000 for the land; $560,000 for the building; $416,000 for the equipment; and $144,000 for the tools. Prepare the entry to record the purchase.

Exercise 12-5
Alternative amortization methods—straight-line and double-declining balance

LO³

Check figure:
b. 2007: $4,575

On January 2, 2005, Simmons Company installed a computerized machine in its factory at a cost of $42,300. The machine's useful life was estimated at four years with a $6,000 trade-in value. Calculate the machine's amortization each year of its estimated useful life under the (a) straight-line and (b) double-declining-balance methods. Simmons' year-end is December 31.

Exercise 12-6
Alternative amortization methods—units-of-production

LO³

Check figure:
2007: 10,520

Refer to the information in Exercise 12-5. Assume that the machine was estimated to produce a total of 181,500 units. Actual units produced were:

2005:	38,300
2006:	41,150
2007:	52,600
2008:	49,450

Calculate the machine's amortization each year under the units-of-production method.

Exercise 12-7
Calculating amortization

LO³

Check figure:
b. $11,920

JenStar Trading purchased a truck on January 1, 2005, for $29,800 cash. Its estimated useful life is five years or 240,000 kilometres with an estimated salvage value of $5,800.

Required
Calculate amortization expense for the year ended December 31, 2005, using each of the following methods:
a. straight-line
b. double-declining balance
c. units-of-production (assume 38,000 kilometres were actually driven in 2005).

On January 3, 2005, Labtech purchased computer equipment for $147,000. The equipment will be used in research and development activities for four years and then sold at an estimated salvage value of $30,000. Prepare a schedule with headings as shown below. Calculate amortization and book values for each year of the equipment's life assuming the straight-line and double-declining-balance methods. Labtech's year-end is December 31.

Exercise 12-8
Alternative amortization methods

 LO³

Check figure:
DDB Amortization expense
2007: $6,750

	Straight-Line Method		Double-Declining-Balance Method	
Year	Amortization Expense	Book Value at December 31	Amortization Expense	Book Value at December 31

Refer to the information in Exercise 12-8. Calculate amortization and book values assuming the computer equipment is amortized based on a total of 6,500 hours of use. Assume actual usage each year was:

Exercise 12-9
Alternative amortization methods

 LO³

Check figure:
Book value 2008: 30,000

Year	Actual Usage in Hours
2005	1,350
2006	1,780
2007	2,400
2008	2,980

At December 31, 2004, Creo Products' balance sheet showed total capital assets of $485,000 and total accumulated amortization of $135,989 as detailed in the Capital Asset Subledger below. Creo Products calculates amortization to the nearest whole month.

Exercise 12-10
Calculating amortization

 LO³

		Cost Information					Amortization	
Description	Date of Purchase	Amortization¹ Method	Cost²	Salvage	Life	Balance of Accum. Amort. Dec. 31, 2004	Amortization Expense for 2005	Balance of Accum. Amort. Dec. 31, 2005
Building	May 2, 1999	S/L	$325,000	$125,000	10 yr.	$113,333		
Land	May 2, 1999	N/A	120,000	N/A	N/A	-0-		
Truck	Jan. 25, 2002	DDB	40,000	5,000	8 yr.	22,656		

¹ S/L—Straight-Line; DDB—Double-Declining-Balance; N/A—not applicable
² There have been no disposals or betterments since the date of purchase.

Required
1. Complete the schedule by calculating amortization expense for 2005 for each asset and then determining the balance of accumulated amortization at December 31, 2005 (round to the nearest whole dollar).
2. Why has amortization not been calculated on the land?

Check figure:
1. Amortization expense,
truck: $4,336

Refer to Exercise 12-10. Assume that the only other assets at December 31, 2004, were total current assets of $169,000. Prepare the asset section of Creo Products' classified balance sheet at December 31, 2004.

Exercise 12-11
Balance sheet presentation

 LO³

Check figure:
Total assets = $518,011

Exercise 12-12
Income statement effects of alternative amortization methods

LO³

Check figure:
b. Amortization expense
Year 3: $21,448

Shamrock Enterprises recently paid $156,800 for equipment that will last five years and have a salvage value of $35,000. By using the machine in its operations for five years, the company expects to earn $57,000 annually, after deducting all expenses except amortization. Complete the following schedule assuming each of (a) straight-line amortization and (b) double-declining-balance amortization.

	Year 1	Year 2	Year 3	Year 4	Year 5	5-Year Totals
Income before amortization.......						
Amortization expense...............						
Net income.............................						

Exercise 12-13
Alternative amortization methods

LO³

Check figure:
DDB amort. expense 2006: $9,500

On January 3, 2005, Barrow Company installed a computerized machine in its factory at a cost of $53,000. The machine's useful life was estimated at four years with a $17,000 trade-in value. Barrow's year-end is December 31. Calculate annual amortization under the straight-line and double-declining-balance methods and complete the following schedule for each year of the asset's estimated useful life (round to the nearest dollar):

	Straight-Line			Double-Declining-Balance		
Year	Amort. Expense	Accum. Amort.	Book Value, Dec. 31	Amort. Expense	Accum. Amort.	Book Value, Dec. 31

Exercise 12-14
Alternative amortization methods—units-of-production

LO³

Check figure:
Amort. expense 2008: $1,800

Refer to the information in Exercise 12-13. The total estimated units of production for the computerized machine purchased on January 3, 2005, was 80,000 units. Calculate annual amortization under the units-of-production method and complete a schedule similar to Exercise 12-13 assuming the actual production each year was:

Year	Actual Production in Units
2005	26,000
2006	21,000
2007	29,000
2008	18,000
Total	94,000

Exercise 12-15
Partial period amortization—nearest month

LO⁴

Check figure:
DDB 2006: $13,917

Refer to the information in Exercises 12-13 and 12-14. Assume that the computerized equipment was purchased on *March 12, 2005* (instead of January 3, 2005). Calculate annual amortization to the nearest whole month under the straight-line, double-declining-balance, and units-of-production methods and complete a schedule with the following headings (round to the nearest whole dollar):

	Amortization		
Year	Straight-Line	Double-Declining-Balance	Units-of-Production

Exercise 12-16
Partial period amortization—half-year rule

LO⁴

Check figure:
DDB 2007: $2,875

Repeat Exercise 12-15 calculating amortization using the half-year rule.

On April 1, 2005, Rodgers Backhoe Co. purchased a trencher for $250,000. The machine was expected to last five years and have a salvage value of $25,000.

Required
Calculate amortization expense for 2005 and 2006 to the nearest month, using (a) the straight-line method, and (b) the double-declining-balance method. Rodgers Backhoe has a December 31 year-end.

Exercise 12-17
Alternative amortization methods
—partial year's amortization

  LO⁴

Check figure:
a. 2006 $45,000

BodySmart Fitness Club used straight-line amortization for a machine that cost $21,750, under the assumption it would have a four-year life and a $2,250 trade-in value. After two years, BodySmart determined that the machine still had three more years of remaining useful life, after which it would have an estimated $1,800 trade-in value.

Required
1. Calculate the machine's book value at the end of its second year.
2. Calculate the amount of amortization to be charged during each of the remaining years in the machine's revised useful life.

Exercise 12-18
Revising amortization rates

LO⁵

Check figure:
2. $3,400

On April 3, 2005, Billows Equipment purchased a machine for $89,000. It was assumed that the machine would have a five-year life and a $19,000 trade-in value. Early in January of 2008, it was determined that the machine would have a seven-year useful life and the trade-in value would be $10,000. Billows uses the straight-line method to the nearest month for calculating amortization.

Required
Record amortization at December 31, 2008, Billows' year-end. Round to the nearest whole dollar.

Exercise 12-19
Revising amortization rates—
change in useful life
and salvage value

LO⁵

Check figure:
Revised amortization = $9,529

The Jinks O'Neill Company owns a building that appeared on its balance sheet at December 31, 2005, at its original $561,000 cost less $420,750 accumulated amortization. The building has been amortized on a straight-line basis under the assumption that it would have a 20-year life and no salvage value. On January 11, 2006, major structural repairs were completed on the building at a cost of $67,200. The repairs did not increase the building's capacity, but they did extend its expected life for seven years beyond the 20 years originally estimated.

Required
a. Determine the building's age as of December 31, 2005.
b. Give the entry to record the repairs on January 11, 2006, which were paid with cash.
c. Determine the book value of the building after the repairs were recorded.
d. Give the entry to record the amortization at December 31, 2006. Round to the nearest whole dollar.

Exercise 12-20
Revising amortization
rates—betterment

LO²,⁵

Check figure:
c. $207,450

McGraw Company purchased equipment costing $107,000 on March 3, 2005, under the assumption it would have a five-year life and a $17,000 trade-in value. On February 20, 2009, a major overhaul on the equipment required the installation of a new motor. The total cost of the installation was $28,000 and the useful life was adjusted to a total of seven years and a $15,000 trade-in value. McGraw uses the straight-line method to the nearest month for calculating amortization.

Required
1. Record the installation of the new motor on February 20, 2009 (McGraw paid cash).
2. Record amortization for the years 2005, 2006, 2007, and 2008.
3. Record amortization at December 31, 2009, McGraw's year-end. Round to the nearest whole dollar.

Exercise 12-21
Revising amortization
rates—betterment

 LO²,⁵

Check figure:
3. Amortization for 2009
= $16,333

Exercise 12-22
Disposal of capital assets

LO⁶

Check figures:
b. Gain $1,750
c. Loss $3,650

Gildan Activewear sold a van on March 1, 2005. The accounts showed adjusted balances on February 28, 2005, as follows:

Van	$38,500
Accumulated Amortization, Van	21,850

Required
Record the sale of the van assuming the cash proceeds were:
a. $16,650
b. $18,400
c. $13,000
d. $0 (the van was scrapped).

Exercise 12-23
Partial year's amortization; disposal of capital asset

LO⁴,⁶

Check figures:
a. Gain $1,875
b. Loss $3,125

Plum Co. purchased and installed a machine on January 1, 2005, at a total cost of $92,750. Straight-line amortization was taken each year for four years, based on the assumption of a seven-year life and no salvage value. The machine was disposed of on July 1, 2009, during its fifth year of service. Plum's year-end is December 31.

Required
Present the entries to record the partial year's amortization on July 1, 2005, and to record the disposal under each of the following unrelated assumptions:
a. The machine was sold for $35,000 cash.
b. Plum received an insurance settlement of $30,000 resulting from the total destruction of the machine in a fire.

Exercise 12-24
Exchanging capital assets

LO⁶

Check figure:
b. Loss $29,000

On October 6, 2005, Greenbelt Construction traded in an old tractor for a new truck, receiving a $56,000 trade-in allowance and paying the remaining $164,000 in cash. The old tractor cost $190,000, and straight-line amortization of $105,000 had been recorded as of October 6, 2005, under the assumption that it would last eight years and have a $22,000 salvage value.

Required
a. What was the book value of the old tractor?
b. What is the gain or loss on the exchange?
c. What amount should be debited to the new Truck account?
d. Record the exchange.

Exercise 12-25
Recording capital asset disposal or exchange

LO⁶

Check figures:
a. Loss $3,125
b. Gain $625
c. Loss $1,375
d. Gain $5,625

On January 2, 2005, Hammond Service Co. disposed of a machine that cost $42,000 and had been amortized $22,625. Present the journal entries to record the disposal under each of the following unrelated assumptions:
a. The machine was sold for $16,250 cash.
b. The machine was traded in on new tools having a $58,500 cash price. A $20,000 trade-in allowance was received, and the balance was paid in cash.
c. The machine plus $34,000 was exchanged for a new van having a fair value of $52,000.
d. The machine was traded for vacant land adjacent to the shop to be used as a parking lot. The land had a fair value of $37,500, and Hammond paid $12,500 cash in addition to giving the seller the machine.

Exercise 12-26
Amortization of natural resources

LO⁷

Check figure:
Amortization Expense, Ore Deposit $398,310

On April 2, 2005, Northern Mining Co. paid $3,633,750 for an ore deposit containing 1,425,000 tonnes. The company also installed machinery in the mine that cost $171,000, had an estimated seven-year life with no salvage value, and was capable of removing all the ore in six years. The machine will be abandoned when the ore is completely mined. Northern began operations on May 1, 2005, and mined and sold 156,200 tonnes of ore during the remaining eight months of the year. Give the December 31, 2005, entries to record the amortization of the ore deposit and the amortization of the mining machinery.

The SMU Gallery purchased the copyright on an oil painting for $236,700 on January 1, 2005. The copyright legally protects its owner for 19 more years. However, SMU Gallery plans to market and sell prints of the original for the next 12 years. Prepare journal entries to record the purchase of the copyright and the annual amortization of the copyright on December 31, 2005.

Exercise 12-27
Amortization of intangible assets

LO⁸

Check figure:
Amortization Expense,
Copyright $19,725

Corey Boyd has devoted years to developing a profitable business that earns an attractive return. Boyd is now considering the possibility of selling the business to you and has calculated that a fair selling price is $720,000. You agree to pay this price. The following information is available:

Exercise 12-28
Recording goodwill

LO⁹

Account	Account Balance December 31, 2005	Fair Value
Current assets	$249,000	$236,000
Land	38,000	294,000
Building	52,000	69,000
Accumulated amortization, building	46,000	
Equipment	152,000	42,000
Accumulated amortization, equipment	73,000	
Total liabilities	132,500	132,500

Required
1. Prepare the entry to record your purchase of the business on January 1, 2006, assuming you paid cash of $100,000 and borrowed the balance.
2. Assume that on December 31, 2008, management performed an impairment test on the goodwill calculated in Part 1. What is the appropriate entry if the fair value of the company was determined to be $520,000 and the net identifiable assets had a current fair value of $468,500?

Check figure:
1. Goodwill $211,500

On April 16, 2005, Jetta Interiors exchanged cash of $800 and furniture with a cost of $57,000 and related accumulated amortization of $36,000 for furniture with a market value of $29,000. Record the exchange.

*Exercise 12-29
Exchanging similar
non-monetary assets

LO¹⁰

Check figure:
Furniture (new) $21,800

Hannover Holdings had land recorded in its accounting records at an original cost of $130,000. On March 1, 2005, Hannover exchanged this land plus paid $3,000 for a parcel of land with a market value of $140,000. Record the exchange.

*Exercise 12-30
Exchanging similar
non-monetary assets

LO¹⁰

Check figure:
Land (new) $133,000

An asterisk (*) identifies assignment material based on Appendix 12A.

Problems

Problem 12-1A
Real estate costs

LO²

On March 31, 2005, ProSports paid $2,800,000 for a tract of land and two buildings on it. The plan was to demolish Building 1 and build a new store in its place. Building 2 was to be used as a company office and was appraised at a value of $641,300. A lighted parking lot near Building 2 had improvements (Land Improvements 1) valued at $408,100. Without considering the buildings or improvements, the tract of land was estimated to have a value of $1,865,600. ProSports incurred the following additional costs:

Cost to demolish Building 1	$ 422,600
Cost of additional landscaping	167,200
Cost to construct new building (Building 3)	2,019,000
Cost of new land improvements near Building 2 (Land Improvements 2)	158,000

Check figure:
2. Land $2,381,800

Required
1. Prepare a schedule having the following column headings: Land, Building 2, Building 3 Land Improvements 1, and Land Improvements 2. Allocate the costs incurred by ProSports to the appropriate columns and total each column.
2. Prepare a single journal entry dated March 31, 2005, to record all the incurred costs, assuming they were paid in cash on that date.

Problem 12-2A
Balance sheet presentation

LO³

The adjusted balances at December 31, 2005, for Mosaic Services are shown in alphabetical order below:

Accounts payable	42,000	Office supplies	2,900
Accumulated amortization, equipment	81,000	Other operating expenses	698,000
Accumulated amortization, tools	53,000	Patent	17,000
Accumulated amortization, vehicles	122,000	Prepaid rent	60,000
Amortization expense, franchise	14,000	Reg Manning, capital*	47,900
Amortization expense, patent	2,000	Reg Manning, withdrawals	48,000
Cash	36,000	Salaries payable	33,000
Equipment	125,000	Service revenue	942,000
Franchise	38,000	Tools	126,000
Notes payable, due in 18 months	162,000	Vehicles	316,000

The owner, Reg Manning, made no additional investments during the year.

Check figure:
Total assets = $464,900

Required
Prepare a classified balance sheet at December 31, 2005.

Problem 12-3A
Calculating amortization—
partial periods

LO³, ⁴

Check figure:
DDB 2007: $46,000

Nanaimo Touring Company runs boat tours along the west coast of British Columbia. It purchased on March 5, 2005, for cash of $345,000, a cruising boat with a useful life of 10 years or 13,250 hours with a salvage of $80,000. The company's year-end is December 31.

Required
Calculate amortization expense for the fiscal years 2005, 2006, and 2007 by completing a schedule with the following headings (round to the nearest whole dollar):

	Amortization Method¹:		
Year	Straight-Line	Double-Declining-Balance	Units-of-Production²

¹ Amortization is calculated to the nearest month.
² Assume actual hours of service were: 2005, 720; 2006, 1,780; 2007, 1,535.

Refer to the information in Problem 12-3A. Redo the question assuming that amortization for partial periods is calculated using the half-year rule.

Problem 12-4A
Calculating amortization—
partial periods

$LO^{3,4}$

Check figure:
DDB 2007: $49,680

On July 1, 2005, CYBERplex Company purchased for $675,000 equipment having an estimated useful life of six years with an estimated salvage value of $45,000. Amortization is taken for the portion of the year the asset is used. The company has a December 31 year-end.

Required
Complete the following schedules:

Problem 12-5A
Calculating amortization—
partial periods

$LO^{3,4}$

Check figures:
1. 2007 Amortization
   expense $125,000
2. 2007 Amortization
   expense $105,000

	2005	2006	2007
1. Double-declining-balance method			
Equipment			
Less: Accumulated amortization			
Year-end book value			
Amortization expense for the year			
2. Straight-line method			
Equipment			
Less: Accumulated amortization			
Year-end book value			
Amortization expense for the year			

**Alma Company
Partial Balance Sheet
April 30, 2005**

Property, plant, and equipment:		
Land		$1,300,000
Building[1]	$975,000	
Less: Accumulated amortization	715,000	260,000
Equipment[2]	750,000	
Less: Accumulated amortization	318,000	432,000
Total property, plant, and equipment		$1,992,000

[1] The building was purchased on May 3, 1994, and is amortized to the nearest whole month using the straight-line method. Amortization is based on a 15-year life after which it will be demolished and replaced with a new one.

[2] The equipment was purchased on November 3, 2002, and is amortized to the nearest whole month using the double-declining-balance method. The total estimated useful life is 10 years with a salvage value of $250,000.

Problem 12-6A
Calculating amortization

LO^3

Required
1. Calculate *and* record amortization for the year just ended April 30, 2006, for both the building and equipment.
2. Prepare the property, plant, and equipment section of the balance sheet at April 30, 2006.

Check figures:
1. Dr. Amortization Expense,
   Building $65,000
1. Dr. Amortization Expense,
   Equipment $86,400
2. Total PPE = $1,840,600

Problem 12-7A
Capital asset costs; partial year's amortization; alternative methods

LO2, 3, 4

Check figures:
2. $19,575
3. $13,125

New Economy Construction recently negotiated a lump-sum purchase of several assets from a company that was going out of business. The purchase was completed on March 1, 2005, at a total cash price of $787,500 and included a building, land, certain land improvements, and 12 vehicles. The estimated market values of the assets were: building, $408,000; land, $289,000; land improvements, $42,500; and vehicles, $110,500. The company's fiscal year ends on December 31.

Required
1. Prepare a schedule to allocate the lump-sum purchase price to the separate assets that were purchased. Also present the journal entry to record the purchase.
2. Calculate the 2005 amortization expense on the building using the straight-line method to the nearest whole month, assuming a 15-year life and a $25,650 salvage value.
3. Calculate the 2005 amortization expense on the land improvements assuming a five-year life and double-declining-balance amortization calculated to the nearest whole month.

Problem 12-8A
Alternative amortization methods; partial year's amortization

LO3, 4

Check figures:
2005 SL = $15,833
2007 DDB = $43,750
2009 Units = $37,360

A machine that cost $210,000, with a four-year life and an estimated $20,000 salvage value, was installed in Wolfville Company's factory on September 1, 2005. The factory manager estimated that the machine would produce 475,000 units of product during its life. It actually produced the following units: 2005, 21,400; 2006, 122,400; 2007, 119,600; 2008, 118,200; and 2009, 102,000. Wolfville's year-end is December 31.

Required
Prepare a form with the following column headings:

Year	Straight-Line	Units-of-Production	Double-Declining-Balance

Show the amortization for each year and the total amortization for the machine under each amortization method calculated to the nearest whole month.

Problem 12-9A
Calculating amortization; partial year's amortization

LO3, 4

At December 31, 2005, Neopolitan Servicing's balance sheet showed capital asset information as detailed in the schedule below. Neopolitan calculates amortization to the nearest whole month.

		Cost Information				Amortization		
Description	Date of Purchase	Amortization Method	Cost[1]	Salvage	Life	Balance of Accum. Amort. Dec. 31, 2005	Amortization Expense for 2006	Balance of Accum. Amort. Dec. 31, 2006
Office Equip.	March 27/02	Straight-line	$52,000	$14,000	10 yr.			
Machinery	June 4/02	Double-declining-balance	$275,000	$46,000	6 yr.			
Truck	Nov. 13/05	Units-of-production	$113,000	$26,000	250,000 km[2]			

[1] There have been no disposals or betterments since the date of purchase.
[2] Actual kilometres driven were: 2005, 14,000; 2006, 68,000.

Check figures:
Amort. Expense:
Office equip. $3,800;
Machinery $19,638;
Truck $23,664

Required
Complete the schedule.

ACT, Inc., completed the following transactions involving delivery trucks:

2005
Mar. 26   Paid cash for a new delivery truck, $19,415 plus $1,165 provincial sales tax. The truck was estimated to have a five-year life and a $3,000 trade-in value.
Dec. 31   Recorded straight-line amortization on the truck to the nearest whole month.
2006
Dec. 31   Recorded straight-line amortization on the truck to the nearest whole month. However, due to new information obtained early in January, the original estimated useful life of the truck was changed from five years to four years, and the original estimated trade-in value was increased to $3,500.

Required
Prepare journal entries to record the transactions.

Problem 12-10A
Partial year's amortization; revising amortization rates

LO$^{2, 3, 5}$

Check figure:
Dec. 31/06 Amort. Exp. $4,444

The December 31, 2005, adjusted trial balance of BW Technologies showed the following information:

Machinery...	$348,000
Accumulated amortization, machinery[1].......................................	154,000
Office furniture	56,000
Accumulated amortization, office furniture[2]..................................	31,000

[1] Remaining useful life four years; estimated salvage $40,000
[2] Remaining useful life five years; estimated salvage $7,000.

On July 7, 2006, a highly specialized component costing $52,000 was installed on the machinery to increase its productivity significantly. The useful life of the machinery did not change but the salvage value was adjusted to $60,000. At the beginning of 2006, it was determined that the estimated life of the office furniture should be reduced by two years and the salvage value decreased by $4,000. BW Technologies calculates amortization using the straight-line method to the nearest month.

Required
Prepare the entries to record amortization on the machinery and office furniture for the year ended December 31, 2006 (round calculations to the nearest whole dollar).

Problem 12-11A
Revising amortization rates

LO^5

Check figures:
Amort. Exp., Machinery $43,071;
Amort. Exp., Office Furn. $7,333

Crenshaw Contractors completed these transactions involving the purchase and operation of heavy equipment:

2005
July 1   Paid $255,440 cash for a new front-end loader, plus $15,200 in provincial sales tax and $2,500 for transportation charges. The loader was estimated to have a four-year life and a $34,740 salvage value.
Oct 2   Paid $3,660 to enclose the cab and install air conditioning in the loader. This increased the estimated salvage value of the loader by $1,110.
Dec. 31   Recorded straight-line amortization on the loader (to nearest whole month).
2006
Feb. 17   Paid $920 to repair the loader after the operator backed it into a tree.
June 30   Paid $4,500 to overhaul the loader's engine. As a result, the estimated useful life of the loader was increased by two years.
Dec. 31   Recorded straight-line amortization on the loader (to nearest whole month).

Required
Prepare journal entries to record the transactions.

Problem 12-12A
Revenue and capital expenditures; partial year's amortization; revising amortization rates

LO$^{2, 3, 4, 5}$

Check figures:
Dec. 31/05 Amort. Exp.,
Equip. $29,970;
Dec. 31/06 Amort. Exp.,
Equip. $48,674

Problem 12-13A

Partial period amortization; disposal of capital assets

$LO^{3, 4, 6}$

McFinley & Sons showed the following selected capital asset balances on December 31, 2005:

Land	$248,000
Building...	329,000
Accumulated amortization, building[1]..	246,000
Equipment	214,000
Accumulated amortization, equipment[2]	93,000

[1] Remaining estimated useful life is eight years with a salvage value of $50,000; amortized using the straight-line method to the nearest whole month.

[2] Total estimated useful life is 10 years with a salvage value of $20,000; amortized using the double-declining-balance method to the nearest whole month.

Check figures:
1. Gain $142,094
2. Loss $82,833

Required

Prepare the entries for each of the following (round final calculations to the nearest whole dollar).

1. The land and building were sold on September 27, 2006, for $470,000 cash.
2. The equipment was sold on November 2, 2006, for $18,000 cash.

Problem 12-14A

Disposal of capital assets

$LO^{2, 3, 4, 6}$

Wolfville purchased a used machine for $167,000 on January 2, 2005. It was repaired the next day at a cost of $3,420 and installed on a new platform that cost $1,080. The company predicted that the machine would be used for six years and would then have a $14,600 salvage value. Amortization was to be charged on a straight-line basis to the nearest whole month. A full year's amortization was charged on December 31, 2005. On September 30, 2010, it was retired.

Check figures:
2. Dec. 31/05 $26,150
3a. Loss $7,637
3b. Gain $14,863
3c. Gain $2,863

Required

1. Prepare journal entries to record the purchase of the machine, the cost of repairing it, and the installation. Assume that cash was paid.
2. Prepare entries to record amortization on the machine on December 31 of its first year and on September 30 in the year of its disposal (round calculations to the nearest whole dollar).
3. Prepare entries to record the retirement of the machine under each of the following unrelated assumptions:
   a. It was sold for $13,500.
   b. It was sold for $36,000.
   c. It was destroyed in a fire and the insurance company paid $24,000 in full settlement of the loss claim.

Problem 12-15A

Partial year's amortization; exchanging capital assets

$LO^{3, 4, 6}$

In 2005, Delcor Company completed the following transactions involving delivery trucks:

July 5   Traded in an old truck and paid $12,800 in cash for furniture. The accounting records on July 5 showed the cost of the old truck at $18,000 and related accumulated amortization of $3,000. The furniture was estimated to have a six-year life and a $3,134 trade-in value. The invoice for the exchange showed these items:

Price of the furniture	$22,550
Trade-in allowance granted on the old truck	(9,750)
Total paid in cash	$12,800

Dec. 31   Recorded straight-line amortization on the furniture (to nearest whole month).

Check figures:
July 5/05: Loss $5,250
Dec. 31/05: Amort. Exp. $1,618

Required

Prepare journal entries to record the transactions.

Wallingford Co. completed the following transactions involving machinery:

Machine No. 15-50 was purchased for cash on April 1, 2005, at an installed cost of $52,900. Its useful life was estimated to be six years with a $4,300 trade-in value. Straight-line amortization was recorded for the machine at the ends of 2005, 2006, and 2007. On March 29, 2008, it was traded for Machine No. 17-95, with an installed cash price of $62,000. A trade-in allowance of $30,210 was received for Machine No. 15-50, and the balance was paid in cash.

Machine No. 17-95's life was predicted to be four years with a trade-in value of $8,200. Double-declining-balance amortization on this machine was recorded each December 31. On October 2, 2009, it was traded for Machine No. BT-311, which had an installed cash price of $537,000. A trade-in allowance of $20,000 was received for Machine No. 17-95, and the balance was paid in cash.

It was estimated that Machine No. BT-311 would produce 200,000 units of product during its five-year useful life, after which it would have a $35,000 trade-in value. Units-of-production amortization was recorded for the machine for 2009, a period in which it produced 31,000 units of product. Between January 1, 2010, and August 21, 2012, the machine produced 108,000 more units. On August 21, 2012, it was sold for $81,200.

Required

Prepare journal entries to record:

a. The amortization expense recorded to the nearest whole month on the first December 31 of each machine's life.

b. The purchase/exchange/disposal of each machine.

Problem 12-16A
Partial year's amortization; alternative methods; exchange/disposal of capital assets

$LO^{3, 4, 6}$

Check figures:
a. Machine 15-50: $6,075;
Machine 17-95: $23,250;
Machine BT-311: $77,810

On February 20, 2005, Winnipeg Industries Ltd. paid $8,700,000 for land estimated to contain 11.6 million tonnes of recoverable ore of a valuable mineral. It installed machinery costing $348,000, which had a 12-year life and no salvage value, and was capable of exhausting the ore deposit in nine years. The machinery was paid for on May 24, 2005, six days before mining operations began. The company removed 744,000 tonnes of ore during the first seven months of operations.

Required

Prepare entries to record:

a. The purchase of the land

b. The installation of the machinery

c. The first seven months' amortization on the mine under the assumption that the land will be valueless after the ore is mined

d. The first seven months' amortization on the machinery, which will be abandoned after the ore is fully mined.

Problem 12-17A
Natural resources

LO^7

Check figures:
c. $558,000
d. $22,320

On November 1, 2005, Gelibrand purchased for $120,000 the copyright to publish the music composed by a local Celtic group. Gelibrand expects the music to be sold over the next five years.

Required

Prepare entries to record:

a. The purchase of the copyright, and

b. The amortization for the year ended December 31, 2005, calculated to the nearest whole month.

Problem 12-18A
Intangible assets

LO^8

Check figure:
b. $4,000

Alternate Problems

Problem 12-1B
Real estate costs

LO^2

In 2005, WebSpeed Technologies paid $1,350,000 for a tract of land on which two buildings were located. The plan was to demolish Building A and build a new factory (Building C) in its place. Building B was to be used as a company office and was appraised at a value of $472,770. A lighted parking lot near Building B had improvements valued at $125,145. Without considering the buildings or improvements, the tract of land was estimated to have a value of $792,585.

WebSpeed incurred the following additional costs:

Cost to demolish Building A	$ 117,000
Cost to landscape new building site	172,500
Cost to construct new building (Building C)	1,356,000
Cost of new land improvements (Land Improvements C)	101,250

Check figure:
2. Dr. Land $1,059,000

Required
1. Prepare a schedule having the following column headings: Land, Building B, Building C, Land Improvements B, and Land Improvements C. Allocate the costs incurred by WebSpeed to the appropriate columns and total each column.
2. Prepare a single journal entry dated June 1 to record all the incurred costs, assuming they were paid in cash on that date.

Problem 12-2B
Balance sheet presentation

LO^3

The adjusted balances at September 30, 2005, for Aidan Consulting are shown in alphabetical order below:

Accounts payable	1,750	Consulting fees earned	346,000
Accounts receivable	2,400	Copyright	3,700
Accumulated amortization, building	28,000	Land	38,000
Accumulated amortization, machinery	46,000	Machinery	64,000
Aidan Cummings, capital	150,140	Notes payable, due October 2010	31,000
Aidan Cummings, withdrawals	23,000	Other operating expenses	298,000
Amortization expense, copyright	540	Prepaid insurance	850
Building	125,000	Salaries expense	49,000
Cash	1,500	Unearned fees	3,100

The owner, Aidan Cummings, made a $75,000 additional investment during the year ended September 30, 2005.

Check figure:
Total assets = $161,450

Required
Prepare a classified balance sheet at September 30, 2005.

Problem 12-3B
Calculating amortization;
partial periods

$LO^{3,4}$

Check figure:
DDB 2007: $32,480

Tundra Tours runs tundra buggy expeditions in northern Manitoba for tourists to catch a glimpse of the abundant caribou, polar bears, and other wildlife. Tundra purchased a tundra buggy on October 19, 2005, for cash of $145,000. Its estimated useful life is five years or 100,000 kilometres with a salvage value estimated at $25,000. Tundra Tours' year-end is December 31.

Required
Calculate amortization expense for each fiscal year of the asset's useful life by completing a schedule with the following headings (round calculations to the nearest whole dollar):

	Amortization Method[1]:		
Year	Straight-Line	Double-Declining-Balance	Units-of-Production[2]

[1] Amortization is calculated to the nearest month.
[2] Assume actual kilometres of use were: 2005, 5,800; 2006, 19,400; 2007, 22,850; 2008, 25,700; 2009, 19,980; 2010, 14,600.

Refer to the information in Problem 12-3B. Redo the question assuming that amortization for partial periods is calculated using the half-year rule.

Problem 12-4B
Calculating amortization;
partial periods

$LO^{3,4}$

Check figure:
DDB 2007: $27,840

On April 2, 2005, CryptoLogic Company purchased machinery for $420,000 having an estimated useful life of 10 years with an estimated salvage value of $40,000. The company's year-end is December 31. Amortization is calculated using the half-year rule.

Required
Complete the following schedules:

Problem 12-5B
Calculating amortization;
partial periods

$LO^{3,4}$

Check figures:
1. 2007 Amortization expense $60,480
2. 2007 Amortization expense $38,000

	2005	2006	2007
1. Double-declining-balance method			
Machinery..	_____	_____	_____
Less: Accumulated amortization	_____	_____	_____
Year-end book value..	_____	_____	_____
Amortization expense for the year	_____	_____	_____
2. Straight-line method			
Machinery..	_____	_____	_____
Less: Accumulated amortization	_____	_____	_____
Year-end book value..	_____	_____	_____
Amortization expense for the year	_____	_____	_____

Problem 12-6B
Calculating amortization

LO^3

Ace Mechanical
Partial Balance Sheet
December 31, 2005

Property, plant, and equipment:

Delivery van[1]...	$125,000	
Less: Accumulated amortization...	82,500	$ 42,500
Machinery[2]...	320,000	
Less: Accumulated amortization...	256,667	63,333
Total property, plant, and equipment................................		$105,833

[1] The delivery van was purchased on January 1, 1996, and is amortized to the nearest whole month using the straight-line method. Its total estimated useful life is eight years with a $15,000 salvage value.

[2] The machinery was purchased on August 1, 2003, and is amortized to the nearest whole month using the double-declining-balance method. The useful life is estimated to be four years with a salvage value of $9,000.

Required
1. Calculate and record amortization for the year just ended December 31, 2006, for both the delivery van and machinery (round calculations to the nearest whole dollar).
2. Prepare the capital asset section of the balance sheet at December 31, 2006.

Check figures:
1. Dr. Amortization Expense, Van $13,750;
1. Dr. Amortization Expense, Machinery $31,667
2. Total PPE = $60,416

Problem 12-7B

Capital asset costs; partial year's amortization; alternative methods

LO 2, 3, 4

Check figures:
2. $7,350
3. $5,438

Willo Company recently negotiated a lump-sum purchase of several assets from a contractor who was planning to change locations. The purchase was completed on September 30, 2005, at a total cash price of $870,000, and included a building, land, certain land improvements, and a heavy general purpose truck. The estimated market values of the assets were: building, $552,750; land, $331,650; land improvements, $100,500; and truck, $20,100. The company's fiscal year ends on December 31.

Required
1. Prepare a schedule to allocate the lump-sum purchase price to the separate assets that were purchased. Also present the journal entry to record the purchase.
2. Calculate the 2005 amortization expense on the building using the straight-line method to the nearest whole month, assuming a 15-year life and a $37,500 salvage value.
3. Calculate the 2005 amortization expense on the land improvements assuming an eight-year life and double-declining-balance amortization to the nearest whole month (round calculations to the nearest whole dollar).

Problem 12-8B

Alternative amortization methods; partial year's amortization

LO 3, 4

Check figures:
2005 SL = $22,360
2010 Units = $15,100
2007 DDB = $34,320

On May 2, 2005, Gibbons Co. purchased and installed a new machine that cost $195,000, with a five-year life and an estimated $27,300 salvage value. Management estimated that the machine would produce 120,000 units of product during its life. Actual production of units was as follows:

2005	16,800
2006	26,400
2007	24,000
2008	22,800
2009	19,000
2010	22,100

Required
Prepare a schedule with the following column headings.

Year	Straight-Line	Units-of-Production	Double-Declining-Balance

Show the amortization for each year (calculated to the nearest whole month) and the total amortization for the machine under each amortization method. For units-of-production, round the amortization charge per unit to two decimal places. Gibbons Co.'s year-end is December 31.

At April 30, 2005, East Coast Helicopter's year-end, the balance sheet showed capital asset information as detailed in the schedule below. East Coast Helicopter calculates amortization for partial periods using the half-year rule.

Problem 12-9B
Calculating amortization; partial year's amortization

$LO^{3,4}$

Cost Information						Amortization		
Description	Date of Purchase	Amortization[1] Method	Cost[1]	Salvage	Life	Balance of Accum. Amort. Apr. 30, 2005	Amortization Expense for 2006	Balance of Accum. Amort. Apr. 30, 2006
Hangar	Oct. 3/02	Straight-line	$52,000	$14,000	20 yr.			
Helicopter	Oct. 28/02	Units-of-Production	$540,000	$180,000	10,000 flying hours[2]			
Tools	Nov. 3/02	Double-declining-balance	$64,000	$15,000	5 yr.			

[1] There have been no disposals or betterments since the date of purchase.
[2] Actual flying hours were (for years ended April 30): 2003, 94; 2004, 1,015; 2005, 928; 2006, 1,059.

Required
Complete the schedule.

Check figures:
Amort. Expense: Hangar $1,900;
Helicopter $38,124; Tools $3,432

Whitty Company completed the following transactions involving the purchase of delivery equipment.

Problem 12-10B
Partial year's amortization; revising amortization rates

$LO^{2,3,5}$

2005
June 26   Paid cash for a new truck, $34,200 plus $1,710 in provincial sales taxes. The truck was estimated to have a four-year life and a $9,000 salvage value.
July 5   Paid $1,890 for special racks installed on the truck. The racks did not increase the truck's estimated trade-in value but did improve the truck's usefulness.
Dec. 31   Recorded straight-line amortization on the truck to the nearest whole month.
2006
Jan. 5   It was determined that the estimated useful life of the truck should be revised to a total of six years and the salvage value changed to $5,050.
Mar. 15   Paid $330 for repairs to the truck's fender damaged when the driver backed into a loading dock.
Dec. 31   Recorded straight-line amortization on the machine to the nearest whole month.

Required
Prepare journal entries to record the transactions.

Check figure:
Dec. 31/06 Amort. Exp. $5,300

The December 31, 2005, adjusted trial balance of Cascades Company showed the following information:

Problem 12-11B
Revising amortization rates

LO^5

Building	$229,000
Accumulated amortization, building[1]	112,000
Equipment	98,000
Accumulated amortization, equipment[2]	32,000

[1] Remaining useful life 15 years; estimated salvage value $50,000
[2] Remaining useful life six years; estimated salvage value $15,000.

On September 28, 2006, a major renovation on the building was completed, costing $152,000 and increasing its estimated salvage value to $120,000. The estimated useful life of the building was not affected by the renovation. At the beginning of 2006, it was determined that the remaining estimated life of the equipment should be 10 years and the salvage value $5,000. Cascades Company calculates amortization using the straight-line method to the nearest month (round calculations to the nearest whole dollar).

Check figures:
Amort. Exp., Building $5,905;
Amort. Exp., Equip. $6,100

Required

Prepare the entries to record amortization on the building and equipment for the year ended December 31, 2006.

Problem 12-12B

Revenue and capital expenditures; partial year's amortization; disposal

$LO^{2,3,4,6}$

Check figures:
2. Dec. 31/05 Amort. Exp. $24,000
    Mar. 29/07 Amort. Exp. $6,000
3a. Gain $6,450
3b. Loss $4,650
3c. Loss $6,750

On January 9, 2005, Gibbons purchased a used machine for $68,400. The next day, it was repaired at a cost of $8,100 and was mounted on a new platform that cost $6,300. Management estimated that the machine would be used for three years and would then have a $10,800 salvage value. Amortization was to be charged on a straight-line basis to the nearest whole month. A full year's amortization was charged on December 31 of the first and second years of the machine's use, and on March 29, 2007, the machine was retired from service.

Required
1. Prepare journal entries to record the purchase of the machine, the cost of repairing it, and the installation. Assume that cash was paid.
2. Prepare entries to record amortization on the machine on December 31, 2005, and on March 29, 2007. Assume amortization is calculated to the nearest whole month.
3. Prepare entries to record the retirement of the machine under each of the following unrelated assumptions:
    a. It was sold for $35,250.
    b. It was sold for $24,150.
    c. It was destroyed in a fire and the insurance company paid $22,050 in full settlement of the loss claim.

Problem 12-13B
Partial period amortization; disposal of capital assets

$LO^{3,4,6}$

Tamboora Industries showed the following selected capital asset balances on January 31, 2005:

Van...	$46,000
Accumulated amortization, van[1]..	29,000
Machinery..	92,000
Accumulated amortization, machinery[2]...	14,600
Equipment	54,000
Accumulated amortization, equipment[3]...	32,000

[1] Remaining estimated useful life is 40,000 kilometres with a salvage value of $7,000; amortized using the units-of-production method.

[2] Total estimated useful life is 10 years with a salvage value of $12,000; amortized using the double-declining-balance method to the nearest whole month.

[3] Remaining estimated useful life is three years with a salvage value of $4,000; amortized using the straight-line method to the nearest whole month.

Check figures:
1. Accum. Amort. $30,125;
2. Accum. Amort. $23,630;
3. Accum. Amort. $34,500

Required
Prepare the entries to record the following disposals:
1. The van was sold on March 2, 2005, for cash of $12,800. It had been driven 4,500 kilometres from January 31, 2005, to the date of sale.
2. The machinery was sold on August 27, 2005, for cash of $68,370.
3. The equipment was sold on June 29, 2005, for cash of $19,800.

On January 1, 2005, Brodie purchased a used machine for $130,000. The next day, it was repaired at a cost of $3,390 and mounted on a new platform that cost $4,800. Management estimated that the machine would be used for seven years and would then have an $18,000 salvage value. Amortization was to be charged on a straight-line basis to the nearest whole month. A full year's amortization was charged on December 31, 2005, through to December 31, 2009, and on April 1, 2010, the machine was retired from service.

Required

1. Prepare journal entries to record the purchase of the machine, the cost of repairing it, and the installation. Assume that cash was paid.
2. Prepare entries to record amortization on the machine on December 31, 2005, and on April 1, 2010 (round calculations to the nearest whole dollar).
3. Prepare entries to record the retirement of the machine under each of the following unrelated assumptions:
   a. It was sold for $30,000.
   b. It was sold for $50,000.
   c. It was destroyed in a fire and the insurance company paid $20,000 in full settlement of the loss claim.

Problem 12-14B
Disposal of capital assets

LO² ³ ⁴ ⁶

Check figures:
2. Dec. 31/05 $17,170
    Apr. 1/10 $4,293
3a. Loss $18,047
3b. Gain $1,953
3c. Loss $28,047

During 2005, Delton Hardware had the following transactions.

2005

Aug. 31   Delton traded in furniture with a cost of $21,000 and accumulated amortization of $12,900 recorded in the accounting records on this date. Delton paid $28,200 in cash for a computer system that was estimated to have a three-year life and a $9,600 trade-in value. The invoice for the exchange showed these items:

Price of the computer equipment	$37,200
Trade-in allowance granted on the furniture	(9,000)
Total paid in cash	$28,200

Sept. 4   Paid $3,690 for upgrades to the computer equipment, which increased its usefulness.
Dec. 31   Recorded straight-line amortization on the computer equipment to the nearest whole month. Round calculations to the nearest whole dollar.

Required
Prepare journal entries to record the transactions.

Problem 12-15B
Partial year's amortization; revising amortization; exchanging capital assets

LO³ ⁴ ⁵ ⁶

Check figures:
Aug. 31/05: Gain $900;
Dec. 31/05: Amort. Exp. $3,477

Montreal Printing Co. completed the following transactions involving printing equipment:
Machine 366-90 was purchased for cash on May 1, 2005, at an installed cost of $48,600. Its useful life was estimated to be four years with a $5,400 trade-in value. Straight-line amortization was recorded for the machine at the end of 2005 and 2006.
On August 5, 2007, it was traded for machine 366-91, which had an installed cash price of $36,000. A trade-in allowance of $27,000 was received and the balance was paid in cash. The new machine's life was estimated at five years with a $6,300 trade-in value. Double-declining-balance amortization was recorded on each December 31 of its life. On February 1, 2010, it was sold for $9,000.
Machine 367-11 was purchased on February 1, 2010, at an installed cash price of $53,100. It was estimated that the new machine would produce 75,000 units during its useful life after which it would have a $5,400 trade-in value. Units-of-production amortization was recorded on the machine for 2010, a period in which it produced 7,500 units of product. Between January 1 and October 3, 2011, the machine produced 11,250 more units. On October 3, 2011, it was sold for $36,000.

Required
Prepare journal entries to record:
1. The amortization expense recorded to the nearest whole month on the first December 31 of each machine's life (for units-of-production, round the rate per unit to two decimal places).
2. The purchase/exchange/disposal of each machine.

Problem 12-16B
Partial year's amortization; alternative methods; exchange/disposal of capital assets

LO³ ⁴ ⁶

Check figures:
1. Machine 366-90: $7,200;
    Machine 366-91: $6,000;
    Machine 367-11: $4,800

Problem 12-17B
Natural resources

Check figures:
3. $86,400
4. $15,000

On May 8, 2005, Hubert Industries paid $1,080,000 for land estimated to contain nine million tonnes of recoverable ore. It installed machinery costing $187,500, which had an eight-year life and no salvage value, and was capable of exhausting the ore deposit in five years. The machinery was paid for on June 28, four days before mining operations began. The company removed 720,000 tonnes of ore during the first six months of operations.

Required
Prepare entries to record:
1. The purchase of the land
2. The installation of the machinery
3. The first six months' amortization on the mine under the assumption that the land will be valueless after the ore is mined, and
4. The first six months' amortization on the machinery, which will be abandoned after the ore is fully mined.

Problem 12-18B
Intangible assets

On Febrary 3, 2005, Letsin Pharmacy Products purchased the patent for a new drug for cash of $184,000. Letsin expects the drug to be sold over the next 10 years.

Required
1. Prepare entries to record the:
   a. purchase of the patent, and
   b. amortization for the year ended December 31, 2005, calculated to the nearest whole month.
2. On December 31, 2005, Letsin's adjusted trial balance showed the following additional asset accounts:

Accounts receivable	238,000
Accumulated amortization, equipment	216,000
Accumulated amortization, building	157,500
Allowance for doubtful accounts	7,000
Cash	86,000
Equipment	398,000
Building	496,000
Land	92,000
Merchandise inventory	113,000

Prepare the asset section of the balance sheet at December 31, 2005, including the patent purchased on February 3, 2005.

Analytical and Review Problem

A & R Problem 12-1

At the last meeting of the executive committee of Kearins, Ltd., the controller was severely criticized by both the president and vice-president of production about the recognition of periodic amortization. The president was unhappy with the fact that what he referred to as "a fictitious item" was deducted, resulting in depressed net income. In his words, "Amortization is a fiction when the assets being amortized are worth far more than we paid for them. What the controller is doing is unduly understating our net income. This in turn is detrimental to our shareholders because it results in the undervaluation of our shares on the market."

The vice-president was equally adamant about the periodic amortization charges; however, she presented a different argument. She said, "Our maintenance people tell me that the level of maintenance is such that our plant and equipment will last virtually forever." She further stated that charging amortization on top of maintenance expenses is double-counting—it seems reasonable to charge either maintenance or amortization but not both.

The time taken by other pressing matters did not permit the controller to answer; instead, you were asked to prepare a report to the executive committee to deal with the issues raised by the president and vice-president.

Required
As the controller's assistant, prepare the required report.

Ethics Challenge

EC 12-1

Marcia Diamond is a small business owner who handles all the books for her business. Her company just finished a year in which a large amount of borrowed funds was invested into a new building addition as well as numerous equipment and fixture additions. Marcia's banker requires that she submit semiannual financial statements for his file so he can monitor the financial health of her business. He has warned her that if profit margins erode, making the loan riskier from the bank's point of view, he might raise the interest rate on the borrowed funds. Marcia knows that her profit margin is likely to decline in this current year. As she posts year-end adjusting entries, she decides to apply the following amortization rule: All capital additions for the current year are considered put into service the first day of the following month.

Required
1. Identify the decisions managers like Ms. Diamond must make in applying amortization methods.
2. Is Marcia's decision an ethical violation, or is it a legitimate decision that managers make in computing amortization?
3. How will Marcia's amortization rule affect the profit margin of her business?

Focus on Financial Statements

GelCo's Capital Asset Subledger at January 1, 2005, appeared as follows:

FFS 12-1

| | Cost Information | | | | | Amortization | |
Description	Date of Purchase[1]	Amort. Method[2]	Original Cost[3]	Salvage	Life	Accum. Amort. Balance Dec. 31, 2004	Amort. Expense for 2005
Land[4]	July 3/02		$140,000				
Building[4]	July 3/02	S/L	227,000	20,000	15 yr.		
Machinery[5]	Mar 20/02	Units	75,000	15,000	250,000 units		
Truck[6]	Mar 01/02	S/L	149,400	15,000	7 yr.		
Furniture[7,8]	Feb 18/02	DDB	12,000	1,500	5 yr.		
Patent	Nov 7/03		51,900	-0-	5 yr.		

Additional information:
[1] GelCo calculates amortization to the nearest whole month.
[2] S/L = Straight-Line; DDB = Double-Declining-Balance; Units = Units-of-Production
[3] There were no disposals or betterments prior to January 1, 2005.
[4] At the beginning of 2005, it was determined that the land and building would be used for five years less than originally estimated due to the need to expand.
[5] Actual units produced: 2002, 45,000; 2003, 55,000; 2004, 52,000; 2005, 65,000.
[6] A major overhaul costing $21,600 was performed on the truck on July 3, 2005, that would extend its useful life by four years (with no material change expected in the salvage value). The overhaul of $21,600 has not been included in the cost of $149,400.
[7] Used office equipment and furniture were purchased on April 10, 2005, for a total of $57,000 at a bankruptcy sale. The appraised value of the office equipment was $48,000 and of the furniture $36,000. The old furniture was given to a charitable organization on April 12, 2005.
[8] The estimated useful lives and salvage values of the April 10 purchases were four years and $5,000 for the office equipment, and five years and $2,000 for the furniture. These assets will be amortized using the DDB method.

Required
a. Complete the Capital Asset Subledger; round calculations to the nearest dollar.
b. Using the information from the Capital Asset Subledger completed in Part (a) and the following December 31, 2005, adjusted account balances, prepare a single-step income statement and statement of owner's equity for the year ended December 31, 2005, along with the December 31, 2005, classified balance sheet: Cash, $15,000; Accounts Receivable, $36,000; Prepaid Insurance, $7,800; Accounts Payable, $34,000; Unearned Revenue, $26,900; Notes Payable due in 2008, $142,000; Ted Gel, Capital, $232,190; Ted Gel, Withdrawals, $102,000; Fees Earned, $475,000; Salaries Expense, $147,000; Insurance Expense, $15,000; Loss on disposal of furniture, $2,592. Ted Gel, the owner, made no investments during 2005.

Current Liabilities

Sometimes, "It's Not What You See; It's What You Don't See"!!!

Current liabilities include accounts payable, salaries and wages payable, interest payable, property taxes payable, income taxes payable, source deductions payable, GST and sales tax payable, as well as many others. According to John Douglas, a Chartered Accountant and Certified Fraud Examiner based in Toronto, Ontario, undisclosed current liabilities may significantly distort the true picture of financial statements used by decision makers such as analysts, banks, and investors, who evaluate the business based on these financial statements.

For example, when current liabilities are omitted, the working capital (current assets less current liabilities), quick ratio, and current ratio become inflated, giving the impression that the business has a favourable liquidity position when in fact the opposite might be true.

Undisclosed current liabilities may also cause net income to be overstated, if the offset to the liability is an income statement item. If, for instance, wages payable are not recorded, then the associated wages expense would also be missing. In this case, current liabilities would be understated, working capital would be overstated, and net income would be overstated.

But why intentionally mislead users of financial statements by hiding liabilities? John Douglas's experience has been that sometimes when businesspeople face extreme pressures, they employ unethical accounting practices. They are required to prepare one set of financial statements to satisfy multiple audiences, each with goals that could be in conflict with the others'. These might include the absentee owner who wants high profits, the bank or other financier who wants high profits, and the operator who may want lower profits (which would result in lower taxable income and therefore less income tax to pay).

John says that sometimes his review of records may find sizeable accruals booked (accidentally or intentionally) in the wrong accounting period, or not booked at all—for example, large accrued payroll liabilities that should have been accrued at year-end but were booked in the first month of the subsequent accounting period. John says that this is then the start of a bigger problem. Now the business has to deal with liabilities and related expenses from a prior period in the current period.

The ultimate discovery of hidden or unrecorded liabilities was one of the contributing factors to the fall of Enron and other companies.

Because current liabilities have to be paid out of current assets, they have an immediate impact on a business. Therefore, it is important to manage these liabilities, and be sure that they are properly and completely recorded, and in the correct period. To do that, you have to understand how current liabilities arise and how to record them in accordance with GAAP.

—John Douglas is a Chartered Accountant and Certified Fraud Examiner who is based in Toronto. He has carried out large and small fraud and other financial investigations, and has appeared in civil and criminal court as an expert witness. His Web site is located at www.johndouglas.ca.

Learning Objectives

LO1 Describe the characteristics of liabilities and explain the difference between current and long-term liabilities.

LO2 Identify and describe known current liabilities.

LO3 Prepare entries to account for short-term notes payable.

LO4 Account for estimated liabilities, including warranties and corporate income taxes.

LO5 Explain how to account for contingent liabilities.

*APPENDIX 13A

***LO6** Explain and account for short-term notes payable issued at a discount.

Chapter Preview

Previous chapters introduced us to liabilities for accounts payable, notes payable, wages, and unearned revenues. In this chapter we define, classify, and measure these liabilities for the purpose of reporting useful information about them to decision makers. We also learn more about liabilities such as warranties, taxes, payroll liabilities, and contingent liabilities. Understanding liabilities is important for both preparers and users of financial information according to John Douglas as described in the opening article.

Characteristics of Liabilities

LO¹ Describe the characteristics of liabilities and explain the difference between current and long-term liabilities.

This section discusses important characteristics of liabilities, how they are classified, and how they are reported.

Defining Liabilities

A **liability** is a future payment of assets or services that a company is presently obligated to make as a result of past transactions or events.[1] This definition includes three crucial elements as portrayed in Exhibit 13.1.

Exhibit 13.1

Characteristics of a Liability

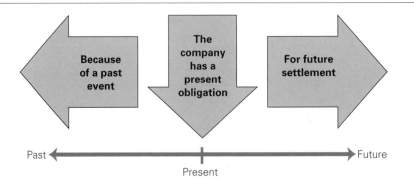

Liabilities do not include *all* expected future settlements. For example, most companies expect to pay wages to their employees in upcoming months and years. But these future amounts are not liabilities because the revenue recognition principle says we record an event only when it occurs. Therefore, a future liability regarding an employee's work will be recorded only when the work has been performed (revenue recognition principle) and in the period in which it occurred (matching principle).

Classifying Liabilities as Current or Long-Term

Information about liabilities is more useful when the balance sheet P.37 identifies them as either current or long-term. Decision makers need to know when obligations are due so they can plan for them and take appropriate action. Improper

---

[1] *CICA Handbook*, section 1000, "Financial Statement Concepts," par. 32.

classification of liabilities can affect key ratios[2] used in financial statement analysis and decision-making.

Current Liabilities

Current liabilities, also called *short-term liabilities*, are obligations expected to be settled:

> 1. Within one year of the balance sheet date, or within the company's next operating cycle, whichever is longer,
> 2. Using current assets or by creating other current liabilities (e.g., replacing an account payable with a note payable).[3]

Examples of current liabilities are accounts payable, short-term notes payable, wages payable, warranty liabilities, lease liabilities, payroll and other taxes payable, unearned revenues, and the portion of long-term debt that is due within the next period.

Current liabilities and their classification on financial statements vary depending on the type of operations performed by the company and the desired detail. For instance, Gildan Activewear Inc. reported current liabilities on its September 29, 2002, balance sheet as shown in Exhibit 13.2. This means that Gildan Activewear expected to pay $91,479,836 of current liabilities using current assets during the year after the balance sheet date of September 29, 2002.

Liabilities:		
Current Liabilities		
Accounts payable and accrued liabilities	$82,167,747	
Income taxes payable	3,063,050	
Current portion of long-term debt	6,249,039	
Total current liabilities		$ 91,479,836
Long-term debt		114,866,404

Exhibit 13.2

Liabilities of Gildan Activewear Inc. at September 29, 2002

www.gildan.com

Long-Term Liabilities

A company's obligations *not* expected to be settled within the longer of one year of the balance sheet date or the next operating cycle are reported as **long-term liabilities**. Long-term liabilities such as long-term notes payable, lease liabilities, and bonds payable are expected to be settled out of current assets that do not yet exist. Sometimes long-term liabilities are reported on the balance sheet as a single item or they can be reported as individual amounts. Gildan Activewear reported long-term debt on its September 29, 2002, balance sheet as shown in Exhibit 13.2. This means Gildan expects to pay $114,866,404 after September 29, *2003*.

Long-term liabilities are discussed in greater detail in Chapter 17 but are introduced here because of their relationship to current liabilities.

---

[2] For example, current liabilities are the denominator in the calculation of both the *current ratio* P. 225 and *acid-test ratio* P. 486. These ratios, commonly referred to as measures of *liquidity*, measure an organization's ability to pay current obligations with specific current assets. If current liabilities are understated because of a misclassification of liabilities, both ratios would overstate the company's liquidity.

[3] *CICA Handbook*, section 1510, "Current Assets and Current Liabilities," par. .03.

Current Portion of Long-Term Debt

The **current portion of long-term debt** is the part of long-term debt that is due within the longer of one year of the balance sheet date or the next operating cycle and is reported under current liabilities. Exhibit 13.2 shows Gildan Activewear's *current portion of long-term debt* as part of current liabilities. This represents the principal amount of debt that will be paid by Gildan Activewear by September 29, 2003, which is *within one year from the balance sheet date*. The portion due after *September 29, 2003*, is reported on the balance sheet as long-term debt. Exhibit 13.3 illustrates the timing of current vs. long-term debt in comparison to the balance sheet date for Gildan Activewear.

Exhibit 13.3

Timing of Current vs. Long-Term Liabilities to Gildan Activewear Inc.'s September 29, 2002, Balance Sheet Date

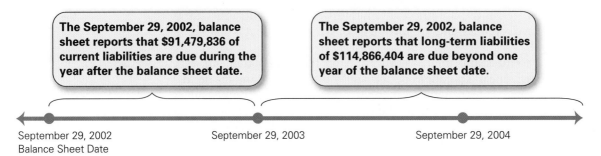

To illustrate further, let's assume a debt of $7,500 is issued on January 1, 2005. It is to be repaid in installments of $1,500 per year for five years each December 31. On December 31, 2005, the first principal payment of $1,500 was made (ignore interest) leaving a principal balance owing on December 31, 2005, of $6,000 (= $7,500 − $1,500). The December 31, 2005, balance sheet reports the $1,500 principal payment due in 2006 as the current portion of long-term debt under current liabilities as shown in Exhibit 13.4. The *remaining* $4,500 long-

Exhibit 13.4

Determining Current vs. Long-Term Portions of Liabilities

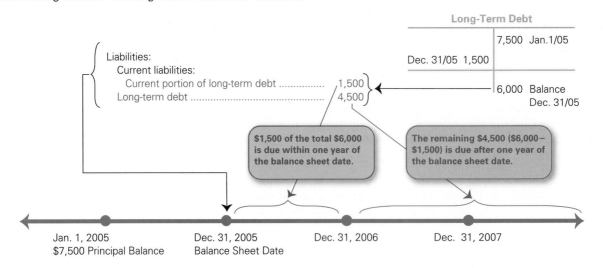

term portion of the principal (= $6,000 total liability − $1,500 current portion) will be reported under long-term liabilities on the December 31, 2005, balance sheet. The sum of the current and long-term portions equals the $6,000 total principal of the liability outstanding on December 31, 2005. No journal entry is necessary to split the current portion from the long-term portion. Instead, we properly classify the amounts for debt as either current or long-term when the balance sheet is prepared.

Dividing a liability between its current and long-term portion involves only the principal amount of the debt and not the anticipated future interest payments. Any interest that has accrued up to the date of the balance sheet is reported as *interest payable* under current liabilities.

Liabilities not having a fixed due date that are payable on the creditor's demand are known as **demand loans**. They are reported as current liabilities because the creditor may *demand* or require payment within a year from the balance sheet date or the company's next operating cycle; whichever is longer.

Balance Sheet Presentation of Current Liabilities

Exhibit 13.5 is based on the December 28, 2002, balance sheet of Loblaw Companies Limited. The actual balance sheet details the assets and shareholders' equity items and contains notes corresponding to items on the balance sheet. Our focus is on the liability section of the balance sheet. Note that current liabilities are listed according to their maturity or due dates similar to the current liabilities listed in Exhibit 13.2.

Loblaw Companies Limited
Balance Sheet
December 28, 2002
($millions)

Assets		$11,110
Liabilities:		
Current liabilities:		
Commercial paper	$ 533	
Accounts payable and accrued liabilities	2,336	
Income taxes	179	
Long-term debt due within one year	106	
Total current liabilities		$ 3,154
Long-term debt		3,420
Other liabilities		412
Total liabilities		$ 6,986
Shareholders' equity		4,124
Total liabilities and shareholders' equity		$11,110

Exhibit 13.5

Balance Sheet of Loblaw Companies Limited

1. What is a liability?

2. Is every expected future payment a liability?

3. If a liability is payable in 15 months, is it classified as current or long-term?

Flashback

Answers—p. 692

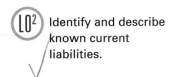

Identify and describe known current liabilities.

Known (Determinable) Liabilities

Accounting for liabilities involves addressing three important questions: Whom to pay? When to pay? How much to pay? Answers to these questions often are decided when a liability is incurred. For example, suppose a company has an account payable to a specific individual for $5,000, due on August 15, 2005. This liability is definite with respect to all three questions. The company *knows* whom to pay, when to pay, and how much to pay; these liabilities are called **known liabilities**. They are set by agreements, contracts, or laws, and are measurable and include accounts payable, payroll, sales taxes, unearned revenues, and notes payable. For other types of liabilities there may be *uncertainty* with respect to one or more of these three questions. This section discusses how we account for *known* liabilities. The next section will look at *uncertain* liabilities.

Trade Accounts Payable

Trade accounts payable, frequently shortened to *accounts payable*, are amounts owed to suppliers with whom we *trade* regarding products or services purchased on credit. Much of our discussion of merchandising activities in earlier chapters dealt with accounts payable. To review, assume Leon's purchases $12,000 of office supplies from Staples on November 14, 2005, on credit, terms n/30. Leon's would record the transaction as follows:

2005			
Nov. 14	Office Supplies	12,000	
	Accounts Payable—Staples		12,000
	To record the purchase of office supplies on credit: terms n/30.		

Because this account payable is due within 30 days (which is within the current period), it is reported as a current liability on the balance sheet.

Payroll Liabilities

Extend Your Knowledge

13-1

A more detailed discussion of payroll liabilities than what follows is included in Chapter 11 of Volume 1. For your convenience, Chapter 11, including end-of-chapter materials, is available in PDF format on the Online Learning Centre.

Payroll represents employee compensation for work performed. **Payroll liabilities** are employee compensation amounts owing to employees. Employers are required by law to deduct (withhold) amounts regarding the employee's income taxes payable and Canada Pension Plan P.574 (CPP) (or Quebec Pension Plan in Quebec) and Employment Insurance P.574 (EI) contributions. Employers may withhold other amounts such as union dues and hospital insurance as authorized by the employee. All amounts withheld are remitted by the employer to the appropriate authorities. The difference between an employee's gross earnings and deductions taken equals an employee's net pay (or take-home pay).

To illustrate the journal entry to record payroll liabilities, assume that on January 5, the end of its first weekly pay period in the year, Chandler Company's payroll records showed that its one office employee and two sales employees had each earned gross pay of $688, $880, and $648 respectively. The payroll records showed the following details:

| | | | Deductions | | | | Payment | Distribution | |
Gross Pay	EI Premium[4]	Income Taxes[4]	Hosp. Ins.	CPP[4]	Union Dues	Total Deductions	Net Pay	Office Salaries	Sales Salaries
688.00	14.45	137.50	40.00	30.72	15.00	237.67	450.33	688.00	
880.00	18.48	203.35	40.00	40.23	15.00	317.06	562.94		880.00
648.00	13.61	124.80	40.00	28.74	15.00	222.15	425.85		648.00
2,216.00	46.54	465.65	120.00	99.69	45.00	776.88	1,439.12	688.00	1,528.00

The journal entries to record the January 5 payroll liabilities are:

Jan. 5	Office Salaries Expense.............................	688.00	
	Sales Salaries Expense.............................	1,528.00	
	EI Payable		46.54
	Employees' Income Tax Payable		465.65
	Employees' Hospital Insurance		
	Payable..................................		120.00
	CPP Payable................................		99.69
	Employees' Union Dues Payable...........		45.00
	Salaries Payable		1,439.12
	To record January 5 payroll.		
5	EI Expense	65.16	
	CPP Expense.......................................	99.69	
	EI Payable		65.16
	CPP Payable		99.69
	To record the employer's payroll taxes;		
	46.54 × 1.4 = 65.16 EI;		
	99.69 × 1 = 99.69 CPP.		

Payroll liabilities are shown on the balance sheet under current liabilities. Bombardier reported "Payroll related liabilities" of $558.1 million as part of its current liabilities at January 31, 2003.

www.bombardier.com

Provincial Sales Tax (PST) and Federal Goods and Services Tax (GST) Payable

Canada has two levels of government, provincial and federal, that impose sales taxes on the same transactions. We will introduce and demonstrate *each independently* to avoid confusion.

Provincial Sales Tax (PST)

Provincial Sales Tax (PST) is a tax levied on sales to the *final* consumers of products. It is calculated as a percentage of the sale price of the item being sold.[5] PST percentages vary across the country, as detailed in Exhibit 13.6. All provinces (except Alberta) require retailers to collect PST from their customers and to forward this tax periodically to the appropriate provincial authority.

To demonstrate, assume that Best Furniture, located in Maidstone, Saskatchewan, is a retailer of household furnishings. Best purchases merchandise inventory from several manufacturers including Holt Industries. Because Best Furniture is

Exhibit 13.6

Provincial Sales Tax Rates

	PST Rate
Alberta..	-0-
British Columbia	7.5%
Manitoba	7%
Northwest Territories	-0-
Nunavut..	-0-
Ontario	8%
Prince Edward Island[5]	10%
Quebec[5]	7.5%
Saskatchewan	6%
Yukon Territory	-0-

Note: For New Brunswick, Nova Scotia, and Newfoundland and Labrador, a Harmonized Sales Tax (HST) is used (see Exhibit 13.7 for explanation of HST).

---

[4] These values are based on the Saskatchewan payroll deductions tables in effect on January 1, 2003.

[5] In Quebec and PEI, PST = PST% × (Sales Price + GST).

not the final consumer, it does not pay PST on purchases made from Holt Industries and its other suppliers. Customers purchasing from Best Furniture are the final consumer and will therefore pay the applicable PST. Best Furniture is required to collect and remit PST charged on sales to its customers. If Best Furniture's total cash sales on July 14, 2005, were $16,000 (cost of sales $12,000), the company would record the following entry (assuming a perpetual inventory system):

2005			
July 14	Cash	16,960	
	Sales...		16,000
	PST Payable		960
	To record cash sales plus applicable PST;		
	16,000 × 6% = 960.		
14	Cost of Goods Sold..	12,000	
	Merchandise Inventory		12,000
	To record cost of sales.		

When Best Furniture *remits* or forwards this tax to the provincial authority, the entry is (assume for simplicity that it is remitted on the same day):

2005			
July 14	PST Payable..	960	
	Cash		960
	To record remittance of sales tax		
	payable to provincial authority.		

Any balance in PST Payable at the end of the period is reported as a current liability on the balance sheet.

Federal Goods and Services Tax (GST)

The federal government levies a **Goods and Services Tax (GST)**, which is a tax on nearly all goods and services sold in Canada. To discuss GST, the related terminology must be understood and is summarized in Exhibit 13.7.

Exhibit 13.7

Terminology Related to GST

Exempt Supplies	GST-exempt services are educational, health care, and financial services.
Harmonized Sales Tax (HST)	A combined GST and PST rate of 15% applied to *taxable supplies*. Currently, New Brunswick, Nova Scotia, and Newfoundland and Labrador apply HST.
Input Tax Credit (ITC)	GST paid by the *registrant* on purchases of *taxable supplies*. Input tax credits are applied against (reduce) GST Payable. Input tax credits are also known as and recorded by the *registrant* as GST Receivable.
Receiver General for Canada	Federal government authority to which GST Payable is remitted.
Registrant	Registered[6] individual or entity selling *taxable supplies* that is responsible for collecting the GST on behalf of the government.
Taxable Supplies	Taxable goods or services on which GST is calculated and includes everything except *zero-rated* and *exempt* supplies.
Zero-Rated Supplies	Goods including groceries, prescription drugs, and medical devices, which have zero GST.

[6] A business with sales of less than $30,000 per year does not have to register for GST purposes.

GST is calculated as 7% of taxable supplies. A registrant collects GST regarding a sale of taxable supplies. The same registrant also *pays* GST on purchases of taxable supplies but records an input tax credit (or GST Receivable) for the amount of GST paid. GST collected less input tax credits (GST paid) equals the balance to be remitted to (or refunded from) the Receiver General for Canada.[7]

We will now demonstrate the collection, payment, and final remittance of GST (for simplicity, PST will be ignored for the moment). On August 3, 2005, Best Furniture purchased $20,000 of merchandise inventory on credit from Holt Industries; terms n/30. Best Furniture records this transaction as:

2005			
Aug. 3	Merchandise Inventory....................................	20,000	
	GST Receivable...	1,400	
	Accounts Payable—Holt Industries		21,400
	To record purchase on credit plus applicable ITC; 20,000 × 7% = 1,400.		

The balance in GST Receivable after posting the August 3 transaction is (assuming a zero beginning balance):

GST Receivable (or ITC)			
Aug. 3	1,400		

On August 6, Best Furniture recorded total sales (all cash) of $45,000 (cost of sales $33,750) as:

2005			
Aug. 6	Cash	48,150	
	Sales..		45,000
	GST Payable		3,150
	To record cash sales plus applicable GST; 45,000 × 7% = 3,150.		
6	Cost of Goods Sold..	33,750	
	Merchandise Inventory		33,750
	To record cost of sales.		

The balance in GST Payable after posting the August 6 transaction is (assuming a zero beginning balance):

GST Payable			
		3,150	Aug. 6

After posting the August 6 transaction, the GST accounts show a net balance *owing* to the Receiver General for Canada of $1,750 (GST Payable of $3,150 less GST Receivable or ITC of $1,400).[8]

---

[7] Businesses are required to remit quarterly, or for larger businesses, monthly. Certain businesses may elect to pay annually.

[8] Some businesses combine GST Receivable and GST Payable to achieve the same net result. For example, if Best Furniture had combined the GST accounts, as shown below, the same $1,750 net balance results.

GST Receivable/Payable			
Aug. 3	1,400	3,150	Aug. 6
		1,750	Balance

Assume Best Furniture remitted the balance to the Receiver General for Canada on August 7. The entry to record this transaction is:

2005			
Aug. 7	GST Payable..	3,150	
	Cash		1,750
	GST Receivable		1,400
	To record remittance of GST to Receiver General for Canada.		

The balances in GST Receivable and GST Payable would be zero after posting the August 7 entry.

If the balance in GST Receivable (ITC) exceeds the balance in GST Payable, Best Furniture would be entitled to receive a refund.

A net credit balance in the GST Payable account at the end of the period would be shown on the balance sheet as a current liability; a net debit balance would appear under current assets as GST Receivable.

Flashback

Answer—p. 692

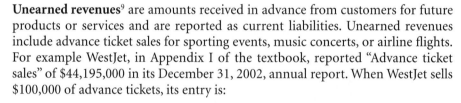

4. Masters Company collected $1,150 including taxes from a customer. Assuming that Masters pays a combined PST/GST rate of 15%, calculate (a) sales, and (b) harmonized sales taxes payable.

Unearned Revenues

Unearned revenues[9] are amounts received in advance from customers for future products or services and are reported as current liabilities. Unearned revenues include advance ticket sales for sporting events, music concerts, or airline flights. For example WestJet, in Appendix I of the textbook, reported "Advance ticket sales" of $44,195,000 in its December 31, 2002, annual report. When WestJet sells $100,000 of advance tickets, its entry is:

Cash	100,000	
Advance ticket sales		100,000
To record airline tickets sold in advance.		

If $40,000 in airline tickets purchased in advance are redeemed at a later date, the entry is:

Advance ticket sales	40,000	
Passenger revenues		40,000
To record redemption of airline tickets sold in advance.		

Unearned revenues also arise with magazine publishers, construction projects, hotel reservations, and custom orders. Unearned revenue accounts are reported as current liabilities.

---

[9] Unearned revenues are also called **deferred revenues**, **collections in advance**, or *customer deposits*.

Mid-Chapter Demonstration Problem

Centrum Cleaning Services, a Montreal business, has a December 31 year-end and prepares financial statements annually. Centrum gathered the following information to prepare the current liability section of its December 31, 2005, balance sheet.

a. Centrum borrowed $48,000 on January 2, 2005. Payments are made annually for five years each January 2.

Year	Annual Payment	Principal Portion of Payment	Interest Portion of Payment	Principal Balance at Year-End
2006	11,395	8,515	2,880	39,485
2007	11,395	9,026	2,369	30,459
2008	11,395	9,567	1,828	20,892
2009	11,395	10,142	1,253	10,750
2010	11,395	10,750	645	-0-

b. Property taxes of $8,650 were unpaid and unrecorded at December 31, 2005.

c. The payroll register showed the following total unpaid amounts as at December 31, 2005.

	Deductions					Pay	Distribution	
Gross Pay	EI Premiums[10]	Income Taxes[10]	United Way	CPP[10]	Total Deductions	Net Pay	Office Salaries	Sales Salaries
7,840.00	164.64*	3,196.25	320.00	384.75*	4,065.64	3,774.36	1,900.00	5,940.00

The employer's portions of EI and CPP are 1.4 times and 1 times the employee's portion respectively.

d. Centrum Cleaning Services operates out of a small building in downtown Montreal. Total services provided to clients during the month of December were $186,000 excluding sales taxes. Assume GST and PST are paid on the fifteenth day of the month following sales.

e. The unadjusted trial balance P. 154 showed Unearned Service Revenue of $7,800. $5,200 of this amount had been earned by December 31.

Required

For each of the above, determine what will be included in the current liabilities section of Centrum's December 31, 2005, balance sheet. Hint: For (d), refer to Exhibit 13.6 to determine the appropriate PST rate.

SOLUTION TO Mid-Chapter Demonstration Problem

a. Two amounts will appear in the current liabilities section as a result of this information:
    Interest payable of $2,880; and
    Current portion of long-term note $8,515.

b. Property taxes payable of $8,650

---

[10] These values are based on the Saskatchewan payroll deduction tables in effect on January 1, 2003.

c. Five amounts will be included in the "Payroll liabilities" amount appearing in the current liabilities section as a result of this information:

EI payable...	$ 395.14*
Employees' income taxes payable	3,196.25
United Way payable	320.00
CPP payable	769.50**
Salaries payable....................................	3,774.36
Total payroll liabilities...........................	$8,455.25

*164.64 × 1.4 = 230.50 Employer's portion plus 164.64 Employees' portion.

**384.75 Employer's portion plus 384.75 Employees' portion.

d. GST = $186,000 × 7%   = $13,020.00
PST = ($186,000 + $13,020) × 7.5% = $\underline{14,926.50}$
Total sales taxes payable $27,946.50

e. Unearned revenue = $7,800 − $5,200 = $ 2,600

Short-Term Notes Payable

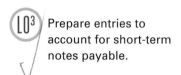

Prepare entries to account for short-term notes payable.

A **short-term note payable** is a written promise to pay a specified amount on a specified future date within one year or the company's operating cycle, whichever is longer, and is reported as a current liability on the balance sheet. Notes payable are interest-bearing to compensate for the time until payment is made. Less common are notes payable issued at a discount, which are discussed in Appendix 13A.

A company often issues a note payable to purchase merchandise inventory and other assets or to replace an account payable. Short-term notes payable also arise when money is borrowed from a bank.

Note Given to Extend Credit Period

A company can substitute an interest-bearing note payable to replace an overdue account payable that does not bear interest.

To illustrate, assume that on November 23, 2005, Weston Holdings asks to extend its past-due $6,000 account payable to TechNology Inc. After some negotiations, TechNology Inc. agrees to accept $1,000 cash and a 60-day, 12%, $5,000 note payable to replace the account payable. Weston Holdings records this transaction as:

2005			
Nov. 23	Accounts Payable—TechNology Inc.	6,000.00	
	Cash		1,000.00
	Notes Payable		5,000.00
	Gave $1,000 cash and a 60-day note to extend due date on account.		

Signing the note changes the form of the debt from an account payable to a note payable.

On December 31, 2005, Weston's year-end, accrued interest on the note (38 days from November 23 to December 31) is recorded as follows:

Dec. 31	Interest Expense...	62.47	
	Interest Payable		62.47
	Accrued interest expense on note;		
	$5,000 × 12% × 38/365.		

To calculate interest, we used the formula in Exhibit 13.8.

Interest	=	**P**rincipal of the Note	×	Annual Interest **R**ate	×	**T**ime
$62.47	=	$5,000	×	12%	×	38/365

Exhibit 13.8

Formula to Calculate Interest (*I* = *Prt*)

The balance sheet presentation on December 31, 2005, of the liabilities regarding the note payable is shown under current liabilities as in Exhibit 13.9. Interest is rounded to the nearest whole dollar for financial statement presentation purposes.

Current liabilities:	
Notes payable, short-term	$5,000
Interest payable	62

Exhibit 13.9

Balance Sheet Presentation of Short-Term Notes Payable and Interest Payable

On the due date[11] of January 22, 2006, Weston pays the note and interest by giving TechNology a cheque for $ 5,098.63; $5,000 represents payment for the note payable and $98.63 is payment of the total interest for the 60-day note calculated at the rate of 12%.

The payment is recorded as:

Jan. 22	Notes Payable..	5,000.00	
	Interest Payable..	62.47	
	Interest Expense..	36.16	
	Cash		5,098.63
	Paid note with interest;		
	$5,000 × 12% × 22/365 = $36.16.		

---

[11] The *due date* or *maturity date* P.533 of a note was discussed in Chapter 10. To review the calculation of the due date, assume the 60-day note above that is dated November 23. The due date or maturity date is January 22 calculated as:

Days in November	30
Minus date of note..	23
Days remaining in November	7
Add days in December..................................	31
	38
Days to equal 60 days or	
Maturity date, January 22	22
Period of the note in days.............................	60

Notice that $62.47 of the total interest being paid is for the interest liability that appeared on the December 31 balance sheet in Exhibit 13.9. $36.16 of the total interest is the interest expense for the accounting period beginning January 1, 2006. The matching principle P.140 requires that the total interest expense be allocated over the term of the note as illustrated in Exhibit 13.10.

Exhibit 13.10

Matching of Interest Expense to the Proper Accounting Periods

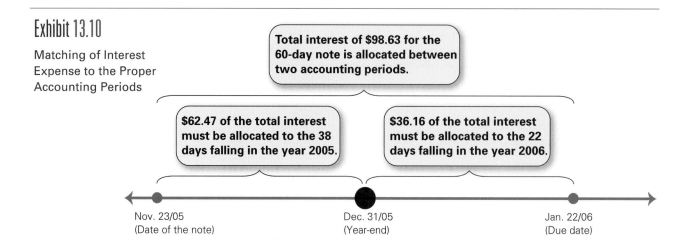

Total interest of $98.63 for the 60-day note is allocated between two accounting periods.

$62.47 of the total interest must be allocated to the 38 days falling in the year 2005.

$36.16 of the total interest must be allocated to the 22 days falling in the year 2006.

Nov. 23/05 (Date of the note)   Dec. 31/05 (Year-end)   Jan. 22/06 (Due date)

Note Given to Borrow from Bank

A bank requires a borrower to sign a promissory note P.533 when making a loan. The borrowing company records its receipt of cash and the new liability with this entry:

Sept. 30	Cash	2,000.00	
	Notes Payable		2,000.00
	Borrowed $2,000 cash with a 60-day, 12%, $2,000 note.		

When the note matures (or becomes due), the borrower repays the note plus interest. Journal entries regarding the accrual of interest expense at the end of the accounting period and repayment of the note on the due date are the same as described in the previous section for a note given to extend a credit period.

Flashback

Answers—p. 692

5. Why does a creditor want a past-due account replaced by a note?

6. A company borrows $10,000 by signing a note payable promising to repay the principal plus interest calculated at the rate of 8% in 180 days. What is the total interest expense?

Estimated (or Uncertain) Liabilities

LO⁴ Account for estimated liabilities, including warranties and corporate income taxes.

An **estimated liability** is a known obligation of an uncertain amount, but one that can be reasonably estimated. Common examples are warranties offered by a seller and income taxes. We discuss each of these in this section. Other examples of estimated liabilities include property taxes and certain contracts to provide future services.

Warranty Liabilities

A warranty is an estimated liability of the seller. A **warranty** obligates a seller to pay for replacing or repairing the product (or service) when it fails to perform as expected within a specified period. Most cars, for instance, are sold with a warranty covering parts for a specified period of time.

To comply with the *matching principle*, the seller reports the expected expense of providing the warranty in the period when revenue from the sale of the product is reported. The seller reports this warranty obligation as a liability, even though there is uncertainty about existence, amount, payee P.533, and date the obligation will be satisfied. The seller's warranty obligation does not require payments unless products fail and are returned for repairs. But future payments are probable and the amount of this liability can be estimated using, for instance, past experience with warranties.

Illustration of Warranty Liabilities

To illustrate, let's consider a dealer who sells a used car for $8,000 on December 1, 2005, with a one-year or 15,000-kilometre warranty covering parts. This dealer's experience shows warranty expense averages 4% of a car's selling price or $320 (= $8,000 × 4%). The dealer records this estimated expense and liability with this entry:

2005			
Dec. 1	Warranty Expense	320	
	Estimated Warranty Liability		320
	To record warranty expense and liability		
	at 4% of selling price.		

This entry alternatively could have been made as part of end-of-period adjustments. Either way, it causes the estimated warranty expense to be reported on the 2005 income statement. Also, it results in a warranty liability on the balance sheet for December 31, 2005.

Suppose the customer returns the car for warranty repairs on January 9, 2006. The dealer performs this work by replacing parts costing $200. The customer was required to pay $180 for labour regarding installation of the parts. The entry to record partial settlement of the estimated warranty liability is:

2006			
Jan. 9	Estimated Warranty Liability	200	
	Cash	180	
	Auto Parts Inventory		200
	Wages Payable...		180
	To record costs of warranty repairs and		
	receipt of cash for labour.		

This entry does not record any additional expense in year 2006 but instead reduces the balance of the estimated warranty liability. Warranty expense was already recorded in 2005, the year the car was sold. The balance in the Estimated Warranty Liability account on January 9, 2006, after posting this entry is:

Estimated Warranty Liability			
Jan. 9/06	200	320	Dec. 1/05
		120	Balance

What happens if total warranty costs turn out to be more or less than the estimated 4% or $320? The answer is that management should monitor actual warranty costs to see whether the 4% rate is accurate. If experience reveals a large difference from estimates, the rate should be changed for future sales. This means while differences are expected, they should be small.

The preceding example illustrated estimating warranty expense based on a percent of sales dollars. Warranty expense can also be based on a percent of *units* sold. The journal entries are the same for both methods of calculating warranty expense. Which method is used depends on whether warranty expense is to be matched to sales dollars or units sold.

Answers—p. 692

7. Estimated liabilities include an obligation to pay:
   a. An uncertain but reasonably estimated amount to a specific entity on a specific date.
   b. A known amount to a specific entity on an uncertain due date.
   c. A known amount to an uncertain entity on a known due date.
   d. All of the above.

8. A car is sold for $15,000 on June 1, 2004, with a one-year warranty covering parts and labour. Warranty expense is estimated at 1.5% of selling price. On March 1, 2005, the car is returned for warranty repairs for parts costing $75 and labour costing $60. The amount recorded as warranty expense at the time of the March 1 repairs is:
   a. $0   d. $135
   b. $60   e. $225
   c. $75

Income Tax Liabilities for Corporations

Financial statements of both single proprietorships and partnerships P.7 do not include income taxes because these organizations do not directly pay income taxes. Instead, taxable income for these organizations is carried to the owners' personal tax return and taxed at that level. But corporations P.7 are subject to income taxes and must estimate their income tax liability when preparing financial statements. We explain this process in this section.

Income tax expense for a corporation creates a liability until payment is made to the government. Because this tax is created through earning income, a liability is incurred when income is earned. This tax must usually be paid monthly under federal regulations. The monthly installment is equal to one-twelfth of the corporation's estimated income tax liability for the year.

Illustration of Income Tax Liabilities

To illustrate, let's consider a corporation that prepares monthly financial statements. Based on its income earned in 2004, this corporation estimates it will owe income taxes of $144,000 in 2005. In January 2005, the following adjusting entry records the estimated income tax:

2005			
Jan. 31	Income Tax Expense..	12,000	
	Income Tax Payable..............................		12,000
	Accrued income tax based on 1/12 of		
	total estimated; $144,000 × 1/12.		

Assume that the tax installment is paid the next day and the entry to record its payment is:

Feb. 1	Income Tax Payable...	12,000	
	Cash		12,000
	Paid income tax installment for January 2005.		

This process of accruing and then paying tax installments continues through the year. By the time annual financial statements are prepared at year-end, the corporation knows its total earned income and the actual amount of income taxes it must pay. This information allows it to update the expense and liability accounts.

Suppose this corporation determines that its income tax liability for 2005 is a total of $156,700. The Income Tax Expense account reflects estimated taxes of $132,000 based on installments recorded at the rate of $12,000 per month for each of January to November. The entry to record the additional income tax for 2005 is as follows:

Dec. 31	Income Tax Expense...	24,700	
	Income Tax Payable...............................		24,700
	To record additional tax expense and liability; $156,700 − $132,000 = $24,700 balance owing.		

This liability of $24,700 is settled when the corporation makes its final payment, assumed to be on January 1, 2006.

9. Why does a corporation accrue an income tax liability for quarterly reports?

Flashback

Answer—p. 692

Contingent Liabilities

A **contingent liability** is a potential future liability caused by a past event. Any future payment of a contingent liability depends on uncertain future events. A typical example is a lawsuit pending in court. Here, a past transaction or event leads to a lawsuit where the result is uncertain because it is to be determined by the court.

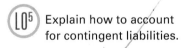
LO5 Explain how to account for contingent liabilities.

Accounting for Contingent Liabilities

Accounting for contingent liabilities depends on the likelihood of a future event occurring along with our ability to estimate the amount owed in the future if it occurs. Typical examples include a lawsuit taken against a company or environmental liability concerns.

There are two main categories of contingent liabilities. Those that are:

1. *Likely* and *the amount can be reasonably estimated,* and
2. *Unlikely.*

The first category includes situations in which the contingency is both likely (probable) and the amount can be reasonably estimated, in which case the amount is recorded on the balance sheet as a liability.[12] These amounts must be accrued because they meet the two criteria of being likely to occur **and** the amount can be reasonably estimated. The journal entry to record a likely contingent liability, which is estimated to be in the amount of $10,000, is:

Contingent Loss..	10,000	
Contingent Liability		10,000
To record a likely and estimable contingent loss.		

Recording this entry prevents income and net assets from being overstated, which is in accordance with the *conservatism principle* P. 360. If the potential future liability is likely but the amount is not measurable then the contingent loss and liability should be disclosed in the notes to the financial statements because this information is relevant to users of financial statements. This is in accordance with the *full disclosure principle* P. 358.

According to the *CICA Handbook*, uncertainties such as warranties and doubtful accounts are not contingencies since they relate to normal business activities.[13]

The second category of contingent liabilities involves situations in which the future event is *unlikely* (remote or slight chance of occurrence). If the occurrence of a contingent loss is unlikely but would have a significant negative effect on the reporting company if the event were to occur, note disclosure is required. The reporting options for contingent liabilities are summarized in Exhibit 13.11.

In practice, accounting for contingencies is extremely difficult to apply. Canadian GAAP permit a business to apply judgement: Is a contingent liability likely? Can the amount be reasonably estimated? Management recognizes that recording and/or disclosing a contingent liability could impact decisions made by users of financial statements. For example, note disclosure regarding a pending lawsuit may cause share prices to decline. In applying judgement, the unethical manager may withhold information regarding uncertain future events.

Gain Contingencies

Contingent gains should never be recorded until they are actually realized. Gain contingencies that are likely are disclosed in the notes to the financial statements but because of conservatism we should avoid any misleading implications about their realization.[14] For example, a plaintiff in a lawsuit should not disclose any expected gain until the courts settle the matter. Disclosure of *unlikely* contingent gains is prohibited.

---

[12] *CICA Handbook*, section 3290, "Contingencies," par. .06.

[13] In the United States, the FASB argues that contingencies include estimated liabilities such as warranties, vacation pay, premiums offered to customers, and income taxes. It claims that all estimated liabilities are contingencies because they represent potential liabilities.

[14] *CICA Handbook*, par. 3290.18.

Exhibit 13.11

Reporting of Contingencies[15]

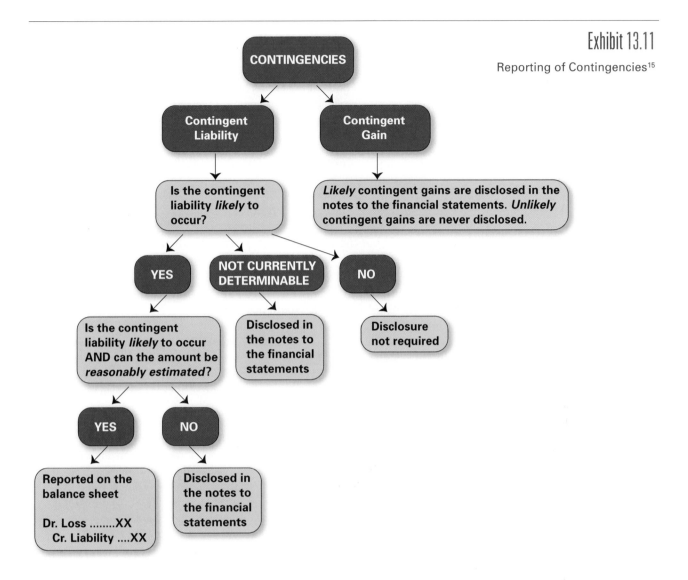

10. A future payment is reported as a liability on the balance sheet if payment is contingent on a future event that:
   a. Is not likely but is reasonably possible and the payment cannot be reasonably estimated.
   b. Is likely and the payment can be reasonably estimated.
   c. Is not likely but the payment is known.

11. Under what circumstances is a future payment reported in the notes to the financial statements as a contingent liability ?

Flashback

Answers—p. 692

---

[15] *CICA Handbook*, section "Contingencies," par. 3290.12–15.

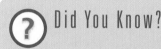 **Did You Know?**

Eco Cops

What's it worth to be able to ski at Lake Louise? What's the cost when beaches are closed due to pollution? What's the life of a seal worth? These questions are part of measuring environmental liabilities of polluters. One method of measuring these liabilities is called contingent valuation, in which people are surveyed and asked to answer questions like these. Their answers are used by regulators to levy hefty fines, assess punitive damages, measure costs of clean-up, and assign penalties for damage to "environmental intangibles."

Summary

LO¹ **Describe the characteristics of liabilities and explain the difference between current and long-term liabilities.** Liabilities are highly probable future settlements of assets or services an entity is presently obligated to make as a result of past transactions or events. Current liabilities are due within one year of the balance sheet date or the next operating cycle, whichever is longer, and are settled using current assets. All other liabilities are long-term liabilities.

LO² **Identify and describe known current liabilities.** Known current liabilities are set by agreements or laws and are measurable with little uncertainty. They include accounts payable, sales taxes payable, unearned revenues, notes payable, payroll liabilities, and the current portion of long-term debt.

LO³ **Prepare entries to account for short-term notes payable.** Short-term notes payable are current

liabilities and most bear interest. When a short-term note is interest-bearing, its face value equals the amount borrowed. This type of note also identifies a rate of interest to be paid at maturity.

LO⁴ **Account for estimated liabilities, including warranties and corporate income taxes.** Liabilities for warranties and corporate income taxes are recorded with estimated amounts and are recognized as expenses when incurred.

LO⁵ **Explain how to account for contingent liabilities.** If an uncertain future payment depends on a probable future event and the amount can be reasonably estimated, the payment is recorded as a liability. If the future payment is reported as a contingent liability, (a) the future event is reasonably possible but not probable, or (b) the event is probable but the amount of the payment cannot be reasonably estimated.

GUIDANCE ANSWERS TO   Flashback

1. Liabilities are probable future settlements of assets or services that an entity is presently obligated to make as a result of past transactions or events.

2. No, an expected future payment is not a liability unless an existing obligation was created by a past event or transaction.

3. In most cases, a liability due in 15 months is classified as long-term. But it is classified as a current liability if the company's operating cycle is 15 months or longer.

4. **a.** Sales = $1,150 ÷ 1.15 = $1,000

   b. HST = $1,150 − $1,000 = $150

5. A creditor might want to have a note payable instead of an account payable in order to (a) start charging interest and/or (b) have positive evidence of the debt and its terms.

6. The interest expense was $10,000 × 8% × 180/365 = $394.52.

7. *a*

8. *a*

9. A corporation accrues an income tax liability for its interim financial statements because income tax expense is incurred when income is earned, not just at the end of the year.

10. *b*

11. A future payment is reported as a contingent liability in the notes to the financial statements if (a) the uncertain future event is likely but the amount of payment cannot be reasonably estimated, or (b) the uncertain future event is not likely but has a reasonable possibility of occurring.

Demonstration Problem

The following series of transactions and other events took place at the Kern Company, located in Saskatchewan, during its calendar reporting year. Describe their effects on the financial statements by presenting the journal entries described in each situation.

a. In September 2005, Kern sold $140,000 of merchandise that was covered by a 180-day warranty. Prior experience shows that the costs of fulfilling the warranty will equal 5% of the sales revenue. Calculate September's warranty expense and the increase in the warranty liability and show how it would be recorded with a September 30 adjusting entry. Also show the journal entry that would be made on October 8 to record an expenditure of $300 cash to provide warranty service on an item sold in September.

b. On October 12, 2005, Kern arranged with a supplier to replace an overdue $10,000 account payable by paying $2,500 cash and signing a note for the remainder. The note matured in 90 days and had a 12% interest rate. Show the entries that would be recorded on October 12, December 31, and the date the note matures.

c. In late December the company learns that it is facing a product liability suit filed by an unhappy customer. The company's lawyer is of the opinion that although the company will likely suffer a loss from the lawsuit it is not possible to estimate the amount of the damages at the present time.

d. Kern Company recorded estimated income taxes each month at the rate of 28% of income before tax. Total income before taxes for the year was $896,000. At year-end, the actual income tax expense was determined to be $273,880. Record the year-end income tax expense adjustment entry for the company.

e. On November 1, Kern Company borrows $5,000 from the bank on a 90-day, 14% note. Record the issuance of the note on November 1, interest accrual on December 31, and repayment of the note with interest on the maturity date.

f. As of November 30, 2005, the account balances for GST Receivable, GST Payable, and PST Payable were $16,800, $9,660, and $8,280 respectively. During December, Kern Company purchased $196,000 of merchandise on credit and recorded credit sales of $295,000 (cost of sales $177,000). Kern Company remits GST and PST on the last day of each month regarding the previous month's transactions. Record the remittance or refund of sales taxes on December 31 as well as summary entries for the purchase and sale of merchandise during December. (Date the summary entries Dec. 31 for simplicity.)

Planning the Solution

○ For (a), calculate the warranty expense for September and record it with an estimated liability. Record the October expenditure as a decrease in the liability.

○ For (b), eliminate the liability for the account payable and create the liability for the note payable. Calculate the interest expense for the 80 days that the note is outstanding in 2005 and record it as an additional liability. Determine the maturity date of the note. Record the payment of the note, being sure to include the interest for the 10 days in 2006.

○ For (c) decide if the contingent liability for the company needs to be disclosed or accrued according to the two necessary criteria: how probable the loss and how reasonably the amount can be estimated.

○ For (d) determine how much of the income tax expense is payable for the current year.

○ For *(e)* record the note. Make the year-end adjustment for 60 days' accrued interest. Record the repayment of the note being sure to include the interest for the 30 days in 2006.

○ For *(f)*, four entries are required. First, prepare separate entries to record the remittance or refund of GST and PST on December 31 based on the November 30, 2005, account balances. Next, prepare the entry to record the purchase of merchandise during December, including GST. Finally, prepare the entry to record the sale of merchandise during December, including GST and appropriate PST for Saskatchewan.

SOLUTION TO **Demonstration Problem**

a. Warranty expense = 5% × $140,000 = $7,000

Sept. 30	Warranty Expense	7,000.00	
	Estimated Warranty Liability		7,000.00
	To record warranty expense and liability		
	at 5% of sales for the month.		
Oct. 8	Estimated Warranty Liability	300.00	
	Cash		300.00
	To record the cost of the warranty service.		

b. Interest expense for 2005 = 12% × $7,500 × 80/365 = $197.26
Interest expense for 2006 = 12% × $7,500 × 10/365 = $24.66

Oct. 12	Accounts Payable	10,000.00	
	Notes Payable		7,500.00
	Cash		2,500.00
	Paid $2,500 cash and gave a 90-day, 12%		
	note to extend the due date on the account.		
Dec. 31	Interest Expense..	197.26	
	Interest Payable		197.26
	To accrue interest on note payable;		
	7,500 × 0.12 × 80/365 = 197.26.		
Jan. 10	Notes Payable...	7,500.00	
	Interest Payable..	197.26	
	Interest Expense	24.66	
	Cash		7,721.92
	Paid note with interest, including accrued		
	interest payable.		

c. The pending lawsuit should be disclosed only in the notes to the financial statements. Although the loss is likely, no liability can be accrued since the loss cannot be reasonably estimated.

d.

Dec 31	Income Tax Expense..	23,000.00	
	Income Taxes Payable.............................		23,000.00
	To record income tax expense; $273,880		
	− ($896,000 × 28% = $250,880) = $23,000.		

e.

Nov. 1	Cash...	5,000.00	
	Notes Payable		5,000.00
	Borrowed cash with a 90-day 14% note.		
Dec. 31	Interest Expense...............................	115.07	
	Interest Payable		115.07
	To record accrued interest;		
	5,000 × 14% × 60/365 = 115.07.		
Jan. 30	Notes Payable.................................	5,000.00	
	Interest Expense...............................	57.53	
	Interest Payable	115.07	
	Cash		5,172.60
	To record payment of note and accrued		
	interest; 5,000 × 14% × 30/365 = 57.53.		

f.

Dec. 31	GST Payable.....................................	9,660	
	Cash	7,140	
	GST Receivable		16,800
	To record refund of GST from Receiver		
	General for Canada; $16,800 − $9,660		
	= $7,140.		
31	PST Payable.....................................	8,280	
	Cash		8,280
	To record remittance of sales tax payable		
	to provincial authority.		
31	Merchandise Inventory	196,000	
	GST Receivable.................................	13,720	
	Accounts Payable.....................		209,720
	To record the purchase of merchandise on		
	credit; $196,000 × 7% = $13,720 GST.		
31	Accounts Receivable	333,350	
	Sales..		295,000
	PST Payable		17,700
	GST Payable		20,650
	To record the sale of merchandise on		
	credit; $295,000 × 7% GST = $20,650 GST;		
	$295,000 × 6% PST = $17,700 PST.		
31	Cost of Goods Sold...............................	177,000	
	Merchandise Inventory		177,000
	To record the cost of sales.		

13A

Short-Term Notes Payable Issued at a Discount

LO⁶ Explain and account for short-term notes payable issued at a discount.

A note often states that the signer of the note promises to pay principal (the amount borrowed) plus interest. In this case, the face value of the note equals principal. These are referred to as interest-bearing notes and were discussed in Chapter 13.

A bank sometimes has a borrower sign a note with a face value that includes *both* principal and interest. In this case, the signer of the note receives *less than* the note's face value. The difference between the borrowed amount and the note's face value is interest. These are **short-term notes issued at a discount**. Since the borrowed amount is less than the note's face value, the difference is called **discount on notes payable**.

To illustrate, let's assume a company needs $2,000 for a specific project and borrows this money from a bank at 12% annual interest by signing a discounted note. The loan is made on December 16, 2005, and is due in 60 days. The face value of the note will *include* interest. Therefore, the borrowing company signs a $2,039.45 note that includes a promise similar to: "I promise to pay $2,039.45 within 60 days after December 16." The note does not refer to the rate used to calculate the $39.45 of interest (= $2,000 × 12% × 60/365) included in the $2,039.45 face value. Because this note lacks a stated interest rate, it is sometimes called a **non-interest-bearing note**.

When recording this note, the company credits the $2,039.45 face value to Notes Payable and debits the $39.45 discount to a contra-liability account. This entry is:

2005			
Dec. 16	Cash..	2,000.00	
	Discount on Notes Payable............................	39.45	
	Notes Payable		2,039.45
	Borrowed $2,000 cash with a 60-day		
	discounted note.		

Discount on Notes Payable is a contra-liability account to the Notes Payable account. If a balance sheet is prepared on December 16, the $39.45 discount is subtracted from the $2,039.45 balance in the Notes Payable account to reflect the $2,000 net amount borrowed as follows:[16]

Note Payable..	$2,039.45	
Less: Discount on Note Payable..	39.45	$ 2,000

---

[16] We approximate the annual interest rate on a short-term loan as:
($ Interest paid ÷ $ Amount received) × (365 days ÷ Loan period in days).

At year-end, the adjusting entry needed to record the accrual of 15 days of interest for 2005 is:

Dec. 31	Interest Expense......................................	9.86	
	Discount on Notes Payable		9.86
	To record accrued interest on note;		
	$2,000 \times 12\% \times 15/365$ or $39.45 \times 15/60$.		

Note that accrued interest is not credited to Interest Payable. Instead, this entry reduces the balance of the contra-liability account from $39.45 to $29.59 (= $39.45 − $9.86). This increases the net note liability to $2,009.86 (= $2,039.45 note less $29.59 discount).

When the note matures, we need an entry both to accrue interest expense for the last 45 days of the note and to record its payment:

2006			
Feb. 14	Interest Expense......................................	29.59	
	Notes Payable...	2,039.45	
	Discount on Notes Payable		29.59
	Cash		2,039.45
	Paid note with interest; $2,000 \times 12\%		
	$\times 45/365$ or $39.45 \times 45/60$.		

Rock Band

Judgement Call

Answer—p. 697

You are a member of a rock band. Your band needs $15,000 to upgrade equipment. You receive loan approvals for $15,000 at two banks. One bank's proposed loan contract reads: "Band promises to pay $15,000 plus interest at 14% in six months." The competing bank's contract reads: "Band promises to pay $16,000 in six months." Which loan do you prefer?

Summary of Appendix 13A

LO6 **Explain and account for short-term notes payable issued at a discount.** Short-term notes payable are current liabilities. The face value of a short-term note payable issued at a discount includes both principal and interest. At the time of signing the note, the debtor receives less than the face value: the face value less the interest portion. When the note is repaid, the entire face value is repaid.

GUIDANCE ANSWER TO *Judgement Call*

Rock Band

Both banks have agreed to give the band $15,000, and both loans require repayment in six months. Provided terms in these contracts are similar, the only potential difference is in the amount of interest the band must pay. The second bank's contract makes this clear—since $15,000 is borrowed and the band must pay $16,000, the interest charged is $1,000. We must calculate interest on the first bank's contract—it is $1,050, calculated as $15,000 \times 14\% \times 6/12$. The band prefers the contract requiring less interest, which is the one reading: "Band promises to pay $16,000 in six months."

Glossary

Collections in advance See *unearned revenues.* (p. 682)

Contingent gain A potential gain that depends on a future event arising out of a past transaction. Contingent gains are never recorded until actually realized. (p. 690)

Contingent liability A potential liability that depends on a future event arising out of a past transaction; it is not an existing liability. (p. 689)

Current liability Obligations due within a year of the balance sheet date or the company's next operating cycle, whichever is longer; paid using current assets or by creating other current liabilities. (p. 675)

Current portion of long-term debt The portion of long-term debt that is due within one year of the balance sheet date; reported under current liabilities on the balance sheet. (p. 676)

Deferred revenues See *unearned revenues.* (p. 682)

Demand loan A liability not having a fixed due date that is payable on the creditor's demand. (p. 677)

Discount on notes payable The difference between the face value of a non-interest-bearing note payable and the amount borrowed; represents interest that will be paid on the note over its life. (p. 696)

Estimated liability An obligation of an uncertain amount that can be reasonably estimated. (p. 686)

Exempt supplies GST-exempt services are educational, health care, and financial services. (p. 680)

Goods and Services Tax (GST) A value-added tax on nearly all goods and services sold in Canada. The tax is levied by the federal government. (p. 680)

Harmonized Sales Tax (HST) A combined GST and PST rate of 15% applied to taxable supplies. Currently, New Brunswick, Nova Scotia, and Newfoundland and Labrador apply HST. (p. 680)

Input Tax Credit (ITC) GST paid by the registrant on purchases of taxable supplies. Input tax credits are applied against (reduce) GST Payable. Also known as *GST Receivable.* (p. 680)

Known liability A company's obligations that have little uncertainty and are set by agreements, contracts, or laws; also called *definitely determinable liabilities.* (p. 678)

Liability A future payment of assets or services that a company is presently obligated to make as a result of past transactions or events. (p. 674)

Long-term liability Obligations of a company that do not require payment within the longer of one year or an operating cycle. (p. 675)

Non-interest-bearing note A note that does not have a stated rate of interest; the interest is included in the face value of the note. (p. 696)

Payroll Employee compensation for work performed. (p. 678)

Payroll liabilities Employee compensation amounts owing to employees and government and other agencies. (p. 678)

Provincial Sales Tax (PST) A consumption tax levied by provincial governments on sales to the final consumers of products; calculated as a percentage of the sale price of the item being sold. (p. 679)

Registrant Registered individual or entity selling taxable supplies that is responsible for collecting the GST on behalf of the government. A business with sales of less than $30,000 per year does not have to register for GST purposes. (p. 680)

Short-term note payable A current obligation in the form of a written promissory note. (p. 684)

Short-term notes issued at a discount See *non-interest-bearing note.* (p. 696)

Taxable supplies Taxable goods or services on which GST is calculated and includes everything except zero-rated and exempt supplies. (p. 680)

Trade accounts payable Amounts owed to suppliers regarding products or services purchased on credit. Commonly referred to as *accounts payable.* (p. 678)

Unearned revenues Amounts received in advance from customers for future products or services. (p. 682)

Warranty An agreement that obligates the seller or manufacturer to repair or replace a product when it breaks or otherwise fails to perform properly within a specified period. (p. 687)

Zero-rated supplies Goods including groceries, prescription drugs, and medical devices that have zero GST. (p. 680)

For more study tools, quizzes, and problem material, refer to the Online Learning Centre at **www.mcgrawhill.ca/college/larson**

Questions

1. What is the difference between a current and a long-term liability?

2. What are the three important questions concerning the certainty of liabilities?

3. What amount does WestJet, in Appendix I, report as the current portion of long-term debt as at December 31, 2002? In what accounting period will this amount be paid?

4. Refer to Leon's balance sheet in Appendix I. Does Leon's show any unearned amounts? If so, what are the account name and the December 31, 2002, balance in the account?

5. What is an estimated liability?

6. Why are warranty liabilities usually recognized on the balance sheet as liabilities even when they are uncertain?

7. Suppose that a company has a facility located in an area where disastrous weather conditions often occur. Should it report a probable loss from a future disaster as a liability on its balance sheet? Why?

Quick Study

Which of the following items would normally be classified as a current liability for a company that has a 15-month operating cycle?
a. A note payable due in 18 months.
b. Salaries payable.
c. A payable that matures in two years.
d. A note payable due in 10 months.
e. The portion of a long-term note that is due to be paid in 12 months.

QS 13-1
Distinguishing between current and long-term liabilities

LO[1]

On January 1, 2005, Tetley Manufacturing borrowed $146,000 from the bank. Interest is calculated at the rate of 10% and the term of the note is four years. Four equal annual payments will be made in the amount of $46,059 each December 31. The payment schedule is shown below:

QS 13-2
Current portion of long-term debt

LO[1]

Year	Annual Payment	Principal Portion of Payment	Interest Portion of Payment	Principal Balance at Year-End
2005	46,059	31,459	14,600	114,541
2006	46,059	34,605	11,454	79,936
2007	46,059	38,065	7,994	41,871
2008	46,059	41,871	4,188	-0-

Show how Tetley Manufacturing will show the note on its year-end:
1. December 31, 2005, balance sheet.
2. December 31, 2006, balance sheet.

MetroConcerts receives $2,000,000 in advance cash ticket sales for a four-date tour for Rita MacNeil. Record the advance ticket sales as a lump sum as of October 31, 2005. The concerts sold out and no additional ticket sales have been recorded. Record the revenue earned for the first concert date, November 16, 2005, assuming each concert date brings in the same amount of revenue.

QS 13-3
Unearned revenue

LO[2]

Palm Computing sells $5,000 of merchandise (with a cost of $4,450) for cash on September 30. The sales tax law requires Palm Computing to collect 15% harmonized sales tax on every dollar of merchandise sold. Record Palm's entries for the $5,000 sale and applicable sales tax.

QS 13-4
Accounting for sales tax payable

LO[2]

Saratoga Designers, located in Quebec, provided $3,400 of services on credit to a client on May 7, 2005. Record Saratoga's entry, including the appropriate GST and PST. Hint: Refer to Exhibit 13.6 for PST rates.

QS 13-5
Sales tax payable

LO[2]

On September 3, 2005, Metcalfe Retailers, operating out of Nunavut, sold $7,350 of goods for cash with a cost of $6,190. Record Metcalfe's entries, including all appropriate sales taxes.

QS 13-6
Sales tax payable

LO[2]

QS 13-7
Payroll liabilities

LO^2

Tecsey's has two employees and the payroll register showed the following information for the biweekly pay-period ended March 23, 2005:

| | | Deductions | | | | Pay | Distribution |
Employee	Gross Pay	EI Premium	Income Taxes	CPP	Total Deductions	Net Pay	Salaries Expense
Bently, A.	2,010.00	42.21	493.75	92.83	628.79	1,381.21	2,010.00
Craig, T.	2,115.00	44.42	532.65	98.03	675.10	1,439.90	2,115.00
Totals	4,125.00	86.63	1,026.40	190.86	1,303.89	2,821.11	4,125.00

Prepare the entry to record the payroll liability on March 23, 2005. Ignore employer's contributions payable on CPP and EI.

QS 13-8
Notes payable

LO^3

Jackson Textiles had an outstanding account in the amount of $14,800 owing to Nordon Manufacturing. On October 1, 2005, Nordon agreed to convert Jackson's account to an 8%, 45-day note having a face value of $14,800. Record Jackson's entries on October 1, 2005, and on the due date.

QS 13-9
Short-term note transactions

LO^3

On December 11, 2005, the Sydner Company borrowed $42,000 and signed a 60-day, 9% note payable. Calculate the accrued interest payable on December 31, 2005.

QS 13-10
Warranty liabilities

LO^4

Vision Wear's product warranties state that defective glasses will be replaced free of charge for the life of the product. Vision Wear estimates that 2% of all items sold will require replacement. Each pair of glasses costs Vision Wear on average $40. During October 2005, Vision Wear sold 1,300 pairs of glasses at an average price of $120 per pair. Record the estimated warranty liability for October.

QS 13-11
Warranty liabilities

LO^4

On December 20, 2005, The Net Department Store sold a computer for $3,500 with a one-year warranty that covers parts and labour. Warranty expense was estimated at 2% of sales. On March 2, 2006, the computer was taken in for repairs covered under the warranty that required $30 in parts and $10 of labour. Prepare the March 2 journal entry to record the warranty repairs.

QS 13-12
Recording an income tax liability

LO^4

Wang Corp. estimates income tax expense to be $285,600 for the year 2005. Record estimated income tax at January 31, 2005, and the payment on February 1, 2005.

QS 13-13
Accounting for contingent liabilities

LO^5

The following legal claims exist for the Doucet Company. Classify the required accounting treatment for each legal situation as (a) a liability should be recorded, or (b) the legal claim need only be described in the notes to the financial statements.
a. Doucet faces a likely loss on a pending lawsuit; however, the amount of the judgement cannot be reasonably estimated.
b. Doucet Company estimates that one lawsuit could result in a damage award of $1,200,000, and it is likely that the plaintiff will win the case.
c. Doucet Company estimates damages of another case at $3,000,000 with a likelihood of losing the case.

QS 13-14
Contingent liabilities

LO^5

BioMed Pharmaceuticals was notified by its lawyers on November 18, 2005, that a lawsuit had been launched against the company. It was the opinion of the lawyers that BioMed would probably lose the case and that the plaintiff would settle for approximately $750,000. How should this be reported?

Jerico Estates received $12,000 from the bank after signing a 60-day discounted note payable with a face value of $12,138 dated May 15, 2005. Record Jerico's entries on May 15 and on the due date.

*QS 13-15
Discounting notes payable

LO⁶

The Snyder Company signs a discounted note dated December 20, 2005, promising to pay $8,200 within 60 days. Record the signing of the note and the interest accrual on December 31, 2005. ($200 of interest is included in the note's face value of $8,200.)

*QS 13-16
Discounting notes payable

LO⁶

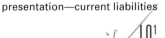

Exercises

The following list of items might appear as liabilities on the balance sheet of a company that has a two-month operating cycle. Identify the proper classification of each item. In the space beside each item write a *C* if it is a current liability, an *L* if it is a long-term liability, or an *N* if it is not a liability.

Exercise 13-1
Classifying liabilities

LO¹

_____ a. Wages payable.
_____ b. Notes payable in 60 days.
_____ c. Mortgage payable (payments due in the next 12 months).
_____ d. Notes receivable in 90 days.
_____ e. Note payable (matures in 5 years).
_____ f. Mortgage payable (payments due after the next 12 months).
_____ g. Notes payable due in 6 to 12 months.
_____ h. Income taxes payable.

The Kotler Company shows the following selected adjusted account balances as at December 31, 2005:

Exercise 13-2
Financial statement presentation—current liabilities

LO¹

Accounts Payable	$ 60,000
Salaries Payable	6,000
Accumulated Amortization, Equipment	18,000
Estimated Warranty Liability	16,000
Mortgage Payable	150,000
Notes Payable, 6 months	12,000

Required
Prepare the current liability section of the Kotler Company's balance sheet. $24,000 in principal is due during 2006 regarding the mortgage payable. For simplicity, order the liabilities from largest to smallest.

Check figure:
Total current liabilities = $118,000

On January 2, 2005, the Bonnet Co. acquired land by issuing a 6%, three-year note for $120,000. The note will be paid in three annual payments of $44,893 each December 31. The payment schedule follows:

Exercise 13-3
Current versus long-term portions of debt

LO¹

Year	Annual Payment	Principal Portion of Payment	Interest Portion of Payment	Principal Balance at Year-End
2005	44,893	37,693	7,200	82,307
2006	44,893	39,955	4,938	42,352
2007	44,893	42,352	2,541	-0-

_____
An asterisk (*) identifies assignment material based on Appendix 13A.

Required
1. Prepare the entry to:
   a. Issue the note on January 2, 2005.
   b. Record the annual payment on December 31, 2005.
2. Show how the note will appear on the December 31, 2005, balance sheet.

Exercise 13-4
Financial statement
presentation—current liabilities

LO¹

The following alphabetized list of selected adjusted account balances is from the records of Elstrada Company on December 31, 2005:

Accounts Payable	$ 20,000
Accumulated Amortization—Equipment	25,000
Estimated Warranty Liability	6,000
GST Payable	7,000
Mortgage Payable, $10,000 due Dec. 31, 2006	120,000
Notes Payable, due April 1, 2006	12,000
Notes Payable, due April 1, 2009	60,000
PST Payable	6,000
Warranty Expense	4,000

Check figure:
Total current liabilities = $61,000

Required
Prepare the current liability section of Elstrada Company's 2005 balance sheet (for simplicity, list the accounts from largest to smallest).

Exercise 13-5
Unearned revenues

LO²

James & Sons is a lucrative paving stone installation business that operates from about April to October each year. Clients arrange for their own paving stones and James & Sons is contracted to provide the installation. Because of the boom in the construction business, James & Sons has pre-booked customers for the next year and a half. Customers must pay 40% at the time of booking and the balance seven days prior to the start of the job. The December 31, 2005, balance sheet shows Unearned Revenues totalling $2,050,000. During 2006, $3,780,000 of cash was collected: $2,124,000 regarding work completed during the year, and the balance representing prepayments.

Required
1. Prepare the entry to record the collection of cash in 2006.
2. Determine the balance in Unearned Revenue at December 31, 2006.

Exercise 13-6
Various liabilities

LO²

Jordan Holdings had the following additional information at its November 30, 2005, year-end:
a. The Unearned Revenue account showed a balance of $48,000, which represented six months of services paid in advance by a client on October 15, 2005.
b. The payroll register showed the following unpaid amounts as at November 30:

EI* Premium	Income Taxes	CPP*	Total Deductions	Net Payable	Office Salaries	Sales Salaries
103.20	1,290.00	157.20	1,550.40	2,749.60	2,500.00	1,800.00

*The employer's portions of EI and CPP are 1.4 times and 1 times the employees' portion respectively.

c. The November utility bill in the amount of $1,380 was unpaid and unrecorded at November 30.

Required
Prepare the appropriate entries at year-end based on the above information.

Gelibrand Architectural Consultants provided $180,000 of consulting services to Carnegy Developments on April 14, 2005, on account.

Required
Journalize Gelibrand's April 14 transaction including applicable PST and GST or HST assuming it is located in:
a. Nova Scotia.
b. British Columbia.
c. Prince Edward Island.
Refer to Exhibit 13.6 for PST rates.

Exercise 13-7
Sales taxes payable

LO²

Check figures:
a. HST Payable 27,000
b. PST Payable 13,500
c. PST Payable 19,260

On October 15, Lentron purchased $2,500 of merchandise on credit. The next day, it recorded sales of $1,700; cost of sales was $1,200. Record the October 15 and October 16 entries assuming each of the geographical areas noted in Exhibit 13.6. A chart similar to the following might be useful in organizing your answer.

Exercise 13-8
Sales tax payable

LO²

Date	Description	Alberta	Etc.

The LaPierre Company purchased some machinery on March 10, 2005, that had a cost of $60,000 (ignore GST/PST). Show the journal entries that would record this purchase and payment under these three separate situations:
a. The company paid cash for the full purchase price.
b. The company purchased the machinery on credit with terms 1/30, n/60. Payment was made on April 9, 2005.
c. The company signed a 10%, one-year note for the full purchase price. The note was paid on March 10, 2006, the maturity date. Ignore year-end accruals.

Exercise 13-9
Asset purchased with a note

LO²,³

Gaudet Systems borrowed $50,000 on September 1, 2005, for 90 days at 8% interest by signing a note.
1. On what date will this note mature?
2. How much interest expense is created by this note?
3. Prepare the journal entries for September 1, 2005, and the maturity date.

Exercise 13-10
Notes payable

LO³

Check figure:
1. November 30

Sobey Co. borrowed $30,000 on December 1, 2005, for 90 days at 10% interest by signing a note.
1. On what date will this note mature?
2. How much interest expense is created by this note in 2005?
3. How much interest expense is created by this note in 2006?
4. Prepare the journal entries on December 1, December 31 (Sobey Co.'s year-end), and the maturity date.

Exercise 13-11
Notes payable with year-end adjustments

LO³

Check figure:
1. March 1

Scheffield Knives extends a lifetime replacement warranty on all units sold. Using past experience, the company estimates that 0.5% of units sold will be returned and require replacement at an average cost of $65 per unit. On January 1, 2005, the balance in Scheffield's Estimated Warranty Liability account was $7,800. During 2005, sales totalled $1,800,000 or 15,000 units. The actual number of units returned and replaced was 52.

Required
a. Prepare the entry to estimate warranty liabilities regarding the units sold for 2005. Assume the adjustment is made on December 31.
b. Record the replacement of the units returned in 2005 (use a date of December 31).
c. Calculate the balance in the Estimated Warranty Liability account at December 31, 2005.
d. What is the warranty expense that will appear on the income statement for the year ended December 31, 2005?

Exercise 13-12
Estimated warranties

LO⁴

Check figures:
c. $9,295
d. $4,875

Exercise 13-13
Warranty expense and liability

LO⁴

Check figure:
4. Ending 2006 balance: $162

On December 6, 2005, Midinski Co. sold a computer for cash of $8,000 (cost $4,200) with a two-year parts and labour warranty. Based on prior experience, Midinski expects eventually to incur warranty costs equal to 5% of the selling price. The fiscal year P.35 coincides with the calendar year P.35. On January 20, 2006, the customer returned the computer for repairs that were completed the same day. The cost of the repairs consisted of $198 for the materials taken from the parts inventory and $40 of labour that was fully paid with cash. These were the only repairs required in 2006 for this computer.

Required
1. How much warranty expense should the company report in 2005 for this computer?
2. How much is the warranty liability for this computer as of December 31, 2005?
3. How much warranty expense should the company report in 2006 for this computer?
4. How much is the warranty liability for this computer as of December 31, 2006?
5. Show the journal entries that would be made to record: (a) the sale (assume a perpetual inventory system); (b) the adjustment on December 31, 2005, to record the warranty expense; and (c) the repairs that occurred in January 2006.

Exercise 13-14
Income taxes payable

LO⁴

Check figure:
5. $692,000

Leskowich Computer Repairs Ltd. prepares statements quarterly.

Part A

Required
1. Based on 2004 results, Leskowich's estimated tax liability for 2005 is $206,400. Leskowich will accrue 1/12 of this amount at the end of each month (assume the installments are paid the next day). Prepare the entry on January 31, 2005, to accrue the tax liability and on February 1 to record the payment.
2. At year-end, December 31, the actual income tax for 2005 was determined to be $199,200. Prepare the adjusting entry on December 31 to record the accrual. Record the payment on January 1, 2006.

Part B

Required
3. Complete the following table assuming the company estimates its tax liability for the year 2005 to be $199,200.

	Jan. – Mar.	Apr. – June	July – Sept.	Oct. – Dec.
Income before tax..........................	$228,000	$136,000	$242,000	$329,000
Estimated income tax expense				
Net income				

4. Assuming that actual tax for the year 2005 was determined to be $243,000, prepare the appropriate adjusting entry at year-end to bring the balance in the Income Tax Expense account to the correct balance.
5. Calculate the company's actual net income for the year 2005.

Exercise 13-15
Accounting for income tax

LO⁴

MacKenzie Company prepares interim financial statements each month. As part of the process, estimated income tax of $2,490 is accrued each month. The estimated income tax is paid the day after the accrual is recorded. The actual amount of tax due at the end of the year is determined to be $31,100.

Required
1. Determine the amount of the adjustment needed on December 31 to produce the proper ending balance in the Income Tax Expense account.
2. Prepare the journal entries to record the: estimated income tax on January 31, 2005; payment of tax on February 1, 2005; and the adjustment to Income Tax Expense on December 31, 2005.

Copeland Company, located in Ontario, is preparing adjusting entries at December 31, 2005. An analysis reveals the following:

a. During December, Copeland Company sold 4,000 units of a product that carries a 60-day warranty. The sales for this product totalled $120,000. The company expects 8% of the units to need repair under warranty and it estimates that the average repair cost per unit will be $16.

b. A disgruntled employee is suing the company. Legal advisors believe that it is probable that the company will have to pay damages, the amount of which cannot be reasonably estimated.

c. The company needs to record previously unrecorded cash sales of $2,000,000 (cost of sales 65%) plus applicable PST and GST.

d. The company recognizes that $40,000 of $100,000 received in advance for products has now been earned.

Required
Prepare any required adjusting entries at December 31, 2005, for each of the above.

Exercise 13-16
Various liabilities

LO²,⁴,⁵

Check figure:
c. PST Payable $160,000

Gladiator Systems received $65,000 after signing a discounted note with a face value of $66,442 on July 15, 2005, for 90 days.

Required
1. On what date will this note mature?
2. How much interest expense is created by this note?
3. Prepare the journal entries for July 15, 2005, and the maturity date.

*Exercise 13-17
Discounted notes payable

LO⁶

Check figure:
1. October 13

Silica Co. received $120,000 after signing a discounted note with a face value of $121,578 on November 20, 2005, for 60 days.

Required
1. On what date will this note mature?
2. How much interest expense is created by this note in 2005?
3. How much interest expense is created by this note in 2006?
4. Prepare the journal entries on November 20, December 31 (Silica Co.'s year-end), and the maturity date.

*Exercise 13-18
Discounted notes payable

LO⁶

Check figure:
1. January 19

Problems

On January 2, 2005, Barrett Company acquired equipment by issuing a 12%, $500,000 note due in four years on December 31, 2008. Annual payments are $164,617 each December 31. The payment schedule is:

Problem 13-1A
Current versus long-term portions of debt

LO¹

Year	Annual Payment	Principal Portion of Payment	Interest Portion of Payment	Principal Balance at Year-End
2005	164,617	104,617	60,000	395,383
2006	164,617	117,171	47,446	278,212
2007	164,617	131,232	33,385	146,980
2008	164,617	146,980	17,637	-0-

An asterisk (*) identifies assignment material based on Appendix 13A.

Required

Using the information provided, complete the following liabilities section of Barrett Company's balance sheet at December 31:

	December 31			
	2005	2006	2007	2008
Current Liabilities:				
Current portion of long-term debt.................				
Interest payable				
Long-term liabilities				
Long-term debt..				

Problem 13-2A

Transactions with short-term notes payable

LO³

The Chernin Company entered into the following transactions involving short-term liabilities during 2005 and 2006:

> **2005**
> Mar. 14   Purchased merchandise on credit from Ferris Inc. for $12,500. The terms were 1/10, n/30 (assume a perpetual inventory system).
> Apr. 14   Chernin paid $3,500 cash and replaced the $9,000 remaining balance of the account payable to Ferris Inc. with a 10%, 60-day note payable.
> May 21   Borrowed $20,000 from Scotia Bank by signing a 12%, 90-day note.
> ?   Paid the note to Ferris Inc. at maturity.
> ?   Paid the note to the bank at maturity.
> Dec. 15   Borrowed $35,000 and signed a 9%, 120-day note with National Bank.
> Dec. 31   Recorded an adjusting entry for the accrual of interest on the note to National Bank.
>
> **2006**
> ?   Paid the note to National Bank at maturity.

Required

1. Determine the maturity dates of the three notes just described.
2. Present journal entries for each of the preceding dates.

Problem 13-3A

Estimated product warranty liabilities

LO⁴

On November 10, 2005, Sullivan Products began to buy and resell high-powered flashlights for $40 each. Sullivan uses the perpetual method to account for inventories. The flashlights are covered under a warranty that requires the company to replace any nonworking flashlight within 90 days. When a flashlight is returned, the company simply throws it away and mails a new one from inventory to the customer. The company's cost for a new flashlight is only $7. The manufacturer has advised the company to expect warranty costs to equal 18% of the units sold. These transactions occurred in 2005 and 2006 (ignore GST and PST):

> **2005**
> Nov. 15   Sold 200 flashlights for $8,000 cash.
>   30   Recognized warranty expense for November with an adjusting entry.
> Dec. 8   Replaced 15 flashlights that were returned under the warranty.
>   15   Sold 550 flashlights.
>   29   Replaced 40 flashlights that were returned under the warranty.
>   31   Recognized warranty expense for December with an adjusting entry.
> **2006**
> Jan. 14   Sold 275 flashlights.
>   20   Replaced 63 flashlights that were returned under the warranty.
>   31   Recognized warranty expense for January with an adjusting entry.

Check figures:
2. $350
3. $560
4. $469

Required

1. How much warranty expense should be reported for November and December 2005?
2. How much warranty expense should be reported for January 2006?
3. What is the balance of the estimated warranty liability as of December 31, 2005?
4. What is the balance of the estimated warranty liability as of January 31, 2006?
5. Prepare journal entries to record the transactions and adjustments.

Part 1

Ontario Cameras manufactures and markets products throughout Canada. It was disclosed in notes to the company's financial statements that estimated warranty costs are accrued at the time products are sold. Assume that in 2005 warranty costs are estimated at $200,000 and that the related warranty work was actually paid for during 2006.

Required

Explain how financial statements are affected due to warranties in 2005 and 2006.

Part 2

Assume that Maclean's collected $3,000,000 during 2005 for magazines that will be delivered in future years. During 2006, Maclean's delivered magazines based on these subscriptions amounting to $900,000.

Required

Explain how financial statements are affected in 2005 and 2006 by these subscriptions.

Problem 13-4A
Determining the effects of various liabilities on financial statements

$LO^{1,4}$

The statement of owner's equity for the year ended June 30, 2005, is shown below for Blanchard Company.

Problem 13-5A
Comprehensive

$LO^{1,2,3,4}$

BLANCHARD COMPANY Statement of Owner's Equity For Year Ended June 30, 2005	
Stan Blanchard, capital, June 30, 2004	$299,000
Add: Net income	60,000
Total	$359,000
Less: Withdrawals	50,000
Stan Blanchard, capital June 30, 2005	$309,000

The liabilities reported on the June 30, 2005, balance sheet were:

Accounts payable	$ 96,000
Notes payable, due 2007	250,000
Total liabilities	$346,000

Stan is selling the business. A potential buyer has hired an accountant to review the accounting records and the following was discovered:

a. Blanchard Company began selling a new product line this past year that offered a warranty to customers. It is expected that $25,000 of warranty work will result next year based on first-year sales. No entry was prepared on June 30 to show this.

b. Annual property taxes of $9,840 are due July 31, 2005; the income statement shows only one month of property expense resulting from an entry correctly recorded on July 31, 2004.

c. Interest on the notes payable is paid quarterly. No entry has been recorded since the last quarterly payment of $4,350 on May 1, 2005.

d. $17,000 of new office furniture was purchased on account and received on June 28. This transaction has not been recorded .

e. Unearned revenue of $46,000 has been included on the income statement.

Required

Using the information provided, prepare a corrected statement of owner's equity and liabilities section of the balance sheet.

Check figure:
Total liabilities = $445,920

Alternate Problems

Problem 13-1B
Current versus long-term
portions of debt

LO[1]

On January 2, 2005, Wimberly Manufacturing acquired machinery by issuing a 10%,
$250,000 note due in four years on January 2, 2009. Annual payments are $78,868 each
January 2. The payment schedule is:

Year	Annual Payment	Principal Portion of Payment	Interest Portion of Payment	Principal Balance at Year-End
2006	78,868	53,868	25,000	196,132
2007	78,868	59,254	19,613	136,878
2008	78,868	65,180	13,688	71,698
2009	78,868	71,698	7,170	-0-

Required
Using the information provided, complete the following liabilities section of Wimberly
Manufacturing's balance sheet:

	December 31			
	2005	2006	2007	2008
Current Liabilities:				
Current portion of long-term debt				
Interest payable...				
Long-term liabilities				
Long-term debt...				

Problem 13-2B
Transactions with short-term
notes payable

LO[3]

Pap Company entered into the following transactions involving short-term liabilities
during 2005 and 2006:

2005
Feb. 4   Purchased merchandise on credit from Shafai Products for $35,200. The
terms were 2/10, n/60. Assume Pap uses a perpetual inventory system.
Mar. 2   Borrowed $120,000 from the First Provincial Bank by signing a note
payable for 30 days at 14%.
Apr. 1   Paid the First Provincial Bank note.
5   Gave Shafai Products $11,200 cash and a $24,000, 30-day, 12% note to
secure an extension on Pap's past-due account.
May 5   Paid the note given to Shafai on April 5.
Nov. 16   Borrowed $108,000 at First Provincial Bank by signing a note payable for
60 days at 10%.
Dec. 1   Borrowed money at the Bank of Montreal by giving a $150,000, 90-day,
15% note payable.
31   Recorded an adjusting entry for the accrual of interest on the note to the
First Provincial Bank.
31   Recorded an adjusting entry for the accrual of interest on the note to the
Bank of Montreal.
2006
Jan. 15   Paid the November 16 note to First Provincial Bank.
Mar. 1   Paid the principal and interest on the December 1 note given to the Bank of
Montreal.

Required
Prepare journal entries to record these transactions for Pap Company.

On November 9, 2005, Hubert Co. began to buy and resell toasters for $35 each. Hubert uses the perpetual method to account for inventories. The toasters are covered under a warranty that requires the company to replace any non-working toaster within 60 days. When a toaster is returned, the company simply throws it away and mails a new one from inventory to the customer. The company's cost for a new toaster is only $14. The manufacturer has advised the company to expect warranty costs to equal 20% of the total units sold. These transactions occurred in 2005 and 2006:

Problem 13-3B
Estimated product warranty liabilities

LO⁴

2005	
Nov. 16	Sold 60 toasters for $2,100 cash.
30	Recognized warranty expense for November with an adjusting entry.
Dec. 10	Replaced six toasters that were returned under the warranty.
20	Sold 140 toasters.
30	Replaced 17 toasters that were returned under the warranty.
31	Recognized warranty expense for December with an adjusting entry.
2006	
Jan. 6	Sold 50 toasters for $1,750 cash.
20	Replaced 26 toasters that were returned under the warranty.
31	Recognized warranty expense for January with an adjusting entry.

Required
1. How much warranty expense should be reported for November and December 2005?
2. How much warranty expense should be reported for January 2006?
3. What is the balance of the estimated warranty liability as of December 31, 2005?
4. What is the balance of the estimated warranty liability as of January 31, 2006?
5. Prepare journal entries to record the transactions and adjustments.

Check figures:
2. $140
3. $238
4. $14

Sam Aryee is the new manager of accounting and finance for a medium-sized manufacturing company. Now that the end of the year is approaching, his problem is determining whether and how to describe some of the company's contingencies and warranty estimates in the financial statements. The general manager, Sue Peebles, raised objections to one contingency and one warranty estimate in his preliminary proposal.

First, Peebles objected to the proposal to report nothing about a patent P.636 infringement suit that the company has filed against a competitor. The manager's written comment on his proposal was, "We KNOW that we have them cold on this one! There is no way that we're not going to win a very large settlement!"

Second, she objected to his proposal to recognize an expense and a liability for warranty service on units of a new product that was just introduced in the company's fourth quarter. Her scribbled comment on this point was, "There is no way that we can estimate this warranty cost. Besides, we don't owe anybody anything until the products break down and are returned for service. Let's just report an expense if and when we do the repairs."

Problem 13-4B
Contingencies and warranties

LO⁴, ⁵

Required
Develop a written response for Aryee to the objections raised by the general manager.

Problem 13-5B
Comprehensive

LO[1, 2, 3, 4]

Picadilly Company's condensed income statement for the year ended November 30, 2005, is shown below.

PICADILLY COMPANY Income Statement For Year Ended November 30, 2005	
Fees earned	$940,000
Operating expenses	830,000
Net income	$110,000

The liabilities reported on the November 30, 2005, balance sheet were:

Accounts payable	$ 36,000
Mortgage payable	300,000
Total liabilities	$336,000

Louise Kinny, the owner, is looking for additional financing. A potential lender has reviewed Picadilly's accounting records and discovered the following:

a. Mortgage payments are made annually each December 1. The December 1, 2005, payment has not yet been made or recorded. A partial amortization schedule for the mortgage follows:

Year	Payment	Interest	Principal	Principal Balance, December 1
2004				300,000
2005	50,000	21,000	29,000	271,000
2006	50,000	18,970	31,030	239,970
2007	50,000	16,800	33,200	206,770

b. Fees earned included $170,000 received for work to be done in January and February 2006.
c. Accrued salaries at November 30, 2005, totalling $23,000 have not been recorded.
d. $14,000 of office supplies purchased on account were received November 28; this transaction was not recorded.
e. Annual property taxes of $15,000 are due each December 1; no property taxes have been included on the income statement.

Required
Using the information provided, prepare a corrected income statement and liabilities section of the balance sheet.

Ethics Challenge

EC 13-1

Mike Thatcher is a sales manager for an automobile dealership in Alberta. Mike earns a bonus each year based on revenue generated by the number of vehicles sold in the year less related warranty expenses. The quality of automobiles sold each year seems to vary since the warranty experience related to vehicles sold is highly variable. The actual warranty expenses have varied over the past 10 years from a low of 3% of an automobile's selling price to a high of 10%. In the past, Mike has tended toward estimating warranty expenses on the high end just to be conservative. It is the end of the year and once again he must work with the dealership's accountant in arriving at the warranty expense accrual for the cars sold this year.

Required
1. Does the warranty accrual decision present any kind of ethical dilemma for Mike Thatcher?
2. Since the warranty experience is not constant, what percent do you think Mike should choose for this year? Justify your response.

Focus on Financial Statements

On August 31, 2005, World Travel Consulting showed the following selected adjusted account balances in alphabetical order:

FFS 13-1

Accounts payable	$ 3,100
Accounts receivable	29,000
Accumulated amortization, building	36,000
Accumulated amortization, equipment	13,000
Building	271,000
Cash	15,000
Equipment	38,000
GST receivable	840
Interest payable	1,400
Land	145,000
Long-term mortgage payable	116,000
Notes payable, due December 1, 2006	26,000
Notes payable, due March 1, 2006	17,000
Office supplies	1,800
Office supplies expense	14,000
Other operating expenses (including amortization)	101,000
Prepaid expenses	8,500
Salaries expense	126,000
Salaries payable	8,200
Sales	642,000

Required

1. Prepare the liability section of the balance sheet at August 31, 2005.
2. Charles World, the owner, is planning on expanding the business and has applied for a $2,000,000 bank loan. John Douglas, the Chartered Accountant and Certified Fraud Examiner featured in the chapter opening vignette on page 672, was contracted by the bank to review the financial statements of World Travel Consulting. John discovered that included in sales were the following:

Advance air ticket sales	114,000
Accommodation prepayments	96,000
Unearned bus tour revenue	36,000

He also noted the following excerpt from the amortization schedule of the long-term mortgage payable:

Year	Principal Balance at August 31
2004	$148,570
2005	116,000
2006	81,800
2007	45,900

Prepare a corrected balance sheet at August 31, 2005.
3. Using your answers from Parts 1 and 2, discuss the implications of John's findings on the financial statements.

Comprehensive Problem

Fast Exterminators
(Review of Chapters 1–13)

Fast Exterminators provides pest control services and sells pest extermination products manufactured by other companies. The following six-column table contains the company's unadjusted trial balance as of December 31, 2005.

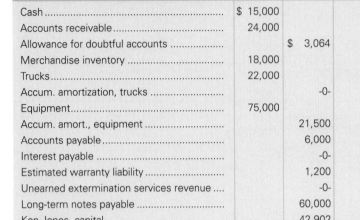

Fast Exterminators Six-Column Table December 31, 2005					
	Unadjusted Trial Balance		Adjustments		Adjusted Trial Balance
Cash	$ 15,000				
Accounts receivable	24,000				
Allowance for doubtful accounts		$ 3,064			
Merchandise inventory	18,000				
Trucks..	22,000				
Accum. amortization, trucks		-0-			
Equipment..	75,000				
Accum. amort., equipment		21,500			
Accounts payable......................................		6,000			
Interest payable		-0-			
Estimated warranty liability		1,200			
Unearned extermination services revenue		-0-			
Long-term notes payable		60,000			
Ken Jones, capital		42,902			
Ken Jones, withdrawals..............................	21,000				
Extermination services revenue...................		70,000			
Interest earned...		436			
Sales		135,000			
Cost of goods sold	81,000				
Amort. expense, trucks..............................	-0-				
Amort. expense, equip................................	-0-				
Wages expense	45,000				
Interest expense	-0-				
Rent expense..	16,000				
Bad debts expense	-0-				
Miscellaneous expenses.............................	6,202				
Repairs expense	11,000				
Utilities expense	5,900				
Warranty expense......................................	-0-				
Totals...	$340,102	$340,102			

The following information applies to the company and its situation at the end of the year:

a. The bank reconciliation P.476 as of December 31, 2005, includes these facts:

Balance per bank	$13,200
Balance per books	15,000
Outstanding cheques...	2,600
Deposit in transit	3,500
Interest earned	44
Service charges (miscellaneous expense)	17

Included with the bank statement was a cancelled cheque that the company had failed to record. (This information allows you to determine the amount of the cheque, which was a payment of an account payable.)

b. An examination of customers' accounts shows that accounts totalling $2,500 should be written off as uncollectible. In addition, it has been determined that the ending balance of the Allowance for Doubtful Accounts account should be $4,300.

c. A truck was purchased and placed in service on July 1, 2005. Its cost is being amortized with the straight-line method using these facts and predictions:

Original cost	$22,000
Expected salvage value	6,000
Useful life (years)...	4

d. Two items of equipment (a sprayer and an injector) were purchased and put into service early in January 2003. Their costs are being amortized with the straight-line method using these facts and predictions:

	Sprayer	Injector
Original cost	$45,000	$30,000
Expected salvage value	3,000	2,500
Useful life (years)...	8	5

e. On October 1, 2005, the company was paid $2,640 in advance to provide monthly service on an apartment complex for one year. The company began providing the services in October. When the cash was received, the full amount was credited to the Extermination Services Revenue account.

f. The company offers a warranty for all of the products it sells. The expected cost of providing warranty service is 2% of sales. No warranty expense has been recorded for 2005. All costs of servicing products under the warranties in 2005 were properly debited to the liability account.

g. The $60,000 long-term note is a five-year, 8% note that was given to National Bank on December 31, 2003.

h. The ending inventory of merchandise was counted and determined to have a cost of $16,300. The difference is due to shrinkage; assume a perpetual inventory system.

Required

1. Use the preceding information to determine the amounts of the following items:
   a. The correct ending balance of Cash and the amount of the omitted cheque.
   b. The adjustment needed to obtain the correct ending balance of the Allowance for Doubtful Accounts.
   c. The annual amortization expense for the truck that was acquired during the year (computed to the nearest month).
   d. The annual amortization expense for the two items of equipment that were used during the year.
   e. The correct ending balances of the Extermination Services Revenue and Unearned Extermination Services Revenue accounts.
   f. The correct ending balances of the accounts for Warranty Expense and Estimated Warranty Liability.
   g. The correct ending balance of the Interest Expense account. (Round amounts to the nearest whole dollar.)
   h. The cost of goods sold for the year.
2. Use the results of requirement 1 to complete the six-column table by first entering the appropriate adjustments for items *(a)* through *(h)* and then completing the adjusted trial balance columns. (Hint: Item *(b)* requires two entries.)
3. Present General Journal entries to record the adjustments entered on the six-column table.
4. Present a single-step income statement P.284, a statement of owner's equity P.37, and a classified balance sheet P.216.

Check figures:
4. Net Income = $12,695
Total assets = $110,350

14

Partnerships

Go For It!

Toronto, ON—What do we say to an 18-year-old who wants some extra spending money? Maybe, "Check the *help wanted* at Zellers, McDonald's, or The Bay." But do we ever say, "What do *you* want to do?" Well, Jennifer Wong did what she wanted to do. Wong decided to block print cotton T-shirts and dresses in her parents' garage to be sold at craft shows and festivals. One would not normally expect much success from such a venture.

Wong's efforts paid off, however. In her first full year of business, at the ripe age of 19, her sales climbed to $110,000. In her second year, with a loan co-signed by her parents, she set up a small factory in a leased building in Scarborough. Jennifer formed a partnership with her friend, Malu Balizar, who invested $10,000 into the business. A partnership agreement was drawn up specifying how profits and losses would be divided between Jennifer and Malu and how the assets would be allocated if they decided to end the partnership. Wong has never looked back. Wong's clothing is funky, flowing, and artsy. Each product is individually hand block printed with evocative designs and symbols, and signed by the artist. Jennifer's clothing isn't cheap—a T-shirt can cost $60 and a dress, $200 to $300—but the style holds up from year to year. Wong says her clothing "is customer driven and says something meaningful about our times." All clothing is made with natural dyes and uses only organic cotton.

Learning Objectives

LO¹ Identify characteristics of partnerships.

LO² Prepare entries when forming a partnership.

LO³ Allocate and record income and loss among partners.

LO⁴ Account for the admission and withdrawal of a partner.

LO⁵ Prepare entries for partnership liquidation

Chapter Preview

There are three common types of business organizations: corporations, partnerships, and proprietorships. In Chapter 1, we briefly discussed the following characteristics of these organizations:

	Sole Proprietorship	Partnership	Corporation
Business entity	yes	yes	yes
Legal entity	no	no	yes
Limited liability	no	no	yes
Unlimited life	no	no	yes
Business taxed	no	no	yes
One owner allowed	yes	no	yes

The opening article revealed Jennifer Wong's choice to form a partnership with her friend Malu, but there are disadvantages as well as advantages to this form of business organization. This chapter focuses on the partnership form of organization.

Partnership Form of Organization

A **partnership** is an unincorporated association of two or more persons to pursue a business for profit as co-owners. General partnerships are governed by provincial law and registration requirements. Many businesses are organized as partnerships. They are especially common in small retail and service businesses. Many professional practitioners such as physicians, lawyers, and accountants also organize their practices as partnerships.

Two forms of partnerships are recognized by Canadian law: *general partnerships* and *limited partnerships*.

Characteristics of General Partnerships

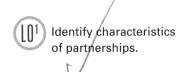

LO¹ Identify characteristics of partnerships.

General partnerships offer certain advantages and disadvantages with their unique characteristics, as described in this section.

Partnership Agreement

Forming a partnership requires that two or more legally competent persons agree to be partners. Their agreement becomes a **partnership contract**. While it should be in writing to protect partners in the event of disagreement or dissolution of the business, the contract is binding even if it is only expressed verbally.[1] Partnership agreements normally include the partners':

- names and contributions,
- rights and duties,
- sharing of income and losses,
- withdrawal provisions,
- dispute procedures,
- procedures for admission and withdrawal of new partners, and
- rights and duties of surviving partners in the event of a partner's death.

---

[1] Some courts have ruled that partnerships are created by the actions of partners even when there is no expressed agreement to form one.

Lawyers prepare partnership contracts but it is common for public accountants to review these contracts and advise partners on tax matters relating to their share of partnership income.

Limited Life

The life of a partnership is limited. Death,[2] bankruptcy, or any event taking away the ability of a partner to enter into or fulfill a contract ends a partnership. A partnership can also be terminated at will by any one of the partners. Conditions of termination may be specified in the partnership contract.

Taxation

A partnership is not subject to taxes on its income. It has the same tax status as a proprietorship. The income or loss of a partnership is allocated to the partners according to the partnership agreement, and is included for determining the taxable income of each partner's tax return.[3] Allocation of partnership income or loss is done each year whether or not cash is distributed to partners.

Co-Ownership of Property

Partnership assets are owned jointly by all partners. Any investment by a partner becomes the joint property of all partners. Partners have a claim on partnership assets based on the balances in their capital accounts.

Mutual Agency

The relationship between partners in a general partnership involves **mutual agency**. This means each partner is a fully authorized agent of the partnership. As its agent, a partner can commit or bind the partnership to any contract within the scope of the partnership's business. For instance, a partner in a merchandising business can sign contracts binding the partnership to buy merchandise, lease a store building, borrow money, or hire employees. These activities are all within the scope of business of a merchandising firm. However, a partner in a law firm, acting alone, cannot bind the other partners to a contract to buy snowboards for resale or rent an apartment for parties. These actions are outside the normal scope of a law firm's business.

Partners can agree to limit the power of any one or more of the partners to negotiate contracts for the partnership. This agreement is binding on the partners and on outsiders who know it exists, but it is not binding on outsiders who do not know it exists. Outsiders unaware of the agreement have the right to assume each partner has normal agency powers for the partnership. Because mutual agency exposes all partners to the risk of unwise actions by any one partner, people should evaluate each potential partner before agreeing to join a partnership.

Unlimited Liability

When a general partnership cannot pay its debts, the creditors can apply their claims to *personal* assets of partners, such as their homes. If a partner does not have enough assets to meet his or her share of the partnership debt, the creditors can apply their claims to the assets of the *other* partners. Because partners can be called on to pay the debts of a partnership, each partner is said to have **unlimited liability** for the partnership's debts. Mutual agency and unlimited liability are two main reasons why most partnerships have only a few members. Unlimited liability is considered a major disadvantage of the partnership form of organization. For a summary of advantages and disadvantages of partnerships see Exhibit 14.1.

---

[2] Partnership agreements may include special provisions regarding the death of a partner so that the partnership can continue after that event.

[3] The *Canada Income Tax Act* requires that proper records be maintained by partnerships and all other forms of business ownership that fall under its provisions.

Exhibit 14.1

Advantages and
Disadvantages of
Partnerships

Partnerships	
Advantages	**Potential Disadvantages**
• Ease of formation	• Unlimited liability for general partnerships creating personal obligations
• Low start-up costs	• Hard to find suitable partners
• Access to more capital sources	• Possible development of conflict among partners
• Broader base of management talent	• Divided authority
• Increased effectiveness from pooling talent	• Partners can legally bind each other without prior approval
• Less bureaucracy than corporations	• Lack of continuity

Limited Partnerships

Some individuals who want to invest in a partnership are unwilling to accept the risk of unlimited liability. Their needs may be met with a **limited partnership**. Limited partnerships are established under provincial statutes that require registration. A limited partnership has two classes of partners: general and limited. At least one partner must be a **general partner** who assumes management duties and unlimited liability for the debts of the partnership. The **limited partners** have no personal liability beyond the amounts they invest in the partnership. A limited partnership is managed by the general partner(s). Limited partners have no active role except as specified in the partnership agreement. A limited partnership agreement often specifies unique procedures for allocating incomes and losses between general and limited partners. The same basic accounting procedures are used for both limited and general partnerships.

Limited Liability Partnerships

Some provinces such as Ontario allow professionals such as lawyers and accountants to form a **limited liability partnership**. This is identified with the words "Limited Liability Partnership" or by "L.L.P." This type of partnership is designed to protect innocent partners from malpractice or negligence claims resulting from the acts of another partner. When a partner provides service resulting in a malpractice claim, that partner has personal liability for the claim. The remaining partners who are not responsible for the actions resulting from the claim are not personally liable. However, all partners are personally liable for other partnership debts. Accounting for a limited liability partnership is the same as for a general partnership.

Flashback

Answers—p. 737

1. Prepare a summary of the characteristics of a general partnership.
2. What is the difference between a *limited partnership* and a *limited liability partnership?*

Basic Partnership Accounting

Accounting for a partnership is the same as accounting for a proprietorship except for transactions directly affecting partners' equity. Because ownership rights in a partnership are divided among partners, partnership accounting:

- Uses a capital account for each partner.
- Uses a withdrawals account for each partner.
- Allocates net income or loss to partners according to the partnership agreement.

This section describes partnership accounting for organizing a partnership, distributing income and losses, and preparing financial statements P.34.

Organizing a Partnership

When partners invest in a partnership, their capital accounts are credited for the invested amounts. Partners can invest both assets and liabilities. Each partner's investment is recorded at an agreed upon value, normally the fair market value P.144 of the assets and liabilities at their date of transfer to the partnership.

LO² Prepare entries when forming a partnership.

To illustrate, on January 11, 2005, Olivia Tsang and David Breck organize as a partnership called The Landing Zone. Their business offers year-around facilities for skateboarding and snowboarding. Tsang's initial net investment in The Landing Zone is $30,000, made up of $7,000 in cash, equipment with a fair value of $33,000, and a $10,000 note payable reflecting a bank loan for the business due in six months. Breck's initial investment is cash of $10,000. These amounts are the values agreed upon by both partners. The entries to record these investments are:

2005				
Jan. 11	Cash..	7,000	
	Equipment	33,000	
	Notes payable		10,000
	Olivia Tsang, Capital		30,000
	To record investment of Tsang.		
11	Cash..	10,000	
	David Breck, Capital		10,000
	To record investment of Breck.		

The balance sheet for the partnership would appear as follows immediately after the initial investment on January 11, 2005:

The Landing Zone
Balance Sheet
January 11, 2005

Assets

Current assets:
Cash.. $17,000

Capital assets:
Equipment 33,000

Total assets................................... $50,000

Liabilities

Notes payable $10,000

Partners' Equity

Olivia Tsang, capital.................	$30,000	
David Breck, capital..................	10,000	
Total partners' equity		40,000
Total liabilities and partners' equity...........		$50,000

After a partnership is formed, accounting for its transactions is similar to a proprietorship. The differences include:

> 1. Partners' withdrawals of assets are debited to their *individual* withdrawals accounts (as opposed to *one* withdrawals account for a sole proprietorship P.7).
> 2. In closing the accounts at the end of a period, *each* partner's capital account is credited or debited for his or her share of net income or loss (as opposed to *one* capital account for a sole proprietorship).
> 3. The withdrawals account of *each* partner is closed to that partner's capital account (as opposed to *one* withdrawals account and *one* capital account for a sole proprietorship).

In the following sections, we will demonstrate that the basic accounting procedures related to the recording of withdrawals and closing of the accounts at the end of a period are similar for a partnership as for a proprietorship.

Dividing Income or Loss

Partners are not employees of the partnership. They are its owners. Partnership agreements generally include a provision for rewarding partners for their service and capital contributions to the partnership. If partners devote their time and services to their partnership, they are understood to do so for profit, not for salary. This means that when partners calculate the net income of a partnership, the amounts that they withdraw from the partnership assets are **not** expenses on the income statement.[4] They are recorded by debiting the partner's withdrawals account. Assume, for example, that on December 15, 2005, Olivia Tsang withdrew $20,000 and David Breck withdrew $18,000. The journal entry to record the withdrawals is:

2005			
Dec. 15	Olivia Tsang, Withdrawals..............................	20,000	
	David Breck, Withdrawals..............................	18,000	
	Cash		38,000
	To record the withdrawal of cash by each partner.		

When net income or loss of a partnership is allocated among partners, the partners can agree to be assigned *salary allowances* as part of their allocation. *These salary allowances simply represent allocations of income; they are not actual distributions of cash.* Partners also can agree that division of partnership earnings includes a return based on the amount invested. These are called *interest allowances.* Their partnership agreement can provide for interest allowances based on their capital balances. For instance, since Tsang contributes three times the investment of Breck, it is only fair that this fact be considered when earnings are allocated between them. Like salary allowances, these interest allowances are *not* expenses on the income statement and they are *not* actual distributions of cash.

---

[4] Withdrawals are frequently called salary allowances but they should not be confused with salary expense. Salaries taken out of the partnership are simply withdrawals.

Partners can agree to any method of dividing income or loss. In the absence of an agreement, the law says that income or loss of a partnership is shared equally by the partners. If partners agree on how they share income but say nothing about losses, then losses are shared in the same way as income. Several methods of sharing partnership income or loss are used. Three frequently used methods divide income or loss using: (1) a stated fractional basis, (2) the ratio of capital investments, or (3) salary and interest allowances and any remainder in a fixed ratio.

LO³ Allocate and record income and loss among partners.

1. Allocated on a Stated Fractional Basis

One way to divide partnership income or loss is to give each partner a fraction of the total. Partners must agree on the fractional share each receives. A fractional basis can be expressed as a ratio, a fraction, or a percentage. As an example, assume a 3:2 ratio as illustrated in Exhibit 14.2. This means that 3/5 or 60% (3 ÷ 5 = 0.60 × 100 = 60%) is allocated to one partner and 2/5 or 40% (2 ÷ 5 = 0.40 × 100 = 40%) is allocated to the other partner.

Assume the partnership agreement of Olivia Tsang and David Breck is based on a ratio of 3:2. This means Tsang receives three-fifths or 60%, and Breck two-fifths or 40%, of partnership income and loss. If their partnership's net income for the year ended December 31, 2005, is $70,000, it is allocated to the partners and the Income Summary account is closed with the following entry:

2005			
Dec. 31	Income Summary	70,000	
	Olivia Tsang, Capital		42,000
	David Breck, Capital		28,000
	To allocate income and close the Income Summary account.		

2. Allocated on the Ratio of Capital Investments

Partners can also allocate income or loss on the ratio of the relative capital investments of each partner. Assume Tsang and Breck agreed to share earnings on the ratio of their beginning capital investments. Since Tsang invested $30,000 and Breck invested $10,000, this means Tsang receives three-fourths [$30,000/($30,000 + $10,000)] or 75% of any income or loss and Breck receives one-fourth [$10,000/($30,000 + $10,000)] or 25%.

3. Allocated Using Salaries, Interest Allowance, and a Fixed Ratio

Service contributions (the amount of work each partner does) and capital contributions of partners often are not equal. Salary allowances can make up for differences in service contributions and interest allowances can make up for unequal capital contributions. When both service and capital contributions are unequal, the allocation of income and loss can include *both* salary and interest allowances.

In the new partnership formed by Olivia Tsang and David Breck, assume both partners agree that Tsang's services are worth an annual salary of $40,000. Since Breck is less experienced in the business, his services are valued at $25,000 annually. To compensate Tsang and Breck fairly given these differences in service and capital contributions, they agree to share income or loss as per Exhibit 14.3.

Exhibit 14.2

Illustration of 3:2 Ratio

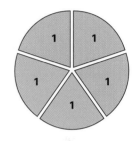

or

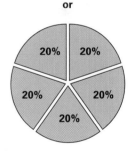

Exhibit 14.3

Partnership Agreement Between Tsang and Breck

1. Annual salary allowances of $40,000 to Tsang and $25,000 to Breck.
2. Interest allowances equal to 10% of each partner's beginning-of-year capital balance.
3. Any remaining balance of income or loss to be shared 3:1.

The provisions for salaries and interest in this partnership agreement are called *allowances*. Allowances are *not* reported as salaries and interest expense on the income statement. They are a means of dividing the income or loss of a partnership so each partner's capital account can be allocated its share.

Illustration When Income Exceeds Allowance

Recall that Tsang's original investment was $30,000 and Breck's $10,000. If The Landing Zone has first-year income of $70,000 and Tsang and Breck apply the partnership agreement as per Exhibit 14.3, they would allocate income or loss as shown in Exhibit 14.4 with the accompanying entry following.

Exhibit 14.4

Allocating Income When Income Exceeds Allowances

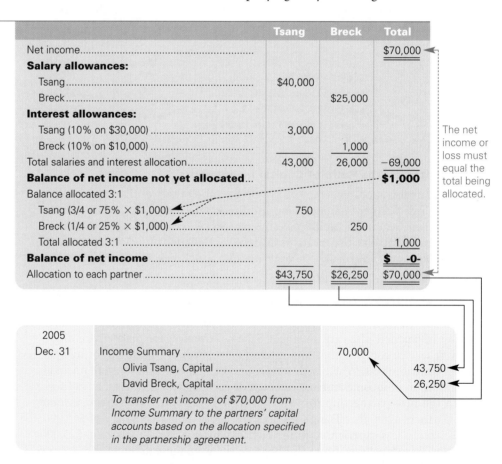

	Tsang	Breck	Total
Net income..			$70,000
Salary allowances:			
Tsang...	$40,000		
Breck...		$25,000	
Interest allowances:			
Tsang (10% on $30,000).............................	3,000		
Breck (10% on $10,000).............................		1,000	
Total salaries and interest allocation...........	43,000	26,000	−69,000
Balance of net income not yet allocated...			**$1,000**
Balance allocated 3:1			
Tsang (3/4 or 75% × $1,000)......................	750		
Breck (1/4 or 25% × $1,000)......................		250	
Total allocated 3:1...................................			1,000
Balance of net income.............................			**$ -0-**
Allocation to each partner...........................	$43,750	$26,250	$70,000

The net income or loss must equal the total being allocated.

2005			
Dec. 31	Income Summary	70,000	
	Olivia Tsang, Capital		43,750
	David Breck, Capital		26,250
	To transfer net income of $70,000 from		
	Income Summary to the partners' capital		
	accounts based on the allocation specified		
	in the partnership agreement.		

Tsang is *allocated* $43,750 and Breck $26,250 of the $70,000 total; they do not *receive* these amounts. Remember that the purpose of the calculation in Exhibit 14.4 is to determine the amount of income or loss to be allocated to each partner's capital account at the end of the accounting period. Therefore, the entry to allocate the $70,000 net income between the partners and to close the Income Summary account on December 31, 2005, is as shown in Exhibit 14.4.

The balance in each of Tsang's and Breck's capital accounts at December 31, 2005, after posting all closing entries P. 207 is reflected in Exhibit 14.5.

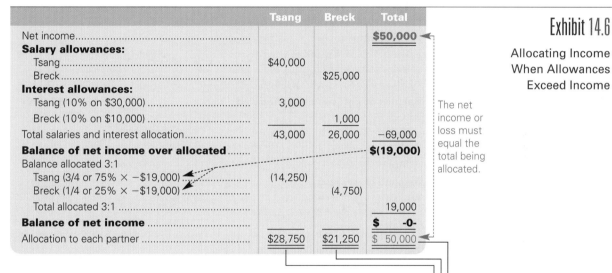

Olivia Tsang, Capital		
	30,000	Jan. 11/05 Partner investment
Dec. 31/05 Withdrawal[5] 20,000	43,750	Dec. 31/05 Allocation of income
	53,750	Post-Closing Balance Dec. 31/05

David Breck, Capital		
	10,000	Jan. 11/05 Partner investment
Dec. 31/05 Withdrawal[5] 18,000	26,250	Dec. 31/05 Allocation of income
	18,250	Post-Closing Balance Dec. 31/05

Exhibit 14.5

Partners' Post-Closing Capital Balances at December 31, 2005

Illustration When Allowances Exceed Income

The method of sharing agreed to by Tsang and Breck must be followed even if net income is less than the total of the allowances. If The Landing Zone's first-year net income is $50,000 instead of $70,000, it is allocated to the partners as shown in Exhibit 14.6. The net income or loss must equal the total being allocated.

	Tsang	Breck	Total
Net income...			**$50,000**
Salary allowances:			
Tsang...	$40,000		
Breck...		$25,000	
Interest allowances:			
Tsang (10% on $30,000)	3,000		
Breck (10% on $10,000)		1,000	
Total salaries and interest allocation......................	43,000	26,000	−69,000
Balance of net income over allocated			**$(19,000)**
Balance allocated 3:1			
Tsang (3/4 or 75% × −$19,000)	(14,250)		
Breck (1/4 or 25% × −$19,000)		(4,750)	
Total allocated 3:1			19,000
Balance of net income			$ -0-
Allocation to each partner	$28,750	$21,250	$ 50,000

Exhibit 14.6

Allocating Income When Allowances Exceed Income

The net income or loss must equal the total being allocated.

Calculations for salaries and interest are identical to those in Exhibit 14.4. When we apply the total allowances against net income, the balance of income is negative. This negative $19,000 balance is allocated in the same manner as a positive balance. The 3:1 sharing agreement means negative $14,250 and negative $4,750 are allocated to the partners to determine the final allocation. In this case, Tsang's capital account is credited with $28,750 and Breck's capital account with $21,250 as reflected in the following closing entry:

2005 Dec. 31	Income Summary	50,000	
	Olivia Tsang, Capital		28,750
	David Breck, Capital		21,250
	To transfer net income of $50,000 from Income Summary to the partners' capital accounts based on the allocation specified in the partnership agreement.		

---

[5] Recall that the closing entry for withdrawals would have been:

2005 Dec. 31	Olivia Tsang, Capital...	20,000	
	David Breck, Capital..	18,000	
	Olivia Tsang, Withdrawals		20,000
	David Breck, Withdrawals		18,000
	To record withdrawals to each partner's capital account.		

Illustration When There is a Net Loss

If The Landing Zone had experienced a loss, then it would have been shared by Tsang and Breck in the same manner as the $50,000 income. The only difference is that they would have begun with a negative amount because of the loss. Specifically, the partners would still have been allocated their salary and interest allowances, further adding to the negative balance of the loss. This *total* negative balance *after* salary and interest allowances would have been allocated 3:1 (75% and 25%) between the partners. These allocations would have been applied against the positive numbers from any allowances to determine each partner's share of the loss. Exhibit 14.7 illustrates how a $6,000 net loss would be divided between Tsang and Breck.

Exhibit 14.7

Allocating a Net Loss

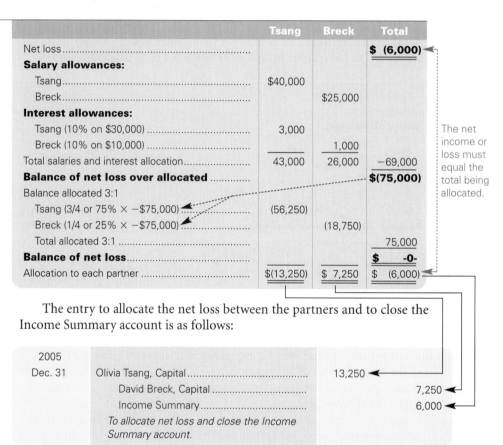

	Tsang	Breck	Total
Net loss			$ (6,000)
Salary allowances:			
Tsang	$40,000		
Breck		$25,000	
Interest allowances:			
Tsang (10% on $30,000)	3,000		
Breck (10% on $10,000)		1,000	
Total salaries and interest allocation	43,000	26,000	−69,000
Balance of net loss over allocated			$(75,000)
Balance allocated 3:1			
Tsang (3/4 or 75% × −$75,000)	(56,250)		
Breck (1/4 or 25% × −$75,000)		(18,750)	
Total allocated 3:1			75,000
Balance of net loss			$ -0-
Allocation to each partner	$(13,250)	$ 7,250	$ (6,000)

The net income or loss must equal the total being allocated.

The entry to allocate the net loss between the partners and to close the Income Summary account is as follows:

2005			
Dec. 31	Olivia Tsang, Capital	13,250	
	David Breck, Capital		7,250
	Income Summary		6,000
	To allocate net loss and close the Income Summary account.		

When a net loss is allocated to the partners' capital accounts, you would expect each partner's capital account to decrease (a debit). However, notice that this entry causes Breck's capital account to increase (a credit) even though the partnership incurred a $6,000 loss. This occurs because Breck's 25% share of the $75,000 negative remaining balance is less than his $26,000 salaries and interest allocation. If the net loss had been, for example, $60,000, both Tsang's and Breck's capital accounts would have decreased as a result of the closing entry.

Flashback

Answers—p. 737

3. Ben and Jerry form a partnership by contributing $70,000 and $35,000, respectively. They agree to an interest allowance equal to 10% of each partner's capital balance at the beginning of the year with the remaining income shared equally. Allocate first-year income of $40,000 to each partner.

4. What fraction does each receive if three partners share on a 1:2:2 basis?

5. What percentage does each receive if three partners share on a 1:2:2 basis?

Partnership Financial Statements

Partnership financial statements are very similar to those of a proprietorship. The **Statement of Partners' Equity** is one exception. It shows each partner's capital balance at the beginning of the period, any additional investments made by each partner, each partner's allocation of the income or loss, withdrawals made by each partner, and the ending capital balance for each partner. To illustrate, Exhibit 14.8 shows the statement of partners' equity for The Landing Zone prepared according to the sharing agreement of Exhibit 14.3. Recall that The Landing Zone's first-year income was $70,000. Also, Tsang withdrew $20,000 and Breck $18,000 at the end of the first year as reflected in the T-accounts of Exhibit 14.5.

The Landing Zone Statement of Partners' Equity For Year Ended December 31, 2005			
	Tsang	Breck	Total
Capital, January 1	-0-	-0-	-0-
Add: Investments by partners	30,000	10,000	40,000
Net income	43,750	26,250	70,000
Total	$73,750	$36,250	$110,000
Less: Partners' withdrawals	(20,000)	(18,000)	(38,000)
Capital, December 31	**$53,750**	**$18,250**	**$72,000**

Exhibit 14.8

Statement of Partners' Equity

The owners' equity section of the balance sheet of a partnership usually shows the separate capital account balance of each partner. In the case of The Landing Zone, both Olivia Tsang, Capital and David Breck, Capital are listed in the partners' equity section along with their balances of $53,750 and $18,250, respectively. This information appears on the December 31, 2005, balance sheet as shown in Exhibit 14.9.

The Landing Zone Balance Sheet December 31, 2005		
Assets		
Current assets:		
Cash		$50,000
Capital assets:		
Equipment	$33,000	
Less: Accumulated amortization	3,000	30,000
Total assets		80,000
Liabilities		
Long-term notes payable		$ 8,000
Partners' Equity		
Olivia Tsang, capital	$53,750	
David Breck, capital	18,250	
Total partners' equity		72,000
Total liabilities and partners' equity		$80,000

Exhibit 14.9

Balance Sheet for The Landing Zone at December 31, 2005

Mid-Chapter Demonstration Problem

Claudia Parker and Tom Poon began a partnership by investing $10,000 and $90,000 respectively. For the year ended September 30, 2005, the partnership earned $50,000.

1. Prepare calculations that show how the income should be allocated to the partners under each of the following plans for sharing net incomes and losses:

   a. The partners fail to agree on a method of sharing income.

   b. The partners agree to share income and losses in their investment ratio.

   c. The partners agree to share income by allowing an $85,000 per year salary allowance to Parker, a $15,000 per year salary allowance to Poon, 10% interest on beginning capital balances, and the remainder equally.

2. After each calculation in (a), (b), and (c), prepare the journal entry to close the Income Summary account to the partners' capital accounts.

Planning the Solution

○ Set up a column for each partner as well as a column to keep track of allocated income.

○ Allocate income to each partner according to the terms of the partnership agreement.

○ Prepare the entry to close the Income Summary to the partners' capital accounts.

SOLUTION TO # Mid-Chapter Demonstration Problem

1a.

	Parker	Poon	Total
$50,000 × 50%...	$25,000	$25,000	**$50,000**

2a.

2005				
Sept. 30	Income Summary	50,000		
	Claudia Parker, Capital.............................			25,000
	Tom Poon, Capital			25,000
	To transfer net income of $50,000 from			
	Income Summary to the partners'			
	capital accounts.			

1b.

	Parker	Poon	Total
[$10,000/($10,000 + $90,000)] × $50,000	$5,000		$ 5,000
[$90,000/($10,000 + $90,000)] × $50,000		$45,000	45,000
Allocation to each partner	$5,000	$45,000	$50,000

2b.

2005			
Dec. 31	Income Summary	50,000	
	Claudia Parker, Capital		5,000
	Tom Poon, Capital		45,000
	To transfer net income of $50,000 from Income Summary to the partners' capital accounts.		

1c.

	Parker	Poon	Total
Net income			**$50,000**
Salary allowances:			
Parker..	$85,000		
Poon...		$15,000	
Interest allowances:			
Parker (10% on $10,000)	1,000		
Poon (10% on $90,000)		9,000	
Total salaries and interest allocation	86,000	24,000	−110,000
Balance of net income over allocated...........			**$(60,000)**
Balance allocated equally:			
Parker (50% × −$60,000)	(30,000)		
Poon (50% × −$60,000)		(30,000)	
Total allocated equally			60,000
Balance of net income			**$ -0-**
Allocation to each partner	$56,000	$(6,000)	$ 50,000

must be equal

2c.

2005			
Dec. 31	Income Summary	50,000	
	Tom Poon, Capital	6,000	
	Claudia Parker, Capital............................		56,000
	To transfer net income of $50,000 from Income Summary to the partners' capital accounts.		

Admission and Withdrawal of Partner

LO⁴ Account for the admission and withdrawal of a partner.

A partnership is based on a contract between individuals. When a partner is added or a partner withdraws, the old partnership ends. Still, the business can continue to operate as a new partnership among the remaining partners. This section looks at how we account for the addition and withdrawal of a partner.

Admission of a Partner

There are two ways in which a new partner is admitted to a partnership. First, a new partner can purchase an interest from one or more current partners. Second, a new partner can invest cash or other assets in the partnership.

Purchase of a Partnership Interest

The purchase of a partnership interest is a *personal transaction between one or more current partners and the new partner* that involves a reallocation of current partners' capital. To become a partner, the purchaser must be accepted by the current partners.

To illustrate, assume that at the end of The Landing Zone's third year, David Breck has a capital balance of $20,000 and he sells *one-half* of his partnership interest to Cris Davis for $18,000 on January 4, 2008. Breck is selling a $10,000 recorded interest (= $20,000 × 1/2) in the partnership. The partnership records this as:

2008			
Jan. 4	David Breck, Capital...	10,000	
	Cris Davis, Capital		10,000
	To record admission of Davis by purchase.		

The effect of this transaction on partners' equity is as follows:

	Olivia Tsang, Capital	David Breck, Capital	Cris Davis, Capital	Total Partners' Equity
Balance **before** January 4 transaction ...	$52,000	$20,000	$ -0-	$72,000
January 4 tranaction..............................	-0-	(10,000)	+10,000	-0-
Balance **after** January 4 transaction	$52,000	$10,000	$10,000	$72,000

Two aspects of this transaction are important. First, the $18,000 Davis paid to Breck is *not* recorded by the partnership. The partnership's assets, liabilities, and total equity are not affected by this transaction. Second, Tsang and Breck must agree if Davis is to become a partner. If they agree to accept Davis, a new partnership is formed and a new contract with a new income-and-loss-sharing agreement is prepared. If Tsang or Breck refuses to accept Davis as a partner, then Davis gets Breck's sold share of partnership income and loss. If the partnership is liquidated, Davis gets Breck's sold share of partnership assets. However, Davis gets no voice in managing the company until being admitted as a partner.

Investing Assets in a Partnership

Admitting a partner by an investment of assets is a *transaction between the new partner and the partnership*. The invested assets become partnership property. To illustrate, if Tsang (with a $52,000 interest) and Breck (with a $20,000 interest) agree to accept Davis as a partner in The Landing Zone with her investment of $28,000, the entry to record Davis' investment is:

2008			
Jan. 4	Cash..	28,000	
	Cris Davis, Capital		28,000
	To record admission of Davis by investment.		

After this entry is posted, both assets (cash) and owners' equity (Cris Davis, Capital) increase by $28,000 as shown in the following schedule:

	Net Assets	Olivia Tsang, Capital	David Breck, Capital	Cris Davis, Capital	Total Partners' Equity
Balance *before* January 4 transaction	$ 72,000	$52,000	$20,000	$ -0-	$ 72,000
January 4 tranaction............................	+28,000	-0-	-0-	+28,000	+28,000
Balance *after* January 4 transaction....	$100,000	$52,000	$20,000	$28,000	$100,000

Davis now has 28% equity in the net assets of the business, calculated as $28,000 divided by the entire partnership equity of $100,000 (= $52,000 + $20,000 + $28,000). However, she does not necessarily have a right to 28% of income. Dividing income and loss is a separate matter on which partners must agree.

Bonus to Old Partners

When the current market value of a partnership is greater than the recorded amounts of equity, the partners usually require a new partner to pay a bonus (premium) for the privilege of joining. This situation exists when the market value of net assets exceeds their book value. To illustrate, let's say Tsang and Breck agree to accept Davis as a partner with a 25% interest in The Landing Zone, but they require Davis to invest $48,000. Recall that the partnership's accounting records show Tsang's equity in the business to be $52,000 and Breck's equity to be $20,000. Davis' equity is determined as follows:

Equities of existing partners ($52,000 + $20,000)	$ 72,000
Investment of new partner	48,000
Total partnership equity..	$120,000
Equity of Davis (25% × $120,000)	$ 30,000

Although Davis invests $48,000, her equity in the recorded net assets of the partnership is only $30,000. The difference of $18,000 is called a bonus (or premium) and is allocated to the existing partners according to their net income/loss share ratio. Assume this to be 50:50. The entry to record this is:

2008			
Jan. 4	Cash..	48,000	
	Cris Davis, Capital		30,000
	Olivia Tsang, Capital		9,000
	David Breck, Capital		9,000
	To record admission of Davis and bonus to old partners; $18,000 × 1/2 = $9,000.		

The effects of this transaction on the accounts are summarized as follows:

	Net Assets	Olivia Tsang, Capital	David Breck, Capital	Cris Davis, Capital	Total Partners' Equity
Balance **before** January 4 transaction..	$ 72,000	$52,000	$20,000	$ -0-	$ 72,000
January 4 tranaction	+48,000	+9,000	+9,000	+30,000	+48,000
Balance **after** January 4 transaction	$120,000	$61,000	$29,000	$30,000	$120,000

Bonus to New Partner

Existing partners can give a bonus (premium) to a new partner so that the new partner gets a larger equity than the amount invested. This usually occurs when additional cash is needed or the new partner has exceptional talents. To illustrate, let's say Tsang and Breck agree to accept Davis as a partner with a 25% interest in the partnership's equity, but they require Davis to invest only $18,000. Davis' equity is determined as:

Equities of existing partners ($52,000 + $20,000)	$72,000
Investment of new partner	18,000
Total partnership equity..	$90,000
Equity of Davis (25% × $90,000)	$22,500

Davis receives a bonus of $4,500 (= $22,500 − $18,000). The entry to record Davis' investment is:

2008				
Jan. 4	Cash...	18,000	
	Olivia Tsang, Capital	2,250	
	David Breck, Capital	2,250	
	Cris Davis, Capital		22,500
	To record Davis' admission and bonus;		
	$4,500 × 1/2 = $2,250.		

The effect of this transaction on the accounts follows:

	Net Assets	Olivia Tsang, Capital	David Breck, Capital	Cris Davis, Capital	Total Partners' Equity
Balance **before** January 4 transaction..	$ 72,000	$52,000	$20,000	$ -0-	$72,000
January 4 tranaction	+18,000	−2,250	−2,250	+22,500	+18,000
Balance **after** January 4 transaction	$90,000	$49,750	$17,750	$22,500	$90,000

Davis' bonus of $4,500 is contributed by the old partners in their income-and-loss-sharing ratio. Davis' 25% equity doesn't necessarily entitle her to 25% of any income or loss. This is a separate matter for agreement by the partners.

Withdrawal of a Partner

There are generally two ways in which a partner withdraws from a partnership. First, the withdrawing partner can sell his or her interest to another person who pays for it in cash or other assets. For this, we debit the withdrawing partner's capital account and credit the new partner's capital account (as already described in our discussion on the purchase of partnership interests). The second case is when cash or other assets of the partnership are given to the withdrawing partner in settlement of his or her equity interest. This section explains the accounting for the second case.

To illustrate, let's assume that on October 31, 2008, Breck withdraws from the partnership of The Landing Zone. The three partners share income and loss equally. The accounts show the following capital balances immediately prior to Breck's withdrawal:

	Olivia Tsang, Capital	David Breck, Capital	Cris Davis, Capital	Total Partners' Equity
Capital balances immediately **prior** to Breck's withdrawal	$84,000	$38,000	$38,000	$160,000

Accounting for the withdrawal depends on whether a bonus is paid or not. We describe three possibilities, summarized as follows:

1. No Bonus

If Breck withdraws and receives cash of $38,000

Oct. 31	David Breck, Capital	38,000	
	Cash		38,000

2. Bonus to Remaining Partners

If Breck withdraws and receives cash of $34,000

Oct. 31	David Breck, Capital	38,000	
	Cash		34,000
	Olivia Tsang, Capital		2,000
	Cris Davis, Capital		2,000

3. Bonus to Withdrawing Partner

If Breck withdraws and receives cash of $40,000

Oct. 31	David Breck, Capital	38,000	
	Olivia Tsang, Capital	1,000	
	Cris Davis, Capital	1,000	
	Cash		40,000

A withdrawing partner is sometimes willing to take less than the recorded value of his or her equity just to get out of the partnership or because the recorded values of some assets are overstated. When this occurs, the withdrawing partner in effect gives a bonus to remaining partners equal to the equity left behind as shown in the second situation above.

The third case shows a bonus to the withdrawing partner. This bonus might arise for two reasons:

- if the recorded equity of the partnership is understated, or
- if the remaining partners want to remove a partner, which may require giving assets of greater value than the withdrawing partner's recorded equity.

Death of a Partner

A partner's death dissolves a partnership if the partnership agreement does not provide otherwise. A deceased partner's estate is entitled to receive his or her equity based on provisions that are stated in the partnership contract. These provisions include methods for: (a) closing of the books to determine income or loss since the end of the previous period up to the date of death, and (b) determining current values for assets and liabilities. The remaining partners and the deceased partner's estate then must agree to a settlement of the deceased partner's equity. This can involve selling the equity to remaining partners or to an outsider, or it can involve withdrawing assets. The journal entries regarding the death of a partner are the same as those for the withdrawal of a partner.

Judgement Call

Answer—p. 737

Lawyer

You are a lawyer hired by the two remaining partners of a three-member partnership. The third partner recently died. The three partners shared income and loss in the ratio of their capital balances, which were equal. The partnership agreement says a deceased partner's estate is entitled to the "partner's percent share of partnership assets." The estate argues it is entitled to one-third of the current value of the partnership's total assets. The remaining partners say the distribution should use the asset's book values, which are only 75% of current value. They also point to partnership liabilities, which equal 40% of the assets' book value, and 30% of current value. How would you resolve this situation?

Liquidation of a Partnership

Partnership liquidation is the process of closing down a business; it involves selling partnership assets, paying business debts, and distributing any remaining cash to owners. When a partnership is liquidated, its business is ended. Four steps are involved:

1. Non-cash assets are sold for cash and a gain or loss on liquidation is recorded.
2. Gain or loss on liquidation is allocated to partners using their income-and-loss ratio.
3. Liabilities are paid.
4. Remaining cash is distributed to partners based on their capital balances.

Partnership liquidation often follows one of two different cases described below.

No Capital Deficiency

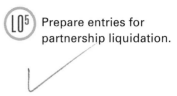

LO⁵ Prepare entries for partnership liquidation.

No capital deficiency means that all partners have credit balances in their capital accounts before final distribution of cash. To illustrate, let's assume Tsang, Breck, and Davis operate their partnership in The Landing Zone for several years, sharing income and losses equally. The partners decide to liquidate on January 15, 2010. On that date, the books are closed, and income from operations is transferred to partners' capital accounts. A summary of account balances immediately *prior* to liquidation are:

		Assets			= Liabilities +	Partners' Equity		
	Cash	Sporting Facilities	Accum. Amort. Sporting Facilities	Land	Accounts Payable	Olivia Tsang, Capital	David Breck, Capital	Cris Davis, Capital
Account balances immediately ***prior*** to liquidation...............	$168,000	$33,000	$18,000	$25,000	$20,000	$70,000	$66,000	$52,000

Following the four-step liquidation process, we first record the sale of the non-cash assets that occurred on January 15 for cash of $46,000. The entry is:

2010			
Jan. 15	Cash..	46,000	
	Accumulated Amortization, Sporting Facilities	18,000	
	Sporting Facilities		33,000
	Land		25,000
	Gain From Liquidation		6,000
	Sold non-cash assets at a gain.		

Second, we record the allocation of the resulting gain from liquidation against the partners' capital accounts:

Jan. 15	Gain From Liquidation	6,000	
	Olivia Tsang, Capital		2,000
	David Breck, Capital		2,000
	Cris Davis, Capital		2,000
	To allocate liquidation gain to partners.		

The balances in the accounts after Steps 1 and 2 are recorded and summarized in Exhibit 14.10.

Step 3 in the liquidation process requires that liabilities be paid. Because creditors have claim to partnership assets before the partners do, they are paid first. The entry to record payment to the creditors is:

Jan. 15	Accounts Payable	20,000	
	Cash		20,000
	To pay claims of creditors.		

Exhibit 14.10 shows the account balances after Step 3, payment of creditors.

Exhibit 14.10

Liquidation of a Partnership—No Capital Deficiency

			Assets			= Liabilities +	Partners' Equity		
		Cash	Sporting Facilities	Accum. Amort., Sporting Facilities	Land	Accounts Payable	Olivia Tsang, Capital	David Breck, Capital	Cris Davis, Capital
	Account balances immediately **prior** to liquidation	$168,000	$33,000	$18,000	$25,000	$20,000	$70,000	$66,000	$52,000
1. & 2.	Sale of non-cash assets for a gain of $6,000	+46,000	−33,000	−18,000	−25,000		+2,000	+2,000	+2,000
	Balance..................................	$214,000	$ −0−	$ −0−	$ −0−	$20,000	$72,000	$68,000	$54,000
3.	Payment of Accounts Payable	−20,000				−20,000			
	Balance..................................	$194,000	$ −0−	$ −0−	$ −0−	$ −0−	$72,000	$68,000	$54,000
4.	Distribution of cash to partners	−194,000					−72,000	−68,000	−54,000
	Final balance..........................	$ −0−	$ −0−	$ −0−	$ −0−	$ −0−	$ −0−	$ −0−	$ −0−

Step 4 in the liquidation process is to *divide the remaining cash of $194,000 among the partners according to their capital account balances* as follows:

Jan. 15	Olivia Tsang, Capital	72,000 ◄	
	David Breck, Capital	68,000 ◄	
	Cris Davis, Capital	54,000 ◄	
	Cash...		194,000
	To distribute remaining cash to partners.		

The account balances after distribution of cash to the partners are summarized in Exhibit 14.10.

Capital Deficiency

Capital deficiency means that at least one partner has a debit balance in his or her capital account before the final distribution of cash. This can arise from liquidation losses, excessive withdrawals before liquidation, or recurring losses in prior periods.

Assume that the partners of The Landing Zone decide to liquidate. Davis' capital account shows a deficiency of $3,000 immediately prior to the final distribution of cash. Davis' capital deficiency means that she owes the partnership $3,000. The final distribution of cash depends on whether the deficient partner can pay the deficiency or not.

Partner Pays Deficiency

Davis should pay $3,000 into the partnership to cover the deficiency. If Davis is willing and able to pay, the partners' capital balances after the payment are:

	Cash	Olivia Tsang, Capital	David Breck, Capital	Cris Davis, Capital
Account balances immediately *prior* to distribution of cash to partners	$24,000	$19,000	$8,000	$(3,000)
Davis pays deficiency	+3,000			+3,000
Balance	$27,000	$19,000	$8,000	$ -0-

The entry to record the final cash distributions to partners is:

Jan. 15	Olivia Tsang, Capital	19,000	
	David Breck, Capital	8,000	
	Cash		27,000
	To distribute remaining cash to partners.		

Partner Cannot Pay Deficiency

Because of unlimited liability in a partnership, a partner's unpaid deficiency is absorbed by the remaining partners with credit balances. If Davis is unable to pay the $3,000 deficiency, it is shared by Tsang and Breck based on their income-and-loss-sharing ratio. Since they share equally, this is recorded as:

Jan. 15	Olivia Tsang, Capital	1,500	
	David Breck, Capital	1,500	
	Cris Davis, Capital		3,000
	To transfer Davis' deficiency to Tsang and Breck.		

After Davis' deficiency is absorbed by Tsang and Breck, the capital account balances of the partners are:

	Cash	Olivia Tsang, Capital	David Breck, Capital	Cris Davis, Capital
Account balances immediately *prior* to distribution of cash to partners	$24,000	$19,000	$8,000	$(3,000)
Transfer Davis' deficiency to Tsang and Breck		−1,500	−1,500	+3,000
Balance	$24,000	$17,500	$6,500	$ -0-

The entry to record the final cash distributions to the partners is:

Jan. 15	Olivia Tsang, Capital	17,500	
	David Breck, Capital	6,500	
	Cash		24,000
	To distribute remaining cash to partners.		

The inability of Davis to cover her deficiency does not relieve her of the liability. If she becomes able to pay at some future date, Tsang and Breck can each collect $1,500 from her. If Davis does not comply, then Tsang and Breck may have to resort to legal action.

The sharing of an insolvent partner's deficit by the remaining partners in their original income-and-loss-sharing ratio is generally regarded as equitable.

Summary

LO¹ **Identify characteristics of partnerships.** A partnership is a voluntary association between the partners that is based on a contract. The life of a partnership is limited by agreement or by the death or incapacity of a partner. Normally, each partner can act as an agent of the other partners and commit the partnership to any contract within the apparent scope of its business. All partners in a general partnership are personally liable for all the debts of the partnership. Limited partnerships include one or more general partners plus one or more (limited) partners whose liabilities are limited to the amounts of their investments in the partnership. The risk of becoming a partner results in part from the fact that partnership characteristics include mutual agency and unlimited liability.

LO² **Prepare entries when forming a partnership.** The initial investment of partnership assets is recorded by debiting the assets contributed at the fair market value and crediting the partners' capital accounts.

LO³ **Allocate and record income and loss among partners.** A partnership's net incomes or losses are allocated to the partners according to the terms of the partnership agreement. The agreement may specify that each partner will receive a given fraction, or that the allocation of incomes and losses will reflect salary allowances and/or interest allowances. When salary and/or interest

allowances are granted, the residual net income or loss usually is allocated equally or on a stated fractional basis.

LO⁴ **Account for the admission and withdrawal of a partner.** When a new partner buys a partnership interest directly from one or more of the existing partners, the amount of cash paid from one partner to another does not affect the total recorded equity of the partnership. The recorded equity of the selling partner(s) is simply transferred to the capital account of the new partner. Alternatively, a new partner may purchase an equity interest in the partnership by investing additional assets in the partnership. When this occurs, part of the new partner's investment may be credited as a bonus to the capital accounts of the existing partners. Also, to gain the participation of the new partner, the existing partners may give the new partner a bonus whereby portions of the existing partners' capital balances are transferred to the new partner's capital account.

LO⁵ **Prepare entries for partnership liquidation.** When a partnership is liquidated, losses and gains from selling the partnership assets are allocated to the partners according to the partnership income-and-loss-sharing ratio. If a partner's capital account has a deficit balance that the partner cannot pay, the other partners must share the deficit in their relative income-and-loss-sharing ratio.

GUIDANCE ANSWERS TO Judgement Call

Lawyer

The partnership agreement apparently fails to mention liabilities or use the term "net assets." Still, to give the estate one-third of total assets is not fair to the remaining partners. This is because if the partner had lived and the partners had decided to liquidate, the liabilities would have had to be paid first. Also, a settlement based on the recorded equity of the deceased partner would fail to recognize excess of current value over book value. These value increases would be realized if the partnership were liquidated. A fair settlement would be a payment to the estate for the balance of the deceased partner's equity based on the *current value of net assets.*

GUIDANCE ANSWERS TO Flashback

1. A summary of the characteristics of a general partnership is as follows:

Partnership agreement	A contract exists between the partners and in its absence, incomes and losses are shared equally.
Limited life	The life of a partnership is limited subject to terms in the partnership contract.
Taxation	A partnership is not subject to tax.
Co-ownership of property	Partnership assets are owned jointly by the partners.
Mutual agency	Each partner is an authorized agent of the partnership.
Unlimited liability	Partners can be called on to pay the debts of the partnership.

2. A limited partnership has one general partner who assumes management duties and unlimited liability for the debts of the partnership; the limited partners have no personal liability beyond the amounts they invest in the partnership. In a limited liability partnership, liability is limited to the partner(s) responsible for any malpractice or negligence claims; innocent partners are not liable. However, all partners in a limited liability partnership are personally liable for other partnership debts.

3.

	Ben	Jerry	Total	
Net income			$40,000	
Interest allowance	$ 7,000	$ 3,500	−10,500	
Remaining balance			**$29,500**	must be
Balance allocated equally	14,750	14,750	29,500	equal
Remaining balance			$ -0-	
Shares of partners	**$21,750**	**$18,250**	**$40,000**	

4. 1/5, 2/5, 2/5

5. 20%, 40%, 40%

Demonstration Problem

Part 1

On a work sheet similar to that shown below, include eight columns to show the effects of the following on the partner's capital accounts over a four-year period.

Date	Transaction	Ries, Capital	Bax, Capital	Royce, Capital	Murdock, Capital	Elway, Capital	Total Partners' Equity

Apr. 13/05	Ries, Bax, and Royce create RB&R Co. Ries and Bax each invest $10,000 while Royce invests $24,000. They agree that each will get a 10% interest allowance on each partner's beginning-of-year capital balance. In addition, Ries and Bax are to receive $5,000 salary allowances. The remainder of the income is to be divided evenly.
Dec. 31/05	The partnership's income for the year is $39,900, and withdrawals at year-end are: Ries, $5,000; Bax, $12,500; and Royce, $11,000.
Jan. 1/06	Ries sells her interest to Murdock for $20,000, who is accepted by Bax and Royce as a partner in the new BR&M Co. The profits are to be shared equally after Bax and Royce each receive $25,000 salaries.
Dec. 31/06	The partnership's income for the year is $35,000, and their withdrawals are: Bax, $2,500; and Royce, $2,000.
Jan. 1/07	Elway is admitted as a partner after investing $60,000 cash in the new Elway & Associates partnership. Elway is given a 60% interest in capital after the other partners transfer $9,180 to his account from each of theirs. A 20% interest allowance (on the beginning-of-year capital balances) will be used in sharing profits, but there will be no salaries. Elway will get 40% of the remainder, and the other three partners will each get 20%. (Note: The interest allowance is to be calculated on each partner's capital balance immediately after the admission of Elway.)
Dec. 31/07	Elway & Associates earns $127,600 for the year, and year-end withdrawals are: Bax, $25,000; Royce, $27,000; Murdock, $15,000; and Elway, $40,000.
Jan. 1/08	Elway buys out Bax and Royce for the balances of their capital accounts, paying them $92,000 cash from personal funds. Murdock and Elway will share future profits on a 1:9 ratio.
Feb.29/08	The partnership has earned $10,000 of income since the beginning of the year. Murdock retires and receives partnership cash equal to her capital balance. Elway takes possession of the partnership assets in his own name, and the business is dissolved.

Part 2

Journalize the transactions affecting the partnership for the year ended December 31, 2006.

Planning the Solution

o Evaluate each transaction's effects on the capital accounts of the partners.

o Each time a new partner is admitted or a partner withdraws, allocate any bonus based on the income-or-loss-sharing agreement.

o Each time a new partner is admitted or a partner withdraws, allocate subsequent net incomes or losses in accordance with the new partnership agreement.

o Prepare the journal entries to record the transactions for the year 2006.

S O L U T I O N   T O   Demonstration Problem

Part 1

Date	Event	Ries, Capital	Bax, Capital	Royce, Capital	Murdock, Capital	Elway, Capital	Total Partners' Equity
Apr. 13/05	Investment	$10,000	$10,000	$24,000			$ 44,000
Dec. 31/05	$39,900 income allocation:						39,900
	− 10% interest	1,000	1,000	2,400			
	− salary allowance	5,000	5,000	-0-			
	− $25,500 remainder equally	8,500	8,500	8,500			
	Withdrawals:	(5,000)	(12,500)	(11,000)			(28,500)
	Balance:	$19,500	$12,000	$23,900			$ 55,400
Jan. 1/06	Ries sells to Murdock	(19,500)			$19,500		-0-
Dec. 31/06	$35,000 income allocation:						35,000
	− salary allowance		25,000	25,000	-0-		
	− ($15,000) remainder equally		(5,000)	(5,000)	(5,000)		
	Withdrawals:		(2,500)	(2,000)	-0-		(4,500)
	Balance:		$29,500	$41,900	$14,500		$ 85,900
Jan. 1/07	Elway admitted as partner		(9,180)	(9,180)	(9,180)	$ 87,540	60,000
Dec. 31/07	$127,600 income allocation:						127,600
	− 20% interest allowance		4,064	6,544	1,064	17,508	
	− remainder 40% Elway; 20% others		19,684	19,684	19,684	39,368	
	Withdrawals:		(25,000)	(27,000)	(15,000)	(40,000)	(107,000)
	Balance:		$19,068	$31,948	$11,068	$104,416	$166,500
Jan. 1/08	Elway buys out Bax and Royce		(19,068)	(31,948)		51,016	-0-
	Balance:		$ -0-	$ -0-	$11,068	$155,432	$166,500
Feb. 29/08	$10,000 income allocation:				1,000	9,000	10,000
	Adjusted balance:				$12,068	$164,432	$176,500
	Murdock retires:				(12,068)	-0-	(12,068)
	Adjusted balance:				$ -0-	$164,432	$164,432
	Partnership dissolved					(164,432)	(164,432)
	Final balance					$ -0-	$ -0-

Part 2

2006				
Jan. 1	Ries, Capital		19,500	
	Murdock, Capital			19,500
	To record entrance of Murdock in place of Ries.			
Dec. 31	Bax, Capital		2,500	
	Royce, Capital		2,000	
	Bax, Withdrawals			2,500
	Royce, Withdrawals			2,000
	To close partners' withdrawal accounts to their capital.			
Dec. 31	Income Summary		35,000	
	Murdock, Capital		5,000	
	Bax, Capital			20,000
	Royce, Capital			20,000
	To close Income Summary to partners' capital.			

Glossary

General partner A partner who assumes unlimited liability for the debts of the partnership; also, the general partner in a limited partnership is responsible for its management. (p. 718)

General partnership A partnership in which all partners have mutual agency and unlimited liability for partnership debts. (p. 716)

Limited liability partnership A partnership in which each partner is not personally liable for malpractice or negligence claims unless the partner was responsible for providing the service that resulted in the claim. (p. 718)

Limited partners Partners who have no personal liability for debts of the partnership beyond the amounts they have invested in the partnership. (p. 718)

Limited partnership A partnership that has two classes of partners: limited partners and general partners. (p. 718)

Mutual agency The legal relationship among the partners whereby each partner is an agent of the partnership and is able to bind the partnership to contracts within the apparent scope of the partnership's business. (p. 717)

Partnership An unincorporated association of two or more persons to pursue a business for profit as co-owners. (p. 716)

Partnership contract The agreement between partners that sets forth the terms under which the affairs of the partnership will be conducted. (p. 716)

Partnership liquidation The dissolution of a business partnership by: (1) selling non-cash assets for cash, (2) allocating the gain or loss according to partners' income-and-loss ratio, (3) paying liabilities, and (4) distributing remaining cash to partners based on capital balances. (p. 732)

Statement of partners' equity A financial statement that shows the total capital balances at the beginning of the period, any additional investment by the partners, the net income or loss of the period, the partners' withdrawals during the period, and the ending capital balances. (p. 725)

Unlimited liability of partners The legal relationship among general partners that makes each of them responsible for paying all the debts of the partnership if the other partners are unable to pay their shares. (p. 717)

For more study tools, quizzes, and problem material,
refer to the Online Learning Centre at
www.mcgrawhill.ca/college/larson

Questions

1. Amey and Lacey are partners. Lacey dies, and her son claims the right to take his mother's place in the partnership. Does he have this right? Why?

2. If a partnership contract does not state the period of time over which the partnership is to exist, when does the partnership end?

3. As applied to a partnership, what does the term *mutual agency* mean?

4. Can partners limit the right of a partner to commit their partnership to contracts? Would the agreement be binding: (a) on the partners, and (b) on outsiders?

5. What does the term *unlimited liability* mean when it is applied to members of a partnership?

6. How does a general partnership differ from a limited partnership?

7. George, Burton, and Dillman have been partners for three years. The partnership is being dissolved. George is leaving the firm, but Burton and Dillman plan to carry on the business. In the final settlement, George places a $75,000 salary claim against the partnership. He contends that he has a claim for a salary of $25,000 for each year because he devoted all of his time for three years to the affairs of the partnership. Is his claim valid? Why?

8. The partnership agreement of Jenny Nelmida and Fei Abella provides for a two-thirds/one-third sharing of income but says nothing about losses. The first year of partnership operations resulted in a loss and Nelmida argues that the loss should be shared equally because the partnership agreement said nothing about sharing losses. What do you think?

9. If the partners in Blume Partnership want the financial statements to show the procedures used to allocate the partnership income among the partners, on what financial statement should the allocation appear?

10. After all partnership assets are converted to cash and all liabilities have been paid, the remaining cash should equal the sum of the balances of the partners' capital accounts. Why?

11. Kay, Kat, and Kim are partners. In a liquidation, Kay's share of partnership losses exceeds her capital account balance. She is unable to meet the deficit from her personal assets, and the excess losses are shared by her partners. Does this relieve Kay of liability?

12. A partner withdraws from a partnership and receives assets of greater value than the book value of his equity. Should the remaining partners share the resulting reduction in their equities in the ratio of their relative capital balances or in their income-and-loss-sharing ratio?

Quick Study

Bowen and Campbell are partners in operating a store. Without consulting Bowen, Campbell enters into a contract for the purchase of merchandise for the store. Bowen contends that he did not authorize the order and refuses to take delivery. The vendor sues the partners for the contract price of the merchandise. Will the partnership have to pay? Why? Does your answer differ if Bowen and Campbell are partners in a public accounting firm?

QS 14-1
Partnership liability

LO^1

Pourier organized a limited partnership and is the only general partner. Hillier invested $20,000 in the partnership and was admitted as a limited partner with the understanding that he would receive 10% of the profits. After two unprofitable years, the partnership ceased doing business. At that point, partnership liabilities were $85,000 larger than partnership assets. How much money can the creditors of the partnership obtain from the personal assets of Hillier in satisfaction of the unpaid partnership debts?

QS 14-2
Liability in limited partnerships

LO^1

Len Peters and Beau Silver form a partnership to operate a catering business. Peters invests $20,000 cash and Silver invests $30,000 cash on March 1, 2005. Prepare the journal entry to record the formation of the partnership.

QS 14-3
Journal entry when forming a partnership

LO^2

Bill Ace and Dennis Bud are partners in AMPAC Company. Net income for the year ended March 31, 2005, is $120,000. How much net income should be allocated to each partner assuming there is no partnership agreement? Prepare the entry to allocate the net income.

QS 14-4
Partnership income allocation

LO^3

Check figure:
To Ace: $60,000

Roger Blythe and Art Beery are partners in a business they started two years ago. Determine each partner's share of the current year's net loss of $84,000 assuming there is no partnership agreement. Prepare the entry to allocate the net loss for the year ended December 31, 2005.

QS 14-5
Partnership income allocation

LO^3

Check figure:
To Blythe: $(42,000)

Lisa Montgomery and Joel Calmar had a partnership and shared incomes and losses based on an agreement that gave Lisa a salary allowance of $45,000 and Joel $10,000 with any unallocated income (loss) shared equally. Prepare the entry to close the Income Summary account at December 31, 2005, assuming a credit balance of $48,000.

QS 14-6
Income allocation

LO^3

Check figures:
To Montgomery: $41,500;
To Calmar: $6,500

QS 14-7
Income allocation

LO³

Assume the same information as in QS 14-6 except that Income Summary had a credit balance of $28,000 at December 31, 2005. Prepare the entry to close the Income Summary account.

Check figures:
To Montgomery: $31,500;
To Calmar: $(3,500)

QS 14-8
Income allocation

LO³ ✓

Assume the same information as in QS 14-6 except that Income Summary had a debit balance of $28,000 at December 31, 2005. Prepare the entry to close the Income Summary account.

Check figures:
To Montgomery: $3,500;
To Calmar: $(31,500)

QS 14-9
Admission of a partner

LO⁴ ✓

Ramos and Briley are equal partners, each with $30,000 in his partnership capital account. Fontaine is admitted to the partnership on October 1, 2005, by an investment of $30,000 for a one-third interest. Make the entry to show Fontaine's admission to the partnership.

QS 14-10
Partner admission through purchase of interest

LO⁴ ✓

On March 12, 2005, Fontaine agrees to pay Ramos and Briley $12,000 each for a one-third interest in the existing Ramos–Briley partnership. At the time Fontaine is admitted, each partner has a $30,000 capital balance. Make the journal entry to record Fontaine's purchase of the partners' interest.

QS 14-11
Partner admission through purchase of interest

LO⁴ ✓

On June 17, 2005, Bishop agrees to invest $30,000 into a partnership for a 40% interest in total partnership equity. At the time Bishop is admitted, the existing partners, Pollard and Mission, each have a $30,000 capital balance. Prepare the entry on June 17 to record Bishop's admission to the partnership. Any bonus is to be shared equally by Pollard and Mission.

QS 14-12
Partner admission through purchase of interest

LO⁴ ✓

On April 21, 2005, Wilson agrees to invest $30,000 into a partnership for a 20% interest in total partnership equity. At the time Wilson is admitted, the existing partners, Beacon and Metcalf, each have a $30,000 capital balance. Prepare the entry on April 21 to record Wilson's admission to the partnership. Any bonus is to be shared equally by Beacon and Metcalf.

QS 14-13
Partner withdrawal

LO⁴ ✓

Lector, Wylo, and Stuart are partners with capital balances of $25,000, $40,000, and $35,000 respectively. They share income and losses equally. Stuart is retiring and has agreed to accept $35,000 cash for his share of the partnership. Record Stuart's withdrawal on November 23, 2005.

QS 14-14
Partner withdrawal

LO⁴ ✓

Assume the same information as in QS 14-13 except that Stuart has agreed to accept $28,000 cash for his share of the partnership. Record Stuart's withdrawal on November 23, 2005. Any bonus is to be shared equally.

Assume the same information as in QS 14-13 except that Stuart has agreed to accept $41,000 cash for his share of the partnership. Record Stuart's withdrawal on November 23, 2005. Any bonus is to be shared equally.

QS 14-15
Partner withdrawal

LO⁴

Oliver, Peter, and Wendell are partners in NewTech Company. Their capital balances are $30,000, $22,000, and $15,000 respectively. They share income and losses in the ratio of 3:2:1. Peter is about to retire and has agreed to accept $30,000 for his share of the partnership. Calculate the capital balances of Oliver and Wendell after Peter's withdrawal.

QS 14-16
Partner withdrawal

LO⁴

Sam, Andrews, and Mary were partners in Gana Company. The partners shared profits and losses 3:2:3, respectively. On April 1, 2005, the partnership showed the following account balances just prior to liquidation:

QS 14-17
Partnership liquidation

LO⁵

	Cash	Equipment	Accum. Amort. Equipment	Sam, Capital	Andrews, Capital	Mary, Capital
Account balances immediately **prior** to liquidation	$32,000	$151,000	$36,000	$65,000	$48,000	$34,000

Equipment was sold for $175,000. Prepare the journal entry to record the final distribution of cash.

Assume the same information as in QS 14-17 except that the *Equipment* was sold for $85,000 on April 1, 2005. Prepare the journal entry to record the final distribution of cash.

QS 14-18
Partnership liquidation

LO⁵

Exercises

For each scenario below, recommend a form of business organization: sole proprietorship, partnership, or corporation. Along with each recommendation explain how business profits would be taxed if the form of organization recommended were adopted by the owners. Also list several advantages that the owners would enjoy from the form of business organization that you recommend.

Exercise 14-1
Forms of organization

LO¹

1. Keith, Scott, and Brian are new university graduates in computer science. They are thinking of starting a Web-page creation company. They all have quite a few university debts and currently do not own any of the computer equipment that they will need to get the company started.
2. Dr. Marble and Dr. Sampson are new graduates from medical residency programs. They are both family practice physicians and would like to open a clinic in an underserved rural area. Although neither has any funds to bring to the new venture, a banker has expressed interest in making a loan to provide start-up funds for the practice.
3. Matthew has been out of school for about five years and has become quite knowledgeable about the commercial real estate market. Matthew would like to organize a company that buys and sells real estate. Matthew feels that he has the expertise to manage the company but needs funds to invest in the commercial property.

Exercise 14-2
Journalizing partnership entries

LO2,3

Check figures:
1. Share of income:
   To Young: $48,000;
   To Olde: $20,000

On February 1, 2005, Tim Young and Gene Olde formed a partnership in the province of Ontario. Young contributed $70,000 cash and Olde contributed land valued at $80,000 and a small building valued at $90,000. Also, the partnership assumed responsibility for Olde's $30,000 long-term note payable associated with the land and building. The partners agreed to share profits as follows: Young is to receive an annual salary allowance of $35,000, both are to receive an annual interest allowance of 10% of their original capital investments, and any remaining profit or loss is to be shared equally. On November 20, 2005, Young withdrew cash of $40,000 and Olde withdrew $30,000. After the adjusting entries and the closing entries to the revenue and expense accounts, the Income Summary account had a credit balance of $68,000.

Required
1. Present General Journal entries to record the initial capital investments of the partners, their cash withdrawals, and the December 31 closing of the Income Summary and withdrawals accounts.
2. Determine the balances of the partners' capital accounts as of the end of 2005.

Exercise 14-3
Income allocation in a partnership

LO3

Check figures:
c. To Newton: $98,700;
   To Scampi: $81,300

Newton and Scampi began a partnership by investing $52,000 and $78,000, respectively. During its first year, the partnership recorded net income of $180,000.

Required
Prepare calculations showing how the income should be allocated to the partners under each of the following plans for sharing net incomes and losses:
a. The partners failed to agree on a method of sharing income.
b. The partners agreed to share incomes and losses in proportion to their initial investments.
c. The partners agreed to share income by allowing an $85,000 per year salary allowance to Newton, a $65,000 per year salary allowance to Scampi, 10% interest on their initial investments, and the balance equally.

Exercise 14-4
Income allocation in a partnership

LO3

Check figures:
1. To Newton: $81,350;
   To Scampi: $63,950
2. To Newton: $(11,400);
   To Scampi: $(28,800)

Assume that the partners of Exercise 14-3 agreed to share net incomes and losses by allowing yearly salary allowances of $85,000 to Newton and $65,000 to Scampi, 10% interest allowances on their investments, and the balance equally.
1. Determine the shares of Newton and Scampi in a first-year net income of $145,300.
2. Determine the partners' shares in a first-year net loss of $40,200.

Exercise 14-5
Income allocation

 LO3

Check figures:
Share of income:
To Sauer: $54,750;
To Curtley: $(24,750)

Ray Sauer and Bim Curtley formed a partnership by investing $20,000 and $100,000 respectively. They agreed to share income based on an allocation to Ray of an annual salary allowance of $65,000, interest allowance to both Ray and Bim equal to 15% of their beginning-of-year capital balance, and any balance based on a 1:3 ratio respectively. At the end of their first year, December 31, 2005, the Income Summary had a credit balance of $30,000. Ray withdrew $7,000 during the year and Bim $24,000.

Required
1. Prepare the entry to close the Income Summary on December 31, 2005.
2. Calculate the balance in each partner's capital account at the end of their first year.

Exercise 14-6
Income allocation

LO3

Alex and Warren are partners who agree that Alex will receive a $50,000 salary allowance after which remaining incomes or losses will be shared equally. If Warren's capital account is credited $4,000 as his share of the net income (loss) in a given period, how much net income (loss) did the partnership earn?

The Hagan–Baden Partnership has total partners' equity of $380,000, which is made up of Hagan, Capital, $300,000, and Baden, Capital, $80,000. The partners share net incomes and losses in a ratio of 75% to Hagan and 25% to Baden. On July 1, Megan is admitted to the partnership and given a 20% interest in equity.

Required
Prepare the journal entry to record the admission of Megan under each of the following unrelated assumptions, in which Megan invests cash of:
a. $95,000
b. $115,000
c. $55,000

Exercise 14-7
Admission of a new partner

 LO⁴

Check figures:
b. Cr Baden, Capital: 4,000
c. Dr Baden, Capital: 8,000

Nels & Larens Consulting showed the following partners' equity at August 31, 2005:

Peter Nels, Capital	$200,000
Meta Larens, Capital	780,000

Peter and Meta share net incomes and losses in a 2:3 ratio respectively. On September 1, 2005, Dana Barth is admitted to the partnership with a cash investment of $420,000.

Required
Prepare the journal entry to record the admission of Dana under each of the following unrelated assumptions, where she is given:
a. a 30% interest in equity
b. a 20% interest in equity
c. a 50% interest in equity

Exercise 14-8
Admission of a new partner

 LO⁴

The partners in the Magesty Partnership have agreed that partner Prince may sell his $70,000 equity in the partnership to Queen, for which Queen will pay Prince $55,000. Present the partnership's journal entry to record the sale on April 30.

Exercise 14-9
Sale of a partnership interest

 LO⁴

Evans, Harris, and Wood have been partners sharing net incomes and losses in a 5:3:2 ratio. On November 30, the date Wood retires from the partnership, the equities of the partners are: Evans, $200,000; Harris, $130,000; and Wood, $50,000. Present General Journal entries to record Wood's retirement under each of the following unrelated assumptions:
a. Wood is paid $50,000 in partnership cash for his equity.
b. Wood is paid $60,000 in partnership cash for his equity.
c. Wood is paid $45,000 in partnership cash for his equity.

Exercise 14-10
Retirement of a partner

 LO⁴

Check figures:
b. Dr Harris, Capital: 3,750
c. Cr Harris, Capital: 1,875

Barb Rusnak, Len Peters, and Doug Morris are partners in RPM Dance Studios. They share net incomes and losses in a 40:40:20 ratio. Doug retires from the partnership on October 14, 2005, and receives $40,000 cash plus a car with a book value of $20,000 (original cost was $42,000).

Required
For each of the following unrelated situations, present the journal entry to record Doug's retirement assuming the equities of the partnership on October 14 are:
a. Rusnak, $150,000; Peters, $200,000; Morris, $60,000
b. Rusnak, $50,000; Peters, $60,000; Morris; $80,000
c. Rusnak, $65,000; Peters, $80,000; Morris; $30,000

Exercise 14-11
Retirement of a partner

LO⁴

Exercise 14-12
Liquidation of a partnership

LO[5]

Bill Weston, Marnie Wolf, and Jacob Bean were partners and showed the following account balances as of December 31, 2005:

	Cash	Equipment	Accum. Amort. Equipment	Accounts Payable	Notes Payable	Bill Weston, Capital	Marnie Wolf, Capital	Jacob Bean, Capital
Account balances December 31, 2005 ...	$13,000	$152,000	$89,000	$7,000	$12,000	$31,000	$14,000	$12,000

Due to several unprofitable periods, the partners decided to liquidate the partnership. The equipment was sold for $56,000 on January 1, 2006. The partners share any income (loss) in the ratio of 2:1:1 for Weston, Wolf, and Bean respectively.

Check figure:
Dr Bill Weston, Capital: 27,500

Required
Prepare the entry to distribute the remaining cash to the partners.

Exercise 14-13
Liquidation of a partnership

LO[5]

Martha Wheaton, Bess Jones, and Sam Dun were partners and showed the following account balances as of December 31, 2005:

	Cash	Building	Accum. Amort. Building	Land	Accounts Payable	Martha Wheaton, Capital	Bess Jones, Capital	Sam Dun, Capital
Account balances December 31, 2005 ...	$46,000	$206,000	$120,000	$52,000	$32,000	$79,000	($13,000)	$86,000

Due to difficulties, the partners decided to liquidate the partnership. The land and building were sold for $170,000 on January 1, 2006. The partners share any income (loss) in the ratio of 2:1:1 for Wheaton, Jones, and Dun respectively.

Check figure:
Dr Martha Wheaton, Capital: 95,000

Required
Prepare the entry to distribute the remaining cash to the partners assuming any deficiencies are paid by the partners.

Exercise 14-14
Liquidation of a partnership

LO[5]

Assume the same information as in Exercise 14-13 except that capital deficiencies at liquidation are absorbed by the remaining partners according to their income (loss) ratio.

Check figure:
Dr Martha Wheaton, Capital: 91,667

Required
Prepare the entry to distribute the remaining cash to the partners. Round calculations to the nearest whole dollar.

Exercise 14-15
Liquidation of a partnership

LO[5]

The Whiz–Bam–Boom partnership began with investments by the partners as follows: Whiz, $115,600; Bam, $88,600; and Boom, $95,800. The first year of operations did not go well, and the partners finally decided to liquidate the partnership, sharing all losses equally. On December 31, after all assets were converted to cash and all creditors were paid, only $30,000 in partnership cash remained.

Check figure:
3b. Dr Boom, Capital: 5,100

Required
1. Calculate the capital account balances of the partners after the liquidation of assets and payment of creditors.
2. Assume that any partner with a deficit pays cash to the partnership to cover the deficit. Present the General Journal entries on December 31 to record the cash receipt from the deficient partner(s) and the final disbursement of cash to the partners.

3. Now make the contrary assumption that any partner with a deficit is not able to reimburse the partnership. Present journal entries: (a) to transfer the deficit of any deficient partners to the other partners, and (b) to record the final disbursement of cash to the partners.

Problems

Matthew Carroll, Wai Wai Lee, and Carole Power invested $66,400, $58,100, and $41,500, respectively, in a partnership. During its first year, the firm recorded net income of $175,500.

Required
Prepare entries to close the firm's Income Summary account as of December 31 and to allocate the net income to the partners under each of the following assumptions:
a. The partners did not produce any special agreement on the method of sharing incomes.
b. The partners agreed to share net incomes and losses in the ratio of their beginning investments.
c. The partners agreed to share income by: providing annual salary allowances of $52,000 to Carroll, $58,000 to Lee, and $45,000 to Power; allowing 10% interest on the partners' beginning investments; and sharing the remainder equally.

Problem 14-1A
Methods of allocating partnership income

LO³

Check figure:
c. Cr Matthew Carroll, Capital: $59,940

Linda Meade and Richard Munez are in the process of forming a partnership to which Meade will devote one-third time and Munez will devote full time. They have discussed the following alternative plans for sharing net incomes and losses.
a. In the ratio of their initial investments, which they have agreed will be $33,000 for Meade and $49,500 for Munez.
b. In proportion to the time devoted to the business.
c. A salary allowance of $3,500 per month to Munez and the balance in accordance with their initial investment ratio.
d. A $3,500 per month salary allowance to Munez, 10% interest on their initial investments, and the balance equally.
The partners expect the business to generate income as follows: Year 1, $20,000 net loss; Year 2, $60,000 net income; and Year 3, $95,000 net income.

Required
Prepare four schedules with the following column headings:

Year	Calculations	Share to Meade	Share to Munez	Total

Complete a schedule for each of the four plans being considered by showing how the partnership net income or loss for each year would be allocated to the partners. Round your answers to the nearest whole dollar.

Problem 14-2A
Allocating partnership incomes and losses; sequential years

LO³

Check figures:
d. Year 1: To Meade: ($31,825);
To Munez: $11,825
d. Year 2: To Meade: $8,175;
To Munez: $51,825
d. Year 3: To Meade: $25,675;
To Munez: $69,325

Betty Iris, Jim Dolan, and Bob Carrow formed the IDC Partnership by making capital contributions of $245,000, $280,000, and $175,000, respectively. They anticipate annual net income of $390,000 and are considering the following alternative plans of sharing net incomes and losses:
a. Equally;
b. In the ratio of their initial investments; or
c. Salary allowances of $95,000 to Iris, $46,000 to Dolan, and $60,000 to Carrow and interest allowances of 12% on initial investments, with any remaining balance shared equally.

Problem 14-3A
Partnership income allocation, statement of partners' equity, and closing entries

LO²,³

Required

1. Prepare a schedule with the following column headings:

Income/Loss Sharing Plan	Calculations	Share to Iris	Share to Dolan	Share to Carrow

Use the schedule to show how a net income of $390,000 would be distributed under each of the alternative plans being considered.

2. Prepare a statement of partners' equity showing the allocation of income to the partners, assuming they agree to use alternative (c) and the net income actually earned for the year ended December 31, 2005, is $390,000. During the year, Iris, Dolan, and Carrow withdraw $40,000, $30,000, and $20,000, respectively.

3. Prepare the December 31, 2005, journal entry to close Income Summary assuming they agree to use alternative (c) and the net income is $390,000. Also, close the withdrawals accounts.

Problem 14-4A
Admission of a partner

LO⁴

Check figures:
b. Dr Wong, Capital $6,187.50
c. Cr Wong, Capital $6,975.00

Wong, Lam, and Lin are partners with capital balances as follows: Wong, $84,000; Lam, $69,000; and Lin, $147,000. The partners share incomes and losses in a 3:2:5 ratio. Goldburg is admitted to the partnership on May 1, 2005, with a 25% equity. Prepare General Journal entries to record the entry of Goldburg into the partnership under each of the following unrelated assumptions:

a. Goldburg invests $100,000.
b. Goldburg invests $72,500.
c. Goldburg invests $131,000.

Problem 14-5A
Withdrawal of a partner

LO⁴

Check figures:
d. Dr Wong, Capital $23,625
e. Cr Wong, Capital $3,656

Wong, Lam, and Lin are partners with capital balances as follows: Wong, $84,000; Lam, $69,000; and Lin, $147,000. The partners share incomes and losses in a 3:2:5 ratio. Lam decides to withdraw from the partnership. Prepare General Journal entries to record the May 1, 2005, withdrawal of Lam from the partnership under each of the following unrelated assumptions:

a. Lam sells his interest to Leung for $168,000 after Wong and Lin approve the entry of Leung as a partner.
b. Lam gives his interest to a son-in-law, Donnelly. Wong and Lin accept Donnelly as a partner.
c. Lam is paid $69,000 in partnership cash for his equity.
d. Lam is paid $132,000 in partnership cash for his equity.
e. Lam is paid $27,250 in partnership cash plus computer equipment that is recorded on the partnership books at $115,000 less accumulated amortization of $83,000 (round calculations to the nearest whole dollar).

Problem 14-6A
Liquidation of a partnership

LO⁵

Pyle, White, and Zin plan to liquidate their partnership. They have always shared losses and gains in a 1:4:5 ratio, and on the day of the liquidation their balance sheet appeared as follows:

Pyle, White, and Zin
Balance Sheet
June 30, 2005

Assets

Cash		$ 27,500
Truck	$235,500	
Less: Accumulated Amortization	55,000	180,500
Total assets		$208,000

Liabilities

Accounts payable		$ 52,150

Partners' Equity

David Pyle, capital	$ 30,500	
Annie White, capital	80,350	
Mike Zin, capital	45,000	
Total partners' equity		155,850
Total liabilities and partners' equity		$208,000

Required

Under the assumption that the other assets are sold and the cash is distributed to the proper parties on June 30, 2005, complete the schedule provided below.

	Cash	Other Assets	Accounts Payable	David Pyle, Capital	Annie White, Capital	Mike Zin, Capital
Account balances June 30, 2005						

Show the sale, the gain or loss allocation, and the distribution of the cash in each of the following unrelated cases:

a. The other assets are sold for $195,250.

b. The other assets are sold for $150,000.

c. The other assets are sold for $85,000, and any partners with resulting deficits can and do pay in the amount of their deficits.

d. The other assets are sold for $75,000, and the partners have no assets other than those invested in the business.

Check figures:
a. Cash to Pyle: $31,975
b. Cash to Pyle: $27,450
c. Cash to Pyle: $20,950
d. Cash to Pyle: $18,400

Tracy Nelson and Bruce Stammers have a partnership and share income and losses in a 3:1 ratio. They decide to liquidate their partnership on December 31, 2005, when the balance sheet shows the following:

Problem 14-7A
Liquidation of a partnership

LO⁵

Nelson and Stammers Consulting
Balance Sheet
December 31, 2005

Assets

Cash..		$ 38,000
Property, plant, and equipment............	$214,000	
Less: Accumulated amortization	83,000	131,000
Total assets...		$169,000

Liabilities

Accounts payable.............................		$ 21,000

Partners' Equity

Tracy Nelson, capital	$102,000	
Bruce Stammers, capital......................	46,000	
Total partners' equity........................		148,000
Total liabilities and partners' equity		$169,000

Required

Prepare the entries on December 31, 2005, to record the liquidation under each of the following independent assumptions:

a. Property, plant, and equipment are sold for $300,000.

b. Property, plant, and equipment are sold for $60,000.

Check figures:
Re: final distribution of cash
a. Dr Nelson, Capital $228,750
b. Dr Nelson, Capital $48,750

Alternate Problems

Paula Jones, Roy Rodgers, and Anne Jackson invested $92,400, $74,800, and $52,800, respectively, in a partnership. During its first year, the firm earned $135,000.

Required

Prepare entries to close the firm's Income Summary account as of December 31 and to allocate the net income to the partners under each of the following assumptions. (Round your answers to the nearest whole dollar.)

a. The partners did not specify any special method of sharing incomes.

b. The partners agreed to share net incomes and losses in the ratio of their beginning investments.

c. The partners agreed to share income by: providing annual salary allowances of $75,000 to Jones, $40,500 to Rodgers, and $45,500 to Jackson; allowing 10% interest on the partners' beginning investments; and sharing the remainder equally.

Problem 14-1B
Methods of allocating partnership income

LO³

Check figure:
c. Cr Roy Rodgers, Capital: $31,980

Problem 14-2B
Allocating partnership incomes
and losses; sequential years

LO³

Harriet Monroe and Ozzie Young are in the process of forming a partnership to which
Monroe will devote one-third time and Young will devote full time. They have discussed
the following alternative plans for sharing net incomes and losses.
  a. In the ratio of their initial investments, which they have agreed will be $49,800 for
  Monroe and $74,700 for Young.
  b. In proportion to the time devoted to the business.
  c. A salary allowance of $5,250 per month to Young and the balance in accordance with
  their initial investment ratio.
  d. A $5,250 per month salary allowance to Young, 10% interest on their initial investments,
  and the balance equally.
The partners expect the business to generate income as follows: Year 1, $30,500 net
income; Year 2, $82,500 net loss; and Year 3, $215,000 net income.

Check figures:
d. Year 1:To Monroe: $(17,495);
    To Young: $47,995
d. Year 2:To Monroe: $(73,995);
    To Young: $(8,505)
d. Year 3:To Monroe: $74,755;
    To Young: $140,245

Required
Prepare four schedules with the following column headings:

Year	Calculations	Share to Monroe	Share to Young	Total

Complete a schedule for each of the four plans being considered by showing how the
partnership income or loss for each year would be allocated to the partners. Round your
answers to the nearest whole dollar.

Problem 14-3B
Partnership income allocation,
statement of partners' equity,
and closing entries

LO²,³

Milton Vacon, Milford Masters, and Marita Ramos formed the VMR Partnership by making
capital contributions of $116,640, $129,600, and $142,560, respectively on January 7, 2005.
They anticipate annual net incomes of $195,000 and are considering the following
alternative plans of sharing net incomes and losses:
  a. Equally;
  b. In the ratio of their initial investments (do not round the ratio calculations); or
  c. Salary allowances of $35,000 to Vacon, $20,000 to Masters, and $45,000 to Ramos;
  interest allowances of 10% on initial investments, with any remaining balance shared
  equally.

Check figures:
1c. To Vacon: $65,371;
    To Masters: $51,667;
    To Ramos: $77,962

Required
1. Prepare a schedule with the following column headings:

Income/Loss Sharing Plan	Calculations	Share to Vacon	Share to Masters	Share to Ramos	Total

Use the schedule to show how a net income of $195,000 would be distributed under each
of the alternative plans being considered. Round your answers to the nearest whole dollar.
2. Prepare a statement of partners' equity showing the allocation of income to the partners, assuming they agree to use alternative (c) and the net income actually earned
for the year ended December 31, 2005, is $195,000. During 2005, Vacon, Masters, and
Ramos withdrew $15,000, $20,000, and $23,000, respectively.
3. Prepare the December 31, 2005, journal entry to close Income Summary, assuming
they agree to use alternative (c) and the net income is $195,000. Also, close the
withdrawals accounts.

Problem 14-4B
Admission of a Partner

LO⁴

Check figures:
b. Dr Burke, Capital $4,500.00
c. Cr Burke, Capital $9,300.00

Burke, Comeau, and LeJeune are partners with capital balances as follows: Burke,
$153,000; Comeau, $51,000; and LeJeune, $102,000. The partners share incomes and
losses in a 1:2:1 ratio. Sung is admitted to the partnership on November 30 with a 20%
equity. Prepare General Journal entries to record the entry of Sung under each of the
following unrelated assumptions:
  a. Sung invests $76,500.
  b. Sung invests $54,000.
  c. Sung invests $123,000.

Burke, Comeau, and LeJeune are partners with capital balances as follows: Burke, $153,000; Comeau, $51,000; and LeJeune, $102,000. The partners share incomes and losses in a 1:2:1 ratio. LeJeune decides to withdraw from the partnership. Prepare General Journal entries to record the November 30 withdrawal of LeJeune from the partnership under each of the following unrelated assumptions:

a. LeJeune sells her interest to Devereau for $42,800 after Burke and Comeau approve the entry of Devereau as a partner.
b. LeJeune gives her interest to a daughter-in-law, Shulak. Burke and Comeau accept Shulak as a partner.
c. LeJeune is paid $102,000 in partnership cash for her equity.
d. LeJeune is paid $129,000 in partnership cash for her equity.
e. LeJeune is paid $36,000 in partnership cash plus manufacturing equipment recorded on the partnership books at $78,000 less accumulated amortization of $45,000.

Problem 14-5B
Withdrawal of a partner

LO⁴

Check figures:
d. Dr Burke, Capital $9,000
e. Cr Burke, Capital $11,000

Poppy, Sweetbean, and Olive, who have always shared incomes and losses in a 3:1:1 ratio, plan to liquidate their partnership. Just prior to the liquidation their balance sheet appeared as follows:

Problem 14-6B
Liquidation of a partnership

LO⁵

Poppy, Sweetbean, and Olive
Balance Sheet
October 15, 2005

Assets

Cash	$ 13,500
Equipment (net)*	237,600
Total assets	$251,100

Liabilities

Accounts payable	$ 56,700

Partners' Equity

Ernie Poppy, capital	$ 91,200	
Lynn Sweetbean, capital	60,000	
Ned Olive, capital	43,200	
Total partners' equity		194,400
Total liabilities and partners' equity		$251,100

*Accumulated amortization = $58,000

Required

Under the assumption that the other assets are sold and the cash is distributed to the proper parties on October 15, 2005, complete the schedule provided below.

	Cash	Equipment (net)	Accounts Payable	Ernie Poppy, Capital	Lynn Sweetbean, Capital	Ned Olive, Capital
Account balances October 15, 2005						

Show the sale, the gain or loss allocation, and the distribution of the cash in each of the following unrelated cases:

a. The equipment is sold for $270,000.
b. The equipment is sold for $170,100.
c. The equipment is sold for $72,600, and any partners with resulting deficits can and do pay in the amount of their deficits.
d. The equipment is sold for $55,200, and the partners have no assets other than those invested in the business.

Check figures:
a. Cash to Olive $49,680
b. Cash to Olive $29,700
c. Cash to Olive $10,200
d. Cash to Olive $0

Problem 14-7B
Liquidation of a partnership

LO⁵

Leslie Bjorn, Jason Douglas, and Tom Pierce have a partnership and share income and losses in a 3:1:1 ratio. They decide to liquidate their partnership on March 31, 2005. The balance sheet appeared as follows on the date of liquidation:

BDP Architects
Balance Sheet
March 31, 2005

Assets

Cash..		$ 79,000
Property, plant, and equipment............	$389,000	
Less: Accumulated amortization	214,000	175,000
Total assets..		$254,000

Liabilities

Accounts payable.............................	$ 46,000

Partners' Equity

Leslie Bjorn, capital.............................	$ 92,000	
Jason Douglas, capital	106,000	
Tom Pierce, capital..............................	10,000	
Total partners' equity........................		208,000
Total liabilities and partners' equity		$254,000

Check figures:
Re: final distribution of cash
a. Dr Bjorn, Capital $257,000
b. Dr Bjorn, Capital $53,000

Required
Prepare the entries on March 31, 2005, to record the liquidation under each of the following independent assumptions:
a. Property, plant, and equipment is sold for $450,000.
b. Property, plant, and equipment is sold for $110,000.
Assume that any deficiencies are paid by the partners.

Analytical and Review Problems

A & R Problem 14-1
Liquidation of a partnership

Prince, Count, and Earl are partners who share incomes and losses in a 1:3:4 ratio. After lengthy disagreements among the partners and several unprofitable periods, the partners decided to liquidate the partnership. Before the liquidation, the partnership balance sheet showed: total assets, $238,000; total liabilities, $200,000; Prince, Capital, $8,000; Count, Capital, $10,000; and Earl, Capital, $20,000. The cash proceeds from selling the assets were sufficient to repay all but $45,000 to the creditors. Calculate the loss from selling the assets, allocate the loss to the partners, and determine how much of the remaining liability should be paid by each partner.

A & R Problem 14-2
Liquidation of a limited partnership

Assume that the Prince, Count, and Earl partnership of A & R 14-1 is a limited partnership. Prince and Count are general partners and Earl is a limited partner. How much of the remaining $45,000 liability should be paid by each partner?

A & R Problem 14-3
Income allocation

Keith Scott and David McPeek agreed to share the annual net incomes or losses of their partnership as follows: If the partnership earned a net income, the first $60,000 would be allocated 40% to Scott and 60% to McPeek to reflect the time devoted to the business by each partner. Income in excess of $60,000 would be shared equally. Also, the partners have agreed to share any losses equally.

Required
1. Prepare a schedule showing how net income of $72,000 for 2005 should be allocated to the partners.
2. Sometime later in 2006, the partners discovered that $80,000 of accounts payable had existed on December 31, 2005, but had not been recorded. These accounts payable relate to expenses incurred by the business. They are now trying to determine the best way to correct their accounting records, particularly their capital accounts.

McPeek suggested that they make a special entry crediting $80,000 to the liability account, and debiting their capital accounts for $40,000 each. Scott, on the other hand, suggested that an entry should be made to record the accounts payable and retroactively correct the capital accounts to reflect the balance that they would have had if the expenses had been recognized in 2005. If they had been recognized, the partnership would have reported a loss of $8,000 instead of the $72,000 net income.

   a. Present the journal entry suggested by McPeek for recording the accounts payable and allocating the loss to the partners.
   b. Give the journal entry to record the accounts payable and correct the capital accounts according to Scott's suggestion. Show how you calculated the amounts presented in the entry.

3. Which suggestion do you think complies with their partnership agreement? Why?

Ethics Challenge

EC 14-1

Paul, Frank, and Basil formed a partnership 10 years ago and Paul is about to retire. Paul is not financially minded but he knows that he is entitled to one-third of partnership assets upon his retirement. Total assets have a book value of $900,000 and Paul feels that he is entitled to his share. Frank and Basil are aware that the market value of the firm's net assets approximates $1,500,000. Frank and Basil plan to form a new partnership.

Required
What are the financial and ethical implications of distributing $300,000 to Paul upon his retirement?

Focus on Financial Statements

FFS 14-1

Les Waruck, Kim Chau, and Leena Manta formed a partnership, WCL Sales, on January 11, 2005, by investing $68,250, $109,200, and $95,550 respectively. The partnership agreement states that incomes and losses are to be shared on the basis of a salary allowance of $40,000 for Waruck, $80,000 for Chau, and $40,000 for Manta, with any remainder shared on the ratio of beginning-of-period capital balance. Following is the December 31, 2005, adjusted trial balance, in alphabetical order:

Account	Balance*	Account	Balance*
Accounts payable	14,000	Leena Manta, capital	95,550
Accounts receivable	46,000	Leena Manta, withdrawals	10,000
Accum. amort., fixtures	3,000	Les Waruck, capital	68,250
Accum. amort., furniture	6,000	Les Waruck, withdrawals	30,000
Allowance for doubtful accounts	1,200	Merchandise inventory	22,000
Amort. expense, fixtures	3,000	Notes payable, due 2008**	34,000
Amort. expense, furniture	6,000	Patent	14,000
Amort. expense, patent	2,000	Prepaid rent	36,000
Bad debt expense	2,800	Rent expense	84,000
Cash	14,000	Sales	102,000
Fixtures	31,000	Sales discounts	3,400
Furniture	69,000	Unearned sales	3,000
Kim Chau, capital	109,200	Wages expense	49,000
Kim Chau, withdrawals	14,000		

*Assume all accounts have a normal balance.
**$7,000 is due during 2006.

Required
Prepare the December 31, 2005, classified balance sheet, showing all appropriate supporting calculations.

Organization and Operation of Corporations

Staying Private

The word *corporation* conjures up images of Canadian giants like the Toronto-Dominion Bank, Alcan Inc., Hudson's Bay Company, Bombardier Inc., or Air Canada. These are examples of *public* corporations, which means ownership is achieved through the purchase of *publicly traded* shares (shares that are bought and sold on a stock exchange). The shareholders, or owners, can be from anywhere across Canada or around the globe. There are, however, corporations that do not trade their shares publicly, like McCain Foods Limited and Birks … these are *private* corporations. Friesens, specializing in book manufacturing and retailing, is also a private corporation. Perhaps more familiar to you than the company's name are some of the books it prints, including the *Company's Coming* cookbook series or, with over 20 million copies printed to date, the incredibly successful book *Love You Forever* from Canadian children's author Robert Munsch.

Friesens' 15 million shares are available only to its 500 employees. Located in Altona, Manitoba, since it was founded in 1907, the community's population of about 3,000 depends heavily on the success of Friesens, its largest employer. David Friesen, the CEO, believes that it is people who make the company a success and with sales of $85 million for 2002, it's tough to argue against that philosophy. To ensure continued success, Friesens has established Friesens Graphic Arts College, accredited by Red River Community College in Winnipeg, to meet the company's growing need for skilled staff. Through the hard work and dedication of the employees (alias owners, alias shareholders!), Friesens' share values have increased an average of 10% per year over the past eight years. And that's good news for the shareholders (the employees!), who receive total annual dividends equal to 8% of the share value.

www.friesens.com

Friesens

Learning Objectives

Chapter Preview

There are three common types of business organizations: corporations, partnerships, and proprietorships. This chapter explains corporations. Corporations are fewest in number but, with dollar sales at least 10 times the combined sales of unincorporated companies, they are very important players in our global economy. Understanding the advantages and disadvantages of the forms of business organization was important for D.W. Friesen, the founder of Friesens described in the opening article. Mr. Friesen chose to incorporate as a privately held company to meet the needs of his community and customers. This chapter begins by providing general information to help us make the decision as to which form of organization best satisfies our needs. We then analyze financial statements for corporations in contrast to those for the unincorporated form of organization. The basic journal entries specific to corporations are illustrated, including those related to issuing shares, dividends, and closing the accounts.

Corporate Form of Organization

LO¹ Identify characteristics of corporations and their organization.

A corporation is an entity that is created by law and is separate from its owners. It has most of the rights and privileges granted to individuals. Owners of corporations are called **shareholders**. Each unit of ownership in a corporation is called a **share**. **Share capital**, also referred to as **capital stock**, is a general term referring to all types (or classes) of a corporation's shares. *Common shares* and *preferred shares*, explained in a later section, are names given to two classes of shares issued (sold) by corporations to shareholders. Corporations can be separated into *privately held* and *publicly held* corporations. A **privately held** corporation, also called **closely held**, does not offer its shares for public sale and usually has few shareholders. A **publicly held** corporation offers its shares for *public sale* and can have thousands of shareholders. **Public sale** refers to trading in an organized stock market such as the Montreal or Toronto stock exchanges.

Characteristics of Corporations

Corporations are important because of advantages created by the unique characteristics of the corporate structure of ownership. We describe these characteristics in this section.

Separate Legal Entity

A corporation is a separate legal entity that conducts its affairs with the same rights, duties, and responsibilities as a person. A corporation takes actions through its agents, who are its officers and managers.

Limited Liability of Shareholders

Because a corporation is a separate legal entity, it is responsible for its own acts and its own debt. Because shareholders are not liable for either, the corporate form of organization is also known as a *limited company*. Shareholders invest in the business by contributing cash or other assets in return for ownership rights in the corporation. If the business fails, the amount contributed by shareholders is the maximum loss to the shareholders. If there are insufficient assets to pay business creditor claims, creditors have no claim on the shareholders' personal assets, an important advantage of the corporate form.

Ownership Rights Are Transferable

Ownership of a corporation is evidenced by shares that are usually easily bought or sold. The transfer of shares from one shareholder to another usually has no effect on the corporation or its operations.[1] Many corporations have thousands or even millions of their shares bought and sold daily in major stock exchanges throughout the world. For example, it is not uncommon for over 2,000,000 Toronto-Dominion Bank shares to trade in one day.

www.td.com

Continuous Life

A corporation's life can continue indefinitely because it is not tied to the physical lives of its owners. This means a corporation can exist as long as it continues to be successful.

Shareholders Are Not Corporate Agents

A corporation acts through its agents, who are the officers or managers of the corporation. Shareholders who are not officers or managers of the corporation do not have the power to bind the corporation to contracts. This is also referred to as *lack of mutual agency* P.717.

Ease of Capital Accumulation

Buying shares in a corporation often is attractive to investors because of the advantages of the corporate form of organization, as summarized in Exhibit 15.1. These advantages make it possible for some corporations to accumulate large amounts of capital from the total investments of many shareholders. Alcan Inc. for example, a Canadian company involved in ventures such as bauxite mining, alumina refining, and power generation, had by 2002 accumulated about $4,703 million from common shareholders who own 321,470,298 shares.[2]

www.alcan.com

Advantages	Disadvantages
Limited liability of shareholders	Government regulation
Ownership rights are easily transferable	Corporate taxation
Continuous life	Separation of management and ownership
Lack of mutual agency	
Ease of capital accumulation	

Exhibit 15.1

Summary of Advantages and Disadvantages of the Corporate Form of Organization

Governmental Regulation

Corporations must meet requirements of provincial or federal incorporation laws. Single proprietorships P.7 and partnerships P.7 escape some of these regulations. Private corporations, however, are exempt from most of the security and corporate legislation reporting requirements. According to the *Canada Business Corporations Act* (CBCA), any publicly traded company with gross revenues of $10 million or assets exceeding $5 million must make public its financial statements, which have been prepared according to Canadian Generally Accepted Accounting Principles P.40. All public corporations that are registered with one of the provincial securities bodies, depending on which province, must file annual audited financial statements within 140–170 days of their fiscal year-end P.35.

Many Canadian companies are listed on U.S. stock exchanges as well and are also required to file their annual reports with U.S. regulators. Some of these companies—such as Nortel, Corel, and Alcan—actually issue their annual reports in U.S. dollars.

---

[1] A transfer of ownership can create significant effects if it brings about a change in who controls the company's activities.
[2] *Annual Report*, Alcan Inc., 2002.

Corporate Taxation

Corporations are subject to the same property, payroll, and consumption taxes (GST P.680 and PST P.679) as proprietorships and partnerships. Corporations are subject to an *additional* tax not levied on either of these two forms, however, that is, income tax expense (normally referred to as just *tax expense*).

The tax situation of a corporation is usually a disadvantage. But in some cases it can be an advantage to shareholders because corporation and individual tax rates are *progressive*. A **progressive tax** means higher levels of income are taxed at higher rates and lower levels of income are taxed at lower rates. This suggests that taxes can be saved or at least delayed if a large amount of income is divided among two or more tax-paying entities. A person who has a large personal income and pays a high rate of tax can benefit if some of the income is earned by a corporation the person owns, so long as the corporation avoids paying dividends or pays tax at a lower rate than the individual's rate.

Corporate income tax is an expense that appears on the income statement. However, income tax expense is *not* an operating expense because income tax expense is determined by government rather than by how the business operates. It is therefore reported as a separate expense as shown in the excerpt below taken from the income statement of Hudson's Bay Company for its year ended January 31, 2003.

www.hbc.com

(thousands of dollars)	
Earnings before income taxes	$153,882
Income taxes	(42,421)
Net earnings	$111,461

Choosing the proper form of entity for a business is crucial. Many factors should be considered including taxes, liability, tax and fiscal year-end, ownership structure, estate planning, business risks, and earnings and property distributions. The chart below gives a summary of several important characteristics of business organizations:

	Proprietorship	Partnership	Corporation
Business entity........................	yes	yes	yes
Legal entity.............................	no	no	yes
Limited liability........................	no	no	yes
Business taxed	no	no	yes
One owner allowed.................	yes	no	yes

Organizing a Corporation

This section describes incorporation and treatment of organization costs.

Incorporation

A corporation may be created under either provincial law or federal laws. Those incorporated federally must comply with the *Canada Business Corporations Act* (CBCA). Most of the provincial laws are modelled after the federal statute. Requirements vary across provinces and from the CBCA, but essentially a legal document known as a charter, articles of incorporation, letters patent, or memorandum of association is completed and signed by the prospective shareholders.

A corporation's charter *authorizes* the number and types (or classes[3]) of shares to be issued. **Authorized shares** are the total number of shares that a corporation is permitted to sell. When all of the legal requirements are satisfied, investors purchase the corporation's shares, meet as shareholders, and elect a board of directors. Directors are responsible for guiding a corporation's affairs.

Organization Costs

The costs of organizing a corporation are **organization costs**. They include legal fees, promoters' fees, and amounts paid to obtain a charter. Assuming a corporation paid $15,000 in organization costs on April 15, 2005, the entry would be:

2002			
April 15	Organization Costs..	15,000	
	Cash..		15,000
	To record payment of costs regarding the		
	organization of the corporation.		

Collectively, organization costs are an intangible asset that benefits the corporation, and the costs are amortized over their estimated useful life. Because organization costs usually are small in amount, the materiality principle P.347 supports an arbitrary short amortization period P.143. Sometimes a corporation gives shares to promoters in exchange for their services in selling shares of the corporation. The entry to record this transaction would credit the appropriate share capital account instead of the Cash account.

Management of a Corporation

Ultimate control of a corporation rests with its shareholders through election of the *board of directors*. Individual shareholders' rights to affect management are limited to a vote in shareholders' meetings, where each shareholder has one vote for each common share owned. This relation is shown in Exhibit 15.2.

Exhibit 15.2

Corporation Authority Structure

A corporation's board of directors is responsible for and has final authority for managing the corporation's activities but usually limits its actions to establishing broad policy and hiring the external auditors and corporate officers. It can

---

[3] There is no limit on the number of classes of shares that can be set out in the articles of incorporation. Shares may be alphabetized by class such as *Class A* and *Class B* or may be assigned names such as *common shares* and *preferred shares*. ClubLink, for instance, is authorized to issue an unlimited number of each of preferred and common shares. Bombardier reported in its January 31, 2003, annual report that it is authorized to issue 12 million each of Series 2 and Series 3 preferred shares, 9.4 million Series 4 preferred shares, and 1,792 million each of Class A and Class B common shares.

act only as a collective body and an individual director has no power to transact corporate business.

A group of shareholders owning or controlling votes of more than a 50% share of a corporation's shares can elect the board and control the corporation. However, in many corporations few shareholders actually get involved in the voting process, which means a much smaller percentage is often able to dominate the election of board members. Shareholders may delegate their voting rights to an agent by signing a document called a **proxy**.

Rights of Shareholders

According to the *Canada Business Corporations Act*, shareholders have three basic rights: the right to vote, the right to receive dividends that have been declared, and the right to receive property of the corporation after its closure. When there is more than one class of shares, each of these three basic rights is assigned to at least one class but not necessarily to all. When a corporation has only one class of shares, those shares are identified as **common shares**. Shareholders are also entitled to receive timely reports on the corporation's financial position and results of operations. These reports take the form of financial statements and are the topic of the next section.

Corporate Financial Statements

LO² Describe and contrast the specialized components of corporate financial statements.

The financial statements for the corporate form of organization are similar to those of unincorporated businesses. The differences all relate to *who owns* each form of business organization. We focus on these differences by comparing the assumed statements for ABC Corporation to those of a single proprietorship, Dell's Servicing.

Income Statement

Exhibit 15.3

Comparison of Income Statements

The income statements in Exhibit 15.3 are identical except for income tax expense. Corporations are required by law to pay tax because they are a separate legal entity. Application of corporate tax rules can be complex. Therefore, to show how tax expense appears on the income statement for a corporation, we have

ABC Corporation Income Statement For Year Ended December 31, 2005		
Revenues		$116
Operating expenses		40
Income from operations		$ 76
Other revenues and expenses:[4]		
Gain on sale of capital assets	$ 7	
Interest revenue	3	
Loss on sale of capital assets	(12)	
Interest expense	(14)	(16)
Income before tax		$ 60
Income tax expense		12
Net income		$ 48

Dell's Servicing Income Statement For Year Ended December 31, 2005		
Revenues		$116
Operating expenses		40
Income from operations		$ 76
Other revenues and expenses:[4]		
Gain on sale of capital assets	$ 7	
Interest revenue	3	
Loss on sale of capital assets	(12)	
Interest expense	(14)	(16)
Net income		$ 60

The income statements are identical except for the $12 of income tax expense.

---

[4] Some companies will divide this section on their income statement between *Other Revenues and Gains* and *Other Expenses and Losses*. The *CICA Handbook* P.59 permits flexibility in this regard.

simplified the calculation and assumed a 20% flat tax rate. The 20% tax rate is applied to *income before tax* (20% $\times$ $60 = $12). The resulting tax expense of $12 is subtracted from *income before tax* to arrive at *net income*. Therefore, the term *net income* for a corporation means income after tax. Because the single proprietorship and partnership forms of business organization are not taxed (the owners are taxed) the net income for these two business organizations excludes income tax expense.

Statement of Retained Earnings

A single proprietorship prepares a Statement of Owner's Equity P.37 to show how equity changed during the accounting period. The equity of the owners, regardless of the form of business organization, changes because of:

- net incomes or losses,
- distributions of income (known as withdrawals for a single proprietorship), and
- owner investments.

A single proprietorship includes all three of these activities in one account, the owner's capital account.

The equity of a corporation also changes because of net incomes or losses, distributions of income (called *dividends*), and owner investments. However, net incomes or losses and dividends are recorded in the *Retained Earnings* account while shareholder (or owner) investments are recorded in a share capital account, either common shares or preferred shares. **Retained Earnings** represents the income to date that has been kept (retained) by the corporation for the purpose of reinvestment. The **Statement of Retained Earnings** shows how retained earnings have changed during an accounting period as shown in Exhibit 15.4.

Exhibit 15.4

Comparison of Statement of Retained Earnings and Statement of Owner's Equity

ABC Corporation Statement of Retained Earnings For Year Ended December 31, 2005	
Retained earnings, January 1	$-0-
Add: Net income	48
Total	$48
Less: Dividends	40
Retained earnings, December 31	$ 8

Dell's Servicing Statement of Owner's Equity For Year Ended December 31, 2005		
Ivor Dell, capital, January 1		$ -0-
Add: Owner investment	$500	
Net income	60	
Total		$560
Less: Withdrawals		40
Ivor Dell, capital, December 31		$520

Notice that both statements include net income (losses) and distributions of income (called *dividends* for a corporation and *withdrawals* for a single proprietorship). Owner investments are included as part of Ivor Dell, Capital, for the single proprietorship but, for the corporation, investments by shareholders are *not* part of Retained Earnings.

Balance Sheet

The balance sheets for the corporation and the single proprietorship are identical except for the equity section. The equity section for the single proprietorship is called *owner's equity* because the equity belongs to the owner. The equity section is called **Shareholders' Equity** for a corporation because the equity belongs to a group of owners known as shareholders. Assume the owner of the single proprietorship invested $500 into the business. This $500 investment is included as part of Ivor Dell, Capital, as shown in Exhibit 15.4. The shareholders of ABC Corporation also invested $500. Their investment is recorded in a share capital account, which is shown on the balance sheet as part of Shareholders' Equity in Exhibit 15.5.

Exhibit 15.5

Comparison of Balance Sheets

ABC Corporation **Balance Sheet** **December 31, 2005**		
Assets		
Cash...		$148
Other assets.............................		600
Total assets...............................		$748
Liabilities......................................		$240
Shareholders' Equity		
Share capital.............................	$500	
Retained earnings.....................	8	
Total shareholders' equity.............................		508
Total liabilities and shareholders' equity..........		$748

Dell's Servicing **Balance Sheet** **December 31, 2005**	
Assets	
Cash...	$160
Other assets.............................	600
Total assets...............................	$760
Liabilities......................................	$240
Owner's Equity	
Ivor Dell, Capital......................	520
Total liabilities and owner's equity	$760

Shareholders' Equity and Owner's Equity include the same transactions in total: net incomes (losses), distributions of income, and owner investments.

In summary, the transactions that affect shareholders' equity for the corporate form of organization are the same as for an unincorporated business. The difference is into which accounts the transactions are recorded. A corporation records net incomes (losses) and dividends in Retained Earnings and shareholder investments are recorded in a share capital account. How we record shareholder investments is the topic of the next section. Dividends are discussed later in the chapter.

 **Flashback**

Answers—p. 778

1. Refer to Exhibit 15.5. Explain why there is a difference of $12 between *Total liabilities and shareholders' equity* on the corporate balance sheet and *Total liabilities and owner's equity* on the single proprietorship balance sheet.

2. Explain the difference between the income statement for a corporation and that for an unincorporated business.

3. How is the Statement of Retained Earnings similar to the Statement of Owner's Equity?

4. Explain the differences between Shareholders' Equity and Owner's Equity on the balance sheets for a corporation and a single proprietorship.

Issuing Shares

When investors buy a corporation's shares, they sometimes receive a *share certificate* as proof they purchased shares. Issuance of certificates is becoming less common. Instead, most shareholders maintain accounts with the corporation or their stockbrokers and never receive certificates. If a corporation's shares are traded on a major stock exchange, the corporation must have a *registrar* who keeps shareholder records and prepares official lists of shareholders for shareholders' meetings and dividend payments.

The selling or issuing of shares by a corporation is referred to as **equity financing** because assets are increased (financed) through shareholder (equity) investment. For instance, assume ABC Corporation issued shares to shareholders in exchange for $100,000 cash. The balance sheet prepared for ABC Corporation immediately after this transaction shows the $100,000 cash having been provided through shareholders' equity.

ABC Corporation **Balance Sheet** **December 31, 2005**	
Assets	
Cash...	$100,000
Total assets	$100,000
Liabilities	$ -0-
Shareholders' Equity	
Share capital	100,000
Total liabilities and shareholders' equity.................	$100,000

The next section introduces us to the terminology and basic accounting for the issuance of common and preferred shares.

Accounting for Shares

Corporations can sell shares either *directly* or *indirectly* to shareholders at the *market value per share*. To **sell shares directly**, a corporation advertises its share issuance directly to potential buyers, which is most common with privately held corporations. To **sell shares indirectly**, a corporation pays a brokerage house (investment banker) to issue its shares. Some brokerage houses **underwrite** an indirect issuance of shares, meaning they buy the shares from the corporation and take all gains or losses from the shares' resale to shareholders.

 Record the issuance of common and preferred shares and describe their presentation in shareholders' equity on the balance sheet.

Market value per share is the price at which a share is bought or sold. Market value is influenced by a variety of factors, including expected future earnings, dividends, growth, and other company and economic events. Market values of frequently traded shares are reported online and in daily newspapers such as *The Globe & Mail*. For example, WestJet Airlines' trading history over a three-year period ending February 2003 is illustrated in a chart format below. The first chart shows the changes in share price over three years. During that time, the market price per share has fluctuated between a low of $6.00 per share to about $20.00 per share. The second chart shows how many shares were trading (called volume) over that same time period.

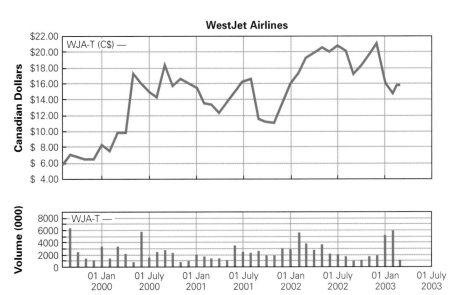

SOURCE: www.tse.com, February 16, 2003.

Market values of shares not actively traded are more difficult to determine. Several techniques are used to estimate the value of these and other shares but most use accounting information as an important input. *We must remember that the buying and selling of shares **between** investors does not impact that corporation's shareholders' equity accounts.*

Common Shares

Recall that if a corporation has only one class of shares, they are known as common shares. Common shares represent *residual equity*, or what is left over after creditors and other shareholders (if any) are paid when a corporation is liquidated (or closed). Common shares have certain rights, which are summarized in Exhibit 15.10 on page 768.

Issuing Common Shares for Cash

Extend Your Knowledge

15-1

The *Canada Business Corporations Act* (CBCA) requires that all shares be of **no par value** or nominal value. Some jurisdictions permit the issuance of *par value* shares. **Par value** is an arbitrary value a corporation places on each share of its share capital. Par value shares are rare in Canada and will be addressed in an Online Learning Centre supplement.

Shares are most commonly issued in exchange for cash. For example, assume that on June 4, 2005, Dillon Snowboards Ltd. was granted a charter to issue an unlimited number of both common and preferred shares. The entry to record Dillon Snowboards' immediate issuance of 30,000 common shares for $300,000 on June 5, 2005, is:

2005			
June 5	Cash..	300,000	
	Common Shares................................		300,000
	Sold and issued 30,000 common shares at $10 per share.		

Many important terms and phrases are used in the shareholders' equity section of a balance sheet. Exhibit 15.6 details each of these using the shareholders' equity section of Dillon Snowboards Ltd. at June 30, 2005, assuming net income for June of $65,000 and no dividend payments.

Exhibit 15.6

Shareholders' Equity of Dillon Snowboards Ltd. at June 30, 2005

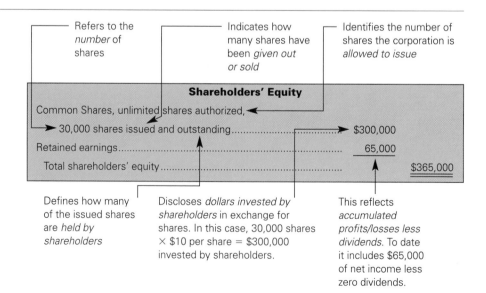

Shares outstanding are explained in detail in Appendix 15A. For simplicity, we will assume that **outstanding shares** (or shares held by shareholders) will be equal to the shares issued (or sold) unless otherwise noted.

Issuing Common Shares for Non-Cash Assets

A corporation can receive assets other than cash in exchange for its shares.[5] The corporation records the assets acquired at the assets' fair market values as of the date of the transaction.[6]

To illustrate, here is the entry to record Dillon Snowboards' receipt of land on July 2, 2005, valued at $105,000 in return for immediate issuance of 4,000 common shares:

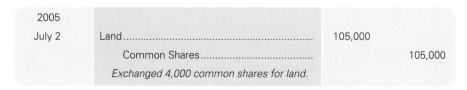

2005			
July 2	Land...	105,000	
	Common Shares.....................................		105,000
	Exchanged 4,000 common shares for land.		

Exhibit 15.7 shows the shareholders' equity of Dillon Snowboards at July 31, 2005, assuming net income earned during July of $82,000.

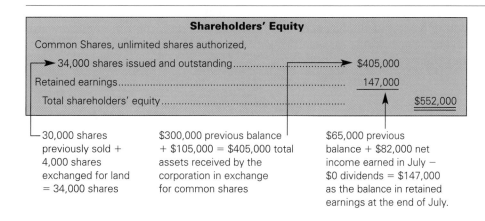

Shareholders' Equity

Common Shares, unlimited shares authorized,	
→ 34,000 shares issued and outstanding................................ →	$405,000
Retained earnings...	147,000
Total shareholders' equity..	$552,000

└ 30,000 shares previously sold + 4,000 shares exchanged for land = 34,000 shares

$300,000 previous balance + $105,000 = $405,000 total assets received by the corporation in exchange for common shares

$65,000 previous balance + $82,000 net income earned in July − $0 dividends = $147,000 as the balance in retained earnings at the end of July.

Exhibit 15.7

Shareholders' Equity of Dillon Snowboards Ltd. at July 31, 2005

5. Refer to Exhibit 15.7. What was the average issue price per common share at July 31, 2005?

6. A company issues 7,000 common shares and a $40,000 note payable in exchange for equipment valued at $105,000. The entry to record this transaction includes a credit to: (a) Retained Earnings for $65,000; (b) Common Shares for $65,000; or (c) Common Shares for $105,000.

Flashback

Answers—p. 778

---

[5] It can also assume liabilities on assets received such as a mortgage on property.
[6] Fair market value is determined by the value of the shares if current, otherwise the value of the assets acquired is used.

Preferred Shares

Preferred shares have special rights that give them priority (or senior status) over common shares in one or more areas. Special rights typically include a preference for receiving dividends and for the distribution of assets if the corporation is liquidated. Because of these special rights, preferred shares are always listed before common shares in the shareholders' equity section. Most preferred shares do not have the right to vote.

Issuing Preferred Shares for Cash

A separate account is used to record preferred shares. To illustrate, if on August 3, 2005, Dillon Snowboards issued 5,000 preferred shares with a dividend preference of $3 per share for a total of $125,000 cash, the entry is:

2005			
Aug. 3	Cash..	125,000	
	Preferred Shares.......................................		125,000
	Issued 5,000 preferred shares for total cash of $125,000.		

Issuing preferred shares for non-cash assets is treated like similar entries for common shares.

The preferred shares account is included as part of contributed capital. The equity section of the balance sheet at August 31, 2005, for Dillon Snowboards assuming net income earned during August of $156,000 would appear as shown in Exhibit 15.8.

Exhibit 15.8

Shareholders' Equity with Common and Preferred Shares

When more than one class of shares has been issued, the shareholders' equity section is classified by grouping the share capital accounts under the heading *Contributed capital*. **Contributed capital** is the total amount of cash and other assets received by the corporation from its shareholders in exchange for common and/or preferred shares.

The notation "$3" is the **dividend preference**, which means preferred shareholders are entitled to dividends at the rate of $3 per year per preferred share when declared.

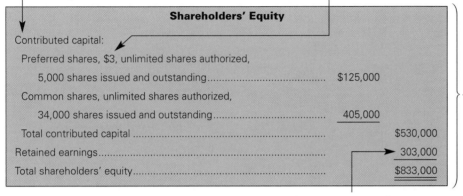

Shareholders' Equity

Contributed capital:	
Preferred shares, $3, unlimited shares authorized,	
5,000 shares issued and outstanding	$125,000
Common shares, unlimited shares authorized,	
34,000 shares issued and outstanding	405,000
Total contributed capital	$530,000
Retained earnings	303,000
Total shareholders' equity	$833,000

Net income of $65,000 for June + $82,000 net income for July + $156,000 net income for August − $-0- dividends = $303,000 as the balance in retained earnings at August 31, 2005.

Exhibit 15.9

Shareholders' Equity on August 31, 2005, Balance Sheet

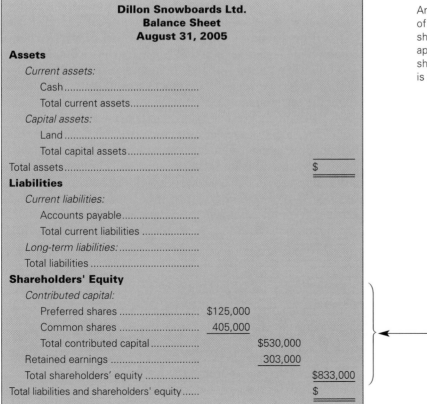

Dillon Snowboards Ltd.
Balance Sheet
August 31, 2005

Assets

Current assets:

Cash	
Total current assets	

Capital assets:

Land	
Total capital assets	
Total assets	$

Liabilities

Current liabilities:

Accounts payable	
Total current liabilities	

Long-term liabilities:

Total liabilities	

Shareholders' Equity

Contributed capital:

Preferred shares	$125,000	
Common shares	405,000	
Total contributed capital		$530,000
Retained earnings		303,000
Total shareholders' equity		$833,000
Total liabilities and shareholders' equity		$

An abbreviated example of how Dillon Snowboards' shareholders' equity might appear within the balance sheet at August 31, 2005, is illustrated in Exhibit 15.9.

Exhibit 15.10

Summary of Rights of Preferred and Common Shareholders

Rights of Preferred Shareholders	Rights of Common Shareholders
1. No voting rights.	1. The right to vote at shareholders' meetings.
2. The right to receive dividends *before* the common shareholders receive a dividend. In other words, a dividend cannot be paid to common shareholders unless preferred shareholders also receive one.	2. The right to share pro rata with other common shareholders in any dividends declared. This means each common share receives the same dividend per share.
3. The right to share equally *before* common shareholders in any assets that remain after creditors are paid when the corporation is liquidated.	3. The right to share equally in any assets that remain after creditors and preferred shareholders are paid when the corporation is liquidated.
4. The right to sell or otherwise dispose of their shares.	4. The right to sell or otherwise dispose of their shares.
	5. The right to purchase additional shares of common shares issued by the corporation in the future, called the **preemptive right**. It protects shareholders' proportionate interest in the corporation. For example, a shareholder who owns 25% of a corporation's common shares has the first opportunity to buy 25% of any new common shares issued. This enables the shareholder to maintain a 25% ownership interest if desired.

Motivation for Preferred Shares

There are several reasons for a corporation to issue preferred shares. One reason is to raise capital without sacrificing control of the corporation. For example, let's suppose the organizers of a company have $100,000 cash to invest and wish to organize a corporation needing $200,000 of capital to get off to a good start. If they sold $100,000 worth of common shares, they would have only 50% control and would need to negotiate with other shareholders in making policy. However, if they issue $100,000 of the common shares to themselves and sell outsiders 1,000 shares of $8 cumulative preferred shares with no voting rights for $100,000, they retain control of the corporation.

A second reason for issuing preferred shares is to increase the return earned by common shareholders. To illustrate, let's suppose a corporation's organizers expect their new company to earn an annual net income of $24,000 on an investment of $200,000. If they sell and issue $200,000 worth of common shares, this income produces a 12% return on the $200,000 of common shareholders' equity ($24,000/$200,000 = 0.12 or 12%). However, if they issue 1,000 shares of $8 preferred shares to outsiders for $100,000 and $100,000 of common shares to themselves, their own return increases to 16% per year, as shown in Exhibit 15.11.

Exhibit 15.11

Return to Common Shareholders

Net after-tax income	$24,000
Less: Preferred dividends at $8 (1,000 preferred shares × $8 dividends per share)	8,000
Balance to Common Shareholders	$16,000
Return to Common Shareholders ($16,000/$100,000)	16%

Common shareholders earn 16% instead of 12% because assets contributed by preferred shareholders are invested to earn $12,000 while the preferred dividend payments amount to only $8,000.

Use of preferred shares to increase return to common shareholders is an example of **financial leverage**. Whenever the dividend rate on preferred shares is less than the rate the corporation earns on the amount invested by preferred shareholders, the effect of issuing preferred shares is to increase (or *leverage*) the rate earned by common shareholders. Financial leverage also occurs when debt is issued and the interest rate paid on it is less than the rate earned from using the assets the creditors lent to the corporation.

There are other reasons for issuing preferred shares. For example, a corporation's preferred shares may appeal to some investors who believe its common shares are too risky or that the dividend rate on common shares is too low. Also, if a corporation's management wants to issue common shares but believes the current market price for common shares is too low, the corporation may issue preferred shares that are *convertible* into common shares. If and when the price of common shares increases, the preferred shareholders can *convert* their shares into common shares. *Convertible preferred shares* are discussed on page 775 of this chapter.

Concert Organizer

You organize music concerts for profit. You've recently decided to move away from concerts targeted at under 5,000 people to those targeted at between 10,000 to 50,000 people. This demands funding. You decide to incorporate because of the increased risk of lawsuits and your desire to issue shares to meet funding demands. It is important to you that you keep control of the company for decisions on whom to schedule and when. What type of share issuance do you offer?

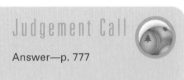

Judgement Call

Answer—p. 777

7. In what ways do preferred shares often have priority over common shares?

8. Increasing the return to common shareholders by issuing preferred shares is an example of: (a) financial leverage; (b) cumulative earnings; or (c) dividends in arrears.

Flashback

Answers—p. 778

Mid-Chapter Demonstration Problem

Roberta Inc. began operations on January 2, 2005, and immediately issued 8,000 of its common shares for cash of $1.50 per share. On January 3, 500 common shares were issued to promoters in exchange for their services in selling shares of the corporation. The shares were valued at a total of $1,000. On January 5, 10,000 common shares were issued in exchange for land valued at $24,925. On January 11, 4,000 preferred shares were issued for cash of $5.00 per share. On January 25, 3,000 more preferred shares were issued for total cash of $15,700.

a. Present the journal entries that the company's accountant would use to record these transactions.

b. Prepare the shareholders' equity section at January 31, 2005, assuming net income earned during the month was $40,000. No dividends had been declared. Roberta Inc. is authorized to issue an unlimited number of preferred and common shares.

c. What was the average issue price per common share as of January 31, 2005?

d. What was the average issue price per preferred share as of January 31, 2005?

SOLUTION TO Mid-Chapter Demonstration Problem

a.

2005			
Jan. 2	Cash..	12,000	
	Common Shares		12,000
	Issued 8,000 common shares for cash;		
	8,000 × $1.50 = $12,000.		
3	Organization Cost	1,000	
	Common Shares		1,000
	Issued 500 common shares for		
	incorporation fees.		
5	Land..	24,925	
	Common Shares		24,925
	Issued 10,000 common shares in		
	exchange for land.		
11	Cash..	20,000	
	Preferred Shares......................		20,000
	Issued 4,000 preferred shares for cash;		
	4,000 × $5.00 = $20,000.		
25	Cash..	15,700	
	Preferred Shares......................		15,700
	Issued 3,000 preferred shares for cash.		

b.

Roberta Inc.
Shareholders' Equity
January 31, 2005

Contributed capital:	
Preferred shares, unlimited shares authorized,	
7,000 shares issued and outstanding..	$35,700
Common shares, unlimited shares authorized;	
18,500 shares issued and outstanding....................................	37,925
Total contributed capital..	$ 73,625
Retained earnings	40,000
Total shareholders' equity	$113,625

c. $37,925/18,500 shares = $2.05 average issue price per common share

d. $35,700/7,000 shares = $5.10 average issue price per preferred share

Dividends

Dividends are a distribution of earnings (also referred to as a distribution of net income). The corporation's board of directors is responsible for making decisions regarding dividends. Dividends cause retained earnings to decrease. The two most common types of dividends are cash dividends and share (or stock) dividends. A share (stock) split is not a type of dividend but has a similar effect on shareholders' equity as share dividends do. Share dividends and splits are discussed in Chapter 16. Cash dividends are explained in the following section.

Cash Dividends

Generally a corporation is permitted to pay cash dividends if retained earnings and cash exist. The decision to pay cash dividends rests with the board of directors and involves more than evaluating retained earnings and cash. The directors, for instance, may decide to keep the cash and invest in the growth of the corporation. Other reasons to keep the cash include meeting emergencies, taking advantage of unexpected opportunities, or paying off debt.

LO⁴ Describe and account for cash dividends.

Many corporations pay cash dividends to their shareholders in regular amounts at regular dates. These cash flows provide a return to investors and almost always affect the shares' market value.

Entries for Cash Dividends

The payment of dividends involves three important dates: declaration, record, and payment date.

Date of declaration is the date the directors vote to pay a dividend creating a legal liability of the corporation to its shareholders. To illustrate, the entry to record a November 9 declaration of a $1 per share dividend by the directors of Z-Tech Ltd. with 5,000 outstanding common shares is:

or

Nov. 9	Cash Dividends	5,000	
	Common Dividends Payable		5,000
	Declared a $1 per share cash dividend on common shares.		

Nov. 9	Retained Earnings	5,000	
	Common Dividends Payable		5,000
	Declared a $1 per share cash dividend on common shares.		

Cash Dividends is a temporary account that gathers information about total dividends declared during the reporting period. It is not an expense account. An alternative to using a Cash Dividends account is to debit Retained Earnings as shown. The sequence of entries using this alternative will be shown to the right. The Common Dividends Payable account reflects the corporation's current liability to its common shareholders.

Date of record is the future date specified by the directors for identifying those shareholders listed in the corporation's records to receive dividends. Persons who own shares on the date of record receive dividends. No journal entry is needed at the date of record.

Date of payment is the date when shareholders receive payment. If a balance sheet is prepared between the date of declaration and date of payment, Common Dividends Payable is reported as a current liability.

For instance, Leon's reported $2,520,000 of dividends payable as at December 31, 2002.

On December 1, Z-Tech's date of payment, the following entry is recorded:

or

Dec. 1	Common Dividends Payable	5,000			Dec. 1	Common Dividends Payable	5,000	
	Cash		5,000			Cash		5,000
	Paid cash dividend to common shareholders.					*Paid cash dividend to common shareholders.*		

At the end of the reporting period, the balance of Z-Tech's Cash Dividends account is closed to Retained Earnings as follows:

or

Dec. 31	Retained Earnings	5,000			Dec. 31	No entry
	Cash Dividends		5,000			*Because Retained Earnings was debited directly on the date of declaration, no closing entry is required when using this alternative approach.*
	To close Cash Dividends account.					

www.opg.com

Because dividends cause retained earnings to decrease, they are subtracted on the Statement of Retained Earnings as shown previously for ABC Corporation in Exhibit 15.4. For example, Ontario Power Generation Inc.'s retained earnings were decreased by $134 million for the year ended December 31, 2002, because of a cash dividend declared and paid to common shareholders.

The entries regarding cash dividends on preferred shares would be recorded in the same way as shown for common shares.

Deficits and Cash Dividends

A corporation with a debit (abnormal) balance in Retained Earnings is said to have a **deficit**. A deficit arises when a company has cumulative losses greater than total profits earned in prior years. A deficit is deducted on a corporation's balance sheet as shown in Exhibit 15.12.

Exhibit 15.12

Rent-A-Wreck Capital Inc. —Deficit Illustrated

www.rentawreck.ca

Rent-A-Wreck Capital Inc. **Shareholders' Equity** **September 30, 2002**	
Share capital	$ 702,173
Deficit	(657,502)

A corporation with a deficit is not allowed to pay a cash dividend to its shareholders in most jurisdictions. This legal restriction is designed to protect creditors of the corporation by preventing distribution of assets to shareholders at a time when the company is in financial difficulty.

Special Features of Preferred Shares

Preferred shares can have a number of special features such as being cumulative or non-cumulative, participating, callable, and convertible. These characteristics are unique to preferred shares and are discussed in this section.

Dividend Preference

In exchange for voting rights, preferred shares usually carry a **dividend preference**, which means a dividend cannot be paid to common shareholders unless preferred shareholders are paid first. The dividend preference is usually expressed as a dollar amount per share as illustrated in Exhibit 15.13.

Exhibit 15.13

Presentation of
Dividend Preference

Stake Technology Ltd. Shareholders' Equity April 30, 2005		
Contributed capital:		
Preferred shares, $2.20, 25,000 shares authorized; 7,000 shares issued and outstanding	$ 84,000	
Common shares, unlimited shares authorized; 80,000 shares issued and outstanding	760,000	
Total contributed capital		$844,000
Retained earnings		49,000
Total shareholders' equity		$893,000

The preferred shareholders
are entitled to receive $2.20
per share annually when
dividends are declared.

A preference for dividends does not guarantee dividends. If the directors do not declare a dividend, neither the preferred nor the common shareholders receive one. However, if dividends are not declared on preferred shares, the undeclared dividends from prior periods plus current dividends may be paid if the preferred shares have a *cumulative* feature. The features known as cumulative and non-cumulative dividends are the topic of the next section.

Cumulative or Non-Cumulative Dividend

Many preferred shares carry a *cumulative* dividend right. **Cumulative preferred shares** have a right to be paid both current and all prior periods' undeclared dividends before any dividend is paid to common shareholders. When preferred shares are cumulative and the directors either do not declare a dividend to preferred shareholders or declare a dividend that does not satisfy the cumulative dividend, then the unpaid dividend amount is called a **dividend in arrears**. Accumulation of dividends in arrears on cumulative preferred shares does not guarantee they will be paid. Some preferred shares are *non-cumulative*. **Non-cumulative preferred shares** have no right to prior periods' unpaid dividends if they were not declared.

LO⁵ Distribute dividends between common and preferred shares.

To illustrate and show the difference between cumulative and non-cumulative preferred shares, refer to the assumed information regarding the shares of Stake Technology Ltd. in Exhibit 15.13.

During the year ended April 30, 2005, the first year of the corporation's operations, the directors declared and paid total cash dividends of $31,400. During the years ended April 30, 2006 and 2007, total dividends declared and paid were $0 and $110,800 respectively. Allocations of total dividends are shown in Exhibit 15.14 under two assumptions:

a. the preferred shares are non-cumulative, and

b. the preferred shares are cumulative.

Exhibit 15.14

Allocation of Dividends Between Preferred and Common Shares

a. If non-cumulative preferred:

	Preferred	Common	Total
Year ended 2005:			
7,000 shares × $2.20/share	$15,400		
Remainder to common		$16,000	$ 31,400
Year ended 2006:	-0-	-0-	$ -0-
Year ended 2007:			
7,000 shares × $2.20/share	15,400		
Remainder to common		$95,400	$110,800

b. If cumulative preferred:

	Preferred	Common	Total
Year ended 2005:			
7,000 shares × $2.20/share	$15,400		
Remainder to common		$16,000	$ 31,400
Year ended 2006:	-0-	-0-	$ -0-
Year ended 2007:			
Dividends in arrears = $15,400			
+ Current year dividends of $15,400	30,800		
Remainder to common		$80,000	$110,800

With non-cumulative preferred shares, the preferred shareholders in Exhibit 15.14 never receive the $15,400 not declared for the year ended 2006. Undeclared dividends are *lost* if preferred shares are non-cumulative.

When preferred shares are cumulative, undeclared dividends are not lost because they go into arrears. In Exhibit 15.14, the $15,400 not declared in 2006 is paid during the year ended 2007 before the common shareholders receive a dividend.

Financial Statement Disclosure of Dividends

A liability for a dividend does not exist until the directors declare a dividend. This means that if a preferred dividend date passes and the corporation's board fails to declare the dividend on its cumulative preferred shares, the dividend in arrears is not a liability. When preparing financial statements, the *full disclosure principle* P. 350 requires the corporation to report the amount of preferred dividends in arrears as of the balance sheet date. This information is usually in a note.

Flashback

Answers—p. 778

9. The Cash Dividends account is normally: (a) reported on the balance sheet as a liability; (b) closed to Income Summary; or (c) closed to Retained Earnings.

10. What three dates are involved in the process of paying a cash dividend?

11. When does a dividend become a legal obligation of the company?

In addition to being cumulative or non-cumulative, preferred shares can have other features. This is the topic of the next section.

Other Features of Preferred Shares

Participating or Non-Participating Dividends on Preferred Shares

Non-participating preferred shares have dividends limited to a maximum amount each year. This maximum is often stated as a specific dollar amount per share. Once preferred shareholders receive this amount, the common shareholders receive any and all additional dividends.

Participating preferred shares have a feature in which preferred shareholders share with common shareholders in any dividends paid in excess of the dollar amount specified for the preferred shares. This participating feature does not apply until common shareholders receive dividends in a ratio equal to the preferred share's dividend. While many corporations are authorized to issue participating preferred shares, they are rarely issued.

Convertible Preferred Shares

Preferred shares are more attractive to investors if they carry a right to exchange preferred shares for a fixed number of common shares. **Convertible preferred shares** give holders the option of exchanging their preferred shares into common shares at a specified rate. This feature offers holders of convertible preferred shares a higher potential return. When a company prospers and its common shares increase in value, convertible preferred shareholders can share in this success by converting their preferred shares into more valuable common shares. Also, these holders benefit from increases in the value of common shares without converting their preferred shares because the preferred share's market value is impacted by changes in the value of common shares.

To illustrate the entries to record the conversion of preferred shares to common, assume that the preferred shares in Exhibit 15.13 were convertible at the rate of two common shares for each preferred share. The average issue price of the preferred shares is used as the basis of the calculation to record the conversion of 1,000 preferred shares into common shares on May 1, 2005:

2005			
May 1	Preferred Shares..	12,000	
	Common Shares.......................................		12,000
	To record the conversion of preferred shares into common; $84,000/7,000 shares = $12/share average issue price; $12/share × 1,000 shares = $12,000.		

This entry transfers $12,000 from the Preferred Shares account to the Common Shares account. Total shareholders' equity does not change.

Callable Preferred Shares

Callable preferred shares, also known as **redeemable preferred shares**, give the issuing corporation the right to purchase (retire) these shares from their holders at specified future prices and dates. Many issues of preferred shares are callable. The amount paid to call and retire a preferred share is its **call price**, or *redemption value*. This amount is set at the time the shares are issued. The call price normally includes the issue price of the shares plus a premium giving holders additional return on their investment. When the issuing corporation calls and retires preferred shares, it must pay the call price *and* any dividends in arrears.

For instance, in Note 11 of its December 31, 2002, annual report, TransCanada Pipelines Limited reports that on or after October 15, 2013, for the Series U shares, and on or after March 5, 2014, for the Series Y shares, the company may redeem the shares at $50 per share.

TransCanada
In business to deliver ™
www.transcanada.com

Flashback

Answer—p. 778

12. A corporation has issued 9,000 shares of $5 cumulative preferred shares for a total of $450,000 and 27,000 common shares for a total of $270,000. No dividends have been declared for 2003 and 2004. During 2005, the corporation declares a $288,000 dividend. The amount paid to common shareholders is: (a) $198,000; (b) $153,000; or (c) $108,000.

Closing Entries for Corporations

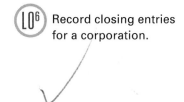

Record closing entries for a corporation.

Recall that the closing process involves closing all temporary accounts. This includes closing revenues and expenses to the Income Summary account. For the corporate form of organization, the balance in the Income Summary account is closed to Retained Earnings. To demonstrate, assume Weber Inc. had a credit balance of $63,000 in its Income Summary account at December 31, 2005, after closing all revenues and expenses. The entry to close the Income Summary account is:

2005			
Dec. 31	Income Summary	63,000	
	Retained Earnings		63,000
	To close net income to Retained Earnings.		

If, instead, Weber Inc. had realized a net loss during the accounting period of $14,000, the balance in the Income Summary account would have been a debit after closing all revenues and expenses. The entry to close the Income Summary account in this instance would be:

2005			
Dec. 31	Retained Earnings...	14,000	
	Income Summary......................................		14,000
	To close net loss to Retained Earnings.		

The final step in the closing process would be to close dividends (unless Retained Earnings had been debited directly as described on page 771). Assuming Weber Inc. had a balance of $10,000 in its Cash Dividends account, the closing entry would be:

2005			
Dec. 31	Retained Earnings...	10,000	
	Cash Dividends		10,000
	To close the Cash Dividends account to		
	Retained Earnings.		

Summary

LO1 Identify characteristics of corporations and their organization. Corporations are separate legal entities and their shareholders are not liable for corporate debts. Shares issued by corporations are easily transferred between shareholders, and the life of a corporation does not end with the incapacity or death of a shareholder. A corporation acts through its agents, who are its officers and managers, not its shareholders. Corporations are regulated by the government and are subject to income taxes.

LO2 Describe and contrast the specialized components of corporate financial statements. The income statement for a corporation is similar to that of an unincorporated organization except for the inclusion of income tax expense. A corporation, like a proprietorship, records net incomes (losses), distributions of net income (in the form of dividends) to its owners (shareholders), and owner (shareholder) investments. Accumulated net incomes less losses and dividends are recorded in Retained Earnings and summarized on the Statement of Retained Earnings. Shareholder investments are recorded in share capital accounts, either common shares or preferred shares, in shareholders' equity on the balance sheet. An unincorporated business records these three activities in the owner's capital account.

LO3 Record the issuance of common and preferred shares and describe their presentation in shareholders' equity on the balance sheet. When only one class of shares is issued, they are called common shares. Shares, both common and preferred, can be issued for cash or other assets. The number of shares authorized, issued, and outstanding, along with the dollar value contributed by the shareholders, is shown under the heading Contributed Capital in the Shareholders' Equity section on the balance sheet. Preferred shares have a priority (or senior status) relative to common shares in one or more areas. The usual areas include preference as to (a) dividends and (b) assets in case of liquidation. They do not have voting rights.

LO4 Describe and account for cash dividends. The board of directors makes all decisions regarding dividends. The date of declaration is the date the liability to pay dividends is created. All shareholders holding shares as of the date of record are eligible to receive the declared dividend. The dividend payment date is when dividends are actually paid.

LO5 Distribute dividends between common and preferred shares. Preferred shareholders usually hold the right to receive dividend distributions before common shareholders. This right is known as dividend preference. When preferred shares are cumulative and in arrears, the amount in arrears must be distributed to preferred shareholders before any dividends are distributed to common shareholders. Preferred shares can also be convertible or callable. Convertibility permits the holder to convert preferred shares to common shares. Callability permits the issuer to buy preferred shares under specified conditions.

LO6 Record closing entries for a corporation. Revenues and expenses are closed to the Income Summary account as for an unincorporated organization. The balance in Income Summary is closed to Retained Earnings. Dividends are closed to Retained Earnings, as well.

GUIDANCE ANSWER TO Judgement Call

Concert Organizer

Because you wish to maintain control of the company, you want to issue shares in a way that does not interfere with your ability to run the company the way you desire. You have two basic options: (1) different classes of common shares, or (2) common and preferred shares. Your objective in this case is to issue a class of shares to yourself that has all or a majority of the voting power. The other class of shares you issue would carry limited or no voting rights. In this way you maintain complete control and are able to raise your necessary funds.

1. All transactions are identical for both organizations except for the $12, which represents the income tax expense imposed on the corporation but not on the unincorporated form of organization.

2. The income statement of a corporation includes Income Tax Expense but the income statement for an unincorporated business does not. This is because a corporation must pay taxes on its income, whereas an unincorporated business does not since it is not a separate legal entity.

3. Both statements include net incomes (losses) less distributions of earnings (called *withdrawals* for an unincorporated organization and *dividends* for the corporation).

4. Shareholders' equity shows investments by the owners (shareholders) separately from net incomes (losses) and dividends. Shareholder investments are recorded in share capital accounts, either common shares or preferred shares, and net incomes (losses) less dividends are summarized in the Retained Earnings account. Owner's equity shows all three activities in one account, the owner's capital account.

5. The average issue price per common share at July 31, 2005, was $405,000/34,000 = $11.91 (rounded).

6. *b*

7. Special rights include a preference for receiving dividends and for the distribution of assets if the corporation's assets are liquidated.

8. *a*

9. *c*

10. The three dates are the date of declaration, date of record, and date of payment.

11. A dividend becomes a legal obligation of the company when it is declared by the board of directors on the date of declaration.

12. *b*

Total dividend	$288,000
To preferred shareholders	135,000*
Remainder to common shareholders	$153,000

*$9,000 × $5 × 3 = $135,000

Demonstration Problem

Barton Corporation was created on January 1, 2005. Barton is authorized by its articles of incorporation to issue 100,000 shares of $10 cumulative preferred shares and an unlimited number of common shares. The following transactions relating to shareholders' equity occurred during the first two years of the company's operations.

2005

Jan. 2   Issued 200,000 common shares at $12 per share.

2   Issued 100,000 common shares in exchange for a building valued at $820,000 and merchandise inventory valued at $380,000.

3   Paid a cash reimbursement to the company's founders for $100,000 of organization costs; these costs are to be amortized over 10 years.

3   Issued 12,000 preferred shares for cash at $110 per share.

Dec. 31   The Income Summary account for 2005 had a $125,000 credit balance before being closed to Retained Earnings; no dividends were declared on either common or preferred shares.

2006

June 4   Issued 100,000 common shares for cash at $15 per share.

Dec. 10   Declared total cash dividends of $540,000 payable on January 10, 2007.

31   The Income Summary account for 2006 had a $1 million credit balance before being closed to Retained Earnings.

Required

1. Prepare the journal entries to record these transactions.

2. Prepare statements of retained earnings for the years ended December 31, 2005 and 2006.

3. Prepare the balance sheet presentation of the organization costs, liabilities, and shareholders' equity as at December 31, 2005 and 2006. Include appropriate notes to the financial statements (regarding any dividends in arrears).

Planning the Solution

○ Record journal entries for the transactions in 2005 and 2006.

○ Close the accounts related to retained earnings at the end of each year.

○ Prepare the statements of retained earnings for the years 2005 and 2006.

○ Determine the balances for the 2005 and 2006 contributed capital accounts for the balance sheet including information about the number of shares issued.

○ Prepare the shareholders' equity section of the 2005 and 2006 balance sheet including a note regarding any dividends in arrears.

SOLUTION TO Demonstration Problem

1.

2005			
Jan. 2	Cash..	2,400,000	
	Common Shares		2,400,000
	Issued 200,000 common shares;		
	200,000 × $12.		
2	Building...	820,000	
	Merchandise Inventory	380,000	
	Common Shares		1,200,000
	Issued 100,000 common shares.		
3	Organization Costs...	100,000	
	Cash		100,000
	Reimbursed the founders for organization		
	costs.		
3	Cash..	1,320,000	
	Preferred Shares		1,320,000
	Issued 12,000 preferred shares;		
	12,000 × $110.		
Dec. 31	Income Summary	125,000	
	Retained Earnings		125,000
	Close the Income Summary account and		
	update Retained Earnings.		
2006			
June 4	Cash..	1,500,000	
	Common Shares		1,500,000
	Issued 100,000 common shares;		
	100,000 × $15.		
Dec. 10	Cash Dividends (or Retained Earnings).............	540,000	
	Preferred Dividend Payable.......................		240,000
	Common Dividend Payable.......................		300,000
	Declared current dividends and dividends		
	in arrears to common and preferred		
	shareholders, payable on January 10, 2007;		
	Preferred = $10/share × 12,000 shares ×		
	2 years; Common = $ 540,000 − $ 240,000.		
31	Income Summary	1,000,000	
	Retained Earnings		1,000,000
	To close the Income Summary account and		
	update Retained Earnings.		
31	Retained Earnings..	540,000	
	Cash Dividends		540,000
	To close to Retained Earnings the Cash		
	Dividends.		

2.

Barton Corporation **Statement of Retained Earnings** **For Years Ended December 31,**	2006	2005
Retained earnings, January 1	$ 125,000	$ -0-
Add: Net income	1,000,000	125,000
Total	$1,125,000	$125,000
Less: Dividends	540,000	-0-
Retained earnings, December 31	$ 585,000	$125,000

3. Balance sheet presentations:

Barton Corporation **Balance Sheet** **As of December 31,**	2006	2005
Assets		
Organization costs	$ 80,000	$ 90,000
Liabilities		
Preferred dividend payable	$ 240,000	$ -0-
Common dividend payable	300,000	-0-
Shareholders' Equity		
Contributed capital:		
Preferred shares, $10 cumulative, 100,000 shares authorized; 12,000 shares issued and outstanding	$1,320,000	$1,320,000
Common shares, unlimited shares authorized; 400,000 shares issued and outstanding in 2006; 300,000 shares issued and outstanding in 2005	5,100,000	3,600,000
Total contributed capital	$6,420,000	$4,920,000
Retained earnings (see Note 1)	585,000	125,000
Total shareholders' equity	$7,005,000	$5,045,000

Note 1: As of December 31, 2005, there were $120,000 of dividends in arrears on the preferred shares.

Book Value Per Share

LO7 Calculate book value and explain its use in analysis.

This section explains how we calculate book value and use it for analysis. We first focus on book value per share for corporations with only common shares outstanding, and then look at book value per share when both common and preferred shares are outstanding.

Book Value Per Share When Only Common Shares Are Outstanding

Book value per common share is the recorded amount of shareholders' equity applicable to common shares divided by the number of common shares outstanding. This ratio is defined in Exhibit 15A.1.

Exhibit 15A.1

Book Value Per Common Share Formula

$$\text{Book value per common share} = \frac{\text{Shareholders' equity applicable to common shares}}{\text{Number of common shares outstanding}}$$

For instance, we can calculate the book value per common share for Dillon Snowboards at June 30, 2005, using data in Exhibit 15.6. Dillon has 30,000 outstanding common shares and the shareholders' equity applicable to common shares is $365,000. Common shares are entitled to total shareholders' equity when there are no preferred shares outstanding. Dillon's book value per common share is $12.17, calculated as $365,000 divided by 30,000 shares.

Book Value Per Share When Both Common and Preferred Shares Are Outstanding

To calculate book value when both common and preferred shares are outstanding, we must first allocate total shareholders' equity between these two kinds of shares. The **book value per preferred share** is calculated first, and its calculation is shown in Exhibit 15A.2.

Exhibit 15A.2

Book Value Per Preferred Share Formula

$$\text{Book value per preferred share} = \frac{\text{Shareholders' equity applicable to preferred shares}}{\text{Number of preferred shares outstanding}}$$

The shareholders' equity applicable to preferred shares equals the preferred share's call price (or average paid-in amount if the preferred share is not callable) plus any cumulative dividends in arrears. The remaining shareholders' equity is the portion applicable to common shares.

To illustrate, let us look at the December 31, 2005, shareholders' equity section of Music Live! as shown in Exhibit 15A.3. The preferred shares of Music Live! are callable at $108 per share, and since no dividends were declared during 2004 and 2005, there are two years of cumulative preferred dividends in arrears.

Music Live! Shareholders' Equity December 31, 2005	
Contributed capital:	
Preferred shares, $7 cumulative, $108 call price, 2,000 shares authorized, 1,000 shares issued and outstanding	$105,000
Common shares, 12,000 shares authorized, 10,000 shares issued and outstanding	260,000
Total contributed capital	$365,000
Retained earnings	82,000
Total shareholders' equity	$447,000

Exhibit 15A.3

Shareholders' Equity with Preferred and Common Shares

The book values of Music Live! preferred and common shares are calculated in Exhibit 15A.4. Note the need to allocate equity to preferred shares before we calculate the book value of common shares.

Total shareholders' equity		$ 447,000
Less equity applicable to preferred shares:		
Call price (1,000 × $108)	$108,000	
Cumulative dividends in arrears (1,000 × $7 × 2)	14,000	(122,000)
Equity applicable to common shares		$ 325,000
Book value per preferred share ($122,000/1,000)		$122.00
Book value per common share ($325,000/10,000)		$32.50

Exhibit 15A.4

Calculating Book Value Per Share

Book value per share is often used in analysis of a company. It is the starting point in many share valuation methods. Other uses include merger negotiations, price setting for public utilities, and loan contracts. The main limitation in using book values is likely differences between book values and market values for both assets and liabilities. Professionals often adjust their analyses and the accounting numbers to reflect these differences.

Investor

You are considering investing in Ride Ltd., a leading manufacturer of snowboards. Ride's current book value per common share is about $4, yet its common shares are priced at about $7 per share on the stock exchange. From this information, can you say whether Ride's net assets are priced higher or lower than their recorded values?

Judgement Call

Answer—p. 784

Flashback

Answers—p. 784

13. A corporation's outstanding shares includes $90,000 of cumulative preferred shares consisting of 1,000 shares and 12,000 common shares. Preferred shares have a call price of $90 and dividends of $18,000 are in arrears. Total shareholders' equity is $630,000. What is the book value per common share?

14. The price at which a share is bought or sold is the (a) call price, (b) redemption value, or (c) market value.

Summary of Appendix 15A

LO⁷ **Calculate book value and explain its use in analysis.** Book value per common share is shareholders' equity applicable to common shares divided by the number of outstanding common shares. Book value per preferred share is shareholders' equity applicable to preferred shares divided by the number of outstanding preferred shares.

G U I D A N C E   A N S W E R   T O   *Judgement Call*

Investor

Book value reflects recorded values. Ride's book value is about $4 per common share. The share price reflects the market's expectation of current and future values.

Ride's market value is about $7 per common share. Comparing these figures suggests that market perception of Ride's value is much higher than its recorded values ($7 vs. $4 per share, respectively).

G U I D A N C E   A N S W E R S   T O   **Flashback**

13.

Total shareholders' equity		$630,000
Less equity applicable to preferred shares:		
Call price (1,000 × $90).....................................	$90,000	
Dividends in arrears..	18,000	108,000
Equity applicable to common shares		$522,000
Book value of common shares ($522,000/12,000)		$43.50

14. *c*

Glossary

Authorized shares The total number of shares that a corporation's charter authorizes it to sell. Federally incorporated companies are authorized to issue an unlimited number. (p. 759)

Book value per common share The recorded amount of shareholders' equity applicable to common shares divided by the number of common shares outstanding. (p. 782)

Book value per preferred share The amount of shareholders' equity applicable to preferred shares (equals the preferred share's call price or issue price if the preferred share is not callable, plus any cumulative dividends in arrears) divided by the number of preferred shares outstanding. (p. 782)

Call price The amount that must be paid to call and retire a preferred share. (p. 775)

Callable preferred shares Preferred shares that the issuing corporation, at its option, may retire by paying a specified amount (the call price) to the preferred shareholders plus any dividends in arrears. (p. 775)

Capital stock See *share capital.* (p. 756)

Closely held shares See *privately held shares.* (p. 756)

Common shares Shares of a corporation when there is only one class of shares. (p. 760)

Contributed capital The total amount of cash and other assets received by the corporation from its shareholders in exchange for common and/or preferred shares. (p. 767)

Convertible preferred shares Preferred shares that give holders the option of exchanging their preferred shares for common shares at a specified rate. (p. 775)

Cumulative preferred shares Preferred shares on which undeclared dividends accumulate until they are paid; common shareholders cannot receive a dividend until all cumulative dividends have been paid. (p. 773)

Date of declaration The date the directors vote to pay a dividend. (p. 771)

Date of payment The date when shareholders receive the dividend payment. (p. 771)

Date of record The future date specified by the directors for identifying those shareholders listed in the corporation's records to receive dividends. (p. 771)

Deficit Arises when a corporation has a debit (abnormal) balance for retained earnings. (p. 772)

Dividend in arrears An unpaid dividend on cumulative preferred shares; it must be paid before any current dividends on the preferred shares and before any dividends on common shares are paid. (p. 773)

Dividend preference The rate per share at which dividends are paid when declared. (p. 773)

Equity financing Obtaining capital, or money, by issuing shares. (p. 762)

Financial leverage Achieving an increased return on common shares by paying dividends on preferred shares or interest on debt at a rate that is less than the rate of return earned with the assets that were invested in the corporation by the preferred shareholders or creditors. (p. 769)

Market value per share The price at which stock is bought or sold. (p. 763)

Non-cumulative preferred shares Preferred shares on which the right to receive dividends is lost for any year that the dividends are not declared. (p. 773)

No par value A class of shares that has not been assigned a par value by the corporate charter. (p. 764)

Non-participating preferred shares Preferred shares on which dividends are limited to a maximum amount each year. (p. 775)

Organization costs The costs of bringing a corporation into existence, including legal fees, promoters' fees, and amounts paid to the incorporating legal jurisdiction. (p. 759)

Outstanding shares The number of shares held by shareholders. (p. 765)

Par value An arbitrary value a corporation places on each of the corporation's shares. (p. 764)

Participating preferred shares Preferred shares with a feature that allows preferred shareholders to share with common shareholders in any dividends paid in excess of the percent stated on the preferred shares. (p. 775)

Preemptive right The right to purchase additional shares of common shares issued by the corporation in the future. (p. 768)

Preferred shares Shares that give their owners a priority status over common shareholders in one or more ways, such as the payment of dividends or the distribution of assets on liquidation. (p. 766)

Privately held shares When a corporation offers its shares to only a few shareholders; shares are not for public sale; also called *closely held shares.* (p. 756)

Progressive tax Higher levels of income are taxed at higher rates and lower levels of income are taxed at lower rates. (p. 758)

Proxy A legal document that gives an agent of a shareholder the power to exercise the voting rights of that shareholder's shares. (p. 760)

Publicly held shares When a corporation offers its shares for public sale, which can result in thousands of shareholders. (p. 756)

Public sale Refers to trading in an organized stock market. (p. 756)

Redeemable preferred shares See *callable preferred shares.* (p. 775)

Retained earnings The cumulative net income less losses and dividends retained by a corporation. (p. 761)

Sell shares directly When a corporation advertises its shares' issuance directly to potential buyers. This is most common with privately held corporations. (p. 763)

Sell shares indirectly When a corporation pays a brokerage house (investment banker) to issue its shares. (p. 763)

Share One unit of ownership in a corporation. (p. 756)

Share capital Refers to all types (or classes) of a corporation's shares; also called *capital stock.* (p. 756)

Shareholder(s) The owners of a corporation. (p. 756)

Shareholders' equity The equity of a corporation; also called *corporate capital.* (p. 761)

Statement of retained earnings A financial statement unique to the corporate form of organization that reconciles retained earnings for the period by taking retained earnings

at the beginning of the period, plus net income for the period (or less net loss), less dividends declared for the period, to arrive at retained earnings at the end of the period. (p. 761)

Underwrite When a brokerage house buys the shares from the corporation and takes all gains or losses from its resale to shareholders. (p. 763)

For more study tools, quizzes, and problem material,
refer to the Online Learning Centre at
www.mcgrawhill.ca/college/larson

Questions

1. Who is responsible for directing the affairs of a corporation?

2. What are organization costs? List examples of these costs.

3. How are organization costs classified on the balance sheet?

4. List the general rights of common shareholders.

5. What is the preemptive right of common shareholders?

6. What is the meaning of the *call price* of a share?

7. Why would an investor find convertible preferred shares attractive?

8. Examine the balance sheet for WestJet Airlines in Appendix I at the end of the book and determine the average issue price per common share at December 31, 2002.

9. Refer to the financial statements for Leon's in Appendix I at the end of the book. How many common shares were issued as at December 31, 2002?

Quick Study

QS 15-1
Characteristics of corporations

LO¹

Of the following statements, which are true for the corporation form of business?
a. Capital often is more easily accumulated than with other forms of organization.
b. It has a limited life.
c. Owners have unlimited liability for corporate debts.
d. It is a separate legal entity.
e. Ownership rights cannot be easily transferred.

QS 15-2
Organization of corporations

LO¹

Bentley Inc. incorporated on January 2, 2005. Total costs regarding organization were $56,000. The organizers accepted cash of $50,000 and common shares for the balance. Record Bentley's entries on January 2 and on December 31, the year-end, assuming the organization costs were to be amortized over five years using the straight-line method.

QS 15-3
Corporate financial statements

LO²

Ludwig Ltd. showed the following amounts for its year just ended October 31, 2005. Prepare a multi-step income statement assuming a tax rate of 25%.

Cost of goods sold	$420,000
Gain on sale of capital assets	4,000
Interest expense	6,200
Operating expenses	162,000
Sales	982,000

From the following list of selected accounts for X-cell Inc., identify the shareholder equity accounts. Use "CC" for contributed capital, "RE" for retained earnings, and "X" if not a shareholder equity account.

QS 15-4
Components of shareholders' equity

LO²

	Cash		Preferred shares
	Common shares		Retained earnings
	Common dividend payable		Preferred dividend payable
	Deficit		Preferred shares, $5 non-cumulative

Vision Consulting began operations on January 1, 2005. Complete the following schedule with journal entries detailing the transactions during 2005 for Vision Consulting under two forms of organization, as a single proprietorship (owned by Ian Smith) and as a corporation.

QS 15-5
Corporate financial statements

LO²

	FORM OF BUSINESS ORGANIZATION	
Transaction	**Single Proprietorship**	**Corporation**
Jan. 1, 2005: The owner(s) invested $10,000 into the new business		
During 2005: Revenues of $50,000 were earned; all cash		
During 2005: Expenses of $30,000 were incurred; all cash		
Dec. 15, 2005: $15,000 cash was distributed to the owner(s)		
Dec. 31, 2005, Year-End: All temporary accounts were closed -Close Revenue account		
-Close Expense account		
-Close Income Summary account to appropriate equity account(s)		
-Close Withdrawal/Cash Dividends Declared account		
Equity section on the balance sheet at December 31, 2005 after the first year of operations.	**Vision Consulting Partial Balance Sheet December 31, 2005**	**Vision Consulting Inc. Partial Balance Sheet December 31, 2005**

Benson Inc. had a credit balance in retained earnings on December 31, 2005, of $48,000. During 2006, Benson recorded net income of $146,000 and declared and paid dividends of $47,000. During 2007, the company recorded a net loss of $15,000. No dividends were declared or paid in 2007. Calculate the balance in retained earnings at December 31, 2007.

QS 15-6
Retained earnings

LO²

QS 15-7
Analyzing retained earnings

LO^2

The retained earnings account for Callaho Inc. is shown below:

Retained Earnings		
50,000	120,000	(Balance Jan. 1/05)
	X	
	300,000	(Balance Dec. 31/05)

1. Calculate X.
2. What does X represent?
3. What caused the debit of $50,000?

QS 15-8
Issuance of common shares

LO^3

On February 1, Excel Corporation issued 37,500 common shares for $252,440 cash. On February 12, an additional 47,000 common shares were issued for cash of $7.25 per share. Present the entries to record these transactions and calculate the average issue price per common share.

QS 15-9
Interpreting journal entries for share issuances

LO^3

Each of these entries was recently recorded by a different corporation. Provide an explanation for the transaction described by each entry.

a.	Apr. 1	Cash..	60,000	
		Common Shares		60,000
b.	Apr. 3	Organization Costs............................	90,000	
		Common Shares		90,000
c.	Apr. 5	Merchandise Inventory......................	90,000	
		Machinery...	130,000	
		Notes Payable.............................		144,000
		Common Shares		76,000

QS 15-10
Issuance of preferred shares

LO^3

On October 3, 2005, Allarco Inc. issued 4,000 of its preferred shares for cash of $15 each. On November 19 the company issued 3,400 preferred shares in exchange for land with a fair market value of $52,480.
a. Prepare the entries for October 3 and November 19.
b. Calculate the average issue price per preferred share.

QS 15-11
Accounting for cash dividends

LO^4

Prepare journal entries to record the following transactions for Desmond Corporation:

Apr. 15	Declared a $48,000 cash dividend payable to common shareholders.
June 30	Paid the dividend declared on April 15.
Dec. 31	Closed the Cash Dividends account.

The shareholders' equity section of the Holden Ltd. balance sheet includes 75,000 shares of $0.40 cumulative preferred shares that had been issued for $375,000 and 200,000 common shares issued for a total of $720,000. Holden did not declare any dividends during the prior year and now declares and pays a $108,000 cash dividend. Determine the amount distributed to each class of shareholders.

QS 15-12
Dividend allocation between classes of shareholders

 LO⁵

Refer to the information in QS 15-12. Repeat the question assuming the preferred shares were non-cumulative.

QS 15-13
Dividend allocation between classes of shareholders

 LO⁵

QS 15-14
Components of shareholders' equity

LO³,⁴,⁵

Reese Corporation
Shareholders' Equity
December 31, 2005

Contributed capital:

Preferred shares, $0.50 cumulative; 20,000 shares authorized, issued, and outstanding	$ 200,000
Common shares, unlimited shares authorized; 150,000 shares issued and outstanding	750,000
Total contributed capital	$ 950,000
Retained earnings	890,000
Total shareholders' equity	$1,840,000

Explain each of the following terms included in the shareholders' equity section above:
a. $0.50 cumulative
b. total contributed capital
c. 20,000 shares authorized
d. 150,000 shares issued and outstanding
e. retained earnings

Peter Puck Inc. showed the following adjusted information on May 31, 2005, its year-end:

QS 15-15
Statement of retained earnings, closing entries for a corporation—net income

LO²,⁶

Assets	Liabilities	Common Shares
120,000	40,500	13,000

Preferred Shares	Retained Earnings	Cash Dividends
7,000	29,000	3,500

Revenues	Expenses	Income Summary
92,000	58,000	

a. Prepare the appropriate closing entries.
b. Prepare a statement of retained earnings for the year ended May 31, 2005.

QS 15-16
Statement of retained
earnings, closing entries
for a corporation—net loss

LO2, 6

Morris Inc. showed the following adjusted information on November 30, 2005, its year-end:

Assets		Liabilities		Common Shares	
95,000			18,000		48,000

Preferred Shares		Retained Earnings		Cash Dividends	
	10,000		42,000	14,000	

Revenues		Expenses		Income Summary	
	87,000	96,000			

    a. Prepare the appropriate closing entries.
    b. Prepare a statement of retained earnings for the year ended November 30, 2005.

QS 15-17
Statement of retained
earnings, closing entries
for a corporation—net loss
and deficit

LO2, 6

Velor Ltd. showed the following adjusted information on August 31, 2005, its year-end:

Assets		Liabilities		Common Shares	
75,000			23,000		48,000

Preferred Shares		Retained Earnings		Cash Dividends	
	10,000		12,000	-0-	

Revenues		Expenses		Income Summary	
	76,000	94,000			

    a. Prepare the appropriate closing entries.
    b. Prepare a statement of retained earnings for the year ended August 31, 2005.

*QS 15-18
Book value per common share

LO7

Courtland Corporation **Shareholders' Equity** **December 31, 2005**	
Contributed capital:	
Preferred shares, $5 cumulative, 10,000 shares authorized, issued and outstanding	$100,000
Common shares, 100,000 shares authorized; 75,000 shares issued and outstanding...................................	375,000
Total contributed capital	$475,000
Retained earnings	445,000
Total shareholders' equity	$920,000

The call price of the preferred shares is $30. Using the information provided, determine
Courtland's book value per common share under the assumption that there are no
dividends in arrears.

*QS 15-19
Book value per common share

LO7

Refer to the information in *QS 15-18. Repeat the question assuming there are three
years of dividends in arrears.

An asterisk (*) identifies assignment material based on Appendix 15A.

Write a brief description of how each of the following eight general characteristics of business organizations applies to corporations and general partnerships.

Exercise 15-1
Characteristics of corporations and partnerships

	Corporations	General Partnerships
1. Life		
2. Owners' liability		
3. Legal status		
4. Tax status of income		
5. Owners' authority		
6. Ease of formation		
7. Transferability of ownership		
8. Ability to raise large amounts of capital		

Tom Seabrink and Joan Miller began a new business on February 14 when each of them invested $125,000 in the company. On December 20, it was decided that $48,000 of the company's cash would be distributed equally between the owners. Two cheques for $24,000 were prepared and given to the owners on December 23. On December 31, the company reported a $96,000 net income.

Prepare two sets of journal entries to record the investments by the owners, the distribution of cash to the owners, the closing of the Income Summary account, and the withdrawals or dividends under these alternative assumptions:
a. the business is a partnership, and
b. the business is a corporation that issued 1,000 common shares.

Exercise 15-2
Comparative entries for partnership and corporation

Prepare journal entries for each of the following selected transactions that occurred during W-Alert Inc.'s first year of operations:

Exercise 15-3
Issuing shares

2005
Jan. 15   Issued 2,000 common shares to the corporation's promoters in exchange for their efforts in creating it. Their efforts are estimated to be worth $45,000.
Feb. 21   15,000 common shares were issued for cash of $20 per share.
Mar. 9   6,000 preferred shares were issued for cash totalling $158,000.
Aug. 15   55,000 common shares were issued in exchange for land, building, and equipment with appraised values of $450,000, $600,000, and $160,000 respectively.

Hanson Inc. began operations on June 5, 2005. Journalize the following shareholders' equity transactions that occurred during the first month of operations:

Exercise 15-4
Issuing shares

2005
June 5   Gave 4,000 common shares to the organizers of the corporation in exchange for accounting and legal services valued at $65,000.
17   Received $17 cash per share for the issuance of 75,000 common shares.
18   Issued 10,000 preferred shares for cash of $30 per share.
19   8,000 common shares were issued to a creditor who was owed $100,000.
26   Issued an additional 5,000 preferred shares for cash totalling $155,000.
30   150,000 common shares were issued in exchange for machinery with a fair market value of $2,000,000. The shares were actively trading on this date at $13.20 per share.

Exercise 15-5
Issuing shares in exchange
for building and land

LO³

On July 25, United Corporation issued 20,000 common shares for a building and land. The market value of the building and land was $300,000. A comparable land site recently sold for $60,000. Give the entry to record the acquisition.

Exercise 15-6
Issuing shares;
shareholders' equity

LO²,³,⁶

Lindsay Ltd. was authorized to issue an unlimited number of common shares. During January 2005, its first month of operations, the following selected transactions occurred:

> Jan. 1 1,000 shares were issued to the organizers of the corporation. The total value of the shares was determined to be $8,000.
>   5 15,000 shares were sold to various shareholders for $9.00 each.
>   10 3,000 shares were issued for total cash of $31,500.
>   20 4,000 shares were issued in exchange for land valued at $32,000. The shares were actively trading on this date at $10.75 per share.
>   31 Closed the Income Summary account, which showed a credit balance of $110,000.

Check figure:
b. Total shareholders'
equity = $327,500

Required
a. Journalize the above transactions.
b. Prepare the shareholders' equity section of the balance sheet of Lindsay Ltd. at January 31, 2005.
c. What was the average issue price per common share?

Exercise 15-7
Share transactions,
shareholders' equity

LO²,³

ABC Inc. was authorized to issue 50,000 $2.00 preferred shares and 300,000 common shares. During 2005, its first year of operations, the following selected transactions occurred:

> Jan. 1 5,000 of the preferred shares were issued at $10.00 per share; cash.
> Feb. 5 15,000 of the common shares were issued for a total of $105,000; cash.
> Mar. 20 3,000 of the common shares were given to the organizers of the corporation regarding their efforts. The shares were valued at a total of $24,000.
> May 15 12,000 preferred shares and 20,000 common shares were issued at $11.00 and $8.00 respectively; cash.
> Dec. 31 The Income Summary account was closed; it showed a debit balance of $235,000. December 31 is ABC Inc.'s year-end.

Check figure:
b. Total shareholders'
equity = $236,000

Required
a. Journalize the above transactions.
b. Prepare the shareholders' equity section of the ABC Inc. balance sheet at December 31, 2005.
c. The preferred shares are described as *"$2.00 preferred shares."* Explain what the $2.00 means.

Exercise 15-8
Cash dividend

LO⁴

On March 1, the board of directors declared a cash dividend of $0.25 per common share to shareholders of record on March 10, payable March 31. There were 75,000 shares issued and outstanding on March 1 and no additional shares had been issued during the month. Record the entries for March 1, 10, and 31.

The December 31, 2005, shareholders' equity section of the balance sheet of Maritime Inc. appears below.

Maritime Inc. Shareholders' Equity December 31, 2005	
Contributed capital:	
Preferred shares, $4.50 cumulative,	
40,000 shares authorized and issued	$2,000,000
Preferred shares, $12 non-cumulative,	
8,000 shares authorized and issued	800,000
Common shares, 400,000 shares authorized and issued	2,000,000
Total contributed capital	$4,800,000
Retained earnings...	890,000
Total shareholders' equity	$5,690,000

Required
All the shares were issued on January 1, 2003 (when the corporation began operations). No dividends had been declared during the first two years of operations (2003 and 2004). During 2005, the cash dividends declared and paid totalled $736,000.
1. Calculate the amount of cash dividends paid during 2005 to each of the three classes of shares.
2. Assuming net income earned during 2005 was $1,500,000, determine the December 31, **2004**, balance in retained earnings.
3. Prepare a statement of retained earnings for the year ended December 31, 2005.

Star Inc. showed the following shareholders' equity as at December 31, 2005:

Star Inc. Shareholders' Equity December 31, 2005	
Contributed capital:	
Preferred shares, $1.50 non-cumulative; 100,000 shares authorized	
75,000 shares issued and outstanding	**A**
Common shares; unlimited shares authorized;	
E shares issued and outstanding..	**B**
Total contributed capital	$3,125,000
Retained earnings	**C**
Total shareholders' equity	**D**

Other information:
a. The preferred shares had sold for an average price of $15.00.
b. The common shares had sold for an average price of $8.00.
c. Retained Earnings at December 31, 2004, was $80,000. During 2005, net income earned was $720,000. The board of directors declared a total cash dividend of $225,000.

Required
Calculate A, B, C, D, and E.

Exercise 15-11

Share transactions, distribution of dividends, shareholders' equity

LO¹, 2, 3, 4, 5

Selected T-accounts for Watson Corporation at December 31, 2005, are duplicated below.

Preferred Shares, $5 cumulative 10,000 shares authorized 8,000 shares issued		
	160,000	Dec. 31/04 Bal.
	160,000	Dec. 31/05 Bal.

Common Shares, 50,000 shares authorized 45,000 shares issued		
	450,000	Dec. 31/04 Bal.
	450,000	Dec. 31/05 Bal.

Retained Earnings		
	105,000	Dec. 31/04 Bal.
	????	Dec. 31/05 Bal.

Note: • Dividends were not paid during 2003 or 2004. Dividends of $4 per common share were declared and paid for the year ended December 31, 2005.
• 2003 was the first year of operations.
• All shares were issued in the first year of operations.

Required

Using the information provided, answer the following questions.

1. What is the total amount of dividends that the preferred shareholders are entitled to receive per year?
2. Are there any dividends in arrears at December 31, 2004? If yes, calculate the dividends in arrears.
3. Calculate total dividends paid during 2005 to the:
   a. Preferred Shareholders.
   b. Common Shareholders.
4. During 2005, the company earned a net income of $340,000. Calculate the balance in the Retained Earnings account at the end of 2005.
5. Calculate Total Contributed Capital at the end of 2005.
6. Calculate Total Shareholders' Equity at December 31, 2005.
7. How many more preferred shares are available for issue at December 31, 2005?
8. What was the average issue price per share of the preferred shares at December 31, 2005?

Exercise 15-12

Allocating dividends between common and cumulative preferred shares

LO⁵

The outstanding share capital of Kuker Realty Corporation includes 47,000 shares of $4 cumulative preferred and 82,000 common shares, all issued during the first year of operations. During its first four years of operation, the corporation declared and paid the following amounts in dividends:

Year	Total Dividends Declared
2005	$ -0-
2006	200,000
2007	420,000
2008	200,000

Determine the total dividends paid in each year to each class of shareholders. Also determine the total dividends paid to each class over the four years.

Exercise 15-13

Allocating dividends between common and non-cumulative preferred shares

LO⁵

Determine the total dividends paid in each year to each class of shareholders of Exercise 15-12 under the assumption that the preferred shares are non-cumulative. Also determine the total dividends paid to each class over the four years.

Match each of the numbered descriptions with the characteristic of preferred shares that it best describes. Indicate your answer by writing the letter for the correct characteristic in the blank space next to each description.

A. Callable or redeemable   D. Non-cumulative
B. Convertible   E. Non-participating
C. Cumulative   F. Participating

_____ 1. The holders of the shares can exchange them for common shares.
_____ 2. The issuing corporation can retire the shares by paying a prearranged price.
_____ 3. The holders of the shares are entitled to receive dividends in excess of the stated rate under some conditions.
_____ 4. The holders of the shares are not entitled to receive dividends in excess of the stated rate.
_____ 5. The holders of the shares lose any dividends that are not declared.
_____ 6. The holders of the shares are entitled to receive current and all past dividends before common shareholders receive any dividends.

Exercise 15-14
Identifying characteristics
of preferred shares

LO^5

Almarat Trading Corporation has the following outstanding shares:

> 15,000 shares, $4.50 cumulative preferred
> 35,000 shares, common

During 2005, Almarat declared and paid $150,000 in dividends. Dividends were in arrears for the previous year (2004) only. No new shares have been issued since the first year of operations.

Required
1. What was the total amount paid to the preferred shareholders as dividends in 2005?
2. What was the total amount paid to the common shareholders as dividends in 2005?

Exercise 15-15
Dividend allocation

LO^5

JetSki Inc. showed the following alphabetized list of adjusted account balances at December 31, 2005:

Accounts Payable	9,200	Income Tax Expense	14,500
Accounts Receivable	14,000	Land	42,000
Accum. Amort., Equip.	3,800	Notes Payable, due in 2008	12,000
Accum. Amort., Warehouse	7,600	Operating Expenses	39,000
Cash	3,000	Preferred Shares	14,000
Cash Dividends	7,000	Retained Earnings	9,900
Common Shares	40,000	Revenue	97,000
Equipment	28,000	Warehouse	46,000

Required
Assuming normal balances, prepare the closing entries at December 31, 2005, JetSki's year-end. Also, calculate the post-closing balance in Retained Earnings at December 31, 2005.

Exercise 15-16
Closing entries for a corporation

LO^6

Check figure:
Retained earnings,
Dec. 31/05 = $46,400

Using the information in Exercise 15-16, prepare a classified balance sheet at December 31, 2005, and then answer each of the following questions (assume that the preferred shares are non-cumulative):
1. What percentage of the total assets is owned by the shareholders?
2. What percentage of JetSki Inc. is equity financed?
3. What percentage of JetSki Inc. is financed by debt?
4. The common shareholders own what percentage of the total assets?
5. What percentage of the assets is financed by the preferred shareholders?
6. What are the advantages to the common shareholders of issuing preferred shares over additional common shares?

Exercise 15-17
Analysis of shareholders' equity

$LO^{1,2,3,4,5,6}$

Check figure:
Total assets = $121,600

Exercise 15-18

Share transactions, distribution of dividends, shareholders' equity, closing

LO 1, 2, 3, 4, 5, 6

The shareholders' equity section of the balance sheet for DWF Inc. showed the following on December 31, 2004:

DWF Inc. Shareholders' Equity December 31, 2004	
Contributed capital:	
Preferred shares, $0.75 cumulative; 80,000 shares authorized;	
60,000 shares issued and outstanding	$300,000
Common shares; 250,000 shares authorized;	
120,000 shares issued and outstanding	240,000
Total contributed capital	$540,000
Retained earnings..	185,000
Total shareholders' equity	$725,000

During the year 2005, DWF Inc. had the following transactions affecting shareholders' equity accounts:

Jan.	3	Sold 20,000 common shares for a total of $43,000 cash
Mar.	1	Sold 5,000 preferred shares at $6.00 each; cash.
June	15	Exchanged 7,000 common shares for equipment with a fair market value of $20,000. The last common share trade was dated March 15 at $6.15.
Dec.	31	Closed the Income Summary account, which showed a credit balance of $350,000.

The board of directors had not declared dividends for the past two years (2004 and 2005).

Check figure:
2. Total shareholders' equity = $1,168,000

Required
1. Journalize the above transactions.
2. Prepare the shareholders' equity section as at December 31, 2005.
3. How many preferred shares are available for issue at December 31, 2005?
4. How many common shares are available for issue at December 31, 2005?

Exercise 15-19

Share transactions, dividend distribution, balance sheet, closing

LO 2, 3, 4, 5, 6

ABC Inc. began a very lucrative consulting operation on October 1, 2005. It is authorized to issue 100,000 shares of $0.50 cumulative preferred shares and 500,000 common shares.

Part A

Required
Prepare journal entries for each of the transactions listed.

Oct.	1	Issued for cash, 1,000 shares of the preferred shares at $4.00 each.
	10	Issued for cash, 50,000 shares of the common stock at $3.00 per share.
	12	The accountant responsible for organizing the corporation accepted 2,500 preferred shares in exchange for her services valued at $11,250.
	15	ABC Inc. purchased land for $155,000, paying cash of $55,000 and borrowing the balance from the bank (to be repaid in two years).
	20	15,000 preferred shares were issued today for total cash proceeds of $70,500.
	24	In addition to the declaration of the annual dividend on the preferred shares, dividends of $22,400 were declared on the common shares today.
	31	Revenues of $750,000 were earned during the month; all cash. Expenses, all cash, totalling $250,000 were incurred in October. Close the Income Summary and dividend accounts.

Part B

Check figure:
B. Total assets = $835,750; Total shareholders' equity = $704,100

Required
Based on the transactions in Part A, prepare the balance sheet as at October 31, 2005.

Kuhn Corp.
Shareholders' Equity
December 31, 2005

Contributed capital:

Preferred shares, $1.50 cumulative, $30 call price, 5,000 shares issued and outstanding	$125,000
Common shares, 40,000 shares issued and outstanding	400,000
Total contributed capital	$525,000
Retained earnings	267,500
Total shareholders' equity	$792,500

Using the information above, calculate the book value per share of the preferred and common shares under these two situations:

a. No preferred dividends are in arrears.
b. Three years of preferred dividends are in arrears.

*Exercise 15-20

Book value per share

LO[7]

Check figures:
a. Book value of common shares = $16.06
b. Book value of common shares = $15.50

Problems

Using the information from the alphabetized post-closing trial balance below, prepare a classified balance sheet for Southgate Inc. as at March 31, 2005. *Be sure to use proper form, including all appropriate subtotals.*

Account Description	Account Balance*
Accounts Payable	$17,000
Accounts Receivable	33,000
Accumulated Amortization	124,000
Cash	24,000
Common Shares 100,000 shares authorized; 25,000 shares were issued at an average price of $7; market price per share on March 31, 2005 was $8	????
Equipment	390,000
Retained Earnings	????
Unearned Consulting Revenue	9,000

Assume that all accounts have normal balances.

Problem 15-1A
Corporate balance sheet preparation

LO[2]

Check figures:
Total assets = $323,000;
Total shareholders' equity = $297,000

An asterisk (*) identifies assignment material based on Appendix 15A.

Problem 15-2A
Retained earnings, dividends

LO²,⁴

The equity sections from the 2005 and 2006 balance sheets of Dylex Corporation appeared as follows:

**Dylex Corporation
Shareholders' Equity
December 31, 2005**

Contributed capital:	
Common shares, unlimited shares authorized,	
96,000 shares issued and outstanding	$ 688,000
Retained earnings	558,608
Total shareholders' equity	$1,246,608

**Dylex Corporation
Shareholders' Equity
December 31, 2006**

Contributed capital:	
Common shares, unlimited shares authorized,	
115,200 shares issued and outstanding	$ 833,920
Retained earnings	459,600
Total shareholders' equity	$1,293,520

On March 16, June 15, September 5, and again on November 22, 2006, the board of directors declared $0.20 per share cash dividends on the outstanding common shares. On October 14, 2006, additional common shares issued were 19,200.

Required

Under the assumption that there were no transactions affecting retained earnings other than the ones given, determine the 2006 net income (net loss) of Dylex Corporation. Show your calculations.

Problem 15-3A
Convertible preferred shares

LO⁴,⁵

**Chandy Corp.
Shareholders' Equity
March 31, 2005**

Contributed capital:	
Preferred shares, $8 cumulative, 2,500 shares	
authorized, issued and outstanding	$250,000
Common shares, unlimited shares authorized,	
40,000 shares issued and outstanding	400,000
Total contributed capital	$650,000
Retained earnings	192,500
Total shareholders' equity	$842,500

Required

a. Refer to the shareholders' equity section above. Assume that the preferred is convertible into common at a rate of eight common shares for each share of preferred. If 1,000 shares of the preferred are converted into common on April 1, 2005, prepare the entry and describe how this affects the shareholders' equity section of the balance sheet (immediately after the conversion).

b. If you are a common shareholder in this company, and the company plans to pay total cash dividends of $300,000, does it make any difference to you whether or not the conversion takes place before the dividend declaration? Why?

Use the information provided below to answer the following questions.

Problem 15-4A
Analyzing shareholders' equity, dividend allocation

LO[2, 5]

Northstar Corp.
Partial Balance Sheet
October 31, 2005

Shareholders' Equity

Contributed capital:

Preferred shares, $2.50 non-cumulative; unlimited shares authorized,

   A   shares issued and outstanding.. $450,000

Common shares, unlimited shares authorized,

   325,000 shares issued and outstanding... **B**

   Total contributed capital .... **C**

Deficit.. **D**

Total shareholders' equity $2,890,000

Other Information:
- All of the shares were issued during the first year of operations (year ended October 31, 2004).
- The common shares were issued for an average price of $8 per share.
- The preferred shares were issued for an average price of $15 per share.
- Retained Earnings at October 31, 2004, was $320,000. No dividends had been paid for the year ended October 31, 2005.

Required
1. Calculate A.
2. Calculate B.
3. Calculate C.
4. Calculate D.
5. Calculate Net Income (Net Loss) for the year ended October 31, 2005.
6. Assume cash dividends of $100,000 were paid during the year ended October 31, 2004. Calculate the total dividends actually paid during the year ended October 31, 2004 to the:
   a. preferred shareholders.
   b. common shareholders.
7. Referring to your answers in (6) above, calculate the dividends *per share* actually received by the:
   a. preferred shareholders.
   b. common shareholders.
8. Are there any dividends in arrears as at October 31, 2005? If yes, calculate the amount of the arrears.
9. Explain the difference between "Retained Earnings" and "Deficit."

Gulf Corp. has the following shares, taken from the shareholders' equity section of its balance sheet dated December 31, 2005.

Problem 15-5A
Dividend allocation

LO[5]

Preferred shares, $2.80 non-cumulative,	
45,000 shares authorized and issued*..	1,800,000
Common shares,	
80,000 shares authorized and issued*..	800,000

All shares were issued during 2003.

During its first three years of operations, Gulf Corp. declared and paid total dividends as shown in the last column of the following schedule.

Required

Part A

Complete the following schedule by filling in the shaded areas.

1. Calculate the total dividends paid in each year to the preferred and to the common shareholders.

Year	Preferred Dividend	Common Dividend	Total Dividend
2003			100,000
2004			250,000
2005			350,000
Total for three years			700,000

2. Calculate the dividends paid *per share* to both the preferred and the common shares in 2005.

Part B

Repeat the requirements in Part A assuming the preferred shares are cumulative.

Problem 15-6A

Share transactions, dividends, statement of retained earnings, shareholders' equity

LO 2, 3, 4, 5, 6

The balance sheet for the Trevor Corporation reported the following components of shareholders' equity on December 31, 2005:

Common shares, unlimited shares authorized, 20,000 shares issued and outstanding	$230,000
Retained earnings	135,000
Total shareholders' equity	$365,000

In 2006, Trevor Corporation had the following transactions affecting shareholders and the shareholder equity accounts:

Jan.	5	The directors declared a $2.00 per share cash dividend payable on Feb. 28 to the Feb. 5 shareholders of record.
Feb.	28	Paid the dividend declared on January 5.
July	6	Sold 750 common shares at $24 per share.
Aug.	22	Sold 1,250 common shares at $17 per share.
Sept.	5	The directors declared a $2.00 per share cash dividend payable on Oct. 28 to the Oct. 5 shareholders of record.
Oct.	28	Paid the dividend declared on September 5.
Dec.	31	Closed the $217,000 credit balance in the Income Summary account.
	31	Closed the Cash Dividends account.

Check figures:

2. Retained earnings, December 31/06 = $268,000
3. Total shareholders' equity = $537,250

Required

1. Prepare journal entries to record the transactions and closings for 2006.
2. Prepare a statement of retained earnings for the year ended December 31, 2006.
3. Prepare the shareholders' equity section of the corporation's balance sheet as of December 31, 2006.

Doucette Corp. was legally incorporated on January 2, 2005. Its articles of incorporation granted it the right to issue an unlimited number of common shares and 100,000 shares of $6 non-cumulative preferred shares. The following transactions are among those that occurred during the first three years of operations:

2005

Jan. 12 Issued 40,000 common shares at $2 each.

20 Issued 6,000 common shares to promoters who provided legal services that helped to establish the company. These services had a fair value of $15,000.

31 Issued 80,000 common shares in exchange for land, building, and equipment, which have a fair market value of $150,000, $200,000, and $20,000 respectively.

Mar. 4 Purchased equipment at a cost of $3,400 cash. This was thought to be a special bargain price. It was felt that at least $4,500 would normally have had to be paid to acquire this equipment.

Dec. 31 During 2005, Doucette Corp. incurred a net loss of $40,000. The Income Summary account was closed.

2006

Jan. 4 Issued 5,000 preferred shares at $30 per share.

Dec. 31 The Income Summary account was closed. Net income for 2006 was $90,000.

2007

Dec. 4 The company declared a cash dividend of $0.05 per share on the common shares payable on December 18 and also declared the required dividend on the preferred shares.

18 Paid the dividends declared on December 4.

31 Net income for the year ended December 31, 2007, was $80,000. The Income Summary and Cash Dividends accounts were closed.

Required

1. Journalize the transactions for the years 2005, 2006, and 2007.

2. Prepare the statement of retained earnings for the year ended December 31, 2007.

3. Prepare the shareholders' equity section as of December 31, 2007.

Problem 15-7A
Share transactions, statement of retained earnings, shareholders' equity, dividend distribution, closing

LO 2, 3, 4, 5, 6

Check figure:
3. Total shareholders' equity = $708,700

The balance sheet for the Oppong Corporation, provincially incorporated in 2003, reported the following components of shareholders' equity on December 31, 2004.

Oppong Corporation
Shareholders' Equity
December 31, 2004

Contributed capital:	
Preferred shares, $0.75 cumulative, unlimited shares authorized;	
20,000 shares issued and outstanding	$140,000
Common shares, unlimited shares authorized;	
75,000 shares issued and outstanding.	262,500
Total contributed capital	$402,500
Retained earnings	135,000
Total shareholders' equity	$537,500

Problem 15-8A
Share transactions, dividends, statement of retained earnings, shareholders' equity

LO 2, 3, 4, 5, 6

In 2005 and 2006, Oppong Corporation had the following transactions affecting shareholders and the shareholder equity accounts:

> **2005**
> Jan. 1   Sold 30,000 common shares at $3.80 per share.
>   5   The directors declared a total cash dividend of $82,500 payable on Feb. 28 to the Feb. 5 shareholders of record. Dividends had not been declared for the years 2003 and 2004. All of the preferred shares had been issued during 2003.
> Feb. 28   Paid the dividends declared on January 5.
> July 1   Sold preferred shares for a total of $56,000. The average issue price was $8 per share.
> Dec. 31   Closed the dividend accounts along with the $206,000 credit balance in the Income Summary account.
> **2006**
> Sept. 5   The directors declared the required cash dividend on the preferred shares and a $0.50 per common share cash dividend payable on Oct. 28 to the Oct. 5 shareholders of record.
> Oct. 28   Paid the dividends declared on September 5.
> Dec. 31   Closed the cash dividend account along with the $194,000 credit balance in the Income Summary account.

Check figures:

2. Retained earnings,
   Dec. 31/06 = $379,750
3. Shareholders' equity,
   Dec. 31/06 = $952,250

Required

1. Prepare journal entries to record the transactions and closings for 2005 and 2006.
2. Prepare a statement of retained earnings for the year ended December 31, 2006.
3. Prepare the shareholders' equity section of the company's balance sheet as of December 31, 2006.

---

*Problem 15-9A
Book value per share

LO⁷

Segura Corporation's common shares are currently selling on a stock exchange at $170 per share, and a recent balance sheet shows the following information:

Segura Corporation Shareholders' Equity April 30, 2005	
Contributed capital:	
Preferred shares, $5 cumulative, 1,000 shares authorized, issued and outstanding	$100,000
Common shares, 4,000 shares authorized, issued, and outstanding	160,000
Total contributed capital	$260,000
Retained earnings	300,000
Total shareholders' equity	$560,000

Check figures:

3. Book value per common
   share = $115.00
4. Book value per common
   share = $112.50
5. Book value per common
   share = $110.00

Required

Preparation component:

1. What is the market value of the corporation's common shares?
2. How much capital was contributed by the residual owners of the company?
3. If no dividends are in arrears, what are the book values per share of the preferred shares and the common shares?
4. If two years' preferred dividends are in arrears, what are the book values per share of the preferred shares and the common shares?
5. If two years' preferred dividends are in arrears and the preferred shares are callable at $110 per share, what are the book values per share of the preferred shares and the common shares?

An asterisk (*) identifies assignment material based on Appendix 15A.

6. If two years' preferred dividends are in arrears and the board of directors declares dividends of $20,000, what total amount will be paid to preferred and common shareholders? What is the amount of dividends per share for the common shares?

Analysis component:

7. What are some factors that may contribute to the difference between the book value of common shares and their market value?

On December 31, 2005, Meloche Inc. showed the following:

*Problem 15-10A
Calculating book value

LO^7

Meloche Inc. **Shareholders' Equity** **December 31, 2005**	
Contributed capital:	
Preferred shares, $2, unlimited shares authorized,	
10,000 shares issued and outstanding*	$110,000
Common shares, unlimited shares authorized,	
25,000 shares issued and outstanding*	162,500
Total contributed capital	$272,500
Retained earnings	340,000
Total shareholders' equity	$612,500

*All of the shares had been issued early in 2004.

Required

Part 1:
Calculate book value per common share and preferred share at December 31, 2005, assuming no dividends were declared for the years ended December 31, 2004 or 2005, and that the preferred shares are:
a. Cumulative,
b. Non-cumulative.

Part 2 (independent of Part 1):
Calculate book value per common share and preferred share at December 31, 2005, assuming total dividends of $32,500 were declared and paid in each of the years ended December 31, 2004 or 2005, and that the preferred shares are:
c. Cumulative,
d. Non-cumulative.

Part 3 (independent of Parts 1 and 2):
e. Calculate book value per common share and preferred share at December 31, 2005, assuming:
– Preferred shares are cumulative, and callable at $15 per share, and
– Dividends were not declared for the years ended December 31, 2004 and 2005.

Check figures:
Book value per common
a. $18.50
c. $20.10
e. $16.90

_____

An asterisk (*) identifies assignment material based on Appendix 15A.

Alternate Problems

Problem 15-1B
Corporate balance sheet preparation

LO²

Check figures:
Total assets = $4,561,000;
Total shareholders'
equity = $3,695,000

Using the information from the alphabetized post-closing trial balance below, prepare a classified balance sheet for JenStar Inc. as at October 31, 2005. Be sure to use proper form, including all appropriate subtotals.

Account Description	Account Balance*
Accounts Payable	$ 158,000
Accounts Receivable	225,000
Accumulated Amortization—Building	833,000
Accumulated Amortization—Machinery	763,000
Building	2,875,000
Cash	355,000
Common shares (unlimited shares authorized; 50,000 shares issued at an average price of $32 per share; market price per share on October 31, 2005, $57)	????
Land	1,000,000
Long-Term Notes Payable (due in 2009)	550,000
Machinery	1,600,000
Office Supplies	85,000
Preferred shares ($1.50 non-cumulative, unlimited shares authorized; 30,000 shares issued at an average price of $40 per share; market price per share on October 31, 2005, $60)	???
Prepaid Insurance	17,000
Retained Earnings	???
Unearned Fees	28,000
Wages Payable	130,000

Assume all accounts have normal balances.

Problem 15-2B
Retained earnings, dividends

LO²,⁴

The equity sections from the 2005 and 2006 balance sheets of Henns Corporation appeared as follows:

Henns Corporation
Shareholders' Equity
December 31, 2005

Contributed capital:	
Common shares, unlimited shares authorized,	
350,000 shares issued	$ 8,750,000
Retained earnings	1,960,720
Total shareholders' equity	$10,710,720

Henns Corporation
Shareholders' Equity
December 31, 2006

Contributed capital:	
Common shares, unlimited shares authorized,	
385,000 shares issued	$ 9,660,000
Retained earnings	2,200,500
Total shareholders' equity	$11,860,500

On February 11, May 24, August 13, and again on December 12, 2006, the board of directors declared $0.25 per share cash dividends on the outstanding shares. 15,000 common shares were issued on August 1, 2006, and another 20,000 were issued on November 2, 2006.

Required

Under the assumption that there were no transactions affecting retained earnings other than the ones given, determine the 2006 net income of Henns Corporation. Show your calculations.

Sembaluk Corp.
Shareholders' Equity
November 30, 2005

Contributed capital:

Preferred shares, $11 cumulative,	
2,000 shares authorized and issued..	$ 200,000
Common shares, unlimited shares authorized; 60,000 shares issued............	600,000
Total contributed capital	$ 800,000
Retained earnings	420,000
Total shareholders' equity	$1,220,000

Problem 15-3B
Convertible preferred shares

LO^{4,5}

Required

a. Refer to the shareholders' equity section above. Assume that the preferred shares are convertible into common at a rate of eight common shares for each share of preferred. If 1,000 shares of the preferred are converted into common shares on December 1, 2005, prepare the entry and describe how this affects the shareholders' equity section of the balance sheet (immediately after the conversion).

b. If you are a common shareholder in this company, and it plans to pay total cash dividends of $487,000, does it make a difference to you whether or not the conversion takes place before the dividend declaration? Why?

JenCo Inc.
Partial Balance Sheet
October 31, 2005

Shareholders' Equity

Contributed capital:

Preferred shares, $8 cumulative, unlimited shares authorized,	
45,000 shares issued and outstanding...	**A**
Preferred shares, $5 non-cumulative, unlimited shares authorized,	
B shares issued and outstanding:	3,800,000
Common shares, unlimited shares authorized,	
265,000 shares issued and outstanding..	**C**
Total contributed capital..	**D**
Retained earnings..	**E**
Total shareholders' equity	**F**

Problem 15-4B
Analyzing shareholders' equity, dividend allocation

LO^{2,5}

Required

1. Calculate A assuming an average issue price of $20 per share.
2. Calculate B assuming an average issue price of $100 per share.
3. Calculate C assuming the average issue price was $5 per share.
4. Calculate D.
5. Calculate E assuming that JenCo Inc. showed net incomes (losses) for the years ended October 31, 2002, 2003, 2004, and 2005, of $2,500,000, $1,750,000, $1,300,000, and ($2,200,000) respectively. Dividends totalling $1,200,000 were declared and paid during the first year ended October 31, 2002. No other dividends have been declared to date.
6. Calculate F.
7. Calculate any dividends in arrears as at October 31, 2005 (all of the shares were issued early in 2002).

Problem 15-5B
Dividend allocation

LO⁵

XYZ Corporation has issued and outstanding a total of 40,000 shares of $12 preferred shares and 120,000 of common shares. The company began operations and issued both classes of shares on January 1, 2004.

Required

1. Calculate the total dividends to be paid to each group of shareholders in each year by completing the following chart. Assume that the preferred shares are cumulative.

Year	Dividends Declared and Paid	Preferred Dividends	Common Dividends
2004	600,000		
2005	100,000		
2006	250,000		
2007	1,500,000		

2. Calculate the total dividends to be paid to each group of shareholders in each year by completing the following chart. Assume that the preferred shares are non-cumulative.

Year	Dividends Declared and Paid	Preferred Dividends	Common Dividends
2004	600,000		
2005	100,000		
2006	250,000		
2007	1,500,000		

Problem 15-6B
Share transactions, statement of retained earnings, shareholders' equity, dividend distribution, closing

LO²,³,⁴,⁵,⁶

The balance sheet for Caldwell Corp. reported the following components of shareholders' equity on December 31, 2005:

Common shares, unlimited shares authorized,	
100,000 shares issued and outstanding...	$ 800,000
Retained earnings...	1,080,000
Total shareholders' equity...	$1,880,000

The company completed these transactions during 2006:

Mar.	2	The directors declared a $1.50 per share cash dividend payable on March 31 to the March 15 shareholders of record.
	31	Paid the dividend declared on March 2.
Nov.	11	Issued 12,000 common shares at $13 per share.
	25	Issued 8,000 common shares at $9.50 per share.
Dec.	1	The directors declared a $2.50 per share cash dividend payable on January 2, 2007, to the December 10 shareholders of record.
	31	Closed the $536,000 credit balance in the Income Summary account to Retained Earnings.
	31	Closed the Cash Dividends account.

Check figures:

2. Retained earnings,
   December 31 = $1,166,000
3. Total shareholders' equity
   = $2,198,000

Required

1. Prepare General Journal entries to record the transactions and closings for 2006.
2. Prepare a statement of retained earnings for the year ended December 31, 2006.
3. Prepare the shareholders' equity section of the company's balance sheet as of December 31, 2006.

Problem 15-7B
Share transactions, statement
of retained earnings,
shareholders' equity, dividend
distribution, closing

LO 2, 3, 4, 5, 6

Solar Energy Company Inc. is authorized to issue an unlimited number of common shares and 100,000 shares of $10 non-cumulative preferred. The company completed the following transactions:

2005
Feb. 5   Issued 70,000 common shares at $10 for cash.
      28   Gave the corporation's promoters 3,750 common shares for their services in organizing the corporation. The directors valued the services at $40,000.
Mar. 3   Issued 44,000 common shares in exchange for the following assets with the indicated reliable market values: land, $80,000; buildings, $210,000; and machinery, $155,000.
Dec. 31   Closed the Income Summary account. A $27,000 loss was incurred.
2006
Jan. 28   Issued for cash 4,000 preferred shares at $100 per share.
Dec. 31   Closed the Income Summary account. A $98,000 net income was earned.
2007
Jan. 1   The board of directors declared a $10 per share cash dividend to preferred shares and $0.20 per share cash dividend to outstanding common shares, payable on February 5 to the January 24 shareholders of record.
Feb. 5   Paid the previously declared dividends.
Dec. 31   Closed the Cash Dividends and Income Summary accounts. A $159,000 net income was earned.

Required
1. Prepare General Journal entries to record the transactions.
2. Prepare a statement of retained earnings for the year ended December 31, 2007.
3. Prepare the shareholders' equity section of the balance sheet as of the close of business on December 31, 2007.

Check figures:
2. Retained earnings,
December 31 = $166,450
3. Total shareholders'
equity = $1,751,450

Problem 15-8B
Share transactions, dividends,
statement of retained earnings,
shareholders' equity

LO 2, 3, 4, 5, 6

Francois Corp. began operations in 2004. Its balance sheet reported the following components of shareholders' equity on December 31, 2004:

Francois Corp. Shareholders' Equity December 31, 2004	
Contributed capital:	
Preferred shares, $0.75 non-cumulative, unlimited shares authorized; 100,000 shares issued and outstanding	$1,300,000
Common shares, unlimited shares authorized; 650,000 shares issued and outstanding	2,925,000
Total contributed capital	$4,225,000
Retained earnings	1,135,000
Total shareholders' equity	$5,360,000

The corporation completed these transactions during 2005 and 2006:

2005
Jan. 1   Sold 130,000 common shares at $4.75 per share.
      5   The directors declared its first cash dividend totalling $270,000 payable on Feb. 28 to the Feb. 5 shareholders of record.
Feb. 28   Paid the dividends declared on January 5.
July 1   Issued preferred shares for a total of $675,000. The average issue price was $13.50 per share.
Dec. 31   Closed the dividend accounts along with the Income Summary account, which reflected net income earned during 2005 of $320,000.

2006
Sept. 5   The directors declared a $0.75 cash dividend per preferred share and a $0.25 per common share cash dividend payable on Oct. 28 to the Oct. 5 shareholders of record.
Oct. 28   Paid the dividends declared on September 5.
Dec. 31   Closed the dividend accounts along with the $480,000 debit balance in the Income Summary account.

Check figures:
2. Retained earnings,
   Dec. 31/06 = $397,500
3. Shareholders' equity,
   Dec. 31/06 = $5,915,000

Required
1. Prepare journal entries to record the transactions and closings for 2005 and 2006.
2. Prepare the statement of retained earnings for the year ended December 31, 2006.
3. Prepare the shareholders' equity section of the company's balance sheet as of December 31, 2006.

---

*Problem 15-9B
Book value per share

LO^7

The balance sheet of Global Filter Company Ltd. at November 30, 2005, includes the following information:

Global Filter Company Ltd. Shareholders' Equity November 30, 2005		
Contributed capital:		
Preferred shares, $11 cumulative,		
2,000 shares authorized and issued		$200,000
Common shares, 60,000 shares authorized and issued		600,000
Total contributed capital		$800,000
Retained earnings		120,000
Total shareholders' equity		$920,000

Check figures:
a. Book value per common
   share = $11.80
b. Book value per common
   share = $11.43
c. Book value per common
   share = $10.70

Required
Assume that the preferred shares have a call price of $106. Calculate the book value per share of the preferred and common under each of the following assumptions:
a. No dividends are in arrears on the preferred shares.
b. One year's dividends are in arrears on the preferred shares.
c. Three years' dividends are in arrears on the preferred shares.

An asterisk (*) identifies assignment material based on Appendix 15A.

On December 31, 2005, Abbotsfield Corp. showed the following:

*Problem 15-10B
Calculating book value

L0[7]

**Abbotsfield Corp.
Shareholders' Equity
December 31, 2005**

Contributed capital:		
Preferred shares, $0.75, unlimited shares authorized,		
50,000 shares issued and outstanding*	$400,000	
Common shares, unlimited shares authorized,		
125,000 shares issued and outstanding*	525,000	
Total contributed capital		$ 925,000
Retained earnings		875,000
Total shareholders' equity		$1,800,000

*All of the shares had been issued early in 2004.

Required

Part 1:
Calculate book value per common share and preferred share at December 31, 2005, assuming no dividends were declared for the years ended December 31, 2004 or 2005, and that the preferred shares are:
a. Cumulative,   b. Non-cumulative.

Part 2 (independent of Part 1):
Assume no dividends were declared for the year ended December 31, 2004, and total dividends of $50,000 were declared and paid for the year ended December 31, 2005. Calculate book value per common share and preferred share at December 31, 2005, if preferred shares are:
c. Cumulative,   d. Non-cumulative.

Part 3 (independent of Parts 1 and 2):
e. Calculate book value per common share and preferred share at December 31, 2005, assuming:
  – Preferred shares are cumulative and callable at $12 per share, and
  – there were no dividends in arrears.

Check figures:
Book value per common
a. $10.60
c. $11.00
e. $9.60

Analytical and Review Problem

A & R 15-1

Fargo Inc. showed the following income statement information for its first three years of operation:

For the Years Ended December 31			
	2006	2005	2004
Net Sales	$5,000,000	$4,000,000	$3,000,000
Cost of Goods Sold	3,000,000	2,400,000	1,650,000
Operating Expenses	1,400,000	1,300,000	900,000
Other Revenues (Expenses)	(200,000)	(220,000)	50,000
Income Tax Expense	80,000	16,000	100,000

An asterisk (*) identifies assignment material based on Appendix 15A.

Partial information regarding Fargo's shareholders' equity for the past three years follows:

	Dec. 31 2006	Dec. 31 2005	Dec. 31 2004
Contributed capital:			
Preferred shares, $2 non-cumulative; 100,000 shares authorized; 20,000* shares issued and outstanding...	$400,000	$400,000	$400,000
Common shares, 500,000 shares authorized; 100,000* shares issued and outstanding...	550,000	550,000	550,000
Total contributed capital	?	?	?
Retained earnings**	?	?	?
Total shareholders' equity	?	?	?

* *Issued on January 1, 2004*
***Cash dividends of $100,000 were declared and paid for the year ended Dec. 31, 2004. Dividends were not declared for the years ended Dec. 31, 2005, or Dec. 31, 2006.*

Required
1. Calculate Gross Profit, Operating Income, Income Before Tax, and Net Income for the years ended December 31, 2004, 2005, and 2006.
2. Calculate Contributed Capital as at December 31, 2004, 2005, and 2006.
3. Calculate Retained Earnings as at December 31, 2004, 2005, and 2006.
4. Calculate Total Shareholders' Equity as at December 31, 2004, 2005, and 2006.

Ethics Challenge

EC 15-1

Jack and Bill are partners in a computer software company. They developed a word processing program that is remarkably similar to a Corel product. Jack telephones Bill at home one evening and says, "We should convert our partnership into a corporation before we launch this new word processing software. Let's withdraw most of our assets from the business before forming a corporate entity. If we are sued by Corel, our liability will be to our business assets." Bill feels a little uneasy and replies, "Let's meet at 9 A.M. sharp to discuss this matter."

Focus on Financial Statements

FFS 15-1

Barry Bowtie incorporated his business under the name BowTie Fishing Expeditions Corp. on March 1, 2005. It was authorized to issue 30,000 $2 cumulative preferred shares and an unauthorized limit of common shares. During March, the following shareholder equity transactions occurred:
a. 50,000 common shares were issued for cash of $3 per share.
b. 10,000 preferred shares were issued for $5,000 cash plus equipment with a fair market value of $37,000.
c. The corporation reported net income for the month of $190,000.
d. Total cash dividends of $45,000 were declared payable on April 15 to shareholders of record on March 31.

Part A

Required

Using the information provided in (a) through (d) plus the following March 31, 2005, selected account balances[1], prepare the statement of retained earnings for the month ended March 31, 2005, along with the March 31, 2005, balance sheet:

Accounts Payable	$17,000	Customer Deposits	28,000
Accounts Receivable	36,000	Equipment	140,000
Accumulated Amortization, Building	12,000	Estimated Warranty Liabilities	3,400
Accumulated Amortization, Equipment	2,000	Furniture	75,000
		Land	105,000
Accumulated Amortization, Furniture	5,000	Notes Payable[2]	90,000
		Patent	12,000
Allowance for Doubtful Accounts	1,200	Prepaid Rent	9,000
Building	148,600		
Cash	15,000		

1. This list of accounts is incomplete; you will have to add several accounts based on the information provided in (a) through (d).
2. The note payable is due in principal installments of $30,000 beginning March 1, 2006.

Part B

Required

Use your answer from Part A to answer each of the following questions:
1. What percentage of the total assets is equity financed?
2. What percentage of BowTie Fishing is financed by debt?
3. The common shareholders own what percentage of the total assets?
4. What percentage of the assets is financed by the preferred shareholders?

Corporate Reporting:
Income, Earnings Per Share, and Retained Earnings

The Power of Share Capital

Boardwalk Equities Inc. had its humble beginnings in 1984 when two brothers, aged 22 and 17, bought a rundown 16-unit walk-up apartment building in Calgary, Alberta, borrowing the down payment from their father. Six months later, after renovations were complete, they sold the project for almost twice the purchase price. Sam and Van Kolias reinvested the sale proceeds into another building. However, it was not until 1994, when the brothers went public, that they realized their potential through the revenue-generating power of share capital. At December 31, 2002, Boardwalk showed more than 50 million common shares issued in exchange for over $266 million. Sam and Van have invested those funds into revenue-producing assets. Their revenues have grown from $408,000 in 1994 to more than $249 million in 2002. Shareholders are pleased because earnings per share, an important ratio shown as part of the income statement, went from $0.09 per share in 1996 to $0.23 per share in 2002 and retained earnings over the same period grew from $385,000 to $35,229,000. Boardwalk Equities Inc. was named by *Profit Magazine* as Canada's fastest-growing company over the period 1994 to 1999. In addition, it has received the Business Builder Award for new job creation and the Hewlett–Packard Innovative Technology Award for being a leader in exploring the best use of new technology to achieve growth. Boardwalk Equities Inc. has come a long way in a decade and the new millennium looks promising.

www.bwalk.com

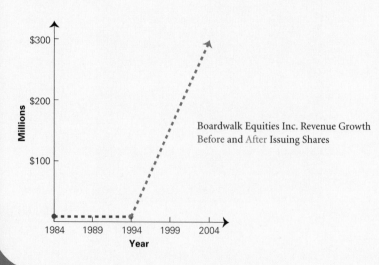

Boardwalk Equities Inc. Revenue Growth
Before and After Issuing Shares

Learning Objectives

LO¹ Explain the form and content of a comprehensive corporate income statement.

LO² Describe and account for share dividends, share splits, and retirement of shares.

LO³ Calculate earnings per share and describe its use.

LO⁴ Explain the items reported in retained earnings.

*APPENDIX 16A

*⃰**LO⁵** Record the purchase and reissue of treasury shares.

Chapter Preview

Corporations constantly evaluate their performance and make decisions to keep pace with changes in their global marketplace. This ongoing process often results in activities that include income-related transactions that go beyond a company's continuing, normal operations. The income statement needs to provide useful information to help users understand both current and past transactions, and to predict future performance. The first section of this chapter focuses on the reporting of additional income information. The next section describes share transactions that impact the calculation of an important ratio, earnings per share, that is included as part of the corporate income statement. Earnings per share is described in more detail in the third section of the chapter. The final section describes special issues regarding the statement of retained earnings. Understanding these topics helps us read, interpret, and use financial statements for decision making, and helps shareholders when they evaluate the performance of companies like Boardwalk Equities, as described in the opening article.

Reporting Income Information

LO¹ Explain the form and content of a comprehensive corporate income statement.

The basic corporate income statement of Exhibit 16.1 shows the revenues, expenses, and income generated by the company's **continuing operations**. Prior chapters have explained the nature of the items and measures included in income from these continuing operations.

Exhibit 16.1

Corporate Income Statement Showing Continuing Operations

Amanda Corporation
Income Statement
For Year Ended December 31, 2005

Sales		$100
Cost of goods sold		40
Gross profit		$ 60
Operating expenses		18
Income from operations		$ 42
Other revenues and expenses:¹		
Gain on sale of capital assets	$4	
Interest revenue	3	
Loss on sale of capital assets	(7)	
Interest expense	(2)	(2)
Income before tax		$ 40
Income tax expense		10
Net income		$ 30

Continuing operations

When a company's activities include income-related transactions that are not part of a company's continuing, normal operations, the income statement needs to be expanded to include different sections to provide more useful information to users. The most important of these additional sections include: *discontinued operations, extraordinary items,* and *earnings per share.* Discontinued operations and extraordinary items will be discussed in this section. Earnings per share is

---

¹ Some companies will divide this section on the income statement between *Other Revenues and Gains* and *Other Expenses and Losses.* The *CICA Handbook* permits flexibility in this regard.

described in detail in a later section. Exhibit 16.2 shows the additional income statement items as reported for CanComp for its year ended December 31, 2005.

Exhibit 16.2

Comprehensive Income Statement for a Corporation

CanComp Corporation Income Statement For Year Ended December 31, 2005			
Net sales		$8,440,000	① Continuing operations
Cost of goods sold		5,950,000	
Gross profit		$2,490,000	
Operating expenses		570,000	
Operating income		$1,920,000	
Other revenues and expenses:			
Loss on relocating a plant		(45,000)	
Income from continuing operations before income tax		$1,875,000	
Income tax expense		397,000	
Income from continuing operations		$1,478,000	
Discontinued operations:			② Discontinued operations
Income from operating Division A (net of $180,000 income taxes)	$420,000		
Loss on disposal of Division A (net of $66,000 tax benefit)	(154,000)	266,000	
Income before extraordinary items		$1,744,000	
Extraordinary items:			③ Extraordinary items
Gain on sale of land taken by government (net of $61,200 income taxes)		142,000	
Net income		$1,886,000	
Earnings per common share			④ Earnings per share
(200,000 outstanding shares):			
Income from continuing operations		$ 7.39	
Income from discontinued operations		1.33	
Income before extraordinary item		$ 8.72	
Extraordinary item		0.71	
Net income (basic earnings per share)		$ 9.43	

Many companies have several different lines of business or operating *segments* that deal with different groups of customers. A **segment of a business** is a part of a company's operations that serves a particular line of business or class of customers and is of interest to users of financial statements. For instance, ClubLink reports two operating segments in Note 15 of its 2002 financial statements: golf club operations and golf resort operations. Lions Gate Entertainment reports its operations in five business segments: Motion Pictures, Television, Animation, Studio Facilities, and CineGate.

www.clublink.com

www.lionsgatefilms.com

Discontinued Operations

When an operating segment of the business is discontinued, a **discontinued operation** results and two items must be reported in a separate section of the income statement:[2]

> **1.** The gain or loss from selling or closing down a segment, and
>
> **2.** The income from operating the discontinued segment prior to its disposal.

---

[2] *CICA Handbook*, section 1700.

The income tax effects of each are also reported net of tax separate from continuing operations as shown in Section 2 of Exhibit 16.2. When an amount is shown **net of tax**, it means that it has been adjusted for the income tax effect. The income tax effect can be an additional expense or a benefit (reduction of total tax expense). For example, in the case of the $420,000 reported in Section 2 as the *Income from Operating Division A*, it is *net of $180,000 income tax expense*. This means that the gross income (or before-tax amount) was $600,000 ($420,000 net amount + $180,000 income tax expense). For the *Loss on Disposal of Division A*, the $154,000 is reported net of a *$66,000 tax benefit*. Because a loss reduces net income, it also reduces income tax expense—therefore a tax *benefit* results.

www.molson.com

The purpose of reporting discontinued operations separately is to clearly isolate the results of discontinued operations from continuing operations. Additional information regarding the transaction must be disclosed in the notes to the financial statements.[3] For instance, on its income statement for the year ended March 31, 2002, and in Note 8, Molson Inc. reported as a discontinued operation the sale completed on July 25, 2001, of its Sports and Entertainment business consisting of the Montreal Canadiens and the Molson Centre.

Extraordinary Items

Section 3 of the income statement in Exhibit 16.2 reports **extraordinary items**. The *CICA Handbook* identifies an **extraordinary gain or loss** as an item that has all of the following three characteristics:

- It is not expected to occur frequently over several years,
- It does not typify the normal business activities of the entity, and
- It does not depend primarily on decisions or determinations by management or owners.[4]

Reporting extraordinary items in a separate category helps users predict future performance, without the effects of extraordinary items. Extraordinary items, like gains or losses resulting from discontinued segments, are reported net of income tax expense or benefit.

Few items qualify as extraordinary because they must meet both criteria of *unusual* and *infrequent*. An **unusual gain or loss** is abnormal or otherwise unrelated to the ordinary activities and environment of the business. An **infrequent gain or loss** is one that is not expected to occur again. The list of items usually considered extraordinary include:

- Expropriation (taking away) of property by a foreign government.
- Condemning of property by a domestic government body.
- Prohibition against using an asset by a newly enacted law.
- Losses or gains from an unusual and infrequent calamity ("act of God").

www.transalta.com

Only one Canadian company reported any extraordinary items that were in conformance with GAAP in 2000, and none in 2001.[5] TransAlta Corporation reported an extraordinary loss, net of income tax benefits, of $209.7 million related to its discontinued use of regulatory accounting for its Alberta Generation operations. In its place, TransAlta commenced application of Canadian GAAP, consistent with deregulation of the electricity generation industry in Alberta.

---

[3] *CICA Handbook*, section 3475, "Discontinued Operations."
[4] *CICA Handbook*, section 3480.
[5] This information was reported on page 477 of the CICA's 2001 *Financial Reporting in Canada*.

Gains or losses that result from the risks of normal business activities are not extraordinary and are reported in continuing operations *but* below the normal revenues and expenses. The following are examples of items *not* considered extraordinary:

- Write-downs of inventories.
- Write-offs of receivables.
- Gains or losses from exchanging foreign currencies.
- Effects of labour strikes.
- Accrual adjustments on long-term contracts.
- Sale of equipment.

Flashback

Answers—p. 833

1. Which of the following is an extraordinary item? (a) A settlement paid to a customer injured while using a company's product; (b) A loss from damages to a plant caused by a meteorite; or (c) A loss from selling old equipment.

2. Identify the four major sections of the income statement that are potentially reported.

Farmer

You are a farmer with an orchard in Kentville, Nova Scotia. This winter, a bad frost wiped out about half your trees. You are currently preparing an income statement for a bank loan. Can you claim the loss of apple trees as extraordinary and separate from continuing operations?

Judgement Call

Answer—p. 833

Additional Share Transactions

In order to discuss completely the earnings per share section of the comprehensive income statement in Exhibit 16.2, we need to understand share transactions that occur in addition to the issuance of those discussed in Chapter 15. These additional share transactions impact the calculation of earnings per share and include share dividends, share splits, and the retirement of shares. We describe these in the next section.

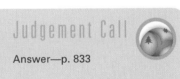

Describe and account for share dividends, share splits, and retirement of shares.

Share Dividends

In Chapter 15, we described cash dividends. However, a corporation's directors can also declare a **share dividend**, also called a *stock dividend*, in which a company distributes additional shares to its shareholders without receiving any payment in return. Share dividends and cash dividends are different: A share dividend does not reduce a corporation's assets and shareholders' equity, while a cash dividend does both. A share dividend simply transfers a portion of equity from retained earnings to contributed capital. This is sometimes described as *capitalizing* retained earnings because it increases a company's contributed capital.

Reasons for Share Dividends

If share dividends do not affect assets or total shareholders' equity, then why declare and distribute them? Reasons include the following:

1. Directors are said to use share dividends to keep the market price of the shares affordable. For example, if a profitable corporation grows but does not pay cash dividends, the price of its common shares continues to increase. The price of such shares may become so high that it discourages some investors from buying them. When a corporation declares a share dividend, it increases the number of outstanding shares and lowers the market price of its shares.

2. Issuing share dividends conserves cash for business expansion that might lead to positive returns on shareholder investment.

3. A share dividend provides evidence of management's confidence that the company is doing well.

Entries for Share Dividends

To illustrate share dividends, we use the shareholders' equity section of the balance sheet for X-Quest Ltd., shown in Exhibit 16.3, just *before* the company's declaration of a share dividend.

Exhibit 16.3

Shareholders' Equity Before the Share Dividend

X-Quest Ltd. **Shareholders' Equity** **December 31, 2005**	
Contributed capital:	
Common shares, unlimited shares authorized, 10,000 shares issued and outstanding	$108,000
Retained earnings	35,000
Total shareholders' equity	$143,000

Let's assume the directors of X-Quest Ltd. declare a 10% share dividend on December 31, 2005. This share dividend of 1,000 shares, calculated as 10% of its 10,000 outstanding shares P. 765, is to be distributed on January 20 to the shareholders of record on January 15. The *Canada Business Corporations Act* requires that the value to be assigned to a share dividend be equal to the market value P. 144 of the shares on the date of declaration. Since the market price of X-Quest's shares on December 31 is $15 per share, the dividend declaration is recorded as:

or

Dec. 31	Share Dividends	15,000	
	Common Share Dividends Distributable		15,000
	To record declaration of a share dividend of 1,000 common shares.		

Dec. 31	Retained Earnings	15,000	
	Common Share Dividends Distributable		15,000
	To record declaration of a share dividend of 1,000 common shares.		

The debit is recorded in the temporary (contra equity) account called Share Dividends. This account serves the same purpose as the Cash Dividends account. As shown above, an alternative entry is to debit Retained Earnings directly to eliminate the need to close the Share Dividends account at the end of the accounting period. The $15,000 credit is an increase to a contributed capital account called Common Share Dividends Distributable. This account balance exists only until the shares are actually issued.

A share dividend is *never a liability* because shareholders will be given shares in the future; shareholders receiving a share dividend are *not* owed any assets. Share dividends affect equity accounts only. The shareholders' equity section of X-Quest's December 31, 2005, balance sheet immediately *after* the declaration of the share dividend appears in Exhibit 16.4.

Exhibit 16.4

Shareholders' Equity After Declaring a Share Dividend

X-Quest Ltd. Shareholders' Equity December 31, 2005	
Contributed capital:	
Common shares, unlimited shares authorized, 10,000 shares issued and outstanding	$108,000
Common share dividends distributable, 1,000 shares	15,000
Total contributed capital	$123,000
Retained earnings	20,000
Total shareholders' equity	$143,000

As part of the year-end closing process, X-Quest Ltd. closes the Share Dividends account to Retained Earnings with the following entry:

Dec. 31	Retained Earnings	15,000	
	Share Dividends		15,000
	To close the Share Dividends account.		

Note that if Retained Earnings had been debited on the date of declaration instead of Share Dividends, the above closing entry would not be required. No entry is made on the date of record for a share dividend. On January 20, the date of distribution,[6] X-Quest distributes the new shares to shareholders and records this with the entry:

Jan. 20	Common Share Dividends Distributable	15,000	
	Common Shares		15,000
	To record distribution of a 1,000-share common share dividend.		

The combined effect of these two share dividend entries is to transfer (or capitalize) $15,000 of retained earnings to contributed capital. Share dividends have no effect on *total* shareholders' equity as shown in Exhibit 16.5. Nor do they affect the percent of the company owned by individual shareholders.

---

[6] For a share dividend, additional shares are issued (no cash is paid). Therefore, January 20 is referred to as the date of distribution and not the date of payment.

Exhibit 16.5

Shareholders' Equity Before and After Distribution of Share Dividend

	X-Quest Ltd. Shareholders' Equity	
	Dec. 31, 2005, Before Declaration of Share Dividend	Jan. 20, 2006, After Declaration of Share Dividend
Contributed capital:		
Common shares, unlimited shares authorized,		
Dec. 31, 2005: 10,000 shares issued and outstanding	$108,000	
Jan. 20, 2006: 11,000 shares issued and outstanding		$123,000
Retained earnings	35,000	20,000
Total shareholders' equity	$143,000	$143,000

Share Splits

A **share split** is the distribution of additional shares to shareholders according to their percent ownership. When a share split occurs, the corporation calls in its outstanding shares and issues more than one new share in exchange for each old share.[7] Splits can be done in any ratio including two-for-one (expressed as 2:1), three-for-one (expressed as 3:1), or higher. There are no journal entries for a share split but note disclosure is required and should state the number of shares distributed. For example:

> Note 6: As a result of a two-for-one share split declared by the board of directors, the company issued an additional 200,000 common shares on July 1, 2005.

To illustrate the effect of a share split on shareholders' equity, assume the information in Exhibit 16.6 for CLT Inc. at December 31, 2005, immediately prior to the declaration of a share split. CLT Inc.'s board of directors declared a 3:1 share split on December 31, 2005, to be issued on January 4, 2006. Notice that the share split simply replaces the 20,000 shares issued on December 31, 2005, with 60,000 shares on January 4, 2006. A share split does not affect individual shareholders' percent ownership. The Contributed Capital and Retained Earnings accounts are unchanged by a split. The only effect of a share split on the accounts is a change in

Exhibit 16.6

Shareholders' Equity for CLT Inc. Before and After Share Split

	CLT Inc. Shareholders' Equity	
	Dec. 31, 2005 Before Share Split	Jan. 4, 2006 After Share Split
Contributed capital:		
Common shares, unlimited shares authorized,		
Dec. 31, 2005: 20,000 shares issued and outstanding	$240,000	
Jan. 4, 2006: 60,000 shares issued and outstanding		$240,000
Retained earnings	90,000	90,000
Total shareholders' equity	$330,000	$330,000

[7] To reduce administrative cost, most splits are done by issuing new certificates to shareholders for the additional shares they are entitled to receive. The shareholders keep the old certificates.

the number of common shares. However, the market will respond by reducing the market value of the shares in proportion to the share split. For example, if CLT Inc.'s shares were trading on December 31, 2005, for $21 per share, the market value would be reduced to about $7 ($21 ÷ 3) per share after the share split.

A **reverse share split** is the opposite of a share split. It increases both the market value per share and the issued value per share. It does this by specifying the ratio to be less than one-to-one, such as one-for-two. This means shareholders end up with fewer shares after a reverse share split.

3. Which of the following statements is correct?
  a. A share split increases the market value per share.
  b. Share dividends and share splits have the same effect on the total assets and retained earnings of the issuing corporation.
  c. A share dividend does not transfer corporate assets to the shareholders but does require that retained earnings be capitalized.
4. What distinguishes a share dividend from a share split?
5. What amount of retained earnings is capitalized for a share dividend?

Flashback

Answers—p. 833

Repurchase of Shares

Under the *Canada Business Corporations Act*, a corporation may repurchase shares of its own outstanding share capital. Shares can be repurchased and then retired; this is referred to as a retirement or **cancelling of shares**.

For example, Note 8 of Leon's 2002 financial statements included in Appendix I at the end of the text states that Leon's repurchased and cancelled 163,500 of its common shares at a net cost of $4,902,000.

Retiring shares reduces the number of issued shares. Purchases and retirements of shares are allowed under the CBCA only if they do not jeopardize the interests of creditors and shareholders and are therefore limited by the balance of retained earnings. Corporations buy back their own shares for several reasons: they can repurchase shares to avoid a hostile takeover by an investor, or they can buy shares to maintain a strong or stable market. By buying shares, management shows its confidence in the price of its shares.

Retiring Shares

To demonstrate the accounting for the **retirement of shares**, assume that Delta Inc. originally issued its common shares at an average price per share of $12.[8] If, on May 1, the corporation purchased and retired 1,000 of these shares at the same price for which they were issued, the entry would be:

May 1	Common Shares	12,000	
	Cash		12,000
	Purchased and retired 1,000 common shares equal to the average issue price; $12 × 1,000 shares.		

---

[8] Shares are often issued at different amounts per share. Therefore when retiring shares, the average issue price per share is used to determine the amount to be debited to the share capital account. Average issue price per share is equal to Total share capital ÷ Total number of shares.

If, on June 1, the corporation retires 500 common shares, paying $11, which is less than the $12 average issue price, the entry would be:

June 1	Common Shares	6,000	
	Cash		5,500
	Contributed Capital from Retirement		
	of Common Shares		500
	Purchased and retired 500 common shares		
	at less than the average issue price;		
	$12 × 500 shares = $6,000;		
	$11 × 500 shares = $5,500.		

The Contributed Capital from Retirement of Common Shares account is reported as a separate item in the contributed capital section of shareholders' equity. *No gain is ever reported from the retirement of shares.* Why? Because the repurchase of shares affects balance sheet accounts, specifically shareholders' equity accounts, not income statement accounts. When shares are repurchased, the transaction is between shareholders and the corporation (balance sheet); it is not an operating activity (income statement).

Now assume that on July 5 the corporation pays $15 to retire 2,000 common shares, which is *more than* the average issue price of $12. The entry would be:

July 5	Common Shares	24,000	
	Contributed Capital from Retirement		
	of Common Shares	500	
	Retained Earnings	5,500	
	Cash		30,000
	Purchased and retired 2,000 common		
	shares at more than the average issue		
	price; $12 × 2,000 shares = $24,000;		
	$15 × 2,000 shares = $30,000.		

When shares are retired at a price *greater* than their average issue price, Retained Earnings is debited for the excess paid over the purchase price. However, if there is a balance in the Contributed Capital from Retirement account, this account must be debited *first* to the extent of its balance.

A corporation may also repurchase shares with the intent to reissue them. This is referred to as a *treasury share* transaction. Treasury share transactions are discussed in more detail in Appendix 16A.

Now that we understand share dividends, share splits, and the retirement of shares, we are ready to explore earnings per share, the topic of the next section.

Mid-Chapter Demonstration Problem

Airies Travel Inc. showed the following in its shareholders' equity section on the August 31, 2005, balance sheet:

Contributed capital:	
Common shares, unlimited shares authorized,	
10,000 shares issued and outstanding*	$150,000
Retained earnings..	80,000
Total shareholders' equity..	$230,000

*All of the common shares had been issued for an average price of $15.00 per share calculated as $150,000 ÷ 10,000 shares.

Part 1

On September 3, 2005, Airies' board of directors declared a 20% share dividend to shareholders of record on September 17 to be distributed on September 24. The share price on each of these dates was:

Date	Market price per share
Sept. 3, 2005	$15.20
17, 2005	15.25
24, 2005	12.30

Several months later, the board declared a two-for-one share split effective June 12, 2006.

Required

a. Prepare the journal entries, if applicable, for September 3, 17, and 24, along with June 12.

b. Prepare a comparative shareholders' equity section immediately before and after the share dividend, similar to Exhibit 16.5. Assume no other changes to retained earnings.

c. Prepare a comparative shareholders' equity section immediately before and after the share split, similar to Exhibit 16.6.

Part 2

Required

Assuming the information for Airies Travel Inc. only at August 31, 2005, record the following entries:

a. On September 16, 2005, Airies Travel repurchased and retired 500 of its common shares, paying $15.00 per share.

b. Airies repurchased and retired 1,000 of its shares on November 5, 2005, paying $14.50 per share.

c. Airies paid $16.20 per share on July 14, 2006, to repurchase and retire 1,000 of its shares.

SOLUTION TO Mid-Chapter Demonstration Problem

Part 1

a.

2005			
Sept. 3	Share Dividends	30,400	
	Common Share Dividends Distributable.......		30,400
	Declared a 20% share dividend;		
	10,000 × 20% = 2,000 shares;		
	2,000 shares × $15.20/share = 30,400.		
17	No entry.		
24	Common Share Dividends Distributable	30,400	
	Common Shares..		30,400
	Distributed 2,000 shares regarding the		
	share dividend declared on September 3.		
2006			
June 12	No entry.		
	Note disclosure is required stating that an		
	additional 12,000 shares are to be distributed		
	as a result of the two-for-one share split.		

b.

	Before Share Dividend	After Share Dividend
Contributed capital:		
Common shares, unlimited shares authorized,		
Before share dividend: 10,000 shares issued and outstanding.........	$150,000	
After share dividend: 12,000 shares issued and outstanding		$180,400
Retained earnings	80,000	49,600
Total shareholders' equity	$230,000	$230,000

c.

	Before Share Split	After Share Split
Contributed capital:		
Common shares, unlimited shares authorized,		
Before share split: 12,000 shares issued and outstanding.	$180,400	
After share split: 24,000 shares issued and outstanding		$180,400
Retained earnings	49,600	49,600
Total shareholders' equity	$230,000	$230,000

Part 2

a.

2005			
Sept. 16	Common Shares	7,500	
	Cash		7,500

To record repurchase of common shares;
500 × $15.00 = $7,500

b.

Nov. 5	Common Shares	15,000	
	Contributed Capital from Retirement		
	of Common Shares		500
	Cash		14,500

To record repurchase of common shares;
1,000 × $14.50 = $14,500;
1,000 × ($15.00 − $14.50) = $500.

c.

2006			
July 14	Common Shares	15,000	
	Contributed Capital from Retirement		
	of Common Shares	500	
	Retained Earnings	700	
	Cash		16,200

To record repurchase of common shares;
1,000 × $16.20 = $16,200;
1,000 × ($16.20 − $15.00) = $1,200.

Earnings Per Share (EPS)

There is one final section to analyze on the income statement in Exhibit 16.2: *earnings per share.* **Earnings per share**, commonly abbreviated as **EPS**, is the amount of income earned by each share of a company's outstanding common shares. Earnings per share information is included on the face of the income statement in accordance with accounting standards. Earnings per share is useful because it reports a company's earnings in terms of a single common share. The **basic earnings per share** formula is shown in Exhibit 16.7.

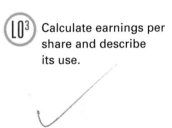

LO³ Calculate earnings per share and describe its use.

$$\text{Basic earnings per share} = \frac{\text{Net income} - \text{Preferred dividends}}{\text{Weighted-average common shares}}$$

Exhibit 16.7

Basic Earnings Per Share Formula

It should be noted that *only dividends actually declared in the current year are subtracted.* The exception is when preferred shares are cumulative, in which case annual dividends are deducted regardless of whether they have been declared or not. Dividends in arrears P. 773 are not relevant when calculating earnings per share.

Earnings Per Share When There Is No Change in Common Shares Outstanding

Consider Lescon Inc., with shares issued as shown in Exhibit 16.8.

Exhibit 16.8

Shareholders' Equity of Lescon Inc. at December 31, 2005

Lescon Inc. Shareholders' Equity December 31, 2005	
Contributed capital:	
Common shares, unlimited shares authorized,	
500,000 shares issued and outstanding	$6,500,000
Retained earnings	480,000
Total shareholders' equity	$6,980,000

Exhibit 16.9 illustrates the earnings per share presentation for Lescon Inc. for the year ended December 31, 2005, calculated as $750,000/500,000 shares = $1.50.

Exhibit 16.9

Income Statement with Earnings Per Share Information

Lescon Inc. Income Statement For Year Ended December 31, 2005	
Sales	$8,500,000
Cost of goods sold	4,600,000
Net income	$ 750,000
Earnings per common share	$1.50

Leon's Furniture Limited reported basic earnings per share of $1.96 for the year ended December 31, 2002, as shown in its annual report found in Appendix I at the end of this textbook. WestJet reported basic earnings per share of $0.70 for the same period.

When common shares outstanding are constant throughout the year, the calculation of earnings per share is straightforward because the denominator of the ratio, weighted-average common shares outstanding, is equal to the reported number of shares outstanding. The next section demonstrates the calculation of earnings per share when shares outstanding *changes* during the year.

Earnings Per Share When There Are Changes in Common Shares Outstanding

The number of shares outstanding can change because of:

- The issuance of additional shares,
- Share dividends,
- Share splits, and/or
- The retirement of shares.

We consider the effect of each on the denominator of the earnings per share calculation.

When Shares Are Sold or Purchased in the Period

When a company sells or repurchases shares during the year, the denominator of the basic earnings per share formula must equal the *weighted-average number of outstanding shares.* The idea behind this calculation is to measure the average amount of earnings to the average number of shares outstanding during the year. Why do we need a weighted-average calculation? To illustrate, assume you have $100 to invest in a 12% savings account at the bank. What is the earning power of your investment? The earning power is dependent on how long the money is in the savings account. If you deposit the money on January 1, 2005, the interest revenue earned by December 31, 2005, is $12 ($100 × 12%). If the money is invested on December 1, 2005, $1 ($100 × 12% × 1/12) of earnings would be realized by December 31, 2005. The earning power of an investment is greater the longer the funds are invested. Shares represent investments made by shareholders in the corporation. The longer those investments are in the company, the greater their potential impact on earnings.

Assume Lescon Inc. reported net income of $880,000 for the year ended December 31, 2006. During 2006, Lescon issued 50,000 preferred and 40,000 additional common shares and retired 30,000 common shares, as shown in Exhibit 16.10. Dividends were declared on the preferred shares only.

Lescon Inc. Shareholders' Equity December 31, 2006	
Contributed capital:	
Preferred shares, $5 cumulative, unlimited shares authorized,	
50,000 shares issued and outstanding	$1,000,000
Common shares, unlimited shares authorized,	
510,000 shares issued and outstanding*	7,200,000
Total contributed capital	$8,200,000
Retained earnings	1,110,000
Total shareholders' equity	$9,310,000

Exhibit 16.10

Shareholders' Equity of Lescon Inc. at December 31, 2006

500,000 shares were issued and outstanding on January 1, 2006; 40,000 common shares were issued on April 1, 2006; 30,000 common shares were repurchased and retired on November 1, 2006.

To calculate the weighted-average number of shares outstanding, we need to determine the number of months that each group of common shares was outstanding during the year. Exhibit 16.11 shows us how to calculate Lescon's weighted-average number of shares outstanding for the year 2006.

Time Period	Outstanding Shares	Fraction of Year Outstanding	Weighted Average
January–March	500,000	× 3/12	= 125,000
April–October	540,000	× 7/12	= 315,000
November–December	510,000	× 2/12	= 85,000
Weighted-average outstanding shares			525,000

Exhibit 16.11

Calculating Weighted-Average Number of Shares Outstanding

We can then calculate Lescon's basic earnings per share for the year ended December 31, 2006, as:

Basic earnings per share = $\dfrac{\$880{,}000 \text{ net income} - \$250{,}000 \text{ preferred dividends declared*}}{525{,}000}$

= $\underline{\$1.20}$

Note: Because the preferred shares are cumulative, the annual dividends of $250,000 would be subtracted even if the dividends had not been declared.

Lescon reports the $1.20 basic earnings per share number on the face of its December 31, 2006, income statement, similar to that shown in Exhibit 16.9.

Share Dividends or Splits in the Period

The number of outstanding shares is also affected by a share split or share dividend. Earnings for the year are spread over a larger number of shares as a result of a share dividend or share split. This affects our calculation of the weighted-average number of shares outstanding. We handle a share split or share dividend by restating the number of shares outstanding during the year to reflect the share split or dividend *as if it had occurred at the beginning of the year.*

To illustrate, let's assume Lescon declared a two-for-one share split effective December 1, 2006. The calculations in Exhibit 16.11 would change as shown in Exhibit 16.12. Notice that the only change in calculating weighted-average shares outstanding is the additional multiplication. This shows the split as if it had occurred at the beginning of the year. The December outstanding shares already reflect the split and do not require any adjustment.

Exhibit 16.12

Calculating Weighted-Average Number of Shares Outstanding With Share Split

Time Period	Outstanding Shares	Effect of Split	Fraction of Year	Weighted Average
January–March	500,000	× 2	× 3/12	= 250,000
April–October	540,000	× 2	× 7/12	= 630,000
November	510,000	× 2	× 1/12	= 85,000
December	1,020,000	× 1	× 1/12	= 85,000
Weighted-average outstanding shares				1,050,000

Lescon's basic earnings per share for the year 2006 under the assumption of the two-for-one share split is:

$$\text{Basic earnings per share} = \frac{\$880,000 \text{ net income} - \$250,000 \text{ preferred dividends declared}}{1,050,000}$$

$$= \$0.60$$

Exhibit 16.13 shows the calculation of weighted-average shares outstanding if the two-for-one share split had been a 10% share dividend. The December outstanding shares already reflect the share dividend and do not require any adjustment.

Exhibit 16.13

Calculating Weighted-Average Number of Shares With Share Dividend

Time Period	Outstanding Shares	Effect of Share Dividend	Fraction of Year	Weighted Average
January–March	500,000	× 1.10	× 3/12	= 137,500
April–October	540,000	× 1.10	× 7/12	= 346,500
November	510,000	× 1.10	× 1/12	= 46,750
December	561,000	× 1	× 1/12	= 46,750
Weighted-average outstanding shares				577,500

Earnings per share under the assumption of the 10% share dividend would be:

$$\text{Basic earnings per share} = \frac{\$880,000 \text{ net income} - \$250,000 \text{ preferred dividends declared}}{577,500}$$

$$= \$1.09^*$$

rounded to two decimal places

Earnings Per Share and Extraordinary Items

Exhibit 16.14 shows how extraordinary items are reported in the income statement along with the corresponding earnings per share presentation for Gallivan Inc.

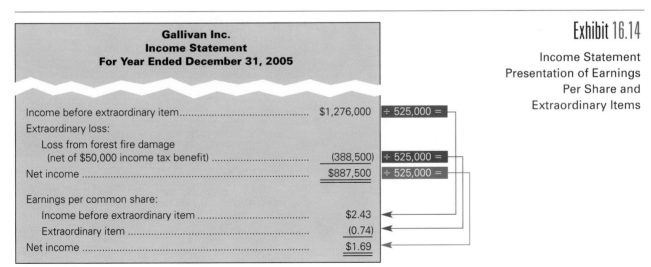

Gallivan Inc.
Income Statement
For Year Ended December 31, 2005

Income before extraordinary item	$1,276,000	÷ 525,000 =
Extraordinary loss:		
Loss from forest fire damage (net of $50,000 income tax benefit)	(388,500)	÷ 525,000 =
Net income	$887,500	÷ 525,000 =
Earnings per common share:		
Income before extraordinary item	$2.43	
Extraordinary item	(0.74)	
Net income	$1.69	

Exhibit 16.14

Income Statement Presentation of Earnings Per Share and Extraordinary Items

Assume there are no preferred shares and the weighted-average number of common shares outstanding is 525,000 shares.

The next section discusses some additional income reporting issues and how they impact the statement of retained earnings P. 761.

Flashback

Answers—pp. 833–834

6. During 2005, FDI reports net income of $250,000 and pays $70,000 in current year preferred dividends. On January 1, 2005, the company had 25,000 outstanding common shares and retired 5,000 shares on July 1, 2005. The 2005 basic earnings per share is: (a) $8; (b) $9; or (c) $10.

7. In addition to the facts in Flashback (6), assume a 3:1 share split occurred on August 1, 2005. The 2005 weighted-average number of common shares outstanding is: (a) 60,000; (b) 117,500; or (c) 67,500.

8. How are share splits and share dividends treated in calculating the weighted-average number of outstanding common shares?

Statement of Retained Earnings

Recall that the statement of retained earnings shows the details of how the Retained Earnings account changes over the accounting period. Retained earnings are part of the shareholders' claim on the company's net assets. A common error is to think that retained earnings represent cash. Retained earnings are not cash. Retained earnings do not imply that there is a certain amount of cash available to pay shareholders, nor any other asset. They simply describe how much of the assets are owned by the shareholders as a result of earnings that have been *retained* for the purpose of reinvestment.

The statement of retained earnings is often combined with the income statement, as shown in Exhibit 16.15.

Exhibit 16.15

Statement of Retained Earnings Presented in Combination with the Income Statement

Petro Inc.	
Statement of Income and Retained Earnings	
For Year Ended December 31, 2005	
Sales	$9,000,000
Cost of goods sold	6,500,000
Net income	$1,250,000
Retained earnings, January 1	1,200,000
Less: Cash dividends	(350,000)
Retained earnings, December 31	$2,100,000
Earnings per common share..	$5.25

For additional examples of how the statement of retained earnings is combined with the income statement, refer to the WestJet and Leon's Furniture statements provided in Appendix I at the end of this textbook.

The next section describes important items affecting retained earnings. It also explains how we include these as part of the statement of retained earnings.

Restricted Retained Earnings

To protect creditors' interests in assets of a corporation, incorporating acts sometimes place *restrictions* on retained earnings. **Restrictions** are limits that identify how much of the retained earnings balance is not available for dividends or the repurchase of shares. Restrictions are usually disclosed in the notes to the financial statements. There are three kinds of restrictions:

(LO⁴) Explain the items reported in retained earnings.

1. *Statutory restrictions* are imposed by a regulatory body. For example, dividends are limited to the balance of retained earnings.

2. *Contractual restrictions* occur when certain contracts, such as loan agreements, restrict retained earnings such that the payment of dividends is limited to a certain amount or percent of retained earnings.

3. *Voluntary restrictions* are placed on retained earnings by a corporation's directors to limit dividends because of a special need for cash, such as for the purchase of new facilities.

Accounting Changes

Another issue that can affect retained earnings is that of accounting changes. There are three types of accounting changes but only two have the potential to impact retained earnings. Exhibit 16.16 summarizes accounting changes and their appropriate treatment:

Accounting Change	Accounting Treatment
1. Change in Accounting Policy or Principle	- Retroactive restatement of financial statements, - Disclosure requiring description of change and effect on financial statements,
2. Correction of Error(s) in Prior Financial Statements	- New policy or corrected amount is reported in current year's operating results, and - Charged or credited (net of tax) to opening balance of Retained Earnings.
3. Change in Estimate	Accounted for in period of change and future.

Exhibit 16.16

Guidelines for the Treatment of Accounting Changes[9]

1. Change in Accounting Policy or Principle

A *change in accounting principle* occurs if, for example, a company changes from FIFO to the weighted-average method for calculating the cost of sales and merchandise inventory. A change in accounting principle is represented by a change from an existing accounting policy or principle to an alternative one. *Consistency* P.40 requires a company to continue applying the same accounting principles once they are chosen to ensure financial statements are comparable from one accounting period to the next. A company can change from one acceptable accounting principle to another as long as the change improves the usefulness of information in its financial statements. The accounting treatment for a change in accounting policy or principle is noted in Exhibit 16.16.

---

[9] *CICA Handbook*, section 1506.

2. Correction of Error(s) in Prior Financial Statements

Sometimes errors occur. For instance, assume Lashburn Ltd. makes an error in a 2005 journal entry for the purchase of land by incorrectly debiting an expense account for $240,000. This error was discovered in 2006 and requires correction as per the guidelines outlined in Exhibit 16.16. The entry to record the correction is:

2006			
Dec. 31	Land..	240,000	
	Income Tax Payable* ($240,000 × 25%)		60,000
	Retained Earnings		180,000
	To adjust for error in 2005 journal entry		
	that expensed the purchase of land.		

*Assuming a flat tax rate of 25% for simplicity.

To correct the error, the 2005 financial statements are restated, appropriate note disclosure is included explaining the error, and retained earnings is restated as per Exhibit 16.17. There is no effect on the current year's operating results in this particular instance.

Exhibit 16.17

Presentation of Accounting Changes on the Statement of Retained Earnings

Lashburn Ltd. Statement of Retained Earnings For Year Ended December 31, 2006	
Retained earnings, December 31, 2005, as previously stated.........................	$4,745,000
Add: Correction of error:	
Cost of land incorrectly expensed **(net of $60,000 income taxes expense).................................**	**180,000**
Retained earnings, December 31, 2005, as adjusted	$4,925,000
Add: Net income...	1,162,500
Less: Cash dividends	240,000
Retained earnings, December 31, 2006	$5,847,500

3. Change in Estimate

Many items reported in financial statements are based on estimates. Future events are certain to reveal that some of these estimates were inaccurate even when based on the best data available at the time. Because these inaccuracies are not the result of mistakes, they are considered to be a **change in accounting estimate** and *not* accounting errors. For example, if the estimated useful life of a capital asset changed because of new information, this would be identified as a change in estimate.

Flashback

Answer—p. 834

9. A company that has used FIFO for the past 15 years decides to switch to LIFO. Which of the following statements describes the effect of this event on past years' net income?

a. The cumulative effect is reported as an adjustment to ending retained earnings for the prior period.

b. The cumulative effect is ignored as it is a change in an accounting estimate.

c. The cumulative effect is reported only on the current year's income statement.

Summary

LO¹ **Explain the form and content of a comprehensive corporate income statement.** Corporate income statements are similar to those for proprietorships and partnerships except for the inclusion of income taxes. The income statement consists of four potential sections: (1) continuing operations, (2) discontinued segments, (3) extraordinary items, and (4) earnings per share.

LO² **Describe and account for share dividends, share splits, and retirement of shares.** Both a share dividend and a share split divide a company's outstanding shares into smaller pieces. The total value of the company is unchanged, but the price of each new share is smaller. Share dividends and share splits do not transfer any of the corporation's assets to shareholders and do not affect assets, total shareholders' equity, or the equity attributed to each shareholder. Share dividends are recorded by capitalizing retained earnings equal to the market value of the distributed shares. Share splits are not recorded with journal entries but do require note disclosure. When a corporation purchases its own previously issued outstanding shares for the purpose of retirement, the share capital account is debited based on the original issue price. If the amount paid

by the corporation is less than the original issue price, the excess is credited to the Contributed Capital from Retirement of Shares account. If the amount paid is greater than the original issue price, Contributed Capital from Retirement of Shares is debited to the extent a credit balance exists in that account and any remaining amount is debited to Retained Earnings.

LO³ **Calculate earnings per share and describe its use.** Corporations calculate basic earnings per share by dividing net income less any preferred dividends by the weighted-average number of outstanding common shares.

LO⁴ **Explain the items reported in retained earnings.** Retained earnings are sometimes restricted to limit dividends and reacquisition of shares or to protect creditors. Corporations may voluntarily restrict retained earnings as a means of informing shareholders why dividends are not larger. Accounting changes that affect retained earnings of prior years include (1) change in accounting policy/procedure, and (2) correction of an error. A change in accounting estimate, also a type of accounting change, does not impact retained earnings of prior years.

GUIDANCE ANSWER TO *Judgement Call*

Farmer

The frost loss is probably not extraordinary. Nova Scotia experiences enough frost damage that it would be difficult to argue that

this event is both unusual and infrequent. Nevertheless, you would want to highlight the frost loss, and hope the bank would view this uncommon event separately from your continuing operations.

GUIDANCE ANSWERS TO   Flashback

1. *b*

2. The four major sections are Income from Continuing Operations, Discontinued Segments, Extraordinary Items, and Earnings per Share.

3. *c*

4. A share dividend increases the number of shares issued and outstanding and requires a journal entry to transfer (or capitalize) a portion of retained earnings to contributed capital. A share split does not involve a journal entry and simply increases the number of shares issued and outstanding.

5. Retained earnings equal to the market value of the distributable shares should be capitalized.

6. *a*

Calculations: ($250,000 − $70,000)/22,500* = $8.00

Time Period	Outstanding Shares	Fraction of Year Outstanding	Weighted Average
January–June	25,000	× 6/12	= 12,500
July–December	20,000	× 6/12	= 10,000
Weighted-average outstanding shares			22,500

7. *c*

Calculations:

Time Period	Outstanding Shares	Effect of Split	Fraction of Year	Weighted Average
January–June	25,000	× 3	× 6/12	= 37,500
July	20,000	× 3	× 1/12	= 5,000
August–December	60,000	× 1	× 5/12	= 25,000
Weighted-average outstanding shares				67,500

8. The number of shares previously outstanding is retroactively restated to reflect the share split or share dividend as if it had occurred at the beginning of the year.

9. *a*

Demonstration Problem

X-On Ltd. began 2005 with the following balances in its shareholders' equity accounts:

Common shares, unlimited shares authorized,	
500,000 shares issued and outstanding	$3,000,000
Retained earnings	2,500,000

The following share-related transactions occurred during the year:

Date	Transaction
March 1	Issued at $20 per share 100,000 $2.50 non-cumulative preferred shares with an unauthorized limit.
May 1	Issued 50,000 common shares at $15 per share.
Sept. 1	Repurchased and retired 150,000 common shares at $16 per share.
Nov. 30	Declared and distributed a 3:1 share split on the common shares.

Required

a. Calculate the weighted-average number of shares outstanding using the information above.

b. Using the information provided, prepare an income statement for 2005 similar to Exhibit 16.2:

Cumulative effect of a change in amortization method (net of $26,000 tax benefit)	$ (136,500)
Operating expenses (related to continuing operations)	(2,072,500)
Extraordinary gain on expropriated land (net of $71,000 tax expense)	275,500
Gain on disposal of discontinued operation's assets (net of $8,600 tax expense)	37,500
Gain on sale of investment in shares	400,000
Loss from operating discontinued operations (net of $40,000 tax benefit)	(182,500)
Income taxes on income from continuing operations	(660,000)
Revenues	5,375,000
Loss from sale of plant assets*	(650,000)

*The assets were items of equipment replaced with new technology.

Planning the Solution

○ Based on the shares outstanding at the beginning of the year and the transactions during the year, calculate the weighted-average number of outstanding shares for the year.
○ Calculate earnings per share.
○ Assign each of the listed items to an appropriate income statement category.
○ Prepare an income statement similar to Exhibit 16.2, including separate sections for continued operations, discontinued operations, extraordinary items, and earnings per share.

SOLUTION TO Demonstration Problem

a. Calculate the weighted-average number of outstanding shares:

Time Period	Outstanding Shares	Effect of Split	Fraction of Year	Weighted Average
January–April	500,000	× 3	× 4/12	= 500,000
May–August	550,000	× 3	× 4/12	= 550,000
September–November	400,000	× 3	× 3/12	= 300,000
December	1,200,000	× 1	× 1/12	= 100,000
Weighted-average outstanding shares				1,450,000

b. Prepare an income statement for 2005:

X-On Ltd.
Income Statement
For Year Ended December 31, 2005

Revenues		$5,375,000
Operating expenses		2,072,500
Income before tax		$3,302,500
Income tax expense		660,000
Income from operations		$2,642,500
Other revenues and expenses:		
Gain on sale of investment in shares	$ 400,000	
Loss from sale of plant assets	(650,000)	(250,000)
Income from continuing operations		$2,392,500
Discontinued operations:		
Loss from operating discontinued operation		
(net of $40,000 tax benefit)	$(182,500)	
Gain on disposal of discontinued operation's assets		
(net of $8,600 tax)	37,500	(145,000)
Income before extraordinary items		$2,247,500
Extraordinary items:		
Extraordinary gain on expropriated land		
(net of $71,000 tax)		275,500
Net income		$2,523,000
Earnings per share		
(1,450,000 average shares outstanding):		
Income from continuing operations		$1.65[1]
Loss from discontinued segment		(0.10)[2]
Income before extraordinary gain		$1.55
Extraordinary gain		0.19[3]
Net income		$1.74

[1] $2,392,500/1,450,000 = $ 1.65
[2] $(145,000)/1,450,000 = $(0.10)
[3] $275,500/1,450,000 = $ 0.19

APPENDIX

Treasury Shares

LO5 Record the purchase and reissue of treasury shares.

In some provincial jurisdictions, a corporation may buy back shares without having to retire them. These reacquired shares are called **treasury shares**. Treasury shares *have been issued* but *are not outstanding* since they are not held by shareholders; instead they are held by the corporation. Because voting rights and dividend entitlements apply to outstanding shares only, treasury shares are not entitled to receive dividends or vote.

Purchasing Treasury Shares

The *Treasury Shares* account is a contra shareholders' equity account. Therefore, purchasing treasury shares for cash reduces the corporation's assets and shareholders' equity by equal amounts.[10] We illustrate these effects on the balance sheet of Cyber Corporation. Exhibit 16A.1 shows Cyber's account balances before any treasury shares are purchased.

Exhibit 16A.1

Balance Sheet Before Purchasing Treasury Shares

Cyber Corporation Balance Sheet May 1, 2005	
Assets	
Cash	$ 30,000
Other assets	95,000
Total assets	$125,000
Liabilities	$ -0-
Shareholders' equity	
Common shares, 10,000 shares authorized, issued and outstanding	$100,000
Retained earnings	25,000
Total liabilities and shareholders' equity	$125,000

On May 2, 2005, Cyber purchased 1,000 of its own common shares at $11.50 per share. The entry to record this purchase is:

May 2	Treasury Shares, Common	11,500	
	Cash		11,500
	Purchased 1,000 treasury shares at $11.50 per share.		

Exhibit 16A.2 shows the effects of this transaction on Cyber's balance sheet.

---

[10] We describe the *cost method* of accounting for treasury shares. It is the method most widely used. The *par value* method is another method explained in advanced courses.

Exhibit 16A.2

Balance Sheet
After Purchasing
Treasury Shares

Cyber Corporation
Balance Sheet
May 2, 2005

Assets

Cash	$ 18,500
Other assets	95,000
Total assets	$113,500

Liabilities	$ -0-

Shareholders' equity

Contributed capital:

Common shares 10,000 shares, authorized and issued;		
9,000 shares outstanding	$100,000	
Retained earnings, of which $11,500 is restricted by		
treasury shares purchased	25,000	
Total	$125,000	
Less: 1,000 treasury shares	11,500	
Total shareholders' equity		$113,500
Total liabilities and shareholders' equity		$113,500

The treasury share purchase reduces Cyber's cash and total equity by $11,500. This purchase does not reduce the balance of either the Common Shares account or the Retained Earnings account. Note that there are only 9,000 shares outstanding (10,000 issued less 1,000 in treasury). The retained earnings description tells us it is partly restricted.

Reissuing Treasury Shares

Treasury shares can be reissued. They can be sold at cost, above cost, or below cost.

If, on May 20, Cyber reissues 100 of the treasury shares at $11.50 per share, their cost on May 1, the entry is:

May 20	Cash	1,150	
	Treasury Shares, Common		1,150
	Reissued 100 treasury shares at cost.		

If, on June 3, 400 treasury shares are reissued at $12 per share, which is above their cost on May 1, the entry is:

June 3	Cash	4,800	
	Treasury Shares, Common		4,600
	Contributed Capital, Treasury Shares		200
	Reissued 400 treasury shares above cost;		
	400 × $11.50 = $4,600; 400 × $12 = $4,800.		

The Contributed Capital, Treasury Shares account is reported as a separate item in the contributed capital section of shareholders' equity. No gain is ever reported from the sale of treasury shares.

If, on July 10, 300 treasury shares are reissued at $11 per share, which is below their cost on May 1, the entry is:

July 10	Cash..	3,300	
	Contributed Capital, Treasury Shares...................	150	
	Treasury Shares, Common		3,450
	Reissued 300 treasury shares below cost;		
	300 × $11.50 = $3,450; 300 × $11 = $3,300.		

The debit to the Contributed Capital, Treasury Shares account cannot exceed the credit balance present in the account (in this case, the July 10 debit of $150 does not exceed the June 3 credit balance of $200; a credit of $50 remains). In a case where the credit balance in the contributed capital account is eliminated, the remaining difference between the cost and the selling price is debited to Retained Earnings.

For example, if, on July 15, 100 treasury shares are reissued at $10 per share, the entry is:

July 15	Cash..	1,000	
	Contributed Capital, Treasury Shares.................	50	
	Retained Earnings	100	
	Treasury Shares, Common		1,150
	Reissued 100 treasury shares below cost.		

Flashback

Answers—p. 838

10. Purchase of treasury shares: (a) has no effect on total assets; (b) reduces total assets and total shareholders' equity by equal amounts; or (c) is recorded with a debit to Retained Earnings.

11. Southern Inc. purchases shares of Northern Corp. Should these shares be classified as treasury shares by either company?

12. How do treasury shares affect the number of shares authorized, issued, and outstanding?

Summary

LO5 Record the purchase and reissue of treasury shares. When a corporation purchases its own previously issued outstanding shares, the cost of these shares is debited to Treasury Shares. The balance of Treasury Shares is subtracted from total shareholders' equity in the balance sheet. If treasury shares are later reissued, the amount of any proceeds in excess of cost is credited to Contributed Capital, Treasury Shares. If the proceeds are less than cost, the difference is debited to Contributed Capital, Treasury Shares to the extent a credit balance exists in that account. Any remaining amount is debited to Retained Earnings.

GUIDANCE ANSWERS TO  Flashback

10. *b*

11. No. The shares are an investment for Southern Inc. and issued and outstanding shares for Northern Corp.

12. Treasury shares do not affect the number of either authorized or issued shares. They reduce the amount of outstanding shares only.

Glossary

Basic earnings per share Calculated with the formula: (Net income − Preferred dividends) ÷ Weighted-average common shares. (p. 825)

Cancelling of shares See *retirement of shares*. (p. 821)

Changes in accounting estimates Corrections to previous estimates or predictions about future events and outcomes, such as salvage values and the useful lives of operating assets; the changes are accounted for in the current and future periods. (p. 832)

Continuing operations That section of an income statement that shows the revenues, expenses, and income generated by the company's day-to-day operating activities. (p. 814)

Discontinued operations When a company with operations in different segments sells a segment, the sold segment is known as a discontinued operation. (p. 815)

Earnings per share The amount of income earned by each share of a company's outstanding common shares; commonly abbreviated as *EPS*. (p. 825)

EPS See *earnings per share*. (p. 825)

Extraordinary gain or loss A gain or loss that is reported separately from continuing operations because it is not expected to occur frequently over several years, does not typify the normal business activities of the entity, and does not depend primarily on decisions or determinations by management or owners. Gains and losses that occur infrequently are not extraordinary. (p. 816)

Extraordinary item See *extraordinary gain or loss*. (p. 816)

Infrequent gain or loss A gain or loss that is not expected to occur again, given the operating environment of the business. (p. 816)

Net of tax An amount reported net of tax means the income tax expense (benefit) has already been subtracted. (p. 816)

Restrictions Legal or contractual limitations that cause a portion of the retained earnings balance not to be available for dividends or the repurchase of shares. No journal entry is required but note disclosure is necessary. (p. 831)

Retirement of shares Occurs when a corporation repurchases and cancels its own shares. (p. 821)

Reverse share split An act by a corporation to call in its shares and replace each share with less than one new share; reverse splits are opposite of share splits as they increase both the market value per share and the issued value per share. (p. 821)

Segment of a business A component of a company's operations that serves a particular line of business or class of customers and that has assets, activities, and financial results of operations that can be distinguished from other parts of the business. (p. 815)

Share dividend A corporation's distribution of its own shares to its shareholders without receiving any payment in return. Also called a *stock dividend*. (p. 817)

Share split An act by a corporation to call in its shares and replace each share with more than one new share; a share split will decrease the market value per share and also the book value per share. (p. 820)

Treasury shares Shares that were reacquired and are still held by the issuing corporation. (p. 836)

Unusual gain or loss A gain or loss that is abnormal or otherwise unrelated to the ordinary activities and environment of the business. (p. 816)

For more study tools, quizzes, and problem material, refer to the Online Learning Centre at
www.mcgrawhill.ca/college/larson

Questions

1. Where on the income statement would a company report an unusual gain that is not expected to occur more often than once every two years?

2. What is the difference between a share dividend and a share split?

3. What effects does declaring a share dividend have on the corporation's assets, liabilities, and total shareholders' equity? What effects does the distribution of the shares have?

4. Refer to the financial statements for Leon's in Appendix I at the end of the book. What is the balance of retained earnings as of December 31, 2002? What amount of dividends was declared during 2002?

5. How are earnings per share results calculated for a corporation with a simple capital structure?

6. Refer to the financial statements for WestJet in Appendix I. Did basic EPS increase or decrease from 2001 to 2002?

7. After taking five years' straight-line amortization expense for an asset that was expected to have an eight-year useful life, a company decided that the asset would last another six years. Is this decision a change in accounting principle? How would the financial statements describe this change?

*8. How does the purchase of treasury shares affect the purchaser's assets and total shareholders' equity?

*9. Why do legal jurisdictions place limits on purchases of treasury shares?

An asterisk (*) identifies assignment material based on Appendix 16A.

Quick Study

QS 16-1
Income statement categories

LO[1]

Using the numbers to represent each section of a comprehensive income statement, identify where each of items (a) through (l) should be reported:

1. Continuing operations
2. Discontinued operations
3. Extraordinary items
4. Earnings per share

a. Gain on sale of Division E _____
b. Operating expenses _____
c. Extraordinary loss _____
d. Loss on sale of equipment _____
e. Interest revenue _____
f. Amortization expense _____
g. Earnings per share _____
h. Cost of goods sold _____
i. Loss from operating Division E _____
j. Income tax expense _____
k. Gain on sale of warehouse _____
l. Interest expense _____

QS 16-2
Accounting for a share dividend

LO[2]

Information taken from Jamestown Corp.'s balance sheet as of April 1, 2005, follows:

Common shares, 375,000 shares authorized, 150,000 shares issued and outstanding..	$1,102,500
Retained earnings...	633,000

On April 1, Jamestown declares and distributes a 10% share dividend. The market value of the shares on this date is $25. Prepare the shareholders' equity section for Jamestown immediately following the share dividend (assume all dividends are debited directly to Retained Earnings).

QS 16-3
Share split

LO[2]

Vector Ltd. showed the following shareholders' equity account balances on December 31, 2005:

Common shares, 100,000 shares authorized; 28,000 shares issued and outstanding..	$476,000
Retained earnings...	85,000

On January 2, 2006, Vector declared a 3:1 share split. Prepare a comparative shareholders' equity section immediately before and after the share split similar to Exhibit 16.6.

QS 16-4
Repurchase and retirement of shares

LO[2]

On September 2, Garrett Corporation purchased and retired 2,000 of its own shares for $18,000. The shares had been issued at an average price of $5. Prepare the September 2 entry for the purchase and retirement of the shares (assuming this is the first retirement ever recorded by Garrett).

QS 16-5
Repurchase and retirement of shares

LO[2]

Amex Inc. had 180,000 common shares issued and outstanding as at December 31, 2005. The shares had been issued for $9.80 each. On September 12, 2006, Amex repurchased and retired 40,000 of these shares at $9.10 each. Record the entry assuming this is the first retirement ever recorded by Amex.

QS 16-6
Repurchase and retirement of shares

LO[2]

Refer to the information in QS 16-5. Amex repurchased and retired 20,000 shares at $11.40 on December 17, 2006. Record the entry.

The Nelson Corp. earned a net income of $450,000. The number of common shares outstanding all year long was 200,000 and preferred shareholders received a dividend totalling $10,000. Calculate the basic earnings per share for Nelson Corp.

QS 16-7
Basic earnings per share

LO³

Bellevue Ltd. reported net income of $860,000 for its year ended December 31, 2005. Calculate earnings per share given the following additional information at December 31, 2005:

Preferred shares, $2 cumulative, 50,000 shares authorized; 26,000 shares issued and outstanding	$ 286,000
Common shares, 300,000 shares authorized, 160,000 shares issued and outstanding*	544,000
Retained earnings**	180,000

* There was no change in the outstanding shares during the year.
**Dividends totalling $100,000 were declared during 2005. There were no dividends in arrears.

QS 16-8
Earnings per share

LO³

On January 1, Harmon Corp. had 100,000 common shares outstanding. On February 1, Harmon Corp. issued 40,000 additional common shares. On June 1, another 80,000 common shares were issued. Calculate Harmon Corp.'s weighted-average shares outstanding.

QS 16-9
Weighted average
shares outstanding

LO³

On January 1, 2005, Wonsto Mining Corp. had 580,000 common shares issued and outstanding. On April 30, it issued an additional 220,000 shares and on October 1 it repurchased and cancelled 100,000 shares. Calculate Wonsto's weighted-average shares outstanding for the year ended December 31, 2005. Round calculations to the nearest whole share.

QS 16-10
Weighted-average
common shares
outstanding—repurchase

LO³

On January 1, Harrell Corp. had 75,000 common shares issued and outstanding. On April 1, it issued 24,000 additional shares and on June 2, declared and distributed a 20% share dividend. Calculate Harrell's weighted-average outstanding shares for the year.

QS 16-11
Weighted average
common shares
outstanding—share dividend

LO³

On January 1, Star Corp. had 50,000 common shares issued and outstanding. On April 1, it issued 4,000 additional shares and on June 5, declared and distributed a two-for-one share split. Calculate Star's weighted-average outstanding shares for the year.

QS 16-12
Calculating weighted
average shares
outstanding—share split

LO³

QS 16-13
Accounting for estimate changes and error adjustments

LO⁴

Answer the questions about each of the following items related to a company's activities for the year:
a. After using an expected useful life of seven years and no salvage value to amortize its office equipment over the preceding three years, the company decided early this year that the equipment would last only two more years. How should the effects of this decision be reported in the current financial statements?
b. An account receivable in the amount of $180,000 was written off two years ago. It was recovered this year. The president believes this should be reported as an error. How should the proceeds be reported in the current year's financial statements?

QS 16-14
Accounting changes

LO⁴

Barton Inc. changed the method of calculating amortization on its equipment from straight-line to double-declining-balance during 2005. The cumulative effect of the change is an additional expense of $46,000 related to prior years. The tax benefit is $13,000. Record the entry on December 31, 2005.

*QS 16-15
Purchase and sale of treasury shares

LO⁵

On May 3, Nicholson Corp. purchased 3,000 of its own shares for $27,000. On November 4, Nicholson reissued 750 treasury shares for $7,080. Prepare the November 4 journal entry Nicholson should make to record the sale of the treasury shares.

*QS 16-16
Treasury shares

LO⁵

Arcon Ltd. had 45,000 common shares issued and outstanding that had been issued for $7.50 each. On September 25, 2005, Arcon repurchased 15,000 shares at $7.80 per share. 10,000 of these shares were reissued to employees of the company on November 14 at $3.00 per share. Record the entries on September 25 and November 14 (assuming this is the first repurchase ever recorded by Arcon).

Exercises

Exercise 16-1
Income statement categories

LO¹

Check figure:
Income before extraordinary items = $124,860

The following list of items was extracted from the December 31, 2005, trial balance of Wesson Corp. Using the information contained in this listing, prepare Wesson's multiple-step income statement for 2005. You need not complete the earnings per share calculations.

	Debit	Credit
Salaries expense	$ 66,700	
Income tax expense (continuing operations)	68,380	
Loss from operating Division C (net of $10,200 tax benefit)	24,000	
Sales		$700,240
Total effect on prior years' income of change from declining-balance to straight-line amortization (net of $9,600 tax)		32,400
Extraordinary gain on provincial condemnation of land owned by Wesson Corp. (net of $24,800 tax)		68,000
Amortization expense	62,100	
Gain on sale of Division C (net of $19,700 tax)		66,000
Cost of goods sold	420,200	

An asterisk (*) identifies assignment material based on Appendix 16A.

In preparing the annual financial statements for Elite Electronics Inc., the correct manner of reporting the following items was not clear to the company's employees. Explain where each of the following items should appear in the financial statements.

a. After amortizing office equipment for three years based on an expected useful life of eight years, the company decided this year that the office equipment should last seven more years. As a result, the amortization for the current year is $8,000 instead of $10,000.

b. This year, the accounting department of the company discovered that last year, an installment payment on the five-year note payable had been charged entirely to interest expense. The after-tax effect of the charge to interest expense was $15,400.

c. The company keeps its repair trucks for several years before disposing of the old trucks and buying new trucks. On June 1 of this year, for the first time in 10 years, it sold old trucks for a gain of $19,900. New trucks were purchased in August of the same year.

Exercise 16-2
Classifying income items not related to continuing operations

During 2005, Magna Data Inc. sold its interest in a chain of wholesale outlets. This sale took the company out of the wholesaling business completely. The company still operates its retail outlets. Following is a lettered list of sections of an income statement:

a. Income from continuing operations
b. Income from operating a discontinued operation
c. Gain or loss from disposing of a discontinued operation
d. Extraordinary gain or loss

Indicate where each of the nine income-related items for the company would appear on the 2005 income statement by writing the letter of the appropriate section in the blank beside each item.

Exercise 16-3
Income statement categories

			Debit	Credit
____	1.	Amortization expense	$ 262,500	
____	2.	Gain on sale of wholesale operation		
		(net of $225,000 income taxes)		$ 675,000
____	3.	Loss from operating wholesale operation		
		(net of $185,000 tax benefit).....................................	555,000	
____	4.	Salaries expense	540,000	
____	5.	Sales..		2,700,000
____	6.	Gain on expropriation of company		
		property (net of $110,000 income taxes)		330,000
____	7.	Cost of goods sold	1,380,000	
____	8.	Income taxes expense..	207,000	

Use the data for Magna Data Inc. in Exercise 16-3 to present a multiple-step income statement for 2005. You need not complete the earnings per share calculations.

Exercise 16-4
Income statement presentation

LO¹

Check figure:
Income from continuing operations (after tax) = $310,500

Exercise 16-5
Share dividends

Delware Inc.'s shareholders' equity section at December 31, 2004, showed the following information:

Common shares, unlimited shares authorized,	
150,000 shares issued and outstanding	$1,850,000
Retained earnings	475,000

On January 15, 2005, Delware's board of directors declared a 5% share dividend to the shareholders of record on January 20 to be distributed on January 30. The market price of the shares on each of these dates was:

January 15...............................	$15.00
20...............................	14.50
30...............................	14.75

Check figure:
2. Retained earnings = $1,012,500

Required
1. Prepare the required entries for January 15, 20, and 30.
2. Prepare the shareholders' equity section at January 31, 2005, assuming net income earned during January 2005 was $650,000.

Exercise 16-6
Share splits

Jostin Inc.'s shareholders' equity section at October 31, 2005, showed the following information:

Common shares, unlimited shares authorized,	
500,000 shares issued and outstanding...	$600,000
Retained earnings	75,000

On November 15, 2005, Jostin's board of directors declared a 3:1 share split to the shareholders of record on November 20 to be distributed on November 29. The market price of the shares on each of these dates was:

November 15...............................	$1.50
20...............................	0.48
29...............................	0.52

Check figure:
2. Retained earnings = $200,000

Required
1. Prepare the required entries for November 15, 20, and 29.
2. Prepare the shareholders' equity section at November 30, 2005, assuming net income earned during November 2005 was $125,000.

Information taken from City Vending Inc.'s January 31, 2005, balance sheet follows:

Common shares, 600,000 shares authorized,	
30,000 shares issued and outstanding	$540,000
Retained earnings	105,800

On February 1, 2005, the company repurchased and retired 400 common shares (the first retirement the company has recorded).

Required
Prepare General Journal entries to record the repurchase and retirement under each of the following independent assumptions.
The shares were repurchased for:
a. $12 per share
b. $18 per share
c. $24 per share

Exercise 16-7
Retirement of shares

LO²

Check figure:
c. Dr Common Shares $7,200

Fargo Inc. showed the following shareholders' equity information at December 31, 2004:

Common shares, 2,000,000 shares authorized;	
500,000 shares issued and outstanding	$1,255,600
Retained earnings	640,000

On April 1, 2005, 200,000 common shares were issued at $2.50 per share. On November 1, the board of directors declared a 15% share dividend to shareholders of record on November 15; the distribution date was December 1. The market prices of the shares on November 1, November 15, and December 1 were $2.60, $2.20, and $2.45, respectively. On December 15, 300,000 shares were repurchased at $2.65 and retired. Net income earned during the year was $490,000.

Required
Prepare the company's shareholders' equity section at December 31, 2005.

Exercise 16-8
Share dividend, retirement of shares, shareholders' equity

LO²

Check figure:
Shareholders' equity
Dec. 31/05 = $2,090,600

The Precision Company of Canada Inc. had the following balances in its shareholders' equity accounts at December 31, 2004:

Common shares, unlimited shares authorized;	
200,000 shares issued and outstanding	$3,000,000
Retained earnings	500,000

During 2005, the following shareholders' equity transactions occurred:

Apr. 15	Repurchased and retired 15,000 common shares at $13 per share.
May 1	Repurchased and retired 25,000 common shares at $17 per share.
Nov. 1	The board of directors declared a 2:1 share split effective on this date.

Required
1. Prepare journal entries to account for the transactions during 2005.
2. Prepare the company's shareholders' equity section at December 31, 2005, assuming a net loss for the year of $170,000.

Exercise 16-9
Share split, retirement of shares

LO²

Check figure:
2. Retained earnings,
Dec. 31/05 = $310,000

Exercise 16-10
Share dividends, share splits,
retirements, shareholders' equity

Jetset Inc. showed the following shareholders' equity account balances at December 31, 2004:

Common shares, unlimited authorized shares,	
680,000 shares issued and outstanding	$3,400,000
Retained earnings	1,800,000

During 2005, the following selected transactions occurred:

Apr.	1	Repurchased and retired 280,000 common shares at $5.25 per share; this is the first retirement recorded by Jetset.
June	1	Declared a 2:1 share split to shareholders of record on June 12, distributable June 30.
Dec.	1	Declared a 10% share dividend to shareholders of record on December 10, distributable December 20. The market prices of the shares on December 1, December 10, and December 20 were $2.75, $2.40, and $2.60 respectively.
	20	Distributed the share dividend declared December 1.
	31	Closed the credit balance of $810,000 in the Income Summary account.

Check figure:
Shareholders' equity,
Dec. 31/05 = $4,540,000

Required
a. Journalize the transactions above.
b. Prepare the shareholders' equity section at December 31, 2005.

Exercise 16-11
Reporting earnings per share

LO¹,³

Northside Corporation's 2005 income statement, excluding the earnings per share portion of the statement, was as follows:

Revenues...		$475,000
Expenses:		
Amortization...	$ 51,900	
Income taxes	65,100	
Other expenses	205,000	322,000
Income from continuing operations.................................		$153,000
Loss from operating discontinued business segment		
(net of $23,500 tax benefit)	$ 56,000	
Loss on sale of business segment (net of $9,400 tax benefit)........	22,000	(78,000)
Income before extraordinary items...................................		$ 75,000
Extraordinary gain (net of $18,400 taxes)		43,200
Net income		$118,200

Check figure:
EPS = $1.18

The weighted-average number of common shares outstanding during the year was 100,000. Present the earnings per share portion of the 2005 income statement.

Exercise 16-12
Weighted-average shares
outstanding and earnings
per share

LO³

Check figure:
Weighted-average outstanding
shares = 84,000

Carefree Footwear Inc. reported $261,400 net income in 2005 and declared preferred dividends of $43,000. The following changes in common shares outstanding occurred during the year:

Jan.	1	60,000 common shares were outstanding.
June	30	Sold 20,000 common shares.
Sept.	1	Declared and issued a 20% common share dividend.

Calculate the weighted-average number of common shares outstanding during the year and earnings per share.

Kingsley Production Corp. reported $741,500 net income in 2005 and declared preferred dividends of $66,500. The following changes in common shares outstanding occurred during the year.

Jan. 1   60,000 common shares were outstanding.
Mar. 1   Sold 20,000 common shares.
Aug. 1   Purchased and retired 4,000 shares.
Dec. 1   Declared and issued a two-for-one share split.

Calculate the weighted-average number of common shares outstanding during the year and earnings per share. Round calculations to the nearest whole share.

Exercise 16-13
Weighted-average shares outstanding and earnings per share

LO^3

Check figure:
Weighted-average
outstanding shares = 150,001

A company reported $1,350,000 of net income for 2005. It also declared $195,000 of dividends on preferred shares for the same year. At the beginning of 2005, the company had 270,000 outstanding common shares. These two events changed the number of outstanding shares during the year:

Apr. 30   Sold 180,000 common shares for cash.
Oct. 31   Purchased and cancelled 108,000 common shares.

a. What is the amount of net income available for distribution to the common shareholders?
b. What is the weighted-average number of common shares for the year?
c. What is the basic earnings per share value for the year?

Exercise 16-14
Weighted-average shares outstanding and earnings per share

LO^3

Check figure:
b. Weighted-average
outstanding shares = 372,000

A company reported $480,000 of net income for 2005. It also declared $65,000 of dividends on preferred shares for the same year. At the beginning of 2005, the company had 50,000 outstanding common shares. These three events changed the number of outstanding shares during the year:

June 1   Sold 30,000 common shares for cash.
Aug. 31   Purchased and retired 13,000 common shares.
Oct.   1   Completed a three-for-one share split.

a. What is the amount of net income available for distribution to the common shareholders?
b. What is the weighted-average number of common shares for the year?
c. What is the basic earnings per share value for the year?

Exercise 16-15
Weighted-average shares outstanding and earnings per share

LO^3

Check figure:
c. EPS = $2.19

Allar Corporation showed the following shareholders' equity account balances at December 31, 2004:

Common shares, unlimited shares authorized,	
70,000 shares issued and outstanding	$680,000
Retained earnings	94,000

Exercise 16-16
Statement of retained earnings

$LO^{2,4}$

Check figure:
b. Total shareholders'
equity = $878,000

Allar Corporation issued long-term debt during 2005 that requires a retained earnings restriction of $60,000. Share dividends declared but not distributed during 2005 totalled 7,000 shares capitalized for a total of $70,000.
a. Prepare a statement of retained earnings for the year ended December 31, 2005, assuming net income earned during the year was $104,000.
b. Prepare the shareholders' equity section at December 31, 2005.
c. What is the maximum amount of dividends that Allar Corporation can declare during 2006?

Exercise 16-17
Accounting for a change in
accounting principle

LO⁴

Canadian Home Company Ltd. put an asset in service on January 1, 2003. Its cost was $225,000, its predicted service life was six years, and its expected salvage value was $22,500. The company decided to use double-declining-balance amortization. After consulting with the company's auditors, management decided to change to straight-line amortization in 2005, without changing either the predicted service life or salvage value.

Required
Explain how and where this change should be accounted for.

Exercise 16-18
Accounting changes

LO⁴

Selected information regarding the accounts of Redware Corp. follows:

Common dividends declared and paid during 2005	$200,000
Cumulative effect of change in accounting estimate (net of $12,000 tax)	(56,000)
Net income for the year ended December 31, 2005	570,000
Preferred dividends declared and paid during 2005	120,000
Retained earnings, December 31, 2004 (as originally reported)	980,000

Prepare a statement of retained earnings for the year ended December 31, 2005.

*Exercise 16-19
Reporting a treasury shares
purchase

LO⁵

On October 10, 2005, the shareholders' equity account balances for Affiliated Systems, Inc., showed the following:

Common shares, unlimited shares authorized, 36,000 shares issued, and outstanding	$468,000
Retained earnings	432,000

On October 11, 2005, the corporation repurchased for treasury 4,500 common shares at $30 per share.

Required
Prepare the shareholders' equity section on October 11, 2005, after the repurchase.

Check figure:
Total shareholders'
equity = $765,000

*Exercise 16-20
Journal entries for treasury
shares transactions

LO⁵

Use the information in Exercise 16-19 to develop the accountant's journal entries to record these events for Affiliated Systems, Inc.:
a. The purchase of the treasury shares on October 11.
b. The sale of 1,500 treasury shares on November 1 for cash at $38 per share.
c. The sale of all the remaining treasury shares on November 25 for cash at $24 per share.

Check figure:
c. Dr. Retained Earnings $6,000

*Exercise 16-21
Treasury shares

LO⁵

Winsley Inc. began 2005 with the following balances in its shareholders' equity accounts:

Common shares, 500,000 shares authorized; 200,000 shares issued and outstanding	$3,000,000
Retained earnings	5,000,000

All of the outstanding shares were issued for $15.

An asterisk (*) identifies assignment material based on Appendix 16A.

Required
Prepare journal entries to account for the following transactions during 2005:

> June 30   Purchased 30,000 treasury shares at $20 per share.
> Aug. 31   Sold 10,000 treasury shares at $20 per share.
> Nov. 30   Sold 15,000 treasury shares at $22 per share.

Problems

The following table shows the balances from various accounts in the adjusted trial balance for Depew Corp. as of December 31, 2005:

Problem 16-1A
Presenting items in an income statement

LO[1]

		Debit	Credit
a.	Interest earned..		$ 12,000
b.	Amortization expense, equipment..	$ 36,000	
c.	Loss on sale of office equipment..	24,750	
d.	Accounts payable..		42,000
e.	Other operating expenses	97,500	
f.	Accumulated amortization, equipment		73,500
g.	Gain from settling a lawsuit		42,000
h.	Cumulative effect of change in accounting principle (pre-tax)		63,000
i.	Accumulated amortization, buildings		163,500
j.	Loss from operating a discontinued operation (pre-tax)............	19,500	
k.	Gain on appropriation of land and building by government (pre-tax)...		28,500
l.	Sales		970,500
m.	Amortization expense, buildings..	54,000	
n.	Correction of overstatement of prior year's sales (pre-tax)	15,000	
o.	Gain on sale of discontinued operation's assets (pre-tax)..		33,000
p.	Loss from settling a lawsuit...	24,000	
q.	Income taxes expense..	?	
r.	Cost of goods sold...	487,500	

Required
Answer each of these questions by providing detailed schedules:
1. Assuming that the company's income tax rate is 30%, what are the tax effects and after-tax measures of the items labelled as pre-tax?
2. What is the amount of the company's income from continuing operations before income taxes? What is the amount of the company's income tax expense? What is the amount of the company's income from continuing operations?
3. What is the amount of after-tax income associated with the discontinued operation?
4. What is the amount of income before extraordinary items?
5. What is the amount of net income for the year?

Problem 16-2A
Earnings per share calculations
and presentation

LO¹,³

Except for the earnings per share statistics, the 2006, 2005, and 2004 income statements of Clear Printing Corp. were originally presented as follows:

	2006	2005	2004
Sales	$998,900	$687,040	$466,855
Costs and expenses	383,570	234,500	157,420
Income from continuing operations	$615,330	$452,540	$309,435
Loss on discontinued operations	(107,325)	—	—
Income (loss) before extraordinary items	$508,005	$452,540	$309,435
Extraordinary gains (losses)	—	80,410	(156,191)
Net income (loss)	$508,005	$532,950	$153,244

Information on Common Shares*

Shares outstanding on December 31, 2003	14,400
Purchase and retirement of shares on March 1, 2004	− 1,440
Sale of shares on June 1, 2004	+ 6,240
Share dividend of 5% on August 1, 2004	+ 960
Shares outstanding on December 31, 2004	20,160
Sale of shares on February 1, 2005	+ 2,880
Purchase and retirement of shares on July 1, 2005	− 720
Shares outstanding on December 31, 2005	22,320
Sale of shares on March 1, 2006	+ 8,280
Purchase and retirement of shares on September 1, 2006	− 1,800
Share split of 3:1 on October 1, 2006	+57,600
Shares outstanding on December 31, 2006	86,400

*No preferred shares have been issued.

Check figures:
Weighted-average outstanding
shares:
1. a. 17,682
   b. 22,440
   c. 85,860

Required

1. Calculate the weighted-average number of common shares outstanding during
   a. 2004   **b.** 2005 and   **c.** 2006.
2. Present the earnings per share portions of:
   a. the 2004 income statement;
   b. the 2005 income statement; and
   c. the 2006 income statement.

Problem 16-3A
Earnings per share

LO³

Jaspur Corp.'s financial statements for the current year ended December 31, 2005, have been completed and submitted to you for review. The shareholders' equity account balances a year ago, at December 31, 2004, are as follows:

Preferred shares, $2.80 non-cumulative, 10,000 shares authorized, issued and outstanding	$498,700
Common shares, unlimited shares authorized, 120,000 shares issued and outstanding	946,900
Retained earnings	450,530

The only share transactions during 2005 were the purchase and retirement of 24,000 common shares on July 1 and the sale of 12,000 common shares on October 31. Jaspur's 2005 net income was $286,200. A cash dividend on the preferred shares was declared on December 1, but was not paid as of December 31. Earnings per share for 2005 were calculated as follows:

$$\frac{\text{Net income}}{\text{Common shares outstanding on Dec. 31, 2005}} = \frac{\$286,200}{108,000} = \$2.65$$

Required

1. Explain what is wrong with the earnings per share calculation, indicating what corrections should be made to both the numerator and the denominator.
2. Explain how your answer to requirement 1 would be different if there had not been a cash dividend declaration to preferred shares and if the purchase and retirement of 24,000 common shares had taken place on January 2, 2005.

The income statement for Davidson Inc.'s year ended December 31, 2005, was prepared by an inexperienced bookkeeper. As the new accountant, your immediate priority is to correct the statement. All amounts included in the statement are before tax (assume a rate of 30%). Davidson Inc. had 100,000 common shares issued and outstanding throughout the year, as well as 20,000 shares of $0.50 cumulative preferred shares issued and outstanding. Retained earnings at December 31, 2004, was $137,000.

Problem 16-4A
Combined statement of income and retained earnings

LO 1, 3, 4

Davidson Inc. Income Statement December 31, 2005		
Revenues:		
Sales..	$480,000	
Gain on sale of equipment	6,000	
Interest revenue...	2,800	
Extraordinary gain...	59,000	
Operating income on discontinued operation	12,100	$559,900
Expenses:		
Cost of goods sold	$145,000	
Selling and administrative expenses	75,000	
Sales discounts	4,900	
Loss on sale of discontinued operation....................	15,000	
Dividends...	50,000	289,900
Net income..		$270,000
Earnings per share..		$2.70

Required

Prepare a corrected multiple-step income statement and statement of retained earnings including earnings per share information. Round earnings per share calculations to the nearest whole cent.

Check figures:
Income before discontinued operation = $184,730;
Earnings per common share = $2.14

The accounts for the Hansen Corporation reported the following shareholders' equity account balances on December 31, 2004:

Problem 16-5A
Dividends, retirement, statement of retained earnings, shareholders' equity

LO 2, 3, 4

Preferred shares, $3 cumulative, unlimited shares authorized............................	$	-0-
Common shares, unlimited shares authorized,		
20,000 shares issued and outstanding		230,000
Retained Earnings		135,000

In 2005, Hansen Corporation had the following transactions affecting shareholders and the shareholders' equity accounts:

Jan. 1 Purchased and retired 2,000 common shares at $15 per share.
      14 The directors declared a 10% share dividend distributable on February 5 to the January 30 shareholders of record. The shares were trading at $19 per share.
      30 Date of record regarding the 10% share dividend.
Feb. 5 Date of distribution regarding the 10% share dividend.
July 6 Sold 5,000 preferred shares at $25 per share.
Sept. 5 The directors declared a total cash dividend of $20,000 payable on October 5 to the September 20 shareholders of record.
Oct. 5 The cash dividend declared on September 5 was paid.
Dec. 31 Closed the $194,000 credit balance in the Income Summary account to Retained Earnings.
      31 Closed the dividend accounts.

Required

1. Prepare journal entries to record the transactions and closings for 2005.
2. Prepare a statement of retained earnings for the year ended December 31, 2005.
3. Prepare the shareholders' equity section of the company's balance sheet as of December 31, 2005.

Check figure:
3. Total shareholders' equity = $634,000

Problem 16-6A
Dividends, retirement, statement of retained earnings, shareholders' equity

$LO^{2,3,4}$

TJ Enterprises Inc. had the following shareholders' equity account balances at December 31, 2004:

Preferred shares, $1.75, non-cumulative,	
Authorized: 20,000 shares	
Issued and outstanding: 5,000 shares	$ 25,000
Common shares,	
Authorized: Unlimited	
Issued and outstanding: 85,000 shares	102,748
Retained earnings	29,000

The board of directors declared and paid the annual cash dividend on the preferred shares on June 30, 2005, and a 12% common share dividend was declared and distributed on the same day when the market price per common share was $1.50. On October 1, 2005, 20,000 of the common shares were repurchased at $1.55 each and then cancelled. Net income earned during 2005 was $146,000.

Check figures:
1. Retained earnings,
Dec. 31/05 = $144,750
2. Total contributed capital,
Dec. 31/05 = $118,248

Required
Using the information provided, prepare the:
1. Statement of retained earnings for the year ended December 31, 2005.
2. Shareholders' equity section of the balance sheet at December 31, 2005.

Problem 16-7A
Retirement of shares, retained earnings analysis

$LO^{2,4}$

Check figure:
1. Outstanding shares
Oct. 5 = 22,200

The equity sections from the 2005 and 2006 balance sheets of TRP Corporation appeared as follows:

TRP Corporation **Shareholders' Equity** **December 31, 2005**	
Contributed capital:	
Common shares, 50,000 shares authorized;	
20,000 shares issued and outstanding	$140,000
Retained earnings	160,000

TRP Corporation **Shareholders' Equity** **December 31, 2006**	
Contributed capital:	
Common shares, 50,000 shares authorized;	
22,200 shares issued and outstanding	$173,900
Retained earnings	200,000

The following transactions occurred during 2006:

Jan.	5	A $0.50 per share cash dividend was declared, and the date of record was five days later.
Mar.	20	1,500 common shares were repurchased and retired at $7 per share.
Apr.	5	A $0.50 per share cash dividend was declared, and the date of record was five days later.
July	5	A $0.50 per share cash dividend was declared, and the date of record was five days later.
	31	A 20% share dividend was declared when the market value was $12 per share.
Aug.	14	The share dividend was issued.
Oct.	5	A $0.50 per share cash dividend was declared, and the date of record was five days later.

Required
1. How many shares were outstanding on each of the cash dividend dates?
2. How much net income did the company earn during 2006?

Waichu Corporation, provincially incorporated, reported the following shareholders' equity account balances on December 31, 2004:

Common shares, unlimited shares authorized, 20,000 shares issued and outstanding...	$230,000
Retained Earnings...	135,000

In 2005, Waichu Corporation had the following transactions affecting shareholders and the shareholder equity accounts:

Jan.	1	Purchased 2,000 treasury shares at $20 per share.
	5	The directors declared a $2.00 per share cash dividend payable on Feb. 28 to the Feb. 5 shareholders of record.
Feb.	28	Paid the dividend declared on January 5.
July	6	Sold 750 of the treasury shares at $24 per share.
Aug.	22	Sold 1,250 of the treasury shares at $17 per share.
Dec.	31	Closed the $194,000 credit balance in the Income Summary account to Retained Earnings.
	31	Closed the Cash Dividends account.

Required
1. Prepare journal entries to record the transactions and closings for 2005.
2. Prepare a statement of retained earnings for the year ended December 31, 2005.
3. Prepare the shareholders' equity section of the company's balance sheet as of December 31, 2005.

Alternate Problems

The following table shows the balances from various accounts in the adjusted trial balance for Barbour Corp. as of December 31, 2005:

		Debit	Credit
a.	Accumulated amortization, buildings...		$ 200,000
b.	Interest earned		10,000
c.	Cumulative effect of change in accounting principle (pre-tax)........		46,000
d.	Sales..		1,320,000
e.	Income taxes expense	?	
f.	Loss on condemnation of property (pre-tax)	32,000	
g.	Accumulated amortization, equipment...		110,000
h.	Other operating expenses..	164,000	
i.	Amortization expense, equipment	50,000	
j.	Loss from settling a lawsuit	18,000	
k.	Gain from settling a lawsuit...		34,000
l.	Loss on sale of office equipment...	12,000	
m.	Loss from operating a discontinued operation (pre-tax)................	60,000	
n.	Amortization expense, buildings	78,000	
o.	Correction of overstatement of prior year's expense (pre-tax).......		24,000
p.	Cost of goods sold	520,000	
q.	Loss on sale of discontinued operation's assets (pre-tax).............	90,000	
r.	Accounts payable		66,000

Required

Answer each of these questions by providing detailed schedules:

1. Assuming that the company's income tax rate is 25%, what are the tax effects and after-tax measures of the items labelled as "pre-tax"?
2. What is the amount of the company's income from continuing operations before income taxes? What is the amount of the company's income taxes expense? What is the amount of the company's income from continuing operations?
3. What is the amount of after-tax income associated with the discontinued operation?
4. What is the amount of income before extraordinary items?
5. What is the amount of net income for the year?

Problem 16-2B

Earnings per share calculations and presentation

LO[1,3]

The original income statements for Titus, Inc., presented the following information when they were first published in 2004, 2005, and 2006:

	2006	2005	2004
Sales	$400,000	$300,000	$250,000
Expenses	270,000	215,000	160,000
Income from continuing operations	$130,000	$ 85,000	$ 90,000
Loss on discontinued segment			(26,145)
Income before extraordinary items	$130,000	$ 85,000	$ 63,855
Extraordinary gain (loss)	(37,125)	14,100	
Net income	$ 92,875	$ 99,100	$ 63,855

The company also experienced some changes in the number of outstanding common shares over the three years through the following events:*

Outstanding shares on December 31, 2003	10,000
2004	
Treasury shares purchase on July 1	− 1,000
Issuance of new shares on September 30	+ 3,500
20% share dividend on December 1	+ 2,500
Outstanding shares on December 31, 2004	15,000
2005	
Issuance of new shares on March 31	+ 4,000
Treasury shares purchase on October 1	− 1,500
Outstanding shares on December 31, 2005	17,500
2006	
Issuance of new shares on July 1	+ 3,000
Treasury shares purchase on October 1	− 1,750
2:1 split on November 1	+18,750
Outstanding shares on December 31, 2006	37,500

*No preferred shares have been issued.

Check figure:

Weighted average outstanding shares:

1. a. 12,450
   b. 17,625
   c. 37,125

Required

1. Calculate the weighted average of the outstanding common shares as of the end of:
   a. 2004;
   b. 2005; and
   c. 2006.
2. Present the earnings per share portions of:
   a. the 2004 income statement;
   b. the 2005 income statement; and
   c. the 2006 income statement.

Computex Corporation has tentatively prepared its financial statements for the year ended December 31, 2005, and has submitted them to you for review. The shareholders' equity account balances at December 31, 2005, are as follows:

Problem 16-3B
Earnings per share

LO³

Preferred shares, $2.50 cumulative, 30,000 shares authorized, 18,000 shares issued and outstanding..	$520,100
Common shares, unlimited shares authorized; 132,000 shares issued and outstanding..	777,840
Retained earnings..	996,200

Computex Corporation's 2005 net income was $600,000 and no cash dividends were declared. The only share transaction that occurred during the year was the sale of 24,000 common shares on March 31, 2005. Earnings per share for 2005 was calculated as follows:

$$\frac{\text{Net income}}{\substack{\text{Common plus preferred shares} \\ \text{outstanding on Dec. 31}}} = \frac{\$600,000}{132,000 + 18,000} = \$4.00$$

Required

1. Explain what is wrong with the earnings per share calculation, indicating what corrections should be made to both the numerator and the denominator.
2. Explain how your answer to requirement 1 could be different if the preferred shares were not cumulative and if the issuance of 24,000 shares had been a share dividend.

After returning from vacation, the accountant of Bosworth Inc. was dismayed to discover that the income statement for the year ended December 31, 2005, was prepared incorrectly. All amounts included in the statement are before tax (assume a rate of 40%). Bosworth Inc. had 200,000 common shares issued and outstanding throughout the year as well as 70,000 $2.00 cumulative preferred shares. Dividends had not been paid for the past two years (2003 and 2004). Retained earnings at December 31, 2004, was $342,000.

Problem 16-4B
Combined statement of income and retained earnings

LO¹, ³, ⁴

Bosworth Inc. Income Statement December 31, 2005		
Revenues:		
Sales	$1,800,000	
Gain on sale of discontinued operation.......................................	240,000	
Accumulated amortization, equipment.......................................	45,000	
Operating income on discontinued operation.............................	636,000	$2,721,000
Expenses:		
Cost of goods sold...	$ 480,000	
Selling and administrative expenses..	180,000	
Sales returns and allowances	14,000	
Extraordinary loss	80,000	
Dividends...	95,000	849,000
Net income		$1,872,000
Earnings per share..		$9.36

Required

Prepare a corrected multiple-step income statement and statement of retained earnings including earnings per share information. Round all earnings per share calculations to the nearest whole cent.

Check figures:
Income before discontinued operation = $675,600;
Earnings per share = $5.07

Problem 16-5B

Dividends, share split, retirement, statement of retained earnings, shareholders' equity

LO 2, 3, 4

The shareholders' equity accounts for Caldwell Corp. showed the following balances on December 31, 2004:

Preferred shares, $2.50 non-cumulative, unlimited shares authorized............ $ –0–	
Common shares, unlimited shares authorized,	
100,000 shares issued and outstanding	800,000
Retained earnings...	1,080,000

The company completed these transactions during 2005:

Jan. 10   Purchased and retired 20,000 common shares at $12 cash per share.
Mar. 2   The directors declared a $1.50 per share cash dividend payable on March 31 to the March 15 shareholders of record.
    31   Paid the dividend declared on March 2.
Apr. 10   The directors announced a 3:1 share split to the April 20 shareholders of record. The shares were trading just prior to the announcement at $12.50 per share.
Nov. 11   Issued 12,000 preferred shares at $25 per share.
Dec. 31   Closed the $136,000 debit balance in the Income Summary account to Retained Earnings.
    31   Closed the Cash Dividends account.

Check figure:
3. Total shareholders' equity = $1,684,000

Required
1. Prepare General Journal entries to record the transactions and closings for 2005.
2. Prepare a statement of retained earnings for 2005.
3. Prepare the shareholders' equity section of the company's balance sheet as of December 31, 2005.

Problem 16-6B

Dividends, retirement, statement of retained earnings, shareholders' equity

LO 2, 3, 4

BusCom Corp. had the following shareholders' equity account balances at December 31, 2004:

Preferred shares, $0.50, cumulative,	
Authorized: 100,000 shares	
Issued and outstanding: 45,000 shares	$360,000
Common shares,	
Authorized: Unlimited	
Issued and outstanding: 300,000 shares	898,200
Retained earnings...	218,000

On November 1, 2005, the board of directors declared and paid the current year's cash dividend on the preferred shares plus the two years of dividends in arrears. On the same day, a 10% common share dividend was declared and distributed; the market price per common share was $3.50. On December 1, 2005, 100,000 of the common shares were repurchased at $3.60 each and then cancelled. Net income earned during 2005 was $479,000.

Check figures:
1. Retained earnings, Dec. 31/05 = $468,500
2. Total contributed capital, Dec. 31/05 = $1,059,200

Required
Using the information provided, prepare the:
1. Statement of retained earnings for the year ended December 31, 2005.
2. Shareholders' equity section of the balance sheet at December 31, 2005.

The equity sections from the 2004 and 2005 balance sheets of Thornhill Corporation appeared as follows:

Problem 16-7B
Retirement of shares, retained earnings analysis

LO^{2,4}

Thornhill Corporation
Shareholders' Equity
December 31, 2004

Contributed capital:
Common shares, 15,000 shares authorized,
8,500 shares issued and outstanding.. $200,000
Retained earnings 135,000
Total shareholders' equity $335,000

Thornhill Corporation
Shareholders' Equity
December 31, 2005

Contributed capital:
Common shares, 15,000 shares authorized,
9,000 shares issued and authorized... $230,235
Retained earnings 147,600
Total shareholders' equity $377,835

The following events occurred during 2005:

Feb. 15   A $0.40 per share cash dividend was declared, and the date of record was five days later.
Mar. 2   500 common shares were purchased for retirement at $23.53 per share.
May 15   A $0.40 per share cash dividend was declared, and the date of record was five days later.
Aug. 15   A $0.40 per share cash dividend was declared, and the date of record was five days later.
Oct. 4   A 12.5% share dividend was declared when the market value was $42 per share.
      20   The dividend shares were issued.
Nov. 15   A $0.40 per share cash dividend was declared, and the date of record was five days later.

Required
1. How many shares were outstanding on each of the cash dividend dates?
2. How much net income did the company earn during 2005?

Check figure:
1. Outstanding shares
Nov. 15 = 9,000

Lavigne Corp. reported the following shareholders' equity account balances on December 31, 2004:

*Problem 16-8B
Dividends, treasury shares transactions

LO^{4,5}

Common shares, unlimited shares authorized;
100,000 shares issued and outstanding... $ 800,000
Retained earnings 1,080,000

An asterisk (*) identifies assignment material based on Appendix 16A.

The company completed these transactions during 2005:

Jan. 10	Purchased 20,000 treasury shares at $12 cash per share.
Mar. 2	The directors declared a $1.50 per share cash dividend payable on March 31 to the March 15 shareholders of record.
31	Paid the dividend declared on March 2.
Nov. 11	Sold 12,000 of the treasury shares at $13 per share.
25	Sold 8,000 of the treasury shares at $9.50 per share.
Dec. 1	The directors declared a $2.50 per share cash dividend payable on January 2, 2006, to the December 10 shareholders of record.
31	Closed the $536,000 credit balance in the Income Summary account to Retained Earnings.
31	Closed the Cash Dividends account.

Check figures:
2. Retained earnings = $1,238,000
3. Total shareholders' equity = $2,038,000

Required
1. Prepare General Journal entries to record the transactions and closings for 2005.
2. Prepare a statement of retained earnings for 2005.
3. Prepare the shareholders' equity section of the company's balance sheet as of December 31, 2005.

Analytical and Review Problem

A & R 16-1

The following adjusted trial balance information (with accounts in alphabetical order) for Willis Tour Co. Inc. as at December 31, 2005, was made available after its second year of operations:

Account	Debit	Credit
Accounts Payable		$ 5,000
Accumulated Amortization, Office Equipment		16,000
Cash	$ 35,000	
Common Shares, 20,000 authorized; 10,000 issued and outstanding		25,000
Dividends Payable		9,000
Gain on Appropriation of Land and Building (net of $10,000 tax)		40,000
Income Tax Expense	14,000	
Income Tax Payable		4,000
Loss on Sale of Office Equipment	27,000	
Notes Payable (due in 18 months)		17,000
Office Equipment	112,000	
Operating Expenses	391,000	
Preferred Shares, $0.50 non-cumulative; 5,000 shares authorized; 2,000 shares issued and outstanding		20,000
Prepaid Rent	45,000	
Retained Earnings		29,000
Ticket Sales		459,000
Totals	$624,000	$624,000

Required
Willis follows the practice of debiting retained earnings directly for the annual dividend declaration. Prepare a multiple-step income statement, statement of retained earnings, and a classified balance sheet for Willis Tour Co. Inc. using the information provided. Include the appropriate presentation for earnings per share.

JenStar's management team has decided that its income statement would be more useful if amortization were calculated using the double-declining-balance method instead of the straight-line method. This change in accounting principle adds $156,000 to net income in the current year. As the auditor of the company, you are reviewing the decision to make the change in accounting principle. You review the equipment in question and realize that it is a piece of high-tech equipment and the risk of obsolescence in the near future is relatively high. You are also aware that all members of top management receive year-end bonuses based on net income.

Required
As an auditor in this situation, would you support the change in principle or ask management to continue using the straight-line method? Justify your response.

Focus on Financial Statements

FFS 16-1

LR Enterprises Inc. had the following shareholders' equity account balances at December 31, 2004:

Preferred shares, $1.75, non-cumulative,	
Authorized: 100,000 shares	
Issued and outstanding: 45,000 shares...	$ 675,000
Common shares,	
Authorized: Unlimited	
Issued and outstanding: 800,000 shares...	1,320,000
Retained earnings	645,000

Sales during 2005 totalled $1,560,000 and operating expenses were $998,000. Assume that income tax is accrued at year-end at the rate of 30% of annual operating income. On March 1, 2005, 200,000 of the common shares were repurchased at $1.70 each and then cancelled. The board of directors declared and paid the annual cash dividend on the preferred shares on December 1 and an 8% common share dividend was declared and distributed on the same day when the market price per common share was $1.80.

Required

Preparation component:
Use the information provided to prepare:
1. An income statement for the year ended December 31, 2005, including appropriate earnings per share information.
2. A statement of retained earnings for the year ended December 31, 2005.
3. A classified balance sheet at December 31, 2005, assuming the following adjusted account balances: Cash, $168,000; Accounts Receivable, $102,000; Allowance for Doubtful Accounts, $3,500; Prepaid Insurance, $36,000; Land, $1,000,000; Building, $500,000; Accumulated Amortization, Building, $241,000; Machinery, $1,909,600; Accumulated Amortization, Machinery, $653,850; Furniture, $78,000; Accumulated Amortization, Furniture, $44,000; Accounts Payable, $41,000; Notes Payable (due March 2007), $27,000.

Analysis component:
4. What percent of the assets is financed by debt?
5. What percent of the assets is financed by equity?

Bonds and Long-Term Notes Payable

Get Real!

Montreal, Que.—Yvette Bourque has overcome odds before. Several years ago she had a plan to open a natural foods store near Montreal. But she needed money. She took plans for her store to the local bank. "The banker criticized my business plan and told me to get real," says Bourque. "That really got to me."

Bourque turned to her family and friends for startup money. Motivated by the banker's remark, Bourque is now the proud owner of Get Real! "I sell *real* food like farm-raised seafood and natural and organic produce. It's successful beyond my wildest expectations. It's like a dream." Get Real! now offers a line of more than 2,000 products.

But Bourque faced another obstacle. "I wanted to open two more stores. One in Quebec City and one in Ottawa." Again, Bourque met with several bankers to get a loan. "Every bank wanted me to come to four meetings and prepare five sets of forecasts. Only then will they make a loan proposal, and none of them were acceptable to me. They viewed my plans as risky and I had little collateral."

Then Bourque got an idea. "I remembered when Ben & Jerry's was a tiny ice-cream parlor and advertised its shares on its ice-cream cartons. But I didn't want the headache of shareholders." Bourque decided to issue bonds on her own and got a lawyer to draw up papers. "I put up posters in the store and printed notices on my grocery bags offering bonds for sale. I also added the notice to my regular newspaper ads." For just the $25 par value, people could buy one of my 8% bonds.

"I was flooded with requests. Some people viewed the bonds as an investment, others as a novelty. In the backroom, I typed in names and addresses and printed up bond certificates. When people sent me a cheque, I sent the bonds." Bourque ended up raising over $200,000. "I'm really fired up! I've already rented a location in Ottawa, and I'm close to a deal in Quebec City." Thanks to one banker, Get Real! is a *real* success.

Learning Objectives

LO1 Compare bond versus share financing.

LO2 Explain the types of bonds and their issuing procedures.

LO3 Prepare entries to record bonds issued at par.

LO4 Determine the price of a bond.

LO5 Prepare entries to record bonds issued at a discount.

LO6 Prepare entries to record bonds issued at a premium.

LO7 Record the retirement of bonds.

LO8 Explain and record notes.

*APPENDIX 17B

*LO9 Prepare entries to record lease liabilities.

Chapter Preview

In Chapters 15 and 16, we learned that companies can get funds through equity financing: by issuing shares and by increasing retained earnings through profitable operations. This chapter discusses another major source of funds—debt financing: issuing bonds. Companies and governments issue bonds to finance their activities. In return for money, bonds promise to repay the amount borrowed plus interest. This chapter explains the basics of bonds and the accounting for their issuance and retirement. We explain how present value concepts affect both the accounting and reporting of bonds. The chapter also describes long-term notes and installment notes. Understanding how bonds and notes are used to the advantage of a company, as shown in the opening article, is an important goal of this chapter.

Basics of Bonds

A **bond** is a written promise to pay an amount identified as the *par value* of the bond along with interest at a stated annual rate. A bond is a liability to the borrowing or issuing corporation. The **par value** of the bond, also called the *face amount* or *face value*, is paid at a specified future date known as the *maturity date of the bond*. The total amount of interest P.533 paid each year is determined by multiplying the par value of the bond by the bond's stated rate of interest. The stated interest rate, sometimes called the **contract rate**, *nominal rate*, or *coupon rate*, is quoted as an annual rate. Interest can be paid annually, semi-annually, or for some other fraction of the year. For example, let's suppose a company issues a $1,000 bond with a contract interest rate of 8% to be paid semi-annually. For this bond, the annual interest of $80 (= 8% × $1,000) is paid in two semi-annual payments of $40 each. The document that specifies the issuer's name, the bond's par value, the contract interest rate, and the maturity date is called a **bond certificate**.

This section explains both advantages and disadvantages of bond financing.

Certificate Number
0001

$2,000,000.00

Issuing Company

Interest Rate

Maturity Date

Principal Amount

ABC COMPANY INC.
(incorporated under
the laws of Canada)

CUSIP TO FOLLOW

12.0% Debentures

ABC Company Inc. (the "Company"), for value received, hereby promises to pay to the registered holder (the "Holder"), John Doe on February 28, 2008, or on such earlier date as the principal amount hereof may become payable in accordance with the conditions herein set out and with the provisions of the Trust Indenture hereinafter mentioned, on presentation and surrender of this Debenture, the sum of $ 2,000,000.00.

in lawful money of Canada, at the office of the Trustee at Any town, Saskatchewan and to pay interest thereon from and including the date of issue at the Interest Rate, payable after as well as before maturity and after as well as before default judgment, with interest on amounts in default at the same rate, on each interest payment date.

As interest becomes due on this Debenture, (excepting interest payable at maturity which may be paid upon presentation and surrender of such Debentures for payment at the offices of the Trustee in Anytown), the Fund shall cause to be sent by prepaid first class mail a cheque for such interest (less any tax required by law to be withheld therefrom) payable to the order of the Holder and addressed to him at his last address appearing on the register, unless the Holder otherwise directs. In the case of joint Holders the cheque shall be payable to/or issued to the order of all such joint Holders and addressed to them at the last address appearing on the register, unless such joint Holders otherwise direct. If more than one address appears on the register in respect of such joint Holders, the cheque shall be made to the first address so appearing. In the event of non-receipt of any cheque for interest by the Holder, the Fund will cause to be issued a replacement cheque for like amount upon being furnished with such evidence of non-receipt as it shall reasonably require and upon being indemnified to its satisfaction, acting reasonably.

This Debenture is one of the Debentures in lawful money of Canada issued under a Trust Indenture (herein referred to as the "Trust Indenture") dated as of February 28, 2003 made between the Company and XYZ Trust Company, as Trustee. The aggregate principal amount of Debentures which may be authorized under the Trust Indenture is $40,000,000. Reference is made hereby to the Trust Indenture and any instruments supplemental thereto for a statement and description of the terms and conditions upon which this Debenture is issued and the rights and remedies of the Holders of the Debentures, the Fund and the Trustee with respect thereto, all to the same effect as if the provisions of the Trust Indenture and of any instruments supplemental thereto were herein set forth, to all of which provisions the registered Holder of this Debenture, by acceptance hereof assents.

The Debentures are issuable as fully registered Debentures in denominations of One Thousand ($1,000) Dollars and integral multiples thereof only. Upon compliance with the provisions of the Trust Indenture, Debentures of any authorized denominations may be exchanged for an equal aggregate principal amount of Debentures in any other authorized denomination or denominations.

All Debentures issued under the Trust Indenture rank equally and rateably without priority or preference.

The Debenture may only be transferred upon compliance with the conditions prescribed in the Trust Indenture on one of the registers to be kept at the principal office of the Trustee in Anytown and at such other place or places (if any) and/or by such other registrar or registrars (if any) as the Fund with the approval of the Trustee may designate, by the registered holder hereof or his executors or administrators or other legal representatives, or his or their attorney duly appointed by an instrument in writing in form and execution satisfactory to the Trustee and/or other registrar may prescribe, and then, only if such transfer shall have been duly entered on one of the appropriate registers or noted on this Debenture by a proper registrar.

The Trust Indenture contains provisions making binding upon all Holders of Debentures outstanding thereunder resolutions passed at meetings of such Holders held in accordance with such provisions and instruments in writing signed by the Holders of a specified percentage of the principal amount of the Debentures outstanding.

This Debenture shall not become obligatory for any purpose until it shall have been certified by the Trustee for the time being under the Trust Indenture

Unless otherwise defined, all initially capitalized terms used herein shall have the meaning ascribed to such terms in the Trust Indenture.

IN WITNESS WHEREOF ABC Company has caused this Debenture to be signed by its duly authorized officers as of the 28 day of February, 2003

ABC Company Inc.

By

By

Trustee

Trustee

PRINTED IN CANADA   SM / Border Style 40FR / Color Red 485   BRITISH AMERICAN BANK NOTE COMPANY LIMITED   Specimen_debenture (p2680tor03) / 1ˢᵗ proof / Oct 6ᵗʰ, 2003

Advantages of Bonds

LO¹ Compare bond versus share financing.

There are three main advantages of bond financing over share financing.

1. *Bonds do not affect shareholder control.* Shares reflect an ownership right in the corporation, whereas a bond does not. A *bondholder* has lent the company money and therefore has a *receivable* from the bond issuer.

2. *Interest on bonds is tax deductible.* Bond interest is tax deductible, but dividends to shareholders are not. To illustrate the importance of this, let's assume a company that pays tax at the rate of 40% issued $1,000,000 of bonds that pay interest at 10%. Interest expense will be $100,000 (= $1,000,000 × 10%). Because interest expense is tax deductible, the company's income tax expense will be reduced by the amount of the interest expense times the tax rate or $40,000 (= $100,000 × 40%). Because the corporation saves $40,000 in taxes, the true cost (or after-tax cost) of borrowing is $60,000 (= $100,000 interest expense less $40,000 tax saving). If the same amount of money were raised by issuing shares, instead of bonds, $100,000 paid out as dividends would not be tax deductible and the net costs of raising the $1,000,000 would be the full amount of the dividends.

3. *Bonds can increase return on equity.* Return on equity is net income available to common shareholders divided by common shareholders' equity.[1] When a company earns a higher return with the borrowed funds than it is paying in interest, it increases its return on equity. This process is called *financial leverage.*

To illustrate the effect on return on equity, let's look at Magnum Skates Corp. Magnum's income before tax is $100,000 per year and it has no interest expense. It has $1 million in equity, and is planning a $500,000 expansion to meet increasing demand for its product. Magnum predicts the $500,000 expansion will provide $125,000 in additional income before paying any interest and tax. Magnum is considering three plans:

- Plan A is to not expand.
- Plan B is to expand, and raise $500,000 from issuing shares.
- Plan C is to sell $500,000 worth of bonds paying 10% annual interest, or $50,000.

Exhibit 17.1 shows us how these three plans affect Magnum's net income, equity, and return on equity (net income ÷ equity).

Exhibit 17.1

Financing With Bonds or Shares

	Plan A: Do Not Expand	Plan B: Increase Equity	Plan C: Issue Bonds
Income before interest expense and tax..........	$ 100,000	$ 225,000	$ 225,000
Interest expense...	—	—	(50,000)
Income before tax...	$ 100,000	$ 225,000	$ 175,000
Equity...	$1,000,000	$1,500,000	$1,000,000
Return on equity (net income ÷ equity) ..	**10.0%**	**15.0%**	**17.5%**

---

[1] Ratios are discussed in more detail in Chapter 20.

Analysis of these plans shows that the corporation will earn a higher return on equity if it expands. The preferred plan of expansion is to issue bonds. Why? Even though the projected income before tax under Plan C of $175,000 is smaller than the $225,000 under Plan B, the return on equity is larger because of less shareholder investment. This is an important example of **financial leverage** and proves a general rule: Return on equity increases when the expected rate of return from the new assets is greater than the rate of interest on the bonds. Issuing bonds also allows the current owners to remain in control.

Disadvantages of Bonds

There are two main disadvantages of bond financing over share financing.

> 1. *Bonds **require** payment of **both** annual interest and par value at maturity.* Bond payments can be a burden when a company's income is low. Shares, on the other hand, do not require payment of dividends because they are declared at the discretion of the board of directors.
> 2. *Bonds can decrease return on equity.* When a company earns a lower return with the borrowed funds than it is paying in interest, it decreases its return on equity. This is a risk of bond financing and is more likely to arise when a company has periods of low income.

A company must weigh the risks of these disadvantages against the advantages of bond financing when deciding how to finance operations.

Types of Bonds

Bonds appear on the balance sheets of companies such as Air Canada, Bell Canada Enterprises, Bombardier, Canadian Tire, and Magna International. We describe the more common kinds of bonds in this section.

Secured and Unsecured Bonds

Secured bonds have specific assets of the issuing company pledged (or *mortgaged*) as *collateral* (a guarantee). This arrangement gives bondholders added protection if the issuing company fails to pay interest or par value. In the event of non-payment, secured bondholders can demand that the secured assets be sold and the proceeds used to pay the bond obligation.

Unsecured bonds, also called **debentures**, are supported by the issuer's general credit standing. Because debentures are unsecured, a company generally must be financially strong to issue debentures successfully at a favourable rate of interest.

 LO2 Explain the types of bonds and their issuing procedures.

Term and Serial Bonds

Term bonds make up a bond issue that becomes due at a single specified date. **Serial bonds** comprise a bond issue whose component parts mature at several different dates (in series). For instance, $1 million of serial bonds might mature at the rate of $100,000 each year from Year 6 until all the bonds are fully repaid in Year 15.

Registered Bonds and Bearer Bonds

Bonds issued in the names and addresses of their owners are **registered bonds**. The issuing company makes bond payments by sending cheques to these registered owners.

Bonds payable to whomever holds them (the *bearer*) are called **bearer bonds**, or *unregistered bonds*. Since there may be no record of sales or exchanges, the holder of a bearer bond is presumed to be its rightful owner. As a result, lost or stolen bearer bonds are difficult to replace.

Many bearer bonds are also **coupon bonds**. This term reflects interest coupons that are attached to these bonds. Each coupon matures on a specific interest payment date. The owner detaches each coupon when it matures and presents it to a bank or broker for collection.

Convertible and Callable Bonds

Bondholders can exchange **convertible bonds** for a fixed number of the issuing company's common shares. Convertible bonds offer bondholders the potential to participate in future increases in the share's market value. If the shares do not appreciate and the bonds are not converted, bondholders continue to receive periodic interest and will receive the par value when the bond matures. In most cases, the bondholders decide whether and when to convert the bonds to shares. **Callable** or **redeemable bonds** have an option under which they can be retired at a stated dollar amount prior to maturity. In the case of callable bonds, the issuer has the option of retiring them; in the case of redeemable bonds, it is the purchaser who has the option of retiring them.

A summary of types of bonds and their features is presented in Exhibit 17.2.

Exhibit 17.2

Summary of Bond Features

Types of Bonds	Explanation
1. Secured or Unsecured a. Secured b. Unsecured (called debentures)	a. Assets are pledged as a guarantee of payment by the issuing company. b. Backed not by specific assets but only by the earning capacity and credit reputation of the issuer.
2. Term and Serial a. Term b. Serial	a. Principal of all bonds is due in a lump sum at a specified single date. b. Principal is due in installments at several different dates.
3. Registered and Bearer a. Registered b. Bearer	a. Bonds issued registered in the names of the buyers. Ownership records are kept up to date. b. Bonds payable to whomever possesses them. No records are kept for change of ownership. Many are coupon bonds, meaning that interest is paid to the holder of attached coupons.
4. Convertible, Callable, Redeemable a. Convertible b. Callable c. Redeemable	a. Bonds that allow the buyer to exchange the bond for common shares at a fixed ratio. b. Bonds that may be called for early retirement at the option of the issuing corporation. c. Bonds that may be retired early at the option of the purchaser.

Bond Issuing Procedures

Issuing company bonds usually requires approval by both the board of directors and shareholders and is governed by provincial and federal laws that require registration with a securities commission. Registration with the securities commission requires that it be informed of the number of bonds authorized, their par value, and the contract interest rate. Bonds are typically issued in par value units of $1,000 or $5,000.

The legal document (contract) identifying the rights and obligations of both the bondholders and the issuer is called the **bond indenture**. The issuing company normally sells the bonds to an investment firm such as BMO Nesbitt Burns, called an *underwriter*, which resells them to the public or directly to investors. The bondholders' interests are represented and protected by a *trustee* who monitors the issue to ensure it complies with the obligations in the bond indenture. Most trustees are large banks or trust companies.

BMO Nesbitt Burns®
www.bmonesbittburns.com

Bond Trading

The offering of bonds to the public is called *floating an issue*. Because bonds are exchanged in the market, they have a market value (price). For convenience, bond market values are expressed as a percent of their par (face) value. For example, a company's bonds might be trading at 103½, which means they can be bought or sold for 103.5% of their par value. Bonds that trade above par value are said to trade at a **premium**. Bonds trading below par value trade at a **discount**. For instance, if a company's bonds are trading at 95, they can be bought or sold at 95% of their par value.

The **market rate of interest**, or **effective interest rate**, is the amount of interest borrowers are willing to pay and lenders are willing to earn for a particular bond given its risk level. When the contract rate and market rate are equal, the bonds sell at their par value, or 100%. When the contract rate does not equal the market rate, the bonds sell at either above or below their par values (greater or less than 100%) as detailed in Exhibit 17.3.

Contract rate is:		Bond sells:
Above market rate	➡	At a premium (> 100% of face value)
Equal to market rate	➡	At par value (= 100% of face value)
Below market rate	➡	At a discount (< 100% of face value)

Exhibit 17.3

Relation Between Bond Issue Price, Contract Rate, and Market Rate

1. Unsecured bonds supported only by the issuer's general credit standing are called: (a) Serial bonds; (b) Debentures; (c) Registered bonds; (d) Convertible bonds; (e) Bearer bonds.

2. How do you calculate the amount of interest a bond issuer pays each year?

3. When the contract interest rate is above the market interest rate, do bonds sell at a premium or a discount? Do purchasers pay more or less than the par value of the bonds?

Flashback

Answers—p. 894

LO³ Prepare entries to record bonds issued at par.

Issuing Bonds at Par

This section explains accounting for bond issuances at par. We first show the accounting for bonds issued on the stated date and then show how to account for bonds that are issued between interest dates. Later in the chapter we will explain accounting for bonds issued below par and above par.

To illustrate an issuance of bonds at par value, let's suppose Barnes Corp. receives authorization to issue $800,000 of 9%, 20-year bonds. The bonds are dated January 1, 2005, and are due in 20 years on January 1, 2025. They pay interest semi-annually each June 30 and December 31. If all bonds are sold at their par value, Barnes Corp. makes this entry to record the sale:

2005			
Jan. 1	Cash	800,000	
	Bonds Payable		800,000
	Sold bonds at par.		

This entry reflects increases in the company's cash and long-term liabilities.

Six months later, the first semi-annual interest payment is made, and Barnes records the payment as:

2005			
June 30	Bond Interest Expense..................................	36,000	
	Cash..		36,000
	Paid semi-annual interest on bonds;		
	9% × $800,000 × 6/12.		

Barnes pays and records the semi-annual interest every six months until the bonds mature.

When the bonds mature 20 years later, Barnes Corp. records its payment of the maturity value with this entry:

2025			
Jan. 1	Bonds Payable..	800,000	
	Cash..		800,000
	Paid bonds at maturity.		

Issuing Bonds Between Interest Dates

Many bonds are sold on an interest payment date. But when a company sells its bonds at a date other than an interest payment date the purchasers pay the issuer the purchase price plus any interest accrued since the prior interest payment date. This accrued interest is then repaid to the bondholders by the issuing corporation on the next interest date.

To illustrate, let's suppose that Canadian Tire has $100,000 of 9% bonds available for sale on January 1. Interest is payable semi-annually on each June 30 and December 31. If the bonds are sold at par on March 1, two months after the original issue date of January 1, the issuer collects two months' interest from the buyer at the time of the sale. This amount is $1,500 (= $100,000 × 9% × 2/12) as shown in Exhibit 17.4.

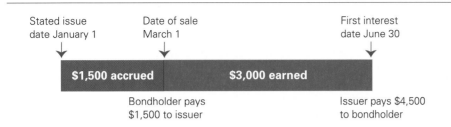

Exhibit 17.4

Accruing Interest Between
Interest Dates

Canadian Tire's entry to record the sale of its bonds on March 1 is:

Mar. 1	Cash	101,500	
	Interest Payable		1,500
	Bonds Payable		100,000
	Sold $100,000 of bonds at par with two		
	months' accrued interest.		

Liabilities for interest payable and the bonds are recorded in separate accounts.

When the June 30 semi-annual interest date arrives, Canadian Tire pays a full six months' interest of $4,500 (= $100,000 × 9% × 6/12) to the bondholder. This payment includes the four months' interest of $3,000 earned by the bondholder from March 1 to June 30 plus the repayment of two months' accrued interest collected by Canadian Tire when the bonds were sold, as shown in Exhibit 17.4 above.

Canadian Tire's entry to record this first interest payment is:

June 30	Interest Payable..	1,500	
	Bond Interest Expense....................................	3,000	
	Cash..		4,500
	Paid semi-annual interest on the bonds.		

The practice of collecting and then repaying accrued interest with the first interest payment is done to simplify the bond issuer's administrative efforts. To understand this, suppose Canadian Tire sold bonds on 20 different dates between the original issue date and the first interest payment date. If Canadian Tire did not collect accrued interest from buyers, it would need to pay 20 different amounts of cash to various bondholders on the first interest payment date. The extra recordkeeping this would involve is avoided by having each buyer pay accrued interest at the time of purchase. Issuers then pay interest of equal amounts to all purchasers, regardless of when the bonds were purchased.

Bond Pricing

Prices for bonds that are traded on an organized exchange are published in newspapers and available through online services. This information includes the bond price (called *quote*), its contract rate, and its market rate (called *yield*). Only a fraction of bonds outstanding are actually traded on an organized exchange, however; many others are rarely traded. To calculate the price of a bond, we need to apply present value concepts. This can be done using special bond pricing tables or through calculating the present value of a bond's cash flows. The *market* interest rate is used to find the present value of a bond. The *contract* interest rate is used to calculate the cash interest payments produced by the bond. This section explains how we use *present value concepts* to price a *discount bond* and a *premium bond*.

LO4 Determine the price
of a bond.

Extend Your Knowledge

17-1

Present Value of a Discount Bond

The issue price of bonds is found by calculating the present value of the bond's future cash payments. To illustrate, Fila Corp. announces an offer to issue bonds with a $100,000 par value, an 8% annual contract rate with interest payable *semi-annually*, and a three-year life. The market rate for Fila's bonds is 10%, meaning the bonds will sell at a discount since the contract rate (8%) is less than the market rate (10%).[2] When calculating the present value of the Fila bond, we work with semi-annual compounding periods because the time between interest payments is six months. This means the annual market rate of 10% is equal to a semi-annual rate of 5% and the three-year life of the bonds is equal to six semi-annual periods.

The two steps involved in calculating the issue price are to find the present value of the:

1. $100,000 maturity payment and
2. Six interest payments of $4,000 each (= $100,000 × 8% × 6/12).

These present values can be determined by using present value functions found on business calculators, by keying in present value formulas on basic calculators that have a power key, or by using present value tables.[3] Appendix 17A lists two present value tables for those who choose not to use calculators to find the present value factors. Table 17A.1 is used to calculate the present value of the single $100,000 maturity payment, and Table 17A.2 is used to calculate the present value of the $4,000 series of equal interest payments that form an *annuity*. An **annuity** is a series of equal payments occurring at equal time intervals.

The bond price is calculated as the present value of the principal plus the present value of the cash interest payments. The present value is found by multiplying the cash flow amounts by the corresponding table values as shown in Exhibit 17.5.

Exhibit 17.5

Calculating Fila's Bond Price

Cash Flow	Table	Table Value	Amount	Present Value
$100,000 par value	17A.1	0.7462	$100,000	$ 74,620
$4,000 interest payments	17A.2	5.0757	4,000	20,303*
Issue price of bond...................				**$94,923**[4]

*Rounded to the nearest whole dollar.

This analysis shows that if 5% is the semi-annual market rate for Fila bonds, the maximum price that buyers will pay (and the minimum price the issuer will accept) is $94,923. At this price the cash flow for the Fila bonds will provide investors a 5% semi-annual rate of return (or 10% annual return) on the $94,923 they have lent Fila.

---

[2] The difference between the contract rate and the market rate of interest on a new bond issue is usually a fraction of a percent. However, here we use a difference of 2% to emphasize the effects.

[3] Many inexpensive calculators provide present value functions for easy calculation of bond prices.

[4] Because of rounding, the present value tables will often result in a slightly different bond price than using the present value function on a calculator. In this case, a calculator would indicate a bond price of $94,924.

Present Value of a Premium Bond

Assume that Hydro Quebec issues bonds with a $50,000 par value, a 14% annual contract rate with interest payable *annually*, and a four-year life. The market rate for Hydro Quebec bonds is 12% on the issue date, meaning the bonds will sell at a premium because the contract rate (14%) is greater than the market rate (12%). This means buyers of these bonds will bid up the market price until the yield equals the market rate. We estimate the issue price of Hydro Quebec bonds by using the market rate to calculate the present value of its future cash flows. Recall that the Fila bond paid interest semi-annually, every six months. In contrast, interest is paid annually on the Hydro Quebec bonds. Therefore, when calculating the present value of the Hydro Quebec bond, we work with *annual* compounding periods because 12 months or one year is the time between interest payments.

The two-step process for calculating the issue price of a bond sold at a premium is the same as shown previously for a discount and is summarized in Exhibit 17.6.

Cash Flow	Table	Table Value	Amount	Present Value
$50,000 par value...............................	17A.1	0.6355	$50,000	$ 31,775
$7,000 interest payments..................	17A.2	3.0373	7,000	21,261*
Issue price of bond				**$53,036**[5]

Rounded to the nearest whole dollar.

Exhibit 17.6

Calculating Hydro Quebec Bond Price

This analysis shows that if 12% is the annual market rate for Hydro Quebec bonds, the maximum price that buyers will pay (also the minimum price the issuer will accept) is $53,036.

Issuing Bonds at a Discount

A **discount on bonds payable** occurs when a company issues bonds with a contract rate less than the market rate. This means the issue price is less than the bonds' par value (or < 100%).

To illustrate, let's assume that the Fila bonds discussed earlier are issued on December 31, 2005, at the discounted price of $94,923 (94.923% of par value). Fila records the bond issue as follows:

LO⁵ Prepare entries to record bonds issued at a discount.

2005			
Dec. 31	Cash	94,923	
	Discount on Bonds Payable	5,077	
	Bonds Payable		100,000
	Sold bonds at a discount on the original issue date.		

These bonds obligate the issuer to pay out two different future cash flows:

1. $100,000 face amount at the end of the bonds' three-year life, and
2. $4,000 interest (8% × $100,000 × 6/12) at the end of each six-month interest period of the bonds' three-year life.

_____

[5] Using the present value function on a calculator would result in a bond price of $53,037.

The pattern of cash flows for Fila's bonds is shown in Exhibit 17.7.

Exhibit 17.7

Cash Flows of Fila's Bonds

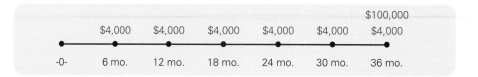

These bonds are reported in the *long-term liability* section of the issuer's December 31, 2005, balance sheet, as shown in Exhibit 17.8.

Exhibit 17.8

Balance Sheet Presentation of Bond Discount

Long-term liabilities:		
Bonds payable, 8%, due December 31, 2008	$100,000	
Less: Discount on bonds payable	**5,077**	$94,923

The discount is deducted from the par value of the bonds to produce the **carrying** *(or book)* **value** of the bonds payable. The Discount on Bonds Payable is a *contra liability account.* The book value of the bonds at the date of issue is always equal to the cash price of the bonds. You will learn in the next section that the carrying value of bonds issued at a discount or premium changes over the life of the bond issue.

Amortizing a Bond Discount

The issuer (Fila) received $94,923 for its bonds and will pay bondholders the $100,000 face amount after three years plus interest payments totalling $24,000 (= $4,000 × 6 interest payments). Because the $5,077 discount is eventually paid to bondholders at maturity, it is part of the cost of using the $94,923 for three years. The upper portion of Exhibit 17.9 shows that the total interest cost of $29,077 is the difference between the total amount repaid to bondholders ($124,000) and the amount borrowed from bondholders ($94,923). Alternatively, we can calculate total bond interest expense as the sum of the interest payments and the bond discount. This alternative calculation is shown in the lower portion of Exhibit 17.9.

Exhibit 17.9

Total Bond Interest Expense for Bonds Issued at a Discount

Amount repaid:	
Six interest payments of $4,000...	$ 24,000
Par value at maturity...	100,000
Total repaid to bondholders...	$124,000
Less: Amount borrowed from bondholders...	94,923
Total bond interest expense...	$ 29,077
Alternative Calculation	
Six payments of $4,000	$ 24,000
Add: Discount	5,077
Total bond interest expense...	$ 29,077

Accounting for Fila's bonds must include two procedures:

1. Allocating the total bond interest expense of $29,077 across the six six-month periods in the bonds' life, and
2. Updating the carrying value of the bonds at each balance sheet date.

To allocate the total bond interest expense over the life of the bonds, known as amortizing the bond discount, either the straight-line or effective interest method can be used. Both methods reduce the discount on the bonds over the life of the bonds.

Straight-Line Method

The **straight-line method** of allocating interest allocates an equal portion of the total bond interest expense to each of the six-month interest periods.

To apply the straight-line method to Fila's bonds, we divide the total expense of $29,077 by 6 (the number of semi-annual periods in the bonds' three-year life). This gives us a total bond interest expense of *$4,846 per period*.[6] Alternatively, we can find this number by dividing the $5,077 original discount by 6. The resulting $846 is the amount of discount to be amortized in each interest period. When the $846 of amortized discount is added to the $4,000 cash interest payment, the total bond interest expense for each six-month period is $4,846.

The issuer records bond interest expense and updates the balance of the bond liability for each semi-annual cash payment with this entry:

2006			
June 30	Bond Interest Expense......................................	4,846	
	Discount on Bonds Payable		846
	Cash...		4,000
	To record six months' interest and discount amortization.		

Fila incurs a $4,846 bond interest expense each period but pays only $4,000. The $846 unpaid interest each period is part of the amount to be repaid when the bond becomes due ($5,077 discount + $94,923 issue price = $100,000 total face amount to be paid at maturity).

The $846 credit to the Discount on Bonds Payable account *increases* the bonds' carrying value as shown in Exhibit 17.10. This increase occurs because we *decrease* the balance of the Discount on Bonds Payable (contra) account, which is subtracted from the Bonds Payable account. Exhibit 17.10 shows this pattern of decreases in the Discount on Bonds Payable account (the unamortized discount), along with increases in the bonds' carrying value.

---

[6] For simplicity, all calculations are rounded to the nearest whole dollar. ***Do the same when solving the exercises and problems at the end of the chapter.***

Exhibit 17.10

Bond Discount and Carrying Value Under Straight-Line

Period Ending	(A) Cash Interest Paid $100,000 × 4%	(B) Period Interest Expense $29,077/6	(C) Discount Amort. $5,077/6	(D) Unamortized Discount	(E) Carrying Value 100,000 − (D)
Dec. 31/05				$5,077	$ 94,923
Jun. 30/06	4,000	4,846	846	4,231[1]	95,769
Dec. 31/06	4,000	4,846	846	3,385[2]	96,615
Jun. 30/07	4,000	4,846	846	2,539	97,461
Dec. 31/07	4,000	4,846	846	1,693	98,307
Jun. 30/08	4,000	4,846	846	847	99,153
Dec. 31/08	4,000	4,847[3]	847[3]	–0–	100,000
Totals	$24,000	$29,077	$5,077		

[1] 5,077 − 846 = 4,231
[2] 4,231 − 846 = 3,385
[3] Adjusted for rounding.

We can summarize the following points in applying straight-line amortization to the discount on Fila's bonds over its life of six semi-annual periods:

1. The $94,923 cash received from selling the bonds equals the $100,000 par value of the bonds less the initial $5,077 discount from selling the bonds for less than par.

2. Semi-annual bond interest expense of $4,846 equals total bond interest expense of $29,077 divided by six semi-annual periods (alternatively calculated as the periodic cash interest paid of $4,000 plus the periodic discount amortization of $846).

3. Semi-annual credit of $846 to the Discount on Bonds Payable account equals the total discount of $5,077 divided by six semi-annual periods.

4. Semi-annual $4,000 interest payment equals the bonds' $100,000 par value multiplied by the 4% semi-annual contract rate.

5. Carrying (or book) value of bonds continues to grow each period by the $846 discount amortization until it equals the par value of the bonds when they mature as shown in Exhibit 17.10.

Effective Interest Method

The straight-line method yields changes in the bonds' carrying value (see Exhibit 17.10) while the amount for bond interest expense does not change (always equal to $4,846 for Fila bonds). This gives the impression of a changing interest rate when users divide a constant bond interest expense over a changing carrying value. As a result, the straight-line method should only be used when its results do not differ materially from those obtained by using the effective interest method.

The **effective interest method** allocates bond interest expense over the life of the bonds in a way that yields a constant rate of interest. *This constant rate of interest is the market rate at the issue date.* The effect of selling bonds at a premium or discount is that the issuer incurs the prevailing market rate of interest at issuance and not the contract rate. Bond interest expense for a period is found by multiplying the balance of the liability at the end of the last period by the bonds' original market rate. An amortization table can be constructed to help us keep track of interest allocation and the balances of bond-related accounts.

Exhibit 17.11 shows an amortization table for the Fila bonds. The key difference between the effective interest and straight-line methods lies in the calculation of bond interest expense. Instead of assigning an equal amount of interest to each interest period, the effective interest method assigns an increasing amount of interest over the Fila bonds' life because the balance of the liability increases over these three years. But both methods allocate the same $29,077 of total expense across the three years.

Exhibit 17.11

Effective Interest Amortization
of Bond Discount

Period Ending	(A) Cash Interest Paid $100,000 × 4%	(B) Period Interest Expense E × 5%	(C) Discount Amort. B – A	(D) Unamortized Discount	(E) Carrying Value 100,000 – (D)
Dec. 31/05				$5,077	$94,923
Jun. 30/06	$4,000	$4,746[1]	$746	4,331	95,669
Dec. 31/06	4,000	4,783[2]	783	3,548	96,452
Jun. 30/07	4,000	4,823	823	2,725	97,275
Dec. 31/07	4,000	4,864	864	1,861	98,139
Jun. 30/08	4,000	4,907	907	954	99,046
Dec. 31/08	4,000	4,954[3]	954	–0–	100,000
	$24,000	$29,077	$5,077		

[1] 94,923 × 0.05 = 4,746
[2] 95,669 × 0.05 = 4,783
[3] Adjusted for rounding.

Column (A) is the bonds' par value ($100,000) multiplied by the semi-annual contract rate (4%).

Column (B) is the bonds' prior period carrying value multiplied by the semi-annual market rate (5%).

Column (C) is the difference between bond interest expense and interest paid, or [(B) – (A)].

Column (D) is the prior period's unamortized discount less the current period's discount amortization.

Column (E) is the bonds' par value less unamortized discount, or [$100,000 – (D)].

The amortization table shows how the balance of the discount (column D) is amortized by the effective interest method until it reaches zero. The bonds' carrying value changes each period until it equals par value at maturity. Total bond interest expense is $29,077, comprising $24,000 of semi-annual cash interest payments and $5,077 of the original discount below par value.

Except for differences in amounts, journal entries recording the expense and updating the liability balance are the same under the effective interest method and the straight-line method. For instance, the entry to record the interest payment at the end of the first interest period is:

2006 June 30	Bond Interest Expense	4,746	
	Discount on Bonds Payable		746
	Cash		4,000
	To record six months' interest and discount amortization.		

We use the numbers in Exhibit 17.11 to make similar entries throughout the three-year life of the bonds. We can also use information in this exhibit to prepare comparative balance sheet information. For example, we prepare the bonds payable section of long-term liabilities for 2007 and 2006 as shown in Exhibit 17.12. Note that the carrying value of the bonds payable increases as the discount on bonds payable gets smaller.

Exhibit 17.12

Balance Sheet Presentation of Bond Discount

	Dec. 31 2007	Dec. 31 2006
Long-term liabilities:		
Bonds payable, 8%, due December 31, 2008	$100,000	$100,000
Less: Discount on bonds payable	1,861	3,548
Carrying value	$ 98,139	$ 96,452

Flashback

Answers—p. 894

Use this information to answer Flashback Questions 4, 5, and 6: Five-year, 6% bonds with a $100,000 par value are issued at a price of $91,893. Interest is paid semi-annually, and the market rate is 8% on the issue date.

4. Are these bonds issued at a discount or a premium? Explain why.

5. What is the issuer's journal entry to record the sale?

6. What is the amount of bond interest expense recorded at the first semi-annual cash payment using the (a) straight-line method and (b) effective interest method?

Issuing Bonds at a Premium

LO⁶ Prepare entries to record bonds issued at a premium.

When bonds carry a contract rate greater than the market rate, the bonds sell at a price greater than par value (or > 100%). The difference between par and market value is the **premium on bonds**. Buyers bid up the price of bonds above the bonds' par value until it reaches a level yielding the market rate.

To illustrate, let's assume that the Hydro Quebec bonds discussed earlier are issued on December 31, 2005, at 106.072 (106.072% of par value), which amounts to $53,036. Hydro Quebec records the bond issue with this entry:

2005 Dec. 31	Cash	53,036	
	Premium on Bonds Payable		3,036
	Bonds Payable		50,000
	Sold bonds at a premium on the original issue date.		

Hydro Quebec's bonds obligate it to pay out two different future cash flows:

1. $100,000 face amount at the end of the bonds' four-year life.

2. $7,000 (= 14% × $100,000) at the end of each annual interest period of the bonds' four-year life.

The pattern of cash flows for Hydro Quebec bonds is shown in Exhibit 17.13.

Exhibit 17.13

Cash Flows of Hydro
Quebec Bonds

These bonds are reported in the long-term liability section of the issuer's December 31, 2005, balance sheet, as shown in Exhibit 17.14.

Long-term liabilities:		
Bonds payable, 14%, due December 31, 2009	$50,000	
Add: Premium on bonds payable	**3,036**	$53,036

Exhibit 17.14

Balance Sheet Presentation
of Bond Premium

The premium is added to the par value of the bonds to produce the carrying (book) value of the bonds payable. The Premium on Bonds Payable is an adjunct (also called accretion) liability account.

Amortizing a Bond Premium

The issuer (Hydro Quebec) receives $53,036 for its bonds and will pay bondholders the $50,000 face amount after four years have passed plus interest payments totalling $28,000. Because the $3,036 premium is not repaid to bondholders at maturity, it reduces the expense of using the $53,036 for four years.

The upper portion of Exhibit 17.15 shows that total bond interest expense of $24,964 is the difference between the total amount repaid to bondholders ($78,000) and the amount borrowed from bondholders ($53,036). Alternatively, we can calculate total bond interest expense as the sum of the interest payments less the bond premium. The premium is subtracted because it will not be paid to the bondholders when the bonds mature. This alternative calculation is shown in the lower portion of Exhibit 17.15. Total bond interest expense is allocated over the four annual periods with either the straight-line or the effective interest method.

Amount repaid:	
Four interest payments of $7,000	$28,000
Par value at maturity	50,000
Total repaid to bondholders..	$78,000
Less: Amount borrowed from bondholders...............................	53,036
Total bond interest expense..	$24,964
Alternative Calculation	
Four payments of $7,000...	$28,000
Less: Premium...	3,036
Total interest expense..	$24,964

Exhibit 17.15

Total Bond Interest
Expense for Bonds
Issued at a Premium

Straight-Line Method

We explained how the straight-line method allocates an equal portion of total bond interest expense to each of the bonds' interest periods. To apply the straight-line method to Hydro Quebec's bonds, we divide the four years' total bond interest expense of $24,964 by 4 (the number of annual periods in the bonds' life). This gives us a total bond interest expense of $6,241 per period.

The issuer records bond interest expense and updates the balance of the bond liability for each annual cash payment with this entry:

2006			
Dec. 31	Bond Interest Expense....................................	6,241	
	Premium on Bonds Payable	759	
	Cash..		7,000
	To record annual interest and premium amortization.		

This is the entry made at the end of each of the four annual interest periods. The $759 debit to the Premium on Bonds Payable account decreases the bonds' carrying value. Exhibit 17.16 shows an amortization table using the straight-line method for the Hydro Quebec bonds.

Exhibit 17.16

Bond Premium and Carrying Value Under Straight-Line

Period Ending	(A) Cash Interest Paid $50,000 × 14%	(B) Period Interest Expense 24,964/4	(C) Premium Amort. 3,036/4	(D) Unamortized Premium	(E) Carrying Value $50,000 + (D)
Dec. 31/05				$3,036	$53,036
Dec. 31/06...	7,000	6,241	759	2,277[1]	52,277
Dec. 31/07	7,000	6,241	759	1,518[2]	51,518
Dec. 31/08...	7,000	6,241	759	759	50,759
Dec. 31/09	7,000	6,241	759	–0–	50,000
Totals...	$28,000	$24,964	$3,036		

[1] 3,036 − 759 = 2,277
[2] 2,277 − 759 = 1,518

Effective Interest Method

Exhibit 17.17 shows an amortization table using the effective interest method for the Hydro Quebec bonds.

Exhibit 17.17

Effective Interest Amortization of Bond Premium

Period Ending	(A) Cash Interest Paid $50,000 × 14%	(B) Period Interest Expense (E) × 12%	(C) Premium Amort. (A) – (B)	(D) Unamortized Premium	(E) Carrying Value $50,000 + (D)
Dec. 31/05				$3,036	$53,036
Dec. 31/06	7,000	6,364[1]	636	2,400	52,400
Dec. 31/07	7,000	6,288[2]	712	1,688	51,688
Dec. 31/08	7,000	6,203	797	891	50,891
Dec. 31/09	7,000	6,109[3]	891	–0–	50,000
Totals	$28,000	$24,964	$3,036		

[1] 53,036 × 0.12 = 6,364
[2] 52,400 × 0.12 = 6,288
[3] Adjusted for rounding.

Column (A) is the bonds' par value ($50,000) multiplied by the annual contract rate (14%).

Column (B) is the bonds' prior period carrying value multiplied by the annual market rate (12%).

Column (C) is the difference between interest paid and bond interest expense, or [(A) – (B)].

Column (D) is the prior period's unamortized premium less the current period's premium amortization.

Column (E) is the bonds' par value plus unamortized premium, or [$50,000 + (D)].

The amount of cash paid (Column A) is larger than bond interest expense (Column B) because the cash payment is based on the higher 14% contract rate.

The effect of premium amortization on the bond interest expense and the bond liability is seen in the journal entry on December 31, 2006, when the issuer makes the first interest payment:

2006			
Dec. 31	Bond Interest Expense	6,364	
	Premium on Bonds Payable	636	
	Cash		7,000
	To record annual interest and premium amortization.		

Similar entries are recorded at each payment date until the bonds mature at the end of 2009. The effective interest method yields decreasing amounts of bond interest expense and increasing amounts of premium amortization over the bonds' life.

Summary of Bond Discount and Premium Behaviour

The Fila and Quebec Hydro bond examples have shown that bond discounts and premiums behave in opposite ways over the term of a bond and therefore impact the bond's carrying value differently. The graphs presented in Exhibit 17.18 summarize these behaviour patterns.

Exhibit 17.18

Graphic Comparison of Bond Discount and Premium Behaviour

BEHAVIOUR OF A BOND DISCOUNT—FILA BONDS

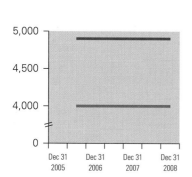

Interest expense is constant over the term of the bond but **greater than** interest paid each period.

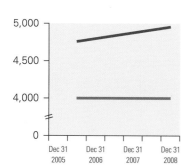

Interest expense is **increasing** over the term of the bond **and greater than** interest paid each period.

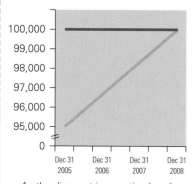

As the discount is amortized each period, the **carrying value of the bond increases** as it approaches par value.

BEHAVIOUR OF A BOND PREMIUM— HYDRO QUEBEC BONDS

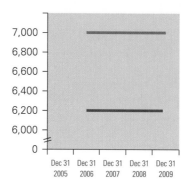

Interest expense is constant over the term of the bond but **less than** interest paid each period.

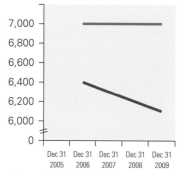

Interest expense is **decreasing** over the term of the bond **and less than** interest paid each period.

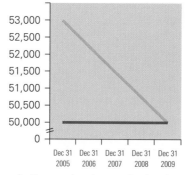

As the premium is amortized each period, the **carrying value of the bond decreases** as it approaches par value.

Straight-Line Amortization

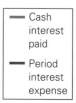

- Cash interest paid
- Period interest expense

vs. Effective Interest Amortization

Carrying vs. Par Value

- Carrying value
- Par value

Accruing Bond Interest Expense

If a bond's interest period does not coincide with the issuing company's accounting period, an adjusting entry is necessary to recognize bond interest expense accruing since the most recent interest payment.

To illustrate, let's assume that the Hydro Quebec bonds described in Exhibit 17.17 were issued on December 31, 2005. If Hydro Quebec's year-end is April 30, four months of bond interest and premium amortization accrue (from December 31, 2005, to April 30, 2006). An adjusting entry is needed to capture:

1. Four months of interest equal to $2,121 (= $6,364 from Column B of Exhibit 17.17 × 4/12), and

2. Four months of premium amortization equal to $212 (= $636 from Column C of Exhibit 17.17 × 4/12).

The resulting interest payable is $2,333, the sum of the $2,121 interest expense and $212 premium amortization (also calculated as $7,000 from Column A of Exhibit 17.17 × 4/12). We record these effects with this adjusting entry:

2006			
Apr. 30	Bond Interest Expense....................................	2,121	
	Premium on Bonds Payable	212	
	Interest Payable		2,333
	To record four months' accrued interest and premium amortization.		

Similar entries are made on each April 30 year-end throughout the three-year life of the bonds.

When the $7,000 cash payment occurs on the December 31, 2006, interest date, the journal entry recognizes the bond interest expense and amortization for May through December, a total of eight months. It must also eliminate the interest payable liability created by the April 30 adjusting entry. In this case we make the following entry to record payment on December 31, 2006:

2006			
Dec. 31	Interest Payable..	2,333	
	Bond Interest Expense ($6,364 × 8/12)	4,243	
	Premium on Bonds Payable ($636 × 8/12).....	424	
	Cash..		7,000
	To record eight months' interest and amortization and eliminate the accrued interest liability.		

Answers—p. 894

Use this information to solve Flashback Questions 7, 8, and 9: On December 31, 2005, a company issued 16%, 10-year bonds with a par value of $100,000. Interest is paid on June 30 and December 31. The bonds are sold at an issue price of $110,592 to yield a 14% annual market rate.

7. Are these bonds issued at a discount or a premium? Explain why.

8. Using the effective interest method of allocating bond interest expense, the issuer records the second interest payment (on December 31, 2006) with a debit to Premium on Bonds Payable in the amount of: (a) $7,470; (b) $7,741; (c) $259; (d) $530; or (e) $277.

9. How are the bonds reported in the long-term liability section of the issuer's balance sheet as of December 31, 2006?

10. On May 1, a company sells 9% bonds with a $500,000 par value that pay semi-annual interest on each January 1 and July 1. The bonds are sold at par value plus interest accrued since January 1. The bond issuer's entry to record the first semi-annual interest payment on July 1 includes: (a) A debit to Interest Payable for $15,000; (b) A debit to Bond interest expense for $22,500; or (c) A credit to Interest Payable for $7,500.

Mid-Chapter Demonstration Problem

On February 1, 2005, Enviro-Engineering Inc. has available for issue a $416,000 5% two-year bond. Interest is to be paid quarterly beginning May 1, 2005.

Required

Part 1
Calculate the issue price of the bonds assuming a market interest rate of:
a. 5%   **b.** 4%   **c.** 8%

Part 2
Assuming the bonds were issued on April 1, 2005, at a market interest rate of 5%, prepare the entries for the following dates:
a. April 1, 2005 (date of issue)   **b.** May 1, 2005 (interest payment date)

Part 3
Assuming the bonds were issued on Feb. 1, 2005, at a market interest rate of 4%:
a. Prepare an amortization schedule using the straight-line method.
b. Record the entries for the following dates:
   i. February 1, 2005 (date of issue)
   ii. May 1, 2005 (interest payment date)
   iii. May 31, 2005 (Enviro's year-end)

Part 4

Assuming the bonds were issued on February 1, 2005, at a market interest rate of 8%:

a. Prepare an amortization schedule using the effective interest method.

b. Record the entries for the following dates:

   i.   February 1, 2005 (date of issue)

   ii. May 1, 2005 (interest payment date)

   iii. May 31, 2005 (Enviro's year-end)

Preparing the Solution:

- ○ Calculate the issue price of the bonds using the PV tables in Appendix 17A.
- ○ Record the journal entries for bonds issued at par (market interest rate of 5%).
- ○ Using the straight-line method, prepare an amortization schedule for a bond issued at a premium (market rate of 4%).
- ○ Using the straight-line amortization schedule, record the journal entries for bonds issued at a premium.
- ○ Using the effective interest method, prepare an amortization schedule for a bond issued at a discount (market interest rate of 8%).
- ○ Using the effective interest amortization schedule, record the journal entries for bonds issued at a discount.

SOLUTION TO Mid-Chapter Demonstration Problem

Part 1

a. $416,000

b.

PV of face amount (Table 17A.1):	$416,000 ×	0.9235 =	$384,176
PV of interest annuity (Table 17A.2):	$ 5,200* ×	7.6517 =	39,789
			$423,965

*$416,000 × 5% × 3/12 = $5,200

c.

PV of face amount (Table 17A.1):	$416,000 ×	0.8535 =	$355,056
PV of interest annuity (Table 17A.2):	$ 5,200* ×	7.3255 =	38,093
			$393,149

*$416,000 × 5% × 3/12 = $5,200

Part 2—Issued at a market interest rate of 5% (par).

a.

2005			
April 1	Cash	419,467	
	Interest Payable ($416,000 × 5% × 2/12)......		3,467
	Bonds Payable		416,000

b.

May 1	Interest Payable..	3,467	
	Bond Interest Expense		
	($416,000 × 5% × 1/12)	1,733	
	Cash		5,200

Part 3—Issued at a market interest rate of 4% (premium).

a.

Period Ending	(A) Cash Interest Paid $416,000 × 5% × 3/12	(B) Period Interest Expense $33,635/8	(C) Premium Amort. $7,965/8	(D) Unamortized Premium	(E) Carrying Value $416,000 + (D)
Feb. 01/05.............................				7,965	423,965
May 01/05.............................	5,200	4,204	996	6,969	422,969
Aug. 01/05	5,200	4,204	996	5,973	421,973
Nov. 01/05.............................	5,200	4,204	996	4,977	420,977
Feb. 01/06.............................	5,200	4,204	996	3,981	419,981
May 01/06.............................	5,200	4,204	996	2,985	418,985
Aug. 01/06	5,200	4,204	996	1,989	417,989
Nov. 01/06.............................	5,200	4,204	996	993	416,993
Feb. 01/07.............................	5,200	4,207*	993	0	416,000
Totals	41,600	33,635	7,965		

Adjusted for rounding.

b.

	2005			
i.	Feb. 1	Cash	423,965	
		Premium on Bonds Payable		7,965
		Bonds Payable...		416,000
ii.	May 1	Bond Interest Expense...............................	4,204	
		Premium on Bonds Payable	996	
		Cash		5,200
iii.	May 31	Bond Interest Expense ($4,204 × 1/3)	1,401	
		Premium on Bonds Payable ($996 × 1/3).......	332	
		Interest Payable ($5,200 × 1/3).............		1,733

Part 4—Issued at a market interest rate of 8% (discount).

a.

Period Ending	(A) Cash Interest Paid $416,000 × 5% × 3/12	(B) Period Interest Expense (E) × 8% × 3/12	(C) Discount Amort. (B) − (A)	(D) Unamortized Discount	(E) Carrying Value $416,000 − (D)
Feb. 01/05				22,851	393,149
May 01/05	5,200	7,863	2,663	20,188	395,812
Aug. 01/05	5,200	7,916	2,716	17,472	398,528
Nov. 01/05	5,200	7,971	2,771	14,701	401,299
Feb. 01/06	5,200	8,026	2,826	11,875	404,125
May 01/06	5,200	8,082	2,882	8,993	407,007
Aug. 01/06	5,200	8,140	2,940	6,053	409,947
Nov. 01/06	5,200	8,199	2,999	3,054	412,946
Feb. 01/07	5,200	8,254*	3,054	0	416,000
Totals	41,600	64,451	22,851		

*Adjusted for rounding.

b.

	2005			
i.	Feb. 1	Cash	393,149	
		Discount on Bonds Payable	22,851	
		Bonds Payable		416,000
ii.	May 1	Bond Interest Expense	7,863	
		Discount on Bonds Payable		2,663
		Cash		5,200
iii.	May 31	Bond Interest Expense ($7,916 × 1/3)	2,639	
		Discount on Bonds Payable ($2,716 × 1/3)		906*
		Interest Payable ($5,200 × 1/3)		1,733

*Adjusted for rounding.

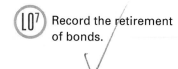

LO7 Record the retirement of bonds.

Bond Retirements

This section describes the retirement of bonds: (1) at maturity, (2) before maturity, and (3) by converting them to shares.

Bond Retirement at Maturity

The carrying value of bonds at maturity will always equal their par value. Both Exhibits 17.11 (a discount) and 17.17 (a premium) show that the carrying value of these bonds at the end of their life equals the bonds' par value.

The entry to record the retirement of the Hydro Quebec bonds in Exhibit 17.17 at maturity, assuming interest is already paid and recorded, is:

2009			
Dec. 31	Bonds Payable..	50,000	
	Cash..		50,000
	To record retirement of bonds at maturity.		

Bond Retirement Before Maturity

Companies sometimes wish to retire some or all of their bonds prior to maturity. For instance, if interest rates decline significantly, a company may wish to replace old high-interest paying bonds with new low-interest bonds. Two common ways of retiring bonds before maturity are to:

1. Exercise a call option, or
2. Purchase them on the open market.

In the first instance, a company can reserve the right to retire bonds early by issuing callable bonds. This means the bond indenture gives the issuing company an option to call the bonds before they mature by paying the par value plus a *call premium* to the bondholders. In the second case, the issuer retires bonds by repurchasing them on the open market at their current price. When there is a difference between the bonds' carrying value and the amount paid in a bond retirement transaction, the issuer records a gain or loss equal to the difference. Any unrecorded discount or premium up to the date of the call must be recorded to bring the carrying value of the bond up to date.

To illustrate bond retirement before maturity, let's assume a company has issued callable bonds with a par value of $100,000. The call option requires the issuer to pay a call premium of $3,000 to bondholders in addition to the par value. Immediately after the June 30, 2005, interest payment, the bonds have a carrying value of $104,500. On July 1, 2005, the issuer calls these bonds and pays $103,000 to bondholders. The issuer recognizes a $1,500 gain from the difference between the bonds' carrying value of $104,500 and the retirement price of $103,000. The entry to record this bond retirement is:

July 1	Bonds Payable..	100,000	
	Premium on Bonds Payable	4,500	
	Gain on Retirement of Bonds		1,500
	Cash..		103,000
	To record retirement of bonds before maturity.		

A company generally must call all of its bonds when it exercises a call option. But a company can retire as many or as few bonds as it desires through open market transactions. If it retires less than the entire set of bonds, it recognizes a gain or loss for the difference between the carrying value of those bonds retired and the amount paid to acquire them.

Flashback

Answer—p. 894

11. Six years ago, a company issued $500,000 of 6%, eight-year bonds at a price of 95. The current carrying value is $493,750. The company retired 50% of the bonds by buying them on the open market at a price of 102½. What is the amount of gain or loss on retirement of these bonds?

Bond Retirement by Conversion to Shares

Convertible bonds are those that give bondholders the right to convert their bonds to a specified number of common shares. When conversion occurs, the carrying value of bonds is transferred from long-term liability accounts to contributed capital accounts and no gain or loss is recorded.

To illustrate, on January 1 the $100,000 par value bonds of Converse Corp., with a carrying value of $100,000, are converted to 15,000 common shares. The entry to record this conversion is:

Jan. 1	Bonds Payable..	100,000	
	Common Shares		100,000
	To record retirement of bonds by		
	conversion into common shares.		

Notice that the market prices of the bonds and shares have no bearing on this entry. Any related bond discount or premium must also be removed. For example if there had been a $4,000 balance in Discount on Bonds Payable, it must be credited as shown in the following entry:

Jan. 1	Bonds Payable..	100,000	
	Discount on Bonds Payable		4,000
	Common Shares		96,000
	To record retirement of bonds by		
	conversion into common shares.		

Long-Term Notes Payable

Like bonds, companies issue notes payable to finance operations. But, unlike signing a bond, signing a note payable is typically a transaction with a single lender such as a bank, insurance company, or pension fund. A note is initially measured and recorded at its selling price. Over the life of a note, the amount of interest expense allocated to each period is calculated by multiplying the interest rate of the note by the beginning-of-period balance of the note.

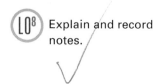

Interest-Bearing Notes

LO⁸ Explain and record notes.

Let's assume Taco Bell buys on January 2, 2005, equipment with a fair market value of $45,000 by issuing an 8%, three-year note with a face value of $45,000 to the equipment seller. The company records the purchase with this entry:

2005			
Jan. 2	Equipment...	45,000	
	Notes Payable...		45,000
	Issued a $45,000, three-year, 8% note payable for equipment.		

The company (note issuer) reports annual interest expense equal to the original interest rate times each year's beginning balance of the note over the life of the note. Exhibit 17.19 shows this interest expense calculation and allocation.

Exhibit 17.19

Interest-Bearing Note—
Interest Paid at Maturity

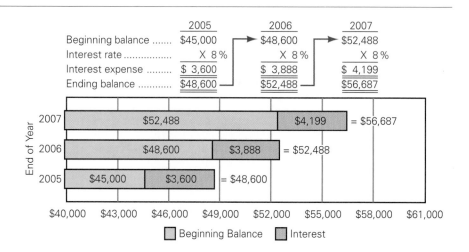

Interest is calculated by multiplying each year's beginning balance by the original 8% interest rate. Interest is then added to the beginning balance to calculate the ending balance. A period's ending balance becomes next period's beginning balance. Because the balance grows by compounding, the amount of interest allocated to each year increases over the life of the note. The final ending balance of $56,687 equals the original $45,000 borrowed plus total interest of $11,687. A note like this one that delays interest payments is more common for lower-risk companies who wish to delay cash payments until some later period. It is often backed with assets as collateral.

Flashback

Answer—p. 894

12. On January 1, 2005, a company signs a $6,000 three-year note payable bearing 6% annual interest. The original principal and all interest is paid on December 31, 2007. Interest is compounded annually. How much interest is allocated to year 2006? (a) $0; (b) $360; (c) $381.60; (d) $741.60.

Installment Notes

An **installment note** is an obligation requiring a series of periodic payments to the lender. Installment notes are common for franchises and other businesses where costs are large and the owner desires to spread these costs over several periods. For example, in Note 4 of its 2002 financial statements found in Appendix I at the back of this textbook, WestJet reports the installment details regarding loans totalling $231,670,000 at December 31, 2002.

To illustrate, let's assume CanBowl, a bowling establishment, borrows $60,000 from a bank to purchase AMF and Brunswick bowling equipment. CanBowl signs an 8% installment note with the bank requiring three annual payments and records the note's issuance as:

2004			
Dec. 31	Cash	60,000	
	Notes Payable..		60,000
	Borrowed $60,000 by signing an 8% installment note.		

Payments on an installment note normally include the interest expense accruing to the date of the payment plus a portion of the amount borrowed (the *principal*). Generally, we can identify two types of payment patterns:

1. Accrued interest plus equal principal payments, and
2. Equal payments.

The remainder of this section describes these two patterns and how we account for them.

Accrued Interest plus Equal Principal Payments

This payment pattern creates cash flows that decrease in size over the life of the note. This decrease occurs because each payment reduces the note's principal balance, yielding less interest expense for the next period.

To illustrate, let's assume the $60,000, 8% note signed by CanBowl requires it to make three payments at the end of each year equal to *accrued interest plus $20,000 of principal*. Exhibit 17.20 describes these payments, interest, and changes in the balance of this note.

This table shows that total interest expense is $9,600 and total principal is $60,000. This means total cash payments are $69,600. Notice the decreasing total payment pattern, decreasing accrued interest, and constant principal payments of $20,000.

Exhibit 17.20

Installment Note—Accrued Interest plus Equal Principal Payments

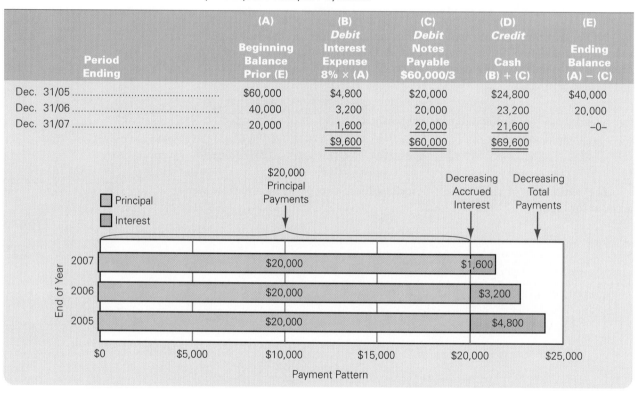

Period Ending	(A) Beginning Balance Prior (E)	(B) *Debit* Interest Expense 8% × (A)	(C) *Debit* Notes Payable $60,000/3	(D) *Credit* Cash (B) + (C)	(E) Ending Balance (A) − (C)
Dec. 31/05	$60,000	$4,800	$20,000	$24,800	$40,000
Dec. 31/06	40,000	3,200	20,000	23,200	20,000
Dec. 31/07	20,000	1,600	20,000	21,600	–0–
		$9,600	$60,000	$69,600	

CanBowl (borrower) records the effects of the first payment with this entry:

2005 Dec. 31	Interest Expense	4,800	
	Notes Payable	20,000	
	Cash		24,800
	To record first installment payment.		

After all three payments are recorded, the balance of the Notes Payable account is zero.

Equal Total Payments

Installment notes that require the borrower to make a series of equal payments consist of changing amounts of interest and principal.

To illustrate, let's assume the previous $60,000 note requires CanBowl to make three equal total payments at the end of each year. Table 17A.2 is used to calculate the series of three payments equal to the present value of the $60,000 note at 8% interest. We go to Row 3 of the table and go across to the 8% column, where the table value is 2.5771. We solve for the payment by dividing $60,000 by 2.5771. The resulting $23,282 payment includes both interest and principal. Exhibit 17.21 shows that while all three payments are equal, the accrued interest decreases each year because the principal balance of the note is declining. As the amount of interest decreases each year, the amount applied to the principal increases.

Exhibit 17.21

Installment Note—Equal Total Payments

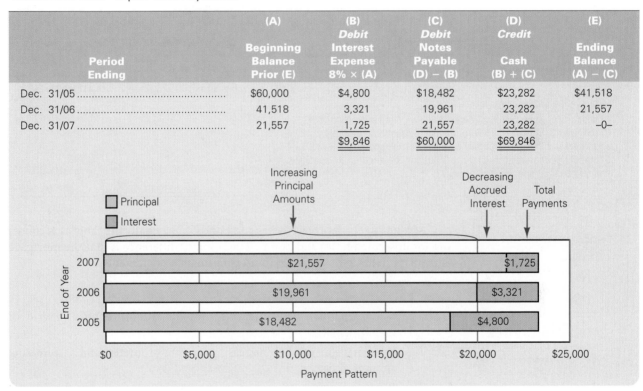

Period Ending	(A) Beginning Balance Prior (E)	(B) *Debit* Interest Expense 8% × (A)	(C) *Debit* Notes Payable (D) − (B)	(D) *Credit* Cash (B) + (C)	(E) Ending Balance (A) − (C)
Dec. 31/05	$60,000	$4,800	$18,482	$23,282	$41,518
Dec. 31/06	41,518	3,321	19,961	23,282	21,557
Dec. 31/07	21,557	1,725	21,557	23,282	–0–
		$9,846	$60,000	$69,846	

The amounts in Exhibit 17.21 are used to show how we record the journal entry for the first payment toward this note:

2005			
Dec. 31	Interest Expense	4,800	
	Notes Payable	18,482	
	Cash		23,282
	To record first installment payment.		

The borrower records similar entries for each of the remaining payments. After three years, the Notes Payable account balance is zero.

It is interesting to compare the two payment patterns graphed in Exhibits 17.20 and 17.21. The series of equal total payments leads to a greater amount of interest expense over the life of the note. This is because the first three payments in Exhibit 17.21 are smaller and do not reduce the principal as quickly as the first three payments in Exhibit 17.20.

Mortgage Notes

A **mortgage** is a legal agreement that helps protect a lender if a borrower fails to make the required payments on bonds or notes. A mortgage gives the lender the right to be paid out of the cash proceeds from the sale of a borrower's specific assets identified in the mortgage. A separate legal document, called a *mortgage contract*, describes the terms of a mortgage.

Mortgage notes include a mortgage contract pledging title to specific assets as security for the note. This contract usually requires the borrower to pay all property taxes on the mortgaged assets, to maintain them properly, and to carry adequate insurance against fire and other types of losses. These requirements are designed to keep the property from losing value and avoid diminishing the lender's security. Mortgage notes are especially popular in the purchase of homes and in the acquisition of plant assets by companies.

For example, Note 6 to Boardwalk Equities Inc.'s December 31, 2002, financial statements states:

6. MORTGAGES PAYABLE		
AS AT	December 31, 2002	December 31, 2001
(a) Revenue producing properties		
Mortgages payable bearing interest at a weighted average of 5.87% (December 31, 2001—6.15%) per annum, payable in monthly principal and interest installments totalling $8.9 million (December 31, 2001—$7.7 million), mature from 2003 to 2020 and are secured by specific charges against specific properties.		
	$1,305,349	$1,106,546

Accounting for mortgage notes and bonds is essentially the same as accounting for unsecured notes and bonds. The primary difference is that the mortgage agreement needs to be disclosed to users of financial statements.

Flashback

Answers—p. 894

13. Which of the following is true for an installment note requiring a series of equal payments?

   a. Payments consist of an increasing amount of interest and a decreasing amount of principal.

   b. Payments consist of changing amounts of principal, but the interest portion remains constant.

   c. Payments consist of a decreasing amount of interest and an increasing amount of principal.

14. How is the interest portion of an installment note payment calculated?

15. When a borrower records a periodic interest payment on an installment note, how are the balance sheet and income statement affected?

Lease Liabilities

Leasing is one alternative to purchasing an asset and, in certain situations, is reported like a known liability P.678. A company can lease an asset by agreeing to make a series of rental payments to the property owner, called the *lessor*. Because a lease gives the asset's user (called the *lessee*) exclusive control over the asset's usefulness, the lessee can use it to earn revenues. A lease creates a liability if it has essentially the same characteristics as a purchase of an asset on credit. Appendix 17B illustrates basic accounting for leases.

Summary

LO1 Compare bond versus share financing. Bond financing is used to fund business activities. Advantages of bond financing versus common shares include (a) no effect on shareholders' control, (b) tax savings, and (c) increased earnings due to financial leverage. Disadvantages include (a) required interest and principal payments, and (b) decreased earnings when operations turn less profitable.

LO2 Explain the types of bonds and their issuing procedures. An issuer's bonds usually are sold to many investors. Certain bonds are secured by the issuer's assets, while other bonds, called debentures, are unsecured. Serial bonds mature at different points in time while term bonds mature together. Registered bonds have each bondholder's name and address recorded by the issuing company, while bearer bonds are payable to whomever holds the bonds. Convertible bonds are exchangeable by bondholders for shares of the issuing company's shares. Callable bonds can be retired by the issuer at a set price. Bonds are often issued by an underwriter, and a bond certificate is evidence of the issuer's obligation.

LO3 Prepare entries to record bonds issued at par. When bonds are issued at par, Cash is debited and Bonds Payable is credited for the bonds' par value. At the bonds' interest payment dates, Bond Interest Expense is debited and Cash credited for an amount equal to the bonds' par value multiplied by the bonds' contract rate. The cash paid to bondholders on semi-annual interest payment dates is calculated as one-half of the result of multiplying the par value of the bonds by their contract rate.

LO4 Determine the price of a bond. The price of a bond is determined by summing the present values of two amounts. One amount is the present value of the interest payments (an annuity) and the second amount is the present value of the face value of the bond that is received at the bond's maturity date. Both amounts are discounted to present value using the market rate of interest.

LO5 Prepare entries to record bonds issued at a discount. Bonds are issued at a discount when the contract rate is less than the market rate. This is the same as saying the issue (selling) price is less than par. When this occurs, the issuer records a credit to Bonds Payable (at par) and debits both to Discount on Bonds Payable and to Cash. The amount of bond interest expense assigned to each period is calculated using either the straight-line or effective interest method. Straight-line can only be used if the results are not materially different from the effective interest method. Bond interest expense using the effective interest method equals the bonds' beginning-of-period carrying value multiplied by the original market rate at time of issuance.

LO6 Prepare entries to record bonds issued at a premium. Bonds are issued at a premium when the contract rate is higher than the market rate. This means that the issue (selling) price is greater than par. When this occurs, the issuer records a debit to Cash and credits both to Premium on Bonds Payable and to Bonds Payable (at par). The amount of bond interest expense assigned to each period is calculated using either the straight-line or effective interest method. The balance of the Premium on Bonds Payable is allocated to reduce bond interest expense over the life of the bonds.

LO7 Record the retirement of bonds. Bonds are retired at maturity with a debit to Bonds Payable and a credit to Cash for the par value of the bonds. Bonds can be retired early by the issuer by exercising a call option or by purchases on the open market. The issuer recognizes a gain or loss for the difference between the amount paid out and the bonds' carrying value. Alternatively, bondholders can retire bonds early by exercising a conversion feature on convertible bonds.

LO8 **Explain and record notes.** Notes can require repayment of principal and interest (a) at the end of a period of time, or (b) gradually over a period of time in either equal or unequal amounts. Notes repaid over a period of time are called installment notes and usually follow one of two payment patterns: (a) decreasing payments of interest plus equal amounts of principal, or (b) equal total payments. Interest is allocated to each period in a note's life by multiplying its carrying value by its interest rate.

GUIDANCE ANSWERS TO  Flashback

1. *b*

2. Multiply the par value of the bonds by the contract rate of interest.

3. The bonds sell at a premium, and the purchasers pay more than the par value of the bonds.

4. The bonds are issued at a discount, meaning issue price is less than par value. A discount occurs because the bonds' contract rate is less than their market rate.

5.

Cash..	91,893	
Discount on Bonds Payable.....................	8,107	
Bonds Payable		100,000

6. a. $3,811 [Interest paid of $3,000 ($100,000 × 0.06 × 6/12) + amortization of bond discount of $811 (= $8,107/10)]

   b. $3,676 (Beginning balance of $91,893 times 4% market interest rate.)

7. The bonds are issued at a premium, meaning issue price is greater than par value. A premium occurs because the bonds' contract rate is greater than their market rate.

8. *e.* (On Jun. 30, 2006: $110,592 × 7% = $7,741 bond interest expense; $8,000 − $7,741 = $259 premium amortization; $110,592 − $259 = $110,333 ending balance. On Dec. 31, 2006: $110,333 × 7% = $7,723 bond interest expense; $8,000 − $7,723 = $277 premium amortization.)

9.

Bonds payable, 16%, due December 31, 2015................	$100,000	
Add: Premium on bonds payable	10,056*	$110,056

*Beginning premium balance of $10,592 less $259 and $277 amortized on Jun. 30, 2006, and Dec. 31, 2006.

10. *a*

11. $9,375 loss (Difference between repurchase price of $256,250 [50% of ($500,000 × 102.5%)] and carrying value of $246,875 [50% of $493,750].)

12. *c* [$6,000 + ($6,000 × 0.06)] × 0.06 = $381.60

13. *c*

14. The interest portion of an installment payment equals the beginning balance for the period multiplied by the original interest rate.

15. On the balance sheet, the balances of the liability and cash are decreased. On the income statement, interest expense is increased.

Demonstration Problem

The Staley Tile Corp. patented and successfully test-marketed a new product. However, to expand its ability to produce and market the product, the company needed to raise $800,000 of additional financing. On January 1, 2005, the company borrowed the money under these arrangements:

a. Staley signed a $400,000, 10% installment note that will be repaid with five equal annual installments. The payments will be made on December 31 of 2005 through 2009.

b. Staley issued five-year bonds with a par value of $400,000. The bonds have a 12% annual contract rate and pay interest on June 30 and December 31. The annual market interest rate for the bonds was 10% on January 1, 2005.

Required

1. For the installment note, prepare an amortization table and present the entry for the first payment.
2. For the bonds:
   (a) calculate the issue price of the bonds;
   (b) present the January 1, 2005, entry to record issuing the bonds;
   (c) prepare an amortization table using the effective interest method;
   (d) present the June 30, 2005, entry to record the first payment of interest; and
   (e) present an entry to record retiring the bonds at the call price of $416,000 on January 1, 2007.

Planning the Solution

- For the installment note, divide the borrowed amount by the annuity table factor for 10% and five payments. Prepare a table similar to Exhibit 17.21 and use the numbers in the table to prepare the required entries.
- For the bonds, calculate the issue price by using the market rate to find the present values of the bonds' cash flows (use a calculator or tables found in Appendix 17A). Then, use this result to record issuing the bonds. Next, develop an amortization table like Exhibit 17.17, and use it to get the numbers that you need for the journal entry. Finally, use the table to find the carrying value as of the date of the retirement of the bonds that you need for the journal entry.

SOLUTION TO Demonstration Problem

Part 1

Period Ending	(A) Beginning Balance	(B) Debit Interest Expense +	(C) Debit Notes Payable =	(D) Credit Cash*	(E) Ending Balance
2005	$400,000	$ 40,000	$ 65,519	$105,519	$334,481
2006	334,481	33,448	72,071	105,519	262,410
2007	262,410	26,241	79,278	105,519	183,132
2008	183,132	18,313	87,206	105,519	95,926
2009	95,926	9,593	95,926	105,519	-0-
Total		$127,595	$400,000	$527,595	

*$400,000 ÷ 3.7908 = $105,519

2005 Dec. 31			
	Interest Expense	40,000	
	Notes Payable	65,519	
	Cash		105,519
	To record first installment payment.		

Part 2

a.

PV of face amount (Table 17A.1):	$400,000 × 0.6139	=	$245,560
PV of interest annuity (Table 17A.2):	$ 24,000* × 7.7217	=	185,321
			$430,881

*$400,000 × 12% × 6/12 = $24,000

b.

2005			
Jan. 1	Cash	430,881	
	Premium on Bonds Payable..................		30,881
	Bonds Payable		400,000
	Sold bonds at a premium.		

c.

Period Ending	(A) Cash Interest Paid $400,000 × 12% × 6/12	(B) Period Interest Expense (E) × 10% × 6/12	(C) Premium Amort. (A) − (B)	(D) Unamortized Premium	(E) Carrying Value $400,000 + (D)
Jan. 1/05				30,881	430,881
June 30/05..	24,000	21,544	2,456	28,425	428,425
Dec. 31/05..	24,000	21,421	2,579	25,846	425,846
June 30/06..	24,000	21,292	2,708	23,138	423,138
Dec. 31/06..	24,000	21,157	2,843	20,295	420,295
June 30/07..	24,000	21,015	2,985	17,310	417,310
Dec. 31/07..	24,000	20,866	3,134	14,176	414,176
June 30/08..	24,000	20,709	3,291	10,885	410,885
Dec. 31/08..	24,000	20,544	3,456	7,429	407,429
June 30/09..	24,000	20,371	3,629	3,800	403,800
Dec. 31/09..	24,000	20,200*	3,800	-0-	400,000
Totals	240,000	209,119	30,881		

*Adjusted for rounding.

d.

2005			
June 30	Bond Interest Expense......................................	21,544	
	Premium on Bonds Payable	2,456	
	Cash		24,000
	Paid semi-annual interest on the bonds.		

e.

2005			
Jan. 1	Bonds Payable..	400,000	
	Premium on Bonds Payable	20,295	
	Cash		416,000
	Gain on Retirement of Bonds		4,295
	To record the retirement of bonds (carrying value determined as of December 31, 2006).		

PV Tables

Table 17A.1

Present Value of 1 Due in *n* Periods

Periods	Rate											
	1%	2%	3%	4%	5%	6%	7%	8%	9%	10%	12%	15%
1	0.9901	0.9804	0.9709	0.9615	0.9524	0.9434	0.9346	0.9259	0.9174	0.9091	0.8929	0.8696
2	0.9803	0.9612	0.9426	0.9246	0.9070	0.8900	0.8734	0.8573	0.8417	0.8264	0.7972	0.7561
3	0.9706	0.9423	0.9151	0.8890	0.8638	0.8396	0.8163	0.7938	0.7722	0.7513	0.7118	0.6575
4	0.9610	0.9238	0.8885	0.8548	0.8227	0.7921	0.7629	0.7350	0.7084	0.6830	0.6355	0.5718
5	0.9515	0.9057	0.8626	0.8219	0.7835	0.7473	0.7130	0.6806	0.6499	0.6209	0.5674	0.4972
6	0.9420	0.8880	0.8375	0.7903	0.7462	0.7050	0.6663	0.6302	0.5963	0.5645	0.5066	0.4323
7	0.9327	0.8706	0.8131	0.7599	0.7107	0.6651	0.6227	0.5835	0.5470	0.5132	0.4523	0.3759
8	0.9235	0.8535	0.7894	0.7307	0.6768	0.6274	0.5820	0.5403	0.5019	0.4665	0.4039	0.3269
9	0.9143	0.8368	0.7664	0.7026	0.6446	0.5919	0.5439	0.5002	0.4604	0.4241	0.3606	0.2843
10	0.9053	0.8203	0.7441	0.6756	0.6139	0.5584	0.5083	0.4632	0.4224	0.3855	0.3220	0.2472
11	0.8963	0.8043	0.7224	0.6496	0.5847	0.5268	0.4751	0.4289	0.3875	0.3505	0.2875	0.2149
12	0.8874	0.7885	0.7014	0.6246	0.5568	0.4970	0.4440	0.3971	0.3555	0.3186	0.2567	0.1869
13	0.8787	0.7730	0.6810	0.6006	0.5303	0.4688	0.4150	0.3677	0.3262	0.2897	0.2292	0.1625
14	0.8700	0.7579	0.6611	0.5775	0.5051	0.4423	0.3878	0.3405	0.2992	0.2633	0.2046	0.1413
15	0.8613	0.7430	0.6419	0.5553	0.4810	0.4173	0.3624	0.3152	0.2745	0.2394	0.1827	0.1229
16	0.8528	0.7284	0.6232	0.5339	0.4581	0.3936	0.3387	0.2919	0.2519	0.2176	0.1631	0.1069
17	0.8444	0.7142	0.6050	0.5134	0.4363	0.3714	0.3166	0.2703	0.2311	0.1978	0.1456	0.0929
18	0.8360	0.7002	0.5874	0.4936	0.4155	0.3503	0.2959	0.2502	0.2120	0.1799	0.1300	0.0808
19	0.8277	0.6864	0.5703	0.4746	0.3957	0.3305	0.2765	0.2317	0.1945	0.1635	0.1161	0.0703
20	0.8195	0.6730	0.5537	0.4564	0.3769	0.3118	0.2584	0.2145	0.1784	0.1486	0.1037	0.0611
25	0.7798	0.6095	0.4776	0.3751	0.2953	0.2330	0.1842	0.1460	0.1160	0.0923	0.0588	0.0304
30	0.7419	0.5521	0.4120	0.3083	0.2314	0.1741	0.1314	0.0994	0.0754	0.0573	0.0334	0.0151
35	0.7059	0.5000	0.3554	0.2534	0.1813	0.1301	0.0937	0.0676	0.0490	0.0356	0.0189	0.0075
40	0.6717	0.4529	0.3066	0.2083	0.1420	0.0972	0.0668	0.0460	0.0318	0.0221	0.0107	0.0037

Table 17A.2

Present Value of an Annuity of 1 per Period

Periods	Rate											
	1%	2%	3%	4%	5%	6%	7%	8%	9%	10%	12%	15%
1	0.9901	0.9804	0.9709	0.9615	0.9524	0.9434	0.9346	0.9259	0.9174	0.9091	0.8929	0.8696
2	1.9704	1.9416	1.9135	1.8861	1.8594	1.8334	1.8080	1.7833	1.7591	1.7355	1.6901	1.6257
3	2.9410	2.8839	2.8286	2.7751	2.7232	2.6730	2.6243	2.5771	2.5313	2.4869	2.4018	2.2832
4	3.9020	3.8077	3.7171	3.6299	3.5460	3.4651	3.3872	3.3121	3.2397	3.1699	3.0373	2.8550
5	4.8534	4.7135	4.5797	4.4518	4.3295	4.2124	4.1002	3.9927	3.8897	3.7908	3.6048	3.3522
6	5.7955	5.6014	5.4172	5.2421	5.0757	4.9173	4.7665	4.6229	4.4859	4.3553	4.1114	3.7845
7	6.7282	6.4720	6.2303	6.0021	5.7864	5.5824	5.3893	5.2064	5.0330	4.8684	4.5638	4.1604
8	7.6517	7.3255	7.0197	6.7327	6.4632	6.2098	5.9713	5.7466	5.5348	5.3349	4.9676	4.4873
9	8.5660	8.1622	7.7861	7.4353	7.1078	6.8017	6.5152	6.2469	5.9952	5.7950	5.3282	4.7716
10	9.4713	8.9826	8.5302	8.1109	7.7217	7.3601	7.0236	6.7101	6.4177	6.1446	5.6502	5.0188
11	10.3676	9.7868	9.2526	8.7605	8.3064	7.8869	7.4987	7.1390	6.8052	6.4951	5.9377	5.2337
12	11.2551	10.5753	9.9540	9.3851	8.8633	8.3838	7.9427	7.5361	7.1607	6.8137	6.1944	5.4206
13	12.1337	11.3484	10.6350	9.9856	9.3936	8.8527	8.3577	7.9038	7.4869	7.1034	6.4235	5.5831
14	13.0037	12.1062	11.2961	10.5631	9.8986	9.2950	8.7455	8.2442	7.7862	7.3667	6.6282	5.7245
15	13.8651	12.8493	11.9379	11.1184	10.3797	9.7122	9.1079	8.5595	8.0607	7.6061	6.8109	5.8474
16	14.7179	13.5777	12.5611	11.6523	10.8378	10.1059	9.4466	8.8514	8.3126	7.8237	6.9740	5.9542
17	15.5623	14.2919	13.1661	12.1657	11.2741	10.4773	9.7632	9.1216	8.5436	8.0216	7.1196	6.0472
18	16.3983	14.9920	13.7535	12.6593	11.6896	10.8276	10.0591	9.3719	8.7556	8.2014	7.2497	6.1280
19	17.2260	15.6785	14.3238	13.1339	12.0853	11.1581	10.3356	9.6036	8.9501	8.3649	7.3658	6.1982
20	18.0456	16.3514	14.8775	13.5903	12.4622	11.4699	10.5940	9.8181	9.1285	8.5136	7.4694	6.2593
25	22.0232	19.5235	17.4131	15.6221	14.0939	12.7834	11.6536	10.6748	9.8226	9.0770	7.8431	6.4641
30	25.8077	22.3965	19.6004	17.2920	15.3725	13.7648	12.4090	11.2578	10.2737	9.4269	8.0552	6.5660
35	29.4086	24.9986	21.4872	18.6646	16.3742	14.4982	12.9477	11.6546	10.5668	9.6442	8.1755	6.6166
40	32.8347	27.3555	23.1148	19.7928	17.1591	15.0463	13.3317	11.9246	10.7574	9.7791	8.2438	6.6418

Lease Liabilities

LO⁹ Prepare entries to record lease liabilities.

There are two types of leases: operating leases and capital leases. An **operating lease** is a short-term lease that does not require the lessee to record the right to use the property as an asset or to record any liability for the future lease payments. An operating lease is a form of off-balance-sheet financing. The lessee has an obligation to make future lease payments but is not required to report this liability on the balance sheet. Note disclosure of the future commitments of the lease agreement is all that is required. Accounting for operating leases is relatively uncomplicated. No recognition is given to the signing of an operating lease. The term of an operating lease is only a portion of the asset's operating life. Therefore, the leased asset remains on the books of lessor because the lessor retains all the risks of ownership. To illustrate accounting for an operating lease, assume that Ledgers Company leases an automobile from O'Regan Company for a payment of $3,000 on the first day of each month beginning February 2005.

Books of Ledgers Company (the lessee)

Feb. 1	Rent Expense	3,000.00	
	Cash		3,000.00
	Paid rental fee for February.		

Books of O'Regan Company (the lessor)

Feb. 1	Cash	3,000.00	
	Rental Revenue......................................		3,000.00
	Received rental fee for February.		

A lease qualifies as a **capital lease** if the lease terms meet any of the following criteria:

- The present value of the minimum lease payments is 90% or more of the fair value of the property at the inception of the lease.
- The lease term is 75% or more of the asset's economic life.
- Ownership transfers to the lessee at the end of the lease term.
- The lease has a bargain purchase option allowing the lessee to purchase the asset at less than the fair market value.

The lessee must report a leased asset and a lease liability if the lease qualifies as a capital lease. A capital lease is a lease agreement transferring the risks and benefits associated with ownership to the lessee. This type of lease spans a number of years and creates a long-term liability that is paid off in a series of payments. A capital lease is the economic equivalent of a purchase with financing arrangements.

When a capital lease is entered into, the lessee records a leased asset and amortizes it over its useful life. The corresponding interest portion of the lease liability is allocated (amortized) to interest expense over the years of the lease. This interest allocation process is the same as that for notes payable.

In summary, with a capital lease both an asset and a liability are reported on the balance sheet of the lessee and both interest expense and amortization expense are reported on the income statement. With an operating lease, the lessee reports rent expense on the income statement; there is nothing to be shown on the balance sheet for an operating lease.

To illustrate accounting for a capital lease, assume that Ledgers Company leases equipment from O'Regan Company at $3,000 per year for four years beginning January 2, 2005, with payments due at the end of each year. An 8% interest rate is assumed and the lease qualifies as a capital lease. Ledgers must record the capital asset at $9,936, the present value of the lease payments ($3,000 payment times the present value of an annuity factor of 3.3121).

2005			
Jan. 2	Leased Equipment	9,936	
	Lease Liability		9,936
	To recognize leased asset and		
	related liability.		

Ledgers recognizes two expenses related to this equipment. The first expense is amortization of the leased asset over the asset's useful life.

Dec. 31	Amortization Expense	2,484	
	Accumulated Amortization,		
	Leased Asset		2,484
	To recognize leased asset and related		
	liability ($9,936 ÷ 4 years); assuming		
	straight-line amortization and a zero		
	salvage value.		

The second expense to be recognized is the interest expense on the lease liability. A portion of each $3,000 payment is interest expense and the remainder is a reduction of the lease liability.

(A) Year	(B) Lease liability at start of year	(C) Payment	(D) Interest expense (B) × (0.08)	(E) Reduction in lease liability (C) − (D)	(F) Lease liability at end of year (B) − (E)
2005................	9,936	3,000	795	2,205	7,731
2006................	7,731	3,000	618	2,382	5,349
2007................	5,349	3,000	428	2,572	2,777
2008................	2,777	3,000	223*	2,777	–0–

*Adjusted for rounding.

The entry to record the lease payment at the end of 2005 is:

Dec. 31	Lease Liability...	2,205	
	Interest Expense	795	
	Cash..		3,000
	To record annual payment of the lease.		

The balance sheet presentation of the leased asset at the end of 2005 is as follows:

Assets:		
Equipment...	$9,936	
Less: Accumulated amortization	2,484	$7,452
Liabilities:		
Current liabilities:		
Lease liability—current portion		$2,382
Long-term liabilities:		
Lease liability		$5,349

Summary of Appendix 17B

LO⁹   **Prepare entries to record lease liabilities.** Lease liabilities are one type of long-term liability often used as an alternative to purchase assets. Capital leases are recorded as assets and liabilities. Other leases, called operating leases, are recorded as rent expense when the asset is issued.

Glossary

Annuity A series of equal payments occurring at equal time intervals. (p. 870)

Bearer bonds Bonds that are made payable to whomever holds them (called the *bearer*); also called *unregistered bonds*. (p. 866)

Bond A written promise to pay an amount identified as the par value of the bond along with interest at a stated annual amount; usually issued in denominations of $1,000. (p. 862)

Bond certificate A document containing information about the bond, such as the issuer's name, the bond's par value, the contract interest rate, and the maturity date. (p. 862)

Bond indenture The contract between the bond issuer and the bondholders; it identifies the rights and obligations of the parties. (p. 867)

Callable bonds Bonds that give the issuer an option of retiring them at a stated dollar amount prior to maturity. (p. 866)

Capital lease A lease that gives the lessee the risks and benefits normally associated with ownership. (p. 898)

Carrying value The net amount at which bonds are reflected on the balance sheet; equals the par value of the bonds less any unamortized discount or plus any unamortized premium; also called the *book value* of the bonds. (p. 872)

Contract rate The interest rate specified in the bond indenture; it is multiplied by the par value of the bonds to determine the amount of interest to be paid each year; also called the *coupon rate*, the *stated rate*, or the *nominal rate*. (p. 862)

Convertible bonds Bonds that can be exchanged by the bondholders for a fixed number of shares of the issuing company's common shares. (p. 866)

Coupon bonds Bonds that have interest coupons attached to their certificates; the bondholders detach the coupons when they mature and present them to a bank or broker for collection. (p. 866)

Debentures See *unsecured bonds*. (p. 865)

Discount/Discount on bonds payable The difference between the par value of a bond and its lower issue price; arises when the contract rate is lower than the market rate. (pp. 867, 871)

Effective interest method Allocates interest expense over the life of the bonds in a way that yields a constant rate of interest; interest expense for a period is found by multiplying the balance of the liability at the beginning of the period by the bonds' original market rate. (p. 874)

Effective interest rate See *market rate of interest*. (p. 867)

Financial leverage When a company earns a higher return with borrowed funds than it is paying in interest, the result is an increase in return on equity. (p. 865)

Installment note An obligation requiring a series of periodic payments to the lender (p. 839)

Market rate of interest The interest rate that borrowers are willing to pay and that lenders are willing to earn for a particular bond given its risk level. Also called the *effective interest rate*. (p. 867)

Mortgage A legal agreement that protects a lender by giving the lender the right to be paid out of the cash proceeds from the sale of the borrower's specific assets identified in the mortgage. (p. 892)

Operating lease A short-term lease that does not require the lessee to record the right to use the property as an asset or to record any liability for future lease payments. (p. 898)

Par value of a bond The amount that the bond issuer agrees to pay at maturity and the amount on which interest payments are based; also called the *face amount* or *face value*. (p. 862)

Premium/Premium on bonds The difference between the par value of a bond and its higher issue price; arises when the contract rate is higher than the market rate. (pp. 867, 876)

Redeemable bonds Bonds that give the purchaser an option of retiring them at a stated dollar amount prior to maturity. (p. 866)

Registered bonds Bonds owned by investors whose names and addresses are recorded by the issuing company; the interest payments are made with cheques to the registered owners. (p. 865)

Secured bonds Bonds that have specific assets of the issuing company pledged as collateral. (p. 865)

Serial bonds Bonds that mature at different dates with the result that the entire debt is repaid gradually over a number of years. (p. 865)

Straight-line method (interest allocation) A method of amortization that allocates an equal amount of interest to each accounting period in the life of bonds. (p. 873)

Term bonds Bonds that are scheduled for payment (mature) at a single specified date. (p. 865)

Unsecured bonds Bonds that are backed by the issuer's general credit standing; unsecured bonds are almost always more risky than unsecured bonds; also called *debentures*. (p. 865)

 **Online LearningCentre** with POWERWEB

For more study tools, quizzes, and problem material, refer to the Online Learning Centre at **www.mcgrawhill.ca/college/larson**

Questions

1. What is the difference between notes payable and bonds payable?

2. What is the primary difference between a share and a bond?

3. What is the main advantage of issuing bonds instead of obtaining funds from the company's owners?

4. What is a bond indenture? What provisions are usually included in an indenture?

5. What are the duties of a trustee for bondholders?

6. What obligation does Yvette Bourque have to the investors who purchased $200,000 of bonds to finance her natural foods store?

7. Refer to the annual report for WestJet presented in Appendix I. Is there any indication that the company has issued bonds?

8. What are the *contract* and *market interest rates* for bonds?

9. What factors affect the market interest rates for bonds?

10. If you know the par value of bonds, the contract rate, and the market interest rate, how can you estimate the market value of the bonds?

11. Does the straight-line or effective interest method produce an allocation of interest that creates a constant rate of interest over a bond's life? Explain your answer.

12. What is the cash price of a $2,000 bond that is sold at 98¼? What is the cash price of a $6,000 bond that is sold at 101½?

13. Why does a company that issues bonds between interest dates collect accrued interest from the bonds' purchasers?

14. Describe two alternative payment patterns for installment notes.

15. Refer to the annual report for WestJet presented in Appendix I. How many long-term loans are outstanding? What is the total dollar amount? Are these loans secured?

*16. How would a lease create an asset and a liability for the lessee?

Quick Study

When solving the exercises and problems
1. Round all dollar amounts to the nearest whole dollar, and
2. Assume that none of the companies uses reversing entries.

QS 17-1
Calculating bond interest

LO¹

A $15,000 bond with a contract interest rate of 6% was issued on March 1, 2005. Calculate the cash paid on the first interest payment date if interest is paid:
a. annually
b. semi-annually
c. quarterly
d. monthly

QS 17-2
Bond financing

LO¹

Curtis Ltd. issued $100,000 of 8% bonds at face value on October 1, 2005. Interest is paid each March 31 and September 30. If Curtis's tax rate is 40%, what is the annual after-tax borrowing cost (a) in dollars and (b) in percentage terms?

QS 17-3
Bond terms and identifications

LO²

Match the following terms and phrases by entering the letter of the phrase that best describes each term in the blank next to the term.

_____	Serial bonds	_____	Secured bonds
_____	Convertible bonds	_____	Debentures
_____	Registered bonds	_____	Bond indenture
_____	Bearer bonds		

a. Issuer records the bondholders' names and addresses.
b. Unsecured; backed only by the issuer's general credit standing.
c. Varying maturity dates.
d. Identifies the rights and responsibilities of the issuer and bondholders.
e. Can be exchanged for shares of the issuer's common shares.
f. Unregistered; interest is paid to whomever possesses them.
g. Specific assets of the issuer are mortgaged as collateral.

An asterisk (*) identifies assignment material based on Appendix 17B.

Web Inc. showed the following on its December 31, 2005, balance sheet:

Long-term liabilities:	
Bonds payable, 5%, due June 30, 2010	$745,000

Interest is paid quarterly each March 31, June 30, September 30, and December 31.
Prepare the entries for:
a. March 31, 2006
b. June 30, 2010

QS 17-4
Recording bonds issued at par

LO³

Presley Corp. issued $200,000 of 6% bonds on November 1, 2005, at par value. The bonds were dated October 1, 2005, and pay interest each April 30 and October 31. Record the issue of the bonds on November 1, 2005.

QS 17-5
Issue of bonds at par between interest dates

LO³

On August 1, 2005, Blancard Inc. issued $520,000 of 10%, seven-year bonds. Interest is to be paid semi-annually. Calculate the issue price of the bonds if the market interest rate was:
a. 12%
b. 10%
c. 14%

QS 17-6
Calculating the price of a bond using PV tables

LO⁴

On February 1, 2005, Seemac Corp. issued $750,000 of 11%, eight-year bonds. Interest is to be paid quarterly. Calculate the issue price of the bonds if the market interest rate was:
a. 10%
b. 11%
c. 12%

QS 17-7
Calculating the price of a bond using business calculator PV function

LO⁴

Refer to QS 17-5. Record the entry for the issuance of the bonds if they had been issued at 97 on October 1, 2005.

QS 17-8
Issue of bonds at a discount

LO⁵

Simone Corp. issued $300,000 of par value bonds on October 1, 2005. The bonds pay interest each March 31 and September 30. Record this transaction if the bonds were issued at 101.

QS 17-9
Issue of bonds at a premium

LO⁶

Alberta Industries Ltd. issued 10%, 10-year bonds with a par value of $200,000 and semi-annual interest payments. On the issue date, the annual market rate of interest for the bonds was 12%, and the selling price was $177,059. The straight-line method is used to allocate the interest.
a. What is the total amount of bond interest expense that will be recognized over the life of the bonds?
b. What is the total bond interest expense recorded on the first interest payment date?

QS 17-10
Bond transactions—discount

LO⁵

QS 17-11

Bond transactions—premium

LO⁶

Dawson Limited issued 12%, 10-year bonds with a par value of $60,000 and semi-annual interest payments. On the issue date, the annual market rate of interest for the bonds was 10%, and they sold for $67,478. The effective interest method is used to allocate the interest.

a. What is the total amount of bond interest expense that will be recognized over the life of the bonds?

b. What is the amount of bond interest expense recorded on the first interest payment date?

QS 17-12

Retiring bonds before maturity

LO⁷

On July 1, 2005, Loudre Ltd. exercises a $4,000 call option on its outstanding bonds that have a carrying value of $206,000 and par value of $200,000. Loudre exercises the call option immediately after the semi-annual interest is paid on June 30, 2005. Record the journal entry to show the retirement of the bonds.

QS 17-13

Bond retirement by share conversion

LO⁷

On January 1, 2005, the $1,000,000 par value bonds of Sinclair Corporation with a carrying value of $950,000 are converted to 500,000 common shares. Journalize the conversion of the bonds.

Use the following information for QS 17-14 to 17-18:

On March 1, 2005, JenStar Inc. issued at par an $80,000, 6%, three-year bond. Interest is to be paid quarterly beginning May 31, 2005. JenStar's year-end is July 31. A partial payment schedule is shown below:

Period Ending	Cash Interest Paid*	Carrying Value
Mar. 1/05		$80,000
May 31/05	$ 1,200	80,000
Aug. 31/05	1,200	80,000
Aug. 31/07	1,200	80,000
Nov. 30/07	1,200	80,000
Feb. 29/08**	1,200	80,000
Total	$14,400	

*$80,000 × 6% × 3/12
**Leap year

QS 17-14

Issuance of bond at par

LO³

Record the issuance of the bond on March 1, 2005.

QS 17-15

Recording payment of bond interest

LO³

Record the payment of interest on May 31, 2005.

Record the accrual of bond interest on July 31, 2005, JenStar's year-end, and the subsequent payment of interest on August 31, 2005.

Assume JenStar Inc. issued the bonds at par on April 1, 2005, instead of March 1. Record the issuance of the bond on April 1, 2005, and the first interest payment on May 31, 2005.

Record the entries on February 28, 2008, regarding the final interest payment and retirement of the bond.

Use the following information for QS 17-19 to 17-23:

Holiday Corporation issued a $95,000, 7%, four-year bond on September 1, 2005, for cash of $92,300. Interest is to be paid semi-annually beginning March 1, 2006. Assume a year-end of April 30. The amortization schedule, using the straight-line method, is shown below:

Period Ending	(A) Cash Interest Paid $95,000 × 7% × 6/12	(B) Period Interest Expense 29,300/8	(C) Discount Amort. 2,700/8	(D) Unamortized Discount	(E) Carrying Value $95,000 − (D)
Sept. 1/05				2,700	92,300
Mar. 1/06	3,325	3,663	338	2,362	92,638
Sept. 1/06	3,325	3,663	338	2,024	92,976
Mar. 1/07	3,325	3,663	338	1,686	93,314
Sept. 1/07	3,325	3,663	338	1,348	93,652
Mar. 1/08	3,325	3,663	338	1,010	93,990
Sept. 1/08	3,325	3,663	338	672	94,328
Mar. 1/09	3,325	3,663	338	334	94,666
Sept. 1/09	3,325	3,659*	334*	-0-	95,000
Totals	**26,600**	**29,300**	**2,700**		

Adjusted for rounding.

Record the issuance of the bond on September 1, 2005.

Record the payment of bond interest on March 1, 2006.

QS 17-21
Accrual of bond interest

LO⁵

Record the accrual of bond interest and discount amortization on April 30, 2006, the year-end, and the subsequent payment of interest on September 1, 2006.

QS 17-22
Balance sheet presentation

LO⁵

Show how the bonds would appear on the balance sheet in the long-term liabilities section at April 30, 2006.

QS 17-23
Retirement of bonds

LO⁷

Record the entries on September 1, 2009, regarding the final interest payment and retirement of the bond.

Use the following information for QS 17-24 to 17-26:

Bozena Inc. issued a $200,000, 8%, three-year bond on November 1, 2005, for cash of $194,792. Interest is to be paid quarterly. The annual market rate of interest is 9%. Assume a year-end of December 31. The amortization schedule, using the effective interest method, is shown below:

Period Ending	(A) Cash Interest Paid $200,000 × 8% × 3/12	(B) Period Interest Expense (E) × 9% × 3/12	(C) Discount Amort. (B) – (A)	(D) Unamortized Discount	(E) Carrying Value $200,000 – (D)
Nov. 1/05				5,208	194,792
Feb. 1/06	4,000	4,383	383	4,825	195,175
Aug. 1/08	4,000	4,478	478	492	199,508
Nov. 1/08	4,000	4,492*	492	-0-	200,000
Totals	**48,000**	**53,208**	**5,208**		

Adjusted for rounding.

QS 17-24
Issuance of bonds at a discount

LO⁵

Record the issuance of the bond on November 1, 2005.

QS 17-25
Accrual of bond interest

LO⁵

Record the accrual of bond interest at year-end, December 31, 2005, and the subsequent payment on February 1, 2006.

QS 17-26
Retirement of bonds

LO⁷

Record the entries on November 1, 2008, regarding the final interest payment and the retirement of the bond.

Use the following information for QS 17-27 to 17-29:

On May 1, 2005, Darroch Corporation issued a $386,000, 15%, four-year bond for cash of $394,600. Interest is to be paid semi-annually. Assume a year-end of August 31. The amortization schedule, using the straight-line method, is shown below:

Period Ending	(A) Cash Interest Paid $386,000 × 15% × 6/12	(B) Period Interest Expense 223,000/8	(C) Premium Amort. 8,600/8	(D) Unamortized Premium	(E) Carrying Value $386,000 + (D)
May 1/05				8,600	394,600
Nov. 1/05	28,950	27,875	1,075	7,525	393,525
May 1/06	28,950	27,875	1,075	6,450	392,450
Nov. 1/06	28,950	27,875	1,075	5,375	391,375
May 1/07	28,950	27,875	1,075	4,300	390,300
Nov. 1/07	28,950	27,875	1,075	3,225	389,225
May 1/08	28,950	27,875	1,075	2,150	388,150
Nov. 1/08	28,950	27,875	1,075	1,075	387,075
May 1/09	28,950	27,875	1,075	-0-	386,000
Totals	**231,600**	**223,000**	**8,600**		

Record the issuance of the bond on May 1, 2005.

QS 17-27
Issuance of bonds at a premium

LO[6]

Record the accrual of bond interest and premium amortization on August 31, 2005, the year-end, and the subsequent payment of interest on November 1, 2005.

QS 17-28
Accrual of bond interest

LO[6]

Record the entries on May 1, 2009, regarding the final interest payment and retirement of the bond.

QS 17-29
Retirement of bonds

LO[7]

Use the following information for QS 17-30 to 17-32:

Henderson Inc. issued a $652,000, 14% 10-year bond on October 1, 2005, for cash of $697,701. Interest is to be paid quarterly. The annual market rate of interest is 12.75%. Assume a year-end of February 28. A partial amortization schedule, using the effective interest method, is shown below.

Period Ending	(A) Cash Interest Paid $652,000 × 14% × 3/12	(B) Period Interest Expense (E) × 12.75% × 3/12	(C) Premium Amort. (A) − (B)	(D) Unamortized Premium	(E) Carrying Value $652,000 + (D)
Oct. 1/05				45,701	697,701
Jan. 1/06	22,820	22,239	581	45,120	697,120
Apr. 1/06	22,820	22,221	599	44,521	696,521
July 1/06	22,820	22,202	618	43,903	695,903
Oct. 1/06	22,820	22,182	638	43,264	695,264
Apr. 1/15	22,820	20,966	1,854	3,888	655,888
July 1/15	22,820	20,906	1,914	1,975	653,975
Oct. 1/15	22,820	20,845	1,975	-0-	652,000
Totals	**912,800**	**867,099**	**45,701**		

QS 17-30
Issuance of bonds at a premium

LO[6]

Record the issuance of the bond on October 1, 2005.

QS 17-31
Accrual of bond interest

LO[6]

Record the accrual of bond interest and premium amortization on February 28, 2006, the year-end, and the subsequent payment of interest on April 1, 2006.

QS 17-32
Retirement of bonds

LO[7]

Record the entries on October 1, 2015, regarding the final interest payment and retirement of the bond.

QS 17-33
Installment note with equal payments

LO[8]

Calvin Corp. borrowed $80,000 from a bank and signed an installment note that calls for five annual payments of equal size, with the first payment due one year after the note was signed. Use Table 17A.2 or a calculator to calculate the size of the annual payment for each of the following annual interest rates:
a. 5%
b. 7%
c. 10%

QS 17-34
Calculating the amount due on an interest-bearing note

LO[8]

On January 1, 2005, the Pareto Company borrowed $80,000 in exchange for an interest-bearing note. The note plus interest compounded at an annual rate of 8% is due on December 31, 2007. Determine the amount that Pareto will pay on the due date.

On January 1, 2005, Sharma Ltd. issued $300,000 of 20-year bonds that pay 8% interest semi-annually on June 30 and December 31. The bonds were sold to investors at their par value.
a. How much interest will Sharma pay to the holders of these bonds every six months?
b. Show the journal entries that Sharma would make to record: (1) the issuance of the bonds on January 1, 2005; (2) the first interest payment on June 30, 2005; and (3) the second interest payment on December 31, 2005.

Exercise 17-1
Bonds issued at par

LO³

On March 1, 2005, Sharma Ltd. issued bonds dated January 1, 2005. The bonds have a $300,000 par value, mature in 20 years, and pay 8% interest semi-annually on June 30 and December 31. The bonds were sold to investors at their par value plus the two months' interest that had accrued since the original issue date.
a. How much accrued interest was paid to Sharma by the purchasers of these bonds on March 1, 2005?
b. Show the journal entries that Sharma would make to record: (1) the issuance of the bonds on March 1, 2005; (2) the first interest payment on June 30, 2005; and (3) the second interest payment on December 31, 2005.

Exercise 17-2
Journal entries for bond issuance with accrued interest

LO³

South Corporation had a $1,350,000, 5% bond available for issue on September 1, 2005. Interest is to be paid quarterly beginning November 30. All of the bonds were issued at par on October 1. Prepare the appropriate entries for:
a. October 1, 2005
b. November 30, 2005
c. December 31, 2005 (South Corporation's year-end)
d. February 28, 2006

Exercise 17-3
Bonds issued at par between interest dates

LO³

North Corporation had a $428,000, 7% bond available for issue on April 1. Interest is to be paid on the last day of each month. On April 14 and 25, bonds with a face value of $325,000 and $103,000, respectively, were issued at par. Record the entries for April 14, 25, and 30.

Exercise 17-4
Bonds issued at par between interest dates

LO³

On October 1, 2005, Allar Inc. has available for issue $618,000 bonds due in four years. Interest at the rate of 4% is to be paid quarterly. Calculate the issue price if the market interest rate is:
a. 5%
b. 4%
c. 3%

Exercise 17-5
Calculating the issue price using business calculator PV function

LO⁴

Check figure:
b. $618,000

Willard Inc. has available for issue a $1,396,000 bond due in seven years. Interest at the rate of 11% is to be paid semi-annually. Calculate the issue price if the market interest rate is:
a. 9.5%
b. 11%
c. 12%

Exercise 17-6
Calculating the issue price using business calculator PV function

LO⁴

Check figure:
b. $1,396,000

Exercise 17-7

Calculating the present value of a bond and recording the issuance

$LO^{4,5}$

Check figure:
e. Discount = $23,055

The Kitchener Corp. issued bonds on March 1, 2005, with a par value of $150,000. The bonds mature in 15 years and pay 8% annual interest in two semi-annual payments. On the issue date, the annual market rate of interest for the bonds turned out to be 10%.
a. What is the size of the semi-annual interest payment for these bonds?
b. How many semi-annual interest payments will be made on these bonds over their life?
c. Use the information about the interest rates to decide whether the bonds were issued at par, at a discount, or at a premium.
d. Estimate the market value of the bonds as of the date they were issued.
e. Present the journal entry that would be made to record the bonds' issuance.

Exercise 17-8

Straight-line allocation of interest for bonds sold at a discount

LO^5

Check figure:
b. Total interest expense = $16,915

Bourque Ltd. issued bonds with a par value of $50,000 on January 1, 2005. The annual contract rate on the bonds is 8%, and the interest is paid semi-annually on June 30 and December 31. The bonds mature after three years. The annual market interest rate at the date of issuance was 12%, and the bonds were sold for $45,085.
a. What is the amount of the original discount on these bonds?
b. How much total bond interest expense will be recognized over the life of these bonds?
c. Present an amortization table for these bonds; use the straight-line method of allocating the interest and amortizing the discount.

Exercise 17-9

Effective interest method allocation of interest for bonds sold at a discount

LO^5

Check figure:
b. Total interest expense = $8,723

Burlington Corporation issued bonds with a par value of $30,000 on January 1, 2005. The annual contract rate on the bonds is 8%, and the interest is paid semi-annually. The bonds mature after three years. The annual market interest rate at the date of issuance was 10%, and the bonds were sold for $28,477.
a. What is the amount of the original discount on these bonds?
b. How much total bond interest expense will be recognized over the life of these bonds?
c. Present an amortization table for these bonds; use the effective interest method of allocating the interest and amortizing the discount.

Exercise 17-10

Straight-line amortization table and accrued interest

LO^5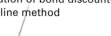

Check figure:
a. Total interest expense = $39,052

Howard Corp. issued bonds with a par value of $100,000 and a five-year life on May 1, 2005. The contract interest rate is 7%. The bonds pay interest on October 31 and April 30. They were issued at a price of $95,948. Howard Corp.'s year-end is December 31.
a. Prepare an amortization table for these bonds that covers their entire life. Use the straight-line method of allocating interest.
b. Show the journal entries that the issuer would make to record the entries on: October 31, 2005; December 31, 2005; and April 30, 2006.

Exercise 17-11

Amortization of bond discount—straight-line method

LO^5

On November 1, 2005, Inca Ltd. issued a $600,000, 5%, two-year bond. Interest is to be paid semi-annually each May 1 and November 1.

Required
a. Calculate the issue price of the bond assuming a market interest rate of 6% on the date of the bond issue.
b. Using the straight-line method, prepare an amortization schedule similar to Exhibit 17.10.

On October 1, 2005, Zayed Inc. issued a $735,000, 7%, seven-year bond. Interest is to be paid annually each October 1.

Required
a. Calculate the issue price of the bond assuming a market interest rate of 9% on the date of the bond issue.
b. Using the straight-line method, prepare an amortization schedule similar to Exhibit 17.10.

Exercise 17-12
Amortization of bond discount—straight-line method

LO[5]

Check figures:
a. $660,993
b. Total interest expense = $434,157

Refer to the amortization schedule prepared in Exercise 17-12. Zayed Inc. has a November 30 year-end.

Required

Part 1
Record the following entries:
a. issuance of the bonds on October 1, 2005,
b. adjusting entry to accrue bond interest and discount amortization on November 30, 2005,
c. payment of interest on October 1, 2006.

Part 2
Show how the bond will appear on the balance sheet under long-term liabilities at November 30, 2009.

Exercise 17-13
Recording bonds issued at a discount—straight-line amortization

LO[5]

Check figure:
a. Discount = $74,007

Refer to the information in Exercise 17-12.

Required
a. Calculate the issue price of the bond assuming a market interest rate of 8% on the date of the bond issue.
b. Using the effective interest method, prepare an amortization schedule similar to Exhibit 17.11.

Exercise 17-14
Amortization of bond discount—effective interest method

LO[5]

Check figures:
a. $696,742
b. Total interest expense = $398,408

Refer to the amortization schedule prepared in Exercise 17-14. Assume a year-end of September 30.

Required

Part 1
Record the following entries:
a. issuance of the bonds on October 1, 2005,
b. accrual of interest on September 30, 2006, the year-end,
c. payment of interest on October 1, 2006.

Part 2
Show how the bonds will appear on the balance sheet under long-term liabilities at September 30, 2008.

Exercise 17-15
Recording bonds issued at a discount—effective interest amortization

LO[5]

Check figure:
a. Discount = $38,258

On January 1, 2005, Sharma Ltd. issued $300,000 of 20-year bonds that pay 8% interest semi-annually on June 30 and December 31. Assume the bonds were sold at: (1) 98; and (2) 102. Journalize the issuance of the bonds at 98 and 102.

Exercise 17-16
Journal entries for bond issuances

LO[5,6]

Check figure:
b. Premium = $6,000

Exercise 17-17
Computing the present value of a bond and recording the issuance

$LO^{4,6}$

Check figure:
e. Cash = $29,900

Allen Ice Ltd., issued bonds on September 1, 2005, with a par value of $25,000. The bonds mature in 15 years and pay 8% annual interest in two semi-annual payments. On the issue date, the annual market rate of interest for the bonds turned out to be 6%.

a. What is the semi-annual interest payment for these bonds?
b. How many semi-annual interest payments will be made on these bonds over their life?
c. Use the information about the interest rates to decide whether the bonds were issued at par, at a discount, or at a premium.
d. Estimate the market value of the bonds as of the date they were issued.
e. Present the journal entry that would be made to record the bonds' issuance.

Exercise 17-18
Effective interest method allocation of interest for bonds sold at a premium

LO^6

Check figure:
b. Total interest expense = $12,370

Power Ltd. issued bonds with a par value of $40,000 on January 1, 2005. The annual contract rate on the bonds was 12%, and the interest is paid semi-annually. The bonds mature after three years. The annual market interest rate at the date of issuance was 10%, and the bonds were sold for $42,030.

a. What is the amount of the original premium on these bonds?
b. How much total bond interest expense will be recognized over the life of these bonds?
c. Present an amortization table for these bonds (similar to Exhibit 17.17); use the effective interest method of allocating the interest and amortizing the premium.

Exercise 17-19
Amortization of bond premium—straight-line method

LO^6

On November 1, Lendrome Inc. issued a $300,000, 5%, two-year bond. Interest is to be paid quarterly each February 1, May 1, August 1, and November 1.

Required
a. Calculate the issue price of the bond assuming a market interest rate of 4% on the date of the bond issue.
b. Using the straight-line method, prepare an amortization schedule similar to Exhibit 17.16.

Exercise 17-20
Amortization of bond premium—straight-line method

LO^6

Check figures:
a. $776,063
b. Total interest expense = $319,087

Refer to the information in Exercise 17-12.

Required
a. Calculate the issue price of the bond assuming a market interest rate of 6% on the date of the bond issue.
b. Using the straight-line method, prepare an amortization schedule similar to Exhibit 17.16.

Exercise 17-21
Recording bonds issued at a premium—straight-line amortization

LO^6

Check figures:
1c. Premium = $4,888
2. Premium = $16,621

Refer to the amortization schedule prepared in Exercise 17-20. Assume a November 30 year-end.

Required

Part 1
Record the following entries:
a. issuance of the bonds on October 1, 2005,
b. adjusting entry to accrue bond interest and premium amortization on November 30, 2005,
c. payment of interest on October 1, 2006.

Part 2
Show how the bond will appear on the balance sheet under long-term liabilities at November 30, 2009.

Refer to the information in Exercise 17-12.

Required
a. Calculate the issue price of the bond assuming a market interest rate of 5%.
b. Prepare an amortization schedule similar to Exhibit 17.17 using the effective interest method.

Exercise 17-22
Amortization of bond premium—
effective interest method

Check figures:
a. $820,075
b. Total interest expense
= $275,075

Refer to the amortization schedule prepared in Exercise 17-22. Assume a November 30 year-end.

Required

Part 1
Record the following entries:
a. issuance of the bonds on October 1, 2005.
b. adjusting entry to accrue bond interest and premium amortization on November 30, 2005.
c. payment of interest on October 1, 2006.

Part 2
Show how the bond will appear on the balance sheet under long-term liabilities at November 30, 2010.

Exercise 17-23
Recording bonds issued
at a premium—effective interest
amortization

Check figure:
a. Cash = $820,075

On January 1, 2005, Dutch Ltd., issued $700,000 of 10%, 15-year bonds at a price of 95 1/2. Interest is to be paid semi-annually. Three years later, on January 1, 2008, the corporation retired 30% of these bonds by buying them on the open market at 105 3/4. All interest had been properly accounted for and paid through December 31, 2007, the day before the purchase. The straight-line method was used to allocate the interest and amortize the original discount.
a. How much money did the company receive when it first issued the entire group of bonds?
b. How large was the original discount on the entire group of bonds?
c. How much amortization did the company record on the entire group of bonds between January 1, 2005, and December 31, 2007?
d. What was the carrying value of the entire group of bonds as of the close of business on December 31, 2007? What was the carrying value of the retired bonds on this date?
e. How much money did the company pay on January 1, 2008, to purchase the bonds that it retired?
f. What is the amount of the gain or loss from retiring the bonds?
g. Provide the General Journal entry that the company would make to record the retirement of the bonds.

Exercise 17-24
Retiring bonds payable

LO⁷

Check figure:
g. Loss = $19,635

Denston Inc. showed the following on its December 31, 2005, balance sheet:

Bonds payable, convertible..	$5,000,000	
Less: Unamortized discount	18,000	$4,982,000

Required
1. Assuming the bonds are convertible into 500,000 common shares, journalize the conversion on January 1, 2006, when the market value per common share was $10.25.
2. How will the conversion of bonds into common shares affect the elements of the balance sheet (assets, liabilities, equity)?

Exercise 17-25
Conversion of bonds payable

LO⁷

Exercise 17-26
Conversion of bonds payable

Tungston Inc.'s December 31, 2005, adjusted trial balance shows the following:

Account Description	Balance*
Bonds payable, convertible	$3,000,000
Premium on bonds payable	40,000

Assume normal balances.

Required
1. What is the carrying value of the bonds on December 31, 2005?
2. The bonds were converted into 150,000 common shares on January 1, 2006. Journalize the entry assuming the market value per common share on this date was $18.15.

Exercise 17-27
Installment note with payments of accrued interest and equal amounts of principal

Check figure:
b. Total interest expense = $2,000

On December 31, 2005, Morgan Inc. borrowed $16,000 by signing a four-year, 5% install-ment note. The note requires annual payments of accrued interest and equal amounts of principal on December 31 of each year from 2006 through 2009.
a. How much principal will be included in each of the four payments?
b. Prepare an amortization table for this installment note like the one presented in Exhibit 17.20.

Exercise 17-28
Journal entries for an installment note with payments of accrued interest and equal amounts of principal

Use the data in Exercise 17-27 to prepare journal entries that Morgan Inc. would make to record the loan on December 31, 2005, and the four payments starting on December 31, 2006, through the final payment on December 31, 2009.

Exercise 17-29
Installment note with equal payments

Check figure:
b. Total interest expense = $1,280

On December 31, 2005, Van Gurp Corp. borrowed $10,000 by signing a four-year, 5% installment note. The note requires four equal payments of accrued interest and principal on December 31 of each year from 2006 through 2009.
a. Calculate the size of each of the four equal payments.
b. Prepare an amortization table for this installment note like the one presented in Exhibit 17.20.

Exercise 17-30
Journal entries for an installment note with equal payments

Use the data in Exercise 17-29 to prepare journal entries that Van Gurp Corp. would make to record the loan on December 31, 2005, and the four payments starting on December 31, 2006, through the final payment on December 31, 2009.

On December 31, 2005, a day when the available interest rate was 10%, Kowloon Printing Company leased equipment with an eight-year life. The contract called for a $6,000 annual lease payment at the end of each of the next five years, with the equipment becoming the property of the lessee at the end of that period. Prepare entries to record: (a) the leasing of the equipment, (b) the recognition of interest expense on the lease liability on December 31, 2006, (c) amortization expense for 2006 assuming straight-line and a zero salvage value, (d) the December 31, 2006 lease payment, and (e) prepare an amortization schedule.

*Exercise 17-31
Liabilities from leasing

LO⁹

Check figures:
a. 22,745
c. 2,843

Problems

Howlett Inc. issued bonds on January 1, 2005, that pay interest semi-annually on June 30 and December 31. The par value of the bonds is $40,000, the annual contract rate is 8%, and the bonds mature in 10 years.

Required
For each of these three situations, (a) determine the issue price of the bonds and (b) show the journal entry that would record the issuance, assuming the market interest rate at the date of issuance was
1. 6%
2. 8%
3. 10%

Problem 17-1A
Calculating bond prices and recording issuance with journal entries

LO³,⁵,⁶

Check figures:
1a. $45,952
2a. $40,000
3a. $35,016

The Abbott Corporation issued $125,000 of bonds that pay 6% annual interest with two semi-annual payments. The date of issuance was January 1, 2005, and the interest is paid on June 30 and December 31. The bonds mature after 10 years and were issued at the price of $108,014.

Required
1. Prepare a General Journal entry to record the issuance of the bonds.
2. Calculate the cash payment, discount amortization amount using straight-line amortization, and bond interest expense to be recognized every six months.
3. Determine the total bond interest expense that will be recognized over the life of these bonds.
4. Show the beginning and ending balances of the Discount on Bonds Payable account for the first four semi-annual periods.
5. Prepare the first two years of an amortization table based on the straight-line method of allocating the interest.
6. Present the journal entries that Abbott would make to record the first two interest payments. Assume a December 31 year-end.

Problem 17-2A
Straight-line method of allocating bond interest and amortizing a bond discount

LO⁵

Check figure:
1. Cash = $108,014

An asterisk (*) identifies assignment material based on Appendix 17B.

Problem 17-3A

Effective interest method of allocating bond interest and amortizing a bond discount

LO⁴,⁵

Check figure:
1. $46,490

Martin Corp. issued $50,000 of bonds that pay 4% annual interest with semi-annual payments. The date of issuance was January 1, 2005, and the interest is paid on June 30 and December 31. The bonds mature after four years. The market interest rate was 6%.

Required

Preparation component:
1. Calculate the issue price of the bond.
2. Prepare a General Journal entry to record the issuance of the bonds.
3. Determine the total bond interest expense that will be recognized over the life of these bonds.
4. Prepare the first two years of an amortization table based on the effective interest method.
5. Show the beginning and ending balances of the discount on bonds payable account for the first four amortization periods.
6. Present the journal entries Martin would make to record the first two interest payments.

Analysis component:
7. Now assume that the market interest rate on January 1, 2005, was 3% instead of 6%. Without presenting any specific numbers, describe how this change would affect the amounts presented on Martin's financial statements.

Problem 17-4A

Amortization of bond discount—straight-line method (using business calculator PV function)

LO⁴,⁵

Check figures:
a. $237,157
b. Total interest expense = $105,843

On February 1, 2005, Blanchard Inc. issued a $245,000, 10%, four-year bond. Interest is to be paid quarterly beginning May 1, 2005.

Required
a. Calculate the issue price of the bond assuming a market interest rate of 11%.
b. Using the straight-line method, prepare an amortization schedule similar to Exhibit 17.10.

Problem 17-5A

Recording bonds issued at a discount—straight-line amortization

LO⁵

Check figures:
1a. Cash = $237,157
1b. Cash = $6,125

Refer to the amortization schedule prepared in Problem 17-4A. Assume Blanchard Inc. has a June 30 year-end.

Required

Part 1
Record the following entries:
a. issuance of the bonds on February 1, 2005,
b. payment of interest on May 1, 2005,
c. adjusting entry to accrue bond interest and discount amortization on June 30, 2005,
d. payment of interest on August 1, 2005.

Part 2
Show how the bonds will appear on the balance sheet under liabilities at June 30, 2008.

Problem 17-6A

Amortization of bond discount—effective interest method (using business calculator PV function)

LO⁴,⁵

Check figures:
a. $175,643
b. Total interest expense = $69,157

On June 1, 2005, Ibach Inc. issued a $180,000 12%, three-year bond. Interest is to be paid semi-annually beginning December 1, 2005.

Required
a. Calculate the issue price of the bond assuming a market interest rate of 13%.
b. Using the effective interest method, prepare an amortization schedule similar to Exhibit 17.11.

Refer to the amortization schedule prepared in Problem 17-6A. Assume Ibach Inc. has a January 31 year-end.

Required

Part 1
Record the following entries:
a. issuance of the bonds on June 1, 2005,
b. payment of interest on December 1, 2005,
c. adjusting entry to accrue bond interest and discount amortization on January 31, 2006,
d. payment of interest on June 1, 2006.

Part 2
Show how the bonds will appear on the balance sheet under long-term liabilities at January 31, 2007.

Problem 17-7A
Recording bonds issued at a discount—effective interest method

LO^5

Check figures:
1a. Cash = $175,643
1b. Cash = $10,800

Briggs Ltd., issued bonds with a par value of $80,000 and a five-year life on January 1, 2005. The bonds pay interest on June 30 and December 31. The contract interest rate is 8.5%. The bonds were issued at a price of $81,625. The market interest rate was 8% on the original issue date.

Required
1. Calculate the total bond interest expense over the life of the bonds.
2. Prepare an amortization table using the effective interest method similar to Exhibit 17.17.
3. Show the journal entries that Briggs Ltd. would make to record the first two interest payments assuming a December 31 year-end.
4. Use the original market interest rate to calculate the present value of the remaining cash flows for these bonds as of December 31, 2007. Compare your answer with the amount shown on the amortization table as the balance for that date and explain your findings.

Problem 17-8A
Bond premium amortization and finding the present value of remaining cash flows—effective interest method

LO^6

Check figure:
2. Total interest expense = $32,375

On March 1, 2005, Gabriella Inc. issued a $200,000, 8%, three-year bond. Interest is payable semi-annually beginning September 1, 2005.

Required

Part 1
a. Calculate the bond issue price assuming a market interest rate of 7% on the date of issue.
b. Using the effective interest method, prepare an amortization schedule.
c. Record the entry for the issuance of the bond on March 1, the adjusting entry to accrue bond interest and related amortization on April 30, 2005, Gabriella's year-end, and the payment of interest on September 1, 2005.

Part 2
d. Calculate the bond issue price assuming a market interest rate of 8.5% on the date of issue.
e. Using the effective interest method, prepare an amortization schedule.
f. Record the entries for the issuance of the bond on March 1, the adjusting entry to accrue bond interest and related amortization on April 30, 2005, Gabriella's year end, and the payment of interest on September 1, 2005.

Problem 17-9A
Bonds issued at a premium and discount—effective interest (using business calculator PV function)

$LO^{4,5,6}$

Problem 17-10A
Recording bonds

LO⁵,⁶,⁷

Valu Inc. has a July 31 year-end. It showed the following partial amortization schedules regarding two bond issues:

Bond Issue A

Period Ending	(A) Cash Interest Paid $340,000 × 9% × 6/12	(B) Period Interest Expense (E) × 8% × 6/12	(C) Amortization (A) − (B)	(D) Unamortized Balance	(E) Carrying Value $340,000 + (D)
June 1/05				21,521	361,521
Dec. 1/05	15,300	14,461	839	20,682	360,682
Dec. 1/11	15,300	13,956	1,344	7,568	347,568
June 1/12	15,300	13,903	1,397	6,171	346,171
Dec. 1/12	15,300	13,847	1,453	4,718	344,718
June 1/13	15,300	13,789	1,511	3,207	343,207
Dec. 1/13	15,300	13,728	1,572	1,635	341,635
June 1/14	15,300	13,665	1,635	-0-	340,000
Totals	**275,400**	**253,879**	**21,521**		

Bond Issue B

Period Ending	(A) Cash Interest Paid $270,000 × 8% × 3/12	(B) Period Interest Expense 233,681/40	(C) Amortization 17,681/40	(D) Unamortized Balance	(E) Carrying Value $270,000 − (D)
Apr. 1/03				17,681	252,319
July 1/03	5,400	5,842	442	17,239	252,761
Apr. 1/11	5,400	5,842	442	3,537	266,463
July 1/11	5,400	5,842	442	3,095	266,905
Oct. 1/11	5,400	5,842	442	2,653	267,347
Jan. 1/12	5,400	5,842	442	2,211	267,789
Apr. 1/12	5,400	5,842	442	1,769	268,231
July 1/12	5,400	5,842	442	1,327	268,673
Oct. 1/12	5,400	5,842	442	885	269,115
Jan. 1/13	5,400	5,842	442	443	269,557
Apr. 1/13	5,400	5,843*	443*	-0-	270,000
Totals	**216,000**	**233,681**	**17,681**		

*Adjusted for rounding.

Required
Answer the following for each bond issue:
a. Were the bonds issued at a premium and/or discount?
b. Journalize the issuance of Bond Issue A and B on June 1, 2005, and April 1, 2003, respectively.
c. What is the contract interest rate for each bond issue?
d. The premium and/or discount is amortized using what method (straight-line and/or effective interest) for each bond issue?
e. Interest of how much is paid how often for each bond issue?
f. What is the term of each bond issue?
g. Show how each of the bonds would appear on the balance sheet under long-term liabilities at July 31, 2011.
h. Calculate the total bond interest expense that would appear on the income statement for the year ended July 31, 2012.
i. Independent of (a) through (h), assume both bond issues were retired on December 1, 2012, at 97. Record the entries.

On November 30, 2005, Secord Ltd. borrowed $50,000 from a bank by signing a four-year installment note bearing interest at 12%. The terms of the note require equal payments each year on November 30, starting November 30, 2006.

Required
1. Calculate the size of each installment payment.
2. Complete an installment note amortization schedule for this note similar to Exhibit 17.21.
3. Present the journal entries that Secord would make to record accrued interest as of December 31, 2005 (the end of the annual reporting period), and the first payment on the note.
4. Now assume that the note does not require equal payments but does require four payments that include accrued interest and an equal amount of principal in each payment. Complete an installment note amortization schedule for this note similar to Exhibit 17.20. Present the journal entries that Secord would make to record accrued interest as of December 31, 2005, (the end of the annual reporting period) and the first payment on the note.

Problem 17-11A
Installment notes

LO^8

Check figure:
2. Total interest expense
= $15,848

Weson Engineering Company leased a machine on January 1, 2005, under a contract calling for four annual payments of $15,000 on December 31, 2005 through 2008. The machine becomes the property of the lessee after the fourth payment. The machine was predicted to have a service life of six years and no salvage value, and the interest rate available to Weson Engineering was 12% on the day the lease was signed. The machine was delivered on January 10, 2005, and was immediately placed in service. On January 4, 2010, it was overhauled at a total cost of $2,500. The overhaul did not increase the machine's efficiency but it did add two additional years to the expected service life. On June 30, 2012, the machine was traded in on a similar new machine having a $42,000 cash price. A $3,000 trade-in allowance was received, and the balance was paid in cash.

Required
1. Determine the initial net liability created by the lease and the cost of the leased asset.
2. Prepare a table showing the calculation of the amount of interest expense allocated to each year the lease is in effect and the carrying amount of the liability at the end of each of those years.
3. Prepare the entry to record the leasing of the machine.
4. Prepare entries that would be made on December 31, 2006, to record the annual amortization on a straight-line basis, and the recording of the lease payment. Also show how the machine and the lease liability should appear on the December 31, 2006, balance sheet.
5. Prepare the entries to record the machine's overhaul in 2010 and amortization at the end of that year.
6. Prepare the entries to record the exchange of the machines on June 30, 2012.

*Problem 17-12A
Lease liabilities

LO^9

Check figure:
2. Total interest expense
= $14,440

Alternate Problems

Stevens Limited issued a group of bonds on January 1, 2005, that pay interest semi-annually on June 30 and December 31. The par value of the bonds is $50,000, the annual contract rate is 10%, and the bonds mature in 10 years.

Required
For each of these three situations, (a) determine the issue price of the bonds, and (b) show the journal entry that would record the issuance, assuming the market interest rate at the date of issuance was:
1. 8%
2. 10%
3. 12%

Problem 17-1B
Calculating bond prices and recording issuance with journal entries

$LO^{3, 5, 6}$

Check figures:
1a. $56,796
2a. $50,000
3a. $44,265

An asterisk (*) identifies assignment material based on Appendix 17B.

Problem 17-2B

Straight-line method of allocating interest and amortizing a bond premium

LO^{4, 6}

Check figure:
1. Cash = $3,890,952

Sontag Corp. issued $3.7 million of bonds that pay 12.9% annual interest with two semi-annual payments. The date of issuance was January 1, 2005, and the interest is paid on June 30 and December 31. The bonds mature after 10 years and were issued at the price of $3,890,952. The market interest rate was 12%.

Required
1. Show how the bond price was calculated and prepare a General Journal entry to record the issuance of the bonds.
2. Calculate the cash payment, premium amortization amount using straight-line amortization, and bond interest expense to be recognized every six months.
3. Determine the total bond interest expense that will be recognized over the life of these bonds.
4. Prepare the first two lines of an amortization table based on the straight-line method.
5. Present the journal entries that Sontag Corp. would make to record the first two interest payments.
6. Show the beginning and ending balances of the premium on bonds payable account for the first four semi-annual periods.

Problem 17-3B

Effective interest method of allocating interest and amortizing a bond discount (using business calculator PV function)

LO^{4, 5}

Check figure:
1. Cash = $785,053

Cape Breton Corp. issued $800,000 of bonds that pay 9.7% annual interest with two semi-annual payments. The date of issuance was January 1, 2005, and the interest is paid on June 30 and December 31. The bonds mature after 10 years and were issued at the price of $785,053. The market interest rate was 10% and the company uses the effective interest method of amortization.

Required
1. Show how the bond price was determined and prepare a General Journal entry to record the issuance of the bonds.
2. Determine the total bond interest expense that will be recognized over the life of these bonds.
3. Prepare the first two lines of an amortization table based on the effective interest method.
4. Present the journal entries that Cape Breton Corp. would make to record the first two interest payments.

Problem 17-4B

Amortization of bond premium—straight-line method (using business calculator PV function)

LO^{4, 6}

Check figures:
a. $640,788
b. Total interest expense = $209,212

On May 1, 2005, Rooniak Corporation issued a $625,000, 12%, three-year bond. Interest is payable quarterly beginning August 1, 2005.

Required
a. Calculate the bond issue price assuming a market interest rate of 11% on the date of issue.
b. Using the straight-line method, prepare an amortization schedule similar to Exhibit 17.16.

Problem 17-5B

Recording bonds issued at a premium—straight-line method

LO⁶

Check figures:
1a. Cash = $640,788
1b. Cash = $18,750

Refer to the amortization schedule prepared in Problem 17-4B. Rooniak Corporation's year-end is August 31.

Required

Part 1
Record the following entries:
a. issuance of the bonds on May 1, 2005,
b. payment of interest on August 1, 2005,
c. adjusting entry to accrue bond interest and premium amortization on August 31, 2005,
d. payment of interest on November 1, 2005.

Part 2
Show how the bond will appear on the balance sheet at August 31, 2007.

On September 1, 2005, Messner Corp. issued a $350,000, 15%, four-year bond. Interest is payable semi-annually beginning March 1, 2006.

Required

a. Calculate the bond issue price assuming a market interest rate of 13.5% on the date of issue.

b. Using the effective interest method, prepare an amortization schedule similar to Exhibit 17.17.

Problem 17-6B

Amortization of bond premium—effective interest method (using business calculator PV function)

LO$^{4, 6}$

Check figures:
a. $365,828
b. Total interest expense = $194,172

Refer to the amortization schedule prepared in Problem 17-6B. Assume a January 31 year-end.

Required

Part 1
Record the following entries:
a. issuance of the bonds on September 1, 2005,
b. adjusting entry to accrue bond interest and premium amortization on January 31, 2006,
c. payment of interest on March 1, 2006.

Part 2
Show how the bond will appear on the balance sheet under long-term liabilities at January 31, 2008.

Problem 17-7B

Recording bonds issued at a premium—effective interest amortization

LO^6

Check figures:
1a. Cash = $365,828
1c. Cash = $26,250

Dipchand Ltd. issued bonds with a par value of $320,000 and a five-year life on January 1, 2005. The bonds pay interest on June 30 and December 31. The contract interest rate is 8%. The market interest rate was 9% on the original issue date.

Required

1. Calculate the issue price and the total bond interest expense over the life of the bonds.
2. Prepare an amortization table using the effective interest method similar to Exhibit 17.11.
3. Show the journal entries that Dipchand would make to record the first two interest payments. Assume a December 31 year-end.
4. Use the original market interest rate to calculate the present value of the remaining cash flows for these bonds as of December 31, 2007. Compare your answer with the amount shown on the amortization table as the balance for that date, and explain your findings.

Problem 17-8B

Bond discount amortization and finding the present value of remaining cash flows—effective interest method (using business calculator PV function)

LO^5

Check figure:
2. Total interest expense = $140,660

On February 1, 2005, Giant Corp. issued an $800,000, 5%, two-year bond. Interest is payable quarterly each May 1, August 1, November 1, and February 1.

Required

Part 1
a. Calculate the bond issue price assuming a market interest rate of 6% on the date of issue.
b. Using the effective interest method, prepare an amortization schedule.
c. Record the entry for the issuance of the bond on February 1, the adjusting entry to accrue bond interest and related amortization on March 31, 2005, Giant Corp.'s year-end, and the payment of interest on May 1, 2005.

Part 2
d. Calculate the bond issue price assuming a market interest rate of 4.5% on the date of issue.
e. Using the effective interest method, prepare an amortization schedule.
f. Record the entries for the issuance of the bond on February 1, the adjusting entry to accrue bond interest and related amortization on March 31, 2005, Giant Corp.'s year-end, and the payment of interest on May 1, 2005.

Problem 17-9B

Bonds issued at a premium and discount—effective interest (using business calculator PV function)

LO$^{4, 5, 6}$

Problem 17-10B
Recording bonds

LO⁵,⁶,⁷

Maritime Inc. has a December 31 year-end. It showed the following partial amortization schedules regarding its two bond issues:

Bond Issue 1

Period Ending	(A) Cash Interest Paid $650,000 × 7% × 3/12	(B) Period Interest Expense (E) × 8% × 3/12	(C) Amortization (B) – (A)	(D) Unamortized Balance	(E) Carrying Value $650,000 – (D)
Sept. 1/06				26,571	623,429
Dec. 1/06	11,375	12,469	1,094	25,477	624,523
Dec. 1/10	11,375	12,876	1,501	4,685	645,315
Mar. 1/11	11,375	12,906	1,531	3,154	646,846
June 1/11	11,375	12,937	1,562	1,592	648,408
Sept. 1/11	11,375	12,967*	1,592	-0-	650,000
Totals	**227,500**	**254,071**	**26,571**		

*Adjusted for rounding.

Bond Issue 2

Period Ending	(A) Cash Interest Paid $780,000 × 11% × 6/12	(B) Period Interest Expense 644,133/16	(C) Amortization 42,267/16	(D) Unamortized Balance	(E) Carrying Value $780,000 + (D)
May 1/04				42,267	822,267
May 1/10	42,900	40,258	2,642	10,563	790,563
Nov. 1/10	42,900	40,258	2,642	7,921	787,921
May 1/11	42,900	40,258	2,642	5,279	785,279
Nov. 1/11	42,900	40,258	2,642	2,637	782,637
May 1/12	42,900	40,263*	2,637	-0-	780,000
Totals	**686,400**	**644,133**	**42,267**		

*Adjusted for rounding.

Required
Answer the following for each bond issue:
a. Were the bonds issued at a premium and/or discount?
b. Journalize the issuance of Bond Issue 1 and 2 on September 1, 2006, and May 1, 2004, respectively.
c. What is the contract interest rate for each bond issue?
d. The premium and/or discount is amortized using what method (straight-line and/or effective interest) for each bond issue?
e. Interest of how much is paid how often for each bond issue?
f. What is the term of each bond issue?
g. Show how each of the bonds would appear on the balance sheet at December 31, 2010.
h. Calculate the total bond interest expense that would appear on the income statement for the year ended December 31, 2011.
i. Independent of (a) through (h), assume both bond issues were retired on December 1, 2010 at 101. Record the entries.

On May 31, 2005, Venice Ltd. borrowed $220,000 from a bank by signing a four-year installment note bearing interest at 14%. The terms of the note require equal semi-annual payments each year beginning on November 30, 2005.

Required
1. Calculate the size of each installment payment.
2. Complete an installment note amortization schedule for this note similar to Exhibit 17.21.
3. Present the journal entries that Venice Ltd. would make to record the first payment on the note, the accrued interest as of December 31, 2005 (the end of the annual reporting period), and the second payment on the note.
4. Now assume that the note does not require equal payments but does require eight payments that include accrued interest and an equal amount of principal in each payment. Complete an installment note amortization schedule for this note similar to Exhibit 17.20. Present the journal entries that Venice Ltd. would make to record the first payment on the note and the accrued interest as of December 31, 2005 (the end of the annual reporting period).

Problem 17-11B
Installment notes

LO^8

Check figure:
2. Total interest expense
= $74,744

Stoney Point Services Company leased a machine on January 1, 2005, under a contract calling for six annual payments of $130,000 on December 31, 2005 through 2010. The machine becomes the property of the lessee after the sixth payment. The machine was predicted to have a service life of seven years and no salvage value, and the interest rate available to Stoney Point Services Company for equipment loans was 9% on the day the lease was signed. The machine was delivered on January 8, 2005, and was immediately placed in service. On January 2, 2008, it was overhauled at a total cost of $29,200. The overhaul did not increase the machine's efficiency but it did add an additional three years to the expected service life. On September 30, 2011, the machine was traded in on a similar new machine having a $330,000 cash price. A $65,000 trade-in allowance was received, and the balance was paid in cash.

Required
1. Determine the initial net liability created by the lease and the cost of the leased asset.
2. Prepare a table showing the calculation of the amount of interest expense allocated to each year the lease is in effect and the carrying amount of the liability at the end of each of those years.
3. Prepare the entry to record the leasing of the machine.
4. Prepare entries that would be made on December 31, 2006, to record the annual amortization on a straight-line basis, and the recording of the lease payment. Also show how the machine and the lease liability should appear on the December 31, 2006, balance sheet.
5. Prepare the entries to record the machine's overhaul in 2008 and amortization at the end of that year.
6. Prepare the entries to record the exchange of the machines on September 30, 2011.

*Problem 17-12B
Lease liabilities

LO^9

Check figure:
2. Total interest expense
= $196,831

Ethics Challenge

EC 17-1

A few years ago, the politicians needed a new headquarters building for their municipal government. The price tag for the building approached $24 million. The politicians felt that the voters were unlikely to approve a bond issue to raise money for the headquarters since approving the bond issue would cause taxes to increase. The politicians opted for a different approach. They had a bank issue $24 million worth of securities to pay for the construction of the building. The municipality then agreed to make a yearly lease payment (comprising repayment of principal and interest) to repay the obligation. Unlike conventional municipal bonds, the lease payments are not binding obligations on the municipal government and, therefore, no voter approval is required.

Required
1. Do you think the actions of the politicians and the investment bankers were ethical in this situation?
2. How does the security issued to pay for the building compare in riskiness to a regular municipal bond issued by a municipal government?

An asterisk (*) identifies assignment material based on Appendix 17B.

Focus on Financial Statements

FFS 17-1

ZedCon Inc. intends to raise $10,000,000 for the purpose of expanding operations internationally. Two options are available:

- Plan 1: Issue $10,000,000 of 5% bonds payable due in 2015, or
- Plan 2: Issue 100,000 common shares at $100 per share.

The expansion is expected to generate additional annual income before interest and tax of $800,000. ZedCon's tax rate is 35%. The assumed adjusted trial balance at December 31, 2006, one year after the expansion under each of Plan 1 and Plan 2, is shown below:

Account	Balance* Plan 1	Balance* Plan 2
Accounts payable	$ 33,000	$ 33,000
Accounts receivable	48,000	48,000
Accumulated amortization, buildings	78,000	78,000
Accumulated amortization, equipment	202,000	202,000
Accumulated amortization, international assets	100,000	100,000
Additional income as a result of expansion	800,000	800,000
Allowance for doubtful accounts	5,200	5,200
Amortization expense	127,000	127,000
Bad debt expense	3,200	3,200
Bonds payable	10,000,000	–0–
Buildings	150,000	150,000
Cash	312,000	812,000
Cash dividends	92,000	92,000
Cash over/short	100	100
Common shares (1,000 shares issued and outstanding)**	100,000	—
Common shares (101,000 shares issued and outstanding)**	—	10,100,000
Cost of goods sold	48,000	48,000
Delivery expense	700	700
Dividends payable	31,000	31,000
Equipment	273,000	273,000
Fees earned	1,050,000	1,050,000
Income tax expense	?	?
Income tax payable	?	?
Interest expense	506,100	6,100
Interest receivable	300	300
Interest revenue	800	800
International property, plant and equipment assets	10,000,000	10,000,000
Land	32,000	32,000
Merchandise inventory	32,000	32,000
Mortgage payable ($14,000 due in 2007)	60,000	60,000
Notes receivable, due October 2010	14,000	14,000
Patent	7,000	7,000
Petty cash	800	800
Retained earnings	25,600	25,600
Salaries expense	916,000	916,000
Sales	59,000	59,000
Sales discounts	1,400	1,400
Unearned fees	19,000	19,000

Assume normal account balances.
**Assume all shares were outstanding for the entire year.*

Required

Preparation component:

1. Prepare a single-step income statement for 2006 (showing salaries expense, amortization expense, cost of goods sold, interest expense, and other expenses) and a classified balance sheet at December 31, 2006, assuming:
   a. Plan 1, and then
   b. Plan 2.

Analysis component:

2. Which financing plan should ZedCon Inc. choose assuming its goal is to:
   a. maximize Earnings Per Share, or
   b. maximize net income.
   Explain your answers showing any relevant calculations (rounded to the nearest whole cent).

18

Accounting for Investments and International Operations

Investing: The Next Generation

Bay Street—It was the worst day in Sara Brempong's young career as a financial analyst. She had just failed to land a major client and her boss removed her from a special analyst training program. Brempong's response? She quit. "Nothing fit," says Brempong. "Here I was, 23 years old, in a stuffy old-boys firm, advising clients twice my age on securities investments. I knew what I was doing, but no one believed in me."

That was five years ago. Today, Brempong is running her own investment firm, Brempong & Brempong. The other Brempong? "Well," laughs Brempong, "I asked my grandfather to sign on as joint partner because, like all the big firms, I thought I needed multiple names for the title of an investment firm." Adds Brempong, "Actually, he is the person who started me on my career. When he gave gifts to us grandchildren, he always tucked in some shares of the manufacturer."

Grandpa must now be proud, for Brempong's upstart firm pulled in over $485,000 in commissions and consulting revenues this past year. And the current year is running 28% ahead of last year. What's the secret? "Two things," says Brempong. "First, I work hard at knowing my investments and client needs. Second, I pursue a niche market for clients." What Brempong does is work tirelessly at attracting young investors, the twenty- and thirty-something crowd. "There is a large untapped market that I've only begun to break into," says Brempong. "Larger investment houses don't pursue these clients—I do." She also relies heavily on analysis of annual reports.

"My fundamental analysis is twofold," says Brempong. "I analyze the financial statements of potential investments to assess their strengths and weaknesses. Then I use their products and services, and ask others about them." Brempong also usually insists on visiting a company before she invests, or recommends investment, in it. "If I'm looking at a camera company, I use its cameras. I ask other people for their opinions too." Still, she cautions, "there is always a risk, but I try to minimize it through smart investing." Seems like Grandpa was a good teacher.

Learning Objectives

LO¹ Describe and explain the purpose of debt and share investments.

LO² Identify and account for temporary investments.

LO³ Identify classes of long-term debt and share investments.

LO⁴ Account for long-term debt investments.

LO⁵ Account for long-term share investments of less than 20% ownership.

LO⁶ Account for long-term share investments of 20% to 50% ownership.

LO⁷ Describe how long-term share investments of more than 50% ownership are reported.

LO⁸ Explain and record foreign exchange transactions.

*APPENDIX 18A

*LO⁹ Prepare consolidated balance sheets and explain how to report any excess of investment cost over book value or minority interests.

Chapter Preview

This chapter focuses on both temporary and long-term investments. Many companies have investments in the form of debt and shares issued by other companies. An increasing number of companies also invests in international operations. We explain how transactions listed in foreign currencies are accounted for and reported. Our understanding of the topics in this chapter is important to our ability to read and interpret financial statements. This knowledge is the type used by Sara Brempong as described in the opening article for investment decisions in shares and bonds.

Purpose of Debt and Share Investments

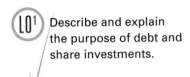

Describe and explain the purpose of debt and share investments.

Corporations frequently purchase debt and shares of other corporations. These are called **intercorporate investments**. A **debt investment** (or **debt security**) such as a bond represents an amount owed and arises when one company lends money to another. A **share investment** (or **equity security**) represents one company's purchase of the shares in another company. The company that purchases as an investment the debt or shares of another is called the **investor**, and the company whose debt (i.e., bonds) or shares (common or preferred) are being purchased is called the **investee**. For instance, if you own shares in WestJet, then you are the investor and WestJet is the investee.

Investments are made in other corporations for various reasons. Examples include:

- To earn greater interest or dividend income on available excess cash than can be earned by leaving the cash in a typical bank account.
- To earn a gain over the original purchase price on the eventual sale of purchased shares.
- To participate in new markets or new technologies.
- To build a favourable business relationship, generally with a major customer or supplier.
- To achieve non-controlling interest with the investee by acquiring enough shares to be influential to the investee's operating, financing, and investing decisions.
- To acquire a controlling interest in the investee.

Temporary Versus Long-Term Investments

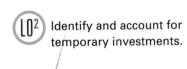

Identify and account for temporary investments.

Temporary investments, also called **short-term investments**, consist of both debt and share investments. They are classified as current assets if they meet two requirements:

1. Management's intention is to convert them into cash within one year or the current operating cycle of the business, whichever is longer, and
2. They can be readily converted to cash.

Also referred to as **marketable securities**, temporary investments include investment certificates, shares, and bonds acquired by the investor to earn a return on excess operating cash. A group of investments held by the investor is known as an **investment portfolio**. The traditional accounting method for temporary investments is *cost*, explained and illustrated in a later section. Leon's, for example, showed marketable securities at December 31, 2002, as follows:

(in thousands)
Current assets:
  Marketable securities....................................... $56,685

Long-term investments are investments not meeting the two requirements for temporary investments. This means long-term investments include investments in bonds and shares that are not marketable or, if marketable, are not intended to be converted into cash in the short term. Long-term investments are reported in the non-current section of the balance sheet, often in their own separate section titled *Long-term investments*.

The next section will illustrate accounting for temporary investments.

Accounting for Temporary Investments

This section explains the basics of accounting for temporary investments in both debt and equity securities. In both cases, the investor records the investment at acquisition cost, which includes the purchase price plus any brokerage fees and commissions. The investor earns interest by investing in debt securities and earns dividend revenue by investing in shares.

Debt Investments

Temporary investments are recorded at cost when purchased. TechCom Company, for instance, purchased short-term notes payable of Transalta Corporation for $4,000 on January 10, 2005. TechCom's entry to record this purchase is:

2005			
Jan. 10	Temporary Investments....................................	4,000	
	Cash..		4,000
	Bought $4,000 of Transalta notes due May 10.		

These notes mature on May 10 and the cash proceeds are $4,000 plus $120 interest. When the proceeds are received, TechCom records this as:

May 10	Cash..	4,120	
	Temporary Investments		4,000
	Interest Revenue		120
	Received cash proceeds from matured notes.		

Share Investments

The cost of an investment includes all costs necessary to acquire it, including commissions paid. TechCom, for instance, purchased 300 Cameco Corporation common shares as a temporary investment. It paid $50 per share plus $375 in commissions. The entry to record this purchase is:

June 2	Temporary Investments...............................	15,375	
	Cash..		15,375
	Bought 300 common shares of Cameco at		
	$50 plus $375 commission.		

Note that the commission is not recorded in a separate account. Why? The cost principle P.41 states that all assets are recorded at their original cost and since the $375 commission is a necessary cost incurred to acquire the asset, it is recorded as part of the asset's cost.

On December 12, TechCom received a $0.40 cash dividend per share on its short-term Cameco share investment. This dividend is credited to a revenue account as follows:

Dec. 12	Cash..	120	
	Dividend Revenue...		120
	Received dividend of $0.40 per share on		
	300 shares of Cameco.		

Balance Sheet Presentation

The *CICA Handbook* requires that temporary investments be reported on the balance sheet at the **lower of cost or market (LCM)** P.360.[1] To calculate the lower of cost or market, the *total cost* of all marketable securities held as temporary investments (the portfolio) is compared with the *total market value* of the portfolio. Comparison on an item-by-item basis is normally not done.

For example, assume that TechCom did not have any temporary investments prior to its purchase of the Cameco shares on June 2, 2005. Later during 2005, TechCom purchased two other temporary investments in marketable securities: Alcan and Imperial Oil common shares. On December 31, 2005, the lower of cost or market is determined by comparing the total cost and total market value of the entire portfolio, as follows:

Temporary Investments	Cost	Market	LCM
Alcan Inc. common shares	$42,600	$43,500	
Imperial Oil common shares.....................	30,500	28,200	
Cameco common shares..........................	15,375	14,500	
Total	$88,475	$86,200	$86,200

The difference between the $88,475 cost and the $86,200 market value amounts to a $2,275 loss of market value.

Since all of the temporary investments were purchased during 2005, this $2,275 market value decline occurred entirely during 2005. The following adjusting entry on December 31, 2005, records the loss:

---

[1] *CICA Handbook,* section 3010, par. 05.

2005			
Dec. 31	Loss on Market Decline of Temporary Investments...................................	2,275	
	Allowance to Reduce Temporary Investments to Market		2,275
	To record the decline in the value of temporary investments.		

The Loss on Market Decline of Temporary Investments account is shown on the income statement as part of Other Revenues and Expenses. The Allowance to Reduce Temporary Investments to Market account is a contra asset account. It is subtracted from the Temporary Investments account so that Temporary Investments is reported at the lower of cost or market on the balance sheet. For example, TechCom would report its temporary investments at December 31, 2005, as shown in Exhibit 18.1.

Current assets:	
Temporary investments, at market value (cost is $88,475)	$86,200

Exhibit 18.1

Statement Presentation of Temporary Investments

In this example, notice that the $2,275 loss recorded during 2005 is equal to the December 31, 2005, balance in the allowance account. This occurs because we have assumed that no investments were owned prior to 2005. Therefore, the allowance account had a zero balance on December 31, 2004.

If an additional loss occurs in a future year, the allowance account balance after recording that loss probably will not equal the amount of that loss. To see why this is true, assume that on December 31, 2006, the total cost of TechCom's temporary investments portfolio is $108,475 and the total market value is $104,700 (assume additions to the investment portfolio during 2006). In other words, market value is $3,775 less than cost. For the market value of $104,700 to appear on the balance sheet, the balance in the Allowance account must be $3,775 as illustrated below:

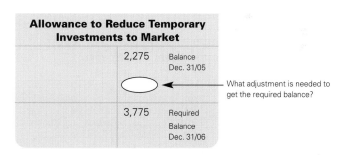

Because the allowance account already has a credit balance of $2,275 as a result of the adjusting entry made on December 31, 2005, the adjusting entry to record the 2006 loss is:

2006			
Dec. 31	Loss on Market Decline of Temporary Investments.....................................	1,500	
	Allowance to Reduce Temporary Investments to Market		1,500
	To record the decline in the value of temporary investments.		

Thus, the loss recorded in 2006 is $1,500 and the December 31, 2006, balance in the allowance account is $3,775.

Because temporary investments in marketable equity securities must be reported at the lower of cost or market, market value increases above cost are not recorded as gains until the investments are sold. However, if a portfolio of temporary investments has been written down to a market value below cost, later increases in market value up to the original cost are reported on the income statement.

For example, assume that on December 31, 2007, the market value of TechCom's temporary investments is $144,500, which is $500 less than the cost of $145,000 shown below:

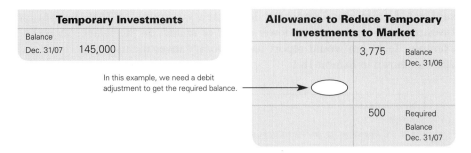

Since the allowance account had a credit balance of $3,775 at the end of 2006, the December 31, 2007, adjusting entry is:

2007			
Dec. 31	Allowance to Reduce Temporary Investments to Market	3,275	
	Gain on Market Recovery of Temporary Investments		3,275
	To adjust the Allowance account from $3,775 to $500.		

Notice that the only entries that change the allowance (contra asset) account balance are the end-of-period adjusting entries. The entries to record purchases and sales of investments during a period do not affect the allowance account.

Investors can obtain the market price of debt and share investments from a number of sources. The following example of share transactions was obtained online from a newspaper.

(Trades of 100,000 or more shares worth at least $1 million)					
Stock	**Symbol**	**Buyer**	**Seller**	**Volume (000s)**	**Price**
CIBC	CM	TD Securit	TD Securit	100	42.20
Cott Corp	BCB	NesBurns	NesBurns	111	26.20
Iamgold	IMG	NesBurns	NesBurns	396	7.34
Norske Skog	NS	NesBurns	NesBurns	316	4.89
Nortel Netwk	NT	CSFB	CSFB	500	3.67
Royal Bank	RY	CIBC World	CIBC World	121	56.55
Suncor Enr	SU	CIBC World	CIBC World	126	25.82
TD Bank	TD	CIBC World	CIBC World	118	34.11
Wstrn Oil	WTO	NesBurns	NesBurns	123	23.75

SOURCE: www.globeandmail.com, February 18, 2003.

Real-time prices in a variety of formats are available from other online sources such as the following graphs.

SOURCE: www.tse.com, February 18, 2003.

1. How are temporary investments reported on the balance sheet—at cost or market values?
2. Normally, how often would an adjusting entry to record LCM be entered?
3. What happens when a previously written down portfolio increases in value?

Flashback

Answers—p. 945

Long-Term Investments

Similar to the accounting for temporary investments, a long-term investment is recorded at its total cost when purchased (including costs such as brokerage fees, if any). Long-term investments include investments in bonds and shares that are not marketable or that, although marketable, are not intended to serve as a ready source of cash. After the purchase, the accounting treatment for long-term investments depends on the class of the investments. There are four classes:

LO³ Identify classes of long-term debt and share investments.

1. Debt investments intended to be held for the long term,
2. Share investments where the investor owns less than 20% of the voting shares of the investee,
3. Share investments where the investor owns 20% to 50% of the voting shares of the investee, and
4. Share investments where the investor owns more than 50% of the voting shares of the investee.

4. What are the requirements for a security to be classified as a long-term investment?

Flashback

Answer—p. 945

We next describe each of these four investment classes and how to account for them.

Debt Investments Held for the Long Term

LO⁴ Account for long-term debt investments.

Long-term debt investments are those that a company intends and is able to hold until maturity. Debt investments are recorded at cost when purchased. Also, long-term debt investments require us to record interest revenue as it accrues.

Illustration of Long-Term Debt Investment

Music City paid $29,500 plus a brokerage fee of $500 to buy Power Corp. 7% bonds payable with a $30,000 par value on September 1, 2005. The bonds pay interest semi-annually on August 31 and February 28. Music City intends to hold the bonds until they mature on August 31, 2007. The entry to record this purchase is:

2005			
Sept. 1	Investment in Power Corp. Bonds....................	30,000	
	Cash		30,000
	Purchased bonds to be held to maturity.		

On December 31, 2005, at the end of its accounting period, Music City accrues interest receivable in the following entry:

Dec. 31	Interest Receivable...	700	
	Interest Revenue		700
	$30,000 × 7% × 4/12.		

The $700 reflects 4/12 of the annual interest. This is the portion earned by Music City during 2005. Exhibit 18.2 shows the financial statement effects of Music City's investment transactions during 2005.

Exhibit 18.2

Financial Statement Effects of Debt Securities

On the income statement for 2005	
Interest revenue	$ 700
On the December 31, 2005, balance sheet	
Assets:	
Current Assets:	
Interest receivable..	$ 700
Long-term investments:	
Investment in Power Corp. bonds	30,000

On February 28, 2006, Music City records receipt of the semi-annual interest as:

2006			
Feb. 28	Cash..	1,050	
	Interest Receivable		700
	Interest Revenue		350
	Received six months' interest on		
	Power Corp. bonds; $30,000 × 7% × 6/12.		

When the bonds mature, the entry to record proceeds from the matured bonds is (assuming interest is recorded separately):

2007			
Aug. 31	Cash...	30,000	
	Investment in Power Corp. Bonds.............		30,000
	Received cash from matured bonds.		

This illustration reflects the *cost method*. The cost method is required in practice for recording and reporting long-term investments in long-term debt investments.

Illustration of Bonds Acquired at a Premium or Discount

A premium or discount P.867 results when the cost of a long-term debt investment is either higher or lower than the maturity value of the debt investment. When the investment is long-term, the premium or discount is amortized over the investment's remaining life so that each period includes some amortization in the calculation of interest revenue. The procedures for amortizing premiums or discounts on bond investments are the same as for bonds payable illustrated in Chapter 17. The difference is that the amount of the premium or discount to be amortized is credited or debited *directly to the investment account*. As a result, on the maturity date of the bonds, the investment account balance will equal the par value of the bonds.

To illustrate, assume that Hydro Quebec issued $100,000 of 12%, 5-year bonds on January 1, 2005, when the market rate of interest was 10%. Interest is payable semi-annually on June 30 and December 31. Assume that Bell Canada Enterprises (BCE) purchased the entire bond issue. Exhibit 18.3 shows the entries made on the date of issue and on the first payment date for both Hydro Quebec (the investee) and BCE (the investor). On January 1, 2005, BCE recorded the investment at cost including the premium. If the bonds had been purchased at a discount, the amount of the discount would have been deducted from the cost. Income on the bond investment is recognized when interest is received on June 30. A premium paid by BCE reduces the amount of interest BCE earns.[2] The premium is amortized against the investment account over the life of the bonds using the effective interest method. For example the interest earned on June 30 is calculated by multiplying the carrying value at the beginning of the period by the market rate of interest adjusted for the portion of the year the carrying value was outstanding ($107,720 × 0.10 × 6/12 = $5,386). The difference between the cash received and the interest earned is the amount of bond premium to be amortized ($6,000 − $5,386 = $614). At the end of an accounting period, a company should accrue any interest that has been earned but not yet received.

Exhibit 18.3

Accounting for Debt Investments—Investor and Investee

	Books of BCE—Investor			Books of Hydro Quebec—Investee		
2005						
Jan. 1	Investment in Hydro Que. Bonds	107,720		Cash	107,720	
	Cash..		107,720	Premium on Bonds Payable		7,720
	To record purchase of Hydro Quebec bonds.			Bonds Payable		100,000
				To record issue of 12% five-year bonds.		
June 30	Cash	6,000		Bond Interest Expense	5,386	
	Investment in Bonds		614	Premium on Bonds Payable	614	
	Interest Revenue........................		5,386	Cash		6,000
	To record receipt of semi-annual interest earned and amortization of premium.			*To record payment of semi-annual interest earned and amortization of premium.*		

---

[2] Recall from Chapter 17 that a discount would have the opposite effect.

Share Investments Less Than 20%

LO⁵ Account for long-term share investments of less than 20% ownership.

Long-term investments in the voting shares of another company are classified according to the investor's ability to *significantly influence* the operating and financial policies of the investee. **Significant influence** is the ability of the investor to influence the investee even though the investor owns less than 50% of the investee's voting shares. Percent ownership in the investee's shares is one way to determine influence. As a general rule, significant influence does not exist for investments of less than 20% of the voting shares of another company, which is the topic of discussion in this section.

We use the **cost method** to account for long-term investments in which the investor does *not* have significant influence over the investee. This is identical to how we accounted for temporary share investments as illustrated at the beginning of this chapter. First, these investments are recorded at cost. Second, dividends received are credited to Dividend Revenue and reported in the income statement. Third, when the shares are sold, proceeds from the sale are compared with the cost of the investment and any gain or loss on the sale is reported in the income statement.

Share Investments of 20% to 50%

LO⁶ Account for long-term share investments of 20% to 50% ownership.

Investors that hold 20% to 50% of an investee's shares are said to have significant influence. The **equity method** of accounting and reporting is used for long-term share investments with significant influence.[3] Under the equity method, shares are recorded at cost when they are purchased. To illustrate, Micron Company purchased 3,000 shares (30%) of JVT common shares for a total cost of $70,650 on January 1, 2005. The entry to record this purchase on Micron's books is:

2005			
Jan. 1	Investment in JVT Common Shares.............	70,650	
	Cash...		70,650
	Purchased 3,000 shares.		

Under the equity method, the investor records its share of the investee's earnings and dividends. This means that when JVT closes its books and reports net income of $20,000 for 2005, Micron records its 30% share of those earnings in its investment account as:

Dec. 31	Investment in JVT Common Shares.............	6,000	
	Earnings from Investment in JVT..............		6,000
	To record 30% equity in investee's		
	earnings of $20,000.		

The debit reflects the increase in Micron's equity in JVT caused by JVT's $20,000 increase in equity through net income. Micron must debit the investment account for its proportionate share in that equity (JVT's net income). The credit shows the source of the increase in the investment account.

If the investee incurs a net loss instead of a net income, the investor records its share of the loss and reduces (credits) its investment account.

The receipt of cash dividends is not recorded as revenue when using the equity method because the investor has already recorded its share of the earnings reported by the investee. When the investee pays dividends its retained earnings are reduced by the

---

[3] Note that in situations where there is a large number of small share holdings, significant influence is possible for an investor that owns less than 20% of the investee. Also, an investor may not be able to exert significant influence with a shareholding of greater than 20% if another shareholder owns a 51% block of shares in the investee.

amount of the dividend. The investee's equity is reduced and therefore the investment of the investor must also be reduced. Dividends received from an investee change the form of the investor's asset from a shares investment to cash. This means dividends reduce the balance of the investment account, but increase cash. To illustrate, JVT declared and paid $10,000 in cash dividends on its common shares. Micron's entry to record its 30% share of these dividends received on January 9, 2006, is:

2006			
Jan. 9	Cash..	3,000	
	Investment in JVT Common Shares..........		3,000
	To record receipt of 30% of $10,000		
	dividend paid by JVT.		

The book value of an investment in equity securities when using the equity method is equal to the cost of the investment plus the investor's equity in the undistributed earnings of the investee. Once we record the above transactions for Micron, its investment account appears as in Exhibit 18.4.

Date	Explanation	Debit	Credit	Balance
2005				
Jan. 1	Investment...	70,650		70,650
Dec. 31	Share of earnings	6,000		76,650
2006				
Jan. 9	Share of dividends..................................		3,000	73,650

Exhibit 18.4

Investment in JVT Common Shares Ledger Account

If a balance sheet were prepared on this date, Micron would report its investment in JVT on the balance sheet after total current assets but before capital assets. Any investment revenue would be reported on the income statement as shown in the bottom section of Exhibit 18.5.

Partial Balance Sheet		
Assets		
Total current assets....................................	$	×××,×××
Long-term investments.............................		73,650
Capital assets...		×××,×××
Total assets		$×,×××,×××
Partial Income Statement		
Income from operations................................	$	×××,×××
Other revenues and expenses:		
Earnings from equity investment...............		6,000

Exhibit 18.5

Statement Presentation of Long-Term Investment and Investment Revenue

Recording the Sale of An Equity Investment

When an investment in equity securities is sold, the gain or loss is calculated by comparing proceeds from the sale with the book value of the investment on the date of sale. Care should be taken to ensure that the investment account is brought up to date in terms of earnings and dividends before recording the sale. If Micron sells its JVT shares for $80,000 on January 10, 2006, the entry to record the sale is:

Jan. 10	Cash...	80,000	
	Investment in JVT Common Shares..........		73,650
	Gain on Sale of Investments.....................		6,350
	Sold 3,000 shares for $80,000.		

Comparison of Entries for Cost and Equity Methods

Exhibit 18.6 uses a side-by-side comparison to emphasize the differences between the cost and equity methods of accounting for share investments. It is assumed that:

1. Maclean Company purchases a 20% interest in the shares of Lee Corp. for $30,000. If Maclean does not have significant influence over Lee Corp., the investment should be accounted for using the cost method. If Maclean can significantly influence Lee Corp., then the investment should be accounted for using the equity method.
2. Lee earns a $40,000 net income during the first year of operations, and
3. Lee pays a dividend of $8,000.

Exhibit 18.6

Illustration of Cost and Equity Methods

	Cost Method			Equity Method		
1.	Investment in Lee Corp. Shares	30,000		Investment in Lee Corp. Shares	30,000	
	Cash		30,000	Cash		30,000
	To record purchase of 20% interest for $30,000.					
2.	No entry			Investment in Lee Corp. Shares	8,000	
				Earnings from Investment in Lee Corp.		8,000
	To record 20% share of investee's $40,000 net income.					
3.	Cash	1,600		Cash	1,600	
	Dividend Revenue		1,600	Investment in Lee Corp. shares		1,600
	To record 20% share of $8,000 dividends received from Lee Corp.					

Share Investments of More Than 50%

LO7 Describe how long-term share investments of more than 50% ownership are reported.

An investor with a long-term share investment that represents more than 50% of the investee's voting shares has *control* over the investee. **Control** is more than influence. The controlling investor can dominate all other shareholders in electing the corporation's board of directors P. 759 and has control over the investee corporation's management. The controlling corporation (investor) is known as the **parent company** and the company whose shares are held by the parent is referred to as a **subsidiary** (investee).

A company owning all the outstanding shares of a subsidiary can take over the subsidiary's assets, cancel the subsidiary's shares, and merge the subsidiary into the parent company, creating potential financial, legal, and tax advantages.

When a business operates as a parent company with subsidiaries, separate accounting records are maintained by each entity. From a legal viewpoint, the parent and each subsidiary are still separate entities with all the rights, duties, and responsibilities of individual companies. However, investors in the parent company are indirect investors in the subsidiaries. To evaluate their investments, parent company investors must consider the financial status and operations of the subsidiaries as well as the parent. This information is provided in *consolidated financial statements.*

Consolidated financial statements show the financial position, results of operations, and cash flows of all companies under the parent's control, including all subsidiaries. These statements are prepared as if the company were organized as one entity. The parent uses the equity method in its accounts, but the investment account is *not* reported on the parent's consolidated financial statements. Instead, the individual assets and liabilities of the parent and its subsidiaries are combined on one balance sheet. Their revenues and expenses also are combined on one income statement and their cash flows are combined on one cash flow statement. The detailed procedures for preparing consolidated financial statements are included in advanced courses. Some of the basic procedures are provided in Appendix 18A.

> **5.** Identify the three categories of long-term share investments, describing the criteria for each.

Flashback

Answer—p. 945

Accounting Summary for Investments in Securities

Exhibit 18.7 summarizes the accounting for investments in securities. Recall that many investments can be classified as either short-term or long-term depending on management's intent and ability to convert them into cash in the future.

Class of Investment	Accounting Method
Temporary Investments	
Debt investments	Lower of cost or market (without
Share investments	amortization of premium/discount)
Long-Term Debt and Share Investments	
Debt investments	Cost (with amortization of premium/discount)
Share investments with insignificant influence (<20%)	Cost method
Share investments with significant influence (20–50%)	Equity method
Share investments with controlling influence (>50%)	Equity method (using consolidation)

Exhibit 18.7

Accounting for Debt and Share Investments

Reporting Long-Term Investments

Long-term investments are stated at cost with market value disclosed even if market value is below cost as long as the decline in value is temporary. However, when there has been a loss in value that is other than temporary, the individual investment is written down to recognize the loss.[4] The credit is made directly to the investment account and, in contrast to temporary investments, no allowance account is used. The write-down (loss) would be included in determining net income. When a long-term investment has been written down to recognize the loss, the new carrying value is deemed to be the new cost basis for subsequent accounting purposes. A subsequent increase in value would be recognized only when realized (i.e., when the shares are sold). For purposes of calculating the gain or loss on sale of the investment, the cost of the investment sold should be calculated on the basis of the average carrying value (= Total cost of the shares ÷ Number of shares held).[5]

---

[4] *CICA Handbook*, section 3050, par. 20.

[5] Ibid., section 3050, par. 27.

Mid-Chapter Demonstration Problem

The following transactions relate to Brown Company's long-term investment activities during 2005 and 2006. Brown did not own any long-term investments prior to 2005. Show the appropriate journal entries and the portions of each year's balance sheet and income statement that describe these transactions.

2005

Sept. 9 Purchased 1,000 shares of Packard Inc. common shares for $80,000 cash. These shares represent 30% of Packard's outstanding shares.

Oct. 2 Purchased as a long-term investment 2,000 shares of MT&T common shares for $60,000 cash. These shares represent less than a 1% ownership in MT&T.

17 Purchased as a long-term investment 1,000 shares of Four Seasons Hotels common shares for $40,000 cash. These shares are less than 1% of Four Seasons Hotels' outstanding shares.

Nov. 1 Received $5,000 cash dividend from Packard.

30 Received $3,000 cash dividend from MT&T.

Dec. 15 Received $1,400 cash dividend from Four Seasons.

31 Packard's 2005 net income was $70,000.

31 Market values for the investments in marketable equity securities are: Packard, $84,000; MT&T, $48,000; and Four Seasons Hotels, $45,000.

2006

Jan. 1 Packard Inc. was taken over by other investors, and Brown sold its shares for $108,000 cash.

May 30 Received $3,100 cash dividend from MT&T.

June 15 Received $1,600 cash dividend from Four Seasons.

Aug. 17 Sold the MT&T shares for $52,000 cash.

19 Purchased 2,000 shares of Loblaw common shares for $50,000 as a long-term investment. The shares represent less than a 5% ownership in Loblaw.

Dec. 15 Received $1,800 cash dividend from Four Seasons.

31 Market values of the investments in marketable equity securities are: Four Seasons Hotels, $39,000 and Loblaw, $48,000.

Planning the Solution

○ Account for the investment in Packard using the equity method.

○ Account for the investments in MT&T, Four Seasons Hotels, and Loblaw as long-term investments in securities using the cost method.

○ Prepare the information for the two balance sheets by including the appropriate assets and shareholders' equity accounts.

SOLUTION TO Mid-Chapter Demonstration Problem

Journal entries during 2005:

Sept. 9	Investment in Packard Common Shares	80,000	
	Cash		80,000
	Acquired 1,000 shares representing a 30% equity in Packard, Inc.		
Oct. 2	Investment in MT&T Common Shares	60,000	
	Cash		60,000
	Acquired 2,000 shares as a long-term investment in securities available for sale.		
17	Investment in Four Seasons Hotels Common Shares	40,000	
	Cash		40,000
	Acquired 1,000 shares as a long-term investment in securities available for sale.		
Nov. 1	Cash	5,000	
	Investment in Packard Common Shares		5,000
	Received dividend from Packard, Inc.		
30	Cash	3,000	
	Dividend Revenue		3,000
	Received dividend from MT&T.		
Dec. 15	Cash	1,400	
	Dividend Revenue		1,400
	Received dividend from Four Seasons Hotels.		
31	Investment in Packard Common Shares	21,000	
	Earnings from Investment in Packard		21,000
	To record our 30% share of Packard's annual earnings of $70,000.		

	Cost (Book Value)	Fair (Market) Value
Packard	$ 96,000	$84,000
MT&T	60,000	48,000
Four Seasons Hotels	40,000	45,000
Total	$100,000	$93,000

Given the usual fluctuations in market prices, it is reasonable to assume that the reduction is temporary. Therefore, no adjustment is necessary.

December 31, 2005, balance sheet items:

Assets	
Long-term investments:	
Equity securities, at cost (market value $93,000)	$100,000
Investment in Packard, Inc. (market value $84,000)	96,000
Total	$196,000

Income statement items for the year ended December 31, 2005:

Other revenues and expenses	
Dividend revenue	$ 4,400
Earnings from equity method investment...	21,000

Journal entries during 2006:

Jan.	1	Cash...	108,000	
		Investment in Packard Common Shares		96,000
		Gain on Sale of Investments......................		12,000
		Sold 1,000 shares for cash.		
May	30	Cash...	3,100	
		Dividend Revenue......................................		3,100
		Received dividend from MT&T.		
June	15	Cash...	1,600	
		Dividend Revenue......................................		1,600
		Received dividend from Four Seasons Hotels.		
Aug.	17	Cash...	52,000	
		Loss on Sale of Investments	8,000	
		Investment in MT&T Common Shares		60,000
		Sold 2,000 shares for cash.		
	19	Investment in Loblaw Common Shares	50,000	
		Cash..		50,000
		Acquired 2,000 shares as a long-term investment in securities available for sale.		
Dec.	15	Cash...	1,800	
		Dividend Revenue......................................		1,800
		Received dividend from Four Seasons Hotels.		

	Cost	Fair (Market) Value
Four Seasons	$40,000	$39,000
Loblaw..	50,000	48,000
Total...	$90,000	$87,000

December 31, 2006, balance sheet items:

Assets	
Long-term investments:	
Equity securities, at cost (market value $87,000)..	$90,000

Income statement items for the year ended December 31, 2006:

Other revenues and expenses	
Dividend revenue	$ 6,500
Gain on sale of investments..	12,000
Loss on sale of investments	(8,000)

Investments in International Operations

Many companies, from small entrepreneurs to large corporations, conduct business internationally. The operations of some large corporations take place in so many different countries that they are called **multinational businesses**. Many of us, for example, think of Alcan, Bombardier, and Nortel as primarily Canadian companies. Yet these companies earn over three-quarters of their sales from outside Canada. Others corporations such as Magna, McCain Foods, CAE Elecronics, and Molson are also major players in the world of international business.

Accounting for sales or purchases listed in a foreign currency is an accounting challenge that arises when companies have international operations. For ease in discussion of this challenge, we use companies with a base of operations in Canada and with a need to prepare financial statements in Canadian dollars. This means the *reporting currency* of these companies is the Canadian dollar.

LO8 Explain and record foreign exchange transactions.

Exchange Rates Between Currencies

Markets for the purchase and sale of foreign currencies exist all over the world. In these markets, Canadian dollars can be exchanged for U.S. dollars, British pounds, Japanese yen, or any other legal currencies. The price of one currency stated in terms of another currency is called a **foreign exchange rate**.

Exhibit 18.8 lists foreign exchange rates for selected currencies at August 31, 2003. In recent years the Canadian currency has risen relative to the other currencies in the list but has fallen relative to the U.S. currency. We say that a currency is strong if it is rising in relation to the currency of other countries. We see in Exhibit 18.8 that the exchange rate for British pounds into Canadian dollars was $2.18455 on that date. This rate means that one British pound could be purchased for Cdn$2.18455. Foreign exchange rates fluctuate due to changing economic and political conditions. These include the supply of and demand for currencies and expectations about future events.

Country (unit)	Price in Canadian dollars
Britain (pound)	$2.18455
U.S. (dollar)	1.385
India (rupee)	0.030187
Sweden (krona)	0.165582
Mexico (peso)	0.125226
Japan (yen)	0.011867
Taiwan (dollar)	0.040592
Europe (euro)	1.52156

Rates for August 31, 2003, http://www.x-rates.com/calculator.html

Exhibit 18.8

Foreign Exchange Rates for Selected Currencies

Sales or Purchases Listed in a Foreign Currency

When a Canadian company makes a credit sale to an international customer, accounting for the sale and the account receivable requires special treatment when the terms of the sale require payment in a foreign currency.

Consider the case of the Canadian-based manufacturer, Quebec Company, which makes credit sales to London Outfitters, a British retail company. A sale occurred on December 12, 2005, for a price of £10,000, payment due on

February 10, 2006. Quebec Company keeps its accounting records in Canadian dollars. To record the sale, Quebec Company must translate the sale price from pounds to dollars. This is done using the exchange rate on the date of the sale. Assuming the exchange rate on December 12, 2005, is $2.36, Quebec records this sale as:

Dec. 12	Accounts Receivable—London Outfitters	23,600	
	Sales (£10,000 × $2.36)		23,600
	To record a sale at £10,000, when the exchange rate equals $2.36.		

Quebec Company prepares its annual financial statements on December 31, 2005. On that date, the current exchange rate increases to $2.38. This means the current dollar value of Quebec Company's receivable is $23,800 (= 10,000 × $2.38). This amount is $200 greater than the amount recorded on December 12. Generally accepted accounting principles require a receivable to be reported in the balance sheet at its current dollar value. Quebec Company must make the following entry to record the increase in the dollar value of this receivable:

Dec. 31	Accounts Receivable—London Outfitters	200	
	Foreign Exchange Gain or Loss		200
	To record the increased value of the British pound on the receivable.		

Quebec Company receives London Outfitters' payment of £10,000 on February 10, 2006. Quebec Company immediately exchanges the pounds for Canadian dollars. On this date, the exchange rate for pounds is $2.35. This means Quebec Company receives only $23,500 (= 10,000 × $2.35). It records the cash receipt and the loss associated with the decline in the exchange rate as follows:

Feb. 10	Cash...	23,500	
	Foreign Exchange Gain or Loss	300	
	Accounts Receivable—London Outfitters ...		23,800
	Received foreign currency payment of an account and converted it into dollars.		

Gains and losses from foreign exchange transactions are accumulated in the Foreign Exchange Gain or Loss account and reported on the income statement as other revenues and expenses.

Accounting for credit purchases from an international supplier is treated in the same way as a credit sale to an international customer.

Flashback

Answer—p. 945

6. If a Canadian company makes a credit sale of merchandise to a French customer and the sales terms require payment in euros:

    a. The Canadian company incurs an exchange loss if the foreign exchange rate between euros and dollars increases from $1.50123 at the date of sale to $1.52156 at the date the account is settled.

    b. The French company may eventually need to record an exchange gain or loss.

    c. The Canadian company may be required to record an exchange gain or loss on the date of the sale.

Summary

LO1 **Describe and explain the purpose of debt and share investments.** *Debt investments* reflect a creditor relationship and include investments in notes, bonds, and certificates of deposit. Debt investments are issued by governments, companies, and individuals. *Share investments* reflect an ownership relationship and include shares issued by corporations. Companies invest in securities to earn income and gains, participate in new markets or new technologies, build relationships, and/or acquire non-controlling interest or controlling interest in the investee.

LO2 **Identify and account for temporary investments.** Temporary debt and share investments are current assets that meet two criteria: they are expected to be converted into cash within one year or the current operating cycle of the business, whichever is longer; they are readily converted to cash and are sometimes called marketable securities. All other security investments are long-term investments.

Temporary investments are recorded at cost, and any dividends or interest earned is recorded as revenue. Temporary investments are reported on the balance sheet at the lower of cost or market. Write-downs to market are credited to an allowance account and the loss is reported on the income statement. When temporary investments are sold, the difference between the net proceeds from the sale (sales price less brokerage fees) and the cost of the temporary investment is recognized as a gain or a loss.

LO3 **Identify classes of long-term debt and share investments.** Long-term debt and share investments are classified into one of four groups: (a) debt securities, (b) share investments of less than 20% of the investee's shares, (c) share investments of 20% to 50% of the investee's shares, and (d) share investments of more than 50% of the investee's shares.

LO4 **Account for long-term debt investments.** Debt investments held to maturity are reported at cost when purchased. Interest revenue is recorded as it accrues. The cost of long-term debt investments is adjusted for amortization of any difference between cost and maturity value.

LO5 **Account for long-term share investments of less than 20% ownership.** Share investments are recorded at cost when purchased. When the investor does not have either controlling or significant influence over the financing and operating policies of the investee (usually owning less than 20% of voting shares) the cost method must be used. Investments remain in the accounts at cost and any gains and losses realized on the sale of these investments are reported in the income statement. Revenue is recognized as dividends are received.

LO6 **Account for long-term share investments of 20% to 50% ownership.** The equity method is used when an investor has a significant influence over an investee. This usually exists when an investor owns 20% or more of the investee's voting shares, but not exceeding 50% ownership. The equity method means an investor records its share of the investee's earnings with a debit to the investment account and a credit to a revenue account. Dividends received satisfy the investor's equity claims and reduce the investment account balance.

LO7 **Describe how long-term share investments of more than 50% ownership are reported.** If an investor owns more than 50% of another company's voting shares and controls the investee, the investor's financial reports are prepared on a consolidated basis using the equity method. These reports are prepared as if the company were organized as one entity. The individual assets and liabilities of the parent and its subsidiaries are combined on one balance sheet. Similarly, their revenues and expenses are combined on one income statement and their cash flows are combined on one cash flow statement.

LO8 **Explain and record foreign exchange transactions.** A foreign exchange rate is the price of one currency stated in terms of another. A company with transactions in a foreign currency when the exchange rate changes between the time of the transactions and their settlement will experience an exchange gain or loss. When a company makes a credit sale to a foreign customer and sales terms call for payment in a foreign currency, the company must translate the foreign currency into dollars to record the receivable. If the exchange rate changes before payment is received, foreign exchange gains or losses are recognized in the year they occur.

GUIDANCE ANSWERS TO  Flashback

1. At the lower of cost or market.
2. Usually, only once per year, at the year-end.
3. The allowance is reduced and the offsetting credit is recorded in the income statement as a gain to a maximum of the balance in the allowance account.
4. A share investment is classified as a long-term investment if it is not marketable or, if marketable, it is not held as an available source of cash to meet the needs of current operations.

5. Long-term share investments are placed in one of the following three categories:
   a. Insignificant (non-influential, less than 20% of outstanding shares).
   b. Significant Influence (20% to 50% of outstanding shares).
   c. Controlling Influence (holding more than 50% of outstanding shares).
6. *a*

Demonstration Problem

Boudreau Corp. is a Canadian corporation that has customers in several foreign countries. Following are some of Boudreau's 2005 and 2006 transactions (ignore cost of sales):

2005

June 6   Sold merchandise to Lejeune Inc. of France for 125,000 euros to be received in 60 days. The exchange rate for euros was $1.50938.

July 21   Sold merchandise for $8,880 cash to Vongurp Corp. of Sweden. The exchange rate for krona was $0.16571 on this date.

Aug. 1   Received Lejeune Inc.'s payment for its purchase of June 6 and exchanged the euros for dollars. The current foreign exchange rate for euros into dollars was $1.51067.

Oct. 25   Sold merchandise on credit to British Imports, Ltd., a company located in London, England. The price of £3,000 was to be paid 90 days from the date of sale. On Nov. 18, the exchange rate for pounds into dollars was $1.7730.

Nov. 30   Sold merchandise for 350,000 yen to Yamoto Inc. of Japan, payment in full to be received in 60 days. On November 30, the foreign exchange rate for yen was $0.007710.

Dec. 31   Prepared adjusting entries to recognize exchange gains or losses on the annual financial statements. Rates for exchanging foreign currencies on this day included the following:

Yen (Japan)   0.007897

Pounds (Britain)   1.7125

2006

Jan. 23   Received full payment from British Imports for the sale of October 25 and immediately exchanged the pounds for dollars. The exchange rate for pounds was $1.7628.

29   Received Yamoto's full payment for the sale of November 30 and immediately exchanged the yen for dollars. The exchange rate for yen was $0.007779.

Required

1. Prepare General Journal entries to account for these transactions of Boudreau Corp. (For simplicity, ignore cost of sales.)

2. Calculate the foreign exchange gain or loss to be reported on Boudreau's 2005 income statement.

3. What actions might Boudreau consider to reduce its risk of foreign exchange gains or losses?

Planning the Solution

○ Account for each transaction.

○ Calculate any foreign exchange gain or loss at year-end by multiplying the number of foreign currency units by the difference between the foreign exchange rate on the transaction date and the year-end foreign exchange rate.

○ Calculate any foreign exchange rate on the date cash is received by multiplying the number of foreign currency units by the difference between the foreign exchange rate on the cash collection date and the foreign exchange rate at the previous year-end.

SOLUTION TO Demonstration Problem

Part 1

2005			
June 6	Accounts Receivable—Lejeune Inc.	188,672.50	
	Sales		188,672.50
	(125,000 × $1.50938 = $188,672.50)		
July 21	Cash..	8,880.00	
	Sales		8,880.00
Aug. 1	Cash (125,000 × $1.51067)...................	188,833.75	
	Foreign Exchange Gain or Loss		161.25
	Accounts Receivable—Lejeune Inc...........		188,672.50
Oct. 25	Accounts Receivable—British Imports, Ltd.	5,319.00	
	Sales		5,319.00
	(3,000 × $1.7730 = $5,319)		
Nov. 30	Accounts Receivable—Yamoto Inc.	2,698.50	
	Sales		2,698.50
	(350,000 × $0.007710 = $2,698.50)		
Dec. 31	Foreign Exchange Gain or Loss	181.50	
	Accounts Receivable—British Imports, Ltd.		181.50
	(3,000 × $1.7730) = $5,319.00		
	(3,000 × $1.7125) = 5,137.50		
	$ 181.50		
31	Accounts Receivable—Yamoto Inc.	65.45	
	Foreign Exchange Gain or Loss		65.45
	(350,000 × $0.007710) = $2,698.50		
	(350,000 × $0.007897) = 2,763.95		
	$ 65.45		
2006			
Jan. 23	Cash (3,000 × $1.7628)...................	5,288.40	
	Foreign Exchange Gain or Loss		150.90
	Accounts Receivable—British Imports, Ltd.		5,137.50
	($5,319.00 − $181.50 = $5,137.50)		
29	Cash (350,000 × $0.007779).................	2,722.65	
	Foreign Exchange Gain or Loss	41.30	
	Accounts Receivable—Yamoto Inc.		2,763.95
	($2,698.50 + $65.45 = $2,763.95)		

Part 2
Net foreign exchange gain in 2005 income statement:

August 1 (foreign exchange gain)	$161.25
December 31 (foreign exchange loss)	(181.50)
December 31 (foreign exchange gain).......................	65.45
Total (net foreign exchange gain).............................	$ 45.20

Part 3
To reduce the risk of foreign exchange gain or loss, Boudreau could attempt to negotiate foreign customer sales that are denominated in Canadian dollars. To accomplish this, Boudreau may be willing to offer favourable terms, such as price discounts or longer credit terms.

18A Parent and Subsidiary Corporations

Consolidated Balance Sheets

LO⁹ Prepare consolidated balance sheets and explain how to report any excess of investment cost over book value or minority interests.

When parent and subsidiary balance sheets are consolidated, duplications in items are eliminated so that the combined figures do not show more assets and equities than actually exist. For example, a parent's investment in a subsidiary is evidenced by shares that are carried as an asset in the parent company's records. However, these shares actually represent an equity in the subsidiary's assets. Therefore, if the parent's investment in a subsidiary and the subsidiary's assets were both shown on the consolidated balance sheet, the same resource would be counted twice. To prevent this, the parent's investment and the subsidiary's capital accounts are offset and eliminated in preparing a consolidated balance sheet.

Likewise, a single enterprise cannot owe a debt to itself. To prevent such double counting, intercompany debts and receivables are also eliminated in preparing a consolidated balance sheet.

Consolidation at Time of Acquisition

When a parent's and a subsidiary's assets are combined in the preparation of a consolidated balance sheet, a work sheet is normally used to organize the data. For example, Exhibit 18A.1 shows a work sheet to consolidate the accounts of Par Inc. and its subsidiary called Sub Inc. In the work sheet, the account balances are on December 31, 2005, which was the day Par Inc. acquired Sub Inc. On that day, Par Inc. paid cash to purchase all of Sub Inc.'s outstanding common shares. The shares had a book value of $115,000, or $11.50 per share, on the books of Sub Inc. In this first illustration, we assume that Par Inc. paid $115,000, or book value, for the outstanding shares.

In Exhibit 18A.1, notice that the Eliminations columns include two sets of debits and credits. One set is identified by the letter (a), and the other set is identified by the letter (b).

Elimination (a)

On the day it acquired Sub Inc., Par Inc. lent Sub Inc. $10,000 to use in the subsidiary's operations. In exchange for the cash, Sub Inc. signed a promissory note to Par Inc. This intercompany debt was in reality a transfer of funds within the consolidated entity. Therefore, since it did not increase the total assets and total liabilities of the affiliated companies, elimination (a) prevents these balances from appearing on the consolidated balance sheet. To understand this elimination, recall that the subsidiary's promissory note appears as a $10,000 debit in Par Inc.'s Notes Receivable account. Then, observe that the first credit in the Eliminations column exactly offsets or eliminates this item. Next, recall that the

Exhibit 18A.1

Consolidated Work Sheet for 100% Owned Subsidiary—Shares Purchased at Book Value

Par Inc. and Sub Inc. Work Sheet for a Consolidated Balance Sheet December 31, 2005			Eliminations		Consolidated Amount
	Par Inc.	Sub Inc.	Debit	Credit	
Assets					
Cash	5,000	15,000			20,000
Notes receivable	10,000			(a) 10,000	
Investment in Sub Inc.	115,000			(b)115,000	
Other assets..................................	190,000	117,000			307,000
	320,000	132,000			327,000
Liabilities and Equities					
Accounts payable	15,000	7,000			22,000
Notes payable		10,000	(a) 10,000		
Common shares.............................	250,000	100,000	(b)100,000		250,000
Retained earnings	55,000	15,000	(b) 15,000		55,000
	320,000	132,000	125,000	125,000	327,000

subsidiary's note appears as a credit in its Notes Payable account. In the Eliminations columns, the $10,000 debit completes the elimination of this intercompany debt.

Elimination (b)

When a parent company buys a subsidiary's shares, the investment is recorded in the accounts of the parent as an asset. This investment represents an equity in the subsidiary's net assets. However, you must not show both the subsidiary's (net) assets and the parent company's investment in the subsidiary on a consolidated balance sheet. To do so would be to double count those resources. On the work sheet, the credit portion of elimination (b) prevents double counting of Sub Inc.'s net assets.

After the intercompany items are eliminated on a work sheet as in Exhibit 18A.1, the assets of the parent and the subsidiary and the remaining equities in these assets are combined and carried into the work sheet's last column. The combined amounts are then used to prepare a consolidated balance sheet that shows all the assets and equities of the parent and its subsidiary.

Parent Company Buys Less Than 100% and Pays More Than Book Value

A parent company often purchases less than 100% of a subsidiary's shares and commonly pays a price that is either more or less than book value. To illustrate, assume Par Inc. purchased only 80% of Sub Inc.'s outstanding shares. Also assume that Par Inc. paid $13 per share, a price that was $1.50 more than the shares's book value.

The entry to eliminate the parent's investment and the subsidiary's shareholders' equity accounts is complicated by (1) the minority interest in the subsidiary and (2) the excess over book value paid by the parent company for the subsidiary's shares.

Minority Interest

When the parent owns less than 100% of the subsidiary's shares, the subsidiary has other shareholders who own a **minority interest** in its assets and share in its earnings.

The equity of the minority interest must be recognized in the consolidated work sheet. This is done in the process of eliminating the shareholders' equity balances of the subsidiary, as shown in Exhibit 18A.2. In this case, the minority shareholders have a 20% interest in the subsidiary. Therefore, on the work sheet, 20% of the subsidiary's shareholders' equity amounts [($100,000 + $15,000) × 20% = $23,000] is reclassified as the minority interest.

Exhibit 18A.2

Consolidated Work Sheet—80% of Subsidiary Shares Purchased at More Than Book Value

Par Inc. and Sub Inc.
Work Sheet for a Consolidated Balance Sheet
December 31, 2005

	Par Inc.	Sub Inc.	Eliminations Debit	Eliminations Credit	Consolidated Amount
Assets					
Cash	16,000	15,000			31,000
Notes receivable	10,000			(a) 10,000	
Investment in Sub Inc.	104,000			(b)104,000	
Other assets..................................	190,000	117,000			307,000
Excess of cost over book value.......			(b) 12,000		12,000
	320,000	132,000			350,000
Liabilities and Equities					
Accounts payable..........................	15,000	7,000			22,000
Notes payable		10,000	(a) 10,000		
Common shares.............................	250,000	100,000	(b)100,000		250,000
Retained earnings	55,000	15,000	(b) 15,000		55,000
Minority Interest............................				(b) 23,000	23,000
	320,000	132,000	137,000	137,000	350,000

Excess of Investment Cost over Book Value

In Exhibit 18A.2, we assume that Par Inc. paid $13 per share for its 8,000 shares of Sub Inc. Therefore, the cost of these shares exceeded their book value by $12,000, calculated as follows:

Cost of shares (8,000 shares at $13 per share)	$ 104,000
Book value (8,000 shares at $11.50 per share)	92,000
Excess of cost over book value	$ 12,000

After the work sheet of Exhibit 18A.2 was completed, the consolidated amounts in the last column were used to prepare the consolidated balance sheet of Exhibit 18A.3. The minority interest usually is shown as a separate item between the liabilities and shareholders' equity sections, as shown in Exhibit 18A.3.

Par Inc. and Sub Inc.
Consolidated Balance Sheet
December 31, 2005

Assets

Cash	$ 31,000
Other assets	307,000
Goodwill from consolidation	12,000
Total assets	$350,000

Liabilities and Shareholders' Equity

Liabilities:

Accounts payable		$ 22,000
Minority interest		23,000
Shareholders' equity:		
Common shares	$250,000	
Retained earnings	55,000	
Total shareholders' equity		305,000
Total liabilities and shareholders' equity		$350,000

Next, observe that the $12,000 excess of cost over book value that Par Inc. paid for Sub Inc.'s shares appears on the consolidated balance sheet as an asset called "Goodwill from consolidation." There are several reasons why a parent might pay more than book value for its equity in a subsidiary: (1) certain of the subsidiary's assets are carried on the subsidiary's books at less than fair value; (2) certain of the subsidiary's liabilities are carried at book values that are greater than fair values; and (3) the subsidiary's earnings prospects may be good enough to justify paying more than the net fair (market) value of its assets and liabilities. In this illustration, we assume that the book values of Sub Inc.'s assets and liabilities are equal to their fair values. However, Sub Inc.'s expected earnings justified paying $104,000 for an 80% equity in the subsidiary's net assets (assets less liabilities).

When a company pays more than book value because the subsidiary's assets are undervalued, the cost in excess of book value must be allocated to those assets and liabilities so that they are restated at fair values. After the subsidiary's assets and liabilities have been restated to reflect fair values, any remaining cost in excess of book value is reported on the consolidated balance sheet as "Goodwill from consolidation."

Occasionally, a parent company pays less than book value for its interest in a subsidiary. The probable reason for a price below book value is that some of the subsidiary's assets are carried on its books at amounts in excess of fair value. The CICA has ruled that the excess of book value over cost should be allocated to reduce the balance sheet valuations of the overvalued assets.

Earnings and Dividends of a Subsidiary

As you already learned, a parent uses the equity method in its books to account for its investment in a subsidiary. As a result, the parent's recorded net income and Retained Earnings account include the parent's equity in the net income earned by the subsidiary since the date of acquisition. Also, the balance of the parent's Investment in Subsidiary account increases (or decreases) each year by an amount equal to the parent's equity in the subsidiary's earnings (or loss) less the parent's share of any dividends paid by the subsidiary.

For example, assume that Sub Inc. earned $12,500 during 2006, its first year as a subsidiary, and at year-end paid out $7,500 in dividends. Par Inc. records its 80% equity in these earnings and dividends as follows:

Dec. 31	Investment in Sub Inc.	10,000	
	Earnings from Investment in Subsidiary...		10,000
	To record 80% of the $12,500 net income		
	reported by Sub Inc.		
31	Cash	6,000	
	Investment in Sub Inc.............................		6,000
	To record the receipt of 80% of the $7,500		
	dividends paid by Sub Inc.		

Consolidations After Acquisition

Exhibit 18A.4 shows the December 31, 2006, work sheet to consolidate the balance sheets of Par Inc. and Sub Inc. To simplify the illustration, it is assumed that Par Inc. had no transactions during the year other than to record its equity in Sub Inc.'s earnings and dividends. Also, the other assets and liabilities of Sub Inc. did not change, and the subsidiary had not paid its note to Par Inc.

Compare Exhibit 18A.4 with Exhibit 18A.2 to see the changes in Par Inc.'s balance sheet (the first column). Par Inc.'s cash increased from $16,000 to $22,000 because of the dividends received from Sub Inc. The Investment in Sub Inc. account increased from $104,000 to $108,000 as a result of the equity method

Exhibit 18A.4

Work Sheet for a Consolidated Balance Sheet, One Year After Acquisition

Par Inc. and Sub Inc.
Work Sheet for a Consolidated Balance Sheet
December 31, 2006

	Par Inc.	Sub Inc.	Eliminations Debit	Eliminations Credit	Consolidated Amount
Assets					
Cash	22,000	20,000			42,000
Notes receivable	10,000			(a) 10,000	
Investment in Sub Inc.	108,000			(b)108,000	
Other assets....................................	190,000	117,000			307,000
Excess of cost over book value.......			(b) 12,000		12,000
	330,000	137,000			361,000
Liabilities and Equities					
Accounts payable............................	15,000	7,000			22,000
Notes payable		10,000	(a) 10,000		
Common shares...............................	250,000	100,000	(b)100,000		250,000
Retained earnings	65,000	20,000	(b) 20,000		65,000
Minority interest.............................				(b) 24,000	24,000
	330,000	137,000	142,000	142,000	361,000

entries during the year. Finally, Par Inc.'s Retained Earnings increased by $10,000, which was the parent's equity in the subsidiary's earnings.

In the second column of Exhibit 18A.4 note only two changes: (a) Sub Inc.'s cash balance increased by $5,000, which is the difference between its $12,500 net income and $7,500 payment of dividends; and (2) retained earnings also increased from $15,000 to $20,000, which is explained by the $12,500 net income less $7,500 dividends. Note that the $20,000 balance is eliminated on the work sheet.

The minority interest set out on the December 31, 2006, work sheet is greater than on the December 31, 2005, work sheet. The minority shareholders have a 20% equity in Sub Inc. So, the $24,000 shown on the December 31, 2006, work sheet is 20% of Sub Inc.'s Common Shares and Retained Earnings balances on December 31, 2006. This $24,000 is $1,000 greater than the beginning-of-year minority interest because the subsidiary's retained earnings increased $5,000 during the year; the minority shareholder's share of this increase is 20%, or $1,000.

Other Consolidated Statements

In addition to the balance sheet, the consolidated financial statements include a consolidated income statement, consolidated retained earnings statement, and consolidated cash flow statement. However, you can have a general understanding of these statements without further discussion of the procedures to prepare them. At this point, you need only recognize that all duplications in items are eliminated. Also, when one affiliate records profit on sales to the other affiliate, the profit is eliminated in the consolidated statements. Finally, the amounts of net income and retained earnings that are reported in consolidated statements are equal to the amounts recorded by the parent under the equity method.

Summary of Appendix 18A

LO⁹ Prepare consolidated balance sheets and explain how to report any excess of investment cost over book value or minority interests.
Consolidated balance sheets are prepared by combining the accounts of the separate corporations as if they were a single entity. When the purchase price of a subsidiary's identifiable assets exceeds book values, the book values should be revalued. Any remaining excess

of the purchase price over the revalued net assets should be shown on the consolidated financial statements as goodwill. In combining these accounts, the effects of intercompany transactions must be eliminated to avoid double counting. Since 100% of subsidiary net assets are reported on the consolidated balance sheet, any claim not represented by the parent company is to be reported as a minority interest.

Glossary

Consolidated financial statements Financial statements that show the results of all operations under the parent's control, including those of any subsidiaries; assets and liabilities of all affiliated companies are combined on a single balance sheet, revenues and expenses are combined on a single income statement, and cash flows are combined on a single cash flow statement as if the business were in fact a single company. (p. 939)

Control When an investor can dominate all other shareholders in electing the corporation's board of directors and has control over the investee corporation's management. (p. 938)

Cost method An accounting method used for long-term investments where the investor does not have significant influence over the investee. (p. 936)

Debt investment Represents an amount owed and arises when one company lends money to another, such as in the case of a bond. Also called *debt security*. (p. 928)

Debt security See *debt investment*. (p. 928)

Equity method An accounting method used for long-term investments when the investor has significant influence over the investee; the investment account is initially debited for cost and then is increased to reflect the investor's share of the investee's earnings and decreased to reflect the investor's receipt of dividends paid by the investee. (p. 936)

Equity security See *share investment*. (p. 928)

Foreign exchange rate The price of one currency stated in terms of another currency. (p. 943)

Intercorporate investments Debt and shares of one corporation purchased by another corporation. (p. 928)

Investee The company whose debt or shares are being purchased. (p. 928)

Investment portfolio A group of investments held by the investor. (p. 929)

Investor The company that purchases as an investment the debt or shares of another. (p. 928)

Long-term investments Investments in shares and bonds that are not marketable or, if marketable, are not intended to be converted into cash in the short term; also funds earmarked for a special purpose, such as land or other assets not used in the company's operations. (p. 929)

Lower of cost or market (LCM) The required method of reporting temporary investments in marketable securities in the balance sheet at the lower of the total cost of all the investments (called the *portfolio*) or their market value on the balance sheet date. (p. 930)

Marketable securities See *temporary investments*. (p. 928)

Minority interest Investors who do not own more than 50% of the voting shares in a corporation. (p. 950)

Multinational business A company that operates in a large number of different countries. (p. 943)

Parent company A corporation that owns a controlling interest in another corporation (more than 50% of the voting shares is required). (p. 938)

Share investment Represents one company's purchase of the shares in another company. Also called *equity security*. (p. 928)

Short-term investments See *temporary investments*. (p. 928)

Significant influence The ability of the investor to influence the investee even though the investor owns less than 50% of the investee's voting shares. (p. 936)

Subsidiary A corporation that is controlled by another corporation (the parent) because the parent owns more than 50% of the subsidiary's voting shares. (p. 938)

Temporary investments Current assets that management generally expects to convert into cash within twelve months (or the operating cycle if longer); can be either debt or equity securities. (p. 928)

For more study tools, quizzes, and problem material,
refer to the Online Learning Centre at
www.mcgrawhill.ca/college/larson

Questions

1. Under what conditions should investments be classified as current assets? As long term assets?

2. Jones Company sold a temporary investment for $8,500. Two months earlier, Jones acquired this investment for $7,200. How should Jones Company account for the difference in these amounts?

3. What valuation should be reported on a balance sheet for temporary investments?

4. Identify the classes for long-term investments.

5. On a balance sheet, what valuation must be reported for long-term debt investments that were initially purchased at par value?

6. How is interest recognized on long-term debt investments?

7. When share investments are accounted for using the cost method, when should revenue be recognized?

8. In accounting for common share investments, when should the equity method be used?

9. When share investments are accounted for using the equity method, when should revenue be recognized? What accounts are debited and credited?

10. Using the equity method, dividends received are not recorded as revenue. Explain why this is true.

11. Under what circumstances would a company prepare consolidated financial statements?

12. What is a basic problem of accounting for international operations?

13. If a Canadian company makes a credit sale to a foreign customer and the customer is required to make payment in Canadian dollars, can the Canadian company have an exchange gain or loss as a result of the sale?

14. A Canadian company makes a credit sale to a foreign customer, and the customer is required to make payment in a foreign currency. The foreign exchange rate was $1.40 on the date of the sale and is $1.30 on the date the customer pays the receivable. Will the Canadian company record an exchange gain or an exchange loss?

15. In the chapter's opening scenario, how does Brempong employ fundamental analysis of companies she invests in or makes recommendations on?

Quick Study

QS 18-1
Short- and long-term investments

$LO^{2,3,7}$

Fill in the blanks using terms from the following list:

cost	equity	long-term	subsidiary
current	interest earned	parent company	

1. Temporary investments are classified as _____ assets.
2. Share investments giving an investor significant influence are recorded using the _____ method.
3. Debt investments held for the long term are presented on the balance sheet at _____.
4. Accrual of interest on bonds held as investments will require a credit to _____.
5. The controlling investor is called the _____ and the investee company is called the _____.

QS 18-2
Distinguishing short- and long-term investments

LO^2

Which of the following are true of long-term investments?
a. They are held as an investment of cash available for current operations.
b. They may include debt investments held for the long term.
c. They may include bonds and shares that are not intended to serve as a ready source of cash.
d. They may include investments in marketable securities.
e. They will be sold within one accounting period.

QS 18-3
Temporary debt investments

LO^2

Shinko Inc. purchased bonds with a face value of $5,000 at 98 as a short-term investment. Shinko paid a brokerage fee of $300. At what amount should Shinko record the cost of the investment?

QS 18-4
Temporary share investments

LO^2

On May 2, Sysco Industries Inc. made a temporary investment in 300 common shares of Computer Web Corp. The purchase price was $40.50 per share and the broker's fee was $350. On July 28, Sysco received $2.50 per share in dividends. Prepare the May 2 and July 28 journal entries.

QS 18-5
Debt investments

LO^4

On April 1, 2005, Demi Dean purchased 8% bonds of Multi Media Inc. as a long-term investment at a cost of $50,000, which equals their par value. The bonds pay interest semi-annually on September 30 and March 31. Prepare the entries to record the September 30 receipt of interest and the December 31 accrual.

QS 18-6
Share investments

LO^2

On April 1, 2005, Martin Corporation purchased 100 shares of Felix Inc.'s voting shares at $50 plus a brokerage fee of $60. Record the purchase of the Felix Inc. shares (using the cost method).

QS 18-7
Share investments

LO⁵

Refer to the information in QS 18-6. Felix Inc. has 1,000 shares outstanding and on July 31, 2005, declared and paid a $4 per share dividend. Record the entry relating to the receipt of the dividend on the books of Martin Corporation.

QS 18-8
Share investments

LO⁵

On January 2, 2005, Nassau Corp. paid $500,000 to acquire 10,000 (10%) of Suffolk Corp.'s outstanding common shares as a long-term investment. On March 25, 2007, Nassau sold half of the shares for $260,000. What method should be used to account for this share investment? Prepare entries to record the acquisition and sale of the shares.

QS 18-9
Share investments

LO⁶

When an investor has significant influence over the company whose shares are being acquired, what method should be used to record the investment in shares: (a) Cost, (b) Lower of cost or market, or (c) Equity method?

QS 18-10
Equity method

LO⁶

Use the same facts from QS 18-8, except assume that the shares acquired represented 30% of Suffolk Corp.'s outstanding shares. Also assume that Suffolk Corp. paid a $100,000 dividend on October 12, 2005, and reported a net income of $400,000 for 2005. Prepare the entry to record the receipt of the dividend and the year-end adjustment of the investment account.

QS 18-11
Foreign currency transactions

LO⁸

On November 21, 2005, a Canadian company, NCN, made a sale with credit terms requiring payment in 30 days to a Swedish corporation, Ehler Corp. The amount of the sale was 50,000 Swedish krona. Assuming the exchange rate in Exhibit 18.8 on the date of sale and $0.160121 on December 21, prepare the entries to record the sale and the cash receipt on December 21. *For simplicity, round all final calculations to the nearest dollar.*

QS 18-12
Foreign currency transactions

LO⁸

A Canadian corporation sells a British corporation a product with the transaction listed in British pounds. On August 31, 2005, the date of the sale, the transaction of $21,846 was billed at £10,000, reflecting an exchange rate as shown in Exhibit 18.8. Show the entry to record the sale and also the receipt of the payment on September 28 when the exchange rate has risen to $2.20234.

Exercises

Exercise 18-1
Transactions involving temporary investments

LO²

Prepare General Journal entries to record the following transactions involving the temporary investments of Aryee Corporation., all of which occurred during 2005.
a. On March 21, paid $60,000 to purchase $60,000 of Cordy Corporation 90-day short-term notes payable, which are dated February 21 and pay 10% interest.
b. On April 16, bought 2,000 common shares of Windsor Motors at $25.50 plus a $750 brokerage fee.
c. On May 2, paid $40,000 to purchase $40,000 of 9% notes payable of Bates Corporation, due May 2, 2006.
d. On June 20, received a cheque from Cordy Corporation in payment of the principal and 90 days' interest on the notes purchased in transaction (a).
e. On September 21, received a $1.00 per common share cash dividend on the Windsor Motors shares purchased in transaction (b).
f. On October 6, sold 1,000 Windsor Motors common shares for $28 per share, less a brokerage fee of $350.
g. On November 2, received a cheque from Bates Corporation for six months' interest on the notes purchased in transaction (c).

Prepare General Journal entries to record the following transactions involving the temporary investments of Baker Inc., all of which occurred during 2005:
a. On February 17, paid $200,000 to purchase $200,000 of Regina Inc. 90-day short-term notes payable, which are dated February 17 and pay 6.8% interest.
b. On March 24, bought 800 shares of Landry Inc. at $26.75 plus a $250 fee.
c. On May 18, received a cheque from Regina Inc. in payment of the principal and 90 days' interest on the notes purchased in transaction (a).
d. On July 30, paid $50,000 to purchase $50,000 of Beakon Inc. 8% notes payable, dated July 30, 2005, and due January 30, 2006.
e. On September 1, received a $0.50 per common share cash dividend on the Landry Salvage shares purchased in transaction (b).
f. On October 8, sold 400 shares of Landry Inc. common shares for $32 per share, less a $175 brokerage fee.
g. On October 30, received a cheque from Beakon Inc. for three months' interest on the notes purchased in transaction (d).

Exercise 18-2
Transactions involving temporary investments

LO²

Roe Inc. temporary investments in equity securities as of December 31, 2005, are as follows:

Exercise 18-3
Temporary investments—LCM

LO²

	Cost	Market
Nortel common shares............................	$17,600	$19,450
Northern Electric common shares...........	42,750	42,050
Imperial Oil common shares	25,200	24,250
Inco Limited common shares.................	34,800	31,950

Roe Inc. had no temporary investments prior to 2005.

Required
Calculate the lower of cost or market of Roe Inc.'s temporary investments and, if necessary, prepare a journal entry to record the decline in market value of these temporary investments.

Refer to the data in Exercise 18-3.

Required
Illustrate how the temporary investments will be reported on the balance sheet on December 31, 2005.

Exercise 18-4
Temporary investments

LO²

The cost and market value of temporary investments of IP Corporation on December 31, 2005, and December 31, 2006, are as follows:

Exercise 18-5
Temporary investments—LCM

LO²

Temporary Investments	Cost	Market
On December 31, 2005..........................	$23,500	$22,000
On December 31, 2006..........................	26,500	24,250

Required
Prepare a journal entry on December 31, 2006, to adjust the balance in the allowance account that is contra to the Temporary Investments account. Assume IP Corporation had no temporary investments prior to 2005.

Exercise 18-6

Temporary debt investments

LO²

On Jan. 1, 2005, Burns Corp. purchased 75 bonds that mature in 10 years from Hanna Corporation at 98½. Burns Company plans to resell these bonds within the current period. Each bond has a par value of $1,000 and a contract interest rate of 10 percent. A brokerage fee of $1,000 is paid. The bonds pay interest semi-annually on June 30 and December 31.

Required
a. Prepare the journal entry to record the purchase of the bonds.
b. Assume that Burns Corp. prepares monthly financial statements. Journalize any necessary adjusting entry on January 31, 2005.

Exercise 18-7

Classifying debt and share investments

LO³

During 2005, Lomas Inc.'s investments in securities included five items. These securities, with their December 31, 2005, market values, are as follows:
a. Vancouver Inc. common shares: 33,500 shares; $345,450 cost; $372,375 market value. Lomas owns 35% of Vancouver Inc.'s voting shares and has a significant influence over Vancouver Inc.
b. Mackenzie Corp. bonds payable: $500,500 cost; $515,000 market value. Lomas intends and is able to hold these bonds until they mature in 2010.
c. Calgary Carpet Inc. common shares: 18,300 shares; $102,400 cost; $109,300 market value. These shares are marketable and they are held as an investment of cash available for operations.
d. Lee Inc. common shares: 12,000 shares; $169,750 cost; $181,000 market value. The goal of this investment, which amounts to 4% of Lee's outstanding shares, is to earn dividends over the next few years.
e. Parsons Inc. common shares: 24,000 shares; $102,300 cost; $97,625 market value. The goal of this investment is an expected increase in market value of the shares over the next three to five years. Parsons has 40,000 common shares outstanding.

State whether each of these investments should be classified as a current asset or as a long-term investment. Also, for each of the long-term items, indicate in which of the four types of long-term investments the item should be classified. Assume that Lomas had no long-term investments prior to 2005. Show how the long-term investments would be reported in the year-end financial statements.

Exercise 18-8

Long-term debt investments

LO⁴

On May 1, 2005, Culvert Inc. purchased 75 bonds that mature in 10 years from Hanna Corporation. Each bond has a par value of $1,000 and a contract interest rate of 10 percent. The bonds pay interest semi-annually on June 30 and December 31. The bonds are acquired at 85.95.

Required
a. Prepare the journal entry to record the purchase of the bonds assuming that Culvert plans to hold these bonds for the long term.
b. Prepare the entry to record the first interest receipt and any amortization of discount or premium. Show the amortization as a separate entry and assume that the market rate of interest is 12.5%. Round amounts to the nearest dollar.

Exercise 18-9

Long-term debt investments

LO⁴

Aron Inc. purchased as a long-term investment $40,000 par value bonds of Margaree Corp. for $38,293.60 on July 1, 2005. The bonds are due in five years and have a contract rate of 5%. The market rate is 6%. Prepare the journal entry to record the purchase of the bonds and the collection of the first period's interest on December 31, 2005, at the market rate.

Exercise 18-10

Long-term debt investments

LO⁴

Venice Corp. purchased 50 of Kentville Inc.'s 10-year $1,000 par value bonds on September 1, 2005. The contract rate on these bonds was 12%. Interest is paid semi-annually on June 30 and December 31. The bonds were purchased at par value plus a brokerage fee of $800. Venice intends to hold the bonds as a long-term investment. Prepare journal entries for Venice Corp. to record the purchase and to record the receipt of interest on December 31, 2005.

The following events are for Toronto Inc.:

> **2005**
> Jan. 14   Purchased 18,000 shares of Queen's Inc. common shares for $156,900 plus a broker's fee of $1,000. Queen's has 90,000 common shares outstanding and has acknowledged the fact that its policies will be significantly influenced by Toronto.
> Oct. 1   Queen's declared and paid a cash dividend of $2.60 per share.
> Dec. 31   Queen's announced that net income for the year amounted to $650,000.
>
> **2006**
> April 1   Queen's declared and paid a cash dividend of $2.70 per share.
> Dec. 31   Queen's announced that net income for the year amounted to $733,100.
>   31 Toronto sold 6,000 shares of Queen's for $104,320.

Required
Prepare General Journal entries to record each transaction.

Exercise 18-11
Share investment
transactions; equity method

LO⁶

On June 2, 2005, Comco Inc. (a Canadian corporation) made a credit sale to Phang (a Taiwanese corporation). The terms of the sale required Phang to pay 980,000 Taiwanese dollars on January 3, 2006. Comco prepares quarterly financial statements on March 31, June 30, September 30, and December 31. The foreign exchange rates for Taiwanese dollars during the time the receivable was outstanding were:

June 2, 2005	$0.040114
June 30, 2005	0.040555
September 30, 2005	0.040675
December 31, 2005	0.040246
January 3, 2006	0.040718

Calculate the foreign exchange gain or loss that Comco should report on each of its quarterly income statements during the last three quarters of 2005 and the first quarter of 2006. Also calculate the amount that should be reported on Comco's balance sheets at the end of the last three quarters of 2005. *For simplicity, round final calculations to the nearest dollar.*

Exercise 18-12
Receivables listed in a
foreign currency

 LO⁸

Donham Corporation of Montvale, New Brunswick, sells its products to customers in Canada and in the U.S. On December 3, 2005, Donham sold merchandise on credit to Swensons, Ltd., of Maine, at a price of U.S.$6,500. The exchange rate on that day was U.S.$1 for Cdn$1.3852. On December 31, 2005, when Donham prepared its financial statements, the exchange rate was U.S.$1 for Cdn$1.2964. Swensons paid its bill in full on January 3, 2006, at which time the exchange rate was U.S.$1 for Cdn$1.3041. Donham immediately exchanged the U.S.$6,500 for Canadian dollars. Prepare journal entries on December 3, December 31, and January 3, to account for the sale and account receivable on Donham's books. *For simplicity, round final calculations to the nearest dollar.*

Exercise 18-13
Foreign currency transactions

 LO⁸

Problems

Problem 18-1A
Accounting for temporary investments

LO²

Landers Inc. had no temporary investments prior to 2005 but had the following transactions involving temporary investments in securities during 2005:

Apr.	1	Paid $100,000 to buy 90-day treasury bills, $100,000 principal amount, 5%, dated April 1.
	12	Purchased 3,000 common shares of Dofasco Ltd. at $22.25 plus a $1,948 brokerage fee.
June	9	Purchased 1,800 common shares of Power Corp. at $49.50 plus a $1,235 brokerage fee.
	20	Purchased 700 common shares of Westburne Ltd. at $15.75 plus a $466 brokerage fee.
July	3	Received a cheque for the principal and accrued interest on the treasury bills that matured on June 30.
	15	Received a $0.95 per share cash dividend on the Dofasco common shares.
	28	Sold 1,500 of the Dofasco common shares at $26.00 less a $912 brokerage fee.
Sept.	1	Received a $2.10 per share cash dividend on the Power Corp. common shares.
Dec.	15	Received a $1.35 per share cash dividend on the remaining Dofasco common shares owned.
	31	Received a $1.60 per share cash dividend on the Power Corp. common shares.

Required
Prepare journal entries to record the preceding transactions.

Problem 18-2A
Entries for temporary investments

LO²

Courteau Security Inc. has relatively large idle cash balances and invests them in securities that it holds as temporary investments. Following is a series of events and other facts relevant to the temporary investment activity of the corporation:

2005		
Jan.	15	Paid $100,000 to buy six-month treasury bills, $100,000 principal amount, 8%, dated January 15.
Feb.	7	Purchased 2,200 common shares of Royal Bank at $26.50 plus a $500 commission.
	19	Purchased 1,200 common shares of Imperial Oil at $51.75 plus a $600 commission.
Mar.	1	Paid $50,000 for treasury notes, $50,000 principal amount, 9%, dated March 1, 2005, due March 1, 2006.
	26	Purchased 2,000 common shares of BCE at $13.38 plus a $250 brokerage fee.
June	1	Received a $0.25 per share cash dividend on the Royal Bank common shares.
	17	Sold 1,200 Royal Bank common shares at $27.00 less a $300 brokerage fee.
July	17	Received a cheque for the principal and accrued interest on the treasury bills that matured on July 15.
Aug.	5	Received a $0.50 per share cash dividend on the Imperial Oil common shares.
Sept.	1	Received a cheque for six months' interest on the treasury notes purchased on March 1.
	1	Received a $0.275 per share cash dividend on the remaining Royal Bank common shares.
Nov.	5	Received a $0.45 per share cash dividend on the Imperial Oil common shares.

On December 31, 2005, the market prices of the equity securities held by Courteau Security Inc. were: Royal Bank, $27.50; Imperial Oil, $50.13; and BCE, $13.50.

Required

1. Prepare journal entries to record the temporary investment activity.
2. Prepare a schedule to calculate the lower of cost or market of Courteau's temporary investments.
3. Prepare adjusting entries, if necessary, to record accrued interest on Courteau Security Inc.'s investments in debt obligations and to reduce the marketable equity securities to the lower of cost or market assuming there were no investments made prior to 2005.

On January 1, 2005, Liu Corporation paid $584,361 to acquire bonds of Peverdo with a par value of $650,000. The annual contract rate on the bonds is 5% and interest is paid semi-annually on June 30 and December 31. The bonds mature after four years. The market rate of interest was 8%.

Required

Prepare Liu's entries to record: (a) the purchase of the bonds, (b) the receipt of the first two interest payments.

Problem 18-3A
Accounting for long-term debt investments

LO⁴

Check figure:
Dec. 31 Investment
Revenue, $23,659

Johnson Inc.'s long-term investment portfolio at December 31, 2004, consisted of the following:

Long-Term Investments*	Cost	Fair Market Value
10,000 Xavier Corporation common shares.......	$163,500	$145,000
1,500 Young Inc. common shares.....................	65,000	62,000
120,000 Zed Corp. common shares..................	40,000	35,600

*No adjustments were recorded in 2004 to write cost values down to market.

Problem 18-4A
Entries for long-term investments

LO⁵, ⁶, ⁷

Johnson made the following long-term investment transactions during 2005:

Jan. 17	Sold 750 common shares of Young Inc. for $36,000 less a brokerage fee of $180.
Mar. 3	Purchased 5,000 common shares of Allen Corp. for $300,000 plus a brokerage fee of $1,500. The shares represent a 30% ownership in Allen Corp.
May 12	Purchased 3,000 common shares of Beaton Inc. for $96,000, plus a brokerage fee of $400. The shares represent a 10% ownership in Beaton Inc.
Nov. 28	Purchased a 5% ownership in Davis Corp. by acquiring 10,000 common shares at a total of $89,000 plus a brokerage fee of $445.
Dec. 30	Sold 10,000 shares of Xavier Corporation for $160,000 less a brokerage fee of $800.
31	Allen Corp. announced a net profit of $280,000 for the year.

The market values of Johnson's investments at December 31, 2005, follow:

Allen Corp.	$418,000
Beaton Inc..	92,000
Davis Corp.	90,800
Young Inc.	38,200
Zed Corp.	31,000

Note: Assume any declines in market value are not temporary.

Required

1. Determine what amount should be reported on Johnson's December 31, 2005, balance sheet for its share investments.
2. Prepare a December 31, 2005, adjusting entry, if necessary, to record any LCM or market adjustments.
3. What amount of gain or loss on those transactions relating to securities should be reported on Johnson's December 31, 2005, income statement?

Check figure:
2. Unrealized loss on long-term investments, $9,000

Problem 18-5A
Accounting for share investments

LO⁵,⁶

Hamilton Ltd. was organized on January 2, 2005. The following investment transactions and events subsequently occurred:

> **2005**
> Jan. 6   Hamilton paid $575,500 for 50,000 shares (20%) of Ginto Inc. outstanding common shares.
> Apr. 30   Ginto declared and paid a cash dividend of $1.10 per share.
> Dec. 31   Ginto announced that its net income for 2005 was $480,000. Market value of the shares was $11.80 per share.
>
> **2006**
> Oct. 15   Ginto declared and paid a cash dividend of $0.70 per share.
> Dec. 31   Ginto announced that its net income for 2006 was $630,000. Market value of the shares was $12.18 per share.
>
> **2007**
> Jan. 5   Hamilton sold all of its investment in Ginto for $682,000 cash.

Part 1
Assume that Hamilton has a significant influence over Ginto with its 20% share.

Check figure:
2. Carrying value per share, $14.15

Required
1. Give the entries to record the preceding transactions in Hamilton's books.
2. Calculate the carrying value per share of Hamilton's investment as reflected in the investment account on January 4, 2007.
3. Calculate the change in Hamilton's equity from January 6, 2005, through January 5, 2007, resulting from its investment in Ginto.

Part 2
Assume that even though Hamilton owns 20% of Ginto's outstanding shares, a thorough investigation of the surrounding circumstances indicates that it does not have a significant influence over the investee.

Required
4. Give the entries to record the preceding transactions in Hamilton's books.
5. Calculate the cost per share of Hamilton's investment as reflected in the investment account on January 4, 2007.
6. Calculate the change in Hamilton's equity from January 6, 2005, through January 5, 2007, resulting from its investment in Ginto.

Problem 18-6A
Foreign currency transactions

LO^8

Lupold Inc. is a Canadian corporation that has customers in several foreign countries. The corporation had the following transactions in 2005 and 2006:

2005

May 22 Sold merchandise to Weishaar Imports of Holland for 15,000 euros on credit. The exchange rate for euros was $1.50041.

Aug. 25 Received Weishaar Imports' payment for its purchase of May 22, and exchanged the euros for dollars. The current exchange rate for euros was $1.53211.

Sep. 9 Sold merchandise to Campos Inc. of Mexico for $24,780 cash. The exchange rate for pesos was $0.114002 on this date.

Nov. 29 Sold merchandise on credit to ONI Corp. located in Japan. The price of 1.1 million yen was to be paid 60 days from the date of sale. The exchange rate for yen was $0.009195 on November 29.

Dec. 23 Sold merchandise for 158,000 ringgit to Martinique Corp. of Malaysia, payment in full to be received in 30 days. On this day, the foreign exchange rate for ringgit was $0.375521.

31 Prepared adjusting entries to recognize exchange gains or losses on the annual financial statements. Rates for exchanging foreign currencies on this day included the following:

Peso (Mexico)	$0.125226
Yen (Japan)	0.011867
Ringgit (Malaysia)	0.364473
Euro (EU)	1.52156

2006

Jan. 24 Received full payment from Martinique for the sale of December 23 and immediately exchanged the ringgit for dollars. The exchange rate for ringgit was $0.342125.

30 Received ONI's full payment for the sale of November 29 and immediately exchanged the yen for dollars. The exchange rate for yen was $0.012004.

Required

Preparation component:

1. Prepare General Journal entries to account for these transactions on Lupold's books. *Round calculations to the nearest whole cent.*

2. Calculate the foreign exchange gain or loss to be reported on Lupold's 2005 income statement.

Analysis component:

3. What actions might Lupold consider to reduce its risk of foreign exchange gains or losses?

Check figure:
2. Total foreign exchange gain, $1,669.11

*Problem 18-7A

Consolidated statements,
at acquisition and one year later

LO⁹

On January 1, 2005, Northwood Corporation purchased 80% of Souther Ltd.'s outstanding common shares at $48 per share. On that date, Northwood Corporation had retained earnings of $517,500. Souther Ltd. had retained earnings of $135,000 and had outstanding 15,000 common shares with a book value of $24 per share.

Part A

Required

1. Give the elimination entry to be used on a work sheet for a consolidated balance sheet dated January 1, 2005.
2. Determine the amount of consolidated retained earnings that should be shown on a consolidated balance sheet dated January 1, 2005.

Part B

During the year ended December 31, 2005, Northwood Corporation paid cash dividends of $67,500 and earned net income of $127,500 excluding earnings from its investment in Souther Ltd. Souther Ltd. earned net income of $63,000 and paid dividends of $30,000. Except for Northwood Corporation's Retained Earnings account and the Investment in Souther Ltd. account, the balance sheet accounts for the two corporations on December 31, 2005, are as follows:

	Northwood Corporation	Souther Ltd.
Assets		
Cash	$157,800	$124,200
Notes receivable	54,000	-0-
Merchandise	367,200	178,200
Building, net	348,000	216,000
Land	210,000	189,000
Investment in Souther Ltd.	?	-0-
Total assets	$?	$707,400
Liabilities and Shareholders' Equity		
Accounts payable	$439,500	$260,400
Notes payable	-0-	54,000
Common shares	672,000	225,000
Retained earnings	?	168,000
Total liabilities and shareholders' equity	$?	$707,400

Northwood Corporation lent $54,000 to Souther Ltd. during 2005, for which Souther Ltd. signed a note. On December 31, 2005, the note had not been repaid.

Check figure:

3. Investment in Souther Ltd., Dec. 31, 2005: $602,400

Required

3. Calculate Northwood Corporation's balance in the Investment in Souther Ltd. account at December 31, 2005.
4. Prepare a consolidated work sheet at December 31, 2005.

An asterisk (*) identifies assignment material based on Appendix 18A.

Kelly Systems Inc. had no temporary investments on December 31, 2005, but had the following transactions involving temporary investments in securities during 2006:

Problem 18-1B
Accounting for temporary investments

LO²

Feb.	5	Purchased 3,500 common shares of Sask Inc. at $29.50 plus a $2,507 brokerage fee.
	16	Paid $20,000 to buy six-month treasury bills with a principal amount of $20,000, paying 5%, dated February 16.
Apr.	7	Purchased 1,200 common shares of Gentra Inc. at $13.25 plus a $477 brokerage fee.
June	2	Purchased 2,500 common shares of Zycom Corp. at $32.75 plus a $2,865 brokerage fee.
	30	Received a $1.75 per share cash dividend on the Sask common shares.
Aug.	11	Sold 875 shares of the Sask common shares at $25.00 less a $531 brokerage fee.
	17	Received a cheque for the principal and accrued interest on the treasury bills purchased February 16.
	24	Received a $0.20 per share cash dividend on the Gentra common shares.
Dec.	18	Received a $0.45 per share cash dividend on the Gentra common shares.
	20	Received a $1.00 per share cash dividend on the remaining Sask common shares.

Required
Prepare General Journal entries to record the preceding transactions.

Edwards Ltd. has relatively large idle cash balances and invests them in securities that it holds as temporary investments. Following is a series of events and other facts relevant to the temporary investment activity of the company:

Problem 18-2B
Entries for temporary investments

LO²

2005		
Jan.	11	Paid $50,000 to buy 183-day treasury bills, $50,000 principal amount, 8% dated January 11.
Feb.	2	Purchased 600 common shares of BNR Corp. at $38.50 plus a $230 commission.
	13	Purchased 2,000 common shares of LR Inc. at $9.75 plus a $200 commission.
Mar.	2	Paid $25,000 for treasury notes, $25,000 principal amount, 9% dated March 2, 2005 and due September 2, 2005.
	27	Purchased 1,200 common shares of NT Inc. at $34.63 plus a $350 brokerage fee.
June	5	Received a $0.35 per share cash dividend on the BNR Corp. common shares.
	17	Sold 400 BNR Corp. common shares at $40.00 less a $160 brokerage fee.
July	13	Received a cheque for the principal and accrued interest on the treasury bills that matured on July 13.
Aug.	12	Received a $0.10 per share cash dividend on the LR Inc. common shares.
Sept.	2	Received a cheque for six months' interest plus principal on the treasury notes purchased on March 2.
	8	Received a $0.35 per share cash dividend on the remaining BNR Corp. common shares.
Nov.	12	Received a $0.25 per share cash dividend on the LR Inc. common shares.

On December 31, 2005, the market prices of the equity securities held by Edwards Ltd. were: BNR Corp., $40.13; LR Inc., $8.50; and NT Inc., $34.00.

Required
1. Prepare journal entries to record the temporary investment activity.
2. Prepare a schedule to calculate the lower of cost or market of Edwards Ltd.'s temporary investments.
3. Prepare adjusting entries, if necessary, to record accrued interest on Edwards Ltd.'s investments in debt obligations and to reduce the marketable equity securities to the lower of cost or market assuming there were no investments made prior to 2005.

Problem 18-3B
Accounting for long-term debt investments

LO⁴

Check figure:
Dec. 31 Investment Revenue $4,630

On January 1, 2005, Jake Inc. paid $92,905 to acquire bonds of Foster Inc. with a par value of $90,000. The annual contract rate on the bonds is 11% and interest is paid semi-annually on June 30 and December 31. The bonds mature after four years. The market rate of interest was 10%.

Required
Prepare Jake Inc.'s entries to record: (a) the purchase of the bonds, and (b) the receipt of the first two interest payments.

Problem 18-4B
Accounting for long-term investments

LO⁵, ⁶, ⁷

Bathurst Ltd.'s long-term investment portfolio at December 31, 2004, consisted of the following:

Long-Term Investments	Cost	Fair Market Value
45,000 shares of Roe Inc. common shares	$1,118,250	$1,136,250
17,000 shares of Shore Inc. common shares	616,760	586,500
22,000 shares of Tate Inc. common shares	294,470	303,600

On January 1, 2005, Bathurst's percentages of ownership of voting shares in Roe, Shore, and Tate were 12%, 6%, and 8% respectively. Bathurst made the following long-term investment transactions during 2005:

Jan. 17	Sold 4,250 of Shore Inc. common shares for $144,500 less a brokerage fee of $2,390.
Mar. 24	Purchased 31,000 of Uris Inc. common shares for $565,750 plus a brokerage fee of $9,900. The shares represent a 62% ownership in Uris Inc.
Apr. 5	Purchased 85,000 of Victor Inc. common shares for $267,750 plus a brokerage fee of $4,500. The shares represent a 10% ownership in Victor Inc.
Sept. 2	Sold 22,000 of Tate Inc. common shares for $313,500 less a brokerage fee of $5,400.
27	Purchased 5,000 of Wong Inc. common shares for $101,000 plus a brokerage fee of $2,100. The shares represent a 25% ownership in Wong Inc.
Oct. 30	Purchased 10,000 shares of Xplus Inc. common shares for $97,500 plus a brokerage fee of $2,340. The shares represent a 13% ownership in Xplus Inc.

The fair (market) values of Bathurst's investments at December 31, 2005, are:

Roe Inc.	$1,136,250
Shore Inc.	200,750*
Uris Inc.	545,600
Victor Inc.	269,875
Wong Inc.	109,375
Xplus Inc.	91,250

*Shore Inc.'s market value is believed to be permanently impaired.

Check figure:
2. Unrealized loss on long-term investments, $261,820

Required
1. Determine what amount should be reported on Bathurst's December 31, 2005, balance sheet for its share investments.
2. Prepare a December 31, 2005, adjusting entry, if necessary, to record any LCM or market adjustments.
3. What amount of gain or loss on those transactions relating to investments sold should be reported on Bathurst's December 31, 2005, income statement?

River Corporation was organized on January 2, 2005. River Corporation issued 50,000 common shares for $250,000 on that date. The following investment transactions and events subsequently occurred:

2005		
Jan. 12	River Corporation acquired 12,000 shares of Turner Ltd. at a cost of $250,000. This investment represented 24% of Turner's outstanding shares.	
Mar. 31	Turner Ltd. declared and paid a cash dividend of $1.00 per share.	
Dec. 31	Turner Ltd. announced that its net income for 2005 was $125,000.	
2006		
Aug. 15	Turner Ltd. declared and paid a cash dividend of $0.80 per share.	
Dec. 31	Turner Ltd. announced that its net loss for 2006 was $95,000.	
2007		
Jan. 6	River Corporation sold all of its investment in Turner Ltd. for $230,000 cash.	

Part 1

Assume that River Corporation has a significant influence over Turner Ltd. with its 24% share.

Required

1. Give the entries to record the preceding transactions in River Corporation's books.
2. Calculate the carrying value per share of River Corporation's investment as reflected in the investment account on January 1, 2007.
3. Calculate the change in River Corporation's equity from January 12, 2005, through January 6, 2007, resulting from its investment in Turner Ltd.

Part 2

Assume that even though River Corporation owns 24% of Turner Ltd.'s outstanding shares, a thorough investigation of the surrounding circumstances indicates that it does not have a significant influence over the investee.

Required

4. Give the entries to record the preceding transactions on the books of River Corporation.
5. Calculate the cost per share of River Corporation's investment as reflected in the investment account on January 1, 2007.
6. Calculate the change in River Corporation's equity from January 12, 2005, through January 6, 2007, resulting from its investment in Turner Ltd.

Check figure:
2. Carrying value per share, $19.63

Problem 18-6B
Foreign currency transactions

LO[8]

Global Enterprises Ltd. is a Canadian corporation that has customers in several foreign countries. It showed the following transactions for 2005 and 2006:

> **2005**
>
> July 13 Sold merchandise for 950,000 yen to Shisedu Inc. of Japan, with payment in full to be received in 60 days. On this day, the foreign exchange rate for yen was $0.012514.
>
> Aug. 21 Sold merchandise to Klaus Retailers of France for $9,500 cash. The foreign exchange rate for euros was $1.54189.
>
> Sept. 11 Received Shisedu Inc.'s payment for its purchase of July 13, and exchanged the yen for dollars. The current exchange rate for yen was $0.010681.
>
> Oct. 6 Sold merchandise on credit to Trafalgar Distributors, a company located in London, England. The price of £5,000 is to be paid 90 days from the date of sale. On October 6, the foreign exchange rate for pounds was $2.21694.
>
> Nov. 18 Sold merchandise for 30,000 Australian dollars to Belgique Suppliers of Australia, payment in full to be received in 60 days. The exchange rate for Australian dollars was $0.887613.
>
> Dec. 31 Prepared adjusting entries to recognize exchange gains or losses on the annual financial statements. Rates of exchanging foreign currencies on this day are:
>
> | | |
> |---|---|
> | Pounds (Britain) | $2.18455 |
> | Euro (EU) | 1.52156 |
> | Yen (Japan) | 0.011867 |
> | Dollar (Australia) | 0.898866 |
>
> **2006**
>
> Jan. 4 Received full payment from Trafalgar Distributors for the October 6 sale and immediately exchanged the pounds for dollars. The exchange rate for pounds was $2.22183.
>
>   17 Received full payment in Australian dollars from Belgique Suppliers for the sale of November 18 and immediately exchanged the Australian dollars for Canadian dollars. The exchange rate for Australian dollars was $0.88985.

Check figure:
2. Total foreign exchange loss, $1,565.71

Required

Preparation component:
1. Prepare General Journal entries to account for these transactions on the books of Global Enterprises. *Round calculations to the nearest whole cent.*
2. Calculate the foreign exchange gain or loss to be reported on Global Enterprises' 2005 income statement.

Analysis component:
What actions might Global Enterprises consider to reduce its risk of foreign exchange gains or losses?

*Problem 18-7B
Consolidated statements, at acquisition and one year later

LO[9]

Part A
On January 1, 2005, Larger Inc. purchased 90% of Smaller Inc.'s outstanding common shares at $24 per share. On that date, Larger Inc. had retained earnings of $350,500. Smaller Inc. had retained earnings of $225,000 and had 20,000 common shares outstanding at a book value of $21.25 per share.

Required
1. Give the elimination entry to be used on a work sheet for a consolidated balance sheet dated January 1, 2005.
2. Determine the amount of consolidated retained earnings that should be shown on a consolidated balance sheet dated January 1, 2005.

An asterisk (*) identifies assignment material based on Appendix 18A.

Part B

During the year ended December 31, 2005, Larger Inc. paid cash dividends of $45,000 and earned net income of $90,000 excluding earnings from its investment in Smaller Inc. Smaller Inc. earned net income of $45,000 and paid dividends of $25,000. Except for Larger Inc.'s Retained Earnings account and the Investment in Smaller Inc. account, the balance sheet accounts for the two companies on December 31, 2005, are as follows:

	Larger Inc.	Smaller Inc.
Assets		
Cash	$140,200	$106,800
Notes receivable	45,000	-0-
Merchandise	220,800	175,300
Building, net	284,250	240,000
Land	186,000	183,500
Investment in Smaller Company	?	
Total assets	$?	$705,600
Liabilities and Shareholders' Equity		
Accounts payable	$215,250	$215,600
Notes payable	-0-	45,000
Common shares	675,000	200,000
Retained earnings	?	245,000
Total liabilities and shareholders' equity	$?	$705,600

Larger Inc. lent $45,000 to Smaller Inc. during 2005, for which Smaller Inc. signed a note. On December 31, 2005, the note had not been repaid.

Required

3. Calculate the December 31, 2005, balances in Larger Inc.'s Investment in Smaller Inc. account and Retained Earnings account.
4. Complete a work sheet to consolidate the balance sheets of the two companies.

Check figure:
3. Investment in Smaller Inc., Dec. 31, 2005, $450,000

Analytical and Review Problems

On January 1, 2005, Hinke Ltd. purchased 30% of Deveau Ltd.'s outstanding common shares. The balance in Hinke Ltd.'s Investment in Deveau Ltd. account was $500,000 as of December 31, 2006. The following information is available for years 2005 and 2006 for Deveau Ltd.:

A & R 18-1

	Net Income	Dividends Paid
2005	$300,000	$100,000
2006	$400,000	$100,000

Required

Calculate the purchase price paid by Hinke Ltd. for Deveau Ltd. shares on January 1, 2005.

A & R 18-2

On January 2, Pedro Inc. purchased a 40% interest (7,500 shares) in Zapata Inc.'s common shares for $236,250. The following entries were recorded in 2005 and 2006.

2005			
June 8	Cash...	10,500	
	Dividend Revenue.....................................		10,500
	To record dividends received.		
Dec. 31	Investment in Zapata Inc.	26,250	
	Investment Revenue...............................		26,250
	To record increase in market value of Zapata shares.		
2006			
June 8	Cash...	10,500	
	Dividend Revenue.....................................		10,500
	To record dividends received.		
Dec. 31	Investment in Zapata Inc.	45,750	
	Investment Revenue...............................		45,750
	To record increase in market value of Zapata shares.		

Zapata Inc.'s results for 2005 and 2006 were as follows:

	2005	2006
Net Income..	$70,500	$52,500
Cash Dividends Paid............................	26,250	26,250

Required

a. Identify any errors you feel that Pedro Inc. may have made with respect to the entries shown in the problem.

b. Prepare any correcting entries as of December 31, 2006, assuming the books have not yet been closed.

A & R 18-3

Santana Corp. purchased 20, $1,000 par value, 10% bonds of Winston Corp. on May 1, 2005, intending to hold them for the long term. The bonds are due five and one-half years from the date of purchase. Interest is paid annually on November 1. Assume that any discount or premium on the bond investment is amortized using the straight-line method.

Required

Assume that Santana paid a total cash outlay of $17,040 to acquire the bonds and prepare entries on the following dates:

a. May 1, 2005,

b. November 1, 2005,

c. December 31, 2005 (year-end).

Ethics Challenge

EC 18-1

Jack Phelps is the controller for Jayhawk Corporation. Jayhawk has numerous long-term investments in debt securities. About 18 months ago, the company had significant amounts of idle cash that were invested in 10-year bonds. Management's intent was to dispose of the bonds within two years of the date of purchase. Jack is preparing the year-end financial statements. In accounting for investments, he knows he must designate each investment as temporary or long-term. Since the bonds were purchased, interest rates have risen sharply, meaning that the market values of the bonds have declined significantly. Jack earns a bonus each year that is calculated as a percent of the net income of the corporation.

Required

1. Will Jack's bonus be dependent in any way on the classification of the debt securities?
2. What criteria must Jack consider to classify the securities properly as temporary or long-term?
3. Are there any likely checks in the corporation to review the classification that Jack chooses for the securities?

Focus on Financial Statements

Delta Corporation showed the following adjusted trial balance at its year-end, December 31, 2005:

FFS 18-1

DELTA CORPORATION Adjusted Trial Balance December 31, 2005 (000s)	
Account	**Balance**[1]
Accounts payable	96
Accounts receivable	69
Accumulated amortization—equipment	76
Allowance for doubtful accounts	8
Cash	70
Cash dividends	40
Common shares	100
Cost of goods sold	395
Equipment	101
Fees earned	200
Income tax expense	52
Income taxes payable	7
Interest expense	5
Investment in Cornerstone Inc. common shares[2]	215
Investment in Delta Inc. bonds[3]	56
Investment income	134
Marketable securities[4]	38
Merchandise inventory	28
Notes payable, due March 2010	74
Operating expenses	218
Preferred shares	44
Prepaid rent	6
Retained earnings	82
Sales	460
Unearned fees	12

1. Assume all balances are normal.

2. The Cornerstone Inc. shares are intended to be held for the long term.

3. The Delta Inc. bonds are intended to be held for the long term.

4. The marketable securities are intended to be held for the short term.

Required

Using the information provided, prepare a single-step income statement, a statement of retained earnings, and a classified balance sheet, in thousands.

Reporting and Analyzing Cash Flows

Flying High

Calgary-based WestJet Airlines Ltd. is Canada's leading low-fare airline. Recently, airlines in general have been experiencing decreasing sales for a variety of reasons, but not WestJet. It realized a 42% increase in sales from the year ended December 31, 2001, to December 31, 2002, with a corresponding 41% increase in net income. Some other airlines are decreasing flights to cut costs, while WestJet is expanding its number of destinations to meet the increasing demand for its services. In order to satisfy this growth in its business, WestJet used $321 million of cash for aircraft additions plus another $24 million for other capital asset additions during 2002. The main sources of this cash were the issuance of debt and common shares: specifically, $190 million of long-term debt plus $85 million in common shares. So what is WestJet's secret? Prudent cash management.

WestJet's Director of Treasury Derek Payne says, "As the airline industry by nature is highly cyclical and capital intensive, it is imperative that airlines keep sufficient cash reserves on hand to fund day-to-day operations. Through the use of a mixture of debt, equity, and lease financing, WestJet has utilized appropriate levels of leverage to finance the growth of the airline, without sacrificing the overall strength of its balance sheet. Continuous monitoring of cash flow along with current and projected key financial ratios ensures the company plans financing options prudently. In addition, the strength of WestJet's balance sheet allows for a range of low-cost financing options and allows the company to secure future financing with ease."

In other words, Derek Payne and his colleagues at WestJet ensure cash flow strategies for the uncertainties of tomorrow are planned for today to keep WestJet flying high!

www.westjet.ca

Learning Objectives

LO¹ Explain the purpose and importance of cash flow information.

LO² Distinguish among operating, investing, and financing activities.

LO³ Identify and disclose non-cash investing and financing activities.

LO⁴ Describe the format of the cash flow statement.

LO⁵ Prepare a cash flow statement.

LO⁶ Calculate cash flows from operating activities using the direct method.

LO⁷ Determine cash flows from both investing and financing activities.

*APPENDIX 19A

*LO⁸ Calculate cash flows from operating activities using the indirect method.

Chapter Preview

Profitability is a primary goal of most managers, but it is not the only goal. A company cannot achieve or maintain profits without careful management of cash. Managers and other users of information pay close attention to a company's cash position and the transactions affecting cash. Information about these transactions is reported in the cash flow statement. This chapter explains how we prepare, analyze, and interpret a cash flow statement using the direct method recommended by the *CICA Handbook* P. 59 and by the indirect method that is entrenched in practice. It also discusses the importance of cash flow information for predicting future performance and making managerial decisions. Developing cash flow strategies based upon an understanding of the cash flow statement is especially important as described by Derek Payne, WestJet's Director of Treasury, in the opening article.

Basics of Cash Flow Reporting

This section describes the basics of cash flow reporting including its purpose, measurement, classification, format, and preparation.

Purpose of the Cash Flow Statement

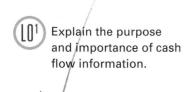

LO¹ Explain the purpose and importance of cash flow information.

The purpose of the **cash flow statement** (CFS) is to report detailed information about the major cash receipts (inflows) and cash payments (outflows) during a period. This includes separately identifying the cash flows related to operating, investing, and financing activities.

The cash flow statement helps financial statement users evaluate the liquidity and solvency of an enterprise and assess the enterprise's ability to generate cash from internal sources, to repay its liabilities, and to reinvest and to make distributions to owners.

We can examine balance sheets at the beginning and end of a year to determine by how much cash has changed, but the cash flow statement gives the details about individual cash flows that helps users answer questions such as:

- How does a company obtain its cash?
- Where does a company spend its cash?
- What is the change in the cash balance?

The cash flow statement addresses these important questions by summarizing, classifying, and reporting a company's periodic cash inflows and outflows; it is an analytical tool used to assess, evaluate, and analyze performance for decision making.

Importance of Cash Flows

Information about cash flows, and its inflows and outflows, can influence decision makers in important ways. For instance, we look more favourably at a company that is financing its expenditures with cash from operations than one that does it by selling its capital assets P. 149. Information about cash flows helps users decide whether a company has enough cash to:

- pay its existing debts as they mature,
- meet unexpected obligations,
- pursue unexpected opportunities
- plan day-to-day operating activities, and
- make long-term investment decisions.

There are many striking examples of how careful analysis and management of cash flows has led to improved financial stability. Call-Net Enterprises Inc., a Canadian telecommunications company, showed a turnaround in cash outflows from operating activities of $27.2 million for the year ended December 31, 2001, to a net cash inflow from operations of $6.1 million for 2002. Call-Net desperately needed to improve its cash flow and was able to do so without bankruptcy protection; instead, it engaged in aggressive cost-cutting measures. Air Canada, on the other hand, showed outflows from operations of $56 million for the quarter ended March 31, 2003, a $27 million deterioration relative to the same quarter in 2002.

Measuring Cash Flows

The cash flow statement details the difference between the beginning and ending balances of cash and *cash equivalents*. While we continue to use the terms *cash flows* and *cash flow statement*, we must remember that both terms refer to cash and cash equivalents.

A **cash equivalent**[1] is an investment that must be:

1. readily convertible to a known amount of cash, and
2. sufficiently close to its maturity date P.533 so its market value is not significantly affected by interest rate changes.

In most cases cash and cash equivalents include cash and temporary investments[2] of three months or less from the date of acquisition. Share investments are not included as cash equivalents because their values are subject to risk of changes in market prices. Cash subject to restrictions that prevent its use for current purposes, such as compensating balances, is also excluded from cash equivalents. Classifying short-term, highly liquid investments as cash equivalents is based on the idea that companies make these investments to earn a return on idle cash balances, yet they can be converted into cash quickly.

Classifying Cash Flows

All individual cash receipts and payments (except cash paid/received for the purchase/sale of cash equivalents) are classified and reported on the statement as operating, investing, or financing activities. A net cash inflow (source) occurs when the receipts in a category exceed the payments. A net cash outflow (use) occurs when the payments in a category exceed receipts.

 Distinguish among operating, investing, and financing activities.

Operating Activities

Operating activities are the principal revenue generating activities of the enterprise.[3] They include the cash effects of transactions that determine net income. But not all items in income, such as unusual gains and losses, are operating activities. We discuss these exceptions later in the chapter.

---

[1] *CICA Handbook* section 1540, "Cash Flow Statements (CFS)," was issued in June 1998 to replace the previously required "Statement of Changes in Financial Position (SCFP)." The revised section is based on International Accounting Standard 7—Cash Flow Statements. The *CICA Handbook* defines cash equivalents as, "short-term, highly liquid investments that are readily convertible to known amounts of cash and which are subject to an insignificant risk of changes in value."

[2] In recent years, cash equivalents have been determined net of short-term borrowings. Short-term borrowings will no longer be deducted.

[3] *CICA Handbook*, section 1540, par. 06.

Examples of **operating activities** are the production and purchase of merchandise, the sale of goods and services to customers, and administrative expenses of the business. Changes in current assets and current liabilities are normally the result of operating activities. Exhibit 19.1 lists the more common cash inflows and outflows from operating activities.

Exhibit 19.1

Cash Flows from Operating Activities

Cash Inflows	Cash Outflows
From customers' cash sales	To employees for salaries and wages
From collection on credit sales	To suppliers for goods and services
From cash dividends received	To governments for taxes and fines
From borrowers for interest	To lenders for interest
From suppliers for refunds	To customers for refunds
From lawsuit settlements	To charities

Investing Activities

Investing activities include the:

a. purchase and sale of capital assets,
b. purchase and sale of investments, other than cash equivalents, and
c. lending and collecting on loans (receivables).

Changes in long-term assets are normally caused by investing activities. Exhibit 19.2 lists examples of cash flows from investing activities. Proceeds from collecting the principal P.533 amounts of loans deserve special attention. If the loan results from sales to customers, its cash receipts are classed as operating activities whether short-term or long-term. But if the loan results from a loan to another party, then its cash receipts from collecting the principal of the note are classed as an investing activity. Collection of interest on a loan, however, is not reported as an investing activity but rather as an operating activity.

Exhibit 19.2

Cash Flows from Investing Activities*

Cash Inflows	Cash Outflows
From selling long-term productive assets	To purchase long-term productive assets
From selling equity investments	To purchase equity investments
From selling debt investments	To purchase debt investments
From collecting principal on loans	To make loans
From selling (discounting) of loans	

*Investing activities exclude transactions in trading securities.

Financing Activities

Financing activities are those that affect a company's owners and creditors. They include (a) obtaining cash from issuing debt and repaying the amounts borrowed, and (b) obtaining cash from or distributing cash to owners. Transactions with creditors that affect net income are classified as operating activities. For example, interest expense on a company's debt is classified as an operating rather than a financing activity because interest is deducted as an expense in calculating net income. Also, cash payments to settle credit purchases of merchandise, whether on account or by note, are operating activities because they are more related to a company's ongoing operations. Changes in long-term debt and equity and short-term debt not involving operating activities are normally a result of financing activities. Exhibit 19.3 lists examples of cash flows from financing activities.

Cash Inflows	Cash Outflows
From issuing its own shares	To pay cash dividends to shareholders
From issuing bonds and notes	To repurchase shares
From issuing short- and long-term liabilities	To repay cash loans
	To cover withdrawals by owners

Exhibit 19.3

Cash Flows from Financing Activities

Non-Cash Investing and Financing Activities

Companies sometimes enter into direct exchange transactions in which non-current balance sheet items are exchanged but cash is not affected. Yet because of their importance and the full disclosure principle P. 358, these important non-cash investing and financing activities are disclosed in a note to the cash flow statement. One example of such a transaction is the purchase of long-term assets by giving a long-term note payable. Exhibit 19.4 lists some transactions that are disclosed as non-cash investing and financing activities.[4]

 Identify and disclose non-cash investing and financing activities.

- Retirement of debt by issuing shares.
- Conversion of preferred shares P. 766 to common shares.
- Purchase of long-term asset by issuing note payable.
- Exchange of non-cash assets for other non-cash assets.
- Purchase of non-cash assets by issuing shares or debt.
- Declaration and issuance of share dividend.

Exhibit 19.4

Examples of Non-Cash Investing and Financing Activities

To illustrate, let's assume Burton Company purchases machinery for $12,000 by paying cash of $5,000 and trading in old machinery with a market value of $7,000. The cash flow statement reports only the $5,000 cash outflow for the purchase of machinery. This means the $12,000 investing transaction is only partially described in the body of the cash flow statement. Yet this information is potentially important to users in that it changes the makeup of assets.

Companies disclose non-cash investing and financing activities not reported in the body of the cash flow statement in either (1) a note, or (2) a separate schedule attached to the statement. In the case of Burton Company, it could either describe the transaction in a note or include a small schedule at the bottom of its statement that lists the $12,000 asset investment along with financing of $5,000 and a $7,000 trade-in of old machinery.

---

[4] *CICA Handbook*, section 1540, par. 47.

Judgement Call

Answer—p. 995

Community Activist

You are a community activist trying to raise public awareness of pollution emitted by a local manufacturer. The manufacturer complains about the high costs of pollution controls and points to its recent $4 million annual loss as evidence. But you also know its net cash flows were a positive $8 million this past year. How are these results possible?

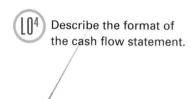

LO⁴ Describe the format of the cash flow statement.

Format of the Cash Flow Statement

Accounting standards require companies to include a cash flow statement in a complete set of financial statements. Refer to the cash flow statement that forms part of WestJet's complete set of financial statements in Appendix I at the end of the textbook.

Exhibit 19.5 shows us the usual format that reports cash inflows and cash outflows from three activities: operating, investing, and financing. The statement explains how transactions affect the beginning-of-period cash (and cash equivalents) balance to produce its end-of-period balance.

Exhibit 19.5

Format of the Cash Flow Statement

Company Name
Cash Flow Statement
Period Covered

Cash flows from operating activities:
 [List of individual inflows and outflows]
 Net cash inflow (outflow) from operating activities .... $ ###
Cash flows from investing activities:
 [List of individual inflows and outflows]
 Net cash inflow (outflow) from investing activities ....   ###
Cash flows from financing activities:
 [List of individual inflows and outflows]
 Net cash inflow (outflow) from financing activities ....   ###
Net increase (decrease) in cash (and cash equivalents) .... $ ###

Cash (and cash equivalents) balance at beginning of period ....   ###
Cash (and cash equivalents) balance at end of period .... $ ###

Note disclosure of *non-cash investing and financing transactions*, for example, "Note 4. Purchased new equipment by issuing bonds"

Flashback

Answers—p. 995

1. Does a cash flow statement disclose payments of cash to purchase cash equivalents? Does it disclose receipts of cash from selling cash equivalents?
2. Identify the categories of cash flows reported separately on the cash flow statement.
3. Identify the category for each of the following cash flow activities: (a) purchase of equipment for cash; (b) payment of wages; (c) issuance of common shares for cash; (d) receipt of cash dividends from share investment; (e) collection of cash from customers; (f) issuance of bonds for cash.

Preparing the Cash Flow Statement

The information we need to prepare a cash flow statement comes from:

- comparative balance sheets at the beginning and end of the period,
- an income statement for the period, and
- a careful analysis of additional information.

Preparation of a cash flow statement involves five steps:

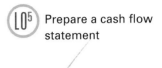

LO⁵ Prepare a cash flow statement

1. Calculate the net increase or decrease in cash and cash equivalents;
2. Calculate and report net cash inflows (outflows) from operating activities using either the
   a. direct or
   b. indirect method.
3. Calculate and report net cash inflows (outflows) from investing activities.
4. Calculate and report net cash inflows (outflows) from financing activities.
5. Calculate net cash flow by combining net cash inflows (outflows) from operating, investing, and financing activities and then prove it by adding it to the beginning cash balance to show it equals the ending cash balance.

Non-cash investing and financing activities are disclosed in a note to the statement or in a separate schedule to the statement, as shown at the bottom of Exhibit 19.5.

The remaining sections of this chapter explain these important steps in preparing the cash flow statement using the 2005 income statement of Genesis Corp. along with its December 31, 2004 and 2005, balance sheets shown in Exhibit 19.6. Our objective with the cash flow statement is to explain the increase or decrease in cash during 2005.

Exhibit 19.6

Financial Statements

In addition to providing its income statement and comparative balance sheet, Genesis Corp. also discloses additional information about year 2005 transactions:

a. All accounts payable balances result from merchandise purchases.

b. Capital assets costing $70,000 are purchased by paying $10,000 cash and issuing $60,000 of bonds payable.

c. Capital assets with an original cost of $30,000 and accumulated amortization of $12,000 are sold for $12,000 cash. This yields a $6,000 loss.

d. Proceeds from issuing 3,000 common shares are $15,000.

e. Paid $18,000 to retire bonds with a book value of $34,000. This yields a $16,000 gain from bond retirement.

f. Cash dividends of $14,000 are declared and paid.

GENESIS CORP.
Income Statement
For Year Ended December 31, 2005

Sales		$ 590,000
Cost of goods sold	$300,000	
Wages and other operating expenses	216,000	
Interest expense	7,000	
Income taxes expense	15,000	
Amortization expense	24,000	(562,000)
Loss on sale of capital assets		(6,000)
Gain on retirement of bonds		16,000
Net income		$ 38,000

GENESIS CORP.
Balance Sheet
December 31, 2005 and 2004

	2005	2004
Assets		
Current assets:		
Cash	$ 17,000	$ 12,000
Accounts receivable	60,000	40,000
Merchandise inventory	84,000	70,000
Prepaid expenses	6,000	4,000
Total current assets	$167,000	$126,000
Long-term assets:		
Capital assets	$250,000	$210,000
Less: Accumulated amortization	(60,000)	(48,000)
Total assets	$357,000	$288,000
Liabilities		
Current liabilities:		
Accounts payable	$ 35,000	$ 40,000
Interest payable	3,000	4,000
Income taxes payable	22,000	12,000
Total current liabilities	$ 60,000	$ 56,000
Long-term liabilities:		
Bonds payable	90,000	64,000
Total liabilities	$150,000	$120,000
Shareholders' Equity		
Contributed capital:		
Common shares	$ 95,000	$ 80,000
Retained earnings	112,000	88,000
Total shareholders' equity	207,000	168,000
Total liabilities and shareholders' equity	$357,000	$288,000

1. Calculate the Net Increase or Decrease in Cash

The increase or decrease in cash equals the current period's cash balance minus the prior period's cash balance. This is the *bottom line* figure for the cash flow statement and is a helpful check on the accuracy of our work. To illustrate, the summarized cash account of Genesis Corp. in Exhibit 19.7 shows a net increase in cash of $5,000 for the year ended December 31, 2005 ($17,000 balance, Dec. 31, 2005, less the $12,000 balance, Dec. 31, 2004).

Exhibit 19.7
Summarized Cash Account

Summarized Cash Account

Balance, Dec. 31/04	12,000		
Receipts from customers	570,000	319,000	..........Payments for merchandise
Proceeds from asset sales	12,000		Payments for wages and
Proceeds from share issuance	15,000	218,000	....................operating expenses
		8,000	........................Interest payments
		5,000	.............................Tax payments
		10,000	.................Payments for assets
		18,000	............Payments to retire bonds
		14,000	....................Dividend payments
Balance, Dec. 31/05	17,000		

2. Calculate and Report Net Cash Inflows (Outflows) from Operating Activities

On the income statement, net income is calculated using accrual basis accounting P. 140. Accrual basis accounting recognizes revenues when earned and expenses when incurred. But revenues and expenses do not necessarily coincide with the receipt and payment of cash. Both the *direct* and *indirect* methods convert accrual net income to the same amount of cash provided by operating activities. The CICA recommends and encourages the use of the direct method because it provides greater detail regarding operating cash flows. The **direct method** separately lists each major item of operating cash receipts (such as cash received from customers) and each major item of operating cash payments (such as cash paid for merchandise). The cash payments are subtracted from cash receipts to determine the net cash inflows (outflows) from operating activities. The operating activities section is a restatement of net income from an accrual basis (as reported on the income statement) to a cash basis.

The **indirect method** calculates the net cash inflows (outflows) from operating activities by adjusting accrual net income to a cash basis. Unlike the direct method, it does not report individual items of cash inflows and cash outflows from operating activities. Instead, the indirect method reports the necessary adjustments to reconcile net income to net cash inflows (outflows) from operating activities.

Although the direct method is *recommended* by the CICA, the indirect method is still used by many companies because the direct method is not *required*. We illustrate the direct method in this chapter by preparing the operating activities section of the cash flow statement for Genesis. The indirect method will be demonstrated in Appendix 19A.

Extend Your Knowledge

19-1

Direct Method of Reporting Operating Cash Flows

LO⁶ Calculate cash flows from operating activities using the direct method.

We calculate cash flows from operating activities under the direct method by adjusting accrual based income statement items to a cash basis. The usual approach is to adjust income statement accounts related to operating activities for changes in their related balance sheet accounts:

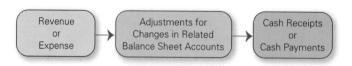

In preparing the operating section for Genesis Corp. using the direct method as highlighted in Exhibit 19.8, we first look at its cash receipts and then its cash payments drawing on the income statement and balance sheets in Exhibit 19.6.

Exhibit 19.8

Cash Flow Statement— Direct Method of Reporting Operating Cash Flows

Genesis Corp.
Cash Flow Statement
For Year Ended December 31, 2005

Cash flows from operating activities:		
Cash received from customers...	$ 570,000	
Cash paid for merchandise	(319,000)	
Cash paid for wages and other operating expenses.................	(218,000)	
Cash paid for interest..	(8,000)	
Cash paid for taxes	(5,000)	
Net cash inflow from operating activities		$20,000
Cash flows from investing activities:		
Cash received from sale of capital assets................................	$ 12,000	
Cash paid for purchase of capital assets..................................	(10,000)	
Net cash inflow from investing activities		2,000
Cash flows from financing activities:		
Cash received from issuing shares	$ 15,000	
Cash paid to retire bonds...	(18,000)	
Cash paid for dividends...	(14,000)	
Net cash outflow from financing activities................................		(17,000)
Net increase in cash...		$ 5,000
Cash balance at beginning of 2005		12,000
Cash balance at end of 2005		$17,000

Note: Non-cash investing and financing activity
During the period capital assets were acquired with issuance of $60,000 of bonds.

Operating Cash Receipts

Exhibit 19.6 and the additional information from Genesis identify only one potential cash receipt—that of sales to customers. This section starts with sales from the income statement and adjusts it as necessary to give us cash received from customers.

Cash Received from Customers   If all sales are for cash, the amount of cash received from customers is equal to sales. But when sales are on account, we must adjust the amount of sales revenue for the change in Accounts Receivable. For example, an increase in Accounts Receivable must be deducted from sales because sales revenue relating to Accounts Receivable has been recorded for which the cash has not yet been received. This is shown in Exhibit 19.9.

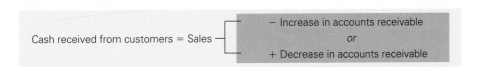

Exhibit 19.9

Formula to Calculate Cash
Received from Customers—
Direct Method

It is often helpful to use *account analysis* for this purpose. To illustrate, the T-account below reconstructs the cash receipts and payments. The balance sheet in Exhibit 19.6 shows that the beginning balance is $40,000 and the ending balance is $60,000. The income statement shows sales of $590,000.

Accounts Receivable			
Balance, Dec. 31/04	40,000		
Sales	590,000	570,000	= Collections
Balance, Dec. 31/05	60,000		

Cash receipts from customers are $570,000, calculated as $40,000 + $590,000 − [?] = $60,000. As summarized in Exhibit 19.9, this calculation can be rearranged to express cash received as equal to sales of $590,000 less a $20,000 increase in accounts receivable.

The cash flow statement for Genesis in Exhibit 19.8 reports the $570,000 cash received from customers as a cash inflow from operating activities.

Other Cash Receipts   While cash receipts of Genesis are limited to collections from customers, we sometimes see other types of cash receipts involving rent, interest, and dividends. We calculate cash received from these items by subtracting an increase or adding a decrease in the related receivable.

Operating Cash Payments

Exhibit 19.6 and the additional information from Genesis identify four operating expenses. We analyze each of these expenses to calculate its operating cash payment for the cash flow statement.

Cash Paid for Merchandise   We calculate cash paid for merchandise by analyzing both cost of goods sold and merchandise inventory. When the balances of Merchandise Inventory and Accounts Payable change, we must adjust cost of goods sold for changes in both of these accounts to calculate cash paid for merchandise. This adjustment has two steps. First, we use the change in the balance of Merchandise Inventory along with the amount of cost of goods sold to calculate cost of purchases for the period. An increase in inventory implies that we bought more than was sold and we add the increase in inventory to cost of goods sold to calculate cost of purchases. A decrease in inventory implies that we bought less than was sold and we subtract the decrease in inventory from cost of goods sold to calculate cost of purchases.

The second step uses the change in the balance of Accounts Payable along with the amount of cost of purchases to calculate cash paid for merchandise. A decrease in Accounts Payable implies that we paid for more goods than were acquired this period and we add the Accounts Payable change to cost of purchases to calculate cash paid for merchandise. An increase in Accounts Payable implies that we paid for less than the amount of goods acquired, and we subtract the Accounts Payable change from purchases to calculate cash paid for merchandise.

First, we use account analysis of merchandise inventory to calculate cost of purchases. We do this by reconstructing the Merchandise Inventory account:

Merchandise Inventory			
Balance, Dec. 31/04	70,000		
Purchases =	314,000	300,000	Cost of goods sold
Balance, Dec. 31/05	84,000		

The beginning balance is $70,000, and its ending balance is $84,000. The income statement shows cost of goods sold is $300,000. We can then determine the cost of purchases as $314,000 (equal to cost of goods sold of $300,000 plus the $14,000 increase in inventory).

Our second step is to calculate cash paid for merchandise by adjusting purchases for the change in accounts payable. Reconstructing Accounts Payable:

Accounts Payable			
		40,000	Balance, Dec. 31/04
Payments =	319,000	314,000	Purchases
		35,000	Balance, Dec. 31/05

This account shows us that its beginning balance of $40,000 plus purchases of $314,000 minus an ending balance of $35,000 gives us cash paid of $319,000 (or $40,000 + $314,000 − [?] = $35,000). Alternatively, we can express cash paid for merchandise as equal to purchases of $314,000 plus the $5,000 decrease in accounts payable.

We summarize the two-step adjustment to cost of goods sold to calculate cash paid for merchandise in Exhibit 19.10.

Exhibit 19.10

Two Steps to Calculate Cash Paid for Merchandise— Direct Method

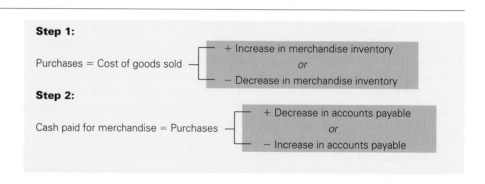

Exhibit 19.8 shows that the $319,000 cash paid by Genesis for merchandise is reported on the cash flow statement as a cash outflow for operating activities.

Cash Paid for Wages and Operating Expenses (Excluding Amortization) and Other Non-Cash Expenses   The income statement of Genesis shows wages and other operating expenses of $216,000 (see Exhibit 19.6). To calculate cash paid for wages and other operating expenses, we adjust this amount for changes in their related balance sheet accounts.

We begin by looking for prepaid expenses and accrued liabilities relating to wages and other operating expenses in the beginning and ending balance sheets of Genesis in Exhibit 19.6. These balance sheets show that Genesis has prepaid expenses but no accrued liabilities. This means its adjustment to this expense item is limited to the change in prepaid expenses. The amount of adjustment is calculated by assuming all cash paid for wages and other operating expenses is initially debited to Prepaid Expenses. This assumption allows us to reconstruct the Prepaid Expenses account:

Prepaid Expenses			
Balance, Dec. 31/04	4,000		
Payments =	218,000		Wages and other
		216,000	operating expenses
Balance, Dec. 31/05	6,000		

This account shows that prepaid expenses increased by $2,000 in the period. This means cash paid for wages and other operating expenses exceeded the reported expense by $2,000. Alternatively, we can express cash paid for wages and other operating expenses of Genesis as equal to its expenses of $216,000 plus the $2,000 increase in prepaid expenses.

Exhibit 19.11 summarizes the adjustments to wages (including salaries) and other operating expenses. While the balance sheet of Genesis did not report accrued liabilities, we add these to the exhibit to explain the adjustment to cash when they do exist. If accrued liabilities decrease, it implies we paid for more goods or services than received this period, and we must add the change in accrued liabilities to the expense amount to get cash paid for these goods or services. If accrued liabilities increase, it implies we paid less than was acquired and we must subtract the change in accrued liabilities from the expense amount to get cash paid.

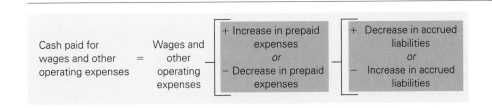

Exhibit 19.11

Formula to Calculate Cash Paid for Wages and Operating Expenses— Direct Method

Cash Paid for Both Interest and Income Taxes   Our analysis for calculating operating cash flows for interest and taxes is similar to that for operating expenses. Both require adjustments to the amounts on the income statement for changes in their related balance sheet accounts.

We begin with the income statement of Genesis showing interest expense of $7,000 and income taxes expense of $15,000. To calculate the cash paid, we adjust interest expense for the change in interest payable and we adjust income taxes expense for the change in income taxes payable. These calculations involve reconstructing both liability accounts:

Interest Payable				Income Taxes Payable			
		4,000	Balance, Dec. 31/04			12,000	Balance, Dec. 31/04
Interest paid =	8,000	7,000	Interest expense	Income taxes paid =	5,000	15,000	Income taxes expense
		3,000	Balance, Dec. 31/05			22,000	Balance, Dec. 31/05

These accounts reveal cash paid for interest of $8,000 and cash paid for income taxes of $5,000. The formulas to calculate these amounts are shown in Exhibit 19.12.

Exhibit 19.12

Formulas to Calculate Cash Paid for Both Interest and Taxes—Direct Method

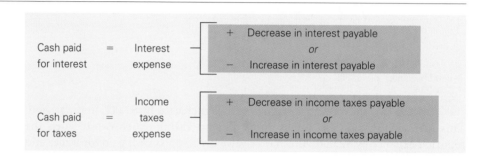

Both of these cash payments are reported as operating cash outflows on the cash flow statement for Genesis in Exhibit 19.8.

Analysis of Other Operating Expenses

Genesis reports three other operating expenses on its income statement: $24,000 of amortization, a $6,000 loss on sale of assets, and a $16,000 gain on retirement of debt. We consider each of these for its potential cash effects.

Amortization Expense   Amortization expense for Genesis is $24,000. It is known as a non-cash expense because there are no cash flows associated with amortization. Amortization expense is an allocation of the amortizable cost of a purchased asset. The cash outflow associated with purchasing a capital asset is reported as part of investing activities when it is paid. This means amortization expense is never reported on a cash flow statement using the direct method.

Loss on Sale of Assets   Sales of assets frequently result in gains and losses reported as part of net income. But the amount of recorded gain or loss does not reflect cash flows in these transactions. Asset sales result in cash inflow equal to the actual cash received, regardless of whether the asset was sold at a gain or a loss. This cash inflow is reported under investing activities. This means the loss or gain on a sale of assets is never reported on a cash flow statement using the direct method.

Gain on Retirement of Bonds   Retirements of bonds usually yield gains and losses reported as part of net income. But the amount of recorded gain or loss does not reflect cash flows in these transactions. Bond retirement results in cash outflow equal to the actual amount paid to settle the bond, regardless of whether the bond was retired at a gain or loss. This cash outflow is reported under financing activities. This means the loss or gain from retirement of a bond is never reported on a cash flow statement using the direct method.

Direct Method Format of Operating Activities Section

Exhibit 19.8 shows the cash flow statement for Genesis using the direct method. Major items of cash inflows and cash outflows are listed separately in the operating activities section. The format requires that operating cash outflows be subtracted from operating cash inflows to get net cash inflows (outflows) from operating activities.

4. Is the direct or indirect method of reporting operating cash flows more informative? Explain. Which method is more common in practice?

5. Net sales in a period are $590,000, beginning accounts receivable are $120,000, and ending accounts receivable are $90,000. What amount is collected from customers in the period?

6. The Merchandise Inventory account balance decreases in a period from a beginning balance of $32,000 to an ending balance of $28,000. Cost of goods sold for the period is $168,000. If the Accounts Payable balance increases $2,400 in the period, what is the amount of cash paid for merchandise?

7. Reported wages and other operating expenses incurred total $112,000. At the end of the prior year, prepaid expenses totalled $1,200, and this year the balance is $4,200. The current balance sheet shows wages payable of $5,600, whereas last year's did not show any accrued liabilities. How much is paid for wages and other operating expenses this year?

Flashback

Answers—p. 995

Mid-Chapter Demonstration Problem

Mitchell Corporation
Comparative Balance Sheet Information

Assets	Dec. 31, 2005	Dec. 31, 2004
Cash	$ 15,000	$ 20,000
Accounts receivable	23,000	25,000
Merchandise inventory	37,000	34,000
Prepaid expenses	6,000	8,000
Long-term investments	39,000	40,000
Capital assets	191,000	170,000
Accumulated amortization	(31,000)	(25,000)
Total assets	$280,000	$272,000
Liabilities and Shareholders' Equity		
Accounts payable	$ 38,000	$ 30,000
Accrued liabilities	68,000	65,000
Bonds payable	100,000	90,000
Common shares	40,000	37,000
Retained earnings	34,000	50,000
Total liabilities and shareholders' equity	$280,000	$272,000

Mitchell Corporation Income Statement For Year Ended December 31, 2005	
Sales	$250,000
Cost of goods sold	165,000
Gross profit	$ 85,000
Operating expenses	40,000
Operating income before taxes	$ 45,000
Gain on sale of investment	8,000
Income before taxes	$ 53,000
Income taxes	14,800
Net income	$ 38,200

Required

a. Calculate sales adjusted to a cash basis.

b. Calculate cost of goods sold adjusted to a cash basis.

c. How much cash was paid for operating expenses?

d. How much cash was provided by operating activities?

SOLUTION TO Mid-Chapter Demonstration Problem

a.

Sales revenue reported per income statement	$250,000	
Adjustments to cash basis:		
Decrease in accounts receivable	2,000	(source of cash)
Sales adjusted to a cash basis	$252,000	

b.

Cost of goods sold per income statement	$165,000	
Adjustments to cash basis:		
Increase in inventory	3,000	(use of cash)
Increase in accounts payable	(8,000)	(source of cash)
Cost of goods sold adjusted to a cash basis	$160,000	

c.

Operating expenses per income statement	$ 40,000	
Adjustments to a cash basis:		
Decrease in prepaid expenses	(2,000)	(non-cash expense)
Increase in accrued liabilities	(3,000)	(increase in expense not using cash)
Amortization	(6,000)	(non-cash expense)
Cash paid for operating expenses	$ 29,000	

d.

Sales adjusted to a cash basis	$252,000
Less: Cost of goods sold adjusted to a cash basis	(160,000)
Cash paid for operating expenses	(29,000)
Cash paid for income tax	(14,800)
Cash inflow from operating activities	$ 48,200

3. Cash Flows from Investing Activities

The third major step in preparing the cash flow statement is to calculate and report net cash flows from investing activities. We normally do this by identifying changes in all non-current asset accounts. Changes in these accounts are then analyzed using available information to determine their effect, if any, on cash. Results of this analysis are reported in the investing activities section of the statement. *Reporting of investing activities is identical under the direct method and indirect method.*

  Determine cash flows from both investing and financing activities.

Investing activities include transactions such as those listed in Exhibit 19.2. Information to calculate cash flows from investing activities is usually taken from beginning and ending balance sheets and from the income statement. Information provided earlier in the chapter about the transactions of Genesis reveals it both purchased and sold capital assets during the period. Both transactions are investing activities.

Capital Asset Transactions

We use a three-step process in determining net cash inflows (outflows) from investing activities: (1) identify changes in investing-related accounts; (2) explain these changes using reconstruction analysis; (3) report cash flow effects.

For capital assets, we need to deal with both the Capital Asset account and its related Accumulated Amortization account. Comparative balance sheet information for these accounts is in Exhibit 19.6. The first step reveals a $40,000 increase in capital assets from $210,000 to $250,000, and a $12,000 increase in accumulated amortization from $48,000 to $60,000. We need to explain these changes.

The second step begins by reviewing ledger accounts and any additional information at our disposal. A capital asset account is affected by both purchases and sales of capital assets. An accumulated amortization account is increased by amortization and reduced by removing accumulated amortization on asset disposals. Items (b) and (c) from the additional information reported with Exhibit 19.6 on page 980 for Genesis are relevant for these accounts. To explain changes in these accounts and to help us understand the cash flows effects, we prepare *reconstructed entries*. A reconstructed entry is our reproduction of an entry from a transaction, *it is not the actual entry made by the preparer.* Item (b) reports that Genesis purchased capital assets costing $70,000 by issuing $60,000 in bonds payable to the seller and paying $10,000 in cash. The reconstructed entry for our analysis of item (b) is:

Capital Assets	70,000	
Bonds Payable		60,000
Cash		**10,000**

This entry reveals a $10,000 cash outflow for assets purchased. It also reveals a non-cash investing and financing transaction involving $60,000 bonds given up for $60,000 of capital assets.

Item (c) on page 980 reports that Genesis sold capital assets costing $30,000 (with $12,000 of accumulated amortization) for cash received of $12,000, resulting in a loss of $6,000. The reconstructed entry for item (c) is:

Cash	**12,000**	
Accumulated Amortization	12,000	
Loss on Sale of Capital Assets	6,000	
Capital Assets		30,000

This entry reveals a $12,000 cash inflow for assets sold. The $6,000 loss is calculated by comparing the asset book value to the cash received, and does not reflect any cash inflow or outflow.

We can also reconstruct the entry for amortization expense using information from the income statement:

Amortization Expense..	24,000	
Accumulated Amortization...		24,000

This entry shows that amortization expense results in no cash flow effects.

These reconstructed entries are reflected in the ledger accounts for both capital assets and accumulated amortization.

Capital Assets				
Balance, Dec. 31/04	210,000			
Purchases	70,000	30,000		Sale
Balance, Dec. 31/05	250,000			

Accumulated Amortization, Capital Assets				
			48,000	Balance, Dec. 31/04
Sale		12,000	24,000	Amort. expense
			60,000	Balance, Dec. 31/05

In performing an actual cash flow analysis we have the entire ledger and additional information at our disposal. Here, for brevity, we are given the additional information for reconstructing accounts and verifying that our analysis of the investing-related accounts is complete.

The third step is to make the necessary disclosures on the cash flow statement. Disclosure of the two cash flow effects in the investing section of the statement appears as (also see Exhibit 19.8):

Genesis Corp.
Cash Flow Statement
For Year Ended December 31, 2005

Cash flows from investing activities:
Cash received from sale of capital assets................................. $ 12,000
Cash paid for purchase of capital assets................................. (10,000)

Note: Non-cash investing and financing activity
During the period capital assets were acquired with issuance of $60,000 of bonds.

The $60,000 portion of the purchase described in item (b) on page 980 and financed by issuance of bonds is a non-cash investing and financing activity and can be reported in a note to the statement as shown above.

We have now reconstructed these accounts by explaining how the beginning balances of both accounts are affected by purchases, sales, and amortization in yielding their ending balances.

Flashback
Answer—p. 995

8. Equipment costing $80,000 with accumulated amortization of $30,000 is sold at a loss of $10,000. What is the cash receipt from the sale? In what category of the cash flow statement is it reported?

4. Cash Flows from Financing Activities

The fourth step in preparing the cash flow statement is to calculate and report net cash flows from financing activities. We normally do this by identifying changes in all notes payable (current and non-current), non-current liabilities, and equity accounts. These accounts include Long-Term Debt, Notes Payable, Bonds Payable, Owner's Capital, Common Shares, and Retained Earnings. Changes in these accounts are then analyzed using available information to determine their effect, if any, on cash. Results of this analysis are reported in the financing activities section of the statement. *Reporting of financing activities is identical under the direct method and indirect method.*

Financing activities include those described in Exhibit 19.3. Information provided on page 980 about the transactions of Genesis reveals four transactions involving financing activities. We already analyzed one of these, the $60,000 issuance of bonds payable to purchase capital assets as a non-cash investing and financing activity. The remaining three transactions are retirement of bonds, issuance of common shares P. 764, and payment of cash dividends. We again use a three-step process in determining net cash inflows (outflows) from financing activities: (1) identify changes in financing-related accounts; (2) explain these changes using reconstruction analysis; and (3) report cash flow effects.

Bonds Payable Transactions

Comparative balance sheet information from Exhibit 19.6 for bonds payable is our starting point. The first step reveals an increase in bonds payable from $64,000 to $90,000. We need to explain this change.

The second step is to review the bonds payable ledger account and any additional information available. Item (e) on page 980 is relevant to bonds payable and reports that bonds with a carrying value of $34,000 are retired for $18,000 cash, resulting in a $16,000 gain. The reconstructed entry for our analysis of item (e) is:

Bonds Payable	34,000	
Gain on Retirement of Debt...		16,000
Cash...		**18,000**

This entry reveals an $18,000 cash outflow for retirement of bonds. It also shows a $16,000 gain from comparing the bonds payable carrying value with the cash received. This gain does not reflect any cash inflow or outflow.

Item (b) also involves bonds payable. It reports that Genesis purchased capital assets costing $70,000 by issuing $60,000 in bonds payable to the seller and paying $10,000 in cash. We already reconstructed its entry for our analysis of investing activities. Recall it increased bonds payable by $60,000 and is reported as a non-cash investing and financing transaction. These reconstructed entries are reflected in the ledger account for bonds payable:

Bonds Payable			
		64,000	Balance, Dec. 31/04
Retired bonds	34,000	60,000	Issued bonds
		90,000	Balance, Dec. 31/05

The third step is to make the necessary disclosures on the cash flow statement. Disclosure of the cash flow effect from the bond retirement in the financing section of the statement appears as (also see Exhibit 19.8):

Genesis Corp.
Cash Flow Statement
For Year Ended December 31, 2005

Cash flows from financing activities:
Cash paid to retire bonds .... (18,000)

Common Shares Transactions

We use comparative balance sheet information from Exhibit 19.6 for the first step in analyzing the Common Shares account. This reveals an increase in common shares from $80,000 to $95,000. We need to explain this change.

Our second step is to review the Common Shares ledger account and any additional information available. Item (d) on page 980 reports that it issued 3,000 common shares for $5 per share. The reconstructed entry for our analysis of item (d) is:

Cash **15,000**
Common shares 15,000

This entry reveals a $15,000 cash inflow from the issuance of shares. This reconstructed entry is reflected in the ledger account for common shares:

Common Shares		
	80,000	Balance, Dec. 31/04
	15,000	Issued shares
	95,000	Balance, Dec. 31/05

The third step is to make the necessary disclosure on the cash flow statement. Disclosure of the cash flow effect from share issuance in the financing section of the statement appears as (also see Exhibit 19.8):

Genesis Corp.
Cash Flow Statement
For Year Ended December 31, 2005

Cash flows from financing activities:
Cash received from issuing shares .... $ 15,000

Retained Earnings Transactions

The first step in analyzing the Retained Earnings account is to review comparative balance sheet information from Exhibit 19.6. We need to explain the increase in retained earnings from $88,000 to $112,000.

Our second step is to analyze the Retained Earnings account and any additional information available. Item (f) on page 980 reports that cash dividends of $14,000 were paid. The reconstructed entry for our analysis of item (f) is:

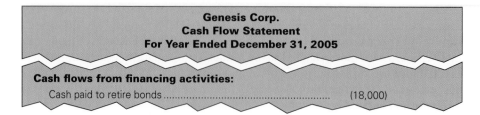

Retained Earnings.................	14,000		OR	Cash Dividends.....................	14,000	
Cash		**14,000**		**Cash**		**14,000**

This entry reveals a $14,000 cash outflow to pay cash dividends.[5] We must also remember that retained earnings is affected by net income from the income statement. Net income was already dealt with under the operating section of the cash flow statement. This reconstruction analysis is reflected in the ledger account for retained earnings:

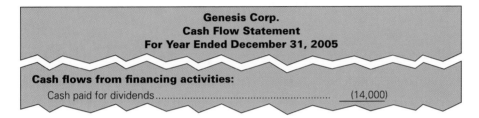

Retained Earnings			
		88,000	Balance, Dec. 31/04
Cash dividend	14,000	38,000	Net income
		112,000	Balance, Dec. 31/05

The third step is to make the necessary disclosure on the cash flow statement. Disclosure of the cash flow effect from the cash dividend appears in the financing section of the statement as (also see Exhibit 19.8):

Genesis Corp.
Cash Flow Statement
For Year Ended December 31, 2005

Cash flows from financing activities:
Cash paid for dividends.. (14,000)

5. Proving Cash Balances

We have now explained all of the cash inflows and outflows of Genesis, along with one non-cash investing and financing transaction. Our analysis has reconciled changes in all non-cash balance sheet accounts. The fifth and final step in preparing the statement is to report the beginning and ending cash balance and prove the net change in cash as explained by operating, investing, and financing net cash flows. This step is highlighted below for Genesis:

Genesis Corp.
Cash Flow Statement
For Year Ended December 31, 2005

Cash flows from operating activities:
Cash received from customers	$ 570,000	
Cash paid for merchandise	(319,000)	
Cash paid for wages and other operating expenses	(218,000)	
Cash paid for interest	(8,000)	
Cash paid for taxes	(5,000)	
Net cash inflow from operating activities		$20,000

Cash flows from investing activities:
Cash received from sale of capital assets	$ 12,000	
Cash paid for purchase of capital assets	(10,000)	
Net cash inflow from investing activities		2,000

Cash flows from financing activities:
Cash received from issuing shares	$ 15,000	
Cash paid to retire bonds	(18,000)	
Cash paid for dividends	(14,000)	
Net cash outflow from financing activities		(17,000)
Net increase in cash		$ 5,000
Cash balance at beginning of 2005		12,000
Cash balance at end of 2005		$17,000

Note: Non-cash investing and financing activity
During the period capital assets were acquired with issuance of $60,000 of bonds.

---

[5] *Share dividends* are a non-cash financing activity.

The statement shows that the $5,000 net increase in cash from $12,000 at the beginning of the period to $17,000 at the end is reconciled by net cash flows from operating ($20,000 inflow), investing ($2,000 inflow), and financing ($17,000 outflow) activities.

Judgement Call

Answer—p. 995

Reporter
You are a newspaper reporter covering a workers' strike. Management grants you an interview and complains about recent losses and negative cash flows. It shows you financial numbers revealing a recent $600,000 net loss that included a $930,000 extraordinary loss. It also shows you the company's total net cash outflow of $550,000, which included net cash outflows of $850,000 for investing activities and $350,000 for financing activities. What is your initial reaction to management's complaints?

Summary

LO¹ Explain the purpose and importance of cash flow information. The main purpose of the cash flow statement is to report the major cash receipts and cash payments for a period. This includes identifying cash flows as relating to operating, investing, or financing activities. Many business decisions involve evaluating cash flows. Users' evaluations include focusing on the transactions that cause cash inflows (outflows).

LO² Distinguish among operating, investing, and financing activities. Operating activities include the cash effects of transactions and events that determine net income. Investing activities include: (a) purchase and sale of long-term assets, (b) the purchase and sale of short-term investments other than cash equivalents, and (c) lending and collecting on loans. Financing activities include: (a) getting cash from issuing debt and repaying the amounts borrowed, and (b) getting cash from or distributing cash to owners and giving owners a return on investment.

LO³ Identify and disclose non-cash investing and financing activities. For external reporting, a company must supplement its cash flow statement with a description of its non-cash investing and financing activities. These activities are disclosed either in a note to the statement or in a separate schedule usually reported at the bottom of the statement.

LO⁴ Describe the format of the cash flow statement. The cash flow statement reports cash receipts and disbursements into one of three categories: operating, investing, or financing activities. Cash inflows and cash outflows are reported for each category.

LO⁵ Prepare a cash flow statement. Preparation of a cash flow statement involves five steps: (1) calculate the net increase or decrease in cash, (2) calculate net cash inflows (outflows) from operating activities, (3) calculate net cash inflows (outflows) from investing activities, (4) calculate net cash inflows (outflows) from financing activities; and (5) report the beginning and ending cash balance and prove it is explained by operating, investing, and financing net cash flows. Non-cash investing and financing activities are disclosed either in a note or in a separate schedule to the statement.

LO⁶ Calculate cash flows from operating activities using the direct method. The direct method for reporting net cash inflows (outflows) from operating activities, recommended by the CICA, involves separately listing the major classes of operating cash inflows and outflows. The operating cash outflows are then subtracted from operating cash inflows to get the net inflow or outflow from operating activities.

LO⁷ Calculate cash flows from both investing and financing activities. Cash flows from both investing and financing activities are determined by identifying the cash flow effects of transactions affecting each balance sheet account related to these activities.

GUIDANCE ANSWERS TO Judgement Call

Community Activist

There could be several explanations for an increase in net cash flows when a loss is reported. Possibilities include: (1) early recognition of expenses relative to revenues generated (research and development), (2) valuable long-term cash sales contracts not yet recognized in income, (3) issuances of debt or shares to finance expansion, (4) selling of assets, (5) delayed cash payments, and (6) prepayment on sales. Your analysis of this manufacturer needs to focus on the components of both net income and net cash flows, and their implications for future performance.

Reporter

Your initial course of action is to verify management's claims about poor performance. A $600,000 loss along with a $550,000 decrease in net cash flows seemingly supports its claim. But closer scrutiny reveals a different picture. You calculate its cash flow from operating activities at a positive $650,000, calculated as [?] − $850,000 − $350,000 = $(550,000). You note also that net income before the extraordinary loss is a positive $330,000, calculated as [?] − $930,000 = $(600,000). This is powerful information to open discussions. A serious and directed discussion is likely to reveal a far more positive picture of this company's financial performance.

GUIDANCE ANSWERS TO  Flashback

1. No. The cash flow statement reports changes in the sum of cash plus cash equivalents. It does not report transfers between cash and cash equivalents.

2. The three categories of cash inflows and outflows are operating activities, investing activities, and financing activities.

3. **a.** Investing

   b. Operating

   c. Financing

   d. Operating

   e. Operating

   f. Financing

4. The direct method is most informative because it separately lists each major item of operating cash receipts and each major item of operating cash payments. The indirect method is used most often.

5. $590,000 + ($120,000 − $90,000) = $620,000

6. $168,000 − ($32,000 − $28,000) − $2,400 = $161,600

7. $112,000 + ($4,200 − $1,200) − $5,600 = $109,400

8. $80,000 − $30,000 − $10,000 = $40,000

   The $40,000 cash receipt is reported as an investing activity.

Demonstration Problem

Umlauf Inc.'s beginning and ending balance sheet, income statement, and supplementary information follow.

Required

Prepare a cash flow statement using the direct method for the year ended 2005.

Umlauf Inc. **Comparative Balance Sheet Information**		
		December 31
Assets	**2005**	**2004**
Cash...	$ 43,050	$ 23,925
Accounts receivable	34,125	39,825
Merchandise inventory	156,000	146,475
Prepaid expenses	3,600	1,650
Equipment	135,825	146,700
Accumulated amortization	(61,950)	(47,550)
Total assets..	$310,650	$311,025
Liabilities and Shareholders' Equity		
Accounts payable	28,800	33,750
Income taxes payable..	5,100	4,425
Dividends payable	-0-	4,500
Bonds payable	-0-	37,500
Common shares	168,750	168,750
Retained earnings...	108,000	62,100
Total liabilities and shareholders' equity	$310,650	$311,025

An examination of the company's statements and accounts showed:

a. All sales were made on credit.

b. All merchandise purchases were on credit.

c. Accounts Payable balances resulted from merchandise purchases.

d. Prepaid expenses relate to other operating expenses.

e. Equipment costing $21,375 with accumulated amortization of $11,100 was sold for cash.

f. Equipment was purchased for cash.

g. The change in the balance of Accumulated Amortization resulted from amortization expense and from the sale of equipment.

h. The change in the balance of Retained Earnings resulted from dividend declarations and net income.

Umlauf Inc.
Income Statement
For Year Ended December 31, 2005

Sales (see note *a*)...		$446,100
Cost of goods sold (see notes *b* and *c*)	$222,300	
Other operating expenses (see note *d*)	120,300	
Amortization expense	25,500	
Income taxes expense...	13,725	(381,825)
Loss on sale of equipment (see note *e*)..		(3,300)
Loss on retirement of bonds..		(825)
Net income (see note *h*)		$ 60,150

Planning the Solution

○ Prepare a blank cash flow statement with sections for operating, investing, and financing activities using the direct method format.

○ Calculate cash received from customers, cash paid for merchandise, and cash paid for other operating expenses and taxes as illustrated in the chapter.

○ Calculate the cash paid for equipment and the cash received from the sale of equipment according to the supplementary information provided, the amount for amortization expense, and the change in the balances of equipment and accumulated amortization. Use a T-account to help chart the effects of the sale and purchase of the equipment on the balances of the equipment account and the accumulated amortization account.

○ Calculate the effect of net income on the change in the retained earnings balance. Note the effect of dividends on the change in retained earnings.

○ Enter the cash effects of the entry in the appropriate section of the statement.

○ Total each section of the statement, determine the total change in cash, and add the beginning balance to get the ending balance.

S O L U T I O N   T O   Demonstration Problem

Calculations:

(1) Sales..	$446,100
Add decrease in accounts receivable..	5,700
Cash received from customers	$451,800
(2) Cost of goods sold	$222,300
Plus increase in merchandise inventory..	9,525
Purchases..	$231,825
Plus decrease in accounts payable	4,950
Cash paid for merchandise..	$236,775
(3) Other operating expenses..	$120,300
Plus increase in prepaid expenses	1,950
Cash paid for other operating expenses	$122,250
(4) Income taxes expense	$ 13,725
Less increase in income taxes payable	(675)
Payments of income taxes..	$ 13,050
(5) Cost of equipment sold..	$ 21,375
Accumulated amortization of equipment sold...	(11,100)
Book value of equipment sold..	$ 10,275
Loss on sale of equipment..	(3,300)
Cash receipt from sale of equipment..	$ 6,975
Cost of equipment sold..	$ 21,375
Less decrease in the equipment account balance	(10,875)
Cash paid for new equipment	$ 10,500

Equipment					Accumulated Amortization, Equipment		
Balance, Dec. 31/04	146,700					47,550	Balance, Dec. 31/04
Purchase	10,500	21,375		Sale	Sale 11,100	25,500	Amort. expense
Balance, Dec. 31/05	135,825					61,950	Balance, Dec. 31/05

(6) Loss on retirement of bonds	$ 825
Carrying value of bonds retired..	37,500
Cash payment to retire bonds	$38,325
(7) Net income	$60,150
Less increase in retained earnings	45,900
Dividends declared	$14,250
Plus decrease in dividends payable	4,500
Cash paid for dividends..	$18,750

Umlauf Inc.
Cash Flow Statement
For Year Ended December 31, 2005

Cash flows from operating activities:

Cash received from customers	$ 451,800	
Cash paid for merchandise	(236,775)	
Cash paid for other operating expenses	(122,250)	
Cash paid for income taxes	(13,050)	
Net cash inflow from operating activities		$ 79,725

Cash flows from investing activities:

Cash received from sale of office equipment	$ 6,975	
Cash paid for store equipment	(10,500)	
Net cash outflow from investing activities		(3,525)

Cash flows from financing activities:

Cash paid to retire bonds payable	$ (38,325)	
Cash paid for dividends	(18,750)	
Net cash outflow from financing activities		(57,075)
Net increase in cash		$ 19,125
Cash balance at beginning of year		23,925
Cash balance at end of year		$ 43,050

Note to Student: Remember that the cash flow statement explains the change in the Cash account balance from one period to the next.

Umlauf Inc.
Comparative Balance Sheet Information

	December 31	
Assets	**2005**	**2004**
Cash	$ 43,050	$ 23,925
Accounts receivable	34,125	39,825
Merchandise inventory	156,000	146,475
Prepaid expenses	3,600	1,650
Equipment	135,825	146,700
Accumulated amortization	(61,950)	(47,550)
Total assets	$310,650	$311,025
Liabilities and Shareholders' Equity		
Accounts payable	28,800	33,750
Income taxes payable	5,100	4,425
Dividends payable	-0-	4,500
Bonds payable	-0-	37,500
Common shares	168,750	168,750
Retained earnings	108,000	62,100
Total liabilities and shareholders' equity	$310,650	$311,025

Cash Flows from Operating Activities—Indirect Method

Indirect Method of Reporting Operating Cash Flows

LO⁸ Calculate cash flows from operating activities using the indirect method.

We draw on the financial statements of Genesis Corp. in Exhibit 19.6 to illustrate application of the indirect method. The indirect method of reporting begins with net income of $38,000 for Genesis and then adjusts it to get net cash inflows (outflows) from operating activities. Exhibit 19A.1 highlights the results of the indirect method of reporting operating cash flows for Genesis. The net cash inflows from operating activities are $20,000. This amount is the same as that for the direct method of reporting operating cash flows (see Exhibit 19.8). *The two methods always yield the same net cash inflows (outflows) from operating activities.* Only the calculations and presentation are different.

Exhibit 19A.1

Cash Flow Statement—Indirect Method of Reporting Operating Cash Flows

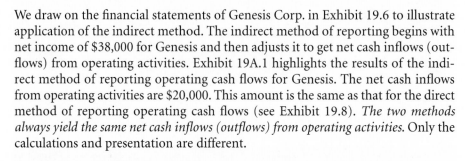

Genesis Corp.
Cash Flow Statement
For Year Ended December 31, 2005

Cash flows from operating activities:		
Net income		$ 38,000
Adjustments to reconcile net income to net cash provided by operating activities:		
Increase in accounts receivable	(20,000)	
Increase in merchandise inventory	(14,000)	
Increase in prepaid expenses	(2,000)	
Decrease in accounts payable	(5,000)	
Decrease in interest payable	(1,000)	
Increase in income taxes payable	10,000	
Amortization expense	24,000	
Loss on sale of capital assets	6,000	
Gain on retirement of bonds	(16,000)	
Net cash inflow from operating activities		$ 20,000
Cash flows from investing activities:		
Cash received from sale of capital assets	$ 12,000	
Cash paid for purchase of capital assets	(10,000)	
Net cash inflow from investing activities		2,000
Cash flows from financing activities:		
Cash received from issuing shares	$ 15,000	
Cash paid to retire bonds	(18,000)	
Cash paid for dividends	(14,000)	
Net cash outflow from financing activities		(17,000)
Net increase in cash		$ 5,000
Cash balance at beginning of 2005		12,000
Cash balance at end of 2005		$ 17,000

The indirect method does not report individual operating cash inflows or cash outflows. Instead, the indirect method adjusts net income for three types of adjustments:

1. Adjustments for changes in non-cash current assets and current liabilities relating to operating activities.

2. Adjustments to income statement items involving operating activities that do not affect cash inflows or outflows during the period.

3. Adjustments to eliminate gains and losses resulting from investing and financing activities (those not part of operating activities).

This section describes each of these three types of adjustments in applying the indirect method.

Adjustments for Changes in Non-Cash Current Assets

Changes in non-cash current assets are normally the result of operating activities. Under the indirect method for reporting operating cash flows:

> **Decreases in non-cash current assets are added to net income.**

> **Increases in non-cash current assets are subtracted from net income.**

To demonstrate, we now look at the individual non-cash current assets of Genesis as shown in Exhibit 19.6.

Accounts Receivable   Accounts Receivable of Genesis *increased* $20,000 in the period, from a beginning balance of $40,000 to an ending balance of $60,000. This increase implies Genesis collected less cash than its reported sales amount for this period. It also means some of these sales were in the form of accounts receivable, leaving Accounts Receivable with an increase. This lesser amount of cash collections compared with sales is reflected in the Accounts Receivable account as shown here:

Accounts Receivable			
Balance, Dec. 31/04	40,000		
Sales, 2005	590,000	570,000	= Collections
Balance, Dec. 31/05	60,000		

This $20,000 increase in Accounts Receivable is subtracted from net income as part of our adjustments to get net cash inflows from operating activities. Subtracting it adjusts sales to the cash receipts amount.

Merchandise Inventory   Merchandise Inventory *increased* $14,000 in the period, from a beginning balance of $70,000 to an ending balance of $84,000. This increase implies Genesis had a greater amount of cash purchases than goods sold this period. This greater amount of cash purchases ended up in the form of inventory, resulting in an inventory increase. This greater amount of cash purchases compared to the amount subtracted from income as cost of goods sold is reflected in the Merchandise Inventory account increase:

Merchandise Inventory			
Balance, Dec. 31/04	70,000		
Purchases =	314,000	300,000	Cost of goods sold
Balance, Dec. 31/05	84,000		

The $14,000 increase in inventory is subtracted from net income as part of our adjustments to get net cash inflows from operating activities.

Prepaid Expenses   Prepaid Expenses *increased* $2,000 in the period, from a beginning balance of $4,000 to an ending balance of $6,000. This increase implies Genesis' cash payments exceeded its operating expenses incurred this period. These larger cash payments ended up increasing the amount of prepaid expenses. This is reflected in the Prepaid Expenses account:

Prepaid Expenses			
Balance, Dec. 31/04	4,000		
Payments =	218,000		
		216,000	Wages and other operating expenses
Balance, Dec. 31/05	6,000		

This $2,000 increase in prepaid expenses is subtracted from net income as part of our adjustments to get net cash inflows from operating activities. Subtracting it adjusts operating expenses to the cash payments amount.

Adjustments for Changes in Current Liabilities

Changes in current liabilities P. 219 are normally the result of operating activities. Under the indirect method for reporting operating cash flows:

> **Increases in current liabilities are added to net income.**

> **Decreases in current liabilities are subtracted from net income.**

To demonstrate, we now analyze the individual current liabilities of Genesis as shown in Exhibit 19.6.

Accounts Payable   Accounts Payable of Genesis *decreased* $5,000 in the period, from a beginning balance of $40,000 to an ending balance of $35,000. This decrease implies its cash payments exceeded its merchandise purchases by $5,000 for the period. This larger amount for cash payments compared to purchases is reflected in the Accounts Payable account:

Accounts Payable			
		40,000	Balance, Dec. 31/04
Payments =	319,000	314,000	Purchases
		35,000	Balance, Dec. 31/05

The $5,000 decrease in Accounts Payable is subtracted from net income as part of our adjustments to get net cash inflows from operating activities.

Interest Payable   Interest Payable *decreased* $1,000 in the period, from a beginning balance of $4,000 to an ending balance of $3,000. This decrease indicates cash payments for interest exceeded interest expense for the period by $1,000. This larger cash payment compared to the reported interest expense is reflected in the Interest Payable account:

Interest Payable		
	4,000	Balance, Dec. 31/04
Interest paid = 8,000	7,000	Interest expense
	3,000	Balance, Dec. 31/05

The $1,000 decrease in Interest Payable is subtracted from net income as part of our adjustments to get net cash inflows from operating activities.

Income Taxes Payable   Income Taxes Payable *increased* $10,000 in the period, from a beginning balance of $12,000 to an ending balance of $22,000. This increase implies the amount owed for income taxes exceeded the cash payments for the period by $10,000. This smaller cash payment compared to income taxes owed is reflected in the Income Taxes Payable account:

Income Taxes Payable		
	12,000	Balance, Dec. 31/04
Income taxes paid = 5,000	15,000	Income taxes expense
	22,000	Balance, Dec. 31/05

The $10,000 increase in income taxes payable is added to net income as part of our adjustments to get net cash inflows from operating activities.

Adjustments for Operating Items Not Providing or Using Cash

The income statement usually includes certain expenses that do not reflect cash outflows in the period. Examples are amortization of capital assets, amortization of bond discount, and bad debts expense. The indirect method for reporting operating cash flows requires that:

> **Expenses with no cash outflows are added back to net income.**

To see this logic, recall that items such as amortization and bad debts are recorded with debits to expense accounts and credits to non-cash accounts. There is no cash effect in these entries. Yet because items such as amortization expense are proper deductions in calculating accrual income, we need to add them back to net income when calculating net cash flows from operations. Adding them back cancels their deductions.

Similarly, when net income includes revenues that do not reflect cash inflows in the period, the indirect method for reporting operating cash flows requires that:

> **Revenues with no cash inflows are subtracted from net income.**

For example, a sale on credit is recorded as a debit to accounts receivable and a credit to sales. This transaction increases net income yet there is no cash inflow. Therefore, we need to subtract transactions with no cash inflows from accrual net income to determine the actual cash generated from (or used in) operating activities.

We now look at the individual operating items of Genesis that fit this category and do not provide or use cash.

Amortization   Amortization expense P. 143 is the only operating item for Genesis that does not affect cash flows in the period. Our discussion indicates that we must add $24,000 amortization expense back to net income as part of our adjustments to get net cash inflows from operating activities.

Adjustments for Non-Operating Items

The income statement sometimes includes losses that are not part of operating activities. Examples are a loss from sale of a capital asset and a loss from retirement of a bond payable. Under the indirect method for reporting operating cash flows:

> **Non-operating losses are added back to net income.**

To see the logic, consider items such as a capital asset sale and bond retirement. We record these transactions by recognizing the cash, removing capital asset or bond accounts, and recognizing the loss or gain. The cash received or paid is not part of operating activities but is recorded under either investing or financing activities. There is no operating cash flow effect. But because the non-operating loss is a deduction in calculating accrual income, we need to add it back to net income when calculating the net cash flow effect from operations. Adding it back cancels the deduction.

Similarly, when net income includes gains that are not part of operating activities, under the indirect method for reporting operating cash flows:

> **Non-operating gains are subtracted from net income.**

These net income adjustments are part of calculations to get net cash provided by operating activities. We now look at the individual non-operating items of Genesis.

Loss on Sale of Capital Assets   Genesis reports a $6,000 loss on sale of capital assets in its income statement. This loss is a proper deduction in calculating net income, but it is *not part of operating activities*. Instead, a sale of capital assets is part of investing activities. This means the $6,000 non-operating loss is added back to net income as part of our adjustments to get net cash inflows from operating activities. Adding it back cancels the recorded loss. Earlier in the chapter we explained how the cash inflow from the capital asset sale was reported in investing activities.

Gain on Retirement of Bonds   There is a $16,000 gain on retirement of bonds reported in the income statement of Genesis. This gain is properly included in net income, but it is *not part of operating activities*. This means the $16,000 non-operating gain is subtracted from net income as part of our adjustments to get net cash inflows from operating activities. Subtracting it cancels the recorded gain. Earlier in the chapter we describe how the cash outflow to retire the bond was reported in financing activities.

Extend Your Knowledge

19-2

While the calculations in determining net cash inflows (outflows) from operating activities are different for the direct and indirect methods, the result is identical. Both methods yield the same $20,000 figure for net cash inflows (outflows) from operating activities; see Exhibits 19.8 (direct method) and 19A.1 (indirect method). A spreadsheet can be used to organize information needed to prepare a cash flow statement.

Cash or Income

Did You Know?

The difference between net income and operating cash flows can be large. For example, Alcan reported a net income of $374 million for the year ended December 31, 2002, but operating cash flows were $1,614 million. Alcan is a Canadian company that reports in U.S. dollars.

9. Determine the net cash inflows (outflows) from operating activities using the following data:

Flashback

Answers—p. 1005

Net income	$74,900
Decrease in accounts receivable	4,600
Increase in inventory	11,700
Decrease in accounts payable	1,000
Loss on sale of equipment	3,400
Payment of dividends	21,500

10. Why are expenses such as amortization added to net income when cash flow from operating activities is calculated by the indirect method?

11. A company reports net income of $15,000 that includes a $3,000 gain on the sale of capital assets. Why is this gain subtracted from net income in calculating cash flow from operating activities using the indirect method?

Summary

LO⁸ **Calculate cash flows from operating activities using the indirect method.** The indirect method for reporting net cash inflows (outflows) from operating activities starts with net income and then adjusts it for three items: (1) changes in non-cash current assets and current liabilities related to operating activities, (2) revenues and expenses not creating cash inflows (outflows), and (3) gains and losses from investing and financing activities.

GUIDANCE ANSWERS TO  Flashback

9. $74,900 + $4,600 − $11,700 − $1,000 + $3,400 = $70,200

10. In the calculation of net income, expenses such as amortization are subtracted because these expenses do not require current cash outflows. Therefore, adding these expenses back to net income eliminates non-cash items from the net income number, converting it to a cash basis.

11. In the process of reconciling net income to net cash inflows (outflows) from operating activities, a gain on the sale of capital assets is subtracted from net income because a sale of capital assets is not an operating activity; it is an investing activity.

Glossary

Cash equivalent An investment that must be readily convertible to a known amount of cash, and sufficiently close to its maturity date so its market value is not significantly affected by interest rate changes. (p. 975)

Cash flow statement A financial statement that reports the cash inflows and outflows for an accounting period, and that classifies those cash flows as operating activities, investing activities, and financing activities. (p. 974)

Direct method A calculation of the net cash inflows (outflows) from operating activities that lists the major classes of operating cash receipts, such as receipts from customers, and subtracts the major classes of operating cash disbursements, such as cash paid for merchandise. This method is encouraged by the CICA. (p. 981)

Financing activities Transactions with a company's owners and creditors that include getting cash from issuing debt and repaying the amounts borrowed, and getting cash from or distributing cash to owners and giving owners a return on investments. (p. 976)

Indirect method A calculation that starts with net income or loss and then adjusts this figure by adding and subtracting items that are necessary to yield net cash inflows or outflows from operating activities. (p. 981)

Investing activities The acquisition and disposal of long-term assets and other investments that are not classified as cash equivalents. (p. 976)

Operating activities The principal revenue-producing activities that are not investing or financing activities. Operating activities involve the production or purchase of merchandise and the sale of goods and services to customers, including expenditures related to administering the business. (p. 976)

For more study tools, quizzes, and problem material,
refer to the Online Learning Centre at
www.mcgrawhill.ca/college/larson

Questions

1. What is the purpose of a cash flow statement?

2. What are cash equivalents and why are they included with cash when preparing a cash flow statement?

3. What is the direct method of reporting cash flows from operating activities?

4. What is the indirect method of reporting cash flows from operating activities?

5. If a company reports a net income for the year, is it possible for the company to show a net cash outflow from operating activities? Explain your answer.

6. Explain how sales are converted from an accrual basis to a cash basis.

7. Explain how cost of goods sold is converted from an accrual basis to a cash basis.

8. When a cash flow statement is prepared by the direct method, what are some examples of items reported as cash flows from operating activities?

9. Is amortization an inflow of cash?

10. On June 3, a company borrowed $50,000 by giving its bank a 60-day, interest-bearing note. On the June 30 cash flow statement, where should this item be reported?

11. What are some examples of items reported on a cash flow statement as investing activities?

12. A company purchases land for $100,000, paying $20,000 cash and borrowing the remainder on a long-term note payable. How should this transaction be reported on a cash flow statement?

13. Refer to WestJet's Cash Flow Statement shown in Appendix I. What activity comprised the largest investing activity resulting in cash outflows for the year ended 2002?

14. What are some examples of items reported on a cash flow statement as financing activities?

15. If a corporation pays cash dividends, where on the corporation's cash flow statement should the payment be reported?

16. Refer to WestJet's Cash Flow Statement shown in Appendix I. What activities comprised WestJet's two largest cash flows from financing activities for the fiscal year ended 2002?

*17. Refer to WestJet's Cash Flow Statement shown in Appendix I.
(a) Which method was used to calculate net cash provided by operating activities? (b) The balance sheet shows that there was an increase in receivables from fiscal year 2001 to fiscal year 2002. WestJet does not disclose the details of changes in current assets and current liabilities but only shows the net increase in non-cash working capital. How were receivables handled in the calculation of net cash provided by operating activities?

*18. Explain why non-cash expenses and losses are added to net income in calculating cash provided by operating activities using the indirect method.

An asterisk (*) identifies assignment material based on Appendix 19A.

QS 19-1
Classifying transactions by activity

LO^2

Classify the following cash flows as operating, investing, or financing activities:
1. Paid interest on outstanding bonds.
2. Received interest on investment.
3. Issued common shares for cash.
4. Paid dividends.
5. Paid property taxes on the company offices.
6. Received payments from customers.
7. Collected proceeds from sale of long-term investments.
8. Paid wages.
9. Purchased merchandise for cash.
10. Sold delivery equipment at a loss.

QS 19-2
Classifying transactions by activity

LO^2

Classify each of the following transactions as operating, financing, or investing activities, or none of these classifications and state whether it is an inflow or outflow of cash.
1. Bonds were retired.
2. Land was sold at a gain.
3. Preferred shares were converted into common shares.
4. Machinery was purchased by giving a long-term note to the seller.
5. Common shares were sold for cash.
6. Dividends were received on shares of another company held as an investment.
7. Paid utilities expense.
8. A share dividend was declared and issued on common shares.

QS 19-3
Classifying transactions by activity

LO^2

Classify each of the following events as operating, financing, or investing activities and give a reason for your choice.
1. Change in Accounts Receivable.
2. Change in Equipment account.
3. Change in Accumulated Amortization.
4. Change in Accrued Wages.
5. Change in Bonds Payable.
6. Proceeds from sale of land.

QS 19-4
Identifying non-cash transactions

LO^3

Identify which of the following are non-cash financing and investing transactions.
1. Long-term bonds were retired by issuing common shares.
2. Recorded amortization expense on the building.
3. A 3:2 share split was declared.
4. A cash dividend was declared and paid.
5. Merchandise was sold on credit.
6. Capital assets were acquired by borrowing from the bank.
7. Borrowed cash from the bank and signed a long-term note payable.
8. Property taxes owed to the city were accrued.

QS 19-5
Calculating cash paid for other expenses

LO^6

Clendenning Ltd. had operating expenses of $968,000 during 2005. Accrued liabilities at the beginning of the year were $27,000, and were $36,000 at the end of the year. Assuming all debits and credits to accrued liabilities are related to operating expenses, what was the total cash paid for operating expenses during 2005?

QS 19-6
Cash flows from operating activities (direct method)

LO^6

Middleton Inc. had sales revenue of $805,000 during 2005. Accounts receivable at the beginning of the year were $20,000 but were $24,000 at the end of the year. How much cash was collected from customers during 2005?

QS 19-7
Cash flows from operating
activities (direct method)

LO⁶

Daum Inc. collected $737,000 cash from customers during 2005. If beginning accounts receivable were $41,000 and credit sales totalled $705,000, what was the balance in ending accounts receivable?

QS 19-8
Calculating cash from customers

LO⁶

Use the following information to answer QS 19-8 through *QS 19-13.

Drinkwater Inc.
Comparative Balance Sheet Information

	June 30	
Assets	**2005**	**2004**
Cash	$ 42,900	$ 17,500
Accounts receivable (net)	26,000	21,000
Inventory	43,400	48,400
Prepaid expenses	3,200	2,600
Furniture	55,000	60,000
Accumulated amortization	(9,000)	(5,000)
Total assets	$161,500	$144,500
Liabilities and Shareholders' Equity		
Accounts payable	$ 8,000	$ 11,000
Wages payable	5,000	3,000
Income taxes payable	1,200	1,800
Notes payable (long-term)	15,000	35,000
Common shares	115,000	90,000
Retained earnings	17,300	3,700
Total liabilities and shareholders' equity	$161,500	$144,500

Drinkwater Inc.
Income Statement
For Year Ended June 30, 2005

Sales		$234,000
Cost of goods sold		156,000
Gross profit		$ 78,000
Operating expenses:		
Amortization expense	$19,300	
Other expenses	28,500	
Total operating expense		47,800
Income from operations		$ 30,200
Income taxes		12,300
Net income		$ 17,900

How much cash was received from customers during 2005?

QS 19-9
Calculating cash paid for
merchandise

LO⁶

Refer to the facts in QS 19-8. How much cash was paid for merchandise during 2005?

Refer to the facts in QS 19-8. How much cash was paid for operating expenses during 2005?

QS 19-10

Calculating cash paid for expenses

LO⁶

Refer to the facts in QS 19-8 and assume furniture that cost $27,000 was sold at its book value and all furniture purchased was for cash. What was the cash inflow related to the sale of furniture?

QS 19-11

Calculating cash from an asset sale

LO⁷

Refer to the facts in QS 19-8 and assume all shares were issued for cash. How much cash is paid for dividends?

QS 19-12

Calculating cash paid for dividends

LO⁷

Refer to the facts in QS 19-8. Using the indirect method, calculate the cash inflow or outflow from operating activities.

*QS 19-13

Calculating cash from operations (indirect method)

LO⁸

The following information for 2005 is extracted from Hartfield Limited:

Net income	$24,500
Accounts receivable decrease	1,000
Inventory increase	1,500
Amortization expense	5,000
Wages payable increase	900

Calculate the cash inflow or outflow from operating activities.

*QS 19-14

Cash flows from operating activities (indirect method)

 LO⁸

The following information for 2005 relates to Day Corp.:

Net income	$49,000
Inventory decrease	3,000
Amortization expense	6,000
Accounts payable decrease	900
Income taxes payable increase	1,200
Loss on sale of capital assets	1,000

Calculate the cash inflow or outflow from operating activities.

*QS 19-15

Cash flows from operating activities (indirect method)

LO⁸

An asterisk (*) identifies assignment material based on Appendix 19A.

Exercises

Exercise 19-1
Classifying transactions on cash flow statement (direct method)

LO[2, 3]

The following occurred during the year. Assuming that the company uses the direct method of reporting cash provided by operating activities, indicate the proper accounting treatment for each item by placing an x in the appropriate column.

	Cash Flow Statement			Note Describing Non-Cash Investing and Financing Activities	Not Reported on Statement or in Footnote
	Operating Activities	Investing Activities	Financing Activities		
a. Long-term bonds payable were retired by issuing common shares	___	___	___	___	___
b. Surplus merchandise inventory was sold for cash	___	___	___	___	___
c. Borrowed cash from the bank by signing a nine-month note payable	___	___	___	___	___
d. Paid cash to purchase a patent	___	___	___	___	___
e. A six-month note receivable was accepted in exchange for a building that had been used in operations	___	___	___	___	___
f. Recorded amortization expense on all capital assets	___	___	___	___	___
g. A cash dividend that was declared in a previous period was paid in the current period	___	___	___	___	___

Exercise 19-2
Calculating cash flows

LO[6]

In each of the following cases, use the information provided about the 2005 operations of Seghal Corp. to calculate the indicated cash flow:

Case A:	Calculate cash received from customers:	
	Sales revenue	$255,000
	Accounts receivable, January 1	12,600
	Accounts receivable, December 31	17,400
Case B:	Calculate cash paid for insurance:	
	Insurance expense	$ 34,200
	Prepaid insurance, January 1	5,700
	Prepaid insurance, December 31	8,550
Case C:	Calculate cash paid for salaries:	
	Salaries expense	$102,000
	Salaries payable, January 1	6,300
	Salaries payable, December 31	7,500

In each of the following cases, use the information provided about the 2005 operations of Clarke Inc. to calculate the indicated cash flow:

Case A: Calculate cash paid for rent:

Rent expense	$ 20,400
Rent payable, January 1	4,400
Rent payable, December 31	3,600

Case B: Calculate cash received from interest:

Interest revenue	$ 68,000
Interest receivable, January 1	6,000
Interest receivable, December 31	7,200

Case C: Calculate cash paid for merchandise:

Cost of goods sold	$352,000
Merchandise inventory, January 1	106,400
Accounts payable, January 1	45,200
Merchandise inventory, December 31	87,600
Accounts payable, December 31	56,000

Exercise 19-3
Calculating cash flows

LO[6]

Use the following income statement and information about changes in non-cash current assets and current liabilities to present the cash flows from operating activities using the direct method:

Exercise 19-4
Cash flows from operating activities (direct method)

LO[6]

Bozena Inc.
Income Statement
For Year Ended December 31, 2005

Sales		$606,000
Cost of goods sold		297,000
Gross profit from sales		$309,000
Operating expenses:		
Salaries expense	$82,845	
Amortization expense	14,400	
Rent expense	12,200	
Amortization expense, patents	1,800	
Utilities expense	6,375	
Total operating expenses		117,620
Gain on sale of equipment		2,400
Income from operations		$193,780
Income taxes		4,000
Net income		$189,780

Changes in current asset and current liability accounts during the year, all of which related to operating activities, were as follows:

Accounts receivable	$13,500 increase
Merchandise inventory	9,000 increase
Accounts payable	4,500 decrease
Salaries payable	1,500 decrease

Check figure:
Net cash inflow from operating activities, $175,080

Exercise 19-5
Organizing the cash flow statement and supporting footnote (direct method)

LO2, 3, 4, 5, 6, 7

Cooke Inc.'s records contain the following information about the 2005 cash flows.

Cash and cash equivalents balance, December 31, 2004	$ 50,000
Cash and cash equivalents balance, December 31, 2005	112,500
Cash received as interest	5,000
Cash paid for salaries	35,000
Bonds payable retired by issuing common shares (there was no gain or loss on the retirement)	375,000
Cash paid to retire long-term notes payable	122,500
Cash received from sale of equipment	50,000
Cash borrowed on six-month note payable	50,000
Land purchased and financed by long-term note payable	212,500
Cash paid for store equipment	47,500
Cash dividends paid	30,000
Cash paid for income taxes	40,000
Cash received from customers	485,000
Cash paid for merchandise	252,500
Amortization expense	145,000

Check figure:
Net cash inflow from operating activities, $162,500

Required
Prepare a cash flow statement using the direct method and a note describing non-cash investing and financing activities.

Exercise 19-6
Analyzing cash inflows and outflows

LO5, 6, 7

(in thousands)	Fraser	Spern	Travis
Cash inflow (outflow) from operating activities	$ 80,000	$ 70,000	$ (34,000)
Cash inflow (outflow) from investing activities:			
Proceeds from sale of capital assets			36,000
Purchase of capital assets	(38,000)	(35,000)	
Cash inflow (outflow) from financing activities:			
Proceeds from issuance of debt			33,000
Repayment of debt	(7,000)		
Net increase (decrease) in cash	35,000	35,000	35,000
Average assets	800,000	650,000	400,000

Required
Which of the three competing corporations is in the strongest relative position as indicated by their comparative cash flow statements?

Exercise 19-7
Preparation of cash flow statement (direct method)

LO2, 5, 6, 7

Check figure:
Net cash inflow from operating activities, $1,510,400

The summarized journal entries on page 1013 show the total debits and credits to the Berezniki Corporation's Cash account during 2005.

Required
1. Use the information to prepare a cash flow statement for 2005. The cash flow from operating activities should be presented according to the direct method. In the statement, identify the entry that records each item of cash flow. Assume that the beginning balance of cash was $133,200.
2. Consult the cash flow statement you have just prepared and answer the following questions:
   a. Of the three activity sections (operating, investing, or financing), which section shows the largest cash flow for the year 2005?
   b. What was the purpose of the largest investing cash outflow in 2005?
   c. Were the proceeds larger from issuing debt or equity in 2005?
   d. Did the corporation have a net cash inflow or outflow from borrowing activity in 2005?

a.	Cash..	1,440,000	
	Common Shares		1,440,000
	Issued common shares for cash.		
b.	Cash..	2,400,000	
	Notes Payable		2,400,000
	Borrowed cash with a note payable.		
c.	Merchandise Inventory...................................	480,000	
	Cash..		480,000
	Purchased merchandise for cash.		
d.	Accounts Payable	1,200,000	
	Cash..		1,200,000
	Paid for credit purchases of merchandise.		
e.	Wages Expense...	600,000	
	Cash..		600,000
	Paid wages to employees.		
f.	Rent Expense	420,000	
	Cash..		420,000
	Paid rent for buildings.		
g.	Cash..	3,000,000	
	Sales		3,000,000
	Made cash sales to customers.		
h.	Cash..	1,800,000	
	Accounts Receivable.................................		1,800,000
	Collected accounts from credit customers.		
i.	Machinery	2,136,000	
	Cash..		2,136,000
	Purchased machinery for cash.		
j.	Long-Term Investments..................................	2,160,000	
	Cash..		2,160,000
	Purchased long-term investments for cash.		
k.	Interest Expense..	216,000	
	Notes Payable..	384,000	
	Cash..		600,000
	Paid notes and accrued interest.		
l.	Cash..	106,400	
	Dividend Revenue.....................................		106,400
	Collected dividends from investments.		
m.	Cash..	210,000	
	Loss on Sale of Long-Term Investments	30,000	
	Long-Term Investments............................		240,000
	Sold long-term investments for cash.		
n.	Cash..	720,000	
	Accumulated Amortization, Machinery.............	420,000	
	Machinery		960,000
	Gain on Sale of Machinery		180,000
	Sold machinery for cash.		
o.	Common Dividend Payable..............................	510,000	
	Cash..		510,000
	Paid cash dividends to shareholders.		
p.	Income Taxes Payable	480,000	
	Cash..		480,000
	Paid income taxes owed for the year.		
q.	Common Shares...	228,000	
	Cash..		228,000
	Purchased and retired common shares for cash.		

Exercise 19-8
Preparation of cash flow
statement (direct method)

LO$^{2, 5, 6, 7}$

Check figure:
Net cash inflow from operating
activities, $138,960

Required
Use the Morpurgo Ltd. financial statements and supplementary information given below
to prepare a cash flow statement for the year ended June 30, 2005, using the direct method.
a. A note is retired at carrying value.
b. The only changes affecting retained earnings during 2005 are net income and cash
dividends paid.
c. New equipment is acquired during 2005 for $58,600.
d. The gain on sale of equipment costing $48,600 during 2005 is $2,000.
e. Prepaid expenses and wages expense affect other expenses on the income statement.
f. All sales and purchases of merchandise were on credit.

Morpurgo Ltd.
Comparative Balance Sheet Information

	June 30	
Assets	**2005**	**2004**
Cash	$ 75,800	$ 35,000
Accounts receivable (net)	80,000	62,000
Inventory	66,800	96,800
Prepaid expenses	5,400	5,200
Equipment	130,000	120,000
Accumulated amortization	(28,000)	(10,000)
Total assets	$330,000	$309,000
Liabilities and Shareholders' Equity		
Accounts payable	$ 26,000	$ 32,000
Wages payable	7,000	16,000
Income taxes payable	2,400	3,600
Notes payable (long-term)	40,000	70,000
Common shares	230,000	180,000
Retained earnings	24,600	7,400
Total liabilities and shareholders' equity	$330,000	$309,000

Morpurgo Ltd.
Income Statement
For Year Ended June 30, 2005

Sales		$655,000
Cost of goods sold		399,000
Gross profit		$256,000
Operating expenses:		
Amortization expense	$58,600	
Other expenses	67,000	
Total operating expenses		125,600
Income from operations		$130,400
Gain on sale of equipment		2,000
Income before taxes		$132,400
Income taxes		45,640
Net income		$ 86,760

*Exercise 19-9
Cash flows from operating
activities (indirect method)

LO^8

Refer to the information about Bozena Inc. presented in Exercise 19-4. Use the indirect
method and calculate the cash inflow (outflow) from operating activities.

An asterisk (*) identifies assignment material based on Appendix 19A.

The account balances for the non-cash current assets and current liabilities of Fefferman Corporation are as follows:

*Exercise 19-10
Cash flows from operating activities (indirect method)

LO⁸

December 31		
	2005	2004
Accounts receivable	$45,000	$37,000
Inventory	32,000	42,000
Prepaid expenses	19,000	17,000
Totals	$96,000	$96,000
Accounts payable	$30,000	$23,000
Salaries payable	9,000	13,000
Interest payable	17,000	14,000
Totals	$56,000	$50,000

During 2005, Fefferman Corporation reported amortization expense of $20,000. All purchases and sales are on account. Net income for 2005 was $90,000.

Required
1. Prepare the operating activities section of the cash flow statement using the indirect method.
2. Explain why cash flows from operating activities are different from net income.

Check figure:
1. Net cash inflow from operating activities, $116,000

Ingrid Inc.'s 2005 income statement showed the following: net income, $728,000; amortization expense, building, $90,000; amortization expense, equipment, $16,400; and gain on sale of capital assets, $14,000. An examination of the company's current assets and current liabilities showed that the following changes occurred because of operating activities: accounts receivable decreased $36,200; merchandise inventory decreased $104,000; prepaid expenses increased $7,400; accounts payable decreased $18,400; other payables increased $2,800. Use the indirect method to calculate the cash flow from operating activities.

*Exercise 19-11
Cash flows from operating activities (indirect method)

LO⁸

Check figure:
1. Net cash inflow from operating activities, $937,600

An asterisk (*) identifies assignment material based on Appendix 19A.

*Exercise 19-12
Classifying transactions on cash flow statement (indirect method)

LO⁸

The following events occurred during the year. Assuming that the company uses the indirect method of reporting cash provided by operating activities, indicate the proper accounting treatment for each event listed below by placing an x in the appropriate column.

	Cash Flow Statement			Note Describing Non-Cash Investing and Financing Activities	Not Reported on Statement or in Footnote
	Operating Activities	Investing Activities	Financing Activities		
a. Land was purchased by issuing common shares.	_____	_____	_____	_____	_____
b. Recorded amortization expense.	_____	_____	_____	_____	_____
c. Income tax payable increased by 15% from prior year.	_____	_____	_____	_____	_____
d. Declared and paid a cash dividend.	_____	_____	_____	_____	_____
e. Paid cash to purchase merchandise inventory.	_____	_____	_____	_____	_____
f. Sold equipment at a loss.	_____	_____	_____	_____	_____
g. Accounts receivable decreased during the year.	_____	_____	_____	_____	_____

*Exercise 19-13
Preparation of cash flow statement (indirect method)

LO⁸

Refer to the data in Exercise 19-8 and prepare the operating activities section of the cash flow statement using the indirect method.

*Exercise 19-14
Adjustments to derive cash flow from operations (indirect method)

LO⁸

	Adjust by	
	Adding	Subtracting
1. Changes in non-cash current assets:		
a. Increases	_____	_____
b. Decreases	_____	_____
2. Changes in current liabilities		
a. Increases	_____	_____
b. Decreases	_____	_____
3. Amortization of capital assets	_____	_____
4. Amortization of intangible assets	_____	_____
5. Interest expense:		
a. Bond premium amortized	_____	_____
b. Bond discount amortized	_____	_____
6. Sale of non-current asset:		
a. Gain	_____	_____
b. Loss	_____	_____

Indicate by an x in the appropriate column whether an item is added or subtracted to derive cash flow from operating activities.

An asterisk (*) identifies assignment material based on Appendix 19A.

Vogrincic Corporation's balance sheet and income statement are as follows:

Problem 19-1A
Cash flow statement
(direct method)

LO[5, 6, 7]

Vogrincic Corporation Comparative Balance Sheet Information		
	December 31	
Assets	**2005**	**2004**
Cash..	$ 232,000	$ 156,000
Accounts receivable..	124,000	108,000
Merchandise inventory	812,000	712,000
Equipment	444,000	396,000
Accumulated amortization	(208,000)	(136,000)
Total assets..	$1,404,000	$1,236,000
Liabilities and Shareholders' Equity		
Accounts payable..	$ 92,000	$ 128,000
Income taxes payable	36,000	32,000
Common shares	1,040,000	960,000
Retained earnings	236,000	116,000
Total liabilities and shareholders' equity	$1,404,000	$1,236,000

Vogrincic Corporation Income Statement For Year Ended December 31, 2005		
Sales		$2,656,000
Cost of goods sold..		1,592,000
Gross profit		$1,064,000
Operating expenses:		
Amortization expense	$ 72,000	
Other expenses...	668,000	
Total operating expenses		740,000
Income from operations..		$ 324,000
Income taxes		56,000
Net income		$ 268,000

Other information regarding Vogrincic Corporation:
a. All sales are credit sales.
b. All credits to accounts receivable in a period are receipts from customers.
c. All purchases of merchandise are on credit.
d. All debits to accounts payable in a period result from payments for merchandise.
e. Other operating expenses are cash expenses.
f. The only decrease in income taxes payable is for payment of taxes.

Additional information regarding Vogrincic Corporation's activities during 2005:
g. Equipment is purchased for $48,000 cash.
h. 16,000 common shares are issued for cash at $5 per share.
i. Declared and paid $148,000 of cash dividends during the year.

Required
Prepare a cash flow statement for 2005 that reports the cash inflows and outflows from operating activities according to the direct method. Show your supporting calculations.

Check figure:
Net cash inflow from operating
activities, $192,000

Problem 19-2A
Cash flow statement
(direct method)

LO 5, 6, 7

Blanchard Ltd.'s comparative balance sheets at December 31, 2005 and 2004, and its income statement for the year ended December 31, 2005, are as follows:

Blanchard Ltd.
Balance Sheet Information

Assets	December 31 2005	December 31 2004	Net Change
Cash...	$ 80,000	$ 41,600	$ 38,400
Temporary investments..............................	28,800	16,000	12,800
Accounts receivable	147,200	62,400	84,800
Inventory..	190,400	139,200	51,200
Long-term investment................................	-0-	28,800	(28,800)
Land...	128,000	128,000	-0-
Building and equipment.............................	740,800	760,000	(19,200)
Accumulated amortization..........................	(196,800)	(161,600)	(35,200)
Total assets...	$1,118,400	$1,014,400	$104,000
Liabilities and Shareholders' Equity			
Accounts payable	$ 33,200	$ 63,000	$ (29,800)
Dividends payable......................................	2,000	1,000	1,000
Bonds payable	40,000	-0-	40,000
Preferred shares..	136,000	136,000	-0-
Common shares	676,800	676,800	-0-
Retained earnings......................................	230,400	137,600	92,800
Total liabilities and shareholders' equity	$1,118,400	$1,014,400	$104,000

Blanchard Ltd.
Income Statement
For Year Ended December 31, 2005

Sales		$1,440,000
Cost of goods sold..		960,000
Gross profit		$ 480,000
Operating expenses...	$221,200	
Amortization expense	68,800	
Loss on sale of equipment...	6,400	
Income taxes	30,000	
Gain on sale of long-term investment...........................	(19,200)	307,200
Net income		$ 172,800

Other information:
a. All sales are credit sales.
b. All credits to accounts receivable in the period are receipts from customers.
c. All purchases of merchandise are on credit.
d. All debits to accounts payable in the period result from payments for merchandise.
e. Other operating expenses are cash expenses.
f. Income taxes are cash expenses.

During 2005, the following transactions occurred:
1. Purchased equipment for $32,000 cash.
2. Sold the long-term investment on January 1, 2005, for $48,000.
3. Sold equipment for $11,200 cash that had originally cost $51,200 and had $33,600 of accumulated amortization.
4. Issued $40,000 of bonds payable at face value.

Check figure:
Cash inflow from operating activities, $63,000

Required
1. How much cash was paid in dividends?
2. Prepare a cash flow statement for Blanchard Ltd. for the year ended December 31, 2005, using the direct method.

Nissen Corp.'s balance sheet and income statement are as follows:

Nissen Corp.
Comparative Balance Sheet Information

	December 31	
Assets	**2005**	**2004**
Cash	$ 75,425	$107,275
Accounts receivable	91,000	69,475
Merchandise inventory	383,250	353,500
Prepaid expenses	7,525	8,750
Equipment	223,300	154,000
Accumulated amortization	(48,475)	(61,600)
Total assets	$732,025	$631,400
Liabilities and Shareholders' Equity		
Accounts payable	$123,375	$163,275
Short-term notes payable	14,000	8,750
Long-term notes payable	131,250	75,250
Common shares	281,750	218,750
Retained earnings	181,650	165,375
Total liabilities and shareholders' equity	$732,025	$631,400

Nissen Corp.
Income Statement
For Year Ended December 31, 2005

Sales		$694,750
Cost of goods sold		350,000
Gross profit		$344,750
Operating expenses:		
Amortization expense	$ 26,250	
Other expenses	191,100	
Total operating expenses		217,350
Loss on sale of equipment		7,175
Income from operations		$120,225
Income taxes		16,975
Net income		$103,250

Other information regarding Nissen:
a. All sales are credit sales.
b. All credits to accounts receivable in the period are receipts from customers.
c. Purchases of merchandise are on credit.
d. All debits to accounts payable in the period result from payments for merchandise.
e. The only decrease in income taxes payable is for payment of taxes.
f. The other expenses are paid in advance and are initially debited to Prepaid Expenses.

Additional information regarding Nissen's activities during 2005:
g. Loss on sale of equipment is $7,175.
h. Equipment costing $65,625, with accumulated amortization of $39,375, is sold for $19,075.
i. Equipment costing $134,925 is purchased by paying cash of $35,000 and signing a long-term note payable for the balance.
j. Borrowed $5,250 by signing a short-term note payable.
k. Paid $43,925 to reduce a long-term note payable.
l. Issued 3,500 common shares for cash at $18 per share.
m. Declared and paid cash dividends of $86,975.

Required
Prepare a cash flow statement for 2005 that reports the cash inflows and outflows from operating activities according to the direct method. Show your supporting calculations. Also prepare a note describing non-cash investing and financing activities.

Check figure:
Net cash inflow from operating activities, $46,725

Problem 19-4A
Cash flow statement
(direct method)

LO⁵·⁶·⁷

Ibach Corporation began operations on January 1, 2004. Its post-closing trial balance at December 31, 2004 and 2005, is shown below along with some other information.

Ibach Corporation
Post-Closing Trial Balance
(000s)

Account	Dec. 31/05	Dec. 31/04
Cash	1,800	1,150
Receivables	1,750	1,300
Merchandise inventory	1,600	1,900
Property, plant and equipment	1,900	1,700
Accumulated amortization	1,200	1,150
Long-term investments	1,300	1,400
Accounts payable	1,200	900
Accrued liabilities	200	300
Bonds payable	1,400	1,500
Common shares	1,900	1,700
Retained earnings	2,450	1,900

Ibach Corporation
Income Statement
For Year Ended December 31, 2005
(000s)

Revenues:		
Sales		$2,365
Expenses:		
Cost of goods sold	$960	
Other expenses	550	
Income tax expense	180	
Amortization expense	50	
Total expenses		1,740
Net income		$ 625

Other information regarding Ibach Corporation and its activities during 2005:
a. Assume all accounts have normal balances.
b. All accounts payable balances result from merchandise purchases.
c. All sales are credit sales.
d. All credits to accounts receivable are receipts from customers.
e. All debits to accounts payable result from payments for merchandise.
f. All other expenses are cash expenses.
g. Cash dividends were declared and paid during the year.
h. There were no sales of plant assets during the year.
i. Long-term investments were sold for cash at their original cost.

Check figure:
Net cash outflows from investing activities, $100 (thousand)

Required
Using the information provided, prepare a cash flow statement (applying the *direct* method) for the year ended December 31, 2005.

J&G Holidays Inc. began operations on January 1, 2004. Its post-closing trial balance at December 31, 2004 and 2005, is shown below along with some other information.

Problem 19-5A
Cash flow statement
(direct method)

LO^{5,6,7}

J&G Holidays Inc. Post-Closing Trial Balance (000s)		
Account	**Dec. 31/05**	**Dec. 31/04**
Cash	3,600	2,100
Receivables	3,500	2,400
Merchandise inventory	3,400	3,800
Property, plant and equipment	6,200	6,600
Accumulated amortization	2,400	2,300
Accounts payable	2,400	1,800
Accrued liabilities	400	600
Bonds payable	2,800	3,000
Common shares	5,140	3,400
Retained earnings	3,560	3,800

J&G Holidays Inc. Income Statement For Year Ended December 31, 2005 (000s)		
Revenues:		
Sales		$5,500
Expenses:		
Cost of goods sold	$4,200	
Other expenses	1,100	
Amortization expense	400	
Total expenses		5,700
Net loss		$ 200

Other information regarding J&G Holidays Inc. and its activities during 2005:
a. Assume all accounts have normal balances.
b. All accounts payable balances result from merchandise purchases.
c. All sales are credit sales.
d. All credits to accounts receivable are receipts from customers.
e. All debits to accounts payable result from payments for merchandise.
f. All other expenses are cash expenses.
g. Cash dividends were declared and paid during the year.
h. Equipment was sold for cash equal to its book value.

Required
Using the information provided, prepare a cash flow statement (applying the *direct* method) for the year ended December 31, 2005.

Check figure:
Net cash inflows from financing
activities, $1,500 (thousand)

Problem 19-6A
Cash flow statement
(direct method)

LO⁵,⁶,⁷

Soltermann Inc. began operations on January 1, 2004. Its post-closing trial balance at December 31, 2004 and 2005, is shown below along with some other information.

Soltermann Inc. Post-Closing Trial Balance		
Account	**Dec. 31/05**	**Dec. 31/04**
Cash	39,000	48,000
Receivables	26,000	19,000
Merchandise inventory	17,000	22,000
Property, plant and equipment	144,000	119,000
Accumulated amortization	40,000	33,000
Accounts payable	31,000	39,000
Accrued liabilities	7,000	4,000
Long-term notes payable	61,000	25,000
Common shares	31,000	5,000
Retained earnings	56,000	102,000

Soltermann Inc. Income Statement For Year Ended December 31, 2005		
Revenues:		
Sales		$392,000
Expenses and other:		
Cost of goods sold	$302,000	
Other expenses	97,000	
Amortization expense	16,000	
Loss on sale of plant assets	13,000	
Total expenses and other		428,000
Net loss		$ 36,000

Other information regarding Soltermann Inc. and its activities during 2005:
a. Assume all accounts have normal balances.
b. All accounts payable balances result from merchandise purchases.
c. All sales are credit sales.
d. All credits to accounts receivable are receipts from customers.
e. All debits to accounts payable result from payments for merchandise.
f. All debits and credits to accrued liabilities result from other expenses.
g. Cash dividends were declared and paid during the year.
h. Plant assets were sold during the year.
i. Plant assets worth $62,000 were purchased during the year by paying cash of $20,000 and issuing a long-term note payable for the balance.

Check figure:
Net cash outflow from investing activities, $5,000

Required
Using the information provided, prepare a cash flow statement (applying the *direct* method) for the year ended December 31, 2005.

Refer to Vogrincic Corporation's financial statements and related information in Problem 19-1A.

Required
Prepare a cash flow statement for 2005 that reports the cash inflows and outflows from operating activities according to the indirect method.

*Problem 19-7A
Cash flow statement
(indirect method)

LO⁸

Check figure:
Net cash inflow from operating
activities, $192,000

Refer to Blanchard Ltd.'s financial statements and related information in Problem 19-2A.

Required
Prepare a cash flow statement for 2005 that reports the cash inflows and outflows from operating activities according to the indirect method.

*Problem 19-8A
Cash flow statement
(indirect method)

LO⁸

Check figure:
Net cash inflow from investing
activities, $27,200

Refer to the information about Nissen Corp. presented in Problem 19-3A.

Required
Prepare a cash flow statement for 2005 that reports the cash inflows and outflows from operating activities according to the indirect method.

*Problem 19-9A
Cash flow statement
(indirect method)

LO⁸

Check figure:
Net cash inflow from operating
activities, $46,725

Required
Using the information in Problem 19-4A, prepare a cash flow statement for the year ended December 31, 2005, using the indirect method.

*Problem 19-10A
Cash flow statement
(indirect method)

LO⁸

Check figure:
Net cash inflow from financing
activities, $25 (thousand)

Required
Using the information in Problem 19-5A, prepare a cash flow statement for the year ended December 31, 2005, using the indirect method.

*Problem 19-11A
Cash flow statement
(indirect method)

LO⁸

Check figure:
Net cash inflow from financing
activities, $1,500 (thousand)

Required
Using the information in Problem 19-6A, prepare a cash flow statement for the year ended December 31, 2005, using the indirect method.

*Problem 19-12A
Cash flow statement
(indirect method)

LO⁸

Check figure:
Net cash outflow from financing
activities, $10,000

An asterisk (*) identifies assignment material based on Appendix 19A.

Alternate Problems

Problem 19-1B
Cash flow statement
(direct method)

LO⁵,⁶,⁷

Clendenning Inc., a merchandiser, recently completed its 2005 operations. During the year:
a. All sales were credit sales.
b. All credits to accounts receivable in the period were receipts from customers.
c. Purchases of merchandise were on credit.
d. All debits to accounts payable were from payments for merchandise.
e. The other operating expenses were cash expenses.
f. The decrease in income taxes payable was for payment of taxes.

Clendenning Inc.
Comparative Balance Sheet Information

Assets	December 31 2005	2004
Cash	$ 75,495	$ 44,520
Accounts receivable	27,195	32,550
Merchandise inventory	245,490	195,825
Equipment	147,630	107,100
Accumulated amortization	(67,620)	(42,840)
Total assets	$428,190	$337,155
Liabilities and Shareholders' Equity		
Accounts payable	$ 53,865	$ 49,875
Income taxes payable	6,300	9,450
Common shares	289,800	231,000
Retained earnings	78,225	46,830
Total liabilities and shareholders' equity	$428,190	$337,155

Clendenning Inc.
Income Statement
For Year Ended December 31, 2005

Sales		$853,650
Cost of goods sold		390,600
Gross profit		$463,050
Operating expenses:		
Amortization expense	$ 24,780	
Other expenses	251,685	
Total operating expenses		276,465
Income from operations		$186,585
Income taxes		62,790
Net income		$123,795

Additional information regarding Clendenning's activities during 2005:
a. Equipment was purchased for $40,530 cash.
b. Issued 4,200 common shares for cash at $14 per share.
c. Declared and paid $92,400 of cash dividends during the year.

Check figure:
Net cash inflow from operating activities, $105,105

Required
Prepare a cash flow statement for 2005 that reports the cash inflows and outflows from operating activities according to the direct method. Show your supporting calculations.

Arnold Ltd.'s comparative balance sheets at December 31, 2005 and 2004, and its income statement for the year ended December 31, 2005, are as follows:

Problem 19-2B

Cash flows (direct method)

$LO^{5, 6, 7}$

Arnold Ltd. Comparative Balance Sheet Information			
Assets	**December 31 2005**	**December 31 2004**	**Net Change**
Cash..	$ 70,000	$ 36,400	$ 33,600
Temporary marketable investments	25,200	14,000	11,200
Accounts receivable	128,800	54,600	74,200
Inventory...	166,600	121,800	44,800
Long-term investment................................	-0-	25,200	(25,200)
Land...	112,000	112,000	-0-
Building and equipment..............................	648,200	665,000	(16,800)
Accumulated amortization..........................	(172,200)	(141,400)	(30,800)
Total assets...	$ 978,600	$ 887,600	$ 91,000
Liabilities and Shareholders' Equity			
Accounts payable	$ 29,800	$ 54,000	$(24,200)
Dividends payable......................................	1,000	2,000	(1,000)
Bonds payable	35,000	-0-	35,000
Preferred shares..	119,000	119,000	-0-
Common shares	592,200	592,200	-0-
Retained earnings......................................	201,600	120,400	81,200
Total liabilities and shareholders' equity	$ 978,600	$ 887,600	$ 91,000

Arnold Ltd. Income Statement Year Ended December 31, 2005		
Sales		$1,260,000
Cost of goods sold..		840,000
Gross profit		$ 420,000
Operating expenses...	$194,800	
Amortization expense	60,200	
Loss on sale of equipment..............................	5,600	
Income taxes	25,000	
Gain on sale of long-term investment.............	(16,800)	268,800
Net income		$ 151,200

Other information:

a. All sales are credit sales.

b. All credits to accounts receivable in a period are receipts from customers.

c. All purchases of merchandise are on credit.

d. All debits to accounts payable in a period result from payments for merchandise.

e. Other operating expenses are cash expenses.

f. Income taxes are cash expenses.

During 2005, the following transactions occurred:

1. Issued $35,000 of bonds payable at face value.

2. Sold the long-term investment on January 1, 2005, for $42,000.

3. Sold equipment for $9,800 cash that had originally cost $44,800 and had $29,400 of accumulated amortization.

4. Purchased equipment for $28,000 cash.

Required

a. How much was paid in dividends during 2005?

b. Prepare a cash flow statement for Arnold Ltd. for the year ended December 31, 2005, using the direct method.

Check figure:

Cash inflow from operating activities, $57,000

Problem 19-3B
Cash flow statement
(direct method)

LO 5, 6, 7

Yahn Inc., a merchandiser, recently completed its 2005 operations. During the year:
a. All sales were credit sales.
b. All credits to accounts receivable in the period were receipts from customers.
c. Purchases of merchandise were on credit.
d. All debits to accounts payable in the period resulted from payments for merchandise.
e. The decrease in income taxes payable was for payment of taxes.
f. The other expenses were paid in advance and were initially debited to prepaid expenses.

Wolfson Inc.'s balance sheet and income statement follow.

Yahn Inc.
Comparative Balance Sheet Information

Assets	December 31 2005	2004
Cash	$ 191,100	$ 100,170
Accounts receivable	103,740	127,050
Merchandise inventory	636,300	686,280
Prepaid expenses	23,940	26,880
Equipment	389,550	302,400
Accumulated amortization	(152,250)	(130,200)
Total assets	$1,192,380	$1,112,580
Liabilities and Shareholders' Equity		
Accounts payable	$ 164,430	$ 172,830
Short-term notes payable	24,150	15,750
Long-term notes payable	157,500	115,500
Common shares	676,200	630,000
Retained earnings	170,100	178,500
Total liabilities and shareholders' equity	$1,192,380	$1,112,580

Yahn Inc.
Income Statement
Year Ended December 31, 2005

Sales		$1,516,200
Cost of goods sold		819,000
Gross profit		$ 697,200
Operating expenses:		
Amortization expense	$ 51,240	
Other expenses	549,990	
Total operating expenses		601,230
Loss on sale of equipment		2,940
Income from operations		$ 93,030
Income taxes		13,230
Net income		$ 79,800

Additional information regarding Yahn's activities during 2005:
a. Loss on sale of equipment is $2,940.
b. Equipment costing $71,400, with accumulated amortization of $29,190, is sold for $39,270.
c. Equipment costing $158,550 is purchased by paying cash of $53,550 and signing a long-term note payable for the balance.
d. Borrowed $8,400 by signing a short-term note payable.
e. Paid $63,000 to reduce a long-term note payable.
f. Issued 4,200 common shares for cash at $11 per share.
g. Declared and paid cash dividends of $88,200.

Check figure:
Net cash inflow from operating activities, $201,810

Required
Prepare a cash flow statement for 2005 that reports the cash inflows and outflows from operating activities according to the direct method. Show your supporting calculations. Also prepare a note describing non-cash investing and financing activities.

Hayes Corporation began operations on January 1, 2004. Its post-closing trial balance at December 31, 2004 and 2005, is shown below along with some other information.

Problem 19-4B
Cash flow statement
(direct method)

LO[5, 6, 7]

Hayes Corporation
Post-Closing Trial Balance
(millions of dollars)

Account	Dec. 31/05	Dec. 31/04
Cash	18	43
Receivables	92	124
Merchandise inventory	136	87
Property, plant and equipment	2,300	2,992
Accumulated amortization	1,233	1,375
Long-term investments	520	103
Accounts payable	106	135
Accrued liabilities	47	39
Bonds payable	400	200
Common shares	900	700
Retained earnings	380	900

Hayes Corporation
Income Statement
For Year Ended December 31, 2005
(millions of dollars)

Revenues:		
Sales		$8,900
Expenses:		
Cost of goods sold	$6,500	
Other expenses	2,350	
Amortization expense	450	
Total expenses		9,300
Net loss		$ 400

Other information regarding Hayes Corporation and its activities during 2005:
a. Assume all accounts have normal balances.
b. All accounts payable balances result from merchandise purchases.
c. All sales are credit sales.
d. All credits to accounts receivable are receipts from customers.
e. All debits to accounts payable result from payments for merchandise.
f. All other expenses are cash expenses.
g. Cash dividends were declared and paid during the year.
h. Plant assets were sold for cash equal to book value during the year.

Required
Using the information provided, prepare a cash flow statement (applying the *direct* method) for the year ended December 31, 2005.

Check figure:
Net cash inflow from financing activities, $280 (million)

Problem 19-5B
Cash flow statement
(direct method)

LO⁵,⁶,⁷

Beck Corporation began operations on January 1, 2004. Its post-closing trial balance at December 31, 2004 and 2005, is shown below along with some other information.

Beck Corporation Post-Closing Trial Balance (millions)		
Account	**Dec. 31/05**	**Dec. 31/04**
Cash	97	15
Receivables	100	70
Prepaid insurance	12	4
Land	248	248
Equipment	107	149
Accumulated amortization	72	17
Accounts payable	31	14
Salaries payable	4	9
Income tax payable	17	50
Long-term notes payable	35	331
Common shares	160	40
Retained earnings	245	25

Beck Corporation Income Statement For Year Ended December 31, 2005 (millions)		
Revenues:		
Consulting revenue		$1,750
Expenses:		
Salaries expense	$940	
Other expenses	320	
Amortization expense	80	
Income tax expense	70	
Total expenses		1,410
Net income		$ 340

Other information regarding Beck Corporation and its activities during 2005:
a. Assume all accounts have normal balances.
b. All accounts payable balances result from other expenses.
c. All consulting revenue is done on credit.
d. All credits to accounts receivable are receipts from customers.
e. All debits to accounts payable result from payments for other expenses.
f. Share dividends were declared and issued during the year.
g. Equipment was sold for cash equal to its book value.

Check figure:
Net cash inflow from investing activities, $17 (million)

Required
Using the information provided, prepare a cash flow statement (applying the *direct* method) for the year ended December 31, 2005.

Guthrie Inc. began operations on January 1, 2004. Its post-closing trial balance at December 31, 2004 and 2005, is shown below along with some other information.

Problem 19-6B
Cash flow statement
(direct method)

LO[5, 6, 7]

Guthrie Inc. Post-Closing Trial Balance		
Account	**Dec. 31/05**	**Dec. 31/04**
Cash	158,000	163,000
Receivables	314,000	321,000
Merchandise inventory	118,000	97,000
Property, plant and equipment	746,000	681,000
Accumulated amortization	419,000	414,000
Accounts payable	197,000	195,000
Accrued liabilities	14,000	18,000
Long-term notes payable	298,000	188,000
Common shares	200,000	200,000
Retained earnings	208,000	247,000

Guthrie Inc. Income Statement For Year Ended December 31, 2005		
Revenues:		
Sales		$1,284,000
Expenses and other:		
Cost of goods sold	$859,000	
Other expenses	419,000	
Amortization expense	45,000	
Gain on sale of plant assets	(20,000)	
Total expenses and other		1,303,000
Net loss		$ 19,000

Other information regarding Guthrie Inc. and its activities during 2005:
a. Assume all accounts have normal balances.
b. All accounts payable balances result from merchandise purchases.
c. All sales are credit sales.
d. All credits to accounts receivable are receipts from customers.
e. All debits to accounts payable result from payments for merchandise.
f. All debits and credits to accrued liabilities result from other expenses.
g. Cash dividends were declared and paid during the year.
h. Plant assets were sold during the year.
i. Plant assets worth $175,000 were purchased during the year by paying cash of $50,000 and issuing a long-term note payable for the balance.

Required
Using the information provided, prepare a cash flow statement (applying the *direct* method) for the year ended December 31, 2005.

Check figure:
Net cash inflow from investing
activities, $40,000

*Problem 19-7B
Cash flow statement
(indirect method)

LO⁸

Check figure:
Net cash inflow from operating
activities, $105,105

Refer to Clendenning Inc.'s financial statements and related information in Problem 19-1B.

Required
Prepare a cash flow statement for 2005 that reports the cash inflows and outflows from operating activities according to the indirect method.

*Problem 19-8B
Cash flow statement
(indirect method)

 LO⁸

Check figure:
Net cash inflow from investing
activities, $23,800

Refer to Arnold Ltd.'s financial statements and related information in Problem 19-2B.

Required
Prepare a cash flow statement for 2005 that reports the cash inflows and outflows from operating activities according to the indirect method.

*Problem 19-9B
Cash flow statement
(indirect method)

 LO⁸

Check figure:
Net cash inflow from operating
activities, $201,810

Refer to Yahn Inc.'s balance sheets presented in Problem 19-3B.

Required
Prepare a cash flow statement for 2005 that reports the cash inflows and outflows from operating activities according to the indirect method.

*Problem 19-10B
Cash flow statement
(indirect method)

LO⁸

Check figure:
Net cash inflow from financing
activities, $280 (million)

Required
Using the information in Problem 19-4B, prepare a cash flow statement for the year ended December 31, 2005, using the indirect method.

*Problem 19-11B
Cash flow statement
(indirect method)

 LO⁸

Check figure:
Net cash inflow from investing
activities, $17 (million)

Required
Using the information in Problem 19-5B, prepare a cash flow statement for the year ended December 31, 2005, using the indirect method.

*Problem 19-12B
Cash flow statement
(indirect method)

 LO⁸

Check figure:
Net cash inflow from investing
activities, $40,000

Required
Using the information in Problem 19-6B, prepare a cash flow statement for the year ended December 31, 2005, using the indirect method.

_____
An asterisk (*) identifies assignment material based on Appendix 19A.

Analytical and Review Problems

Jacobson Corporation earned an $84,000 net income during 2005. Machinery was sold for $116,000 and a $24,000 loss on the sale was recorded. Machinery purchases totalled $330,000 including a July purchase for which an $80,000 promissory note P.533 was issued. Bonds were retired at their face value, and the issuance of new common shares produced an infusion of cash. Barrie's comparative balance sheets were as follows:

*A & R 19-1
(Indirect method)

Jacobson Corporation Comparative Balance Sheet Information (in thousands)		
	December 31	
Assets	**2005**	**2004**
Cash..	$ 104	$ 84
Accounts receivable...	196	222
Merchandise inventory	324	310
Machinery...	1,350	1,260
Accumulated amortization	(190)	(210)
Total assets..	$1,784	$1,666
Liabilities and Shareholders' Equity		
Accounts payable..	$ 238	$ 286
Notes payable...	272	210
Dividends payable...	32	20
Bonds payable	228	320
Common shares	700	560
Retained earnings...	314	270
Total liabilities and shareholders' equity	$1,784	$1,666

1. What was Jacobson's amortization expense in 2005?
2. What was the amount of cash flow from operating activities?
3. What was the amount of cash flow from investing activities?
4. What was the amount of dividends declared? Paid?
5. By what amount would you expect the total inflows of cash to differ from the total outflows of cash?
6. What was the amount of cash flow from financing activities?

The data below refers to Money Ltd. for the year ended December 31, 2005.

*A & R 19-2
(Indirect method)

Required
For each item, identify both the dollar amount and its classification—that is, whether it would appear as a positive or a negative adjustment to net income in the calculation of cash flow from operations (using the *indirect method*), or as some other inflow or outflow of cash.

1. Declared a $15,000 cash dividend; paid $12,000 during the year.
2. Sold, for $90,000 cash, land that had cost $75,000 two years earlier.
3. Sold for cash 2,000 shares for $6 a share.
4. Bought machinery for $24,000 in exchange for a note due in 18 months.
5. Bought a computer that had a fair value of $35,000 by giving in exchange real estate that had cost $15,000 in an earlier period.
6. Equipment amortization, $18,000.
7. Issued for $250,000 cash on December 31, 2005, 10-year, 10% bonds at an $18,000 discount.
8. Bought its own shares for $7,500 and immediately cancelled them.
9. Paid a lawyer $6,200 for services performed, billed, and recorded correctly in 2004.
10. Reported net income of $63,000 for the year ended December 31, 2005.

An asterisk (*) identifies assignment material based on Appendix 19A.

*A & R 19-3
(Indirect method)

Svekla Inc.'s 2005 cash flow statement appeared as follows:

Cash flows from operating activities:		
Net income		$111,100
Accounts receivable increase	$(14,700)	
Inventory decrease	47,600	
Prepaid expense increase	(4,600)	
Accounts payable decrease	(16,300)	
Income taxes payable increase	4,400	
Amortization expense	12,000	
Loss on disposal of equipment	13,400	
Gain on bond retirement	(7,700)	34,100
Net cash inflows from operating activities		$145,200
Cash flows from investing activities:		
Receipt from sale of office equipment	$ 5,100	
Purchase of store equipment	(33,000)	
Net cash outflows from investing activities		(27,900)
Cash flows from financing activities:		
Payment to retire bonds payable	$(42,300)	
Payment of dividends	(30,000)	
Net cash outflows from financing activities		(72,300)
Net increase in cash		$ 45,000
Cash balance at December 31, 2004		45,400
Cash balance at December 31, 2005		$ 90,400

Svekla Inc.'s beginning and ending balance sheets were as follows:

	December 31	
	2005	**2004**
Debits		
Cash	$ 90,400	$ 45,400
Accounts receivable	114,900	100,200
Merchandise inventory	212,700	260,300
Prepaid expenses	9,000	4,400
Equipment	99,100	108,600
Totals	$526,100	$518,900
Credits		
Accumulated amortization	$ 18,200	$ 30,200
Accounts payable	58,500	74,800
Income taxes payable	10,900	6,500
Dividends payable	-0-	7,500
Bonds payable	-0-	50,000
Common shares	300,000	300,000
Retained earnings	138,500	49,900
Totals	$526,100	$518,900

An examination of the company's statements and accounts showed:
a. All sales were made on credit.
b. All merchandise purchases were on credit.

An asterisk (*) identifies assignment material based on Appendix 19A.

c. Accounts payable balances resulted from merchandise purchases.
d. Prepaid expenses relate to other operating expenses.
e. Equipment that cost $42,500 and was amortized $24,000 was sold for cash.
f. Equipment was purchased for cash.
g. The change in the balance of Accumulated Amortization resulted from amortization expense and from the sale of equipment.
h. The change in the balance of Retained Earnings resulted from dividend declarations and net income.
i. Cash receipts from customers were $772,800.
j. Cash payments for merchandise inventory amounted to $425,400.
k. Cash payments for other operating expenses were $169,800.
l. Income taxes paid were $32,400

Required
Prepare Svekla's income statement for 2005. Show supporting calculations.

The following items include the 2005 and 2004 balance sheet information and the 2005 income statement of the Kushnir Corporation. Additional information about the company's 2005 transactions is presented after the financial statements.

*A & R 19-4
(Indirect method)

Kushnir Corporation Balance Sheet Comparative Information		
	December 31	
Assets	**2005**	**2004**
Cash and cash equivalents	$ 1,000	$ 800
Accounts receivable	4,500	3,100
Merchandise inventory	19,000	16,000
Prepaid expenses	700	600
Long-term investment in shares	10,000	12,000
Land	9,000	4,000
Buildings	60,000	60,000
Accumulated amortization, buildings	38,000	36,000
Equipment	21,000	16,000
Accumulated amortization, equipment	6,000	4,000
Total assets	$81,200	$72,500
Liabilities and Shareholders' Equity		
Notes payable	$ 5,000	$ 3,500
Accounts payable	9,000	10,000
Other accrued liabilities	5,300	4,200
Interest payable	400	300
Taxes payable	300	500
Bonds payable, due in 2007	25,000	22,000
Common shares	16,000	14,000
Retained earnings	20,200	18,000
Total liabilities and shareholders' equity	$81,200	$72,500

An asterisk (*) identifies assignment material based on Appendix 19A.

Kushnir Corporation
Income Statement
Year Ended December 31, 2005

Revenues:

Sales	$120,000	
Gain on sale of equity investment	3,000	
Dividend income	500	
Interest income	400	
Total revenues		$123,900

Expenses and losses:

Cost of goods sold	$ 50,000	
Other expenses	54,800	
Interest expense	2,000	
Income tax expense	2,500	
Amortization expense, buildings	2,000	
Amortization expense, equipment	4,000	
Loss on sale of equipment	600	
Total expenses and losses		115,900
Net income		$ 8,000

Additional information:
1. Received $5,000 from the sale of Icahn Corporation common shares that originally cost $2,000.
2. Received a cash dividend of $500 from the Icahn Corporation.
3. Received $400 cash from the First National Bank on December 31, 2005, as interest income.
4. Sold old equipment for $1,400. The old equipment originally cost $4,000 and had accumulated amortization of $2,000.
5. Purchased land costing $5,000 on December 31, 2005, in exchange for a note payable. Both principal and interest are due on June 30, 2006.
6. Purchased new equipment for $9,000 cash.
7. Paid $3,500 of notes payable.
8. Sold additional bonds payable at par of $3,000 on January 1, 2005.
9. Issued 1,000 common shares for cash at $2 per share.
10. Declared and paid a $5,800 cash dividend on October 1, 2005.

Required
Prepare a cash flow statement for Kushnir Corporation using the indirect method.

Ethics Challenge

EC 19-1

Wendy Geiger is working late on a Friday night in preparation for a meeting with her banker early Monday morning. Her business is just finishing its fourth quarter. In Year 1, the business experienced negative cash flows from operations. In Years 2 and 3, cash flows from operations turned positive. Unfortunately, her inventory costs rose significantly in Year 4 and her net income will probably be down about 25% after this year's adjusting entries. Wendy is hoping to secure a line of credit from her banker, which will be a nice financing buffer. From prior experience with her banker, she knows that a focus of Monday's meeting will be cash flows from operations. The banker will scrutinize the cash flow numbers for Years 1 through 4 and will want a projected number for Year 5. Wendy knows that a steady upward progression of cash flows in Years 1 through 4 will really help her case for securing the line of credit. Wendy decides to use her discretion as owner of the business and proposes several adjusting entries and business actions that will help turn her cash flow number in Year 4 from negative to positive.

Required

1. Identify two possible entries or business actions Wendy might use to improve the cash flow from operations number on the cash flow statement for Year 4.
2. Comment on the ethics and possible consequences of Wendy's decision to propose the adjustments/actions for Year 4.

Focus on Financial Statements

FFS 19-1

Wong Corporation began operations on January 1, 2004. Its adjusted trial balance at December 31, 2004 and 2005, is shown below along with some other information.

Wong Corporation Adjusted Trial Balance (000s)		
Account	Dec. 31/05	Dec. 31/04
Accounts payable	$ 21	$ 32
Accounts receivable	96	100
Accumulated amortization, equipment	21	52
Accumulated amortization, machinery	15	36
Allowance for doubtful accounts	6	12
Amortization expense, equipment	7	7
Amortization expense, machinery	4	4
Cash	50	108
Cash dividends	20	20
Common shares	108	98
Equipment	88	110
Income tax expense	—	19
Machinery	34	64
Notes payable; long term[b]	18	25
Other expenses (including losses)	373	200
Preferred shares	40	40
Retained earnings	79	13
Revenues (including gains)	350	316
Unearned revenue	14	8

Other information regarding Wong Corporation and its activities during 2005:
a. Assume all accounts have normal balances.
b. $9,000 of the notes payable will be paid during 2006.
c. Equipment was purchased for $26,000 cash after selling old equipment for $8,000 cash.
d. Common shares were issued for cash.
e. Cash dividends were declared and paid.
f. Machinery was sold for cash of $10,000.
g. All revenues and other expenses were on credit.

Required

Using the information provided, prepare a statement of retained earnings and a cash flow statement (applying the *direct* or *indirect* method)* for the year ended December 31, 2005, plus a classified balance sheet at December 31, 2005.

Note to Instructor: Solutions are available for both the direct and indirect methods.

Analyzing Financial Statements

The Art of Comparison

Calgary—Five years ago, Bruce Hutten landed his first job with Strategic Financial Analyst (SFA). "I'm pretty excited," Bruce told his friends "I'll be advising clients on important operating, financing, and investment decisions after I finish my training period. My supervisor told me that I had to become skilled at analyzing and interpreting financial statements." SFA provides services to clients that include key ratio analysis of customers, suppliers, and competitors.

"In the beginning, I was pretty overwhelmed when my supervisors talked about tools of analysis such as horizontal and vertical analysis, and there seemed to be a million ratios to learn." Bruce's reaction is typical of many who become entrenched in financial statement analysis. But Bruce took a systematic approach and learned the fundamentals step by step. "I have gained a lot of experience and learned to focus my analysis on the needs of my clients. Some want to assess a firm's liquidity but others are more interested in profitability. I have learned that a ratio in isolation is meaningless; it is important to compare ratios to those of other firms in the same industry."

Learning Objectives

LO¹ Explain the purpose of analysis.

LO² Identify the building blocks of analysis.

LO³ Describe standards for comparisons in analysis.

LO⁴ Identify the tools of analysis.

LO⁵ Explain and apply methods of horizontal analysis.

LO⁶ Describe and apply methods of vertical analysis.

LO⁷ Define and apply ratio analysis.

Chapter Preview

This chapter shows us how to use the information in financial statements to evaluate the financial performance and condition of a company. We describe the purpose of analysis, its basic building blocks, the information available, standards for comparisons, and tools of analysis. Three major analysis tools are emphasized—horizontal analysis, vertical analysis, and ratio analysis. We illustrate the application of each of these tools using Ralco Corporation's financial statements. Understanding financial statement analysis is crucial to sound business decision making.

Basics of Analysis

Financial statement analysis is the application of analytical tools to general-purpose financial statements and related data for making business decisions. It involves transforming data into useful information. Financial statement analysis reduces our reliance on hunches, guesses, and intuition. It reduces our uncertainty in decision making. But it does not lessen the need for expert judgement. Instead, it provides us with an effective and systematic basis for business decisions. This section describes the purpose of financial statement analysis, its information sources, the use of comparisons, and some issues in calculations.

Purpose of Analysis

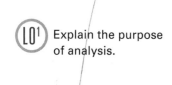

LO¹ Explain the purpose of analysis.

The purpose of financial statement analysis is to help users make better business decisions. These users include decision makers both internal and external to the company.

Internal users P.11 of accounting information are those individuals involved in managing and operating the company. The purpose of financial statement analysis for these users is to provide information helpful in improving the company's efficiency or effectiveness in providing products or services.

External users P.10 of accounting information are *not* directly involved in running the company. External users rely on financial statement analysis to make better and more informed decisions in pursuing their own goals.

We can identify many examples of how financial statement analysis is used. Shareholders and creditors assess future company prospects for investing and lending decisions. A board of directors P.759 analyzes financial statements in monitoring management's decisions. Employees and unions use financial statements in labour negotiations. Suppliers use financial statements in establishing credit terms. Customers analyze financial statements in deciding whether to establish supply relationships. Public utilities set customer rates by analyzing financial statements. Auditors use financial statements in assessing the "fair presentation" of their clients' financial statement numbers. And analyst services such as *Dun & Bradstreet, Moody's,* and *Standard & Poor's* use financial statements in making buy–sell recommendations and setting credit ratings.

The common goal of all these users is to evaluate company performance. This includes evaluation of (1) past and current performance, (2) current financial position, and (3) future performance and risk.

Building Blocks of Analysis

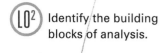

LO² Identify the building blocks of analysis.

Financial statement analysis focuses on one or more elements of a company's financial condition or performance. Our analysis emphasizes four areas of inquiry—with varying degrees of importance. These four areas are described and illustrated in this chapter and are considered the building blocks of financial statement analysis.

- *Liquidity and Efficiency*—ability to meet short-term obligations and to generate revenues efficiently.
- *Solvency*—ability to generate future revenues and meet long-term obligations.
- *Profitability*—ability to provide financial rewards sufficient to attract and retain financing.
- *Market*—ability to generate positive market expectations.

Information for Analysis

We explained how decision makers need to analyze financial statements. Some of these people, such as managers and a few regulatory agencies, are able to receive special financial reports prepared to meet their needs. But most must rely on general purpose financial statements that companies publish periodically. **General purpose financial statements** include the (1) income statement, (2) balance sheet, (3) statement of retained earnings, and (4) cash flow statement, accompanied by notes related to all four statements.

General purpose financial statements are part of **financial reporting**. Financial reporting refers to the communication of relevant financial information to decision makers. It includes financial statements, but it also involves information from filings with the securities commissions, news releases, shareholders' meetings, forecasts, management letters, auditors' reports, and analyses published in annual reports. Financial reporting broadly refers to useful information for decision makers to make investment, credit, and other decisions. It should help users assess the amounts, timing, and uncertainty of future cash inflows and outflows.

Standards for Comparisons

When calculating and interpreting analysis measures as part of our financial statement analysis, we need to decide whether these measures suggest good, bad, or average performance. To make these judgements, we need standards for comparison. Standards for comparison can include:

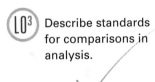

LO3 Describe standards for comparisons in analysis.

- *Intracompany* The company under analysis provides standards for comparisons based on prior performance and relations between its financial items.
- *Competitor* One or more direct competitors of the company under analysis can provide standards for comparison. Care must be exercised, however, in making comparisons with other firms to allow for the financial statement effects that are due to different accounting methods (i.e., different inventory costing systems or different amortization methods).
- *Industry* Industry statistics can provide standards of comparison. Published industry statistics are available from several services such as *Dun & Bradstreet*, *Standard & Poor's*, and *Moody's*.
- *Guidelines (Rules of Thumb)* General standards of comparison can develop from past experiences.

All of these standards of comparison are useful when properly applied. Yet analysis measures taken from a selected competitor or group of competitors are often the best standards of comparison. Also, intracompany and industry measures are important parts of all analyses. Guidelines or rules of thumb should be applied with care, and then only if they seem reasonable in light of past experience and industry norms.

Flashback

Answers—pp. 1067–1068

1. Who are the intended users of general purpose financial statements?
2. What statements are usually included in general purpose financial statements published by corporations?
3. Which of the following are least useful as a basis for comparison when analyzing ratios and turnovers? (a) companies operating in a different economy; (b) past experience; (c) rule-of-thumb standards; (d) averages within a trade or industry.
4. What basis of comparison for ratios is usually best?

Tools of Analysis

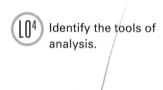

LO4   Identify the tools of analysis.

There are several tools of financial statement analysis. Three of the most common tools are:

- *Horizontal Analysis* Comparison of a company's financial condition and performance across time.
- *Vertical Analysis* Comparison of a company's financial condition and performance to a base amount.
- *Ratio Analysis* Determination of key relations among financial statement items.

The remainder of this chapter describes these tools of analysis and how we apply them.

Horizontal Analysis

LO5   Explain and apply methods of horizontal analysis.

Horizontal analysis is a tool to evaluate the important relations and changes between the items in financial statements *across time*.[1] **Comparative financial statements** show financial amounts in side-by-side columns on a single statement and facilitate the comparison of amounts for two or more successive periods. For instance, WestJet's *annual report* in Appendix I has a comparative statement based on two years of financial performance.

This section explains how we calculate dollar changes and percent changes in comparative statements and illustrates their application to the financial statements of Ralco Corporation.

Calculation of Dollar Changes and Percent Changes

Comparing financial statements over relatively short time periods—two to three years—is often done by analyzing changes in line items. A change analysis usually includes an analysis of absolute dollar amount changes as well as percent changes.

---

[1] The term *horizontal analysis* arises from the left-to-right (or right-to-left) movement of our eyes as we review comparative financial statements across time.

Both analyses are relevant since dollar changes can sometimes yield large percent changes inconsistent with their importance. For instance, a 50-percent change from a base figure of $100 is less important than the same percent change from a base amount of $100,000 in the same statement. Reference to dollar amounts is necessary to retain a proper perspective and for assessing the importance of changes.

We calculate the *dollar change* for a financial statement item as:

$$\text{Dollar change} = \text{Analysis period amount} - \text{Base period amount}$$

where *analysis period* is the point or period of time for the financial statements under analysis, and *base period* is the point or period of time for the financial statements used for comparison purposes. We commonly use the prior year as the base period.

We calculate the *percent change* by dividing the dollar change by the base period amount, and then multiplying this quantity by 100:

$$\text{Percent change} = \frac{\text{Analysis period amount} - \text{Base period amount}}{\text{Base period amount}} \times 100$$

While we can always calculate a dollar change, we must be aware of a few rules in working with percent changes. To illustrate, let's look at four separate cases in the chart below:

Case	Base Period	Analysis Period	Change Analysis Dollar	Change Analysis Percent
A	$ (4,500)	$ 1,500	$ 6,000	—
B	2,000	(1,000)	(3,000)	—
C	—	8,000	8,000	—
D	10,000	-0-	(10,000)	(100%)

When a negative amount appears in the base period and a positive amount in the analysis period (or vice versa), we cannot calculate a meaningful percent change—see cases A and B. Also, when there is no value in the base period, no percent change is identifiable—see case C. Finally, when an item has a value in the base period and zero in the next period, the decrease is 100 percent—see case D.

We commonly round percents and ratios to one or two decimal places, but there is no uniform practice on this matter. Calculations should not be so excessively detailed that important relations are lost among a mountain of decimal points.

Comparative Balance Sheet

One of the most useful comparative statements is the comparative balance sheet. It consists of amounts from two or more balance sheet dates arranged side by side. The usefulness of comparative financial statements is often improved by also showing each item's dollar change and percent change. This type of presentation highlights large dollar and percent changes for decision makers. Exhibit 20.1 shows the comparative balance sheet for Ralco.

Exhibit 20.1

Comparative Balance Sheet

(in thousands)	2005	2004	Amount of Increase or (Decrease) in 2005	Percent of Increase or (Decrease) in 2005
Ralco Corporation				
Balance Sheet				
November 30, 2005, and November 30, 2004				
Assets				
Current assets:				
Cash and short-term investments	$ 85,618	$ 57,000	$28,618	50.2
Accounts receivable				
Trade	50,586	36,327	14,259	39.3
Other...............................	2,264	2,185	79	3.6
Inventory...........................	13,417	7,361	6,056	82.3
Prepaid expenses	1,348	812	536	66.0
Total current assets	$153,233	$103,685	$49,548	47.8
Capital assets (net)......................	38,189	28,605	9,584	33.5
Total assets	$191,422	$132,290	$59,132	44.7
Liabilities				
Current liabilities:				
Accounts payable	$ 8,487	$ 5,391	$ 3,096	57.4
Accrued liabilities.....................	10,722	6,073	4,649	76.6
Income taxes payable.................	4,930	7,400	(2,470)	(33.4)
Total current liabilities	$ 24,139	$ 18,864	$ 5,275	28.0
Long-term debt	2,330	2,192	138	6.3
Total liabilities	$ 26,469	$ 21,056	$ 5,413	25.7
Shareholders' Equity				
Common shares	$ 89,732	$ 68,516	$21,216	31.0
Retained earnings.....................	75,221	42,718	32,503	76.1
Total shareholders' equity	$164,953	$111,234	$53,719	48.3
Total liabilities and				
shareholders' equity	$191,422	$132,290	$59,132	44.7

Our analysis of comparative financial statements begins by focusing on items that show large dollar or percent changes. We then try to identify the reasons for these changes and, if possible, determine whether they are favourable or unfavourable. We also follow up on items with small changes when we expected the changes to be large.

Regarding Ralco's comparative balance sheet, its first line item, "Cash and short-term investments" in Exhibit 20.1 stands out and shows a $28.6 million increase (50.2%). To a large extent, this increase may be explained by the increase in two other items: the $21.2 million increase in Common Shares and the $32.5 million increase in Retained earnings.

Note that Ralco's liabilities increased by $5.4 million. In light of this, the $28.6 million increase in Cash and short-term investments might appear to be an excessive investment in highly liquid assets P. 225 that usually earn a low return. However, the company's very strong and liquid financial position indicates an outstanding ability to respond to new opportunities such as the acquisition of other companies.

Comparative Income Statement

A comparative income statement is prepared similarly to the comparative balance sheet. Amounts for two or more periods are placed side-by-side, with additional columns for dollar and percent changes. Exhibit 20.2 shows Ralco's comparative income statement.

Exhibit 20.2

Comparative Income Statements

Ralco Corporation Income Statement For Years Ended November 30, 2005 and 2004				
(in thousands)	2005	2004	Amount of Increase or (Decrease) in 2005	Percent of Increase or (Decrease) in 2005
Sales	$164,313	$105,027	$59,286	56.4
Cost of goods sold	35,940	24,310	11,630	47.8
Gross profit	$128,373	$ 80,717	$47,656	59.0
Expenses:				
Advertising	34,390	20,579	13,811	67.1
Selling, general and administrative	30,833	18,005	12,828	71.2
Research and development	10,888	6,256	4,632	74.0
Amortization	6,137	4,079	2,058	50.5
Loss (gain) on foreign exchange	1,546	(480)	2,026	—
Total expenses:	$83,794	$ 48,439	$35,355	73.0
Income from continuing operations	$44,579	$ 32,278	$12,301	38.1
Interest income	2,959	2,482	477	19.2
Less: Interest expense	98	93	5	5.4
Income from continuing operations before income taxes	$ 47,440	$ 34,667	$12,773	36.8
Income taxes	14,937	13,814	1,123	8.1
Net income	$ 32,503	$ 20,853	$11,650	55.9

All of the income statement items (except foreign exchange) reflect the company's rapid growth. Especially note the large $13.8 million or 67.1% increase in advertising. This suggests the company's leadership and strong response to competition in the software industry. Although the dollar increase in Interest income was only $0.5 million, this amounted to a 19.2% increase. This is consistent with the increase in Cash and short-term investments reported in the balance sheet.

Output Made Easy

Today's accounting programs and spreadsheets can produce outputs with horizontal, vertical, and ratio analyses. These analyses can include a graphical depiction of financial relations. The key is being able to use this information properly and effectively for business decision making.

Did You Know?

Trend Analysis

Trend analysis, also called *trend percent analysis* or *index number trend analysis*, is used to reveal patterns in data covering successive periods. This method of analysis is a variation on the use of percent changes for horizontal analysis. The difference is that trend analysis does not subtract the base period amount in the numerator. To calculate trend percents we need to:

1. Select a *base period* and assign each item for the base period statement a weight of 100%.
2. Express financial numbers from other periods as a percent of the base period number.

$$\text{Trend percent} = \frac{\text{Analysis period amount}}{\text{Base period amount}} \times 100$$

To illustrate trend analysis, we use selected financial data of Ralco as shown in Exhibit 20.3.

Exhibit 20.3

Revenues and Expenses

	2005	2004	2003	2002	2001
Sales	$164,313	$105,027	$67,515	$52,242	$29,230
Cost of goods sold	35,940	24,310	19,459	7,735	6,015
Gross profit	$128,373	$ 80,717	$48,056	$44,507	$23,215

We select 2001 as the base period and calculate the trend percent for each year and each item by dividing each year's dollar amount by its 2001 dollar amount. For instance, the revenue trend percent for 2004 is 359.3%, calculated as $105,027 ÷ $29,230. The trend percents for the data from Exhibit 20.3 are shown in Exhibit 20.4.

Exhibit 20.4

Trend Percents of Revenues and Expenses

	2005	2004	2003	2002	2001
Sales	562.1%	359.3%	231.0%	178.7%	100%
Cost of goods sold	597.5	404.2	323.5	128.6	100
Gross profit	553.0	347.7	207.0	191.7	100

Exhibit 20.5

Trend Percent Lines for Revenues and Selected Expenses

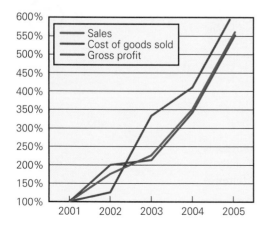

Exhibit 20.5 presents the trend percents from Exhibit 20.4 in a *line graph*. A line graph can help us identify trends and detect changes in direction or magnitude. For example, note that the gross profit line was bending upward from 2001 to 2002 but was essentially flat from 2002 to 2003. The gross profit increased at a lower rate from 2002 to 2003 but was parallel to the sales line from 2002 to 2005.

The line graph in Exhibit 20.5 also helps us understand the relationships between items. For example, the graph in Exhibit 20.5 shows that 2002 through 2005, cost of goods sold increased at a rate that was somewhat more than the increase in sales. Further, the differing trends in these two items had a clear effect on the percentage changes in gross profit. That is, gross profit increased each year at a somewhat slower rate than sales.

Trend analysis of financial statement items also can include comparisons of relations between items on different financial statements. For instance, Exhibit 20.6 shows a comparison of Ralco's total assets and revenues.

	2005	2001	Trend Percent (2005 vs 2001)
Sales	$164.3	$29.2	562.7%
Total assets (fiscal year-end)	191.4	41.9	456.8

Exhibit 20.6

Revenues and Total Assets Data

The rate of increase in total assets was not quite as large as the increase in revenues. Is this change favourable? We cannot say for sure. It might suggest that the company is able to use assets more efficiently than in earlier years. On the other hand, it might mean that the company may realize slower growth in future years. Monitoring this relation is important to see if the company can continue to achieve high revenue growth. An important part of financial analysis is identifying questions and areas of concern such as these. Financial statement analysis often leads the analyst to ask questions, without providing one clear answer. These concerns often direct us to important factors bearing on the future of the company under analysis.

Vertical (or Common-Size) Analysis

Vertical (or common-size) analysis is a tool to evaluate individual financial statement items or groups of items in terms of a specific base amount. We usually define a key aggregate figure as the base, and the base amount is commonly defined as 100%. For instance, an income statement's base is usually revenue and a balance sheet's base is usually total assets. This section explains vertical analysis and applies it to Ralco's statements.[2]

 Describe and apply methods of vertical analysis.

Common-Size Statements

The comparative statements in Exhibits 20.1 and 20.2 show how each item has changed over time, but they do not emphasize the relative importance of each item. We use **common-size financial statements** to reveal changes in the relative importance of each financial statement item. A *common-size percent* is measured by taking each individual financial statement amount under analysis and dividing it by its base amount:

$$\text{Common-size percent} = \frac{\text{Analysis amount}}{\text{Base amount}} \times 100$$

Common-Size Balance Sheet

Common-size statements express each item as a percent of a *base amount*. The base amount for a common-size balance sheet is usually total assets. It is assigned a value of 100%. This also implies the total amount of liabilities plus shareholders' equity equals 100% since this amount equals total assets. Next, we calculate a common-size percent for each asset, liability, and shareholders' equity item where the base amount is total assets as illustrated in Exhibit 20.7.

---

[2] The term *vertical analysis* arises from the up–down (or down–up) movement of our eyes as we review common-size financial statements.

Exhibit 20.7

Common-Size Comparative
Balance Sheet

			Common-Size Percentages	
Ralco Corporation **Balance Sheet** **November 30, 2005, and November 30, 2004**				
(in thousands)	2005	2004	2005	2004
Assets				
Current assets:				
Cash and short-term investments.............	$ 85,618	$ 57,000	44.7	43.1
Accounts receivable				
Trade..	50,586	36,327	26.4	27.4
Other.......................................	2,264	2,185	1.2	1.7
Inventory....................................	13,417	7,361	7.0	5.6
Prepaid expenses.......................	1,348	812	0.7	0.6
Total current assets	$153,233	$103,685	80.0	78.4
Capital assets (net)	38,189	28,605	20.0	21.6
Total assets.................................	$191,422	$132,290	100.0	100.0
Liabilities				
Current liabilities:				
Accounts payable......................	$ 8,487	$ 5,391	4.4	4.1
Accrued liabilities	10,722	6,073	5.6	4.6
Income taxes payable	4,930	7,400	2.6	5.6
Total current liabilities	$ 24,139	$ 18,864	12.6	14.3
Long-term debt...........................	2,330	2,192	1.2	1.6
Total liabilities.............................	$ 26,469	$ 21,056	13.8	15.9
Shareholders' Equity				
Common shares, 60,000 shares issued and outstanding..........................	$ 89,732	$ 68,516	46.9	51.8
Retained earnings	75,221	42,718	39.3	32.3
Total shareholders' equity............	$164,953	$111,234	86.2	84.1
Total liabilities and shareholders' equity	$191,422	$132,290	100.0	100.0

Common-Size Income Statement

Our analysis also usually benefits from an examination of a common-size income statement. The amount of revenues is the base amount and it is assigned a value of 100%. Each common-size income statement item appears as a percent of revenues.

Exhibit 20.8 shows the comparative income statement for 2005 and 2004.

Exhibit 20.8

Common-Size Comparative
Income Statement

Ralco Corporation
Income Statement
For Years Ended November 30, 2005 and 2004

(in thousands)	2005	2004	Common-Size Percentages 2005	2004
Sales	$164,313	$105,027	100.0	100.0
Cost of goods sold	35,940	24,310	21.9	23.1
Gross profit from sales	$128,373	$ 80,717	78.1	76.9
Expenses:				
Advertising	34,390	20,579	20.9	19.6
Selling, general and administrative	30,833	18,005	18.8	17.1
Research and development	10.888	6,256	6.6	6.0
Amortization	6,137	4,079	3.7	3.9
Loss (gain) on foreign exchange	1,546	(480)	0.9	(0.5)
Total expenses	$ 83,794	$ 48,439	51.0	46.1
Income from continuing operations	44,579	32,278	27.1	30.7
Interest income	2,959	2,482	1.8	2.4
Less: Interest expense	98	93	0.1	0.1
Income from continuing operations before income taxes	$ 47,440	$ 34,667	28.8	33.0
Income taxes	14,937	13,814	9.0	13.2
Net income	$ 32,503	$ 20,853	19.8	19.8
Earnings per share	$ 0.63	$ 0.45		
Weighted-average shares outstanding	51,768	46,146		

One of the advantages of calculating common-size percents for successive income statements is in helping us uncover potentially important changes in a company's expenses. For Ralco, the relative size of each expense changed very little from 2004 to 2005. Evidence of no changes is also valuable information for our analysis.

Common-Size Graphics

An income statement readily lends itself to common-size graphical analysis. Revenues affect nearly every item in an income statement. It is also usually helpful for our analysis to know what portion of revenues various geographical regions take up. Exhibit 20.9 shows Ralco's common-size income statement in graphical form. This pie chart highlights the contribution of each component of revenues.

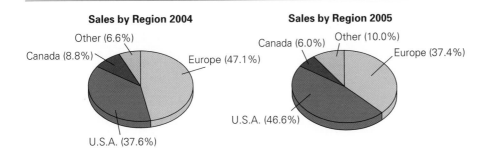

Exhibit 20.9

Common-Size Graphic of
Ralco's Income Statement

Common-size financial statements are useful in comparing different companies because the focus is changed from dollars (which can vary significantly between companies of different sizes) to percentages (which are always expressed as X out of 100, the base is constant). Common-size statements do not reflect the relative sizes of companies under analysis but a comparison of a company's common-size statements with competitors' or industry common-size statistics alerts us to differences that should be explored and explained.

Answers—p. 1068

5. On common-size comparative statements, which of the following is true? (a) Each item is expressed as a percent of a base amount, (b) Total assets are assigned a value of 100%, (c) Amounts from two or more successive periods are placed side-by-side, (d) All of the above are true.

6. What is the difference between the percents shown on a comparative income statement and those shown on a common-size comparative income statement?

7. Trend percents are: (a) shown on the comparative income statement and the comparative balance sheet; (b) shown on common-size comparative statements; or (c) also called index numbers.

Mid-Chapter Demonstration Problem

Use the financial statements of Precision Inc. to satisfy the following requirements:

1. Prepare a comparative income statement showing the percent increase or decrease for 2005 over 2004.

2. Prepare a common-size comparative balance sheet for 2005 and 2004.

Precision Inc. Income Statement For Years Ended December 31, 2005 and 2004		
	2005	**2004**
Sales	$2,486,000	$2,075,000
Cost of goods sold	1,523,000	1,222,000
Gross profit from sales	$ 963,000	$ 853,000
Operating expenses:		
Advertising expense	$ 145,000	$ 100,000
Sales salaries expense	240,000	280,000
Office salaries expense	165,000	200,000
Insurance expense	100,000	45,000
Supplies expense	26,000	35,000
Amortization expense	85,000	75,000
Miscellaneous expenses	17,000	15,000
Total operating expenses	$ 778,000	$ 750,000
Operating income	$ 185,000	$ 103,000
Less interest expense	44,000	46,000
Income before taxes	$ 141,000	$ 57,000
Income taxes	47,000	19,000
Net income	$ 94,000	$ 38,000
Earnings per share	$ 0.99	$ 0.40

Precision Inc.
Balance Sheet
December 31

	2005	2004
Assets		
Current assets:		
Cash	$ 79,000	$ 42,000
Short-term investment	65,000	96,000
Accounts receivable (net)	120,000	100,000
Merchandise inventory	250,000	265,000
Total current assets	$ 514,000	$ 503,000
Capital assets:		
Store equipment (net)	$ 400,000	$ 350,000
Office equipment (net)	45,000	50,000
Buildings (net)	625,000	675,000
Land	100,000	100,000
Total capital assets	$1,170,000	$1,175,000
Total assets	$1,684,000	$1,678,000
Liabilities		
Current liabilities:		
Accounts payable	$ 164,000	$ 190,000
Short-term notes payable	75,000	90,000
Taxes payable	26,000	12,000
Total current liabilities	$ 265,000	$ 292,000
Long-term liabilities:		
Notes payable (secured by mortgage on building and land)	400,000	420,000
Total liabilities	$ 665,000	$ 712,000
Shareholders' Equity		
Contributed capital:		
Common shares	$ 475,000	$ 475,000
Retained earnings	544,000	491,000
Total shareholders' equity	$1,019,000	$ 966,000
Total liabilities and shareholders' equity	$1,684,000	$1,678,000

Planning the Solution

o Set up a four-column income statement; enter the 2005 and 2004 amounts in the first two columns and then enter the dollar change in the third column and the percent change from 2004 in the fourth column.

o Set up a four-column balance sheet; enter the 2005 and 2004 amounts in the first two columns and then calculate and enter the amount of each item as a percent of total assets.

SOLUTION TO Mid-Chapter Demonstration Problem

1.

			Increase (Decrease) in 2005	
	2005	**2004**	**Amount**	**Percent**
Sales	$2,486,000	$2,075,000	$411,000	19.8%
Cost of goods sold	1,523,000	1,222,000	301,000	24.6
Gross profit from sales	$ 963,000	$ 853,000	$110,000	12.9
Operating expenses:				
Advertising expense	$ 145,000	$ 100,000	$ 45,000	45.0
Sales salaries expense	240,000	280,000	(40,000)	(14.3)
Office salaries expense	165,000	200,000	(35,000)	(17.5)
Insurance expense	100,000	45,000	55,000	122.2
Supplies expense	26,000	35,000	(9,000)	(25.7)
Amortization expense	85,000	75,000	10,000	13.3
Other operating expenses	17,000	15,000	2,000	13.3
Total operating expenses	$ 778,000	$ 750,000	$ 28,000	3.7
Operating income	$ 185,000	$ 103,000	$ 82,000	79.6
Less interest expense	44,000	46,000	(2,000)	(4.3)
Income before taxes	$ 141,000	$ 57,000	$ 84,000	147.4
Income taxes	47,000	19,000	28,000	147.4
Net income	$ 94,000	$ 38,000	$ 56,000	147.4
Earnings per share	$ 0.99	$ 0.40	$ 0.59	147.5

Precision Inc.
Income Statement
For Years Ended December 31, 2005 and 2004

2.

			Common-Size Percents	
Precision Inc. **Balance Sheet** **December 31**				
	2005	**2004**	**2005***	**2004***
Assets				
Current assets:				
Cash	$ 79,000	$ 42,000	4.7%	2.5%
Short-term investments	65,000	96,000	3.9	5.7
Accounts receivable (net)	120,000	100,000	7.1	6.0
Merchandise inventory	250,000	265,000	14.8	15.8
Total current assets	$ 514,000	$ 503,000	30.5	30.0
Capital assets:				
Store equipment (net)	$ 400,000	$ 350,000	23.8	20.9
Office equipment (net)	45,000	50,000	2.7	3.0
Buildings (net)	625,000	675,000	37.1	40.2
Land	100,000	100,000	5.9	6.0
Total capital assets	$1,170,000	$1,175,000	69.5	70.0
Total assets	$1,684,000	$1,678,000	100.0	100.0
Liabilities				
Current liabilities:				
Accounts payable	$ 164,000	$ 190,000	9.7	11.3
Short-term notes payable	75,000	90,000	4.5	5.4
Taxes payable	26,000	12,000	1.5	0.7
Total current liabilities	$ 265,000	$ 292,000	15.7	17.4
Long-term liabilities:				
Notes payable (secured by mortgage on building and land)	400,000	420,000	23.8	25.0
Total liabilities	$ 665,000	$ 712,000	39.5	42.4
Shareholders' Equity				
Contributed capital:				
Common shares	$ 475,000	$ 475,000	28.2	28.3
Retained earnings	544,000	491,000	32.3	29.3
Total shareholders' equity	$1,019,000	$ 966,000	60.5	57.6
Total liabilities and equity	$1,684,000	$1,678,000	100.0	100.0

*Columns may not add due to rounding.

Ratio Analysis

LO7 Define and apply ratio analysis.

Ratios are among the most popular and widely used tools of financial analysis. They provide us with clues and symptoms of underlying conditions. Ratios, properly interpreted, identify areas requiring further investigation. A ratio can help us uncover conditions and trends that are difficult to detect by inspecting individual components making up the ratio. Usefulness of ratios depends on how skillfully we interpret them, and interpretation is the most challenging aspect of **ratio analysis**.

A ratio shows a mathematical relation between two quantities. It can be expressed as a percent, a rate, or a proportion. For instance, a change in an account balance from $100 to $250 can be expressed as: (1) 250%, (2) 2.5 times, or (3) 2.5 to 1 (or 2.5:1).

This section describes an important set of financial ratios and shows how to apply them. The selected ratios are organized into the four building blocks of financial statement analysis: (1) liquidity and efficiency, (2) solvency, (3) profitability, and (4) market. Some of these ratios have been previously explained at relevant points in prior chapters.

Liquidity and Efficiency

Liquidity refers to the availability of resources to meet short-term cash requirements. A company's short-term liquidity is affected by the timing of cash inflows and outflows along with its prospects for future performance. **Efficiency** refers to how well a company uses its assets. Efficiency is usually measured relative to how much revenue is generated for a certain level of assets. Inefficient use of assets can yield liquidity problems.

Both liquidity and efficiency are important and complementary in our analysis. If a company fails to meet its current obligations, its continued existence is doubtful. Viewed in this light, all other measures of analysis are of secondary importance. While accounting measurements assume indefinite existence of the company (going concern principle P.41), our analysis must always assess the validity of this assumption using liquidity measures.

For users, a lack of liquidity often precedes lower profitability and opportunity. It can foretell a loss of owner control or loss of investment. When the owner(s) of a proprietorship and certain partnerships possess unlimited liability P.7, a lack of liquidity endangers their personal assets. To creditors of a company, lack of liquidity can yield delays in collecting interest and principal payments P.533 or the loss of amounts due them. A company's customers and suppliers of goods and services are affected by short-term liquidity problems. Implications include a company's inability to execute contracts and potential damage to important customer and supplier relationships. This section describes and illustrates ratios relevant to assessing liquidity and efficiency.

Working Capital and Current Ratio

The amount of current assets P.218 less current liabilities P.219 is called **working capital** or *net working capital*. A company needs an adequate amount of working capital to meet current debts, carry sufficient inventories, and take advantage of cash discounts. A company that runs low on working capital is less likely to meet current obligations or continue operating.

When evaluating a company's working capital, we must look beyond the dollar amount of current assets less current liabilities. We also need to consider the relation between the amounts of current assets and current liabilities. The *current ratio* P.225 describes a company's ability to pay its short-term obligations. The current ratio relates current assets to current liabilities as follows:

$$\text{Current ratio} = \frac{\text{Current assets}}{\text{Current liabilities}}$$

Drawing on information in Exhibit 20.1, Ralco's working capital amounts and current ratios for both 2005 and 2004 are shown in Exhibit 20.10.

(in thousands)	Nov. 30, 2005	Nov. 30, 2004
Current assets	$ 153,233	$103,685
Current liabilities	24,139	18,864
Working capital	**$129,094**	**$84,821**
Current ratio:		
$153,233/$24,139	**6.35 to 1**	
$103,685/$18,864		**5.50 to 1**

Exhibit 20.10

Working Capital and Current Ratio

A high current ratio suggests a strong liquidity position. A high ratio means a company should be able to meet its current obligations. But a company also can have a current ratio that is *too high*. An excessively high ratio means the company has invested too much in current assets compared to its current obligations. Since current assets do not normally generate much additional revenue, an excessive investment in current assets is not an efficient use of funds.

Many users apply a guideline of 2 to 1 for the current ratio in helping evaluate the debt-paying ability of a company. A company with a 2 to 1 or higher current ratio is generally thought to be a good credit risk in the short run. But this analysis is only one step in our process of assessing a company's debt-paying ability. We also need to analyze at least three additional factors:

1. Type of business.
2. Composition of current assets.
3. Turnover rate of current asset components.

Type of Business

The type of business a company operates affects our assessment of its current ratio. A service company that grants little or no credit and carries no inventories other than supplies can probably operate on a current ratio of less than 1 to 1 if its revenues generate enough cash to pay its current liabilities on time. For example, WestJet's current ratio at December 31, 2002, was 0.82 to 1 calculated as its current assets of $143,015,000 divided by its current liabilities of $175,064,000 (refer to WestJet's financial statements in Appendix I at the end of the textbook). On the other hand, a company selling high-priced clothing or furniture requires a higher ratio. This is because of difficulties in judging customer demand and other factors. For instance, if demand falls, this company's inventory may not generate as much cash as expected. A company facing these risks should maintain a current ratio of more than 2 to 1 to protect its creditors. For example, Leon's current ratio at December 31, 2002, was 2.05 to 1 calculated as its current assets of $179,845,000 divided by its current liabilities of $87,605,000 (refer to Leon's financial statements in Appendix I at the end of the textbook).

The importance of the type of business to our analysis implies that an evaluation of a company's current ratio should include a comparison with ratios of other successful companies in the same industry. The industry average ratios for companies in a business similar to Ralco's are shown in Exhibit 20.11. To demonstrate how ratios might be interpreted, we will compare the ratios calculated for Ralco in the following pages against the assumed industry average ratios provided in Exhibit 20.11. In comparing the industry average current ratio of 1.6:1 to Ralco's current ratio of 6.35:1, it appears that Ralco is in a better position to meet its current obligations than its competitors are. However, recall the discussion earlier that an excessively high ratio means that Ralco may have too much invested in current assets, which are generally non-productive. Another important part of our analysis is to observe how the current ratio changes over time. We must also recognize that the current ratio is affected by a company's accounting methods, especially choice of inventory method. For instance, a company using LIFO P.352 tends to report a smaller amount of current assets than if it uses FIFO P.352 when costs are rising. These factors should be considered before we decide whether a given current ratio is adequate.

Exhibit 20.11

2005 Industry Average Ratios

Current ratio	1.6:1	Profit margin	14%
Acid-test ratio	1.1:1	Gross profit ratio	18%
Accounts receivable turnover	16 times	Return on total assets	20%
Days' sales uncollected	21 days	Return on common shareholders' equity	32.7%
Merchandise turnover	5 times	Book value per common share	$8.63
Days' sales in inventory	70 days	Basic earnings per share	$1.79
Total asset turnover	2.3 times	Price–earnings per share	18.2
Debt ratio	35%	Dividend yield	$0.35
Equity ratio	65%		
Times interest earned	50 times		

Composition of Current Assets

The composition of a company's current assets is important to our evaluation of short-term liquidity. For instance, cash, cash equivalents, and temporary investments are more liquid than accounts and notes receivable. Also, short-term receivables normally are more liquid than merchandise inventory. We know cash can be used to pay current debts immediately. But items such as accounts receivable and merchandise inventory must be converted into cash before payments can be made. An excessive amount of receivables and inventory weakens a company's ability to pay current liabilities. One way to take account of the composition of current assets is to evaluate the acid-test ratio. We discuss this in the next section.

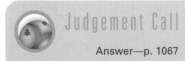

Judgement Call

Answer—p. 1067

Banker

You are a banker, and a company calls on you for a one-year, $200,000 loan to finance an expansion. This company's current ratio is 4:1 with current assets of $160,000. Key competitors carry a current ratio of about 1.9:1. Using this information, do you approve the loan application? Does your decision change if the application is for a 10-year loan?

Acid-Test Ratio

The *acid-test ratio*, also called the *quick ratio*, is a more rigorous test of a company's ability to pay its short-term debts. This ratio focuses on current asset composition. Inventory and prepaid expenses are excluded and only quick assets P.486 are included. Quick assets are cash, temporary investments, accounts receivable, and notes receivable. These are the most liquid types of current assets. We calculate the acid-test ratio as:

$$\text{Acid-test ratio} = \frac{\text{Cash + Temporary investments + Current receivables}}{\text{Current liabilities}}$$

Using the information in Exhibit 20.1, we calculate Ralco's acid-test ratios as shown in Exhibit 20.12.

(in thousands)	Nov. 30, 2005	Nov. 30, 2004
Cash and temporary investments	$ 85,618	$ 57,000
Accounts receivable, trade	50,586	36,327
Total quick assets	$136,204	$ 93,327
Current liabilities	$ 24,139	$ 18,864
Acid-test ratio:		
$136,204/$24,139	5.64 to 1	
$93,327/$18,864		4.95 to 1

Exhibit 20.12

Acid-Test Ratio

A traditional rule of thumb for an acceptable acid-test ratio is 1 to 1. Similar to our analysis of the current ratio, we need to consider other factors. For instance, the working capital requirements of a company are affected by how frequently the company converts its current assets into cash. This implies that our analysis of the company's short-term liquidity should also include analysis of receivables and inventories. We next look at these analyses.

Accounts Receivable Turnover

We can measure how frequently a company converts its receivables into cash by calculating *accounts receivable turnover* P.543. This is calculated as:

$$\text{Accounts receivable turnover} = \frac{\text{Net sales}}{\text{Average accounts receivable}}$$

Accounts receivable turnover is more precise if credit sales are used for the numerator. But net sales (or revenues) are usually used by external users because information about credit sales is typically not reported.

While this ratio is called accounts receivable turnover, short-term notes receivables from customers are normally included in the denominator amount along with accounts receivable.

Average accounts receivable is estimated by averaging the beginning and the ending receivables for the period. If the beginning and ending receivables do not represent the amount normally on hand, an average of quarterly or monthly receivables may be used if available. Ending accounts receivable is sometimes substituted for the average balance in calculating accounts receivable turnover.

This is acceptable if the difference between these figures is insignificant. Also, some users prefer using gross accounts receivable (before subtracting the Allowance for Doubtful Accounts P.522). But many balance sheets report only the net amount of accounts receivable.

Ralco's 2005 accounts receivable turnover is calculated as:

$$\frac{\$164{,}313}{(\$50{,}586 + \$36{,}327)/2} = 3.78 \text{ times}$$

If accounts receivable are collected quickly, then accounts receivable turnover is high. A high turnover is favourable because it means the company need not commit large amounts of capital to accounts receivable. An accounts receivable turnover can be too high. This can occur when credit terms are so restrictive that they negatively affect sales volume. Ralco's accounts receivable turnover of 3.78 times per year is unfavourable in comparison to the industry average of 16 times per year. The industry collects receivables more than four times faster than Ralco does.

Days' Sales Uncollected

We already described how accounts receivable turnover could be used to evaluate how frequently a company collects its accounts. Another measure of this activity is *days' sales uncollected* P.544 defined as:

$$\text{Days' sales uncollected} = \frac{\text{Accounts receivable}}{\text{Net sales}} \times 365$$

This formula takes the usual approach of placing accounts receivable in the numerator. Any short-term notes receivable from customers are also normally included in the numerator.

We illustrate this ratio's application by using Ralco's information in Exhibits 20.1 and 20.2. The days' sales uncollected on November 30, 2005, is:

$$\frac{\$50{,}586}{\$164{,}313} \times 365 = 112.4 \text{ days}$$

Days' sales uncollected is more meaningful if we know the company's credit terms. A rough guideline is that days' sales uncollected should not exceed one and one-third times the days in its: (a) credit period, if discounts are not offered; or (b) discount period, if discounts are offered.

Ralco's days' sales uncollected of 112.4 days is unfavourable when compared to the industry average of 21 days. This means that Ralco has more cash tied up in receivables than its competitors do, reflecting a less efficient use of assets.

Merchandise Inventory Turnover

Working capital (current assets minus current liabilities) requirements are affected by how long a company holds merchandise inventory before selling it. One measure of this effect is the *merchandise turnover* P.376. It provides a measure of a firm's liquidity and how quickly it can convert merchandise inventory to cash. Merchandise turnover is defined as:

$$\text{Merchandise turnover} = \frac{\text{Cost of goods sold}}{\text{Average merchandise inventory}}$$

Using the inventory and cost of goods sold information in Exhibits 20.1 and 20.2, we calculate Ralco's merchandise turnover for 2005 as:

$$\frac{\$35,940}{(\$13,417 + \$7,361)/2} = 3.46 \text{ times}$$

Average inventory is estimated by averaging the beginning and the ending inventories for the period. If the beginning and ending inventories do not represent the amount normally on hand, an average of quarterly or monthly inventories may be used if available.

A company with a high turnover requires a smaller investment in inventory than one producing the same sales with a lower turnover. But merchandise turnover can be too high if a company keeps such a small inventory on hand that it restricts sales volume.

Ralco's merchandise turnover of 3.46 times is unfavourable when compared to the industry average of 5 times. This comparison indicates that Ralco sells its inventory more slowly than its competitors do.

Days' Sales in Inventory

Days' sales in inventory P. 377 is a useful measure in evaluating the liquidity of a company's inventory. Days' sales in inventory is linked to inventory in a similar manner as days' sales uncollected is linked to receivables. Days' sales in inventory is calculated as:

$$\text{Days' sales in inventory} = \frac{\text{Ending inventory}}{\text{Cost of goods sold}} \times 365$$

Applying this formula to Ralco's 2005 financial statements, we calculate days' sales in inventory as:

$$\frac{\$13,417}{\$35,940} \times 365 = 136.3 \text{ days}$$

If the products in Ralco's inventory are in demand by customers, this formula estimates that its inventory will be converted into receivables (or cash) in 136.3 days. If all of Ralco's sales are credit sales, the conversion of inventory to receivables in 136.3 days plus the conversion of receivables to cash in 112.4 days suggest that inventory will be converted to cash in about 248.7 days (= 136.3 + 112.4).

For a business selling perishables such as meat or produce, days' sales in inventory would be very low (1 or 2 days) as compared to a retailer selling slower-moving inventory such as jewellery.

Ralco's days' sales in inventory of 136.3 days is unfavourable when compared to the industry average of 70 days. This means that Ralco has more cash tied up in merchandise inventory than its competitors do.

Total Asset Turnover

Total asset turnover describes the ability of a company to use its assets to generate sales. This ratio is calculated as:

$$\text{Total asset turnover} = \frac{\text{Net sales (or revenues)}}{\text{Average total assets}}$$

In calculating Ralco's total asset turnover for 2005, we follow the usual practice of averaging total assets at the beginning and the end of the year. Taking the information from Exhibits 20.1 and 20.2, this calculation is:

$$\frac{\$164,313}{(\$191,422 + \$132,290)/2} = 1.015 \text{ times}$$

Ralco's total asset turnover of 1.015 times is unfavourable in comparison to the industry average of 2.3 times. This means that Ralco uses its assets less efficiently to generate sales than its competitors do.

Flashback

Answers—p. 1068

8. The following information is from the December 31, 2005, balance sheet of Paff Corp.: cash, $820,000; accounts receivable, $240,000; inventories, $470,000; capital assets, $910,000; accounts payable, $350,000; and income taxes payable, $180,000. Calculate the: (a) current ratio, and (b) acid-test ratio.

9. On December 31, 2004, Paff Corp. (in prior question) had accounts receivable of $290,000 and inventories of $530,000. During 2005, net sales amounted to $2,500,000 and cost of goods sold was $750,000. Calculate the: (a) accounts receivable turnover, (b) days' sales uncollected, (c) merchandise turnover, and (d) days' sales in inventory.

Solvency

Solvency refers to a company's long-run financial viability and its ability to cover long-term obligations. All business activities of a company—financing, investing, and operating—affect a company's solvency. One of the most important components of solvency analysis is the composition of a company's **capital structure**. *Capital structure* refers to a company's sources of financing: shares and/or debt.

Analyzing solvency of a company is different from analyzing short-term liquidity. Analysis of solvency is long-term and uses less precise but more encompassing measures. Analysis of capital structure is one key in evaluating solvency. Capital structure ranges from relatively permanent share capital to more risky or temporary short-term financing. Assets represent secondary sources of security for lenders ranging from loans secured by specific assets to the assets available as general security to unsecured creditors. There are different risks associated with different assets and financing sources.

This section describes tools of solvency analysis. Our analysis is concerned with a company's ability to meet its obligations and provide security to its creditors *over the long run*. Indicators of this ability include *debt* and *equity* ratios, the relation between *pledged assets* and *secured liabilities*, and the company's capacity to earn sufficient income to pay *fixed interest charges*.

Debt and Equity Ratios

One element of solvency analysis is to assess the portion of a company's assets contributed by its owners and the portion contributed by creditors. This relation is reflected in the debt ratio. The *debt ratio* expresses total liabilities as a percent of total assets. The **equity ratio** provides complementary information by expressing total shareholders' equity as a percent of total assets.

Ralco's debt and equity ratios are calculated as:

	Nov. 30, 2005	Ratios	
Total liabilities..	$ 26,469	13.8%	[Debt Ratio]
Total shareholders' equity................................	164,953	86.2	[Equity Ratio]
Total liabilities and shareholders' equity	$191,422	100.0%	

Ralco's financial statements reflect very little debt, 13.8%, compared to the average for its competitors of 35%. The company has only one long-term liability and, at the end of 2005, its liabilities provide only 13.8% of the total assets. A company is considered less risky if its capital structure (equity and long-term debt) comprises more equity. One source of this increased risk is the required payments under debt contracts for interest and principal amounts. Another factor is the amount of financing provided by shareholders. The greater the shareholder financing, the more losses a company can absorb through its shareholders before the remaining assets become inadequate to satisfy the claims of creditors.

From the shareholders' point of view, including debt in the capital structure of a company is desirable so long as risk is not too great. If a company earns a return on borrowed capital that is higher than the cost of borrowing, the difference represents increased income to shareholders. Because debt can have the effect of increasing the return to shareholders, the inclusion of debt is sometimes described as *financial leverage*. We say that a firm is highly leveraged if a large portion of a company's assets is financed by debt.

Pledged Assets to Secured Liabilities

The ratio of pledged assets to secured liabilities is used to evaluate the risk of nonpayment faced by secured creditors. This ratio also is relevant to unsecured creditors. The ratio is calculated as:

$$\text{Pledged assets to secured liabilities} = \frac{\text{Book value of pledged assets}}{\text{Book value of secured liabilities}}$$

The information needed to calculate this ratio is not usually reported in published financial statements. This means that persons who have the ability to obtain information directly from the company (such as bankers and certain lenders) primarily use the ratio.

A generally agreed minimum value for this ratio is about 2 to 1. But the ratio needs careful interpretation because it is based on the *book value* P. 144 of pledged assets. Book values are not necessarily intended to reflect amounts to be received for assets in event of liquidation. Also, the long-term earning ability of a company with pledged assets may be more important than the value of its pledged assets. Creditors prefer that a debtor be able to pay with cash generated by operating activities rather than with cash obtained by liquidating assets.

Times Interest Earned

The *times interest earned* ratio is used to reflect the riskiness of repayments with interest to creditors. The amount of income before the deduction of interest charges and income taxes is the amount available to pay interest charges. We calculate this ratio as:

$$\text{Times interest earned} \; = \; \frac{\text{Income before interest and income taxes}}{\text{Interest expense}}$$

Ralco's times interest earned ratio for 2005 is calculated as:

$$\frac{\$44{,}579 + \$2{,}959}{\$98} \; = \; 485 \text{ times}$$

The larger this ratio, the less risky is the company for lenders. A guideline for this ratio says that creditors are reasonably safe if the company earns its fixed interest charges two or more times each year.

Ralco's times interest earned of 485 times is significantly greater than the industry average of 50 times. This means that Ralco's lenders face little or no risk in terms of collecting the interest owed to them.

Profitability

We are especially interested in the ability of a company to use its assets efficiently to produce profits (and positive cash flows). **Profitability** refers to a company's ability to generate an adequate return on invested capital. Return is judged by assessing earnings relative to the level and sources of financing. Profitability is also relevant to solvency.

This section describes profitability measures and their importance to financial statement analysis. We also explain variations in return measures and their interpretation. We analyze the components of return on invested capital for additional insights into company performance.

Profit Margin

The operating efficiency and profitability of a company can be expressed in two components. The first is the company's *profit margin*. The profit margin reflects a company's ability to earn a net income from sales. Profit margin gives an indication of how sensitive net income is to changes in either prices or costs. It is measured by expressing net income as a percent of revenues (sales and revenues are similar terms). We can use the information in Exhibit 20.2 to calculate Ralco's 2005 profit margin as:

$$\text{Profit margin} \; = \; \frac{\text{Net income}}{\text{Net sales (or revenues)}} \times 100 \; = \; \frac{\$32{,}503}{\$164{,}313} \times 100 = 19.8\%$$

An improved profit margin could be due to more efficient operations resulting in lower cost of goods sold and reduced expenses. It could also be due to higher prices received for products sold. However, a higher profit margin is not always good. For example, a firm can reduce advertising expenses as a percentage of sales, resulting in higher net income for the current year but perhaps in reduced future sales and profits.

To evaluate the profit margin of a company, we must consider the industry in which it operates. For instance, a publishing company might be expected to have a profit margin between 10% and 15%, while a retail supermarket might have a normal profit margin of 1% or 2%.

Ralco's profit margin of 19.5% is favourable in comparison to the 14% industry average. This means that Ralco earns more net income per $1 of sales than its competitors.

The second component of operating efficiency is *total asset turnover*. We described this ratio earlier in this section. Both profit margin and total asset turnover make up the two basic components of operating efficiency. These ratios also reflect on management performance since managers are ultimately responsible for operating efficiency. The next section explains how we use both measures in analyzing return on total assets.

Gross Profit Ratio

Gross profit, also called **gross margin**, is the relation between sales and cost of goods sold. A merchandising company needs sufficient gross profit to cover operating expenses or it will likely fail. To help us focus on gross profit, users often calculate a gross profit ratio. The gross profit ratio, or gross margin ratio, is defined as:

$$\text{Gross profit ratio} = \frac{\text{Gross profit from sales}}{\text{Net sales}} \times 100$$

The gross profit ratios of Ralco for the years 2005 and 2004 were:

	2005	**2004**
Sales......................................	$164,313	$105,027
Cost of goods sold................	35,940	24,310
Gross profit from sales	$128,373	$ 80,717
Gross profit ratio...................	78.13%	76.85%
Calculated as	($128,373/$164,313) × 100	($80,717/$105,027) × 100

This ratio represents the gross profit in each dollar of sales. For example, the calculations above show that Ralco's gross profit ratio in 2004 was 76.85%. This means that each $1 of sales yielded 76.85¢ in gross profit to cover all other expenses. The calculations above show that Ralco's gross profit ratio increased from 2004 to 2005, reflecting a favourable trend. Ralco's gross profit ratio of 78.13% for 2005 is very favourable in comparison to the industry average gross profit ratio of 18%.

Return on Total Assets

The two basic components of operating efficiency—profit margin and total asset turnover—are used to calculate a summary measure. This summary measure is the *return on total assets* calculated as:

$$\text{Return on total assets} = \frac{\text{Net income}}{\text{Average total assets}} \times 100$$

Ralco's 2005 return on total assets is:

$$\frac{\$32,503}{(\$191,422 + \$132,290)/2} \times 100 = 20.1\%$$

Ralco's 20.1% return on total assets is marginally favourable compared to the industry average of 20%. But we need to evaluate the trend in the rate of return earned by the company in recent years and make comparisons with alternative investment opportunities before reaching a conclusion.

The following calculation shows the relation between profit margin, total asset turnover, and return on total assets:

$$\textbf{Profit margin} \quad \times \quad \textbf{Total asset turnover} \quad = \quad \textbf{Return on total assets}$$

or

$$\left(\frac{\textbf{Net income}}{\textbf{Net sales (or revenues)}} \times 100 \right) \times \frac{\textbf{Net sales (or revenues)}}{\textbf{Average total assets}} = \frac{\textbf{Net income}}{\textbf{Average total assets}} \times 100$$

Notice that both profit margin and total asset turnover contribute to overall operating efficiency, as measured by return on total assets. If we apply this formula to Ralco we get:

$$19.8\% \quad \times \quad 1.015 \quad = \quad 20.1\%$$

Return on Common Shareholders' Equity

Perhaps the most important goal in operating a company is to earn net income for its owners. The *return on common shareholders' equity* measures the success of a company in reaching this goal. We calculate this return measure as:

$$\textbf{Return on common shareholders' equity} \quad = \quad \frac{\textbf{Net income} - \textbf{Preferred dividends}}{\textbf{Average common shareholders' equity}} \times 100$$

Recall from Exhibit 20.1 that Ralco did not have any preferred shares P. 766 outstanding. As a result we determine Ralco's return as follows:

$$\frac{\$32,503 - \$0}{(\$164,953 + \$111,234)/2} \times 100 = 23.5\%$$

The denominator in this calculation is the book value of common shares. Book value per share was discussed in Chapter 15. In the numerator, the dividends on cumulative preferred shares must be subtracted whether they are declared or are in arrears. If preferred shares are non-cumulative, the dividends are subtracted only if declared.

Ralco's return on common shareholders' equity of 23.5% is unfavourable when compared to the industry average of 32.7%. This indicates that Ralco's competitors are earning more net income for their owners than Ralco is.

Book Value Per Share

Book value per common share and book value per preferred share were discussed in Appendix 15A. Refer to pages 782 to 784 to review these ratios.

Ralco has no preferred shares, so we calculate only book value per common share. For November 30, 2005, this ratio is calculated as:

$$\text{Book value per common share} = \frac{\text{Shareholders' equity applicable to common shares}}{\text{Number of common shares outstanding}}$$

$$\frac{\$164,953}{60,000} = \$2.75 \text{ book value per common share}$$

This reflects what each share would be worth if Ralco were to be liquidated at amounts reported on the balance sheet at November 30, 2005. The book value can be used as the starting point in share valuation methods or for merger negotiations. The main limitation in using book value is that it reflects original cost and not market value.

Basic Earnings Per Share

Earnings per share was introduced in Chapter 16. Refer to pages 825 to 829 to review this ratio.

Ralco's earnings per share figure was given in Exhibit 20.8. It was calculated as:

$$\text{Basic earnings per share} = \frac{\text{Net income} - \text{Preferred dividends}}{\text{Weighted-average common shares outstanding}}$$

$$\frac{\$32,503 - \$0}{51,768} = \$0.63 \text{ per share}$$

Ralco's earnings per share value of $0.63 is unfavourable in comparison to the industry average of $1.79. This shows that Ralco has realized less earning power per share than its competitors.

Market

Market measures are useful when analyzing corporations having publicly traded shares. These market measures use share price in their calculation. Share price reflects what the market (public) expectations are for the company. This includes both the return and risk characteristics of a company as currently perceived by the market.

Price–Earnings Ratio

The *price–earnings ratio* is the most widely quoted measure of company performance. It measures how investors judge the company's future performance and is calculated as:

$$\text{Price–earnings ratio} = \frac{\text{Market price per share}}{\text{Earnings per share}}$$

Predicted earnings per share P. 825 for the next period is often used in the denominator of this calculation. Reported earnings per share for the most recent period is also commonly used. In both cases, the ratio is an indicator of the future growth of and risk related to a company's earnings as perceived by investors who establish the market price of the shares.

The market price of Ralco's common shares during 2005 ranged from a low of $14.50 to a high of $23.25. Ralco's management reported that it did not expect 2006 revenue growth rates to be as high as those for 2005. Management also indicated that operating expenses as a percentage of revenues might increase. Nevertheless, the price–earnings ratios in 2005 are much higher than many companies'. Using Ralco's $0.63 earnings per share that was reported at the end of 2005, we calculate its price–earnings ratios using both the low and high share prices:

$$\text{Low:} \quad \frac{\$14.50}{\$0.63} = 23.0 \qquad \text{High:} \quad \frac{\$23.25}{\$0.63} = 36.9$$

Ralco's ratios, which are higher than the industry average of 18.2, reflect the expectation of investors that the company will continue to grow at a faster rate than its competitors.

Dividend Yield

We use *dividend yield* as a means of comparing the dividend-paying performance of different investment alternatives. Dividend yield is calculated as:

$$\text{Dividend yield} = \frac{\text{Annual dividends per share}}{\text{Market price per share}} \times 100$$

A low dividend yield is neither bad nor good by itself. Some companies decide not to declare dividends because they prefer to reinvest the cash. Ralco, for instance, does not pay cash dividends on its common shares, but its competitors pay $0.35 per common share on average.

Flashback

Answers—p. 1068

10. Which ratio best reflects the ability of a company to meet immediate interest payments? (a) Debt ratio; (b) Equity ratio; (c) Times interest earned; (d) Pledged assets to secured liabilities.

11. Which ratio measures the success of a company in earning net income for its owners? (a) Profit margin; (b) Return on common shareholders' equity; (c) Price–earnings ratio; (d) Dividend yield.

12. If a company has net sales of $8,500,000, net income of $945,000, and total asset turnover of 1.8 times, what is its return on total assets?

Summary of Ratios

This chapter has presented a variety of ratios that measure liquidity and efficiency, solvency, profitability, and market performance. One purpose of ratio analysis is to provide a standard against which actual performance can be compared. Standards of comparison were discussed earlier in the chapter and may include:

- *Ratios of other firms in the same industry.* Nortel's profit margin, for example, can be compared to Cisco's.
- *Past performance.* WestJet, for example, can compare the current year's net income in relation to sales with that of the past years.
- *Budgeted performance.* BCE can compare various ratios based on actual performance with expected ratios that were budgeted.
- *Subjective standards.* General standards of comparison can develop from past experience. Examples are a 2 to 1 level for the current ratio or 1 to 1 for the acid-test ratio. These guidelines, or rules of thumb, must be carefully applied since context is often crucial.

However all of the foregoing comparison measures involve elements of non-comparability. For example, firms in the same industry may use different accounting methods or one company may be much older than another, making it difficult to compare the costs of assets. Another limitation is that management may engage in year-end transactions that temporarily improve certain ratios. This is an unethical activity called *window dressing*.

A ratio that is significantly higher or lower than standard merely indicates that something may be wrong and should be investigated, but ratios do not provide definitive answers. Ratio analysis is based on current or past performance, but a user may be more interested in future performance. Any conclusions are therefore tentative and must be interpreted in the light of future expectations. Ratio analysis is, however, the beginning of a process of financial analysis and can help describe the financial condition of a company and help a user piece together a story about the relative strength and future potential financial health.

Exhibit 20.13 provides a summary that matches ratios with who generally uses them based on the primary interests of the users.

User	Primary Interest	Key Ratios Emphasized
Short-term creditor	Assess ability of firm to meet cash commitments in the near term	Liquidity and efficiency ratios
Long-term creditor	Assess both short-term and long-term ability to meet cash commitments of interest payments and debt repayment schedules	Solvency ratios
Investor	Assess the firm's ability to make profits, pay dividends, and realize share price increases	Profitability ratios and market ratios

Exhibit 20.13

Matching Ratios to User Needs

Exhibit 20.14 presents a summary of the major financial statement analysis ratios illustrated in this chapter and throughout the book. This summary includes each ratio's title, formula, and common use.

Exhibit 20.14

Financial Statement Analysis Ratios

Ratio	Formula	Measure of:
Liquidity and Efficiency		
Current ratio	$= \dfrac{\text{Current assets}}{\text{Current liabilities}}$	Short-term debt-paying ability
Acid-test ratio	$= \dfrac{\text{Cash + Temporary investments + Current receivables}}{\text{Current liabilities}}$	Immediate short-term debt-paying ability
Accounts receivable turnover	$= \dfrac{\text{Net sales}}{\text{Average accounts receivable}}$	Efficiency of collection
Days' sales uncollected	$= \dfrac{\text{Accounts receivable}}{\text{Net sales}} \times 365$	Liquidity of receivables
Merchandise turnover	$= \dfrac{\text{Cost of goods sold}}{\text{Average merchandising inventory}}$	Efficiency of inventory
Days' sales in inventory	$= \dfrac{\text{Ending inventory}}{\text{Cost of goods sold}} \times 365$	Liquidity of inventory
Total asset turnover	$= \dfrac{\text{Net sales (or revenues)}}{\text{Average total assets}}$	Efficiency of assets in producing sales
Solvency		
Debt ratio	$= \dfrac{\text{Total liabilities}}{\text{Total assets}} \times 100$	Creditor financing and leverage
Equity ratio	$= \dfrac{\text{Total shareholders' equity}}{\text{Total assets}} \times 100$	Owner financing
Pledged assets to secured liabilities	$= \dfrac{\text{Book value of pledged assets}}{\text{Book value of secured liabilities}}$	Protection to secured creditors
Times interest earned	$= \dfrac{\text{Income before interest and taxes}}{\text{Interest expense}}$	Protection in meeting interest payments
Profitability		
Profit margin	$= \dfrac{\text{Net income}}{\text{Net sales (or revenues)}} \times 100$	Net income in each sales dollar
Gross profit ratio	$= \dfrac{\text{Gross profit from sales}}{\text{Net sales}} \times 100$	Gross profit in each sales dollar
Return on total assets	$= \dfrac{\text{Net income}}{\text{Average total assets}} \times 100$	Overall profitability of assets
Return on common shareholders' equity	$= \dfrac{\text{Net income} - \text{Preferred dividends}}{\text{Average common shareholders' equity}} \times 100$	Profitability of owner's investment
Book value per common share	$= \dfrac{\text{Shareholders' equity applicable to common shares}}{\text{Number of common shares outstanding}}$	Liquidation at reported amounts
Book value per preferred share	$= \dfrac{\text{Shareholders' equity applicable to preferred shares}}{\text{Number of preferred shares outstanding}}$	Liquidation at reported amounts
Basic earnings per share	$= \dfrac{\text{Net income} - \text{Preferred dividends}}{\text{Weighted-average common shares outstanding}}$	Net income on each common share
Market		
Price–earnings ratio	$= \dfrac{\text{Market price per share}}{\text{Earnings per share}}$	Market value based on earnings
Dividend yield	$= \dfrac{\text{Annual dividends per share}}{\text{Market price per share}} \times 100$	Cash return to each share

Summary

LO¹ **Explain the purpose of analysis.** The purpose of financial statement analysis is to help users make better business decisions. The common goal of all users is to evaluate a company's (1) past and current performance, (2) current financial position, and (3) future performance and risk.

LO² **Identify the building blocks of analysis.** Financial statement analysis focuses mainly on four areas, the building blocks of analysis: (1) liquidity and efficiency—ability to meet short-term obligations and to generate revenues efficiently; (2) solvency—ability to generate future revenues and meet long-term obligations; (3) profitability—ability to provide financial rewards sufficient to attract and retain financing; and (4) market—ability to generate positive market expectations.

LO³ **Describe standards for comparisons in analysis.** To make conclusions from analysis we need standards for comparisons including: (1) intracompany; (2) competitor; (3) industry; and (4) guidelines (rules of thumb).

LO⁴ **Identify the tools of analysis.** The three most common tools of financial statement analysis: (1) horizontal analysis; (2) vertical analysis; and (3) ratio analysis.

LO⁵ **Explain and apply methods of horizontal analysis.** Horizontal analysis is a tool to evaluate changes in financial statement data across time. Two important tools of horizontal analysis are comparative statements and trend analysis. Comparative statements show amounts for two or more successive periods, often with changes disclosed in both absolute and percent terms. Trend analysis is used to reveal important changes occurring from one period to the next.

LO⁶ **Describe and apply methods of vertical analysis.** In common-size statements, each item is expressed as a percent of a base amount. The base amount for the balance sheet is usually total assets, and the base amount for the income statement is usually net sales. Vertical analysis is a tool to evaluate each financial statement item or group of items in terms of a specific base amount. This base amount is commonly defined as 100%. Two important tools of vertical analysis are common-size statements and graphical analyses.

LO⁷ **Define and apply ratio analysis.** Ratio analysis provides clues and symptoms of underlying conditions. Ratios, properly interpreted, identify areas requiring further investigation. A ratio expresses a mathematical relation between two quantities; examples are a percent, a rate, or a proportion. Selected ratios are organized into the building blocks of analysis: (1) liquidity and efficiency, (2) solvency, (3) profitability, and (4) market.

GUIDANCE ANSWERS TO Judgement Call

Banker

Your decision on the loan application is positive for at least two reasons. First, the current ratio suggests a strong ability to meet short-term obligations. Second, current assets of $160,000 and a current ratio of 4:1 imply current liabilities of $40,000 (one-fourth of current assets) and a working capital excess of $120,000. This working capital excess is 60% of the loan amount. However, if the application is for a 10-year loan, our decision is less optimistic. While the current ratio and working capital suggest a good safety margin, there are indications of inefficiency in operations. In particular, a 4:1 current ratio is more than double its competitors' ratio. This is characteristic of inefficient asset use.

GUIDANCE ANSWERS TO  Flashback

1. General purpose financial statements are intended for the large variety of users who are interested in receiving financial information about a business but who do not have the ability to require the company to prepare specialized financial reports designed to meet their specific interests.

2. General purpose financial statements include the income statement, balance sheet, statement of retained earnings, and cash flow statement, plus notes related to the statements.

3. *a*

4. Data from one or more direct competitors of the company under analysis are usually preferred for developing standards for comparison.

5. *d*

6. Percents on a comparative income statement show the increase or decrease in each item from one period to the next. On a common-size comparative income statement, each item is shown as a percent of net sales for a specific period.

7. *c*

8. (a) $\dfrac{(\$820,000 + \$240,000 + \$470,000)}{(\$350,000 + \$180,000)} = 2.9 \text{ to } 1$

(b) $\dfrac{(\$820,000 + \$240,000)}{(\$350,000 + \$180,000)} = 2 \text{ to } 1$

9. (a) $\$2,500,000/[(\$290,000 + \$240,000)/2] = 9.43 \text{ times}$

(b) $(\$240,000/\$2,500,000) \times 365 = 35 \text{ days}$

(c) $\$750,000/[(\$530,000 + \$470,000)/2] = 1.5 \text{ times}$

(d) $(\$470,000/\$750,000) \times 365 = 228.7 \text{ days}$

10. *c*

11. *b*

12. $\underset{\text{margin}}{\text{Profit}} \times \underset{\text{turnover}}{\text{Total asset}} = \underset{\text{total assets}}{\text{Return on}}$

$[(\$945,000/\$8,500,000) \times 100] \times 1.8 = 20\%$

Demonstration Problem

Use the financial statements of Precision Inc. to calculate and identify the appropriate building block of financial statement analysis for the following ratios as of December 31, 2005:

a. Current ratio

b. Acid-test ratio

c. Accounts receivable turnover

d. Days' sales uncollected

e. Merchandise turnover

f. Debt ratio

g. Pledged assets to secured liabilities

h. Times interest earned

i. Profit margin

j. Total asset turnover

k. Return on total assets

l. Return on common shareholders' equity

Precision Inc.
Comparative Income Statement
For Years Ended December 31, 2005 and 2004

	2005	2004
Sales	$2,486,000	$2,075,000
Cost of goods sold	1,523,000	1,222,000
Gross profit from sales	$ 963,000	$ 853,000
Operating expenses:		
Advertising expense	$ 145,000	$ 100,000
Sales salaries expense	240,000	280,000
Office salaries expense	165,000	200,000
Insurance expense	100,000	45,000
Supplies expense	26,000	35,000
Amortization expense	85,000	75,000
Miscellaneous expenses	17,000	15,000
Total operating expenses	$ 778,000	$ 750,000
Operating income	$ 185,000	$ 103,000
Less interest expense	44,000	46,000
Income before taxes	$ 141,000	$ 57,000
Income taxes	47,000	19,000
Net income	$ 94,000	$ 38,000
Earnings per share	$ 0.99	$ 0.40

Precision Inc.
Comparative Balance Sheet
December 31

	2005	2004
Assets		
Current assets:		
Cash	$ 79,000	$ 42,000
Short-term investments	65,000	96,000
Accounts receivable (net)...	120,000	100,000
Merchandise inventory...	250,000	265,000
Total current assets	$ 514,000	$ 503,000
Capital assets:		
Store equipment (net)	$ 400,000	$ 350,000
Office equipment (net)	45,000	50,000
Buildings (net)	625,000	675,000
Land	100,000	100,000
Total capital assets	$1,170,000	$1,175,000
Total assets	$1,684,000	$1,678,000
Liabilities		
Current liabilities:		
Accounts payable	$ 164,000	$ 190,000
Short-term notes payable	75,000	90,000
Taxes payable	26,000	12,000
Total current liabilities	$ 265,000	$ 292,000
Long-term liabilities:		
Notes payable (secured by mortgage on		
building and land)	400,000	420,000
Total liabilities	$ 665,000	$ 712,000
Shareholders' Equity		
Contributed capital:		
Common shares	$ 475,000	$ 475,000
Retained earnings	544,000	491,000
Total shareholders' equity	$1,019,000	$ 966,000
Total liabilities and shareholders' equity..................................	$1,684,000	$1,678,000

Planning the Solution

○ Calculate the given ratios using the provided numbers; be sure to use the average of the beginning and ending amounts where appropriate.

SOLUTION TO Demonstration Problem

Ratios for 2005:

a. Current ratio: $514,000/$265,000 = 1.9 to 1 (Liquidity and Efficiency)

b. Acid-test ratio: ($79,000 + $65,000 + $120,000)/$265,000 = 1.0 to 1 (Liquidity and Efficiency)

c. Average receivables: ($120,000 + $100,000)/2 = $110,000
   Accounts receivable turnover: $2,486,000/$110,000 = 22.6 times (Liquidity and Efficiency)

  d. Days' sales uncollected: ($120,000/$2,486,000) × 365 = 17.6 days (Liquidity and Efficiency)

  e. Average inventory: ($250,000 + $265,000)/2 = $257,500
Merchandise turnover: $1,523,000/$257,500 = 5.9 times (Liquidity and Efficiency)

  f. Debt ratio: $665,000/$1,684,000 × 100 = 39.5% (Solvency)

  g. Pledged assets to secured liabilities: ($625,000 + $100,000)/$400,000 = 1.8 to 1 (Solvency)

  h. Times interest earned: $185,000/$44,000 = 4.2 times (Solvency)

  i. Profit margin: $94,000/$2,486,000 × 100 = 3.8% (Profitability)

  j. Average total assets: ($1,684,000 + $1,678,000)/2 = $1,681,000
Total asset turnover: $2,486,000/$1,681,000 = 1.48 times (Liquidity and Efficiency)

  k. Return on total assets: $94,000/$1,681,000 × 100 = 5.6%, or 3.8% × 1.48 = 5.6% (Profitability)

  l. Average total equity: ($1,019,000 + $966,000)/2 = $992,500
Return on common shareholders' equity: $94,000/$992,500 × 100 = 9.5% (Profitability)

Glossary

Capital structure A company's source of financing: shares and/or debt. (p. 1058)

Common-size financial statement A statement in which each amount is expressed as a percent of a base amount. In the balance sheet, the amount of total assets is usually selected as the base amount and is expressed as 100%. In the income statement, revenue is usually selected as the base amount. (p. 1045)

Comparative financial statement A financial statement with data for two or more successive accounting periods placed in side-by-side columns, often with changes shown in dollar amounts and percentages. (p. 1040)

Efficiency A company's productivity in using its assets; usually measured relative to how much revenue is generated for a certain level of assets. (p. 1052)

Equity ratio The portion of total assets provided by equity, calculated as equity divided by total assets. (p. 1059)

Financial reporting The process of communicating information that is relevant to investors, creditors, and others in making investment, credit, and other decisions. (p. 1039)

Financial statement analysis The application of analytical tools to general purpose financial statements and related data for making business decisions. (p. 1038)

General purpose financial statements Statements published periodically for use by a wide variety of interested parties; include the income statement, balance sheet, statement of retained earnings, cash flow statement, and notes related to the statements. (p. 1039)

Gross margin See *gross profit*. (p. 1061)

Gross profit The relation between sales and cost of goods sold. (p. 1061)

Horizontal analysis A tool to evaluate changes in financial statement data across time. (p. 1040)

Liquidity The availability of resources to meet short-term cash requirements. (p. 1052)

Profitability A company's ability to generate an adequate return on invested capital. (p. 1060)

Ratio analysis Determination of key relations among financial statement items. (p. 1052)

Solvency A company's long-run financial viability and its ability to cover long-term obligations. (p. 1058)

Vertical analysis The analysis of each financial statement item or group of items in terms of a specific base amount; the base amount is commonly defined as 100% and is usually revenue on the income statement and total assets on the balance sheet. Also called *common-size analysis*. (p. 1045)

Working capital Current assets minus current liabilities. Also known as *net working capital*. (p. 1052)

Online LearningCentre with POWERWEB

For more study tools, quizzes, and problem material,
refer to the Online Learning Centre at
www.mcgrawhill.ca/college/larson

Questions

1. Explain the difference between financial reporting and financial statements.

2. What is the difference between comparative financial statements and common-size comparative statements?

3. Which items are usually assigned a value of 100% on a common-size comparative balance sheet and a common-size comparative income statement?

4. Why is working capital given special attention in the process of analyzing balance sheets?

5. What are three factors that would influence your decision as to whether a company's current ratio is good or bad?

6. Suggest several reasons why a 2 to 1 current ratio may not be adequate for a particular company.

7. Which assets are "quick assets" in computing the acid-test ratio?

8. What does a relatively high accounts receivable turnover indicate about a company's short-term liquidity?

9. What is the significance of the number of days' sales uncollected?

10. Why does merchandise turnover provide information about a company's short-term liquidity?

11. Why is the capital structure of a company, as measured by debt and equity ratios, of importance to financial statement analysts?

12. Why must the ratio of pledged assets to secured liabilities be interpreted with caution?

13. Why would a company's return on total assets be different from its return on common shareholders' equity?

14. What ratios would you calculate for the purpose of evaluating management performance?

15. Refer to the financial statements in Appendix I for WestJet and calculate the percentage change in total revenues from 2001 to 2002.

16. Refer to the financial statements in Appendix I for Leon's and calculate the percentage change in operating expenses from 2001 to 2002.

Quick Study

Which of the following items are means of accomplishing the objective of financial reporting but are not included within general purpose financial statements? (a) Income statements, (b) company news releases, (c) balance sheets, (d) certain reports filed with the CCRA, (e) cash flow statements, (f) management discussions and analyses of financial performance.

QS 20-1
Financial reporting

LO²

Given the following information for Moyers Corporation, determine (a) the common-size percentages for gross profit from sales, and (b) the trend percentages for net sales, using 2004 as the base year.

QS 20-2
Common-size and trend percents

LO⁵,⁶

	2005	2004
Net sales	$114,800	$134,400
Cost of goods sold	60,200	72,800

Peckford Inc. and McKenna Inc. have virtually identical operations, asset balances, liability balances, and physical quantities of inventories. Peckford uses the LIFO inventory valuation method and McKenna uses FIFO. If prices have been rising, which company will have the higher current ratio?

QS 20-3
Identifying ratios

LO³

a. Which two short-term liquidity ratios measure how frequently a company collects its accounts?

b. Which two terms are used to describe the difference between current assets and current liabilities?

c. Which two ratios are the basic components in measuring a company's operating efficiency? Which ratio summarizes these two components?

QS 20-4
Tools of analysis

LO⁷

QS 20-5
Comparing ratios

LO³

What are four possible bases of comparison you can use when analyzing financial state-ment ratios? Which of these is generally considered to be the most useful? Which one is least likely to provide a good basis for comparison?

QS 20-6
Comparing ratios

LO⁷

Baker Corp. uses LIFO and Campbell Inc. uses FIFO during a period of rising prices. What differences would you expect to find with each of the following ratios?
1. Current ratio
2. Profit margin
3. Debt ratio
4. Merchandise turnover
5. Times interest earned

QS 20-7
Building blocks of analysis

LO⁷

Match the ratio to the building block of financial statement analysis to which it relates:
A. Liquidity and efficiency
B. Solvency
C. Profitability
D. Market

1. Gross margin
2. Dividend yield
3. Return on total assets
4. Acid-test ratio
5. Equity ratio
6. Accounts receivable turnover
7. Pledged assets to secured liabilities
8. Book value per common share
9. Days' sales in inventory
10. Times interest earned

QS 20-8
Applying ratio analysis

LO⁷

Use the following information to calculate the current ratio. Explain what the current ratio of a company evaluates. Comment whether the ratio you calculated is favourable or unfavourable in comparison to the industry average in Exhibit 20.11.

Cash	$1,680
Accounts receivable	3,780
Inventory	7,000
Prepaid expenses	840
Equipment	9,000
Accounts payable	4,650
Other current liabilities	1,050

QS 20-9
Applying ratio analysis

LO⁷

Use the information in QS 20-8 to calculate the acid-test ratio. Explain what the acid-test ratio of a company evaluates. Comment whether the ratio you calculated is favourable or unfavourable in comparison to the industry average in Exhibit 20.11.

QS 20-10
Interpreting ratios

LO⁷

For each ratio below identify whether (a) the change in the ratio from 2004 to 2005 would generally be regarded as *favourable* or *unfavourable*, and (b) the 2005 ratio is favourable or unfavourable in comparison to the industry averages in Exhibit 20.11.

Ratio	2005	2004
1. Profit margin	8%	9%
2. Debt ratio	43%	40%
3. Gross profit ratio	33%	45%
4. Acid-test ratio	0.99	1.10
5. Accounts receivable turnover	6.4	5.6
6. Basic earnings per share	$1.18	$1.20
7. Merchandise turnover	3.5	3.3
8. Dividend yield	1%	0.8%

The following facts were extracted from the comparative financial statements of Tamera Corporation:

	2005	2004
Accounts receivable	$ 89,600	$ 67,200
Sales (net)	672,000	616,000

Calculate the accounts receivable turnover for 2005 and identify whether it compares favourably or unfavourably with the industry average in Exhibit 20.11.

QS 20-11
Accounts receivable turnover

Jennifer Inc. reported the following facts in its 2005 annual report: net sales of $9,683 million for 2004 and $9,050 million for 2005; total end-of-year assets of $10,690 million for 2004 and $13,435 million for 2005. Calculate the total asset turnover for 2005 and identify whether it compares favourably or unfavourably with the industry average in Exhibit 20.11.

QS 20-12
Calculating total asset turnover

Exercises

Calculate trend percentages for the following items using 2001 as the base year. Then, state whether the situation shown by the trends appears to be *favourable* or *unfavourable*.

	2005	2004	2003	2002	2001
Sales	$377,600	$362,400	$338,240	$314,080	$302,000
Cost of goods sold	172,720	164,560	155,040	142,800	136,000
Accounts receivable	25,400	24,400	23,200	21,600	20,000

Exercise 20-1
Calculating trend percents

Where possible, calculate percents of increase and decrease for the following accounts of Brewer Ltd.:

	2005	2004
Temporary investments	$203,000	$154,000
Accounts receivable	30,888	35,200
Notes payable	25,000	-0-

Exercise 20-2
Reporting percent changes

Express the following income statement information in common-size percents and assess whether the situation is *favourable* or *unfavourable*.

Exercise 20-3
Calculating common-size percents

Waterford Corporation Income Statement For Years Ended December 31, 2005 and 2004		
	2005	2004
Sales	$1,056,000	$735,000
Cost of goods sold	633,600	382,200
Gross profit from sales	$ 422,400	$352,800
Operating expenses	237,600	148,470
Net income	$ 184,800	$204,330

Exercise 20-4
Evaluating short-term liquidity

LO⁶

Carmon Inc.'s December 31 balance sheets included the following data:

	2005	2004	2003
Cash	$ 51,800	$ 70,310	$ 73,600
Accounts receivable, net	186,800	125,940	98,400
Merchandise inventory	223,000	165,000	106,000
Prepaid expenses	19,400	18,750	8,000
Plant assets, net	555,000	510,000	459,000
Total assets	$1,036,000	$890,000	$745,000
Accounts payable	$ 257,800	$150,500	$ 98,500
Long-term notes payable secured by mortgages on plant assets	195,000	205,000	165,000
Common shares (32,500 shares issued)	325,000	325,000	325,000
Retained earnings	258,200	209,500	156,500
Total liabilities and shareholders' equity	$1,036,000	$890,000	$745,000

Required

Express the balance sheets in common-size percents. Round calculations to two decimal places.

Exercise 20-5
Evaluating short-term liquidity

LO⁷

Refer to Exercise 20-4. Compare the short-term liquidity positions of Carmon Inc. at the end of 2005, 2004, and 2003 by calculating: (a) the current ratio, and (b) the acid-test ratio. Comment on whether the changes were favourable or unfavourable, including a comparison against the industry averages in Exhibit 20.11.

Exercise 20-6
Current and acid-test ratios

LO⁷

Calculate the current and acid-test ratios in each the following cases:

	Case X	Case Y	Case Z
Cash	$ 800	$ 910	$1,100
Temporary investments	-0-	-0-	500
Receivables	-0-	990	800
Inventory	2,000	1,000	4,000
Prepaid expenses	1,200	600	900
Total current assets	$4,000	$3,500	$7,300
Current liabilities	$2,200	$1,100	$3,650

Which case is in the best position to meet short-term obligations most easily? Explain your choice.

Exercise 20-7
Evaluating short-term liquidity

LO⁷

Refer to the information in Exercise 20-4 about Carmon Inc. Carmon's income statement for the years ended December 31, 2005 and 2004, includes the following data:

	2005	2004
Sales	$1,345,000	$1,060,000
Cost of goods sold	$ 820,450	$ 689,000
Other operating expenses	417,100	267,960
Interest expense	22,200	24,600
Income taxes	17,050	15,690
Total costs and expenses	$1,276,800	$ 997,250
Net income	$ 68,200	$ 62,750
Earnings per share	$ 2.10	$ 1.93

Required
For the years ended December 31, 2005 and 2004, assume all sales were on credit and calculate the following: (a) days' sales uncollected, (b) accounts receivable turnover, (c) merchandise turnover, and (d) days' sales in inventory. Comment on whether the changes from 2004 to 2005 were favourable or unfavourable, including a comparison against the industry averages in Exhibit 20.11.

Exercise 20-8
Liquidity of accounts receivable
LO⁷

Federated Merchandise Inc. reported net sales for 2004 and 2005 of $565,000 and $647,000 respectively. The end-of-year balances of accounts receivable were: December 31, 2004, $51,000; and December 31, 2005, $83,000. Calculate the days' sales uncollected at the end of each year and describe any changes in the apparent liquidity of the company's receivables.

Exercise 20-9
Days' sales uncollected and accounts receivable turnover
LO⁷

Both Tate Inc. and Young Inc. produce and market movies and television programs and their fiscal years end December 31. Key comparative figures ($ thousands) for these two organizations follow:

| | Tate Inc. | | Young Inc. | |
Key figures	2005	2004	2005	2004
Accounts receivable, net	$ 82,184	$ 53,081	$ 78,448	$ 69,055
Net sales	282,599	268,945	137,984	136,636

Required
1. Calculate the accounts receivable turnover for Tate Inc. and Young Inc. for 2004 and 2005.
2. How many days of uncollected sales does each company have at December 31, 2005?
3. Which company is more efficient in collecting the accounts receivable?

The following facts were extracted from the comparative financial statements of Ernest Blue Corp.:

Exercise 20-10
Days' sales uncollected and accounts receivable turnover
LO⁷

	2005	2004	2003
Accounts receivable	$ 64,000	$ 48,000	$ 31,000
Sales (net)	480,000	440,000	395,000

Calculate the accounts receivable turnover and days' sales uncollected for 2004 and 2005. Explain why you think the trend is *favourable* or *unfavourable*. Include a comparison against the industry averages in Exhibit 20.11.

	2005	2004	2003
Inventory, Dec. 31	$ 52,000	$ 44,000	$ 38,000
Cost of goods sold	310,000	290,000	245,000
Accounts payable, Dec. 31	40,000	32,000	29,000

Exercise 20-11
Merchandise turnover
LO⁷

Calculate merchandise turnover for 2005 and comment on whether the trend is *favourable* or *unfavourable*.

Refer to Exercise 20-11 and calculate the number of days' sales in inventory for 2004 and 2005. Comment on whether the trend is favourable or unfavourable, including a comparison against the industry average in Exhibit 20.11.

Exercise 20-12
Days' sales in inventory
LO⁷

Exercise 20-13
Evaluating efficient use of assets

LO⁷

Check figure:
2005 = 4.21 times

Godoto Corp. reported net sales of $2,433,000 for 2004 and $3,771,000 for 2005. End-of-year balances for total assets were: 2003, $793,000; 2004, $850,000; and 2005, $941,000. Calculate Godoto's total asset turnover for 2004 and 2005 and comment on the corporation's efficiency in the use of its assets. How does Godoto's total asset turnover compare to the industry average in Exhibit 20.11?

Exercise 20-14
Ratio of pledged assets to secured liabilities

LO⁷

Check figure:
Grant Inc. = 2.37

Use the following information to calculate the ratio of pledged assets to secured liabilities for both companies:

	Grant Inc.	Singh Inc.
Pledged assets	$541,800	$240,800
Total assets	550,000	490,000
Secured liabilities	228,200	229,300
Unsecured liabilities	266,000	390,000

Which company appears to have the riskier secured debt?

Exercise 20-15
Evaluating long-term risk and capital structure

LO⁷

Check figures:
b. 2005 = 2.85
c. 2005 = 4.84

Refer to the information in Exercises 20-4 and 20-7 about Carmon Inc. Compare the long-term risk and capital structure positions of the company at the ends of 2005 and 2004 by calculating the following ratios: (a) debt and equity ratios, (b) pledged assets to secured liabilities, and (c) times interest earned. Comment on whether the changes were favourable or unfavourable, including a comparison against the industry averages in Exhibit 20.11.

Exercise 20-16
Evaluating operating efficiency and profitability

LO⁷

Check figures:
a. 2005: 5.1%
b. 2005: 1.4 times
c. 2005: 7.1%

Refer to the financial statements of Carmon Inc. presented in Exercises 20-4 and 20-7. Evaluate the operating efficiency and profitability of the company by calculating the following: (a) profit margin, (b) total asset turnover, and (c) return on total assets. Comment on whether the changes were favourable or unfavourable, including a comparison against the industry averages in Exhibit 20.11.

Exercise 20-17
Return on total assets

LO⁷

Check figure:
2005 = 11.1%

The following information is available from the financial statements of Rawhide Industries Inc.:

	2005	2004	2003
Total assets, December 31	$190,000	$320,000	$750,000
Net income	28,200	36,400	58,300

Calculate Rawhide's return on total assets for 2004 and 2005. (Round answers to one decimal place.) Comment whether the change in the company's efficiency in using its assets from 2004 to 2005 was favourable or unfavourable, including a comparison against the industry averages in Exhibit 20.11.

Refer to the financial statements of Carmon Inc. presented in Exercises 20-4 and 20-7. This additional information about the company is known:

Exercise 20-18
Evaluating profitability

LO⁷

Common shares market price, December 31, 2005	$30.00
Common shares market price, December 31, 2004	28.00
Annual cash dividends per share in 2005	0.60
Annual cash dividends per share in 2004	0.30

Required
To evaluate the profitability of the company, calculate the following for 2005 and 2004: (a) return on common shareholders' equity, (b) price–earnings ratio on December 31, and (c) dividend yield.

Check figures:
a. 2005: 12.2%
b. 2005: 14.3
c. 2005: 200%

Common-size and trend percentages for a company's sales, cost of goods sold, and expenses follow:

Exercise 20-19
Determining income effects from common-size and trend percents

LO⁵,⁷

	Common-Size Percentages			Trend Percentages		
	2005	2004	2003	2005	2004	2003
Sales	100.0%	100.0%	100.0%	106.5%	105.3%	100.0%
Cost of goods sold	64.5	63.0	60.2	104.1	102.3	100.0
Expenses	16.4	15.9	16.2	96.0	94.1	100.0

Required
Determine whether the company's net income increased, decreased, or remained unchanged during this three-year period.

Problems

The condensed statements of Crane Corp. follow:

Problem 20-1A
Calculating ratios and percents

LO⁵,⁶,⁷

Crane Corp.
Income Statement ($000)
For Years Ended December 31, 2005, 2004, and 2003

	2005	2004	2003
Sales	$148,000	$136,000	$118,000
Cost of goods sold	89,096	85,000	75,520
Gross profit from sales	$ 58,904	$ 51,000	$ 42,480
Selling expenses	$ 20,898	$ 18,768	$ 15,576
Administrative expenses	13,379	11,968	9,735
Total operating expenses	$ 34,277	$ 30,736	$ 25,311
Income before taxes	$ 24,627	$ 20,264	$ 17,169
Income taxes	4,588	4,148	3,481
Net income	$ 20,039	$ 16,116	$ 13,688

Crane Corp.
Balance Sheet ($000)
December 31, 2005, 2004, and 2003

	2005	2004	2003
Assets			
Current assets	$24,240	$18,962	$25,324
Long-term investments	-0-	250	1,860
Plant and equipment	45,000	48,000	28,500
Total assets	$69,240	$67,212	$55,684
Liabilities and Shareholders' Equity			
Current liabilities	$10,100	$ 9,980	$ 9,740
Common shares	40,500	40,500	30,000
Retained earnings	18,640	16,732	15,944
Total liabilities and shareholders' equity	$69,240	$67,212	$55,684

Required

Planning component:
1. Calculate each year's current ratio.
2. Express the income statement data in common-size percents.
3. Express the balance sheet data in trend percents with 2003 as the base year.

Analysis component:
4. Comment on any significant relationships revealed by the ratios and percents.

Problem 20-2A
Calculation and analysis of trend percents

LO⁵

The condensed comparative statements of Glace Bay Corporation follow:

Glace Bay Corporation
Income Statement ($000)
For Years Ended December 31, 2005–1999

	2005	2004	2003	2002	2001	2000	1999
Sales	$797	$698	$635	$582	$543	$505	$420
Cost of goods sold	573	466	401	351	326	305	250
Gross profit from sales	$224	$232	$234	$231	$217	$200	$170
Operating expenses	170	133	122	90	78	77	65
Net income	$ 54	$ 99	$112	$141	$139	$123	$105

Glace Bay Corporation
Balance Sheet ($000)
December 31, 2005–1999

	2005	2004	2003	2002	2001	2000	1999
Assets							
Cash	$ 34	$ 44	$ 46	$ 47	$ 49	$ 48	$ 50
Accounts receivable, net	240	252	228	175	154	146	102
Merchandise inventory	869	632	552	466	418	355	260
Other current assets	23	21	12	22	19	19	10
Long-term investments	0	0	0	68	68	68	68
Plant and equipment, net	1,060	1,057	926	522	539	480	412
Total assets	$2,226	$2,006	$1,764	$1,300	$1,247	$1,116	$902
Liabilities and Equity							
Current liabilities	$ 560	$ 471	$ 309	$ 257	$ 223	$ 211	$136
Long-term liabilities	597	520	506	235	240	260	198
Common shares	625	625	625	510	510	400	400
Retained earnings	444	390	324	298	274	245	168
Total liabilities and equity	$2,226	$2,006	$1,764	$1,300	$1,247	$1,116	$902

Required

Planning component:
1. Calculate trend percentages for the items of the statements using 1999 as the base year.

Analysis component:
2. Analyze and comment on the situation shown in the statements.

The 2005 financial statements of Tooner Corporation follow:

Problem 20-3A
Calculation of financial
statement ratios

LO7

Tooner Corporation
Income Statement
For Year Ended December 31, 2005

Sales	$805,000
Cost of goods sold:	
Merchandise inventory, December 31, 2004	$ 62,800
Purchases	500,700
Goods available for sale	$563,500
Merchandise inventory, December 31, 2005	49,200
Cost of goods sold	514,300
Gross profit from sales	$290,700
Operating expenses	227,800
Operating income	$ 62,900
Interest expense	9,500
Income before taxes	$ 53,400
Income taxes	15,720
Net income	$ 37,680

Tooner Corporation
Balance Sheet
December 31, 2005
Assets

Cash	$ 18,500
Temporary investments	20,400
Accounts receivable, net	43,400
Notes receivable	8,800
Merchandise inventory	49,200
Prepaid expenses	4,800
Plant assets, net	272,100
Total assets	$417,200

Liabilities and Shareholders' Equity

Accounts payable	$ 40,700
Accrued wages payable	5,200
Income taxes payable	5,800
Long-term note payable, secured by mortgage on plant assets	95,000
Common shares, 160,000 shares	160,000
Retained earnings	110,500
Total liabilities and shareholders' equity	$417,200

Assume all sales were on credit. On the December 31, 2004, balance sheet, the assets totalled $360,600, common shares were $160,000, and retained earnings were $89,700.

Required
1. Calculate the following: (a) current ratio, (b) acid-test ratio, (c) days' sales uncollected, (d) merchandise turnover, (e) days' sales in inventory, (f) ratio of pledged plant assets to secured liabilities, (g) times interest earned, (h) profit margin, (i) total asset turnover, (j) return on total assets, and (k) return on common shareholders' equity.
2. Identify whether the ratios calculated above compare favourably or unfavourably to the industry averages in Exhibit 20.11.

Check figures:
1a. 2.81	1g. 6.6
1b. 1.76	1h. 4.7
1c. 19.7	1i. 2.07
1d. 9.2	1j. 9.7
1e. 34.9	1k. 14.5
1f. 2.86	

Problem 20-4A
Analysis of working capital

LO7

Metro Corporation began the month of March with $750,000 of current assets, a current ratio of 2.5 to 1, and an acid-test ratio of 1.1 to 1. During the month, it completed the following transactions:

> Mar. 6   Bought $85,000 of merchandise on account. (The company uses a perpetual inventory system. P.266)
> 11   Sold merchandise that cost $68,000 for $113,000.
> 15   Collected a $29,000 account receivable.
> 17   Paid a $31,000 account payable.
> 19   Wrote off a $13,000 bad debt against Allowance for Doubtful Accounts.
> 24   Declared a $1.25 per share cash dividend on the 40,000 outstanding common shares.
> 28   Paid the dividend declared on March 24.
> 29   Borrowed $85,000 by giving the bank a 30-day, 10% note.
> 30   Borrowed $100,000 by signing a long-term secured note.
> 31   Used the $185,000 proceeds of the notes to buy additional machinery.

Check figure:
March 31 working capital,
$360,000

Required
Prepare a schedule showing Metro's current ratio, acid-test ratio, and working capital after each of the transactions. Round calculations to two decimal places.

Problem 20-5A
Ratio essay

LO5,7

Kerbey Inc. and Telcom Inc. are similar firms that operate within the same industry. The following information is available:

	Kerbey Inc.			Telcom Inc.		
	2005	2004	2003	2005	2004	2003
Current ratio.....................	1.8	1.9	2.2	3.3	2.8	2.0
Acid-test ratio...................	1.1	1.2	1.3	2.9	2.6	1.7
Accounts receivable turnover..........................	30.5	25.2	29.2	16.4	15.2	16.0
Merchandise turnover	24.2	21.9	17.1	14.5	13.0	12.6
Working capital	$65,000	$53,000	$47,000	$126,000	$98,000	$73,000

Required
Write a brief essay comparing Kerbey and Telcom based on the preceding information. Your discussion should include their relative ability to meet current obligations and to use current assets efficiently.

Problem 20-6A
Evaluating ratios

LO7

Harpin Inc. calculated the ratios shown below for 2005 and 2004:

	2005	2004	Change F or U*	Comparison to Industry Average
Current ratio...	1.2:1	1.1:1		
Acid-test ratio.......................................	0.98:1	0.94:1		
Accounts receivable turnover..............	18	21		
Days' sales uncollected	26	35		
Merchandise turnover..........................	7	8		
Days' sales in inventory	55	42		
Total asset turnover	3.6	2.1		
Debt ratio...	75	53		
Times interest earned	2.4	7.1		
Profit margin	17	21		
Gross profit ratio	19	18		

*F = Favourable; U = Unfavourable

Required

1. Identify whether the change in the ratios from 2004 to 2005 is favourable ('F') or unfavourable ('U').

2. Assess whether the 2005 ratios are favourable or unfavourable in comparison to the industry averages shown in Exhibit 20.11.

Alternate Problems

Problem 20-1B
Calculating ratios and percents

 LO[5, 6, 7]

Dexter Corporation Income Statement ($000) For Years Ended December 31, 2005, 2004, and 2003			
	2005	**2004**	**2003**
Sales	$980,000	$824,000	$710,000
Cost of goods sold	545,000	433,000	338,000
Gross profit from sales	$435,000	$391,000	$372,000
Selling expenses	$131,000	$103,500	$109,000
Administrative expenses	98,000	104,500	95,000
Total expenses	$229,000	$208,000	$204,000
Income before taxes	$206,000	$183,000	$168,000
Income taxes	72,100	64,050	58,800
Net income	$133,900	$118,950	$109,200

Dexter Corporation Balance Sheet ($000) December 31, 2005, 2004, and 2003			
	2005	**2004**	**2003**
Assets			
Current assets	$226,000	$125,000	$179,000
Long-term investments	-0-	7,000	27,000
Capital assets	510,000	530,000	392,000
Total assets	$736,000	$662,000	$598,000
Liabilities and Shareholders' Equity			
Current liabilities	$110,000	$ 92,000	$ 77,000
Common shares	196,000	196,000	160,000
Retained earnings	430,000	374,000	361,000
Total liabilities and shareholders' equity	$736,000	$662,000	$598,000

Required

Planning component:

1. Calculate each year's current ratio.
2. Express the income statement data in common-size percents.
3. Express the balance sheet data in trend percents with 2003 as the base year.

Analysis component:

4. Comment on any significant relationships revealed by the ratios and percents.

Problem 20-2B
Calculation and analysis of
trend percentages

LO⁵

Dover Ltd. Income Statement ($000) For Years Ended December 31, 2005–1999							
	2005	**2004**	**2003**	**2002**	**2001**	**2000**	**1999**
Sales	$450	$470	$460	$490	$530	$520	$560
Cost of goods sold	190	197	194	208	219	212	214
Operating expenses	200	207	205	224	231	235	255
Income before taxes	$ 60	$ 66	$ 61	$ 58	$ 80	$ 73	$ 91

Dover Ltd. Balance Sheet ($000) December 31, 2005–1999							
	2005	**2004**	**2003**	**2002**	**2001**	**2000**	**1999**
Assets							
Cash	$ 30	$ 33	$ 32	$ 36	$ 45	$ 42	$ 46
Accounts receivable, net	92	103	99	101	112	110	118
Merchandise inventory	143	149	147	156	159	169	162
Other current assets	20	21	22	24	23	26	28
Long-term investments	80	60	40	87	87	87	90
Plant and equipment, net	362	368	372	287	292	297	302
Total assets	$727	$734	$712	$691	$718	$731	$746
Liabilities and Equity							
Current liabilities	$162	$169	$152	$121	$143	$171	$216
Long-term liabilities	130	145	160	175	190	205	220
Common shares	205	205	205	205	205	205	205
Retained earnings	230	215	195	190	180	150	105
Total liabilities and capital	$727	$734	$712	$691	$718	$731	$746

Required

Planning component:
1. Calculate trend percents for the items of the statements using 1999 as the base year.

Analysis component:
2. Analyze and comment on the situation shown in the statements.

The 2005 financial statements of Myers Corporation follow:

Problem 20-3B
Calculation of financial
statement ratios

LO⁷

Myers Corporation Income Statement For Year Ended December 31, 2005	
Sales	$697,200
Cost of goods sold:	
Merchandise inventory, December 31, 2004	$ 64,800
Purchases	455,800
Goods available for sale	$520,600
Merchandise inventory, December 31, 2005	62,300
Cost of goods sold	$458,300
Gross profit from sales	$238,900
Operating expenses	122,700
Operating income	$116,200
Interest expense	7,100
Income before taxes	$109,100
Income taxes	17,800
Net income	$ 91,300

Myers Corporation Balance Sheet December 31, 2005	
Assets	
Cash	$ 18,000
Temporary investments	14,700
Accounts receivable, net	55,800
Notes receivable (trade)	6,200
Merchandise inventory	62,300
Prepaid expenses	2,800
Plant assets, net	306,300
Total assets	$466,100
Liabilities and Shareholders' Equity	
Accounts payable	$ 32,600
Accrued wages payable	4,200
Income taxes payable	4,800
Long-term note payable, secured by mortgage on plant assets	125,000
Common shares, 180,000 shares	180,000
Retained earnings	119,500
Total liabilities and shareholders' equity	$466,100

Assume that all sales were on credit. On the December 31, 2004, balance sheet, the assets totalled $367,500, common shares were $180,000, and retained earnings were $86,700.

Required
1. Calculate the following: (a) current ratio, (b) acid-test ratio, (c) days' sales uncollected, (d) merchandise turnover, (e) days' sales in inventory, (f) ratio of pledged assets to secured liabilities, (g) times interest earned, (h) profit margin, (i) total asset turnover, (j) return on total assets, and (k) return on common shareholders' equity.
2. Identify whether the ratios calculated above compare favourably or unfavourably to the industry averages in Exhibit 20.11.

Check figures:
1a. 3.84   1g. 16.4
1b. 2.28   1h. 13.1
1c. 3.25   1i. 1.7
1d. 7.2   1j. 21.9
1e. 49.6   1k. 32.3
1f. 2.45

Problem 20-4B
Analysis of working capital

LO⁷

Mason Corporation began the month of March with $286,000 of current assets, a current ratio of 2.2 to 1, and an acid-test ratio of 0.9 to 1. During the month, it completed the following transactions:

Mar. 3 Sold for $55,000 merchandise that cost $36,000. (The company uses a perpetual inventory system P.266.)
     5 Collected a $35,000 account receivable.
    10 Bought $56,000 of merchandise on account.
    12 Borrowed $60,000 by giving the bank a 60-day, 12% note.
    15 Borrowed $90,000 by signing a long-term secured note.
    22 Used the $150,000 proceeds of the notes to buy additional machinery.
    24 Declared a $1.75 per share cash dividend on the 40,000 shares of outstanding common shares.
    26 Wrote off a $14,000 bad debt against Allowance for Doubtful Accounts.
    28 Paid a $45,000 account payable.
    30 Paid the dividend declared on March 24.

Required
Prepare a schedule showing the company's current ratio, acid-test ratio, and working capital after each of the transactions. Round to two decimal places.

Problem 20-5B
Ratio essay

LO⁵,⁷

Bower Inc. and Evans Inc. are similar firms that operate within the same industry. Evans began operations in 2003 and Bower in 1997. In 2005, both companies paid 7% interest to creditors. The following information is available:

	Bower Inc.			Evans Inc.		
	2005	2004	2003	2005	2004	2003
Total asset turnover	3.3	3.0	3.2	1.9	1.7	1.4
Return on total assets	9.2	9.8	9.0	6.1	5.8	5.5
Profit margin	2.6	2.7	2.5	3.0	3.2	3.1
Sales	$800,000	$740,000	$772,000	$400,000	$320,000	$200,000

Required
Write a brief essay comparing Bower and Evans based on the preceding information. Your discussion should include their relative ability to use assets efficiently to produce profits. Also comment on their relative success in employing financial leverage in 2005.

Problem 20-6B
Evaluating ratios

LO⁷

Hartfiled Corporation calculated the ratios shown below for 2005 and 2004:

	2005	2004	Change F or U*	Comparison to Industry Average
Current ratio...	1.3:1	1.4:1		
Acid-test ratio.......................................	1.14:1	1.12:1		
Accounts receivable turnover..............	12	10		
Days' sales uncollected	35	33		
Merchandise turnover..........................	4.8	4.2		
Days' sales in inventory	72	76		
Total asset turnover	2.1	2.3		
Debt ratio...	40	50		
Times interest earned	52	51		
Profit margin	13	11		
Gross profit ratio	16	18		

*F = Favourable; U = Unfavourable

Required
1. Identify whether the change in the ratios from 2004 to 2005 is favourable ('F') or unfavourable ('U').
2. Assess whether the 2005 ratios are favourable or unfavourable in comparison to the industry averages shown in Exhibit 20.11.

Analytical and Review Problems

A & R 20-1

Hope Corporation
Balance Sheet
December 31, 2005

Assets

Cash	$
Accounts receivable, net..	
Merchandise inventory	
Capital assets, net...	
Total assets	$

Liabilities and Shareholders' Equity

Current liabilities	$
12% bonds payable	
Common shares...	
Retained earnings	
Total liabilities and shareholders' equity...	$

Sales (all credit)...	$450,000
Liabilities to total assets...	1 to 2
Income taxes	$1,000
Net income	$36,000
Average collection period...	60.83 days
Capital asset turnover	3 times
Merchandise turnover..	5 times
Expenses (including taxes of 40%)...	$114,000
Current ratio	3 to 1
Total asset turnover	1.5 times
Retained earnings, Jan. 1, 2005..	$10,000

Required
Complete the above balance sheet for Hope Corporation. Round amounts to the nearest $100.

A & R 20-2

Wild Inc. began the month of May with $200,000 of current assets, a 2 to 1 current ratio, and a 1 to 1 acid-test (quick) ratio. During the month, the following transactions were completed (assume a perpetual inventory system):

	Current Ratio			Acid-test Ratio		
	Increase	Decrease	No Change	Increase	Decrease	No Change
a. Bought $50,000 of merchandise on account...................						
b. Credit sales: $70,000 of merchandise costing $40,000............						
c. Collected an $8,500 account receivable...						
d. Paid a $30,000 account payable						
e. Wrote off a $2,000 bad debt against the allowance account...........						
f. Declared a $1 per share cash dividend on the 20,000 common shares outstanding.						
g. Paid the dividend declared in (f).........						
h. Borrowed $25,000 by giving the bank a 60-day, 10% note.						
i. Borrowed $100,000 by placing a 10-year mortgage on the capital assets.						
j. Used $50,000 of proceeds of the mortgage to buy additional machinery.						

Required
1. State the effect of each of the above transactions on the current ratio and the acid-test ratio. Give the effect in terms of increase, decrease, or no change. Use check marks to indicate your answers.
2. For the end of May, calculate the
   i. Current ratio
   i. Acid-test ratio
   iii. Working capital

A & R 20-3

Both Demer Corp. and LitWel Inc. design, produce, market, and sell sports footwear and apparel. Key comparative figures from recent financial statements ($ thousands) for these two organizations follow:

Key figures	Demer	LitWel
Cash and equivalents..	$ 445,421	$ 232,365
Accounts receivable...	1,754,137	590,504
Inventory...	1,338,640	544,522
Retained earnings	2,973,663	992,563
Cost of sales	5,502,993	2,144,422
Income taxes	499,400	84,083
Net sales...	9,186,539	3,478,604
Total assets	5,361,207	1,786,184

Required
1. Calculate common-size percents for the two companies for both years using the selected data provided.
2. Which company incurred a higher percent of net sales as income tax expense?
3. Which company has retained a higher portion of total earnings in the company?
4. Which company has a higher gross margin on sales?
5. Which company is holding a higher percent of total assets as inventory?

Nicole Lukach always asks her advisor in-depth questions before acquiring a company's shares. Nicole is currently considering investing in Nymark Corp. Nymark's annual report contains the following summary of ratios:

A & R 20-4
Ratio analysis

LO⁷

	2005	2004	2003
Sales trend	128.00%	117.00%	100.00%
Selling expenses to sales	9.8%	13.7%	15.3%
Acid-test ratio	0.8 to 1	1.1 to 1	1.2 to 1
Current ratio	2.6 to 1	2.4 to 1	2.1 to 1
Inventory turnover	7.5 times	8.7 times	9.9 times
Accounts receivable turnover	6.7 times	7.4 times	8.2 times
Return on shareholders' equity	9.75%	11.50%	12.25%
Profit margin	3.3%	3.5%	3.7%
Total asset turnover	2.9 times	3.0 times	3.1 times
Return on total assets	8.8%	9.4%	10.1%
Sales to capital assets	3.8 to 1	3.5 to 1	3.3 to 1

Nicole would like answers to the following questions about the trend of events over the three-year period covered in the annual report. Nicole's questions are:
1. Is it becoming easier for Nymark to pay its current debts on time and to take advantage of cash discounts?
2. Is Nymark collecting its accounts receivable more rapidly?
3. Is Nymark's investment in accounts receivable decreasing?
4. Are dollar amounts invested in inventory increasing?
5. Is Nymark's investment in capital assets increasing?
6. Is the shareholders' investment becoming more profitable?
7. Is Nymark using its assets efficiently?
8. Did the dollar amount of selling expenses decrease during the three-year period?

Ethics Challenge

EC 20-1

In your position as controller of Tallman Inc., you are responsible for keeping the board of directors informed about the financial activities and status of the company. At the board meeting, you present the following report:

	2005	2004	2003
Sales trend	147.00	135.00	100.00
Selling expenses to net sales	10.1%	14.0%	15.6%
Sales to capital assets	3.8 to 1	3.6 to 1	3.3 to 1
Current ratio	2.9 to 1	2.7 to 1	2.4 to 1
Acid-test ratio	1.1 to 1	1.4 to 1	1.5 to 1
Merchandise turnover	7.8 times	9.0 times	10.2 times
Accounts receivable turnover	7.0 times	7.7 times	8.5 times
Total asset turnover	2.9 times	2.9 times	3.3 times
Return on total assets	9.1%	9.7%	10.4%
Return on shareholders' equity	9.75%	11.50%	12.25%
Profit margin	3.6%	3.8%	4.0%

After the meeting is over, you overhear the company's CEO holding a press conference with analysts in which she mentions the following ratios:

	2005	2004	2003
Sales trend	147.00	135.00	100.00
Selling expenses to net sales	10.1%	14.0%	15.6%
Sales to capital assets	3.8 to 1	3.6 to 1	3.3 to 1
Current ratio	2.9 to 1	2.7 to 1	2.4 to 1

Required
1. Why do you think the CEO decided to report four ratios instead of the full eleven that you prepared?
2. Comment on the possible consequences of the CEO's decision.

Focus on Financial Statements

FFS 20-1

Drinkwater Inc. reported the following information:

Drinkwater Inc. Adjusted Trial Balance March 31, (in thousands of Canadian dollars)			
	2005	2004	2003
Cash	$ 136,000	$ 98,000	$ 76,000
Accounts receivable	238,000	219,000	206,000
Allowance for doubtful accounts	2,300	2,100	2,000
Merchandise inventory	84,000	71,000	48,000
Prepaid insurance	50	30	25
Notes receivable, due in six months	600	400	150
Property, plant and equipment assets	1,621,100	1,234,670	838,640
Accumulated amortization	325,000	208,000	102,000
Accounts payable	219,000	174,000	145,000
Unearned sales	3,100	750	315
Notes payable, due in 2010	114,000	116,200	77,950
Preferred shares; $1 non-cumulative; 20,000 shares issued and outstanding	100,000	100,000	100,000
Common shares; 50,000 shares issued and outstanding	250,000	250,000	250,000
Retained earnings	772,050	491,550	294,300
Sales	943,000	798,000	503,000
Sales discounts	14,000	11,000	7,000
Cost of goods sold	424,000	335,000	196,000
Other operating expenses	141,000	103,000	50,000
Investment income	9,000	7,000	5,000
Interest expense	5,700	6,500	8,750
Income tax expense	73,000	69,000	49,000

Other information:
1. No shares were issued during the years ended March 31, 2005 and 2004.
2. No dividends were declared or paid during the years ended March 31, 2005 and 2004.
3. The market values per common share at March 31, 2005, and March 31, 2004, were $29 and $25 respectively.
4. Industry averages for 2005 were as provided in the chart on the following page.

Required

1. Using the information provided for Drinkwater Inc., prepare a comparative, single-step income statement and statement of retained earnings for the years ended March 31, 2005 and 2004, as well as a comparative classified balance sheet at March 31, 2005 and 2004.

2. Complete the chart below for Drinkwater Inc. (round all ratios to two decimal places):

	Calculate the Ratio for 2005:	Calculate the Ratio for 2004:	Favourable or Unfavourable Change From Previous Year	Favourable or Unfavourable Relative to Industry Average for 2005	
				Industry Average	Favourable or Unfavourable
a. Current ratio..............................				1.96:1	
b. Acid-test ratio				1.42:1	
c. Accounts receivable turnover......................................				4.35	
d. Days' sales uncollected				95.12	
e. Merchandise turnover................				5.20	
f. Days' sales in inventory				75.08	
g. Total asset turnover				1.8	
h. Debt ratio....................................				21%	
i. Equity ratio.................................				79%	
j. Times interest earned				50.16	
k. Profit margin				30.14	
l. Gross profit ratio				52.16	
m. Return on total assets................				17.20%	
n. Return on common shareholders' equity				31.00%	
o. Book value per common share..				14.91	
p. Book value per preferred share..				$22.00	
q. Basic earnings per share............				$4.32	
r. Price–earnings ratio				6.91	

Financial Statement Information

APPENDIX

I

This appendix includes financial statement information from (a) Leon's Furniture Limited and (b) WestJet Airlines Ltd. All of this information is taken from their annual reports. An **annual report** is a summary of the financial results of a company's operations for the year and its future plans. It is directed at external users of financial information, but also affects actions of internal users.

An annual report is also used by a company to showcase itself and its products. Many include attractive pictures, diagrams, and illustrations related to the company, but the *financial section* is its primary objective. This section communicates much information about a company, with most data drawn from the accounting information system.

The layout of each annual report's financial section that is included in this appendix is:

- Auditor's Report
- Financial Statements
- Notes to Financial Statements

This appendix is organized as follows:

- Leon's: I-1 to I-9
- WestJet: I-10 to I-27

There are questions at the end of each chapter that refer to information in this appendix. We encourage readers to spend extra time with these questions as they are especially useful in reinforcing and showing the relevance and diversity of financial reporting.

More current financial information about these and other Canadian corporations can be found online at www.sedar.com.

This is exciting business

2002 Annual Report / Leon's Furniture Limited

Management's Responsibility for the Financial Statements

The accompanying consolidated financial statements and all information in this annual report are the responsibility of management and have been approved by the Board of Directors.

The accompanying consolidated financial statements have been prepared by management in accordance with Canadian generally accepted accounting principles. Financial statements are not precise since they include certain amounts based upon estimates and judgements. When alternative methods exist, management has chosen those it deems to be the most appropriate in the circumstances. The financial information presented elsewhere in this Annual Report is consistent with that in the financial statements.

Leon's Furniture Limited (Leon's) maintains systems of internal accounting and administrative controls of high quality, consistent with reasonable costs. Such systems are designed to provide reasonable assurance that the financial information is relevant and reliable and that Leon's assets are appropriately accounted for and adequately safeguarded.

The Board of Directors is responsible for ensuring that management fulfils its responsibilities for financial reporting and is ultimately responsible for reviewing and approving the financial statements. The Board carries out this responsibility principally through its Audit Committee.

The Audit Committee is appointed by the Board and reviews the financial statements and annual report; considers the report of the external auditors; assesses the adequacy of the internal controls of the company; examines the fees and expenses for audit services; and recommends to the Board the independent auditors for appointment by the shareholders. The Committee reports its findings to the Board of Directors for consideration when approving the financial statements for issuance to the shareholders.

These consolidated financial statements have been audited by Ernst & Young LLP, the external auditors, in accordance with Canadian generally accepted auditing standards on behalf of the shareholders. Ernst & Young has full and free access to the Audit Committee.

Mark J. Leon
Vice Chairman and C.E.O.

February 21, 2003

Dominic Scarangella
Vice President and C.F.O.

Auditors' Report

To the Shareholders of **Leon's Furniture Limited - Meubles Leon Ltée**

We have audited the consolidated balance sheets of Leon's Furniture Limited - Meubles Leon Ltée as at December 31, 2002 and 2001 and the consolidated statements of income and retained earnings and cash flows for the years then ended. These financial statements are the responsibility of the Company's management. Our responsibility is to express an opinion on these financial statements based on our audits.

We conducted our audits in accordance with Canadian generally accepted auditing standards. Those standards require that we plan and perform an audit to obtain reasonable assurance whether the financial statements are free of material misstatement. An audit includes examining, on a test basis, evidence supporting the amounts and disclosures in the financial statements. An audit also includes assessing the accounting principles used and significant estimates made by management, as well as evaluating the overall financial statement presentation.

In our opinion, these consolidated financial statements present fairly, in all material respects, the financial position of the Company as at December 31, 2002 and 2001 and the results of its operations and its cash flows for the years then ended in accordance with Canadian generally accepted accounting principles.

Ernst & Young LLP

Toronto, Canada,
February 14, 2003

Chartered Accountants

Consolidated Balance Sheets

As at December 31 (in thousands)		2002		2001
ASSETS				
Current				
Cash and cash equivalents	$	29,329	$	19,054
Marketable securities		56,685		80,228
Accounts receivable		31,221		20,724
Inventory		55,047		51,079
Income taxes recoverable		7,563		821
Total current assets		179,845		171,906
Future income tax assets [note 3]		4,010		4,490
Capital assets, net [note 2]		136,584		119,279
	$	320,439	$	295,675
LIABILITIES AND SHAREHOLDERS' EQUITY				
Current				
Accounts payable and accrued liabilities	$	73,151	$	67,953
Customers' deposits		6,664		7,426
Dividends payable		2,520		2,035
Future income tax liabilities [note 3]		5,270		–
Total current liabilities		87,605		77,414
Redeemable share liability [note 7]		199		139
Total liabilities		87,804		77,553
Shareholders' equity				
Common shares [note 8]		9,535		9,325
Retained earnings		223,100		208,797
Total shareholders' equity		232,635		218,122
	$	320,439	$	295,675

See accompanying notes

On behalf of the Board:

Director   Director

Consolidated Statements of Income and Retained Earnings

Years ended December 31 (in thousands, except shares outstanding and earnings per share)	2002	2001
Sales	$ 449,693	$ 425,687
Cost of sales	261,265	248,445
Gross profit	188,428	177,242
Operating expenses (income)		
Salaries and commissions	66,610	62,092
Advertising	27,306	27,263
Rent and property taxes	7,316	7,362
Amortization	8,552	7,742
Employee profit-sharing plan	2,483	2,361
Other operating expenses	25,807	24,790
Interest income	(2,650)	(4,178)
Other income	(10,727)	(13,035)
	124,697	114,397
Income before income taxes	63,731	62,845
Provision for income taxes [note 3]	25,211	26,522
Net income for the year	38,520	36,323
Retained earnings, beginning of year	208,797	192,827
Dividends declared	(19,392)	(7,986)
Excess of cost of share repurchase over carrying value of related shares [note 8]	(4,825)	(12,367)
Retained earnings, end of year	$ 223,100	$ 208,797
Weighted average number of common shares outstanding		
Basic	19,589,298	19,925,675
Diluted	19,956,335	20,265,678
Earnings per share		
Basic	$ 1.96	$ 1.82
Diluted	$ 1.93	$ 1.79

See accompanying notes

Leon's

15

Consolidated Statements of Cash Flows

Years ended December 31 (in thousands)	2002	2001
OPERATING ACTIVITIES		
Net income for the year	$ 38,520	$ 36,323
Add (deduct) items not involving a current cash payment		
Amortization	8,552	7,742
Loss (gain) on sale of capital assets	(6)	12
Future tax expense	5,750	440
Loss (gain) on sale of marketable securities	1,278	(1,072)
	54,094	43,445
Net change in non-cash working capital balances related to operations [note 6]	(17,952)	(10,063)
Cash provided by operating activities	36,142	33,382
INVESTING ACTIVITIES		
Purchase of capital assets	(24,681)	(18,027)
Proceeds on sale of capital assets	11	35
Purchase of marketable securities	(1,180,171)	(1,164,497)
Proceeds on sale of marketable securities	1,202,436	1,163,908
Issuance of series 2002 shares [note 7]	12,104	–
Decrease (increase) in employee share purchase loans [note 7]	(11,825)	83
Cash used in investing activities	(2,126)	(18,498)
FINANCING ACTIVITIES		
Dividends paid	(18,839)	(7,980)
Repurchase of capital stock [note 8]	(4,902)	(12,652)
Cash used in financing activities	(23,741)	(20,632)
Net increase (decrease) in cash and cash equivalents during the year	10,275	(5,748)
Cash and cash equivalents, beginning of year	19,054	24,802
Cash and cash equivalents, end of year	$ 29,329	$ 19,054

See accompanying notes

16

Leon's

1. SUMMARY OF SIGNIFICANT ACCOUNTING POLICIES

These consolidated financial statements of Leon's Furniture Limited - Meubles Leon Ltée [the "Company"] have been prepared by management in accordance with Canadian generally accepted accounting principles. The more significant of these accounting policies are summarized as follows:

Principles of consolidation

The consolidated financial statements include the accounts of the Company and its subsidiaries, all of which are wholly owned.

Revenue recognition

Sales are recognized as revenue for accounting purposes upon the customer either picking up the merchandise ordered or when merchandise is delivered to the customer's home.

Foreign exchange translation

Merchandise imported from the United States is recorded at its equivalent Canadian dollar value upon receipt. United States dollar accounts payable are translated at the year-end exchange rate. Gains and losses resulting from translation of United States dollar accounts payable are included in income.

Cash and cash equivalents

Cash equivalents comprise only highly liquid investments with original maturities of less than ninety days.

Marketable securities

Marketable securities, which consist primarily of bonds with maturities not exceeding eight years and an interest rate range of 2.0% to 6.0%, are stated at the lower of cost and market value. Marketable securities and equity instruments are valued at the lower of cost and market value on an aggregate basis.

Inventory

Inventory is valued at the lower of cost, determined on a first-in, first-out basis, and net realizable value.

Capital assets

Capital assets are initially recorded at cost. Normal maintenance and repair expenditures are expensed as incurred. Amortization is provided over the estimated useful lives of the assets using the following annual rates and bases:

Buildings . . . . 5% straight-line
Equipment . . . . 20% to 30% declining balance
Vehicles . . . . 30% declining balance
Computer hardware and software . . . . 14% straight-line
Leasehold improvements . . . . Over the terms of the leases to a maximum of 15 years

No amortization is provided for assets under construction.

Store pre-opening costs

Store pre-opening costs are expensed as incurred.

Income taxes

The Company follows the liability method for accounting for income taxes. Under the liability method, future tax assets and liabilities are determined based on differences between the financial reporting and tax bases of assets and liabilities and are measured using the substantively enacted tax rates and laws that will be in effect when the differences are expected to reverse.

Earnings per share

Basic earnings per share have been calculated using the weighted average number of common shares outstanding during the year. Diluted earnings per share are calculated using the treasury stock method.

17

Fair value of financial instruments

The fair value of financial instruments held by the Company, comprising cash and cash equivalents, marketable securities, accounts receivable, accounts payable and accrued liabilities, customers' deposits and redeemable share liability approximate their carrying values in these consolidated financial statements.

Stock-based compensation

The Canadian Institute of Chartered Accountants ["CICA"] issued new guidance for accounting for stock-based compensation and other stock-based payments that is effective for fiscal years beginning on or after January 1, 2002 and generally applies to awards granted on or after the date of adoption.

The Management Share Purchase Plan [the "Plan"] represents a compensatory plan under the new CICA guidance. The Company has elected not to recognize compensation costs relating to the Plan [note 7].

2. CAPITAL ASSETS

Capital assets consist of the following:

[in thousands]	2002			2001		
	Cost	Accumulated amortization	Net book value	Cost	Accumulated amortization	Net book value
Land	$ 41,378	$ –	$ 41,378	$ 35,073	$ –	$ 35,073
Buildings	116,832	51,566	65,266	105,325	46,981	58,344
Equipment	17,940	11,712	6,228	16,575	10,678	5,897
Vehicles	13,994	11,533	2,461	13,513	10,680	2,833
Computer hardware and software	6,869	4,335	2,534	5,885	3,614	2,271
Leasehold improvements	26,178	7,461	18,717	21,081	6,220	14,861
	$ 223,191	$ 86,607	$ 136,584	$ 197,452	$ 78,173	$ 119,279

Included in the above balances are assets not being amortized with book values of approximately $5,707,000 [2001 - $1,895,000] due to construction in progress.

3. INCOME TAXES

Significant components of the Company's future tax assets are as follows:

[in thousands]	2002	2001
Future tax assets		
Capital assets	$ 4,010	$ 4,490
Total future tax assets	$ 4,010	$ 4,490

Significant components of the Company's current future tax liabilities are as follows:

[in thousands]	2002	2001
Current future tax liabilities		
Marketable securities	$ (326)	$ –
Accounts receivable	4,940	–
Inventory	656	–
Total current future tax liabilities	$ 5,270	$ –

Significant components of the provision for income taxes are as follows:

[in thousands]	2002	2001
Current tax expense	$ 19,461	$ 26,082
Future income tax expense (benefit) relating to origination and reversal of temporary differences	5,775	(1,111)
Future income tax expense (benefit) relating to tax rate reductions	(25)	1,551
Provision for income taxes	$ 25,211	$ 26,522

The total provision for income taxes in the consolidated financial statements is at a rate different than the combined federal and provincial statutory income tax rate of the current year for the following reasons:

	2002		2001	
Tax at combined federal and provincial tax rate	$ 24,511	38.5%	$ 26,018	41.4%
Tax effect of expenses that are not deductible				
for income tax purposes	23	–	20	–
Tax effect of non-taxable portion of loss (gain) on disposal	159	0.3	(202)	(0.3)
Future tax effect of rate reductions	(25)	–	1,551	2.5
Future tax effect of arising timing differences	(281)	(0.4)	(131)	(0.2)
Federal large corporations tax	21	–	89	0.1
Other, net	803	1.2	(823)	(1.3)
Provision for income taxes	$ 25,211	39.6%	$ 26,522	42.2%

4. COMMITMENTS

[a] The estimated cost to complete construction in progress at three locations [one location in 2001] amounted to approximately $4,143,000 as at December 31, 2002 [2001 - $2,100,000].

[b] The Company is obligated under operating leases to future minimum annual rental payments for certain land and buildings as follows:

[in thousands]

2003	$ 389
2004	251
2005	90
2006	90
2007	90
Thereafter	255
	$ 1,165

[c] The Company has issued approximately $1,900,000 in letters of credit with respect to buildings under construction.

5. FRANCHISE OPERATIONS

As at December 31, 2002, a total of twenty-one franchises [2001 - twenty-one] were in operation representing twenty-two [2001 - twenty-two] stores. Sales by franchise stores during the year ended December 31, 2002, on which the Company earns royalty income, amounted to approximately $129,192,000 [2001 - $119,719,000].

6. CONSOLIDATED STATEMENTS OF CASH FLOWS

[a] The net change in non-cash working capital balances related to operations consists of the following:

[in thousands]	2002	2001
Accounts receivable	$ (10,497)	$ (6,119)
Inventory	(3,968)	(1,908)
Income taxes recoverable	(6,742)	(1,706)
Accounts payable and accrued liabilities	4,017	(1,249)
Customers' deposits	(762)	919
	$ (17,952)	$ (10,063)

[b] Income taxes and interest paid:

[in thousands]	2002	2001
Income taxes paid	$ 26,904	$ 28,583
Interest paid	$ 4	$ 1

[c] During the year, capital assets were acquired at an aggregate cost of $25,862,796 [2001 - $18,487,527], of which $3,908,990 [2001 - $2,726,770] is included in accounts payable and accrued liabilities as at December 31, 2002.

7. REDEEMABLE SHARE LIABILITY

[in thousands]		2002		2001
Authorized				
89,400 convertible, non-voting, series 1994 shares				
350,000 convertible, non-voting, series 1998 shares				
571,000 convertible, non-voting, series 2002 shares				
Issued				
17,874 series 1994 shares [2001 - 40,437] [note 8]	$	228	$	515
299,566 series 1998 shares [2001 - 299,566]		5,272		5,272
421,000 series 2002 shares [2001 - nil]		12,104		–
Less employee share purchase loans		(17,405)		(5,648)
	$	199	$	139

Under the terms of its Management Share Purchase Plan, the Company advanced non-interest bearing loans to certain of its employees in 1994, 1998 and 2002 to allow them to acquire convertible, non-voting, series 1994 shares, series 1998 shares, and series 2002 shares, respectively, of the Company. These loans are repayable through the application against the loans of any dividends on the shares, with any remaining balance repayable on the date the shares are converted to common shares. Each issued and fully paid for series 1994, 1998 and 2002 share may be converted into one common share at any time after the fifth anniversary date of the issue of these shares and prior to the tenth anniversary of such issue. Each share may also be redeemed at the option of the holder or by the Company at any time after the fifth anniversary date of the issue of these shares and prior to the tenth anniversary of such issue. The redemption price is equal to the original issue price of the shares adjusted for subsequent subdivisions of shares plus accrued and unpaid dividends. The purchase prices of the shares are $12.73 per series 1994 share, $17.60 per series 1998 share and $28.75 per series 2002 share.

Dividends paid to series 1994 to 2002 shareholders of approximately $68,000 [2001 - $69,000] have been used to reduce the respective shareholder loans.

During the year ended December 31, 2002, the Company issued 421,000 series 2002 shares for proceeds of approximately $12,104,000. No shares were cancelled during the year ended December 31, 2002. During the year ended December 31, 2001, the Company did not issue or cancel any shares.

Employee share purchase loans have been netted against the redeemable share liability based upon their terms.

This Management Share Purchase Plan represents a compensatory plan. The terms of the series 2002 shares issued under the Plan and related employee share purchase loans collectively give the employees the ability, but not the obligation, to acquire common shares of the Company. The pro forma impact on net income and earnings per share using the fair value method is not material.

8. COMMON SHARES

The Company's common shares consist of the following:

[in thousands]		2002		2001
Authorized				
Unlimited common shares				
Issued				
19,490,144 common shares [2001 - 19,631,081]	$	9,535	$	9,325

During the year ended December 31, 2002, 22,563 convertible, non-voting series 1994 shares [2001 - 7,139] were converted into common shares with a stated value of approximately $287,000 [2001 - $91,000].

During the year ended December 31, 2002, the Company repurchased 163,500 [2001 - 604,600] of its common shares on the open market pursuant to the terms and conditions of Normal Course Issuer Bids at a net cost of approximately $4,902,000 [2001 - $12,652,000]. All shares repurchased by the Company pursuant to its Normal Course Issuer Bids have been cancelled. The repurchase of common shares resulted in a reduction of share capital in the amount of approximately $77,000 [2001 - $285,000]. The excess net cost over the average book value of the shares of approximately $4,825,000 [2001 - $12,367,000] has been shown as a reduction in retained earnings.

WestJet

COAST TO COAST   NEW AIRCRAFT   BETTER AND BIGGER   PLANE TALK   BEST FIGURES OF 2002

WESTJET
Annual Report
The Magazine

The
BEST
of
2002
The Year in Review

FREE

737-700 SERIES
WESTJETéS SUCCESS (itéthe people!)

2002 ANNUAL REPORT

AUDITORS' REPORT TO THE SHAREHOLDERS

We have audited the consolidated balance sheets of WestJet Airlines Ltd. as at December 31, 2002 and 2001 and the consolidated statements of earnings and retained earnings and cash flows for the years then ended. These financial statements are the responsibility of the Corporation's management. Our responsibility is to express an opinion on these financial statements based on our audits.

We conducted our audits in accordance with Canadian generally accepted auditing standards. Those standards require that we plan and perform an audit to obtain reasonable assurance whether the financial statements are free of material misstatement. An audit includes examining, on a test basis, evidence supporting the amounts and disclosures in the financial statements. An audit also includes assessing the accounting principles used and significant estimates made by management, as well as evaluating the overall financial statement presentation.

In our opinion, these consolidated financial statements present fairly, in all material respects, the financial position of the Corporation as at December 31, 2002 and 2001 and the results of its operations and its cash flows for the years then ended in accordance with Canadian generally accepted accounting principles.

[SIGNED] KPMG LLP

Chartered Accountants

Calgary, Canada
February 11, 2003

WESTJET AIRLINES LTD.

Consolidated Balance Sheets

December 31, 2002 and 2001
(Stated in Thousands of Dollars)

	2002	2001
Assets		
Current assets:		
Cash and cash equivalents	$ 100,410	58,942
Accounts receivable	20,532	12,211
Income taxes recoverable	-	779
Prepaid expenses and deposits	19,759	11,643
Inventory	2,314	2,155
	143,015	85,730
Capital assets (note 2)	605,124	300,685
Other long-term assets (note 3)	36,066	6,998
	$ 784,205	$ 393,413
Liabilities and Shareholders' Equity		
Current liabilities:		
Accounts payable and accrued liabilities	$ 67,008	$ 42,019
Income taxes payable	7,982	-
Advance ticket sales	44,195	28,609
Non-refundable guest credits	15,915	12,599
Current portion of long-term debt (note 4)	32,674	8,470
Current portion of obligations under capital lease (note 5)	7,290	3,398
	175,064	95,095
Long-term debt (note 4)	198,996	41,305
Obligations under capital lease (note 5)	16,352	14,400
Future income tax (note 7)	38,037	20,933
	428,449	171,733
Shareholders' equity:		
Share capital (note 6)	211,564	129,268
Retained earnings	144,192	92,412
	355,756	221,680
Commitments and contingencies (notes 5 and 8)		
	$ 784,205	$ 393,413

See accompanying notes to consolidated financial statements.

On behalf of the Board:

[SIGNED] Clive Beddoe, Director
[SIGNED] Wilmot Matthews, Director

WESTJET AIRLINES LTD.

Consolidated Statements of Earnings and Retained Earnings

Years ended December 31, 2002 and 2001
(Stated in Thousands of Dollars, Except Per Share Data)

	2002	2001
Revenues:		
Guest revenues	$ 643,174	$ 452,910
Charter and other	36,822	25,483
	679,996	478,393
Expenses:		
Aircraft fuel	111,737	84,629
Airport operations	88,586	63,881
Maintenance	81,973	72,317
Flight operations and navigational charges	75,759	52,648
Amortization	52,637	34,332
Sales and marketing	44,707	30,862
General and administration	39,791	20,893
Aircraft leasing	35,822	15,284
Inflight	27,284	16,104
Reservations	20,106	17,777
Employee profit share (note 8(b))	15,233	10,311
	593,635	419,038
Earnings from operations	86,361	59,355
Non-operating income (expense):		
Interest income	3,078	2,837
Interest expense	(7,038)	(5,086)
Gain on foreign exchange	346	496
Gain on disposal of capital assets	97	187
	(3,517)	(1,566)
Earnings before income taxes	82,844	57,789
Income taxes (note 7):		
Current	12,626	15,974
Future	18,438	5,105
	31,064	21,079
Net earnings	51,780	36,710
Retained earnings, beginning of year	92,412	55,702
Retained earnings, end of year	$ 144,192	$ 92,412
Earnings per share:		
Basic	$ 0.70	$ 0.53
Diluted	$ 0.69	$ 0.52

See accompanying notes to consolidated financial statements.

WestJet Airlines Ltd.

Consolidated Statements of Cash Flows

Years ended December 31, 2002 and 2001
(Stated in Thousands of Dollars)

	2002	2001
Cash provided by (used in):		
Operations:		
Net earnings	$ 51,780	$ 36,710
Items not involving cash:		
Amortization	52,637	34,332
Gain on disposal of capital assets	(97)	(187)
Future income tax	18,438	5,105
	122,758	75,960
(Increase) decrease in non-cash working capital	38,866	(8,599)
	161,624	67,361
Financing:		
Increase in long-term debt	190,366	8,947
Repayment of long-term debt	(8,471)	(9,461)
Issuance of common shares	84,634	3,878
Share issuance costs	(3,672)	-
Increase in other long-term assets	(32,257)	(2,230)
Decrease in obligations under capital lease	(6,088)	(2,483)
	224,512	(1,349)
Investments:		
Aircraft additions	(320,871)	(60,518)
Other capital asset additions	(24,031)	(26,271)
Other capital asset disposals	234	694
	(344,668)	(86,095)
Increase (decrease) in cash	41,468	(20,083)
Cash, beginning of year	58,942	79,025
Cash, end of year	$ 100,410	$ 58,942

Cash is defined as cash and cash equivalents.

See accompanying notes to consolidated financial statements.

WestJet Airlines Ltd.
Notes to Consolidated Financial Statements

Years ended December 31, 2002 and 2001
(Tabular Amounts are Stated in Thousands of Dollars, Except Per Share Data)

1. **Significant accounting policies:**

(a) Basis of presentation:

These consolidated financial statements include the accounts of the Corporation and its wholly owned subsidiaries, as well as the accounts of HFLP Finance Limited ("HFLP"). The Corporation has no equity ownership in HFLP, however, the Corporation is the primary beneficiary of HFLP's operations (see note 4). All intercompany balances and transactions have been eliminated.

The preparation of financial statements in conformity with accounting principles generally accepted in Canada requires management to make estimates and assumptions that affect the amounts reported in the financial statements and accompanying notes. Actual results could differ from these estimates.

(b) Cash and cash equivalents:

Cash and cash equivalents are comprised of cash and all investments that are highly liquid in nature and generally have a maturity date of three months or less.

(c) Revenue recognition:

Guest revenue is recognized when air transportation is provided. Tickets sold but not yet used are included in the balance sheet as advance ticket sales under current liabilities.

(d) Non-refundable guest credits:

The Corporation, under certain circumstances, may issue future travel credits which are non-refundable and which expire one year from the date of issue. The utilization of guest credits is recorded as revenue when the guest has flown or upon expiry.

(e) Foreign currency:

Monetary assets and liabilities, denominated in foreign currencies, are translated into Canadian dollars at rates of exchange in effect at the balance sheet date. Other assets and revenue and expense items are translated at rates prevailing when they were acquired or incurred. Foreign exchange gains and losses are included in income.

Effective January 1, 2002, the Corporation has adopted the new standard for exchange gains and losses arising on the translation of long-term monetary items that are denominated in foreign currencies as set forth by the Canadian Institute of Chartered Accountants. Under the new standard these gains and losses are recognized on the income statement as they are incurred. The change in accounting policy was applied retroactively with restatement of prior periods. The application of this standard reduced opening retained earnings at January 1, 2002 by $490,000 and reduced basic and diluted earnings per share ("EPS") by $0.01 for the year ended December 31, 2001.

WESTJET AIRLINES LTD.

Notes to Consolidated Financial Statements, Page 2

Years ended December 31, 2002 and 2001
(Tabular Amounts are Stated in Thousands of Dollars, Except Per Share Data)

1. **Significant accounting policies (continued):**

(f) Inventory:

Materials and supplies are valued at the lower of cost and replacement value. Aircraft expendables and consumables are expensed as incurred.

(g) Deferred costs:

Sales and marketing and reservation expenses attributed to advance ticket sales are deferred and expensed in the period the related revenue is recognized. Included in prepaid expenses are $4,161,000 (2001 - $3,643,000) of deferred costs.

(h) Capital assets:

Capital assets are recorded at cost and depreciated to their estimated residual values. Assets under capital leases and leasehold improvements are amortized on a straight-line basis over the term of the lease.

Asset	Basis	Rate
Aircraft net of estimated residual value – 700 series	Cycles	Cycles flown
Aircraft net of estimated residual value – 200 series	Flight hours	Hours flown
Ground property and equipment	Straight-line	5 to 25 years
Spare engines and parts net of estimated residual value – 200 series	Flight hours	Hours flown
Buildings	Straight-line	40 years
Parts – 700 series	Straight-line	20 years

(i) Maintenance costs:

Costs related to the acquisition of an aircraft and preparation for service are capitalized and included in aircraft costs. Heavy maintenance ("D" check) costs incurred on aircraft are capitalized and amortized over the remaining useful service life of the "D" check.

All other maintenance costs are expensed as incurred.

(j) Capitalized costs:

Costs associated with assets under construction are capitalized from inception through to commencement of commercial operations. Interest attributable to funds used to finance the construction of major ground facilities is capitalized to the related asset. Legal and financing costs for the loan facilities are capitalized and amortized over the term of the related loan.

WestJet Airlines Ltd.

Notes to Consolidated Financial Statements, Page 3

Years ended December 31, 2002 and 2001
(Tabular Amounts are Stated in Thousands of Dollars, Except Per Share Data)

---

1. **Significant accounting policies (continued):**

(k) Future income tax:

The Corporation uses the liability method of accounting for future income taxes. Under this method, current income taxes are recognized for the estimated income taxes payable for the current year.   Future income tax assets and liabilities are recognized for temporary differences between the tax and accounting bases of assets and liabilities.

(l) Stock-based compensation plans:

Currently all outstanding stock options of the Corporation have been granted to employees of the Corporation and no compensation cost has been recorded for these awards. Consideration paid by employees on the exercise of stock options is recorded as share capital. The Corporation has disclosed the pro forma effect of accounting for these rewards under the fair value based method (see note 6(f)).

(m) Financial instruments:

The Corporation utilizes derivatives and other financial instruments to manage its exposure to changes in foreign currency exchange rates, interest rates and jet fuel price volatility. Gains or losses relating to derivatives that are hedges are deferred and recognized in the same period and in the same financial category as the corresponding hedged transactions.

(n) Per share amounts:

Basic per share amounts are calculated using the weighted average number of shares outstanding during the year. Diluted per share amounts are calculated based on the treasury stock method, which assumes that any proceeds obtained on exercise of options would be used to purchase common shares at the average price during the period. The weighted average number of shares outstanding is then adjusted by the net change. In computing diluted net earnings per share, 1,339,511 (2001 - 1,319,183) shares were added to the weighted average number of common shares outstanding of 73,942,259 (2001 – 68,889,768) for the year ended December 31, 2002 in determining the dilutive effect of employee stock options.

(o) Comparative figures:

Certain prior period balances have been reclassified to conform with current period's presentation and to comply with a change in accounting policy (see note 1(e)).

WestJet Airlines Ltd.
Notes to Consolidated Financial Statements, Page 4

Years ended December 31, 2002 and 2001
(Tabular Amounts are Stated in Thousands of Dollars, Except Per Share Data)

2. Capital assets:

2002	Cost	Accumulated depreciation	Net book value
Aircraft – 700 series	$ 212,353	$ 786	$ 211,567
Aircraft – 200 series	185,765	72,853	112,912
Ground property and equipment	68,791	13,253	55,538
Aircraft under capital lease	30,966	10,035	20,931
Spare engines and parts – 200 series	28,915	8,850	20,065
Buildings	24,576	1,025	23,551
Parts – 700 series	19,593	1,071	18,522
Leasehold improvements	4,514	1,650	2,864
	575,473	109,523	465,950
Deposits on aircraft	131,464	-	131,464
Assets under construction	7,710	-	7,710
	$ 714,647	$ 109,523	$ 605,124

2001	Cost	Accumulated depreciation	Net book value
Aircraft – 200 series	$ 188,000	$ 49,912	$ 138,088
Ground property and equipment	39,476	7,510	31,966
Spare engines and parts – 200 series	30,166	5,257	24,909
Buildings	23,051	446	22,605
Aircraft under capital lease	18,617	2,980	15,637
Parts – 700 series	12,462	294	12,168
Leasehold improvements	3,539	1,421	2,118
	315,311	67,820	247,491
Deposits on aircraft	53,194	-	53,194
	$ 368,505	$ 67,820	$ 300,685

During the year capital assets were acquired at an aggregate cost of $12,188,000 (2001 - $9,415,000) by means of capital leases and interest costs of nil (2001 - $467,000) were capitalized to assets under construction.

3. Other long-term assets:

Included in other long-term assets is $19,034,000 (2001 - $1,087,000) of unamortized hedge settlements related to the ten leased Boeing Next-Generation aircraft, financing fees of $8,802,000 (2001 – nil), net of accumulated amortization of $123,000 (2001 – nil), related to the facility for the purchase of fifteen Boeing Next-Generation aircraft, security deposits on aircraft and other leaseholds of $7,701,000 (2001 - $4,748,000) and other amounts totaling $529,000 (2001 – $1,163,000).

WestJet Airlines Ltd.
Notes to Consolidated Financial Statements, Page 5

Years ended December 31, 2002 and 2001
(Tabular Amounts are Stated in Thousands of Dollars, Except Per Share Data)

4. Long-term debt:

	2002	2001
$178,777,000 in four individual term loans, amortized on a straight-line basis over a 12 year term, repayable in quarterly principle installments ranging from $913,000 to $955,000, including weighted average interest at 5.28%, guaranteed by the Ex-Im Bank and secured by four aircraft. The first quarterly payments commence February 2003	$ 178,777	$ -
$16,000,000 term loan, repayable in monthly installments of $145,000 including interest at 7.125% (interest rate will be renewed in July 2003 at a fixed rate for up to 5 years), maturing August 2016, secured by the Next-Generation flight simulator and six cross-collateralized aircraft	15,058	15,700
$36,073,000 in eight individual term loans, repayable in monthly installments ranging from $25,000 to $153,000 including weighted average interest at 8.36% with varying maturities ranging between April 2003 through October 2005, secured by seven aircraft	14,626	22,217
$12,000,000 term loan, repayable in monthly installments of $108,000 including interest at 9.03%, maturing April 2011, secured by the hangar facility	11,620	11,858
$11,589,000 term loan, repayable in monthly installments of $1,311,000, including interest of 4.40%, maturing on September 2003	11,589	-
	231,670	49,775
Less current portion	32,674	8,470
	$ 198,996	$ 41,305

The net book value of the assets pledged as collateral for the Corporation's secured borrowings was $292,352,000 as at December 31, 2002 (2001 - $94,485,000).

WestJet Airlines Ltd.

Notes to Consolidated Financial Statements, Page 6

Years ended December 31, 2002 and 2001
(Tabular Amounts are Stated in Thousands of Dollars, Except Per Share Data)

---

4. Long-term debt (continued):

Future scheduled repayments of long-term debt are as follows:

2003	$	32,674
2004		20,009
2005		21,305
2006		16,092
2007		16,187
2008 and thereafter		125,403
	$	231,670

The Corporation has a U.S. $478 million facility with the ING Group which is supported by loan guarantees from the Export-Import Bank of the United States (Ex-Im) for U.S. $478 million for the purchase of fifteen Boeing Next-Generation 737-700 series aircraft. Of these aircraft four were delivered in 2002, with the remaining eleven to be delivered over the course of 2003. HFLP is used as the financial intermediary to facilitate the financing agreement to purchase the aircraft.

This facility will be drawn in Canadian dollars in separate installments with 12 year terms for each new aircraft. Each loan will be amortized on a straight-line basis over the 12 year term in quarterly principal installments, with interest calculated on the outstanding principal balance.

The Corporation is charged a commitment fee of 0.125% per annum on the unutilized and uncancelled balance of the loan guarantee, payable at specified dates and upon delivery of an aircraft. As at December 31, 2002 the unutilized balance was U.S. $364 million.

The Corporation has entered into Forward Starting Interest Rate Agreements at rates between 5.36% and 5.85% on the remaining eleven aircraft to be delivered under this facility.

The Corporation has available a facility with a Canadian chartered bank of $6,000,000 for letters of guarantee. At December 31, 2002, letters of guarantee totaling $4,410,000 have been issued under these facilities. The credit facilities are secured by a fixed first charge on one aircraft, a general security agreement and an assignment of insurance proceeds.

Cash interest paid during the year was $5,836,000 (2001 - $5,570,000).

WESTJET AIRLINES LTD.

Notes to Consolidated Financial Statements, Page 7

Years ended December 31, 2002 and 2001
(Tabular Amounts are Stated in Thousands of Dollars, Except Per Share Data)

---

5. Leases:

The Corporation has entered into operating leases for aircraft, buildings, computer hardware and software licenses and capital leases relating to computer hardware and aircraft. The obligations, on a calendar-year basis, are as follows (see note 8 for additional lease commitments):

	Capital Leases	Operating Leases
2003	$ 8,880	$ 52,715
2004	8,753	51,071
2005	6,256	49,857
2006	2,913	47,341
2007	-	47,206
2008 and thereafter	-	384,276
Total lease payments	26,802	$ 632,466
Less imputed interest at 7.79%	(3,160)	
Net minimum lease payments	23,642	
Less current portion of obligations under capital lease	(7,290)	
Obligations under capital lease	$ 16,352	

6. Share capital:

The non-voting common shares and the non-voting preferred shares are subject to limitations to be fixed by the directors of the Corporation.

(a) Authorized:

Unlimited number of voting common shares

700,000 non-voting performance shares

Unlimited number of non-voting shares

Unlimited number of non-voting first, second and third preferred shares

WestJet Airlines Ltd.
Notes to Consolidated Financial Statements, Page 8

Years ended December 31, 2002 and 2001
(Tabular Amounts are Stated in Thousands of Dollars, Except Per Share Data)

---

6.   Share capital (continued):

(b) Issued:

	2002		2001	
	Number	Amount	Number	Amount
Common shares:				
Balance, beginning of year	69,516,897	$ 129,268	67,497,875	$ 125,390
Common share issue	4,500,000	82,500	-	-
Exercise of options	879,019	2,134	2,019,022	3,878
Issued on rounding of stock split	3,693	-	-	-
Share issuance costs	-	(3,672)	-	-
Tax benefit of issue costs	-	1,334	-	-
Balance, end of year	74,899,609	$ 211,564	69,516,897	$ 129,268

(c) Stock split:

On May 3, 2002, the common shares of the Corporation were split on a three for two basis. All number of shares and per share amounts have been restated to reflect the stock split.

(d) Stock Option Plan:

The Corporation has a Stock Option Plan, whereby up to a maximum of 7,476,330 common shares may be issued to officers and employees of the Corporation subject to the following limitations:

(i)   the number of common shares reserved for issuance to any one optionee will not exceed 5% of the issued and outstanding common shares at any time;

(ii)   the number of common shares reserved for issuance to insiders shall not exceed 10% of the issued and outstanding common shares; and

(iii) the number of common shares issuable under the Plan, which may be issued within a one year period, shall not exceed 10% of the issued and outstanding common shares at any time.

Stock options are granted at a price that equals the market value, have a term of four years and vest over a period of two to three years.

WESTJET AIRLINES LTD.

Notes to Consolidated Financial Statements, Page 9

Years ended December 31, 2002 and 2001
(Tabular Amounts are Stated in Thousands of Dollars, Except Per Share Data)

6. Share capital (continued):

(d) Stock Option Plan (continued):

Changes in the number of options, with their weighted average exercise prices, are summarized below:

	2002		2001	
	Number of options	Weighted average exercise price	Number of options	Weighted average exercise price
Stock options outstanding, beginning of year	5,579,517	$ 11.85	5,037,182	$ 6.43
Granted	1,140,292	20.70	2,681,601	14.64
Exercised	(879,019)	2.43	(2,019,022)	1.92
Cancelled	(31,602)	15.67	(120,244)	13.73
Stock options outstanding, end of year	5,809,188	$ 14.99	5,579,517	$ 11.85
Exercisable, end of year	276,159	$ 3.48	829,329	$ 2.41

The following table summarizes the options outstanding and exercisable at December 31, 2002:

	Outstanding			Exercisable Options	
Range of Exercise Prices	Number Outstanding	Weighted Average Remaining Life (years)	Weighted Average Exercise Price	Number Exercisable	Weighted Average Exercise Price
$2.67 - $4.45	276,159	0.33	$ 3.48	276,159	$ 3.48
$10.99 - $12.67	44,381	2.41	12.15	-	-
$13.65 - $14.68	4,355,706	2.02	14.26	-	-
$15.81 - $20.75	1,132,942	3.31	20.70	-	-
	5,809,188	2.19	$ 14.99	276,159	$ 3.48

Upon filing the Corporation's initial public offering on July 13, 1999, 237,533 options were re-priced from $2.67 per share to $4.45 per share and of this amount 125,033 (2001 – 192,533) were remaining at December 31, 2002. The Corporation committed to the holders of the options that it would pay the differential of $1.78 per share upon exercise of those options.

WestJet Airlines Ltd.

Notes to Consolidated Financial Statements, Page 10

Years ended December 31, 2002 and 2001
(Tabular Amounts are Stated in Thousands of Dollars, Except Per Share Data)

---

6. Share capital (continued):

(e) Employee Share Purchase Plan:

Under the terms of the Employee Share Purchase Plan, employees may contribute up to a maximum of 20% of their gross pay and acquire common shares of the Corporation at the current fair market value of such shares. The Corporation matches the employee contributions and shares may be withdrawn from the Plan after being held in trust for one year. Employees may offer to sell common shares, which have not been held for at least one year, on January 1 and July 1 of each year, to the Corporation for 50% of the then current market price. The Corporation's share of the contributions is recorded as compensation expense and amounted to $10,178,000 (2001 - $6,081,000).

(f) Pro forma disclosure:

The fair value of each option grant is estimated on the date of grant using the Black-Scholes option pricing model with the following weighted average assumptions used for grants in 2002: zero dividend yield; expected volatility of 38%; risk-free rate of 4.5%; and expected life of four years. The weighted average fair value of stock options granted during the year was $8.06 per option.

Had the Corporation accounted for employee stock options issued using the fair value based method, the Corporation's pro forma net earnings and EPS would be as follows:

	As reported 2002	Pro forma 2002
Net earnings	$ 51,780	$ 48,963
Earnings per share:		
Basic	$ 0.70	$ 0.66
Diluted	0.69	0.65

These pro forma earnings reflect compensation cost amortized over the options' vesting period, which varies from two to three years.

WestJet Airlines Ltd.
Notes to Consolidated Financial Statements, Page 11

Years ended December 31, 2002 and 2001
(Tabular Amounts are Stated in Thousands of Dollars, Except Per Share Data)

7. Income taxes:

Income taxes vary upon the amount that would be computed by applying the basic Federal and Provincial tax rate of 38.1% (2001 – 43.7%) to earnings before income taxes as follows:

	2002	2001
Expected income tax provision	$ 31,544	$ 25,445
Add (deduct):		
Non-deductible expenses	518	459
Other	(358)	(729)
Capital taxes	31	251
Large corporations tax	177	-
Future tax rate reductions	(848)	(4,347)
	$ 31,064	$ 21,079

Cash taxes paid during the year were $3,878,000 (2001 – $25,700,000).

The components of the net future income tax liability are as follows:

	2002	2001
Future income tax asset:		
Share issue costs	$ 1,767	$ 1,127
Future income tax liability:		
Capital assets	39,804	22,060
Net future income tax liability	$ 38,037	$ 20,933

8. Commitments and contingencies:

(a) Aircraft:

The Corporation has entered into agreements to lease ten Boeing Next-Generation aircraft, four of which were delivered over the course of 2001, with the remaining six delivered in 2002. Under the terms of these lease agreements, the Corporation received a 737-700 engine for use throughout the period of the leases. Subject to the Corporation's compliance with the terms of the lease agreements, title to the engine will pass to the Corporation at the end of the final lease. The Corporation has also obtained options to lease an additional ten Boeing Next-Generation aircraft to be delivered prior to the end of 2006.

WestJet Airlines Ltd.
Notes to Consolidated Financial Statements, Page 12

Years ended December 31, 2002 and 2001
(Tabular Amounts are Stated in Thousands of Dollars, Except Per Share Data)

---

8. **Commitments and contingencies (continued):**

(a) Aircraft (continued):

The Corporation has also entered into agreements to purchase thirty Boeing Next-Generation aircraft, four of which were delivered over the course of 2002, with the remaining twenty-six to be delivered over the course of 2003 to 2006. This agreement provides the Corporation with the option to purchase an additional forty-four aircraft for delivery prior to the end of 2008.

The remaining estimated amounts to be paid in deposits and purchase prices in U.S. dollars relating to the purchases of the remaining twenty-six aircraft are as follows:

2003	$ 352,244
2004	276,062
2005	151,261
2006	30,603
	$ 810,170

In addition to the existing U.S. $478 million loan guarantee from the Ex-Im Bank (see note 4), the Corporation has received a Preliminary Commitment from the Ex-Im Bank for loan guarantees to support the acquisition of the remaining fifteen Boeing Next-Generation aircraft the Corporation has committed to purchase prior to February 2006.

(b) Employee profit share:

The Corporation has an employee profit sharing plan whereby eligible employees will participate in the pre-tax operating income of the Corporation. The profit share ranges from a minimum of 10% to a maximum of 20% of earnings before employee profit share and income taxes. The amounts paid under the plan are subject to prior approval by the Board of Directors.

(c) Contingencies:

The Corporation is party to legal proceedings and claims that arise during the ordinary course of business. It is the opinion of management that the ultimate outcome of these matters will not have a material effect upon the Corporation's financial position, results of operations or cash flows.

WestJet Airlines Ltd.

Notes to Consolidated Financial Statements, Page 13

Years ended December 31, 2002 and 2001
(Tabular Amounts are Stated in Thousands of Dollars, Except Per Share Data)

9. **Risk management:**

(a) Fuel risk management:

The Corporation has mitigated its exposure to jet fuel price volatility through the use of long-term fixed price contracts and contracts with a fixed ceiling price which it has entered into with a fuel supplier. Any premiums paid to enter into these long-term fuel arrangements are recorded as other long-term assets and amortized to fuel expense over the term of the contracts. As at December 31, 2002, the Corporation had a fixed ceiling price fuel contract that is in effect through to June 2003, at an indicative price of U.S. $18.60 per barrel of crude oil. In 2002, this contract represented 32% (2001 – 42%) of the Corporation's fuel requirements.

(b) Foreign currency exchange risk:

The Corporation is exposed to foreign currency fluctuations as certain ongoing expenses are referenced to U.S. dollar denominated prices. The Corporation periodically uses financial instruments, including forward exchange contracts and options, to manage its exposure. At December 31, 2002 the Corporation did not have any foreign currency financial instruments outstanding.

(c) Interest rate risk:

The Corporation has managed its exposure to interest rate fluctuations on debt financing for the next eleven Boeing Next-Generation aircraft scheduled to be delivered over the course of 2003. The Corporation has managed this exposure by entering into Forward Starting Interest Rate Agreements at rates between 5.36% and 5.85%.

The Corporation has entered into fixed rate debt instruments in order to manage its interest rate exposure on existing debt agreements. These agreements are described in note 4.

(d) Credit risk:

The Corporation does not believe it is subject to any significant concentration of credit risk. Most of the Corporation's receivables result from tickets sold to individual guests through the use of major credit cards and travel agents. These receivables are short-term, generally being settled shortly after the sale. The Corporation manages the credit exposure related to financial instruments by selecting counter parties based on credit ratings, limiting its exposure to any single counter party and monitoring the market position of the program and its relative market position with each counter party.

(e) Fair value of financial instruments:

The carrying amounts of financial instruments included in the balance sheet, other than long-term debt, approximate their fair value due to their short term to maturity.

At December 31, 2002, the fair value of long-term debt was approximately $236 million. The fair value of long-term debt is determined by discounting the future contractual cash flows under current financing arrangements at discount rates which represent borrowing rates presently available to the Corporation for loans with similar terms and maturity.

Chart of Accounts

Assets

Current Assets

101 Cash
102 Petty Cash
103 Cash equivalents
104 Temporary investments
105 Allowance to reduce temporary investments to market
106 Accounts receivable
107 Allowance for doubtful accounts
108 GST receivable
109 Interest receivable
110 Rent receivable
111 Notes receivable
119 Merchandise inventory
120 _____ inventory
124 Office supplies
125 Store supplies
126 _____ supplies
128 Prepaid insurance
129 Prepaid _____
131 Prepaid rent
132 Raw materials inventory
133 Goods in process inventory, _____
135 Finished goods inventory

Long-Term Investments

141 Investment in ____ shares
142 Investment in ____ bonds
144 Investment in _____

Property, Plant, and Equipment

151 Automobiles
152 Accumulated amortization, automobiles
153 Trucks
154 Accumulated amortization, trucks
155 Boats
156 Accumulated amortization, boats
157 Professional library
158 Accumulated amortization, professional library
159 Law library

160 Accumulated amortization, law library
161 Furniture
162 Accumulated amortization, Furniture
163 Office equipment
164 Accumulated amortization, office equipment
165 Store equipment
166 Accumulated amortization, store equipment
167 _____ equipment
168 Accumulated amortization, _____ equipment
169 Machinery
170 Accumulated amortization, machinery
173 Building _____
174 Accumulated amortization, building _____
175 Land
176 Leasehold improvements
179 Land improvements, _____
180 Accumulated amortization, land improvements _____

Natural Resources

185 Mineral deposit
186 Accumulated amortization, mineral deposit

Intangible Assets

191 Patents
192 Leasehold
193 Franchise
194 Copyright
196 Organization costs
198 Goodwill

Liabilities

Current Liabilities

201 Accounts payable
202 Insurance payable
203 Interest payable
204 Legal fees payable
205 Short-term notes payable
206 Discount on short-term notes payable

208 Rent payable
209 Salaries payable
210 Wages payable
214 Estimated warranty liability
215 Income taxes payable
216 Common dividends payable
217 Preferred dividends payable
218 EI payable
219 CPP payable
221 Employees' medical insurance payable
222 Employees' retirement program payable
223 Employees' union dues payable
224 PST payable
225 GST payable
226 Estimated vacation pay liability

Unearned Revenues

230 Unearned consulting fees
231 Unearned legal fees
232 Unearned property management fees
233 Unearned _____

Long-Term Liabilities

251 Long-term notes payable
252 Discount on notes payable
253 Long-term lease liability
255 Bonds payable
256 Discount on bonds payable
257 Premium on bonds payable

Equity

Owners' Equity

301 _____ , capital
302 _____ , withdrawals
303 _____ , capital
304 _____ , withdrawals

Corporate Contributed Capital

307 Common shares

310 Common share dividends distributable
313 Contributed capital from the retirement of common shares
315 Preferred shares

Retained Earnings

318 Retained earnings
319 Cash dividends
320 Share dividends

Revenues

401 _____ fees earned
403 _____ services revenue
405 Commission earned
406 Rent earned
407 Dividends earned
408 Earnings from investment in _____
409 Interest earned
413 Sales
414 Sales returns and allowances
415 Sales discounts

Cost of Sales

502 Cost of goods sold
503 Amortization of mine deposit
505 Purchases
506 Purchases returns and allowances
507 Purchases discounts
508 Transportation-in

Manufacturing Accounts

520 Raw materials purchases
521 Freight-in on raw materials
530 Factory payroll
531 Direct labour
540 Factory overhead
541 Indirect materials
542 Indirect labour
543 Factory insurance expired
544 Factory supervision
545 Factory supplies used
546 Factory utilities
547 Miscellaneous production costs
548 Property taxes on factory building
550 Rent on factory building
551 Repairs, factory equipment
552 Small tools written off
560 Amortization of factory equipment

561 Amortization of factory building

Standard Cost Variance Accounts

580 Direct material quantity variance
581 Direct material price variance
582 Direct labour quantity variance
583 Direct labour price variance
584 Factory overhead volume variance
585 Factory overhead controllable variance

Expenses

Amortization

602 Amortization expense, copyrights
603 Amortization expense, _____
604 Amortization expense, boats
605 Amortization expense, automobiles
606 Amortization expense, building _____
608 Amortization expense, land improvements _____
610 Amortization expense, law library
611 Amortization expense, trucks
612 Amortization expense, _____ equipment
614 Amortization expense, _____

Employee Related Expense

620 Office salaries expense
621 Sales salaries expense
622 Salaries expense
623 _____ wages expense
624 Employees' benefits expense

Financial Expenses

630 Cash over and short
633 Interest expense

Insurance Expenses

635 Insurance expense, delivery equipment
636 Insurance expense, building

637 Insurance expense, _____

Rental Expenses

640 Rent expense
641 Rent expense, office space
642 Rent expense, selling space
645 _____ rental expense

Supplies Expense

650 Office supplies expense
651 Store supplies expense
652 _____ supplies expense

Other Expenses

655 Advertising expense
656 Bad debts expense
659 Collection expense
662 Credit card expense
663 Delivery expense
667 Equipment expense
668 Food and drinks expense
671 Gas and oil expense
673 Janitorial expense
674 Legal fees expense
676 Mileage expense
681 Permits expense
682 Postage expense
683 Property taxes expense
684 Repairs expense, _____
688 Telephone expense
689 Travel and entertaining expense
690 Utilities expense
691 Warranty expense
695 Income taxes expense
696 _____ expense

Gains and Losses

701 Gain on retirement of bonds
702 Gain on sale of machinery
703 Gain on sale of investments
705 Gain on _____
804 Loss on market decline of temporary investments
805 Loss on retirement of bonds
806 Loss on sale of investments
807 Loss on sale of machinery
809 Loss on _____

Clearing Accounts

901 Income summary
902 Manufacturing summary

Credits

Chapter 12, page 606, Cameco logo reproduced courtesy Cameco Corporation.

Chapter 13, page 672, photo © GettyImages

Chapter 14, page 714, photo © Amos Morgan/GettyImages

Chapter 15, page 754, cover image reprinted with permission from Stir Fry © Company's Coming Publishing Limited. Logo courtesy of Friesens Corporation.

Chapter 16, page 812, logo courtesy of Boardwalk Equities, Inc.

Chapter 17, page 860, photo © PhotoDisc

Chapter 18, page 926, photo © Terry Vine/Tony Stone Images

Chapter 19, page 972, photo © WestJet; WestJet logo © WestJet. Both reproduced with permission.

Chapter 20, page 1036, photo © GettyImages

Because of their demonstrated interest in advancing post-secondary accounting education, we would like to say a special thank-you to the following organizations for taking part in interviews and/or providing materials.

Alberta Blue Cross	Institute of Chartered Accountants
Art by Larisa	John N. Douglas CFE CA
BioWare Corp.	Leon's Furniture Ltd.
Cameco	London Drugs
Canada Customs and Revenue Agency	Macrotronics
Certified General Accountants Association	Mrs. Beasley's Cookies Limited
	Rethink Advertising
CIBC	Robert Half Finance & Accounting
Danier Leather Inc.	Rotary International
ECOF—European Classical Oak Furniture	Royal Canadian Mounted Police
	Shell Canada
Edmonton Oilers Hockey Club	Society of Management Accountants
Friesens	WestJet Airlines Ltd.

Index